ENVIRONMENTAL, SOCIAL, GOVERNANCE

The Professional's Guide to the Law and Practice of ESG

BRIAN D. ISRAEL, ELLEN KAYE FLEISHHACKER,
AND TERESA L. JOHNSON, EDITORS

AMERICANBARASSOCIATION
Environment, Energy,
and Resources Section

Cover design by Elmarie Jara/ABA Design

Printed in the United States of America.

27 26 25 24 23 5 4 3 2 1

Library of Congress Cataloging-in-Publication Data

Names: Israel, Brian D., editor. | Fleishhacker, Ellen Kaye, editor. | Johnson, Teresa L., editor.
Title: Environmental, social, governance : the professional's guide to the law and practice of ESG / editors, Brian D. Israel, Ellen Kaye Fleishhacker, Teresa L. Johnson.
Description: 1e. | Chicago : American Bar Association, 2023. | Summary: "First, the book does what any good legal writing should do: it transmutes an awesomely complex subject into a story more easily readable and understandable. The authors achieve that by explaining about how each element of ESG historically came to be, and thereafter elucidating at the more theoretical level, each element's conceptual underpinnings. Second, the book explains and elucidates, with remarkable depth and breadth, the wide array of disparate subjects that ESG encompasses. Third, most notable is the book's well-organized internal structure, which is designed to provide practitioners what they most need -a practical approach"-- Provided by publisher.
Identifiers: LCCN 2023028275 (print) | LCCN 2023028276 (ebook) | ISBN 9781639053292 (hardcover) | ISBN 9781639053308 (ebook)
Subjects: LCSH: Environmental engineering--Law and legislation. | Climatic changes--Law and legislation. | Environmental management--Law and legislation. | Environmental impact analysis--Law and legislation. | Environmental risk assessment--Law and legislation. | Greenhouse gas mitigation--Law and legislation. | Environmental justice. | Environmental law--Social aspects.
Classification: LCC K3585.5.E587 2023 (print) | LCC K3585.5 (ebook) | DDC 344.04/6--dc23/eng/20230616
LC record available at https://lccn.loc.gov/2023028275
LC ebook record available at https://lccn.loc.gov/2023028276

Discounts are available for books ordered in bulk. Special consideration is given to state bars, CLE programs, and other bar-related organizations. Inquire at Book Publishing, ABA Publishing, American Bar Association, 321 N. Clark Street, Chicago, Illinois 60654-7598.

www.shopABA.org

Table of Contents

PART IV

About the Editors

Brian D. Israel is a Partner in Arnold & Porter's Los Angeles and Washington, DC, offices. He is Chair of the firm's Environmental Practice Group, as well as co-lead of the firm's Environmental, Social and Corporate Governance (ESG) working group. Mr. Israel's practice focuses broadly on environmental litigation and counseling—including climate-related issues—and he is one of the nation's leading lawyers for Natural Resource Damages claims. Mr. Israel represents multiple Fortune 500 companies in some of the largest and most complex environmental matters across the country. Mr. Israel has been regularly recognized for his thought leadership and environmental expertise by multiple organizations, including Chambers USA (2013–2023), Legal 500, Best Lawyers, Who's Who Legal, Lawdragon, and the *National Law Journal* (awarded the Energy & Environmental Trailblazer award in 2017).

Prior to joining the firm, Mr. Israel was an Honors Trial Attorney in the Environmental Enforcement Section of the U.S. Department of Justice, where he earned the Distinguished Service Award. Mr. Israel received his BA in Environmental Philosophy from New College, University of South Florida, in 1991, and received his JD from New York University (NYU) in 1995, where he graduated cum laude. Mr. Israel has also received a certificate in Sustainable Capitalism and ESG from the University of California, Berkeley, School of Law. Mr. Israel has spoken and written extensively about environmental law, regulatory reform, energy transition, and ESG issues. He is a principal author of *Natural Resource Damages: A Guide to Litigating and Resolving NRD Cases* (ABA, 2019). Mr. Israel's student note "An Environmental Justice Critique of Risk Assessment" is published in the *NYU Environmental Law Journal.*

Ellen Kaye Fleishhacker, a Partner in Arnold & Porter's San Francisco office, co-leads the firm's Investment Management practice group and the firm's ESG working group. She is also the Co-Managing Partner of the firm. Ms. Fleishhacker's practice focuses on investment management–related matters, including formation, compliance, and transactional matters of private funds, with a special focus on real estate and ESG/impact investment funds. She also represents wealth advisory firms, family offices, and financial institutions on legal, compliance, ESG, and transactional matters associated with their investment management and related operations. In addition, Ms. Fleishhacker works with investors on structuring and negotiating potential investments in private funds, including ESG/impact funds, and other investment vehicles. For over 10 years, she has had a special interest in, and has written and spoken on, legal topics related to impact investing/ESG funds. She received her JD and MBA at the University of California, Berkeley.

Teresa L. Johnson is a Partner in Arnold & Porter's San Francisco office and Co-Chair of the firm's Capital Markets practice. Ms. Johnson serves as a trusted advisor to the C suite and board members, working closely with boards of directors in the boardroom and in committee meetings. In her corporate governance work and thought leadership, Ms. Johnson has focused in particular on board diversity, stakeholder capitalism, and other ESG matters. She is one of the founders of the firm's ESG practice. Ms. Johnson advises clients on securities transactions, compliance, and reporting matters. A "notable practitioner" (Chambers USA: California 2021), Ms. Johnson has been recognized by the *Daily Journal* as one of the top 25 corporate transaction attorneys on the publication's annual list of the "Top 100 Women Lawyers." Ms. Johnson is the 2024 President of the Bar Association of San Francisco and is one of the leaders of the Legal Alliance for Reproductive Rights, a coalition among BASF, the San Francisco City Attorney, and a large cohort of law firms (including Arnold & Porter), which coordinates providing pro bono legal assistance in connection with the exercise of reproductive rights following the *Dobbs* decision.

About the Authors

Robert C. Azarow, a Partner in the New York office of Arnold & Porter, is head of the firm's Financial Services Transactions practice. Mr. Azarow's experience includes serving as lead transaction and regulatory counsel on financial institution mergers and acquisitions, including for privately held and public companies, financial asset acquisitions, branch purchases, acquisitions of strategic partnerships with Fintech companies, and acquisitions of failed financial institutions and distressed assets from the Federal Deposit Insurance Corporation (FDIC). Mr. Azarow also assists financial institutions with their regulatory compliance matters, including response to examination issues and transaction-related matters, as well as regulatory capital compliance, stock repurchase programs, capital distributions, permissible investments and activities, digital payment strategies including use of stablecoin, regulatory agreements for troubled institutions, and regulatory reporting.

Janice Bashford is a Partner in Arnold & Porter's Washington, DC, office. Ms. Bashford brings more than 15 years of experience on Capitol Hill in building strategic partnerships across a range of issues to help clients navigate the legislative process. Ms. Bashford has worked for a U.S. Senator and for three members of Congress in the U.S. House of Representatives. In her prior role as Chief Counsel to Congresswoman Karen Bass, Ms. Bashford played a key role in negotiating and advancing legislation and other initiatives on a range of issues, including financial services, judiciary, appropriations, foreign affairs, and civil and human rights. She also has worked closely with numerous key committees and groups, including the Ways and Means Committee, the Judiciary Committees, the Foreign Affairs Committees, the Congressional Black Caucus, the Bipartisan Women's Caucus, the Congressional Tri-Caucus (the Congressional Black Caucus, the Congressional Hispanic Caucus, and the Congressional Asian-Pacific American Caucus), and the Congressional Caucus on Foster Youth.

Vincent Brown is an Associate in the Legislative practice group in the Washington, DC, office of Arnold & Porter. He received his JD from the American University, Washington College of Law in 2016.

Tyler L. Burgess is a Senior Associate at Arnold & Porter, where her practice focuses on environmental law. She has counseled public companies on ESG disclosures and reporting, advised companies on developing and implementing ESG programs and policies, and conducted ESG due diligence reviews for transactions involving businesses across a wide range of sectors, including healthcare, software, and manufacturing.

Xixi Chen is an Associate in the New York office of Arnold & Porter, where she is a member of the Corporate and Finance group. Her practice involves advising public and private companies on a variety of corporate matters, including mergers and acquisitions, corporate governance, securities offerings, and U.S. Securities and Exchange Commission (SEC) reporting and compliance. She received her JD from the University of Pennsylvania Carey Law School in 2021.

E. Whitney Debevoise is a Partner in Arnold & Porter's Washington, DC, office. Mr. Debevoise's practice involves international financial transactions, banking, public policy, international arbitration, and multijurisdictional litigation. Mr. Debevoise rejoined the firm in 2010, having served as U.S. Executive Director of the World Bank from 2007. Mr. Debevoise has extensive experience in major international financial transactions and the capital markets, including sovereign restructurings and lending facilities with bilateral or multilateral credit support. He has handled significant International Centre for Settlement of Investment Disputes arbitrations and served as an arbitrator in commercial and investor-state cases. In the blockchain and cryptocurrency field, he has represented a country that adopted Bitcoin as an official currency and other clients with respect to the use of electronic wallets.

Mr. Debevoise has written articles on securities regulation, World Trade Organization dispute resolution, debt restructuring, international banking, U.S. export controls, and sovereign immunity. He has lectured at the Harvard and Yale Law Schools, the Tuck School of Business at Dartmouth, the Lauder Institute of the University of Pennsylvania, and the Hungarian Institute for the Training of Bankers. Mr. Debevoise is a summa cum laude graduate of Yale University, with departmental honors in history and Latin American studies, and a graduate of Harvard Law School. He holds an honorary degree from Vermont Law School.

Niels Ersbøll is a Partner and Head of the Brussels Office and Arnold & Porter's EU Antitrust practice. He has more than two decades' experience advising clients on EU competition law in relation to merger control, cartels, restrictive practices, and abuse of dominance. He has extensive experience devising strategy and coordinating complex merger filing submissions to competition authorities worldwide for large multinational clients such as Pfizer, Boston Scientific, and AT&T.

Simon Firth is a Partner in the London office of Arnold & Porter. His practice focuses on funds, investment management, and related regulation. He advises investment managers and sponsors on the establishment, promotion, regulation, and operation of alternative investment funds, as well as on managed account arrangements. Mr. Firth's related transactional work comprises fund seeding and restructuring, and acquisitions and disposals of investment firms. Mr. Firth also regularly advises clients on regulatory matters, including the increasing scope of ESG regulations as it affects financial services firms. Mr. Firth is a regular speaker on investment management and regulatory matters, and frequently contributes articles on industry matters.

Therese M. Fox is an Associate in Arnold & Porter's Corporate and Finance practice group, based in Denver. She represents public and private companies and investors in connection with a variety of corporate and financial matters, including general corporate governance, mergers and acquisitions, and private equity investing. Prior to law school, Ms. Fox worked for Accenture Consulting, where she focused on acquisitions, divestments, and large-scale system migrations for Fortune 100 companies, including one of the largest oil and gas companies globally and one of the largest utility providers in the United States.

Claire Frost is an Associate in the Corporate and Finance group in the New York City office of Arnold & Porter. She has represented clients on a wide range of complex transactions, including mergers and acquisitions, securities offerings, and minority and majority private equity investments. She regularly works with clients across a number of industries, such as life sciences, entertainment, and private equity. She also maintains a pro bono practice, assisting not-for-profit clients and small businesses with their corporate formation and governance.

Kathryn Geoffroy is an Employee Benefits and Executive Compensation Associate at Arnold & Porter in Chicago. Her practice focuses on the design, implementation, and administration of employee benefit plans; employment agreements and compensation arrangements, including equity compensation, for executives and employees; compensation and benefits-related issues in mergers and acquisitions; and related securities, tax, employment, and labor issues. Ms. Geoffroy received her JD from the University of Illinois College of Law.

Jyoti Gill is an Associate in Arnold & Porter's San Francisco office. Ms. Gill's practice focuses on corporate and transactional matters, including mergers and acquisitions, corporate governance, emerging companies and venture capital, and securities law. Ms. Gill received her JD and Business Law Certification from the University of California, Berkeley, where she graduated with Order of the Coif honors. She was a board member of the South Asian Law Students Association and was the recipient of the Jurisprudence Award for being the highest-ranking student in Bankruptcy Law.

Peter Gioello is Counsel in Arnold & Porter's Environmental practice group and focuses on both ESG and environmental, health, and safety risks, issues, and liabilities. He counsels clients on emerging ESG issues such as sustainability reporting and disclosure, ESG due diligence, environmental justice, climate change mitigation and adaptation, product stewardship, and supply chain audits, among other issues. He also focuses on traditional environmental, health, and safety issues, and risks and liabilities as they arise in and relate to major transactions, especially mergers and acquisitions and financing transactions. In 2022, he earned a Certificate in Sustainable Capitalism and ESG from the University of California, Berkeley, School of Law.

Sarah Grey is a Partner in Arnold & Porter's Denver office. Ms. Grey counsels a wide array of clients on regulatory, policy, and compliance matters related to climate change, including the federal Renewable Fuel Standard, California's Low Carbon Fuel Standard, the Clean Air Act (CAA), and other state and international initiatives on transportation-sector greenhouse gas (GHG) emissions. Ms. Grey is a leading strategic advisor on carbon capture, storage, and utilization, and other energy transition–related opportunities, including mandatory and voluntary carbon credit markets and tax credits under the Inflation Reduction Act. She has deep technical expertise on GHG lifecycle accounting and fuels regulatory, compliance, and litigation matters, including enforcement defense matters. Ms. Grey also advises clients on climate risk analysis and disclosure and other ESG issues. She frequently represents clients in the fuels, energy, automobile, and manufacturing industries before the U.S. Environmental Protection Agency and California regulators. Ms. Grey's background includes serving as regulatory counsel for a large biofuels company and its industry trade association, where she managed regulatory, litigation, and legislative matters related to renewable fuels production and regulatory incentives. She also supported the environmental and permitting teams for over 25 facilities, which included negotiating consent decrees and addressing CAA information requests and notices of violations.

Gregory Harrington is a Partner of the law firm Arnold & Porter, based in the Washington, DC, office, where he is co-head of the firm's Sovereign Finance practice. Mr. Harrington received his law degree from the University of Chicago Law School and did his undergraduate studies at The George Washington University. Mr. Harrington regularly advises clients on finance transactions, including the sale of securities in the United States; syndicated and bilateral lending transactions; project finance transactions; and compliance issues under the U.S. securities laws, including the Dodd-Frank Act, Sarbanes-Oxley, and the Foreign Corrupt Practices Act. He has been recognized by Chambers, Legal 500, and International Financial Law Review (aka IFLR) in the areas of Capital Markets and Banking & Finance. Prior to joining Arnold & Porter in Washington, DC, Mr. Harrington practiced in São Paulo, Brazil, from 2000 to 2007. He is a member of the bars of Washington, DC, and New York.

Ryan Hartman is a Partner in Arnold & Porter's Houston office. He represents clients in civil litigation, criminal investigations, and regulatory enforcement actions, and advises companies on strategic transactions, risk management, and compliance. He has represented companies and executives in more than 100 lawsuits, arbitrations, government and internal investigations, regulatory proceedings, and disputes, and previously served as a lawyer and executive at one of the world's largest energy companies.

Daniel M. Hawke, a Partner in Arnold & Porter's Washington, DC, office, is the former chief of the SEC's Market Abuse Unit and director of the SEC's Philadelphia Regional Office. Mr. Hawke counsels clients on all manner of SEC enforcement, examination, and regulatory policy matters. With a focus on complex trading, equity market structure enforcement, and investment advisor compliance issues, Mr. Hawke defends companies and individuals facing SEC enforcement inquiries and litigation. Recognized by the Securities Docket as one of the top 40 "best and brightest" securities defense lawyers in the country, Mr. Hawke has nearly 30 years of combined government and private practice experience. Mr. Hawke represents both individuals and entities in responding to regulatory and enforcement inquiries, preparing for SEC inspections and examinations, conducting internal investigations, and answering corporate governance, internal control, whistleblower, and compliance questions. He has represented public companies, accounting firms, broker-dealers, investment advisors, hedge funds, private equity firms, business development companies, alternative trading systems, and national securities exchanges. He advises board members, corporate executives, compliance officers, professional traders, and other industry participants. Mr. Hawke offers deep insight into and perspective on the SEC, how it operates, and what to expect during an SEC examination or investigation.

Amber Hay is a Partner in Arnold & Porter's Washington, DC, office. Ms. Hay primarily advises traditional financial institutions (banks, savings associations, and credit unions), nonbank financial services companies, as well as financial technology companies on a wide range of regulatory, transactional, and general corporate matters, including matters within the supervisory jurisdiction of the Federal Reserve Board, the Office of the Comptroller of the Currency, the FDIC, the Consumer Financial Protection Bureau, and the Financial Crimes Enforcement Network, as well as state financial regulatory agencies. Ms. Hay routinely advises clients on laws, regulations, and legislative developments related to prudential regulations; virtual currencies (including stablecoins and other digital assets); electronic payments; custodian activities, including those involving digital wallets; and service provider arrangements between banks and nonbanks (e.g., banking as a service and third-party vendor management). Ms. Hay also advises clients in the structuring of corporate transactions and commercial arrangements related to the offering of payments and credit products and services using technology, as well as the acquisition and sale of financial institutions and nonbank financial service companies.

Valarie Hays is a Partner at Arnold & Porter and leads the Chicago office's White Collar Defense & Investigations practice. Prior to joining the firm, Ms. Hays was a federal prosecutor. Ms. Hays represents companies and individuals in government inquiries and complex commercial litigation in federal and state courts. She also conducts corporate internal investigations and advises clients on the execution of their compliance programs across a broad range of industry sectors, including healthcare, financial services, retail, and oil and gas. A first chair trial lawyer, Ms. Hays has tried 17 jury trials over the course of her career and has obtained numerous dismissals and favorable resolutions for her corporate clients.

Elise Henry is an Associate in the Environmental practice group of Arnold & Porter. Ms. Henry's practice focuses on environmental litigation, enforcement matters, and regulatory and compliance counseling. Ms. Henry has experience advising clients under a number of environmental regulations, including the Clean Air Act; the Clean Water Act; and the Comprehensive Environmental Response, Compensation, and Liability Act. Ms. Henry also has experience representing clients in connection with litigation related to onshore and offshore oil and gas operations, as well as toxic tort litigation.

Andrew Johnson is an Associate in the San Francisco office of Arnold & Porter. Mr. Johnson represents public and private companies, officers, and individuals in connection with SEC enforcement actions, securities and stockholder class actions, and complex litigation matters. Prior to his legal career, Mr. Johnson was a Senior Assurance Associate for KPMG LLP, where he primarily focused on financial statement audits of Fortune 500 companies. Mr. Johnson graduated cum laude from the University of California, Hastings College of the Law.

Kardia Leung is a corporate lawyer in the London office of Arnold & Porter. She advises on a wide range of corporate and commercial matters and has represented a number of high-profile clients, including governmental authorities and some of the world's most sophisticated biotechnology and pharmaceutical companies.

Arthur Luk is a Partner at Arnold & Porter, resident in the firm's Washington, DC, office. He represents corporations, directors, officers, executives, and Big 4 accounting firms and individual auditors in investigations conducted by the U.S. Department of Justice, SEC, and Public Company Accounting Oversight Board. Mr. Luk has extensive experience with securities class actions, shareholder derivative suits, and complex commercial litigation in federal and state courts, including insurance coverage disputes and putative class actions arising out of data breaches.

Jonathan S. Martel is a Partner in the Washington, DC, office of Arnold & Porter, where his practice focuses on environmental law, with particular expertise in air quality, climate change, and energy transition matters. He represents clients in regulatory and compliance counseling, participation in agency rulemaking activities, government and citizen enforcement actions, appellate litigation involving challenges to rules, and other litigation matters. He writes and speaks frequently on environmental, air quality, and climate change issues. He served for several years in the Office of General Counsel at the U.S. Environmental Protection Agency, taught at Georgetown Law Center, and served for many years on the Air Quality Committee of the ABA Section of Environment, Energy, and Resources.

Adam Masurovsky is an Associate in Arnold & Porter's Washington, DC, office. Mr. Masurovsky's practice focuses on environmental litigation, regulatory, and compliance matters, as well as international arbitration. Mr. Masurovsky graduated with high honors from The George Washington University Law School in 2020. Prior to law school, Mr. Masurovsky worked for an international conservation and development nongovernmental organization implementing programs throughout eastern and southern Africa.

Jennifer McLellan formerly practiced corporate law in the New York office of Arnold & Porter focusing on a variety of complex business transactions, with an emphasis on cross-border and domestic mergers and acquisitions, and private equity investments and divestments and also advising companies on a wide variety of governance and day-to-day general corporate matters. Ms. McLellan received her JD from the University of Denver Sturm College of Law, where she served as an editor of the *Law Review* and a contributor to The Race to the Bottom Blog.

Paul Nabhan is a Corporate and Finance Associate with Arnold & Porter in New York, New York, primarily focusing on capital markets and structured finance transactions and public company compliance matters. Mr. Nabhan is also a certified public accountant and has previously advised clients on technical accounting matters involving financial instruments, valuation, and standards implementation.

Lazarinka Naydenova is a Senior Associate in the Brussels office of Arnold & Porter. Her practice focuses on all aspects of EU competition law, with particular emphasis on merger control cartels and cooperation agreements. She worked the ex-U.S. processes for Monsanto in its $66 billion acquisition by Bayer, a transaction that won the 2019 GCR Awards for "Global Antitrust Matter of the Year" and "Merger Control Matter of the Year–Europe," and for Fitbit in its acquisition by Google, which won the 2021 edition of the same award. She also represented a client in a dawn raid conducted by the European Commission in relation to an alleged violation of the antitrust rules.

Jane Norberg is a Partner in Arnold & Porter's Washington, DC, office. Ms. Norberg represents public and private companies, financial institutions, individuals, and investment advisors on sensitive whistleblower and other complex matters, including internal and government investigations; response to and defense of specific whistleblower allegations; securities enforcement and white collar defense; whistleblower retaliation claims defense; proactive assessment and structuring of internal compliance mechanisms, policies, and procedures; training boards of directors, management, and workforces on internal reporting and retaliation; and crisis management counseling to mitigate reputational risk. Ms. Norberg also conducts sexual harassment and other sensitive investigations, and educates boards of directors and executives about emerging whistleblower programs such as the Anti-Money Laundering Act whistleblower program and the National Highway Traffic and Safety Administration automotive whistleblower program. Prior to joining Arnold & Porter, Ms. Norberg was Chief of the Office of the Whistleblower at the SEC, where she helped develop and lead the SEC's whistleblower program since near its inception. Under her leadership, the Office's staff expanded and achieved record-breaking growth in both the number of whistleblower tips received and awards issued to whistleblowers under the program. Ms. Norberg has extensive experience and knowledge regarding whistleblower retaliation and is the leading expert on agreements that impede reporting in violation of Exchange Act Rule 21F-17, having directly advised on all whistleblower protection cases brought by the SEC during her tenure. She advised senior SEC leadership on emerging whistleblower issues and policies, as well as reported to Congress regarding the program's activities. Ms. Norberg also had a substantial advisory role related to the amendments to the SEC's whistleblower rules and has advised other domestic and international regulators related to the development of new whistleblower programs. While at the SEC, Ms. Norberg also co-led a diversity and inclusion initiative across the Division of Enforcement.

Nicholas O'Keefe is a Partner in Arnold & Porter's Silicon Valley office. Mr. O'Keefe has more than 25 years of corporate law and M&A experience, with an emphasis on buy-side and sell-side work and takeover defense, including domestic and cross-border deals. His clients include strategics, private equity funds, sovereign wealth funds, and financial advisors. His completed deals range in value from a few million dollars to several billion dollars. Mr. O'Keefe also advises emerging growth and mature issuer clients with respect to general corporate work, corporate governance matters, federal and state securities law matters, and securities transactions. Mr. O'Keefe also has a deep understanding of emerging markets, having spent three years working in the Middle East. His practice in the Middle East included regional and cross-border deals involving Middle East private equity funds, sovereign wealth funds, and regional and U.S. issuers investing in the Middle East.

Erin Grubbs Peña is a former Associate in the Washington, DC, office of Arnold & Porter. She focused on environmental regulatory and compliance counseling. She currently works as environmental and safety legal counsel at Shell USA, Inc.

Jocelyn Porter is an Associate in the Washington, DC, office of Arnold & Porter, where she focuses on general litigation matters along with providing analysis of state legislation. She received her JD from the Indiana University Maurer School of Law in 2021. Before joining Arnold & Porter, she served as a law clerk for the U.S. Court of Appeals for the Seventh Circuit.

William C. Perdue is a Partner in the Appellate and Supreme Court practice group at Arnold & Porter in Washington, DC. He represents clients in a wide variety of industries in appellate and trial-court matters involving novel and complex questions of law. Mr. Perdue litigates cases relating to administrative law, intellectual property, environmental regulation, pharmaceutical regulation, product liability, bankruptcy, government contracts, and the First Amendment. Mr. Perdue also has extensive experience in insurance litigation, including insurance coverage litigation that can implicate ESG issues.

Francesca Pisano is a Senior Associate at Arnold & Porter. She advises clients on a wide range of antitrust issues, including cartel investigations, civil antitrust litigation, and merger and acquisition reviews. In particular, she has represented clients in all phases of merger clearance, before the U.S. Department of Justice and Federal Trade Commission, as well as before federal courts in litigated challenges by the government. Ms. Pisano also provides day-to-day antitrust counseling on a range of issues, including designing effective compliance programs and advising on the intersection of antitrust and ESG initiatives.

Karen Rigberg is of Counsel in Nelson Mullins Riley & Scarborough's Los Angeles office. She represents clients in a variety of strategic business, risk management, and compliance initiatives. Having spent almost 20 years in-house at one of the world's largest automotive companies, she understands that reducing antitrust risk often relies on implementing effective compliance measures within non-lawyer business teams. Her practice includes helping large and small companies comply with antitrust laws and quick and cost-effective use of simple technologies to deploy and maintain the essential elements of a tailored antitrust compliance program, including policies and procedures, resource documents, trainings, governance, monitoring, and assessments. In addition, she maintains a growing library of interactive micro-learning modules that can be quickly customized and periodically delivered to specific employees or project teams, including those working on ESG initiatives.

Sandra Rizzo is a Senior Counsel in the Washington, DC, office of Arnold & Porter. She has represented utility clients such as power generators and transmission owners with regard to energy market and regulatory matters for the majority of her 30-year-plus legal career, primarily before the Federal Energy Regulatory Commission. She has been rated by Chambers and Legal 500 for her work on behalf of energy clients.

Kaitlin Robinson is a Complex Litigation Associate at Arnold & Porter in San Francisco. Her areas of focus are labor and employment and professional responsibility. She also maintains a robust pro bono practice, with an emphasis on reproductive rights. Ms. Robinson received her JD from UC Hastings College of the Law where she served as the executive managing editor of the *Hastings Business Law Journal*. From 2018 to 2019, Ms. Robinson served as a law clerk to the Honorable Laurel Beeler in the U.S. District Court for the Northern District of California.

Tim Roche is an Associate at Arnold & Porter. Mr. Roche's practice focuses on assisting clients in complex civil antitrust litigation, government review of mergers and acquisitions and filing obligations under the Hart-Scott-Rodino Act, as well as counseling clients in relation to antitrust issues before the Federal Trade Commission. Mr. Roche has represented clients in a variety of industries, including health care, pharmaceuticals, oil and gas, and retail.

Michele J. Rowland is a Partner in the Denver office of Arnold & Porter. Ms. Rowland represents clients in mergers, stock and asset purchases, divestitures, minority investments, carve-outs, leveraged buyouts, and joint ventures, and provides corporate counseling to companies and boards of directors. She also represents clients in the structuring, negotiation, and documentation of a broad range of commercial lending transactions, including asset-based loans, working capital facilities, and acquisition financing.

Christian Schultz, a Partner in Arnold & Porter's Washington, DC, office, is the former Assistant Chief Litigation Counsel in the SEC's Division of Enforcement. Mr. Schultz represents public and private companies, financial institutions and accounting firms, and individuals in regulatory investigations, complex financial and securities litigation, SEC and the Public Company Accounting Oversight Board enforcement actions, and white-collar matters. In his 10 years at the SEC, Mr. Schultz investigated potential violations of the federal securities laws and represented the SEC in enforcement actions in federal court and administrative proceedings. He partnered with attorneys, accountants, and industry experts in the SEC's special investigative units—including the Complex Financial Instruments Unit, Market Abuse Unit, and Asset Management Unit—to investigate and litigate potential violations of the securities laws in a broad range of areas, including accounting and issuer disclosure, auditor independence, market manipulation, broker-dealer and investment advisor regulations, compliance failures, insider trading, failure to supervise, complex financial instruments and structured financial products, cryptocurrency and digital asset regulation, and whistleblowing. Mr. Schultz received his JD from the University of Notre Dame Law School, summa cum laude, where he was awarded the 2001 Farabaugh Prize for High Scholarship in Law and served as Executive Note Editor of the *Notre Dame Law Review*. He received his MBA, magna cum laude, from the University of Notre Dame Mendoza School of Business and two BAs, each with honor, from Michigan State University.

Ethan G. Shenkman is a Partner in the Environmental practice group of Arnold & Porter. He is well-known for his work on air quality, climate change policy, and greenhouse gas regulation; counseling clients on issues relating to biofuels, carbon capture and sequestration, methane regulation, and clean energy technologies, as well as National Environmental Policy Act and climate-related litigation. He previously served as Deputy General Counsel at the U.S. Environmental Protection Agency and, prior to that, as Deputy Assistant Attorney General at the U.S. Department of Justice's Environment and Natural Resources Division. Mr. Shenkman is Chambers ranked and an adjunct professor of environmental law at Georgetown.

David Skillman is a Managing Director at Arnold & Porter, where he advises firms on the development of federal law and legislation at the nexus of tax and trade, particularly with regard to areas of key national interest, such as semiconductors, intellectual property, critical minerals, and clean energy. He served for more than a decade as Counsel to a senior member of the Committee on Ways and Means.

Ebony Slaughter-Johnson is an Associate in the Legislative practice group at Arnold & Porter. She is a graduate of Princeton University and Harvard Law School. She is the co-author of several reports produced by the Institute for Policy Studies and contributed to the research, writing, and editing of *The D.C. Reentry Navigator: Empowering You to Succeed with a D.C. Criminal Record*, published by the Public Defender Service for the District of Columbia.

Erik C. Walsh is Counsel in the New York office of Arnold & Porter, where he is a member of the Financial Services group. Mr. Walsh represents financial institutions in enforcement, compliance, and regulatory matters before the federal and state banking agencies, U.S. Department of Justice, and the Office of Foreign Assets Control (OFAC). He regularly represents domestic and foreign institutions in government and internal investigations, particularly in matters involving Bank Secrecy Act/Anti-Money Laundering (BSA/AML) compliance, OFAC sanctions compliance, and bank fraud. Mr. Walsh regularly advises clients on BSA/AML and OFAC policies and procedures; ESG risk management matters; cannabis-related banking issues; and bank examination preparation and remediation. He also has a background in litigation on behalf of a wide variety of clients. Mr. Walsh is a former Senior Counsel in the Enforcement Division of the Federal Reserve Bank of New York.

Sasha Zheng is a Senior Associate in Arnold & Porter's Securities Enforcement & Litigation group, focusing her practice on white-collar inquiries and investigations, securities and stockholder class actions, and corporate governance disputes. She received her JD from Columbia Law School in 2016, where she served as an articles editor for the *Columbia Law Review*.

Foreword

Any movement that powerfully impacts political, regulatory, and economic policy; capital markets; and corporate governance—all at the same time—can fairly be regarded as seismic. If any multinational development merits that characterization, it would be the movement described as "Environmental, Social, and Governance," acronymically shortened to "ESG."

Over the past decade, ESG has evolved and continues to expand in many different spheres and dimensions of endeavor and also at multiple governmental levels. Achieving ESG's goals will require and involve profound changes, nationally and worldwide, in the political, social, and economic spheres. Because the stakes are so phenomenally high, not surprisingly ESG has become a highly controversial hotbed. The issues that ESG implicates transcend purely abstract economic and policy debates conducted at the 30,000-foot level. ESG's focus and most profound impact will be at the ground level, more specifically upon national and international legal, investment, and economic communities. But the controversies now go far beyond that. They have migrated to the political sphere in hitherto unimaginable ways. To cite a few recent examples, certain state officials have advanced proposals to alter public school educational curricula to prohibit classroom teachers from including certain subjects falling within the ESG framework; state legislative proposals that would prohibit state officials from considering ESG when deciding how governmental pension and other public funds should be invested; and a legislative proposal in Congress that would prohibit ESG from being considered when deciding what capital market investments to make. Migrating even further out, the ESG controversy threatens to become an issue in partisan campaigns to win a political party nomination for the U.S. presidency in the forthcoming 2024 election.

Given this highly contentious and unpredictable environment, it is not surprising that considerable ink about ESG continues to be spilled by highly credentialed commentators in all three of ESG's acronymic spheres. Despite the plethora of opinions and viewpoints about this complex subject, one central reality makes it easier for policymakers and practitioners to grasp. The critical perspective to keep in mind is that the entities most immediately impacted by these expansive ESG developments are corporate and other business enterprises, both private and public. Those enterprises will require, on an ongoing basis, sound legal advice and guidance about how best to respond to this rapidly evolving ESG regulatory regime. At the ground level—where the rubber meets the road—the institution best situated to respond to that need is the legal profession.

Viewed from that perspective, of the cascading flow of legal publications addressing ESG, at the end of the day, only a few will stand out. Prominent within that select category will be the ABA publication entitled *Environmental, Social, Governance: The Professional's Guide to the Law and Practice of ESG* (ABA 2023), by Brian D. Israel, Ellen Kaye Fleishhacker, and Teresa L. Johnson. The authors are partners who specialize in ESG in one of the nation's preeminent law firms. Although their book will helpfully inform policymakers and regulators, its primary intended audience consists of practicing attorneys who specialize in the ESG field. For that specific group, this book (I submit) should be required reading.

My reasons for holding that view must be preceded by a disclaimer. I am not, nor do I claim to be, an expert in the broad domain of topics that encompass ESG. My expertise is primarily in the "G" (governance) sphere and was derived from three decades of judicial service, first on the Delaware Court of Chancery and thereafter on the Delaware Supreme Court. Both courts are authoritative expositors of Delaware law that governs disputed issues of corporate and business enterprise governance. That bears importantly on the governance element of ESG, because Delaware is, and for over a century has been, the state of incorporation of a majority of our country's largest publicly held business enterprises. As a consequence, Delaware law has become the nation's most well-developed body of business enterprise governance jurisprudence, and in that area provides guidance to corporate law practitioners throughout the nation. In hundreds of enterprise governance cases in which I ruled as a judge, a central bedrock issue was whether under the business judgment standard of judicial review the company's decision-making fiduciaries (the Board and management), properly exercised their lawful statutory power. That issue frontally implicates the "G" component of ESG. A fundamental thesis espoused by authors Israel, Fleishhacker, and Johnson is that "the business judgment rule provides the theoretical and legal authority for business leaders to implement environmental and social policies, provided these policies can be articulated as valuable to the long-term interests of the corporation."

I now turn to why I believe that over both the short and long run, the book will withstand the test of time and become a prominent work in the ESG field. Although many qualities of this work support that opinion, I limit myself to three.

First, the book does what any good legal writing should do: it transmutes an awesomely complex subject into a story more easily readable and understandable. The authors achieve that by explaining how each element of ESG historically came to be, and thereafter elucidating at the more theoretical level each element's conceptual underpinnings. Readers who are academicians, policymakers, regulators, and practitioners will readily perceive that the book contributes both a solid conceptual foundation for understanding the many interrelated aspects of the ESG movement and a framework for analyzing its potential real-world impacts.

Second, the book explains and elucidates, with remarkable depth and breadth, the wide array of disparate subjects that ESG encompasses. Depth-wise, the book is a legal practitioner's dream, as it contributes highly detailed and nuanced practical advice on the law governing issues ranging from climate change, to animal rights, to diversity, equity, and inclusion, to worker-employee well-being. As for breadth, the book exposes the reader to the detailed ESG legal roadmap, not only within the United States but also in the United Kingdom and the European Union. Moreover, the authors do not shy away from controversial issues that include (to name only a few) environmental justice, voting rights, and economic rights. But the authors accomplish that in a manner designed to enlighten the reader about all sides of any issue, yet also avoids advocating any specific contested viewpoint.

Third, most notable is the book's well-organized internal structure, which is designed to provide practitioners what they most need—a practical approach. The introductory chapter describes the origin and nature of the ESG movement and previews its inherent and varied policy and political controversies. The opening section includes other crosscutting issues, such as the ESG political backlash and the nature of ESG stakeholders. The book next devotes a separate section (serially) to each separate E, S, and G element. Finally, the book ends with a section devoted to the role of the lawyer, where the focus again turns to critical cross-cutting issues such as (for example) organizing internal investigations, conducting ESG due diligence, and the interplay of ESG and antitrust law. The critical message is that these topics should not be regarded as disparate silos that stand alone in a vacuum. Of perhaps greatest importance for practitioners called upon to give practical advice to clients, most chapters conclude with "Key Takeaways." Thus, regardless of the ESG topic, the book provides the reader-practitioner practical suggestions for advising clients how best to navigate the Scylla and Charybdis of ESG's shoals and pitfalls.

In short, the book is comprehensive, well-organized, insightful, and practical. I commend it to anyone charged with confronting ESG issues in their business organization and to practitioners in search of the tools needed to navigating what may be the most challenging business organizational governance issues encountered in our times.

Jack B. Jacobs
Senior Counsel, Young Conaway Stargatt & Taylor
Former Justice, Delaware Supreme Court (2003–2014)

Preface

Stakeholders and Shareholders: ESG Is Not New

While the phrase Environmental, Social, and Governance (ESG) is everywhere, the actual meaning of this term is somewhat elusive, and increasingly controversial. For some, ESG may be about giving primacy to stakeholders (e.g., employees, communities, the environment) over shareholders. Others argue that ESG at its core is not about prioritizing stakeholders *above* shareholders, but rather acknowledging that the corporate entity has many responsibilities *in addition to* its responsibility to its investors and owners.

Even more elusive is the significance of ESG. On one side of the spectrum, ESG is critical to the future of sustainable and strong capitalism. On the other side of the spectrum, ESG signals a distortion of capitalism, or democracy, or both. To some, ESG is about creating long-term value for the corporate entity, including investors. To others—by allegedly placing "values" over "value"—ESG violates the principle behind the original grant of legal status to the corporation.

Our view is that while most companies seek to maximize profits, *all* companies express values, whether or not they use the terms ESG, or sustainability, or diversity and inclusion, or many other terms. Moreover, this is nothing new. Seeing ESG in so many recent headlines suggests that it is a new issue, but that is, in large degree, a question of nomenclature—the term "ESG" may be fairly new, but there is a long history of companies taking values broadly into account.

During World War II, for instance, expenditures for advertisements in the United States increased substantially with many ads broadcasting companies' efforts to support the war effort.[1] From Cadillacs to chemicals to cigarettes, corporations during World War II sought to identify their brand with the larger communal needs of the time, even at the expense of short-term profits.[2] Here's just one example: the Parker Pen Company

[1] The Advertising Age Encyclopedia of Advertising 776 (John McDonough & Karen Egolf, eds., 2003).

[2] Ben Cosgrove, *Fighting Words: Long-winded (and Stunning) Wartime Magazine Ads*, Time (May 19, 2014), https://time.com/99290/fighting-words-magazine-ads-during-world-war-ii/.

advertised in 1944, that "To speed wartime work . . . this is the first duty of the Parker '51'."[3] The ad goes on to say: "Long before Pearl Harbor, Parker *voluntarily* cut its production of fine pens. Today much of our skill and experience is devoted to creating precision fuzes for bombs. . . ."

In this way, today's focus on ESG is merely a current manifestation of a phenomenon that has existed since the beginning of the corporate form, operating within a large community context. ESG is about how companies try to address the risks and opportunities that exist today—from environmental concerns, to employee well-being, to critical social issues of importance, to the communities within which companies operate. And since many of these underlying issues are themselves controversial, how a company addresses these issues may also give rise to controversy.

Navigating Narrow Shoals

Collectively, we, and the other authors of this book, have years of experience advising companies on ESG-related topics. Whether in the boardroom or the courtroom, every day we see companies working hard to formulate, implement, and communicate ESG-related policies in a manner that is effective and protective.

Our goal in this book is to help companies (and the lawyers who advise them) understand the legal/practical considerations related to many ESG issues. And given the highly political and controversial nature of many ESG topics, we also seek to help companies navigate the narrow shoals that are sometimes created (often unnecessarily) by the juxtaposition of shareholders and stakeholders. Companies and their advisors may feel like they are between the proverbial rock and a hard place in trying to address competing agendas advocated by the proponents and opponents of ESG. We offer guidance as to how to weigh those considerations and plot a course consistent with the company's values and strategy.

Our practitioners' guide is organized into five sections:

Part I: ESG Is Here to Stay

In the opening section, we focus on several bigger-picture topics. Chapter 1 provides a brief history of the legal underpinning of stakeholder capitalism, finding that courts have been deferring to corporate values for well over 100 years, although not without limits. Chapter 2, using case studies, identifies categories of stakeholders impacted by ESG-related issues. Chapter 3 is all about the ESG backlash. Specifically, Chapter 3 explores the significant and growing criticism of different aspects of ESG, from both public and private actors, including litigation, legislation, and policy advocacy. Chapter 4 looks to ESG requirements in both the United Kingdom and the European Union, including as a predictor of where the United States may be heading. With this overview, our guide then turns to the specifics of E, S, and G.

[3] *Id.* (emphasis added).

Part II: Environmental: Understanding Risks and Opportunities around Climate and Other Issues

Our opening chapter in this section (Chapter 5) sets the stage by identifying key principles related to climate risk and management. Specifically, this chapter explores various types of climate-related risk to which a company may be subject (physical, transitional, reputational) as well as defining key types of greenhouse gas emissions (Scope 1, Scope 2, and Scope 3) and sector-specific concepts. Chapter 6 provides an overview of climate-related disclosure obligations at the federal and international level. Chapter 7 addresses eight key considerations when setting greenhouse gas emissions targets, ranging from scope, to verification, to offsets. Chapter 8 explores other environmental topics beyond climate change, including biodiversity, animal welfare, plastics, and water. Finally, Chapter 9 provides practical advice for those seeking to communicate about their environmental goals or accomplishments, including an overview of both U.S. and international laws related to green marketing.

Part III: Social: Finding a Path for Complex Social Issues

Our first chapter in this section (Chapter 10) discusses the concept of Diversity, Equity, and Inclusion (DE&I) for companies as well as both the business case for DE&I and the legal and political challenges associated with DE&I initiatives. Chapter 11 explains the concepts of workforce well-being, including the principles of Human Capital Management, disclosure, compensation, benefits, and health. Chapter 12 once again looks to the international stage and provides an overview of the wide-ranging Guidelines for Multinational Enterprises published by the Organisation for Economic Co-operation and Development; these guidelines address a variety of ESG-related topics from human rights to anti-corruption. Chapter 13 provides a practical framework for companies dealing with highly politicized social issues ranging from reproductive rights to LBGTQ+ rights to voting rights. Finally, Chapter 14 explores, at a high level, the issue of environmental justice that overlaps both environmental and social concerns.

Part IV: Governance: Practical Advice for Getting Governance Right

Our first chapter in this section (Chapter 15) provides both legal and practical guidance for the role of the board, including managing ESG-related risks and opportunities, and dealing with a variety of constituents. Chapter 16 discusses management's role in an effective corporate governance framework, with a focus on good governance considerations surrounding a company's evaluation and decision-making about environmental and social issues. Chapter 17 drills down into the emerging tools of ESG management systems, helping a company to track progress towards a company's strategic ESG-related goals. Chapter 18 provides a governance perspective on responding to shareholder initiatives, including a discussion of both legal and practical considerations.

Part V: The Role of the Lawyer: Helping Companies Navigate Uncharted Waters

Our final section addresses wide-ranging legal issues from ESG due diligence, to antitrust, to internal investigations. Our first chapter in this section (Chapter 19) provides a practical overview of ESG considerations in corporate transactions, including due diligence. Chapter 20 turns to internal investigations related to alleged ESG-related misconduct and suggests best practices in setting up investigations as well as responding to whistleblowers. Chapter 21 provides an overview of the fast-moving world of ESG legislative and regulatory activity, from hearings to rulemakings. Chapter 22 turns to ESG investment funds and provides legal best practices for a host of ESG investment fund topics, from marketing, to disclosures, to measurement. Chapter 23 addresses public disclosure of ESG-related issues principally focused on U.S. Securities and Exchange Commission (SEC) requirements. And finally, Chapter 24 addresses the antitrust implications of ESG, including guidance for working with other companies on ESG-related initiatives.

In Conclusion

The core problem with publishing a book about ESG is the dynamic, rapidly changing context of ESG—new developments are happening every day, and keeping up with the latest ESG news can be a full-time job. In all likelihood, this year will see the promulgation of numerous ESG-related regulations (particularly with regard to SEC disclosure and green marketing), increased ESG-related litigation, and further politicization of ESG topics. Knowing how fast-paced the ESG world is today, our aim is to provide practitioners with a multifaceted set of navigational tools designed to be helpful in charting a course through these interesting, challenging, and ever-changing waters.

PART I

ESG Is Here to Stay

1

Leaving the Lights Off: A Short History of the Legal Issues Related to ESG

Brian D. Israel, Ellen Kaye Fleishhacker, and Teresa L. Johnson

I. Part I

Ernie Banks is among the most celebrated players in the history of the Chicago Cubs baseball team. Not only was he the first Black player on the team, but in his 19 years with the Cubs, he was a power hitter as well as a skilled defensive player, first at shortstop and later at first base.[1] In 2008, while reminiscing about his legendary career, he noted that he had never played a single home game at night.[2] "I played all my home games under one light: God's light," he said. The reason for this was simple: Ernie Banks retired from baseball in 1971, a full 17 years before the iconic home of the Chicago Cubs—Wrigley Field—installed artificial lighting. The story of how Wrigley Field came to be the last Major League Baseball park to install artificial lights is also important for framing the legal and practical considerations related to Environmental, Social, and Governance (ESG).

William Shlensky was a lawyer from Chicago. In 1966, he was 27—just beginning his career as an attorney. He was also a serious Cubs fan. He had held stock in the team since he was a child; Shlensky's father had given him two shares of the Chicago Cubs as a gift. As a fan and a shareholder, Shlensky wanted more for his team than to be known as the

[1] *Ernie Banks*, Britannica, https://www.britannica.com/biography/Ernie-Banks (last edited Jan. 27, 2022).

[2] *The Lights of Wrigleyville*, 30 for 30 Podcasts, https://30for30podcasts.com/episodes/the-lights-of-wrigleyville/ (last visited Nov. 17, 2022).

"lovable losers" of the majors. Shlensky wanted the Cubs to win, and he wanted the Cubs to make money. To him (and probably most market observers in the late 1960s) the solution was clear: install lights at Wrigley Field and break the 52-year tradition of the Cubs only playing day games. Wrigley Field had been the only major league ballpark without lights since 1948.[3] As a shareholder attempting to impact corporate behavior, on March 14, 1966, Shlensky sued the directors of the Chicago Cubs corporation for negligence and mismanagement.

At the time, the largest shareholder and president of the Cubs corporation was Philip K. Wrigley, a larger-than-life baseball legend who inherited his father's chewing gum business in 1932. While Mr. Wrigley was a romantic and a purist at heart, he was also fiercely independent and strong-minded. Due to his love of the game and his view of the "club and the park . . . as memorials to [his] father,"[4] Wrigley was determined to protect a unique identity for the Chicago Cubs. Wrigley believed fervently that baseball was an "outdoor, daylight game, where you went out and bought a bag of popcorn and absorbed fresh air and sunshine."[5]

Wrigley was determined to turn this principle into a successful business model. Through the mid-twentieth century, Wrigley sold admission to Cubs games not on the quality of "the beautiful game" to be played but rather on the experience one had in "Beautiful Wrigley Field." "Our idea in advertising the game, and the fun, and the healthfulness of it, the sunshine and the relaxation, is to get the public to see ball games, win or lose," Wrigley said of his marketing strategy.[6] For a while, that worked.

Many older Chicagoans reminisce fondly on the results of Wrigley's insistence on only hosting day games. Harry Caray, famed Cubs announcer, said of the practice, "Ya know, day baseball is a way of life in Chicago. Mom can put Becky and Junior on the L to see a game and have them home before dark."[7] Mike Quigley, a congressman from the 5th District of Illinois, was one of those kids who lived it up in the "good old days."

> Day baseball during the week meant a lot of kids at the ballpark. You could hear them, sort of little-league-type chants: "Hey batter, hey batter. Let's go, Cubbies." I was Junior. I would take the train. I had to make a switchover, but I knew exactly what I had to do. My parents felt that it was safe for me to go. I mean, fourth, fifth, sixth, seventh grade. That's extraordinary. . . . I think there's a different reaction at night.[8]

---

[3] Tim Wiles, *Night Games Gave Access to Baseball to Millions*, NAT'L BASEBALL HALL OF FAME, https://baseballhall.org/discover/night-games-gave-access-to-baseball-to-millions (last visited Oct. 3, 2022).

[4] Andrew Steele, *Philip Wrigley*, SOC'Y FOR AM. BASEBALL RSCH., https://sabr.org/bioproj/person/philip-wrigley/ (last visited Nov. 17, 2022).

[5] *Wrigley Field Lights Chronology*, CHICAGOLOGY, https://chicagology.com/baseball/wrigleylights/ (last visited Nov. 17, 2022).

[6] Steele, *supra* note 4.

[7] *The Lights of Wrigleyville*, *supra* note 2.

[8] *Id.*

As a direct consequence of Mr. Wrigley's decision only to host day games at Wrigley Field, the residents of Wrigleyville enjoyed a nighttime peace that most neighbors of stadiums across the world could only dream of. Rush hour traffic wasn't worsened by thousands of fans commuting to the stadium to see a game. Homeowners of Wrigleyville weren't kept awake by the noise of a screaming crowd. And, of course, the residents of Wrigleyville never had to worry about being kept awake by bright stadium lights. Wrigley himself noted in 1955, "It's a matter of public responsibility. How can anybody sleep with a loudspeaker going, thousands of people hollering, and cars being parked all over their yards? All you need is a louse like me to put in lights and it would wreck things!"[9]

But William Shlensky did not see the theoretical community benefits of Wrigley's decisions as outweighing the private costs to his beloved team. "The directors have a responsibility for producing the most income for the shareholders," Shlensky said later in his life of his motivation to sue Wrigley.[10] Of course, this concept of maximizing shareholder value as the purpose of the corporation is not unfamiliar. The principle was perhaps most famously articulated by another legend from (the University of) Chicago, Milton Friedman. He wrote that corporate executives' responsibility was to conduct a business in accordance with the desires of the corporation's shareholders, "which generally will be to make as much money as possible while conforming to the basic rules of the society."[11]

In his complaint to the Circuit Court of Cook County, Shlensky alleged that Wrigley and the other directors of the Cubs were acting contrary to their responsibility to the shareholders. Shlensky claimed that Wrigley and the other directors were "not motivated by a good faith concern as to the best interests of [the] corporation, but solely" by serving Wrigley's "personal opinions that baseball is a daytime sport and night baseball games will have a deteriorating effect on the surrounding neighborhood."[12]

Shlensky built a strong case that the day-game-only policy was costing the Cubs higher earnings. He cited numerous facts supporting this assertion in his complaint. For example, he noted that the Cubs were the only team in the league that had not yet installed lights for the purposes of increasing attendance and revenue. He demonstrated that Cubs games were better attended when the team was playing on the road at night. Shlensky also compared the Cubs to the White Sox—a team playing the same sport in the same city with about the same weekend daytime attendance. The White Sox had far better weekday attendance when they played at night.

But in the eyes of the courts, none of that amounted to a cause of action. Courts had opined that fraud, illegality, or a conflict of interest were the "only bases for a stockholder's derivative action against . . . directors."[13] After the trial court dismissed his case, Shlensky

[9] *Id.*

[10] Scott Tong, *How a Baseball Lawsuit Helped Define How Corporations Are Governed*, Marketplace (June 16, 2016), https://www.marketplace.org/2016/06/16/profit-wrigley/.

[11] Milton Friedman, *The Social Responsibility of Business Is to Increase Its Profits*, N.Y. Times, Sept. 13, 1970, § 6 (Magazine), at 32, 33.

[12] Shlensky v. Wrigley, 95 Ill.App.2d 173, 176–77 (Ill. App. Ct. 1968).

[13] *Id.* at 177.

argued to the appellate court that his allegations were "sufficient to set forth a cause of action under the principles set out in *Dodge v. Ford Motor Company*, 204 Mich. 459 (Mich. 1919)." In that case, as recounted by the Illinois Appellate Court, Ford's motives for expansion of the business were found to have been to "benefit the public generally and spread the profits out by means of more jobs," which was "not only far from related to the good of the stockholders, but amounted to a change in the ends of the corporation and that this was not a purpose contemplated or allowed by the corporate charter."[14]

In Wrigley's case, however, the Illinois Appellate Court was "not satisfied that the motives assigned to Philip K. Wrigley, and through him to the other directors, [were] contrary to the best interests of the corporation and the stockholders." Instead of adopting Shlensky's theory that keeping lights out of Wrigley Field was an inappropriately benevolent use of Wrigley's operational discretion, the court found Wrigley's actions to be soundly motivated by business judgment.

> [I]t appears to us that the effect on the surrounding neighborhood might well be considered by a director who was considering the patrons who would or would not attend the games if the park were in a poor neighborhood. Furthermore, the long run interest of the corporation in its property value at Wrigley Field might demand all efforts to keep the neighborhood from deteriorating. By these thoughts we do not mean to say that we have decided that the decision of the directors was a correct one. That is beyond our jurisdiction and ability. We are merely saying that the decision is one properly before directors and the motives alleged in the amended complaint showed no fraud, illegality or conflict of interest in their making of that decision.[15]

In the eyes of the court, the well-being of the residents of Wrigleyville was a perfectly valid consideration—not necessarily for the residents' sake, but for the sake of the Cubs brand, which might be damaged by disruption of the neighborhood. The residents of Wrigleyville were all potential Cubs customers; it was only natural that Wrigley and the other directors took into account the residents' perception of the team, as acting contrary to the neighbors' interests might well have damaged the team's interests in the long run. It is this possibility that a director's decision, though sacrificing profits in the short run, might have a long-term positive impact on the corporation that prevented the court in *Wrigley* from ruling in favor of Shlensky.[16]

As discussed below, this concept of deference to directors' reasonable decision-making—sometimes called the business judgment rule—gives directors and executives significant

---

[14] *Id.* at 179.

[15] *Id.* at 180–81.

[16] *Id.* at 183. The court was also unimpressed with the allegations that Wrigley's judgment was contradicted by the views of every other Major League Baseball team. In the eyes of the court, a mere failure to "follow the crowd" is not a dereliction of the duty of the director. Moreover, the court stated that "[d]irectors are elected for their business capabilities and judgment and the courts cannot require them to forego their judgment because of the decisions of directors of other companies."

power to determine the short- and long-term best interests of the corporation. Importantly, the business judgment rule provides the theoretical and legal authority for business leaders to implement environmental and social policies, provided these policies can be articulated as valuable to the long-term interests of the corporation.

The Cubs Epilogue: On August 8, 1988, more than 10 years after Philip Wrigley died, Harry Grossman, a 91-year-old die-hard Cubs fan, turned on the lights at Wrigley Field for the first time ever. Pressing a large red button, Grossman said, "A one . . . a two . . . a three . . . let there be light!" In 2016, from his retirement home in Texas, William Shlensky reflected: "I guess the fact that they finally got lights—my case turned out to be a winner."[17]

II. Part II

The Wrigley Field case is part of a long line of cases—including U.S. Supreme Court decisions—that support corporate directors' discretion to take actions in the public interest even when doing so may sacrifice short-term profits for shareholders.[18] Today, most jurisprudence and commentary on corporate governance focuses on post-1970 Delaware cases (after publication of the seminal Milton Friedman article on shareholder capitalism), but many of the concepts on which stakeholder capitalism are based arose well before that. In *Hawes v. Oakland*, the U.S. Supreme Court reviewed a decision by the directors of the Contra Costa Waterworks Company to give away the corporation's water to the City of Oakland for municipal uses, such as watering parks and flushing sewers. Alleging that the City was only entitled to "receive water free of charge in cases of fire or other great necessity," the plaintiff, on behalf of himself and other stockholders, brought suit against the directors for the "diminution of the dividends which should come to him and other stockholders, and . . . the decrease in the value of their stock" that he alleged was the direct result of the corporation's gift to the City.[19] The directors did not answer the complaint; instead, the City of Oakland, as co-defendant, filed a demurrer, and the ensuing legal contest thus occurred between the plaintiff and the City acting on behalf of itself and the corporation.

The City of Oakland, supporting the directors' decision to allow the City to use its water free of charge for municipal purposes, described the history of the corporation's relationship with the City. The City had, by special ordinance, allowed Contra Costa the exclusive right to use the City's streets to lay pipes and furnish water to the "whole population" of the City.[20] The Court explained in its opinion that, within the company's charter, "there is nothing which forbids the corporation from dealing with the city in the manner it has done," that is conferring reciprocal benefits.[21] Quite to the contrary, the Court noted that "[i]t may

---

[17] Marketplace, *Bill Shlensky on the Cubs*, SoundCloud, https://soundcloud.com/marketplace/bill-shlensky-on-the-cubs (last visited Nov. 17, 2022).

[18] *See generally* Einer Elhauge, *Sacrificing Corporate Profits in the Public Interest*, 80 NYU L. Rev. 733, 763 (2005). This chapter draws deeply from Elhauge's discussion of judicial decisions regarding director discretion, as well as from his analysis of corporate constituency statutes.

[19] Hawes v. Oakland, 104 U.S. 450, 451 (1881).

[20] *Id.* at 462.

[21] *Id.* at 461.

be the exercise of the highest wisdom to let the city use the water in the manner complained of."[22] The Court, like the one in *Wrigley* nearly a century later, emphasized the discretion that Contra Costa's directors had in maintaining their relationship with a variety of stakeholders, including customers. Also as in *Wrigley*, the Court distinguished the judgment of corporate directors from that of the suing stockholder:

> The directors are better able to act understandingly on this subject than a stockholder residing in New York. The great body of the stockholders residing in Oakland or other places in California may take [the directors'] view of it, and be content to abide by the action of the directors.
>
> If this be so, is a bitter litigation with the city to be conducted by one stockholder for the corporation and all other stockholders, because the amount of his dividends is diminished?
>
> This question answers itself. . . .[23]

In sustaining Contra Costa's decision to donate the corporation's water to Oakland, the *Hawes* opinion stands as one of the first to establish a core principle of corporate governance related to ESG—namely, the significant operational discretion of management and directors to prioritize benefits writ large other than shareholder profit.

However, this ability of corporations to act is not without its limits. As referenced above, the *Dodge v. Ford Motor Company* case is illustrative. In this case, Henry Ford and other directors stopped paying special dividends to shareholders in order to fund an expansion of operations that would allow Ford Motor Company to increase employment and lower prices. Henry Ford later testified that his ambition was "to employ still more men, to spread the benefits of this industrial system to the greatest possible number, to help them build up their lives and their homes. To do this we are putting the greatest share of our profits back in the business."[24] The Dodge brothers, who were minority shareholders in the company, sued to enjoin the expansion and to force Ford and the rest of the directors to resume the payouts of the special dividends. The Dodge brothers prevailed. This victory for the Dodge brothers bore some of the strongest language supporting shareholder primacy in case law, including the Michigan Supreme Court's statement that

> [a] business corporation is organized and carried on primarily for the profit of the stockholders. The powers of the directors are to be employed for that end. The discretion of directors is to be exercised in the choice of means to attain that end, and does not extend to a change in the end itself, to the reduction of profits, or to the nondistribution of profits among stockholders in order to devote them to other purposes.
>
> . . . .

[22] *Id.* at 462.

[23] *Id.*

[24] Dodge v. Ford Motor Co., 204 Mich. 459, 505 (1919).

> . . . [I]t is not within the lawful powers of a board of directors to shape and conduct the affairs of a corporation for the merely incidental benefit of shareholders and for the primary purpose of benefiting others. . . .[25]

The court clarified, however, that directorial discretion in achieving profits for shareholders was quite broad:

> There is committed to the discretion of directors, a discretion to be exercised in good faith, the infinite details of business, including the wages which shall be paid to employés [sic], the number of hours they shall work, the conditions under which labor shall be carried on, and the price for which products shall be offered to the public.[26]

The court viewed Ford's possible expansion of the business and lowering of prices as fully within the discretion afforded to the directors, indicating that it was not convinced that such decisions and "the alleged motives" behind those decisions did not "menace the interests of shareholders."[27] The *Dodge* court reiterated that it was outside the purview of a court to make business judgments, stating that "the ultimate results of the larger business cannot be certainly estimated," and that "judges are not business experts."[28]

The problem, in the court's view, was that the Dodge brothers were able to prove that Ford had set aside *too much* cash to follow through with his plan. The decision regarding the dividends did not turn on the sacrifice of profits for an interest other than the shareholders, but rather the choice to hold or distribute those profits.[29] The ruling thus may be limited to situations in which a frustrated stockholder can clearly demonstrate that directors withheld more money from stockholders than they needed for investment in a project or business plan.

In the end, while the court ruled in favor of the minority shareholders, even the court in *Dodge* was not willing to enjoin an operational decision or inquire into the motives behind the business decisions of the majority shareholders. The court was also unwilling to make business judgments about the actual profitability of Ford's expansion. Although the court ordered the company to pay a special dividend to the shareholders due to the large amount of cash the company had on hand, the court declined to interfere with the expansion plan itself, recognizing "that plans must often be made for a long future, for expected competition, for a continuing as well as an immediately profitable venture." Such deference to a company's determinations regarding what may be profitable in the long run continues to inform rulings on derivative suits against corporate directors.

---

[25] *Id.* at 507.

[26] *Id.*

[27] *Id.* at 508.

[28] *Id.*

[29] *See id.* at 509 (noting that "there was a large daily, weekly, monthly, receipt of cash" and that the "contemplated expenditures" for the expansion "were not to be immediately made" and were payable "over a considerable period of time, which created a duty on the directors' part to distribute "a very large sum of money to stockholders" at that).

Fifty years after *Dodge* and one year after *Wrigley*, the Court of Chancery of Delaware heard the case of *Theodora Holding Corp. v. Henderson*, another landmark relevant to the legal underpinnings of ESG.[30] *Theodora* involved a court deciding whether it was proper for corporate defendant Alexander Dawson, Inc. to make a charitable donation of more than $500,000 to a charitable trust that was intended to fund camp for "under privileged children."[31]

In *Theodora Holding*, the court found that a Delaware statute giving corporations the power to "[m]ake donations for the public welfare or for charitable, scientific or educational purposes" supported the propriety of the donation.[32] Moreover, the court indicated that statutory law in almost every state[33] reflected "[t]he recognized obligation of corporations towards philanthropic, educational and artistic causes."[34] The court wrote that "contemporary courts recognize that unless corporations carry an increasing share of the burden of supporting charitable and educational causes that the business advantages now reposed in corporations by law may well prove to be unacceptable to the representatives of an aroused public."[35] The court said that "the Delaware statute . . . must . . . be construed to authorize any reasonable corporate gift of a charitable or educational nature."[36] In applying this reasonableness test, the *Theodora Holding* court relied heavily on tax codes, stating that the donation is being "well within the federal tax deduction limitation of 5%."[37] The court stated:

> It is accordingly obvious . . . that the relatively small loss of immediate income otherwise payable to plaintiff and the corporate defendant's other stockholders, had it not been for the gift in question, is far out-weighed by the overall benefits flowing from the placing of such gift in channels where it serves to benefit those in need of philanthropic or educational support, thus providing justification for large private holdings, thereby benefiting plaintiff in the long run.[38]

---

[30] Theodora Holding Corp. v. Henderson, 257 A.2d 398 (Del. Ch. 1969).

[31] *Id.* at 402. The charitable trust was controlled by an individual defendant who was a director of and had voting control over the corporate defendant. *See id.* at 400–01.

[32] *Id.* at 404.

[33] Every state now has a statute that authorizes unprofitable corporate donations. *See* Elhauge, *supra* note 18, at 738.

[34] *Theodora Holding*, 257 A.2d at 404.

[35] *Id.* The court continued in its advocacy for corporate philanthropy, citing *A.P. Smith Mfg. Co. v. Barlow*, 98 A.2d 581, 585 (N.J. 1953), stating that "the trend towards the transfer of wealth from private industrial entrepreneurs to corporate institutions, the increase of taxes on individual income, coupled with steadily increasing philanthropic needs, necessitate corporate giving for educational needs even were there no statute permitting such gifts" and that "a corporate charitable or educational gift to be valid must merely be within reasonable limits both as to amount and purpose." *Theodora Holding*, 257 A.2d at 404.

[36] *Theodora Holding*, 257 A.2d at 405.

[37] *Id.* This court is not the only court to have used tax codes to help determine the bounds of the reasonableness of acts of corporate philanthropy. *See, e.g.*, Kahn v. Sullivan, 594 A.2d 48, 61 (Del. 1991) (finding that $50 million charitable donation by Occidental Petroleum Corporation for construction of a museum to showcase art owned by Occidental's CEO Armand Hammer and the Armand Hammer Foundation was within *Theodora Holding*'s range of reasonableness based on "the net worth of Occidental, its annual net income before taxes, and the tax benefits to Occidental").

[38] *Theodora Holding*, 257 A.2d at 405.

The scope of director discretion to consider factors other than shareholder benefits has also received significant attention in cases involving corporate takeovers. These cases speak to limits on the consideration that corporate directors may give to stakeholders and constituencies other than shareholders. The Delaware Supreme Court stated in the 1980s, in a case involving Mesa Petroleum Company's hostile takeover bid for Unocal Corporation, that the factors directors may consider in rejecting a takeover bid include "the impact on 'constituencies' other than shareholders (i.e., creditors, customers, employees, and perhaps even the community generally."[39]

Five years later, the Delaware Supreme Court reiterated this ruling in *Paramount Communications, Inc. v. Time*, stating that "directors may consider, when evaluating the threat posed by a takeover bid, . . . 'the impact on "constituencies" other than shareholders. . . .'"[40] The court rejected the argument that "inadequate value" was the only conceivable threat from a hostile offer, and noted that *Unocal*'s "open-ended" approach allowed consideration of other factors, including non-shareholder constituencies and interests such as company culture.[41]

In 2010, the Delaware Chancery Court distinguished *Paramount* in a successful challenge by minority shareholder eBay to actions taken by the majority shareholders of craigslist, acting in their capacity as directors, to restrict eBay's ability to purchase or sell stock.[42] The Chancery Court characterized *Paramount* as a "muted embrace" of directors' efforts to protect "a specific corporate culture."[43] The court said that while *Paramount* involved "the journalistic independence of an iconic American institution"—notably, *Time* magazine—the craigslist directors failed to prove that craigslist possesses "a palpable, distinctive, and advantageous culture that sufficiently promotes stockholder value" to support the restrictions.[44] The court concluded, moreover, that *Paramount* did not hold that corporate directors could protect corporate culture as an end in itself. Instead, "[p]romoting, protecting, or pursuing non-stockholder considerations must lead at some point to value for stockholders."[45] In the craigslist case, the court found that the defendants failed to prove a sufficient connection

---

[39] Unocal Corp. v. Mesa Petroleum Co., 493 A.2d 946, 955 (Del. 1985); *see also* GAF Corp. v. Union Carbide Corp., 624 F. Supp. 1016, 101920 (S.D.N.Y. 1985) ("The exercise of independent, honest business judgment of an enlightened and disinterested Board is the traditional and appropriate way to deal fairly and evenhandedly with both the protection of investors, on the one hand, and the legitimate concerns and interests of employees and management of a corporation who service the interests of investors, on the other."); Mills Acquisition Co. v. Macmillan, Inc., 559 A.2d 1261, 1285 n.35 (Del. 1989) ("Circumstances may dictate that an offer be rebuffed, given the nature and timing of the offer; its legality, feasibility and effect on the corporation and the stockholders; the alternatives available and their effect on the various constituencies, particularly the stockholders; the company's long term strategic plans; and any special factors bearing on stockholder and public interests.").

[40] 571 A.2d 1140, 1153 (Del. 1990).

[41] *Id.* (finding that "the Time board reasonably determined that inadequate value was not the only legally cognizable threat that Paramount's all-cash, all-shares offer could present").

[42] *See* eBay Domestic Holdings, Inc. v. Newmark, 16 A.3d 1 (Del. Ch. 2010).

[43] *Id.* at 32.

[44] *Id.* at 33.

[45] *Id.*

between the company's "culture" and promotion of shareholder value.[46] This line of Delaware cases illustrates that directors have discretion to consider the interests of parties other than shareholders and that courts are inclined to defer to those business judgments, but there is a limit to that discretion and deference.

Moreover, the scope of director discretion to consider non-shareholder constituencies is sharply curtailed when a company has been put up for sale. The Delaware Supreme Court established this principle in *Revlon, Inc. v. MacAndrews & Forbes Holdings, Inc.*, in which the Delaware Supreme Court addressed "for the first time the extent to which a corporation may consider the impact of a takeover threat on constituencies other than shareholders."[47]

In this case, Revlon initiated an active bidding process to sell the company after rejecting a hostile offer by Pantry Pride, Inc., which Revlon's advisors explained would acquire Revlon "through 'junk bond' financing followed by a break-up of Revlon and the disposition of its assets." After the board authorized negotiations with other parties, Pantry Pride continued to make bids to purchase Revlon, but the Revlon board approved a bid from Forstmann Little & Co. that included a "lock-up option" for purchase of two of Revlon's divisions, a "no-shop provision," and a commitment by Forstmann to protect noteholders.[48]

Pantry Pride sued the Revlon directors, seeking to block the Forstmann transaction. The Supreme Court of Delaware agreed with Pantry Pride that the Revlon directors breached their primary duty of loyalty by entering into the Forstmann agreement "on the basis of impermissible considerations at the expense of the shareholders," including the protections for the noteholders. The Revlon board argued that *Unocal* permitted consideration of other corporate constituencies, but the court held that when the board made the decision to put Revlon up for sale (distinguished from the hostile takeover initiated by a third party in *Unocal*), "[t]he duty of the board . . . changed from the preservation of Revlon as a corporate entity to the maximization of the company's value at a sale for the stockholders' benefit."[49] The court stated:

> A board may have regard for various constituencies in discharging its responsibilities, provided there are rationally related benefits accruing to the stockholders. However, such concern for non-stockholder interests is inappropriate when an auction among active bidders is in progress, and the object no longer is to protect or maintain the corporate enterprise but to sell it to the highest bidder.[50]

Revlon, thus, is one of the strictest limitations on record in directorial discretion. In initiating the sale of a company, directors forgo any and all considerations but maximize shareholder value. The concerns of other stakeholders become moot. Later cases, such as

---

[46] *See id.*

[47] 506 A.2d 173, 176 (Del. 1986).

[48] *Id.* at 178–79.

[49] *Id.* at 182.

[50] *Id.* at 182. *Cf. Paramount*, 571 A.2d at 1142 (finding that *Time*'s board did not have "a *Revlon* duty either to auction the company or to maximize short-term shareholder value").

Paramount, emphasize the particular circumstances—a recognition that Revlon's breakup was inevitable—that triggered this limitation on directorial discretion.[51]

The wave of corporate takeovers in the 1980s such as Pantry Pride's takeover of Revlon is credited with leading to states' enactment of "corporate constituency statutes" that authorize corporate boards to take into account the interests of non-stockholder constituencies.[52] Well more than half of the states have such a statute—with one notable exception being Delaware, the leading choice for most large corporations.[53] The other constituencies named in the statutes almost always include employees, customers, and suppliers, and often include creditors and communities.[54] Many of the statutes also mention the state or national economy or society.[55] Two (Arizona and Texas) mention the environment explicitly, and eight statutes allow consideration of other unenumerated constituencies or interests.[56] Some of the statutes also include provisions explicitly authorizing consideration of the long-term as well as short-term interests of stockholders.[57] The influence of constituency statutes is still up for debate—until such time (if any) that these statutes are adopted by Delaware, it is unlikely that they will have a significant impact on corporate governance in the broader market.

Views on the impacts of the constituency statutes on directors' legal obligations vary. Early on, the American Bar Association's Committee on Corporate Laws took the position that the statutes "confirm what the common law has been: directors may take into account the interests of other constituencies but only as and to the extent that the directors are acting in the best interests, long as well as short term, of the shareholders and the corporation."[58] The Committee concluded that broadening the interests corporate directors could consider without reference to their impact on shareholder interests "would conflict with directors' responsibility to shareholders and could undermine the effectiveness of the system that has made the corporation an efficient device for the creation of jobs and wealth."[59]

Numerous other commentators, however, have espoused the view that the constituency statutes allow directors to take actions favoring non-stockholder parties even when

---

[51] *See, e.g.*, *Paramount*, 571 A.2d at 1154 ("Directors are not obliged to abandon a deliberately conceived corporate plan for a short-term shareholder profit unless there is clearly no basis to sustain the corporate strategy."); Ivanhoe Partners v. Newmont Mining Corp., 535 A.2d 1334, 1338 (Del. 1987) ("Newmont was not for sale. Thus, there was no duty of its directors to maximize 'the company's value at a sale for the stockholders' benefit.'").

[52] *See* Principles of Corporate Governance: Analysis and Recommendations § 2.01 Reporter's Note 8; Elhauge, *supra* note 18, at 737; Nathan E. Standley, Note, *Lessons Learned from the Capitulation of the Constituency Statute*, 4 Elon L. Rev. 211 (2012).

[53] *See* Lucian A. Bebchuk et al., *For Whom Corporate Leaders Bargain*, 94 S. Cal. L. Rev. 1467, 1489 (2021) (33 states had constituency statutes during 2000–2019 studied in the article); Standley, *supra* note 52, at 209, 212 (stating that 29 states had constituency statutes in 1999 and 41 at time article was published).

[54] *See* Bebchuk et al., *supra* note 53, at 1491.

[55] *Id.*

[56] *Id.*

[57] *See* Elhauge, *supra* note 18, at 766–67.

[58] Comm. on Corp. L., Am. Bar Ass'n, *Other Constituencies Statutes: Potential for Confusion*, 45 Bus. Law. 2253, 2269 (1990); *see also* Bebchuk et al., *supra* note 53, at 1492.

[59] Comm. on Corp. L., *supra* note 58, at 2268.

stockholders would not reap ancillary benefits.[60] Courts also have interpreted the statutes to give directors room to prioritize other stakeholder interests even when it would not maximize shareholder value.[61] Notwithstanding these interpretations, in practice it does not seem that the corporate constituency statutes have resulted in significant enforceable benefits for non-shareholder constituencies. For example, an analysis of 110 private equity acquisitions between 2000 and 2019 that were governed by constituency statutes found that "[c]orporate leaders used their power to obtain significant benefits for stockholders and themselves but made little use of this power to obtain stakeholder protections," such as limits on employee layoffs or requirements to benefit suppliers, creditors, or the environment.[62]

In recent years, however, there has been increasing attention to the interests of corporate stakeholders generally, rather than focusing only on shareholders. This recent trend towards stakeholder capitalism garnered widespread attention in 2019, when the Business Roundtable released a "Statement on the Purpose of a Corporation" that articulated a "fundamental commitment to all stakeholders" (replacing a statement that "[t]he paramount duty of management and of boards of directors is to the corporation's stockholders").[63] The statement was signed by 181 CEOs. Also, the American Law Institute is currently considering a *Restatement of the Law, Corporate Governance* that would serve as a replacement for the 1994 *Principles of the Law, Corporate Governance*. The tentative draft *Restatement* provisions approved in 2022 include a definition of the objective of a corporation that differentiates between corporations in common-law jurisdictions and in stakeholder jurisdictions (i.e., jurisdictions with constituency statutes). The common-law corporation objective would be "to enhance the economic value of the corporation . . . for the benefit of the corporation's shareholders," with the corporation permitted to consider other factors in achieving this objective, including employees' interests and impacts on the community and the environment.[64] In stakeholder jurisdictions, the objective would be to "enhance the economic value of the corporation . . . for the benefit of the corporation's shareholders and/or, to the extent permitted by state law, for the benefit of employees, suppliers, customers, communities, or any other constituencies."[65] The draft *Restatement* would provide that all corporations, whether common-law or stakeholder, "may devote a reasonable amount of resources to public-welfare, humanitarian, educational, and philanthropic purposes, whether or not doing so enhances the economic

[60] *See* Bebchuk et al., *supra* note 53, at 1492–93 n.104 (citing articles in which authors supported interpretations of constituency statutes that allow directors to "attach independent weight to stakeholder interests and thus sometimes serve such interests even when doing so would not be best for shareholders"); Elhauge, *supra* note 18, at 766–67.

[61] *See* Bebchuk et al., *supra* note 53, at 1493 n.106 (citing cases).

[62] *Id.* at 1524–25.

[63] *See* Press Release, Bus. Roundtable, Business Roundtable Redefines the Purpose of a Corporation to Promote 'An Economy That Serves All Americans' (Aug. 19, 2019), https://www.businessroundtable.org/business-roundtable-redefines-the-purpose-of-a-corporation-to-promote-an-economy-that-serves-all-americans.

[64] *See Restatement of the Law, Corporate Governance*, AM. L. INST., https://www.ali.org/publications/show/corporate-governance-rs/#drafts (last visited Nov. 17, 2022).

[65] Bebchuk et al., *supra* note 53, at 1532 (on "enlightened shareholder" approach).

value of the corporation." Stakeholder capitalism has been embraced by some of the most prominent voices in the corporate establishment, including former Delaware Chief Justice Leo Strine.[66]

While these changing views on corporate governance have been percolating, the profile of environmental and social issues has risen. For example, shareholders have filed shareholder derivative lawsuits alleging that corporate directors breached their fiduciary duties by failing to take concrete steps to implement commitments to diversity.[67] These lawsuits have not been successful thus far,[68] but they are emblematic of the ESG-related pressures that shareholders may exert on companies. Companies also face pressure from shareholder proposals submitted for inclusion in proxy statements. In the 2022 proxy season, 63 percent of shareholder proposals pertained to environmental and social/political topics, with a 38 percent increase in environmental proposals from the 2021 proxy season.[69] ESG-related proposals in 2022 included proposals addressing greenhouse gas emissions reduction disclosures, civil rights audits, and reports on the impacts on employees of legislation restricting access to abortion care.[70]

At the same time, companies also face lawsuits and shareholder proposals by shareholders who contend that companies' policies or actions to achieve social or environmental goals do not align with shareholders' interests. For example, a lawsuit filed in state court in Washington in August 2022 asserts that directors and officers of Starbucks violated federal and state civil rights laws and breached their fiduciary obligations by adopting, implementing, and retaining policies to achieve diversity, equity, and inclusion objectives.[71] In addition, a report on the 2022 proxy season cited a "notable increase" in shareholder proposals submitted by "anti-ESG" entities (54 such proposals, compared to 25 in 2021), including proposals related to workplace diversity and to costs and benefits of companies' climate change-related activities).[72]

---

[66] *See* Leo E. Strine, Jr., *Toward Fair and Sustainable Capitalism* (Roosevelt Inst. Aug. 2020), https://rooseveltinstitute.org/wp-content/uploads/2020/08/RI_TowardFairandSustainableCapitalism_WorkingPaper_202008.pdf.

[67] *See, e.g.*, Klein v. Ellison, No. 20-cv-04439, 2021 U.S. Dist. LEXIS 97965 (N.D. Cal. May 24, 2021) (court granted Oracle defendants' motion to dismiss because plaintiffs did not sufficiently plead demand futility and state law claims were required to be asserted in Delaware Court of Chancery); Lee v. Fisher, No. 20-cv-06163, 2021 U.S. Dist. LEXIS 82804 (N.D. Cal. Apr. 27, 2021), *aff'd*, 34 F.4th 777 (9th Cir. 2022) (court granted Gap defendants' motion to dismiss lawsuit alleging failure to create meaningful diversity on board of directors and within company's leadership on grounds that it was required to be filed in Delaware Court of Chancery); Ocegueda v. Zuckerberg, 526 F. Supp. 3d 637 (N.D. Cal. 2021) (granting motion to dismiss lawsuit against Facebook directors alleging unlawful business practices stemming from lack of diversity, discriminatory advertising, and failure to curb hate speech).

[68] *See* Meredith Mandell, *Placing an Emphasis on the "S" in ESG*, NYSBA (Feb. 17, 2022), https://nysba.org/placing-an-emphasis-on-the-s-in-esg/.

[69] June Hu et al., *2022 Proxy Season Review: Rule 14a-8 Shareholder Proposals*, Harv. L. Sch. Forum on Corp. Governance (Aug. 25, 2022), https://corpgov.law.harvard.edu/2022/08/25/2022-proxy-season-review-rule-14a-8-shareholder-proposals/.

[70] *See* Rob Henry, *The 2022 AGM Season: Which ESG Issues Have Shareholders Targeted?*, PRI Blog (July 25, 2022), https://www.unpri.org/pri-blog/the-2022-agm-season-which-esg-issues-have-shareholders-targeted/10271.article.

[71] Complaint, Nat'l Ctr. for Pub. Pol'y Rsch. v. Schultz, No. 22-2-02945-32 (Wash. Super. Ct. Aug. 30, 2022).

[72] *See* Hu et al., *supra* note 69.

The current corporate climate can put companies in a challenging balancing act, as ESG advocates push companies to focus on stakeholders, while "anti-woke" proponents urge companies to focus on the bottom line and leave ESG considerations on the sidelines. The Balkanized political landscape, with stark divisions between conservative and liberal forces, is drawing battle lines over a wide range of issues, and corporate governance, which previously would not have garnered much attention outside boardrooms and law firms, is becoming a "hot button" issue. Board diversity, pension fund investing guidelines, and net-zero commitments are a few recent examples of surprisingly controversial points, and boards and management have their work cut out for them in navigating an increasingly tricky landscape.[73]

Companies will continue to confront new and evolving social and environmental concerns, and to contend with challenges to their responses to these concerns. The doctrines that companies look to guide their decision-making are also somewhat in flux, as practitioners, scholars, judges, and others consider how companies should balance their duties to shareholders with potential obligations to other stakeholders, and whether long-term benefits outweigh short-term gains. At bottom, however, these dilemmas are not new. These are the same issues that Philip Wrigley weighed in foregoing higher earnings to keep the evenings quiet in the neighborhoods around Wrigley Field.

[73] By way of example, Nasdaq's board diversity disclosure rule has been the subject of litigation in the Fifth Circuit, *see* Alliance for Fair Bd. Recruitment v. SEC, No. 21-60626 (5th Cir. Nov. 22, 2021), as have the California board diversity laws, which the lower courts struck down. *See* Crest v. Padilla, No. 20-STCV-37513, 2022 Cal. Super. LEXIS 11070 (Cal. Super. Ct. Apr. 1, 2022); Crest v. Padilla, No. 19-STCV-27561, 2022 Cal. Super. LEXIS 54310 (Cal. Super. Ct. July 15, 2022). States such as Florida are taking steps to limit public pension funds from taking ESG into account in their investments. Press Release, Ron DeSantis, Governor Ron DeSantis Eliminates ESG Considerations from State Pension Investments (Aug. 23, 2022), https://www.flgov.com/2022/08/23/governor-ron-desantis-eliminates-esg-considerations-from-state-pension-investments/. Commitments to net zero goals have also come under fire—on October 19, 2022, a coalition of 19 state attorneys general announced an investigation into six major banks in connection with their net zero pledges and related limits on fossil fuel lending. Press Release, Eric Schmitt, Mo. Att'y Gen., Missouri Attorney General Leads 19 State Coalition in Launching Investigation into Six Major Banks Over ESG Investing (Oct. 19, 2022), https://ago.mo.gov/home/news/2022/10/19/missouri-attorney-general-leads-19-state-coalition-in-launching-investigation-into-six-major-banks-over-esg-investing. For more discussion of anti-ESG activity, see Chapter 3—ESG Backlash—The Efforts to Constrain ESG.

2

Stakeholders in the ESG Ecosystem

Michele J. Rowland

I. Introduction

Any given company has many stakeholder groups, some of whom, like shareholders, align financially, and others of whom align based on the company's broader purpose and impact on society. Increasingly, there are constituencies that hold no economic interest in a company yet purport to be a stakeholder in the company.

Once the universe of stakeholders is defined by a company, expectations of stakeholder groups (other than shareholders) increasingly factor into a company's calculus of its success and business performance.

Shareholders easily rely on share price and determinable metrics, such as financial statements produced in compliance with generally accepted accounting principles (GAAP) to measure the success or value of a company. Non-shareholder stakeholders have no such standardized measuring stick against which to judge the social performance of a company.

Indeed, non-shareholder stakeholders are not members of a monolithic group with a common purpose or voice. Rather, non-shareholder stakeholders come in many varieties and flavors, each with its own priorities. Non-shareholder stakeholders are voicing the importance of social policies important to them and the roles that companies are expected to play to achieve social policy changes. How then is a company to understand who its stakeholders are and how they align? How is a company to prove success to non-economic stakeholders?

Companies increasingly rely on the voluntary collection, analysis, and disclosure of certain kinds of social information, or ESG data, that are significant to their unique stakeholder groups. For some companies, collection and disclosure of ESG data is required by lenders, investors, or regulators. Other companies anticipate eventual mandated disclosure by the U.S. Securities and Exchange Commission (SEC) or other regulatory schemes.

Stakeholder groups compete for company resources and priority within a company's strategic plan. Boards of directors and management are left without much guidance to weigh their duty to create value for shareholders, and their own fiduciary duties, against their duty to make decisions about the company's impact on society and the expectations of its non-shareholder stakeholders.

This chapter identifies stakeholder groups and discusses how companies are using ESG data collection, analysis, and disclosure to prove performance to stakeholders. Case studies are used in this chapter to illustrate how the interests of non-shareholder stakeholders and ESG awareness inform decisions being made by boards of directors and management groups.

II. ESG Stakeholders

Who are the stakeholders in the ESG ecosystem? In the context of social policy change, constituencies align based on their interests in whether and to what extent companies adopt and administer ESG protocols. These constituencies often have a direct or indirect interest in the behavior of companies and align into the following categories:

- Shareholders
- Boards of directors
- Management
- Employees
- Financial investors and lenders
- Buyers and sellers in merger and acquisition transactions
- Customers
- Vendors
- Manufacturers
- Transportation and logistics
- Suppliers
- Governments (including federal, state, local, and international governments)
- Regulatory agencies
- Nongovernmental organizations (including standards organizations and industry groups)
- Nonprofit organizations
- Third-party consultants and advisors
- The public

III. Stakeholders Have Different Agendas

Stakeholders in the ESG ecosystem have different interests in how and whether a company establishes or achieves ESG goals. How is a board of directors or management team supposed to run a company and create and execute on a strategic plan that both increases shareholder value and serves the goals and priorities of more than a dozen unaligned stakeholder groups? Good question.

A. A Brief History of Shareholder Supremacy vs. Stakeholder Theory

Shareholder primacy under Delaware law mandates that "stockholders' best interests must always, within legal limits, be the end" of business decisions made by directors of a Delaware corporation. The interest of shareholders, which historically has meant "value creation," should be the principal focus of boards of directors and management. This theory, known as "shareholder primacy," is a central tenet of corporate law in Delaware and elsewhere. However, Delaware law and the laws of at least 44 other states permit directors to consider constituencies other than shareholders when making business decisions.

Converse to shareholder primacy is the Stakeholder Theory. Stakeholder Theory is an economic and social theory that interconnects business, its customers, suppliers, investors, and other groups that have an interest in the organization. R. Edward Freeman laid out the framework for the Stakeholder Theory of capitalism in 1984 in his book, *Strategic Management: A Stakeholder Approach*.[1] The Stakeholder Theory is based on the premise that businesses could and should create value for all stakeholders, not just shareholders, and that businesses succeed when the interests of all stakeholders are aligned. The stakeholder view of corporate management integrates business ethics, corporate social responsibility, and market economy to aim to create the most value for the most constituencies with an interest in the organization.

Now comes an open door through which ESG will walk.

B. ESG Is Unlike Socially Responsible Investing of the Past

The underpinnings of ESG are not new. Social policies in different forms, under broad terms such as corporate responsibility and business ethics, have always been considerations of business organizations.[2] The era of socially responsible investing (SRI) finds its roots in the 1980s as companies divested from South Africa and its apartheid regime. SRI was rebooted and rebranded in the early 2000s to advance specific social goals insofar as it identifies the environment and battling climate change and greenhouse gas emissions as a mandate of the mission. The movement followed closely on the heels of the dot-com bubble bursting in the late 1990s and the Enron and WorldCom bankruptcies in the early 2000s, which collectively raised public awareness of weak corporate governance and controls (i.e., the "G" in the ESG model).

C. ESG Encourages Uniform Standards

ESG is unlike social drivers in their prior iterations in that ESG seeks to establish a uniform value set that holds businesses accountable to standards and rewards or punishes behavior when those standards are or are not met.

[1] R. Edward Freeman, Strategic Management: A Stakeholder Approach (1994).

[2] The history and development of ESG as a social driver is discussed more fully in CHAPTER 1—LEAVING THE LIGHTS OFF: A SHORT HISTORY OF THE LEGAL ISSUES RELATED TO ESG.

1. *There is no uniform set of metrics currently*

Defining a uniform set of metrics is a major challenge when imposing social policies on for-profit companies. Several constituencies are trying to establish uniform metrics with which to measure corporate performance (some are discussed later in this chapter); however, until a regulatory scheme is adopted or data disclosure is otherwise mandated, companies are free to apply ESG parameters that show them in the best light. Without a regulated construct, investors and other stakeholders are not able to make an apples-to-apples comparison of companies' performance.

No stakeholders are benefitted if there are no standardized methodologies to produce reliable, consistent, and comparable information. As SEC Chair Gary Gensler wrote in May 2022, "It is important that investors have consistent and comparable disclosures about asset managers' ESG strategies so they can understand what data underlies funds' claims and choose the right investments for them. . . . People are making investment decisions based upon these disclosures, so it's important that they be presented in a meaningful way to investors."[3]

2. *One size does not fit all*

Social policy virtues are ethereal and broad, and span across every industry, region, and market. But, every company is unique and differs from every other company in its customer base, employee base, product or service offering, financial condition, and strategic goals. A social policy virtue might be: It is good to reduce carbon emissions. Corporate decision makers who agree with the virtue are left to their own devices to determine how their company's operations uniquely impact carbon emissions and how the company can reduce its carbon emissions in its industry, with its customers, in its financial condition, with available resources, while achieving its strategic plan and maximizing shareholder value. This will likely continue even after a uniform set of rules is established against which to measure performance.

The ESG movement, unlike prior socially motivated drivers, may be the first large-scale, coordinated movement to establish standardized metrics, assumptions, and methodologies to measure and compare socially favorable behaviors among companies. Applying the metrics at the company level will continue to be a challenge for corporate decision makers.

IV. Stakeholders: The Standard-Setters

There are numerous industry groups and task forces that seek to establish uniform standards by which to measure ESG data, whether related to financial metrics, environmental concerns, or human capital:

- The **Global Reporting Initiative (GRI)** provides "the world's most widely used sustainability reporting standards, which cover topics that range from biodiversity to tax, waste to emissions, and diversity and equality to health and safety. As such, GRI reporting is the enabler for transparency and dialogue between companies and their

[3] Gary Gensler, *Statement on ESG Disclosures Proposal,* U.S. Securities and Exchange Commission (SEC) (May 25, 2022), https://www.sec.gov/news/statement/gensler-statement-esg-disclosures-proposal-052522.

stakeholders."[4] The GRI Standards are aligned with the United Nations (UN) Sustainable Development Goals[5] —the global materiality assessment for our world.[6]

- The **Sustainable Accounting Standards Board (SASB)** is an ESG guidance framework that sets standards for the disclosure of financially material sustainability information by companies to their investors. Since August 2022, the SASB has been under the purview of the International Sustainability Standards Board (ISSB) of the International Financial Reporting Standards (IFRS) Foundation. SASB standards identify the subset of ESG issues most relevant to financial performance in each of 77 industries. They are designed to help companies disclose financially material sustainability information to investors.[7] In June 2023, IFRS Sustainability Disclosure Standards aligned with SASB standards.[8] The SASB also conducts specific research related to three relevant, financially material issues related to human capital management (in industries where sufficient evidence of financial impact and investor interest has been demonstrated): employee health and safety; employee diversity, inclusion, and engagement; and labor practices.
- **Principles for Responsible Investment (PRI)** is an international network of financial investors working together to promote ESG and other social policies, along with long-term financial returns associated with fostering responsible social standards.[9] The PRI was founded in 2005 by then-UN Secretary General Kofi Annan. Today, the PRI works in partnership with the UN Environment Programme Finance Initiative and the UN Global Compact to promote six principles for responsible investment. The PRI's mission statement and six principles "were developed by investors, for investors, in order to develop a more sustainable global financial system." In 2021, more than 3,500 financial institutions worldwide were signatories to the PRI's mission statement. Signatories include asset owners (including pension funds, private equity and venture funds, alternative investment funds, charitable and religious groups, and trusts), investment managers, and service providers. The PRI's mission statement provides:

  > We believe that an economically efficient, sustainable global financial system is a necessity for long-term value creation. Such a system will reward long-term, responsible investment and benefit the environment and society as a whole. The PRI will work to achieve this sustainable global financial system by encouraging adoption of the Principles and collaboration on their implementation; by fostering good governance, integrity and accountability; and by addressing obstacles to a sustainable financial system that lie within market practices, structures and regulation.[10]

---

[4] *See* Global Reporting Initiative (GRI), https://www.globalreporting.org (last visited Mar. 9, 2023).

[5] *See The 17 Goals*, United Nations (UN), https://sdgs.un.org/goals (last visited Mar. 9, 2023).

[6] *Id.*

[7] *See Sustainable Accounting Standards Board (SASB) Standards*, IFRS Found., https://www.sasb.org/standards/download/?lang=en-us (last visited Mar. 9, 2023).

[8] *Id.*

[9] *About Us: About the PRI*, UN Principles for Responsible Investment (PRI), https://www.unpri.org/about-us/about-the-pri (last visited Mar. 6, 2023).

[10] *Id.*

- The **Task Force on Climate-related Financial Disclosures** (**TCFD**) was created by the **Financial Stability Board (FSB)**. The FSB is an international body that monitors and makes recommendations about the global financial system. It created the TCFD to improve and increase reporting of climate-related financial information. The mission of the TCFD is to price "risk" and inform capital allocation decisions. The TCFD gives recommendations on the types of information that companies should disclose to investors, lenders, and insurance underwriters.

V. Stakeholders: The Board of Directors and Management

A. Voluntary vs. Mandatory Disclosures

Companies are moving toward a model that makes social data gathering and disclosure the norm. But we note that in the United States at the time of this publication, ESG and other social policy monitoring is conducted on a largely voluntary basis.

SEC Chair Gensler noted in March 2022 that over 70 percent of Standard and Poor's 500 (S&P 500) companies already report Scope 1 greenhouse gas emissions, and nearly 75 percent of S&P 500 companies report on the percentage of their workforces that are female. Disclosure of carbon dioxide (CO_2) emissions information, diversity statistics, and political contributions among S&P 500 companies has trended reliably up over the last five years.

While many, often larger, better capitalized companies choose to collect this information, many middle-market and smaller companies are resisting the movement to disclose information and to limit the types of information disclosed. They contend that collecting, measuring, and disclosing information is costly and burdensome, and diverts corporate resources.

In order for ESG information gathering and disclosure to gain widespread acceptance, U.S. companies will need first to believe their customers, employees, suppliers, lenders, and other parties involved in their businesses want and expect the information to be disclosed, and that their competitors are disclosing the information. Shy of mandated public disclosures, the market must drive the behavior.

B. Impact on Corporate Decision-Making

1. Costs of Compliance

Whether voluntary or mandatory in nature, ESG reporting has real and embedded costs associated with it, including lost opportunity costs. Companies that collect and disclose ESG information are likely to have fewer resources available to grow organically or achieve other strategic initiatives if internal resources are diverted to ESG data gathering, policy creation, and compliance monitoring.

If fewer resources exist, companies will encounter lost opportunities and incur lost opportunity costs. For example, companies may now find there are more barriers to acquiring strategic targets. The costs of doing a deal will necessarily increase as due diligence of a target company's ESG policies and compliance becomes of greater importance.[11] An acquiring company may decide not to pursue a deal it otherwise would have simply because the acquisition costs do not merit the risk or possible upside of doing the deal. If a deal does go forward, acquiring companies may be assuming liabilities and risk of a target's incomplete data, failure to collect data, failure to administer adequate policies, and ultimate noncompliance with market, regulatory, and stakeholder expectations. Ultimately in a deal, the assumption of greater risk by an acquiring company will have the effect of driving the purchase price down, which reduces net equity to the target's shareholders.

2. *Weighing One Stakeholder Group Against Another*

Is ESG a zero-sum game? Must value creation for the benefit of one stakeholder group decrease value for another? Or, will social policy initiatives contribute to a company's value creation for shareholders? These are the central questions faced by boards of directors and corporate officers, both of whom owe fiduciary and other duties.

The pendulum of corporate decision-making is expected to swing away from shareholder primacy toward Stakeholder Theory as regulators, investors, and other stakeholders make their expectations for corporate behavior known. When making decisions for the organization that are informed by ESG or social policy, directors and management must weigh whether the decision will create value for shareholders or result in a breach of duty owed.

There are two methods for boards of directors and corporate officers to implement ESG initiatives when making operational and strategic decisions, as laid out by Professors Max M. Schanzenbach and Robert H. Sitkoff in their letter to the SEC dated May 5, 2020: (1) decisions not to take action and (2) action-picking.[12] A strategy involving a negative screen on activities means the board of directors and corporate officers will apply ESG factors to screen out undesirable corporate actions (e.g., acquisitions of companies with low ESG scores, certain capital improvements). Employing negative screens on corporate actions leads to diminished returns. As screens are used more broadly, any advantage will be diminished as non-ESG choices become increasingly cheaper and more readily available.[13] Also, a corporation's share price will adjust for the market risk after an initial phase-in of screened behavior. Moreover, negative screens are time-consuming and costly to implement, which reduces the attractiveness of this strategy to boards of directors and corporate officers.[14]

Alternatively, action-picking focuses on actively applying ESG criteria when constructing a growth or acquisition strategy, or making board-level or operational decisions. Action-picking has its own elements of diminishing returns and embedded costs. First, there are costs associated with actively seeking out ESG-favorable opportunities. These costs include

---

[11] *See* Chapter 19—Due Diligence and ESG concerning due diligence in merger and acquisition transactions.

[12] Letter from Max M. Schanzenbach, Seigle Fam. Professor of L., Nw. Pritzker Sch. of L., & Robert H. Sitkoff, John L. Gray Professor of L., Harv. L. Sch., to Sec'y, SEC (May 5, 2020), https://www.sec.gov/comments/s7-04-20/s70420-7153846-216455.pdf.

[13] *Id.*

[14] *Id.*

investigation, analysis, and possibly added tax costs.[15] For this strategy to be profitable, the returns must be large enough to offset the increased real and embedded costs.[16] Second, when employing ESG-focused (or any other focused) behavior, a corporation will incur diversification costs because, by definition, the strategy narrows the opportunities available to the corporation.[17] Third, like with a negative screen strategy, any advantage to a corporation engaged in an action-picking strategy will experience diminished returns as non-ESG choices become cheaper.[18]

C. Overcoming Subjectivity

How should a board of directors weigh ESG factors when they are subjective by their nature? A corporation following best practices will have to resolve the fundamental subjectivity embedded in almost every ESG social initiative. There are differing ESG goals and guidelines established by industry groups that are not in agreement on whether an initiative should be pursued, much less how and to what extent one should pursue the initiative. For example, is nuclear energy a clean alternative energy source that should be pursued and tracked under a corporation's ESG policy, or is nuclear energy so inherently dangerous and potentially harmful to the global population and the environment that a corporation advances its ESG initiatives by not pursuing it?[19]

1. *The Role of Outside Advisors*

Corporate decision-making is often, and rightfully so, guided by advice of outside professionals to the corporation or the board, whether in the form of a fairness opinion, legal counsel, or otherwise. The subjectivity of ESG factors easily lends itself to boards of directors and corporate officers relying on, nay, becoming dependent on, the advice of outside consultants and third parties when making corporate decisions. Directors and corporate officers should be ever mindful to reach their own conclusions after weighing the available information and not fall into the trap of replacing their independent judgment with the advice of third parties. Vigilant corporate counsel will remind directors and officers of this premise often as corporations prepare to enter the era of mandatory ESG reporting and compliance.

Corporate decision-making that takes ESG factors into account, whether voluntarily or by mandate as and when the law evolves, will require a board of directors or corporate officer to answer questions like these: (1) Does the ESG factor improve the corporation's long-term financial returns to shareholders?; (2) Is the corporation trading shareholder value for stakeholder value, and if so, why is the trade defensible?; and (3) Is the corporation exploiting the ESG element for profit, and if so, how does that impact the corporation's ESG "score" or performance metrics?

---

[15] *See* Schanzenbach & Sitkoff, *supra* note 12, Ex. A at 442.

[16] *Id.*

[17] *Id.*

[18] *Id.*

[19] *Id.* Ex. A at 450.

For further discussion on how ESG factors impact boards of directors and corporate officers, see CHAPTER 15—GOVERNANCE: ROLE OF THE BOARD and CHAPTER 16—ROLE OF MANAGEMENT.

VI. Stakeholders: Employees

Employees have and will continue to impact the scope of ESG reporting. It is well established that a company's social value set can help attract and retain employees, can improve employee perception of the workplace, and can increase an employee's perception of his or her impact on the company's place in the world. Now comes the "S" in the ESG model.

Employers often market their social positions, particularly related to ESG issues, to entice highly desirable candidates to work for them and to gain a competitive advantage. Many employers view ESG as a generational necessity also. Companies that are attractive to young talent tend to prioritize and market their ESG initiatives among employment candidates.

There are intangible benefits to a company and all of its stakeholders when the company and its employees have a shared value system and mental model related to social policies and goals. Additionally, there are real and direct benefits to employees and employers when socially relevant workplace data is disclosed.

Socially relevant workplace data includes information related to hiring diversity, diversity in executive ranks, claims of workplace misconduct and hostility, claims of discrimination, board misconduct, and employee retention statistics. Socially relevant workplace data also includes an employer's diversity, equity, and inclusion goals and action plan, and progress made against its plan. In addition to its statistical importance, socially relevant workplace data, when looked at holistically, can indicate the culture of a company.

If and when employers on a large scale are required to disclose socially relevant workplace data, merely requiring the disclosure will cause companies to improve their behavior. Workplace hiring statistics and claims of wrongdoing are often kept in the shadows or quietly settled. Diversity, equity, and inclusion action plans are often touted by employers, but these plans are difficult to measure progress against. Mandating a reporting requirement and specific enforcement guidelines will flesh out acute and systemic problems in an organization. When one's behavior becomes known by others, social pressure, market pressure, and competitive disadvantage can influence positive change. In this case, it is change that can serve all stakeholders in an organization.

Additionally, when ESG workplace data is available in a uniform and usable format, employees and employment candidates can make informed decisions about whether they share the same value set as a company. An employer who hires a candidate with a good "value set" match increases the chances of a longer employment tenure, a happier employee, and ultimately a more profitable employee.

A. Case Study: Activision

The SEC has signaled that, from an enforcement perspective, it will focus on whether a company has misled investors about its efforts to address workplace diversity, workplace hostility, and discrimination, and whether a company has disclosed material and credible allegations of workplace harassment or other misconduct.

In September 2021, the *Wall Street Journal* reported that the SEC was investigating the sufficiency and timeliness of disclosures by Activision Blizzard, Inc. (Activision). Activision is a videogame publishing giant and the maker of "Call of Duty," "World of Warcraft," and "Candy Crush Saga."[20]

Over a period of years, Activision had received complaints from employees and regulators of sexual misconduct, workplace harassment, retaliation, and discrimination, among other complaints. The merits of the claims have been, and are being, addressed in various legal actions and settlements involving Activision. The California Department of Fair Employment and Housing sued Activision in July 2021, claiming, among other things, that "women were subjected to constant sexual harassment, including groping, comments, and advances," and "the company's executives and human resources personnel knew of the harassment and failed to take reasonable steps to prevent the unlawful conduct, and instead retaliated against women who complained."[21] In March 2022, a federal judge approved a settlement with the U.S. Equal Employment Opportunity Commission after the government agency found evidence of sexual harassment, pregnancy discrimination, and related retaliation at the company.[22]

But, the merits of the claims were not the concern of the SEC. Rather, the SEC investigated the sufficiency and timeliness of Activision's disclosures regarding "how the videogame-publishing giant handled employees' allegations of sexual misconduct and workplace discrimination."[23] The SEC issued subpoenas requesting documents, minutes from meetings of the board of directors, personnel files, and communications involving claims of sexual harassment and discrimination, among other documents.[24]

The SEC's investigation came to an end on February 3, 2023, when it announced that Activision agreed to pay $35 million to settle charges for, among other things, its failure to maintain adequate disclosure controls relating to employee complaints. Notably, the SEC did not charge Activision with making misleading statements or omissions. Rather, in its order,[25] the SEC found, among other things, that Activision violated Rule 13a-15(a) of the Securities and Exchange Act of 1934, which requires issuers to maintain disclosure controls and

---

[20] Kirsten Grind & Sarah E. Needleman, *SEC Is Investigating Activision Blizzard Over Workplace Practices, Disclosures*, Wall St. J. (Sept. 20, 2021, 5:27 PM), https://www.wsj.com/articles/sec-is-investigating-activision-blizzard-over-workplace-practices-disclosures-11632165080.

[21] Press Release, Cal. Dep't of Fair Emp. & Hous., DFEH Sues California Gaming Companies for Equal Pay Violations, Sex Discrimination, and Sexual Harassment (July 21, 2021), https://calcivilrights.ca.gov/wp-content/uploads/sites/32/2021/07/BlizzardPR.7.21.21.pdf.

[22] *What You Should Know About: EEOC's Settlement with Activision*, U.S. Equal Emp. Opportunity Comm'n, https://www.eeoc.gov/what-you-should-know-about-eeocs-settlement-activision-blizzard (last visited July 19, 2023).

[23] Grind & Needleman, *supra* note 20.

[24] *See* Valerie Hays et al., *SEC Focus on ESG Has Expanded to Workplace Culture and Sexual Harassment Investigations*, Arnold & Porter Kaye Scholer LLP (Mar. 22, 2022), https://www.arnoldporter.com/en/perspectives/advisories/2022/03/sec-focus-on-esg-has-expanded.

[25] *See* Activision Blizzard, Inc., Exchange Act Release No. 96796, 2023 WL 1765354 (Feb. 3, 2023).

procedures designed to ensure that information required to be disclosed is recorded, processed, summarized, and reported within the required time period.

Activision's annual and quarterly filings with the SEC between 2018 and 2021 had included a risk factor regarding the importance of attracting, retaining, and motivating skilled personnel, emphasizing that the failure to do so could be detrimental to the company's success.[26] The risk factor emphasized the need to *maintain* the company's workforce. The SEC found that Activision violated Rule 13a-15(a) insofar as it lacked controls and procedures designed to ensure that the company's disclosure personnel could access and assess employee complaints and allegations of workplace misconduct. The company's disclosure personnel were therefore unable to assess related risks to the company's business and determine whether such risks warranted disclosure to investors.[27]

There are important takeaways from the Activision matter. The case study is a good reminder to companies to consider the "social" aspect of their disclosures and disclosure controls, including how they interact with other areas of the business, such as human resources, compliance, and legal, that may receive complaints.[28] The action against Activision puts issuers on notice from the Gensler Commission that if they discuss an area as a particular risk to their business (e.g., attracting and retaining workers with a specific skill set) in their filings, then they should ensure that their disclosure controls (1) are broad enough to capture information related to all risk categories and (2) include the timely sharing of information with management or a disclosure committee.[29]

VII. Stakeholder: Government Agencies

A. Case Study: SEC Climate and ESG Task Force

The SEC launched the Climate and ESG Task Force within the Division of Enforcement to develop initiatives to proactively identify ESG-related misconduct consistent with increased investor reliance on climate and ESG-related disclosure and investment. According to the SEC, "[t]he Climate and ESG Task Force is coordinating the effective use of Division resources, including through the use of sophisticated data analysis to mine and assess information across registrants, to identify potential violations including material gaps or misstatements in issuers' disclosure of climate risks under existing rules, and disclosure and compliance issues relating to investment advisers' and funds' ESG strategies."[30] In 2022, the Climate and ESG Task Force initiated at least six ESG-related enforcement actions.[31]

---

[26] See Jane Norberg et al., *What the SEC's Activision Blizzard Settlement Means for ESG Enforcement Trends, Company Disclosures, and Whistleblower Protections*, Arnold & Porter Kaye Scholer LLP (Feb. 23, 2023), https://www.arnoldporter.com/en/perspectives/advisories/2023/02/what-the-secs-activision-blizzard-settlemnt-means.

[27] *Id.*

[28] *Id.*

[29] *Id.*

[30] *Spotlight on Enforcement Task Force Focused on Climate and ESG Issues*, SEC, https://www.sec.gov/spotlight/enforcement-task-force-focused-climate-esg-issues (Nov. 29, 2022).

[31] *Id.*

The SEC has the ability and responsibility to require disclosures, including ESG-related disclosures, that would further its mission to protect investors; promote more fair, orderly, and efficient markets; promote capital formation; and protect the public interest.[32] These responsibilities require the SEC to ensure that market participants have reliable, consistent, and comparable information. Much has been written about whether the information required to be disclosed must be "material," for example, having a quantitative impact on share price or financial performance of a company. This chapter leaves the materiality debate for CHAPTER 23—PUBLIC COMPANY DISCLOSURES. Rather, we note that Congress deemed federal securities disclosures essential because they found that the lack of reliable disclosures was a key contributor to the frenzied speculation that led to the stock market crash of 1929 and the economic devastation that ensued.[33] The SEC has mandated specific disclosures where it deemed them necessary, such as the requirement that public companies disclose when they repurchase their own shares,[34] but more often proscribes general guidelines for disclosure to be applied to unique facts rather than one-size-fits-all mandates. It is reasonable then to suggest that any forthcoming promulgation from the SEC will follow suit and will proscribe guidelines for ESG disclosure, and it will necessarily take years to develop a clear understanding of the implementation and effect of those guidelines.

VIII. Stakeholder: Nongovernmental Industry Groups

Nongovernmental organizations play an important role in solving climate change, and an increasingly important role in bridging gaps between public policy advocates and businesses and investors. There are many task forces and coalitions where industry leaders have come together on a voluntary basis to establish self-imposed standards and goals with respect to reducing carbon emissions and greenhouse gases.

A. Case Study: Commercial Airlines and the International Air Transport Association Pledge

The aviation industry accounts for 12 percent of CO_2 emissions from all transportation sources, compared to 74 percent from road transport, and contributes 2.1 percent of all human-induced CO_2 emissions.[35] Airlines are recidivist polluters. But of course, access to air travel and air cargo services is essential to interstate and international commerce and to our basic personal freedoms to relocate for career or other reasons, to maintain bonds with friends and family, and to broaden our cultural awareness of the world.

Most major airlines are members of the International Air Transport Association (IATA), an industry group that supports aviation with global standards for safety, security, and sustainability. There are 290 member airlines in IATA, including American Airlines, Delta Airlines, and United Airlines.

[32] *See What We Do*, SEC, https://www.sec.gov/about/what-we-do (Nov. 22, 2021).

[33] *See* Securities and Trust Indentures, 15 U.S.C. Ch. 2A; Securities Exchanges, 15 U.S.C. Ch. 2B.

[34] *See* 17 C.F.R. § 240.10b-18.

[35] *See Facts & Figures*, AIR TRANS. ACTION GRP., https://www.atag.org/facts-figures/ (last visited Mar. 9, 2023).

In October 2021, IATA member airlines adopted a resolution at its 2021 IATA General Meeting committing them to achieving net-zero carbon emissions from their operations by 2050 (IATA Pledge).

The aviation sector produces 900 million tons of CO_2 per year, according to IATA. That means that in the period 2021 through 2050, commercial aviation is expected to produce a cumulative total of 21.2 gigatons of CO_2. So then, the aviation industry faces a unique challenge in helping the world achieve net-zero carbon emissions. According to IATA, the solution is multifaceted.

Most flights are powered by jet gasoline, although some partially run on biofuels. When burned, gasoline is converted to CO_2.[36] In order to achieve the IATA Pledge, more sustainable aviation fuels (SAFs), derived from nontraditional feedstocks, agricultural waste, forestry residues, and algae, will need to be incorporated into jet fuel. Currently, commercial aviation fuel is subject to blending limits. But increasing SAF use from less than 0.1 percent of all aviation fuels in 2021 to around 10 percent by 2030 in line with the IATA Pledge will require investment in production capacity and new policies such as fuel taxes, low-carbon fuel standards, and mandatory blending. The technology to process SAFs into usable fuel is advancing, although most SAF technologies are in the early stage, and there is no identifiable SAF lead horse yet. Nonetheless, commercial airlines are showing they are willing to increase their use of SAFs. For example, Wyoming corporation Raven SR Inc. announced on January 17, 2023 a memorandum of understanding to supply Japan Airlines SAFs derived from green waste, municipal solid waste, organic waste, and methane from municipal solid waste over a 10-year period.[37]

Other measures to achieve the IATA Pledge will require incorporating electric and hydrogen technology into airline operations. For example, CNBC, the *Washington Post*, and other media outlets have reported that United Airlines is investing heavily in electric aircraft. The plan, they report, is to have electric aircraft flying regional routes by the end of the decade. Battery-powered aircraft are being developed by Swedish start-up company Heart Aerospace. In July 2021, it was reported that United Airlines placed an order for 100 electric planes. United Airlines has also invested an undisclosed amount in the company through its venture funding arm at the time of the deal. United Airlines has disclosed plans to buy electric air taxis and hydrogen-electric engines, and is investing in the emerging companies developing the new technologies.[38] According to SEC filings, several public aviation companies are reporting that their forecasted budgets include costs associated with incorporating greener technology into their operations. This includes investing in experimental technology, commissioning flights to test electric and hydrogen aircraft engines, and incorporating sonic aircraft into their fleets.

---

[36] See Hannah Ritchie, *Climate Change and Flying: What Share of Global CO_2 Emissions Come From Aviation?*, Our World in Data (Oct. 22, 2020), https://ourworldindata.org/co2-emissions-from-aviation.

[37] *Raven SR Agrees to Supply Sustainable Aviation Fuel to Japan Airlines*, PR Newswire (Jan. 17, 2023), https://www.prnewswire.com/news-releases/raven-sr-agrees-to-supply-sustainable-aviation-fuel-to-japan-airlines-301722984.html.

[38] *See* Ian Thomas, *United Airlines Is Aiming to Have Electric Planes Flying by 2030*, CNBC (Oct. 10, 2022, 11:52 AM), https://www.cnbc.com/2022/10/06/united-airlines-is-aiming-to-have-electric-planes-flying-by-2030.html.

Increasing the use of SAFs and hydrogen and electric technologies in the aviation industry will move the carbon emissions needle, but they alone may not be enough to achieve the IATA Pledge by 2050. IATA's strategy also relies on a system of carbon capture and emissions trading to start the transition away from carbon-emitting fuels, amounting to 19 percent of the total reduction in CO_2 emissions.[39] Through these collective measures, the traveling public will reap the benefits of seemingly rapid developments in technology and will have access to cleaner air travel. After the immense investment being made by airlines and emerging technology companies, however, there is no guarantee that your luggage will not get lost.

IX. Stakeholder: Large Investors, States, Pension Funds, and Retirees

The ESG agenda is a new tool in the toolbox. ESG provides large investors and investment funds with a tool that is being used to shape corporate and government behavior. It can be used to justify a financial firm's divestiture of investments that do not promote the firm's social or political agenda. On the other hand, ESG is being brandished by states and local governments whose political or economic interests are adversely impacted by the ESG agenda. In the crosshairs, we find retirees and pension fund beneficiaries.

A. Case Study: BlackRock

1. *Reallocation, Capital Denial, Divestment*

BlackRock is the world's biggest asset manager, which oversees around $10 trillion for investors.[40] BlackRock has long been touted as a leader in bringing awareness to carbon emissions and climate change and has been a proponent of low-carbon renewable energy.

In 2020, BlackRock's CEO, Larry Fink, sent his annual letter to clients, captioned "*Sustainability as BlackRock's New Standard for Investing*."[41] The letter served as a manifesto for putting ESG at the heart of economic decisions and foretold the firm's new focus for investment strategies and capital reallocation. BlackRock's revised ESG Integration Statement as of December 13, 2022, carries the ESG theme forward: "Our investment conviction is that ESG-integrated portfolios can provide better risk-adjusted returns to investors over the long-term, and that ESG-related data provides an increasingly important set of tools to identify unpriced risks and opportunities within portfolios."[42]

---

[39] Tangi Quemener, *Zero Net Emissions by 2050: A Huge Challenge for Airline Industry*, PHYS.ORG (Oct. 5, 2021), https://phys.org/news/2021-10-net-emissions-huge-airline-industry.html.

[40] Irina Ivanova, *BlackRock Touts Investment in Fossil Fuels After Threat from Texas Official*, CBS NEWS (Feb. 18, 2022, 8:00 AM), https://www.cbsnews.com/news/blackrock-texas-fossil-fuels-boycott.

[41] BlackRock's Global Executive Committee, *BlackRock's 2020 Letter to Clients: Sustainability as BlackRock's New Standard for Investing*, BLACKROCK (2020), https://www.blackrock.com/corporate/investor-relations/2020-blackrock-client-letter.

[42] BLACKROCK, BLACKROCK ESG INTEGRATION STATEMENT 3 (Dec. 13, 2022), https://www.blackrock.com/corporate/literature/publication/blk-esg-investment-statement-web.pdf.

For large investors like BlackRock, complete divestment from fossil fuel companies would be impractical if not impossible. As reported by CBS News, Kirsten Spalding, senior program director of the Ceres Investor Network, which advocates for sustainable investment practices, said on the topic of divestment, "You can't construct robust portfolios without an energy company. So they've got to transform those companies, for sure."[43] Mr. Fink confirmed the same in his 2022 annual letter to CEOs, "BlackRock does not pursue divestment from oil and gas companies as a policy."[44]

While divestment may not be an option for large financial firms, social and political agendas can inform the firms' capital allocation, reallocation, and investment decisions. Do these efforts by BlackRock and other large financial firms come at the expense of oil-producing states like Texas and traditional oil and gas companies? Do these efforts amount to a boycott of Texas's oil companies? If financial firms will transform companies rather than divest their investments in them, what threats do states and lawmakers perceive?

2. *States, Responses*

Texas, Florida, and other states have publicly accused BlackRock and other financial firms of harming companies located in their states by using ESG criteria in their investment decisions. In August 2022, Texas Comptroller Glenn Heger accused 10 financial firms, including BlackRock, BNP Paribas, UBS, and nearly 350 investment funds, of using ESG initiatives to justify boycotting energy companies. Mr. Heger said the focus on ESG in finance had become a proxy for political agendas.[45]

Mr. Heger directed the state's pension funds to divest from these firms, relying on authority of a bill passed by the Texas legislature in 2021 prohibiting state investment with financial actors that "boycott energy companies."[46] Florida and at least six other states have already announced plans to pull funds from the New York-based firm. In October 2022, Louisiana decided to remove almost $800 million in state funds from the asset manager, claiming the firm's "blatantly anti-fossil policies would destroy Louisiana's economy."[47]

However, as a practical matter, Texas and other states' pension funds cannot easily divest from blacklisted firms for a host of reasons, including the redemption gates set by funds in which they are invested and fiduciary duties of the trusts managing assets on behalf of pension fund members.

However, states and lawmakers are finding ways other than divestment to protect their states and constituencies. In 2022, states including Oklahoma, West Virginia, and Kentucky

[43] Ivanova, *supra* note 40.

[44] Larry Fink, *The Power of Capitalism*, BLACKROCK (Dec. 2022), https://www.blackrock.com/corporate/investor-relations/larry-fink-ceo-letter.

[45] Catherine Clifford, Texas Accuses 10 Financial Companies, Including BlackRock, of 'Boycotting' Energy Companies and Orders State Pension Funds to Divest from Holdings, CNBC (Aug. 25, 2022, 2:49 PM), https://www.cnbc.com/2022/08/25/texas-says-10-companies-including-blackrock-boycotting-energy-.html.

[46] S. 13, 2021 Leg., 87th Sess. (Tex. 2021) (enacted), https://capitol.texas.gov/tlodocs/87R/billtext/pdf/SB00013F.pdf.

[47] Saijel Kishan & Danielle Moran, *Republicans Prepare to Ramp Up Their Anti-ESG Campaign in 2023*, BLOOMBERG L. (Dec. 29, 2022, 6:00 AM), https://news.bloomberglaw.com/environment-and-energy/republicans-prepare-to-ramp-up-their-anti-esg-campaign-in-2023.

passed legislation to limit state business with firms that engage in "boycotts" of the oil and gas industry. Following enactment, West Virginia announced it would not award state banking contracts to five firms: JPMorgan, Wells Fargo, Goldman Sachs, BlackRock, and Morgan Stanley.[48]

Florida Governor Ron DeSantis led the effort in 2022 to pass a state resolution specifying that ESG considerations of any kind will not be included in the state of Florida's pension investment management practices.[49] Unlike other states, Florida's approach does not focus on whether industries friendly to the state are being boycotted by investors. Rather, it reaffirms fiduciary duties and prioritizes the highest financial return on investment for Florida taxpayers and retirees. The resolution provides that Florida state pension funds must make investments "based only on pecuniary factors [that] do not include the consideration of the furtherance of social, political, or ideological interests."[50]

As of February 2023, lawmakers in a dozen states this year have proposed bills that would limit access to state contracts and penalize companies for considering ESG factors over financial returns,[51] and more than a dozen Republican state attorneys general have spoken out against ESG financial practices.[52] Governor DeSantis is weighing barring the state and local governments from using environmental, social, governance criteria when issuing municipal bonds, and to require state and local government investments only be guided on potential returns.

There are many takeaways from the battle between BlackRock and its peer firms, on the one hand, and states and lawmakers, on the other hand. The whipsaw will likely continue until we see action at the federal level, whether through Congress, the SEC, the U.S. Department of Labor, or another regulatory scheme, to put a stick in the ground and declare which social values should be advanced, at what cost, and to whom.

Key Takeaways

Every company has a set of stakeholders. But, the list of constituencies claiming to have an interest in for-profit companies is growing.

Increasingly, non-shareholder groups are voicing their expectations that companies achieve social goals—social goals that may or may not be aligned with a board of director's

[48] Carolyn Fortuna, *BlackRock Battles Texas Again Over Divestments*, CleanTechnica (Sept. 5, 2022), https://cleantechnica.com/2022/09/05/blackrock-battles-texas-again-over-divestments/.

[49] Press Release, Fla. Governor Ron DeSantis, Governor Ron DeSantis Eliminates ESG Considerations from State Pension Investments (Aug. 23, 2022), https://www.flgov.com/2022/08/23/governor-ron-desantis-eliminates-esg-considerations-from-state-pension-investments/.

[50] *See also* State Bd. of Admin. of Fla., A Resolution Directing an Update to the Investment Policy Statement and Proxy Voting Policies for the Florida Retirement System Defined Benefit Pension Plan, and Directing the Organization and Execution of an Internal Review 3 (2022), https://www.flgov.com/wp-content/uploads/2022/08/ESG-Resolution-Final.pdf.

[51] Brenna Goth, *State Lawmakers Push Texas-style Business Penalties Against ESG*, Bloomberg L. (Jan. 30, 2023, 5:00 AM), https://news.bloomberglaw.com/esg/state-lawmakers-push-texas-style-business-penalties-against-esg.

[52] Andrew Ramonas & Clara Hudson, *ESG Top of Mind as New State Attorneys General Flex Powers (1)*, Bloomberg L. (Feb. 13, 2023, 1:38 PM), https://news.bloomberglaw.com/esg/esg-top-of-mind-as-new-state-attorneys-general-flex-powers.

duty to create shareholder value and board members' and corporate officers' obligations to fulfill their fiduciary duties.

Boards of directors and management groups are left to their own devices first, to identify their unique stakeholder groups; second, to determine whether a non-shareholder constituency deserves a place in the company's line of sight; and third, to establish a plan and devote resources to address the group's expectations. Boards of directors and management groups are tackling these issues largely on an unregulated, voluntary basis. Moreover, boards of directors and management teams are expected to prove performance to these constituencies where there are no uniform, standardized reporting or measuring systems in place.

Third-party consultants and advisors are new to the party, and are themselves, stakeholders in the ESG ecosystem. Advisors seek to fill the board and management void, and have created a cottage industry in which ESG professionals render their advice to parties who owe fiduciary duties. There are real risks and exposure to boards of directors and corporate officers who fail to fulfill their fiduciary and statutory duties for want of achieving social goals or by accepting third-party professionals' advice unchecked. These risks will continue until we evolve from an environment of voluntary, non-standardized data collection and disclosure to a system of data collection and disclosure that is regulated and that offers a uniform set of determinable metrics against which companies can be measured.

3

ESG Backlash: The Efforts to Constrain ESG

Gregory Harrington

I. Introduction

Notwithstanding significant legislative, regulatory, and public relations gains made by ESG proponents in recent years, these efforts have not been applauded universally. There has been significant and growing criticism of different aspects of these efforts, from both public and private actors, and the backlash has taken multiple forms, including litigation, legislation, and policy advocacy.

The breadth of the backlash defies easy classification of its critics. In fact, many of the critics would likely not consider themselves to be part of *any* backlash and would certainly not see themselves as critics of environmental protection, measures to benefit historically marginalized groups, or good corporate governance. Much of the criticism by these groups is either directed to the methods being used to achieve the stated goals of ESG proponents or to the specifics of proposed legislation or regulation, as opposed to criticism of the goals themselves. They often criticize the means, not the ends.

At the same time, there are other critics who ask, for example, whether the associated costs are worth the perceived benefits, while others ask whether proposed solutions address issues that even require solving.

ESG proponents are often assisted in these efforts by a wide range of third parties with influence over these institutions, including in the case of publicly traded corporations directly by large institutional investors and indirectly by proxy advisory firms. Investment managers, foundations, university endowments, and institutional investors are subject to their own pressures, from both inside and outside their institutions.

One significant criticism made of ESG proponents is the inconsistency of the means with which activists seek to achieve ESG goals with traditional views of shareholder-focused corporate governance and the long-established fiduciary duties of members of boards of directors (under their duty of loyalty) to maximize the economic return to stockholders.

II. Fiduciary Duties and Agency Problems

One method proponents of ESG goals use to affect the decision-making by corporations, investment managers, foundations, university endowments, and similar entities is by influencing the governance process of these institutions. However, critics question whether the persons in charge of these institutions, including members of the boards of directors, boards of trustees, or similar bodies, are permitted to consider ESG factors in their decision-making absent a legal requirement to do so. Members of boards are generally subject to fiduciary obligations under the state law of the jurisdiction of the institution's incorporation or organization, while the powers and decision-making of investment managers (which may or may not be subject to fiduciary obligations) are generally limited by the stated investment purposes of their founding documents (such as a charter), client investment management agreements, or similar arrangements, including for university and other endowments with the terms established by donors of restricted bequests.

A. Fiduciary Duties of Corporate Directors

One aspect of the backlash against ESG efforts is, in fact, a defense of long-established views of corporate governance.

Under Delaware law, it is a central tenet that "directors, rather than shareholders, manage the business and affairs of the corporation."[1] As a result, the power of corporate directors "carries with it certain fundamental fiduciary obligations to the corporation and its shareholders."[2] These fiduciary obligations effectively constrain the actions of directors, ensuring that any act by a director is "twice-tested," first for legal authorization in the form of contract and statute, and second for equity in the form of fiduciary duties.[3]

The fiduciary obligations of corporate directors include the duty of loyalty.[4] Under such a duty, corporate directors must act in the best interests of their company, not their own personal interests.[5] Even more specifically, corporate directors must "maximize the economic value of a for-profit Delaware corporation for the benefit of its stockholders."[6]

[1] Aronson v. Lewis, 473 A.2d 805, 811 (Del. 1984); DE. CODE ANN. tit. 8, § 141(a).

[2] *Id.* at 811 (citing Loft, Inc. v. Guth, 2 A.2d 225 (Del. Ch. 1938)).

[3] *In re* Inv. Bancorp, Inc. Stockholder Litig., 177 A.3d 1208, 1222 (Del. 2017).

[4] *In re* Walt Disney Co. Derivative Litig., 907 A.2d 693, 745 (Del. Ch. 2005).

[5] Cede & Co. v. Technicolor, Inc., 634 A.2d 345, 361 (Del. 1993) ("[T]he duty of loyalty mandates that the best interest of the corporation and its shareholders takes precedence over any interest possessed by a director, officer or controlling shareholder and not shared by the stockholders generally.").

[6] eBay Domestic Holdings, Inc. v. Newmark, 16 A.3d 1, 34 (Del. Ch. 2010).

Proponents of ESG, as a counterpoint, often put forward an alternative view of corporate governance, the so-called "stakeholder" model of corporate governance. Under this model, directors can make decisions to the benefit of constituencies other than the owners of the corporation, the stockholders, even if the benefit given to these constituencies does not convey any benefit, even in the long term, to stockholders. The board would be permitted, notwithstanding their duty of loyalty, to transfer stockholder wealth from the corporation to third parties. In the context of the debate over ESG, this might include the board pushing forward environmental, social, or governance policies of the corporation that arguably confer a benefit on society as a whole but do not necessarily add any value to the corporation itself or its stockholders.

1. *The Uncertain Financial Value of ESG Initiatives*

Critics of ESG proponents argue that corporate directors may breach their fiduciary duty to stockholders by adopting ESG-related initiatives or disclosing ESG-related information.

As an umbrella term encompassing a broad array of environmental, social, and governance criteria, ESG primarily concerns social values, not financial values.[7] Consider, for instance, the claim that climate change supports the pursuit of ESG-related initiatives because of its effect upon a corporation's long-term financial value and assets. Although climate change may generate physical risks, such as adverse weather events, and transition risks, such as costs to firms incurred by complying with future climate laws and regulations, there exists "no universally-accepted measure of what these future changes will be and how they will affect individual companies."[8] In fact, critics argue, there is no evidence of a causal link between climate conservation and superior economic returns.[9]

If the information sought by ESG activists and other stakeholders involved the financial value of a corporation and its assets, then the information would likely be material and is already covered by existing disclosure rules.[10]

Thus, critics argue, the pressure to adopt ESG-related initiatives to serve environmental or social goals is not aligned with a corporate director's fiduciary duties. Rather, it is an attempt to harness corporate power to enhance the interests of employees, customers, communities, and the environment.[11] That is, it is an attempt to take stockholder resources to address what ESG activists see as socially detrimental activity due to the failure of governments to take adequate action. In the words of Davis Soderberg of the National Center for Public Policy, "[a]s a result, these corporations play a much broader role in influencing

[7] Paul G. Mahoney & Julia D. Mahoney, *The New Separation of Ownership and Control: Institutional Investors and ESG*, 2 Colum. Bus. L. Rev. 840, 849 (2021).

[8] *Id.* at 849–50.

[9] Lawrence A. Cunningham et al., *The Proposed SEC Climate Disclosure Rule: A Comment from Twenty-Two Professors of Law and Finance* (July 6, 2022), https://corpgov.law.harvard.edu/2022/07/06/the-proposed-sec-climate-disclosure-rule-a-comment-from-twenty-two-professors-of-law-and-finance/.

[10] Hester M. Peirce, *We Are Not the Securities and Environment Commission - At Least Not Yet*, Securities and Exchange Commission (SEC) (Mar. 21, 2022), https://www.sec.gov/news/statement/peirce-climate-disclosure-20220321.

[11] Lucian A. Bebchuk & Roberto Tallarita, *The Illusory Promise of Stakeholder Governance*, 106 Cornell L. Rev. 91, 100 (2020).

decisions regarding environmental issues, workers' rights, racial equity programs, and other important political topics that ought to be decided through our democratic processes," and as a result lead to "unchecked power for CEOs and corporate board members while skipping over any kind of democratic process in policy-making—like passing legislation in state and federal lawmaking bodies."[12]

2. *The Business Judgment Rule and Breach of Fiduciary Duty*

Another criticism made of efforts by ESG activists with respect to proposed changes to long-established corporate governance principles is that the adoption of certain ESG policies would risk the protections that corporate directors enjoy under the "business judgment" rule.

The business judgment rule serves as a well-established presumption that "in making a business decision the directors of a corporation acted on an informed basis . . . and in the honest belief that the action taken was in the best interests of the company" and its shareholders.[13] In turn, the decisions of a board of directors will be upheld by a reviewing Delaware court unless those actions cannot be "attributed to any rational business purpose."[14] The business judgment rule may be rebutted, however, if a plaintiff can show that the board of directors violated one of its fiduciary duties in connection with a challenged action.[15] And under such circumstances, the burden shifts to a corporation's directors to prove that the challenged action was "entirely fair" to the corporation and its shareholders.[16] ESG critics argue that, because the adoption of certain ESG-related initiatives decisions by corporate directors do not explicitly and directly benefit the corporation or its shareholders, advancing or adopting ESG-related initiatives is not likely protected by the business judgment rule.

Although certain states have enacted constituency statutes that permit directors to consider the interest of constituencies other than the stockholders, Delaware has no such provision. Rather, Delaware law mandates that the "stockholders' best interest must always, within legal limits, be the end. Other constituencies may be considered only instrumentally to advance that end."[17] Thus, when making corporate decisions regarding ESG-related initiatives, corporate directors must first consider their responsibility, under their fiduciary duties, to "promote the value of the corporation for the benefit of its stockholders."[18] If the pursuit of ESG-related investments or initiatives could be construed as acting on behalf of stakeholders other than shareholders or for social or ethical values, then a corporate director or officer's protective presumption under the business judgment rule may be rebutted.

[12] *ESG and the Corruption of Democracy*, NAT'L CTR. FOR PUB. POL'Y RSCH. (Aug. 25, 2021), https://nationalcenter.org/ncppr/2021/08/25/esg-and-the-corruption-of-democracy/.

[13] *Aronson*, 473 A.2d at 812.

[14] Sinclair Oil Corp. v. Levien, 280 A.2d 717, 720 (Del. 1971).

[15] Emerald Partners v. Berlin, 787 A.2d 85, 91 (Del. 2001).

[16] *Walt Disney*, 907 A.2d at 747 (citing *Emerald Partners*, 787 A.2d at 91).

[17] *In re* Trados Inc. S'holder Litig., 73 A.3d 17, 37 (Del. Ch. 2013).

[18] *eBay*, 16 A.3d at 34.

B. Fiduciary Duties of Fund Managers

Similar to corporate directors and officers, investment advisors, plan managers, and trustees who oversee investment funds and fund assets are also subject to a strict set of fiduciary duties established by law. Across all types of funds, these fiduciary duties include the duties of loyalty and care that may be, as critics argue, inconsistent with ESG-related investing and initiatives, and therefore decisions made in support of ESG-related initiatives could result in these individuals facing liability for breach of fiduciary duty.

1. Employee Retirement Income Security Act Plan Managers

The Employee Retirement Income Security Act of 1974 (ERISA) sets minimum standards for voluntarily established retirement and health plans in private industry.[19] Under federal law, plan managers, investment advisors, and trustees who retain management control over plan assets are fiduciaries to a plan.[20] These fiduciary duties include the duties of loyalty and care, which constrain the actions of plan fiduciaries.[21]

Under ERISA's duty of loyalty, a plan fiduciary must act "solely in the interest of the participants and beneficiaries" and for the "exclusive purpose" of benefiting them.[22] Thus, federal codification of the "sole interest rule" establishes a specific and narrow path of considerations for ERISA plan managers when considering investment strategy, including when providing mutual fund or exchange-traded fund selections for self-directed individual accounts.[23] Even more specifically, a plan manager "has a duty to the beneficiaries [and participants] not to be influenced by the interest of any third person or by motives other than the accomplishment of the purposes of the trust [ERISA plan]," according to the Restatement (Third) of Trusts.[24]

Moreover, the Supreme Court has stated that ERISA's fiduciary duties involve a "common investor purpose," which requires the strict pursuit of *financial* benefits for plan beneficiaries, and do not permit the pursuit of nonfinancial or nonmonetary benefits.[25]

If the motive for investing in ESG-related funds involves nonfinancial benefits, such as moral or ethical concerns or the benefit of a nonparticipant or nonbeneficiary stakeholder,

[19] 29 U.S.C. § 1003.

[20] 29 U.S.C. § 1002(21)(A) ("[A] person is a fiduciary with respect to a plan to the extent (i) he exercises any discretionary authority or discretionary control respecting management of such plan or exercises any authority or control respecting management or disposition of its assets."); 29 U.S.C. § 1102(c)(3); 29 U.S.C. § 1105(c)(3).

[21] Cent. States, Se. & Sw. Areas Pension Fund v. Cent. Transp., Inc., 472 U.S. 559, 570–71 (1985).

[22] 29 U.S.C. § 1104(a)(1).

[23] Bernard S. Sharfman, *ESG Investing Under ERISA*, 38 Yale J. Regul. 112, 126 (2020) [hereinafter Sharfman, *ESG Investing*]; Bernard S. Sharfman, *The Conflict Between BlackRock's Shareholder Activism and ERISA's Fiduciary Duties*, 71 Case W. Res. L. Rev. 1241, 1257 (2021).

[24] Max M. Schanzenbach & Robert H. Sitkoff, *Reconciling Fiduciary Duty and Social Conscience: The Law and Economics of ESG Investing by a Trustee*, 72 Stan. L. Rev. 381, 400 (2020) (citing Restatement (Third) of Trusts § 78(l) cmt. f (Am. L. Inst. 2007)).

[25] Fifth Third Bancorp v. Dudenhoeffer, 573 U.S. 409, 421 (2014) ("Read in the context of ERISA as a whole, the term 'benefits' in the provision [§ 1104(a)(1)] must be understood to refer to the sort of *financial* benefits (such as retirement income) that trustees who manage investments typically seek to secure for the trust's beneficiaries.").

then—critics argue—plan managers cannot take such considerations into account.[26] But if a plan manager solely considers ESG-related factors to enhance the risk or return of an investment without regard to nonfinancial considerations or the plan manager's own preferences, then such considerations may be permissible under one's fiduciary obligations.[27]

2. U.S. Department of Labor Proposed Rule Related to Employee Retirement Income Security Act

In October 2021, the Biden administration's U.S. Department of Labor (the "Labor Department") proposed expanding pension fund managers' fiduciary obligations to include ESG-related factors when making investment decisions and exercising shareholder rights.[28] This is in contrast to a rule finalized by the Labor Department in 2020, under the Trump administration, which explicitly limited pension fund fiduciaries to select investments and courses of action solely on "pecuniary factors."[29] Critics argued that the rule, as proposed, would disregard common practice related to trusts and funds. On November 22, 2022, the Labor Department published the final rule (to take effect on January 30, 2023), which took a more neutral position on the consideration of ESG factors than the rule proposed in October 2021.[30]

Critics of permitting ESG-related factors as part of investment decision-making point to, for example, the Uniform Prudent Investor Act (UPIA), a model statute related to investment decision-making by fiduciaries that a majority of states have adopted. Under the UPIA, fiduciaries should consider "the risk and return objectives" of a trust by diversifying investments in accordance with Modern Portfolio Theory.[31] However, the UPIA states that "[n]o form of so-called 'social investing' is consistent with the duty of loyalty if the investment activity entails sacrificing the interests of trust beneficiaries."[32]

Others argue that ESG-focused investing is often poorly understood by retail investors and plan beneficiaries, and that the beneficiaries and participants of pension funds may not want their money invested in unproven ESG-related initiatives and investments. According to one survey by the Financial Industry Regulatory Authority (FINRA) and the University of Chicago, a significant portion of retail investors are unaware of ESG investing, and a quarter incorrectly believe the acronym ESG stands for "Earnings, Stock, Growth."[33] Moreover,

---

[26] Sharfman, *ESG Investing*, *supra* note 23, at 118 (citing Schanzenbach & Sitkoff, *supra* note 24, at 389–90).

[27] Sharfman, *ESG Investing*, *supra* note 23, at 119 (citing Randy Bauslaugh & Hendrik Garz, *Pension Fund Investment: Managing Environmental, Social and Governance (ESG) Factor Integration*, McCarthy Tetrault (May 1, 2019)).

[28] Prudence and Loyalty in Selecting Plan Investments and Exercising Shareholder Rights, 86 Fed. Reg. 57272 (proposed Oct. 14, 2021) (to be codified at 29 C.F.R. pt. 2550).

[29] Financial Factors in Selecting Plan Investments, 85 Fed. Reg. 72846 (Nov. 13, 2020) (to be codified at 29 C.F.R. pts. 2509, 2550).

[30] Prudence and Loyalty in Selecting Plan Investments and Exercising Shareholder Rights, 87 Fed. Reg. 73822 (Dec. 1, 2022) (to be codified at 29 C.F.R. pt. 2550).

[31] Unif. Prudent Investor Act § 2(b), 3 (1994).

[32] Unif. Prudent Investor Act § 5 cmt. (1994).

[33] Gary Mottola et al., Consumer Insights: Money & Investing, Investors Say They Can Change the World, if They Only Knew How: Six Things to Know About ESG and Retail Investors 2 (Mar. 2022), https://www.finrafoundation.org/sites/finrafoundation/files/Consumer-Insights-Money-and-Investing.pdf.

although ESG movements have pushed to curtail U.S. oil production, critics point to studies that show that 61 percent of U.S. residents favor expanding the domestic production of natural gas.[34] And while ESG activists advocate diversifying corporate boards, critics point to studies showing that 74 percent of Americans believe that employers should solely consider a person's qualifications in employment decisions.[35]

Yet, critics say, pension funds are likely to ignore their beneficiaries' and participants' wishes given that their trustees are subject to unique political pressures.[36] Whereas market discipline may operate on other kinds of fund managers, pension fund trustees respond more strongly to political discipline.[37] At times, California Public Employees' Retirement System trustees have even stated that the fund's purpose was social, not financial.[38] And in 2021, a group of Idaho lawmakers, including Idaho's lieutenant governor, requested that the state's pension system divest holdings of large tech and social media platforms that "censor free speech and the free exchange of ideas."[39]

3. *Fiduciary Duties Related to Index Funds*

Critics also argue that the increased inclusion of ESG-related criteria in shareholder proxy voting creates a conflict of interest between fund managers and investors, likely breaching fiduciary obligations. Under the Investment Advisers Act of 1940, investment advisors owe their customers certain fiduciary duties, including the duties of care and loyalty.[40] Under the duty of loyalty, an investment advisor must put the interests of its client ahead of its own and not subordinate its client's interests to its own.[41] In addition, fund managers and investment advisors may not forgo the financial return of all beneficiaries to serve the social goals of some beneficiaries or other supposed stakeholders.[42]

But, critics argue, by advertising and selling index funds that promise diversification, profitability, and the pursuit of ESG objectives, fund managers may be materially misrepresenting their investment vehicles.[43] Because managers of index funds construct, advertise,

---

[34] Alec Tyson & Alison Spencer, *A Majority of Americans Favor Expanding Natural Gas Production to Export to Europe*, Pew Rsch. Ctr. (May 12, 2022), https://www.pewresearch.org/science/2022/05/12/a-majority-of-americans-favor-expanding-natural-gas-production-to-export-to-europe/.

[35] Juliana M. Horowitz, *Americans See Advantages and Challenges in Country's Growing Racial and Ethnic Diversity*, Pew Rsch. Ctr. (May 8, 2019), https://www.pewresearch.org/social-trends/2019/05/08/americans-see-advantages-and-challenges-in-countrys-growing-racial-and-ethnic-diversity/.

[36] Mahoney & Mahoney, *supra* note 7, at 860–61 (citing Roberta Romano, *Public Pension Fund Activism in Corporate Governance Reconsidered*, 93 Colum. L. Rev. 795, 796 (1993)).

[37] *Id.* at 861–62 ("In some instances, these entitlements have a legally protected status that would make it difficult, short of government insolvency, for the state government not to make up shortfalls out of general tax revenues.").

[38] *Id.* at 862 (quoting Mary Williams Walsh, *Calpers Wears a Party, or Union, Label*, N.Y. Times, Oct. 13, 2002, at B1).

[39] *Id.* at 864 (citing *PERSI Responds to Letter Encouraging State to Divest from Big Tech Stocks*, Idaho News (Jan. 25, 2021, 5:10 PM)).

[40] SEC v. Cap. Gains Rsch. Bureau, Inc., 375 U.S. 180, 194 (1963).

[41] Commission Interpretation Regarding Standard of Conduct for Investment Advisers, Investment Advisors Act Release No. 5248, 84 Fed. Reg. 33669 (July 12, 2019) (to be codified at 17 C.F.R. pt. 276).

[42] Mahoney & Mahoney, *supra* note 7, at 843.

[43] Eric C. Chaffee, *Index Funds and ESG Hypocrisy*, 71 Case W. Rsrv. L. Rev. 1295, 1307 (2021).

and sell those funds in accordance with Modern Portfolio Theory, investors expect to achieve the greatest likelihood of returns, while minimizing risk, through diversification.[44] In fact, it is through index funds that retail investors have the ability to diversify their portfolios.[45] By attempting to shift the views of corporate directors to their own, critics argue, ESG activists "create a uniform commitment within companies to ESG-related issues" in contradiction with Modern Portfolio Theory.[46] If fiduciaries have promised to pursue diversification and ESG standardization, then critics question whether they have breached their fiduciary duty and failed to accomplish both goals.[47]

And in many ways, the material misrepresentation of an ESG-specific investment fund is no different than traditional investment vehicles. Consider, for example, an ESG mutual fund promising to exclude fossil fuels from its portfolio but inadvertently investing in oil services providers. Under these circumstances, critics argue, the fund sponsor or investment advisor would have engaged in "greenwashing" by conveying a false impression or providing misleading information about the sustainability of an investment product, even if it arose from an error or omission.

4. *Boycott Bills*

Another aspect of the backlash against the growing wave of ESG-related requirements, particularly as they impact the management of state retirement funds, has been the so-called "boycott bills" or "anti-ESG" requirements imposed by various state governments. These laws take many forms, but some 17 states have adopted legislation or otherwise taken administrative action or initiated litigation that would in some way limit the ability of state government entities to conduct business with companies that have taken measures to retaliate against industries based on ESG criteria.

One example of a "boycott bill" is Texas Senate Bill 13,[48] adopted in May 2021, which would effectively require Texas state-held pension funds to "sell, redeem, divest, or withdraw all publicly traded securities of [any] financial company" that "boycott[s] energy companies." This would impact an estimated $300 billion in invested assets. In August 2022, Texas Comptroller Glenn Hegar announced a list of 10 financial companies (including 1 U.S. firm and 9 European firms) and 350 individual investment funds (but not their parent entities) that would be subject to the divestment provisions.[49]

---

[44] Harry Markowitz, *Portfolio Selection*, 7 J. FIN. 77 (1952).

[45] Chaffee, *supra* note 43, at 1302 (citing Jose Azar, *The Common Ownership Trilemma*, 87 U. CHI. L. REV. 263, 265 (2020)).

[46] *Id.* at 1305.

[47] *Id.* at 1306.

[48] S. 13, 2021 Leg., 87th Sess. (Tex. 2021).

[49] Press Release, Tex. Comptroller of Pub. Accts., Texas Comptroller Glenn Hegar Announces List of Financial Companies that Boycott Energy Companies (Aug. 24, 2022), https://comptroller.texas.gov/about/media-center/news/20220824-texas-comptroller-glenn-hegar-announces-list-of-financial-companies-that-boycott-energy-companies-1661267815099.

An example of an "anti-ESG" requirement, from Florida, is a Resolution adopted in August 2022 by the State Board of Administration of Florida.[50] This Board was created under the state constitution of Florida and primarily acts as an asset management organization responsible for investing and safeguarding the assets of the Florida Retirement System Trust Fund and other funds for the State of Florida. The Resolution established that "the evaluation by the Board of an investment decision must be based only on pecuniary factors" and made clear that pecuniary factors "do not include the consideration of the furtherance of social, political, or ideological interests." The Resolution was meant to counter a proposed rule[51] of the Biden administration's Labor Department that would "remove barriers to [ERISA] plan fiduciaries' ability to consider climate change and other environmental, social and governance factors when they select investments and exercise shareholder rights."[52] The Biden administration's proposed rule is in turn a reversal of a Trump-era rule that required plan fiduciaries to select investments and investment courses of action based solely on consideration of "pecuniary factors."[53] This is discussed in greater detail below.

III. U.S. Securities and Exchange Commission's ESG Climate-Related Proposal

In March 2022, the U.S. Securities and Exchange Commission (SEC or "the Commission") released its long-anticipated proposed amendments on climate-related disclosures. The proposed amendments would require reporting companies (1) to disclose certain climate-related information in a separate section of their registration statement or annual report, and (2) to include certain climate-related financial statement metrics and related disclosure in a note to their consolidated financial statements.

Key highlights of the proposed rule include mandates to disclose:

- Scope 1 and 2 emissions;
- Scope 3 emissions, if material, "or if the registrant has set a GHG emissions target or goal that includes Scope 3 emissions, in absolute terms, not including offsets, and in terms of intensity";
- Internal carbon prices, information about the price and how it is set, if a registrant uses an internal carbon price;
- Both physical and transition risks related to each line item of the consolidated financial statement, unless, as aggregated, the impact is below a materiality threshold of 1 percent of the total line item; and

---

[50] State Bd. of Admin. of Fla., A Resolution Directing an Update to the Investment Policy Statement and Proxy Voting Policies for the Florida Retirement System Defined Benefit Pension Plan, and Directing the Organization and Execution of an Internal Review (2022), https://www.flgov.com/wp-content/uploads/2022/08/ESG-Resolution-Final.pdf.

[51] Prudence and Loyalty in Selecting Plan Investments and Exercising Shareholder Rights, *supra* note 28.

[52] Press Release, U.S. Dep't of Labor, US Department of Labor Proposes Rule to Remove Barriers to Considering Environmental, Social, Governance Factors in Plan Management (Oct. 13, 2021), https://www.dol.gov/newsroom/releases/ebsa/ebsa20211013.

[53] Financial Factors in Selecting Plan Investments, *supra* note 29.

- Information about a registrant's publicly set climate-related targets or goals, including the scope of activities, how the registrant plans to meet its climate targets, relevant data to show the registrant is making progress, and if carbon offsets or renewable energy certificates are being used.

The commissioners' discussion of the rule at the Open Meeting held on March 21, 2022, to discuss the ESG proposal illuminated sharp disagreement between the three commissioners who voted in favor of the proposal and Commissioner Hester Peirce, who voted against. Commissioner Allison Lee, who was at the forefront advocating for enhanced disclosure requirements, described the proposed rule as a watershed moment and highlighted aspects of the proposal that would ensure consistency and reliability across reporting companies.[54]

The SEC's ESG proposal received immediate comment, constructive criticism, and recommended refinements, much of which was meant to improve specific aspects of the Commission's proposal.

On the other hand, there was also immediate backlash against the proposed rule. During the Open Meeting itself, Commissioner Peirce expressed concern in her dissent that the Commission was acting "fast and loose" with the concept of materiality in proposing such sweeping changes related to climate disclosures and that the resultant disclosure requirements would not achieve stated goals of requiring comparable, constituent, and reliable information across registrants. She also stated that instead of following current SEC disclosure mandates "intended to provide investors with an accurate picture of the company's present and prospective performance through managers' own eyes," the ESG proposal would instead tell "corporate managers how regulators, doing the bidding of an array of non-investor stakeholders, expect them to run their companies."[55]

Echoing statements made by Chairman Jay Clayton, Commissioner Peirce said that the SEC's existing rules already "require companies to disclose material risks regardless of the source or cause of the risk."[56] And in foreshadowing litigation then to come, Commissioner Peirce said that the "proposal steps outside our statutory limits by using the disclosure framework to achieve objectives that are not ours to pursue and by pursuing those objectives by means of disclosure mandates that may not comport with First Amendment limitations on compelled speech."[57] She further stated in her dissent that "[t]he Commission today proposes to require companies to disclose information that may not be material to them and recasts materiality to encompass information that investors want based on interests other than their financial interest in the company doing the disclosing."[58]

[54] Statement, Allison Herren Lee, Comm'r, SEC, *Shelter from the Storm: Helping Investors Navigate Climate Change Risk* (Mar. 21, 2022), https://www.sec.gov/news/statement/lee-climate-disclosure-20220321.

[55] Statement, Hester M. Peirce, Comm'r, SEC, *We Are Not the Securities and Environment Commission—At Least Not Yet* (Mar. 21, 2022), https://www.sec.gov/news/statement/peirce-climate-disclosure-20220321.

[56] *Id.*

[57] *Id.*

[58] *Id.*

In a comment letter submitted to the Commission on June 17, 2022, five former Commissioners (including two former Chairmen) summarize their comments by saying: "The Proposal represents an unprecedented and unjustified effort beyond financial materiality and engages the Commission in matters beyond its statutory remit. Should it finalize the Proposal, the Commission endangers its credibility and risks almost certain reversal in court. It thereby endangers its proper mission, namely, the protection of investors, maintenance of fair, orderly, and efficient markets, and the facilitation of capital formation."[59]

Among their specific observations, these former commissioners state that notwithstanding that the "Commission has long limited disclosure obligations to material information, in order to give investors what they need without inundating them with useless or irrelevant information," the SEC's proposal "abandons these prudent pronouncements and the longstanding practice they represent. Instead, the Proposal would require the disclosure of, and in many cases the creation of, mountains of financially immaterial information."[60] Further, they state that "[p]erhaps more fundamentally, the Proposal oversteps the Commission's congressionally delegated regulatory authority. The Commission's rulemaking powers simply do not authorize it to require disclosure of the vast quantities of immaterial information the Proposal contemplates."[61] Echoing Commissioner Peirce's observation that the SEC is "not the Securities and Environment Commission," the former commissioners state that "the Commission has no special competence, let alone expertise, in climate science," noting that "the Commission's heavy reliance on existing disclosure protocols developed by the Task Force on Climate-related Financial Disclosures (TCFD) and frequent citation of international climate organizations underscore that the agency itself does not have the necessary expertise to address these issues, choosing instead to rely on third parties to regulate in this area."[62]

State officials also submitted comments highly critical of the proposal. Scott Fitzgerald, Treasurer of the State of Missouri, in a comment letter dated June 17, 2022, stated that "the Commission proposes hundreds of pages of detailed climate disclosures that, while they may be useful to climate activists and climate-conscious investors, have no conceivable relevance to informed financial investment decisions."[63] Fitzgerald also asserted that "the Proposal unduly interferes with corporation law, which is traditionally the province of the states. Though nominally a disclosure regulation, the Proposal would effectively regulate registrants' internal affairs, requiring massive investments in systems to track and collect information that some outside investors want and that is not necessary to run a business or report to any competent government environmental entity, to the detriment of effective corporate management and remaining investors."[64] He also stated that "[g]iven the demands of

[59] Letter from Richard C. Breeden, Chairman (1989-1993), et al., to Vanessa A. Countryman, Sec'y, SEC, at 6 (June 17, 2022), https://www.sec.gov/comments/s7-10-22/s71022-20132519-303005.pdf.

[60] *Id.* at 2.

[61] *Id.* at 4.

[62] *Id.* at 5.

[63] Letter from Scott Fitzgerald, Mo. State Treasurer, to Vanessa A. Countryman, Sec'y, SEC, at 1 (June 17, 2022), https://www.sec.gov/comments/s7-10-22/s71022-20132271-302800.pdf.

[64] *Id.* at 2.

vocal special interest groups, the Proposal's requiring disclosure of board members' climate expertise, could effectively require yet another 'single purpose' director, i.e., one with 'climate expertise,' restricting the ability of corporations to manage themselves as they see fit under state corporate law."[65]

The attorneys general of 12 states, led by Texas Attorney General Ken Paxton, in a letter dated June 17, 2022, make many of the same arguments against the SEC's proposed rule as other commenters, and state that the "host of new requirements in this Proposed Rule are motivated by a small number of environmental activists who seek to steer the economy away from fossil fuels and to impose controversial environmental, social, and governance (ESG) mandates," and if the SEC were to adopt the proposed rule, it would be usurping the role of the people's elected representatives (i.e., Congress) to set the United States' policy on climate change.[66] They go on to state that "[t]hese requirements are about using the SEC's regulatory authority to steer the economy away from fossil fuels, reduce GHG emissions, and pursue climate-related goals. The role of the SEC, however, is not to mandate the social causes favored by one group of investors (or political administration). It is to protect the average investors who are primarily interested in the financial value of companies regulated by the SEC."[67]

The letter of the attorneys general also questions whether many of the large institutional investors are representing the interests of their small investors, or just their own. Citing a statement in the Commission's release regarding the proposed rule that "[s]everal major institutional investors, which collectively have trillions of dollars in investments under management, have demanded climate-related information from the companies in which they invest," the attorneys general ask whether "these new disclosures originate with a handful of firms that seek to mandate their social preferences as part of corporate governance. Because these institutions manage other people's money, it is unclear whether their ESG advocacy is prompted by their beneficiaries' concerns, or their own priorities."[68]

The letter of the attorneys general also cites the "major questions doctrine," which prohibits regulatory agencies from exploiting ambiguous language in a statute to greatly expand their regulatory authority. The attorneys general cite a holding in *Utility Air Regulatory Group v. EPA*, 573 U.S. 302, 324 (2014), stating that "[w]hen an agency claims to discover in a long-extant statute an unheralded power to regulate a significant portion of the American economy, [courts] typically greet its announcement with a measure of skepticism."[69]

Other dissenters argue that the required disclosures would violate the First Amendment of the U.S. Constitution. The Cato Institute, in a letter dated June 17, 2022, stated its view that because "the rules would mandate disclosures that are not material to the financial performance of the securities, the rules would violate the First Amendment" as compelled speech

[65] *Id.* at 2.

[66] Letter from Ken Paxton, Tex. Att'y Gen., et al., to Vanessa A. Countryman, Sec'y, SEC, at 1 (June 17, 2022), https://www.sec.gov/comments/s7-10-22/s71022-20132121-302606.pdf.

[67] *Id.* at 7.

[68] *Id.* at 8.

[69] *Id.* at 4.

for which the government interests justifying the disclosures are neither "compelling" nor even "substantial."[70] Professor Sean Griffith of Fordham Law School makes similar points in an article published in May 2022, in which he argues that the compelled commercial speech of the SEC's proposed ESG disclosure requirement violates the First Amendment unless the SEC can justify disclosure mandates as a form of investor protection.[71] But, because (as Professor Griffith argues) "the proposed climate rules create controversy by imposing a political viewpoint, by advancing an interest group agenda at the expense of investors generally," they violate the First Amendment.[72]

The Society for Corporate Governance, in a lengthy comment letter dated June 17, 2022, echoes many of the observations of other commenters in questioning the SEC's authority to issue the proposed rule: the problems with materiality thresholds, the gross underestimation of the extraordinary costs to implement the proposed rule, and the proposed rule's focus on the interests of institutional investors instead of marginalized retail investors, among others.[73] In addition, the Society argues that the proposed rule would require reporting companies to analyze hypothetical scenarios "that may occur 10-20, or 30-50, years in the future," thereby "altering the time frames over which companies must gauge and consider materiality."[74]

A comment letter from a group of 22 professors in law and finance, led by Lawrence A. Cunningham of The George Washington University, questions whether the "investor demand" for ESG disclosures is as great as the Commission states in its proposed rule.[75] While acknowledging that widespread investor demand is a credible rationale for SEC regulation, in their letter, these professors express doubt—as did the Society for Corporate Governance—whether this demand is merely from the most vocal segment of the investment industry, which (if so) would provide "a dubious basis for the SEC to claim exercise of its statutory authority in the name of 'investor protection.'"[76] The comment letter states that "[t]he investors demanding climate-related information are overwhelmingly institutional asset managers who are managing other people's money, not their own. This raises the obvious question whether their advocacy is prompted by concern for their beneficiaries' returns or their own profitability."[77] In that connection, the comment letter states that "[t]here is no indication that the SEC has attempted to assess, much less quantify, the potential losses

[70] Letter from the Cato Institute to Vanessa A. Countryman, Sec'y, SEC, at 6 (June 17, 2022), https://www.sec.gov/comments/s7-10-22/s71022-20132199-302715.pdf.

[71] Sean J. Griffith, *What's "Controversial" About ESG? A Theory of Compelled Commercial Speech Under the First Amendment*, FORDHAM L. LEGAL STUD. RSCH. PAPER NO. 4118755 (May 24, 2022), https://papers.ssrn.com/sol3/papers.cfm?abstract_id=4118755.

[72] *Id.* at 1.

[73] Letter from Randi Morrison, Senior Vice President - Commc'ns, & Darla C. Stuckey, President & CEO, Soc'y for Corp. Governance, to Vanessa A. Countryman, Sec'y, SEC (June 17, 2022), https://www.sec.gov/comments/s7-10-22/s71022-20132044-302525.pdf.

[74] *Id.* at 20–21.

[75] Letter from Lawrence A. Cunningham, Corresponding Author, Geo. Wash. Univ., et al., to SEC (Apr. 25, 2022), https://www.sec.gov/comments/s7-10-22/s71022-20126528-287180.pdf.

[76] *Id.* at 2.

[77] *Id.* at 2–3.

to individual investors from self-interested voting or engagement by the asset managers to whom 160 million Americans entrust their savings. That fact alone is a fatal flaw of the Proposal."[78]

Questioning the motivations of institutional investors seeking to market ESG funds to millennial investors, in their comment letter these professors state that "[w]hile index funds may be interested in using climate-friendly voting and engagement as a marketing device, they cannot afford to incur substantial new costs to do so. A mandatory climate disclosure regime requiring publicly traded companies to bear the cost of producing and standardizing the climate-related information would save such funds costs while advancing their agendas."[79] The comment letter also questions the interests of proxy advisors, which invest heavily in nonfinancial products such as climate ratings. Having assigned an ESG rating to a company, the proxy advisor will then turn around and sell "a separate set of services to those companies to improve their ratings."[80]

Professors Paul Mahoney and Julia Mahoney of the University of Virginia Law School, in their article *The New Separation of Ownership and Control: Institutional Investors and ESG*, when in questioning the real goals of ESG advocates, warned that:

> [t]he adoption of ESG disclosure mandates in order to serve environmental or social goals is not well-aligned with the SEC's stated mission of protecting "Main Street investors" and "maintaining fair, orderly, and efficient markets." The SEC has neither the expertise nor the political accountability to pursue climate, diversity, and other public policy goals. Moreover, by appearing to take sides in contentious policy disputes, the SEC risks eroding public trust in its capacity and willingness to serve as an apolitical, technocratic regulator of the capital markets.[81]

They further warned that:

> [o]ur assessment of the future of securities regulation, then, begins with the proposition that the SEC stands at a fork in the road. It may continue to pursue its longstanding mission of investor protection, with a particular emphasis on protecting unsophisticated investors from fraud and agency costs. Alternatively, it may cast its lot with the institutional investors and political activists who wish to further public policy objectives without subjecting them to the transparency and compromises inherent in the normal substantive policy making process. Fairly or not, the latter path may lead investors and the broader public to conclude that the SEC caters to Wall Street rather than Main Street.[82]

[78] *Id.* at 3.

[79] *Id.* at 4–5.

[80] *Id.* at 5.

[81] Mahoney & Mahoney, *supra* note 7, at 842–43.

[82] *Id.* at 845.

In the article, Professors Mahoney and Mahoney voice the concerns of many opponents of the SEC's proposed rule when, in questioning the real goals of ESG advocates, they wrote:

> Why, then, are institutional investors and political activists pressing for the SEC to require an expanded and standardized set of ESG disclosures, given that its rules already require companies to disclose known risks that are material to their future operations and financial position? For political activists, the answer is straightforward—they want to use the information to prod companies to change policies in socially-motivated directions. Standardized disclosures that facilitate the production of an ESG "score" are particularly valuable to political activists. Such disclosures facilitate an ordinal ranking of companies that can serve as a focal point to organize boycotts, demonstrations, and social media campaigns against "brown" companies.[83]

It should be noted that the SEC's proposed rule, and the comments received in response, were released before the U.S. Supreme Court's ruling in *West Virginia v. EPA*, decided June 30, 2022.[84] In that 6–3 ruling, the Supreme Court, pointing to the so-called major questions doctrine, found the Clean Power Plan of the U.S. Environmental Protection Agency (EPA) represented an "extravagant" and "transformative" expansion of the EPA's regulatory authority, which would require "clear congressional authorization."[85] The Supreme Court stated that "[w]e presume that 'Congress intends to make major policy decisions itself, not leave those decisions to agencies.'"[86] This ruling casts doubt on how a court would look at the SEC's final rules on ESG disclosure matters, and critics of the proposed rule will certainly raise the major questions doctrine and *West Virginia v. EPA* to question whether these rules exceed the SEC's authority under the federal securities laws.

IV. Human Capital Management

Another aspect of ESG that has received significant attention is with respect to human capital management, which is concerned with how companies manage their workforces, including senior management. At the heart of human capital management, according to Nasdaq, is "how a company motivates and invests in its workforce" and "recognizes that human capital is a critical asset in driving long-term value," stating further that "there's a clear correlation between human capital management and return on investment."[87] This can include, among other actions by the company, a focus on the financial health of employees; accelerating diversity, equity, and inclusion initiatives; and holding management to high standards of performance.

Efforts to affect companies' human capital management have come from many directions, including legislation, regulation, and public policy.

---

[83] *Id.* at 851-852.

[84] West Virginia v. EPA, 142 S. Ct. 2587 (2022).

[85] *Id.* at 2609–10.

[86] *Id.* at 2609.

[87] *Insights from Nasdaq Governance Solutions, The Path to Strength and Resiliency: Why Human Capital Management Matters*, NASDAQ, https://www.nasdaq.com/solutions/governance/resources/human-capital-management (last visited Oct. 3, 2022).

A. U.S. Securities and Exchange Commission Rulemaking

The SEC's evolution in requiring increased disclosure by public companies of aspects of human capital management has picked up pace in recent years. Since 2006, domestic issuers have been required to disclose, in their annual proxy statement, material information about the compensation objectives and policies for named executive officers.[88] Passage of the Dodd-Frank Wall Street Reform and Consumer Protection Act (the "Dodd-Frank") in 2010 accelerated the trend to require additional human capital management disclosures, including disclosure concerning shareholder approval of executive compensation and "golden parachute" compensation arrangements. Among other disclosure obligations adopted by the SEC as directed under Dodd-Frank are the following:

- *Say-on-Pay.* In 2011, as required under Dodd-Frank, the SEC adopted so-called "say-on-pay" votes.[89] These votes must occur at least once every three years, and reporting companies are also required to hold a "frequency" vote at least once every six years to allow shareholders to decide how often they would like to be presented with the say-on-pay vote. Following that vote, the reporting company is required to publicly disclose how often it will hold the say-on-pay vote. Under these rules, reporting companies also are required to provide additional disclosure regarding "golden parachute" compensation arrangements with certain executive officers in connection with merger transactions.
- *Pay Ratio.* In 2015, and also as required under Dodd-Frank, the SEC adopted a new final rule requiring most reporting companies to disclose annually the pay ratio between its principal executive officer's (PEO) total compensation and the median compensation of its employees.[90] The rule was adopted by the Commission on a narrow 3–2 vote after years of criticism and complaints from both supporters and opponents. The SEC had received over 280,000 comments on the proposed rule.
- *Pay Versus Performance.* Most recently, in August 2022, the SEC issued final rules requiring new "pay for performance" disclosures originally required under Dodd-Frank.[91] The rules were originally proposed in 2015, receiving significant comments, and then reopened for comment in early 2022. The rules are intended to show the relationship between compensation actually paid to a company's PEO and its other named executive officers and the financial performance of the company. The rules require a direct comparison of compensation actually paid to named executive officers and specified financial metrics.

---

[88] Executive Compensation Disclosure, Securities Act Release No. 8765, Exchange Act Release No. 55,009, 71 Fed. Reg. 78338 (Dec. 29, 2006) (to be codified at 17 C.F.R. pts. 228, 229).

[89] *See* Shareholder Approval of Executive Compensation and Golden Parachute Compensation, Securities Act Release No. 9178, Exchange Act Release No. 63,768, 76 Fed. Reg. 6010 (Feb. 2, 2011) (to be codified at 17 C.F.R. pts. 229, 240, 249).

[90] *See* Pay Ratio Disclosure, Securities Act Release No. 9877, Exchange Act Release No. 75,610, 80 Fed. Reg. 50103 (Aug. 18, 2015) (to be codified at 17 C.F.R. pts. 229, 240, 249).

[91] *See* Pay Versus Performance, Exchange Act Release No. 95,607, 87 Fed. Reg. 55134 (Sept. 8, 2022) (to be codified at 17 C.F.R. pts. 229, 232, 240).

While each of these provisions, whether when proposed as part of Dodd-Frank or under the rules proposed by the Commission, received significant comments on the specifics of the proposals, many dissenters argued that the underlying purpose of the law and the rules was not in fact to enhance disclosure by reporting companies to the benefit of investors, but to instead proactively work to change the executive compensation practices of publicly held companies and financial institutions.[92] This pattern, dissenters argue, was back-door federal regulation of corporate activities and further federal encroachment on the traditional state-based system of regulating corporate governance (such as disclosure concerning conflict minerals, mine safety, and resource extraction, and most recently the SEC's proposed environmental disclosures), using as a mechanism the federal securities laws as opposed to state corporate or other regulations. Professor Stephen Bainbridge, writing in 2012, asked "whether these provisions addressed actual corporate governance failures or were simply a sop to populist outrage."[93]

Professors Paul Mahoney and Julia Mahoney of the University of Virginia Law School, in a comment letter concerning the SEC's proposed climate-related financial disclosures, stated that the SEC's

> climate-related and other Environmental, Sustainability and Governance (ESG) disclosure mandates would, if put into force, represent a substantial change in the Commission's approach to its stated mission of protecting "Main Street investors" and "maintaining fair, orderly, and efficient markets." As we discuss in detail in the article,[94] ESG disclosure mandates risk eroding the Commission's reputation as an effective and respected nonpartisan regulator for the simple reason that such mandates may appear to prioritize the social and political views of the largest Wall Street asset management firms over the financial wellbeing of the households whose savings they manage.[95]

Critics have argued that forcing reporting companies to disclose such information, when used together with coordinated boycotts and other public campaigns, backed by activist investors operating under the guise of "socially responsible investing," would effectively force companies to adopt corporate social responsibility programs.[96] In essence, the SEC's disclosure rules would be a method of implementing social policy goals by requiring public

[92] *See, e.g.*, Stephen M. Bainbridge, *Is 'Say on Pay' Justified?*, Regul. (Spring 2009), https://www.shrm.org/ResourcesAndTools/hr-topics/compensation/Documents/v32n1-6.pdf.

[93] Stephen M. Bainbridge, *Executive Compensation, in* Corporate Governance After the Financial Crisis 109 (Oxford Univ. Press, Inc. 2012), https://academic.oup.com/book/12059/chapter-abstract/161388080?redirectedFrom=fulltext.

[94] Referring to their article *The New Separation of Ownership and Control: Institutional Investors and ESG*; *see* Mahoney & Mahoney, *supra* note 7.

[95] Letter from Paul G. Mahoney, David and Mary Harrison, Distinguished Professor of L., Univ. of Va. Sch. of L., & Julia D. Mahoney, John S. Battle Professor of L., Univ. of Va. Sch. of L., to Chair Gensler (June 1, 2021), https://www.sec.gov/comments/climate-disclosure/cll12-8855236-238441.pdf.

[96] Marc Greendorfer, *Discrimination as a Business Policy: The Misuse and Abuse of Corporate Social Responsibility Programs*, 8 Am. U. Bus. L. Rev. 307 (2020).

companies to disclose items less of interest to shareholders and more of interest to a broad array of non-investor "stakeholders." Dissenters point out that this is consistent with President Biden's call during his campaign for "an end to the era of shareholder capitalism—the idea [that] the only responsibility a corporation has is to its shareholders. That's simply not true, it's an absolute farce. They have responsibility to their workers, their community, to their country." James Pethokoukis, writing for the American Enterprise Institute, responded that such a view is "especially common among those who think American capitalism is somehow broken or in a late stage of decline."[97]

B. Diversification of Corporate Boards

Efforts to impact the composition of the boards of directors of public companies are not new. Both the New York Stock Exchange (NYSE)[98] and Nasdaq[99] have for many years required that listed domestic companies maintain certain board committees, such as an audit committee, and that certain directors be "independent."[100] Under the Sarbanes-Oxley Act of 2002, the SEC established its own independence standards for members of audit committees and began requiring public companies to disclose whether at least one member of a reporting company's audit committee is a "financial expert."[101] In adopting its rules regarding the participation of financial experts on audit committees of reporting companies in 2003, the SEC stated that "[t]he strength of the U.S. financial markets depends on investor confidence. Recent events involving allegations of misdeeds by corporate executives, independent auditors and other market participants have undermined that confidence."[102]

In more recent years, advocates have pushed to include "diversity" as an additional board composition requirement. Major successes for this movement have been the enactment, in 2018 and 2020, of statutes in California mandating diversification of boards of publicly traded companies with "principal executive offices" in California, and the adoption, in 2021, of a Nasdaq listing requirement requiring companies with shares listed on Nasdaq to have diverse directors by a certain deadline or otherwise explain their reasons for not doing so. Some other states have followed California's direction on this issue. The NYSE, at the same time, has taken a different path than Nasdaq, launching an initiative in 2019 to identify board-ready candidates from underrepresented groups, but not creating baseline diversity

---

[97] James Pethokoukis, *Two Cheers, Again, for Shareholder Capitalism*, AEI (May 28, 2021), https://www.aei.org/economics/two-cheers-again-for-shareholder-capitalism/.

[98] NYSE, *Audit Committee*, *in* NYSE Company Manual § 303A.06 (2009), https://nyseguide.srorules.com/listed-company-manual/09013e2c85c0074a.

[99] Nasdaq, *Corporate Governance Requirements*, *in* The Nasdaq Stock Market LLC Rules § 5600 (2009), https://listingcenter.nasdaq.com/rulebook/nasdaq/rules/nasdaq-5600-series.

[100] NYSE, *Independent Directors*, *in* NYSE Company Manual § 303A.01 (2009), https://nyseguide.srorules.com/listed-company-manual/09013e2c85c00744.

[101] Disclosure Required by Sections 406 and 407 of the Sarbanes-Oxley Act of 2002, Securities Act Release No. 8177, Exchange Act Release No. 47,235, 68 Fed. Reg. 5109 (Jan. 31, 2003) (to be codified at 17 C.F.R. pts. 228, 229, 249).

[102] *Id.* at 5110.

requirements by its listed companies.[103] Critics of both Nasdaq's Board Diversity Rule and California's board diversification mandates have pursued lawsuits challenging them.

1. *Nasdaq's Board Diversity Rule*

In December 2020, Nasdaq introduced a board diversity rule, which the SEC approved (in amended form) in August 2021. Defining "diverse" directors as those who self-identify as female, members of underrepresented minorities, or LGBTQ+, the rule requires Nasdaq-listed companies to (1) publicly disclose board-level diversity statistics using a standardized template and (2) explain, if the company's board does not have at least two diverse directors, the reason for that lack of diversity in its proxy statement, in its information statement for its annual shareholder meeting, or on the company's website. The rule requires companies to make this disclosure on an annual basis. Nasdaq describes the rule as "a disclosure standard designed to encourage a minimum board diversity objective for companies and provide stakeholders with consistent, comparable disclosures concerning a company's current board composition."

Nasdaq's Board Diversity Rule is the subject of an ongoing, high-stakes court battle in the U.S. Court of Appeals for the Fifth Circuit. The attorneys general of 17 states have faced off against the SEC, the American Civil Liberties Union (ACLU), an "Ad Hoc Coalition of Nasdaq-Listed Companies," and a group of "Investors and Investment Advisers." In an amicus filing, the attorneys general argue that the rule violates the Equal Protection Clause of the Constitution, undermines traditional state authority in the area of corporate governance, and forces companies to violate state anti-discrimination laws. The amici supporting the diversity rule have argued that Nasdaq is a private actor, that board diversity is good for corporations and investors, and that the diversity data reported as a result of the rule will be beneficial to academics and society as a whole.

Opponents challenge the rule as an unconstitutional racial classification, while supporters say that the rule is constitutional, that diversity benefits corporations and investors, and that it facilitates beneficial transparency for the market. Among the rule's opponents are the Alliance for Fair Board Recruitment (AFBR), a recently formed nonprofit whose mission is "to promote the recruitment of corporate board members without regard to race, ethnicity, sex, and sexual identity." The AFBR was formed by Edward Blum, an activist who also has challenged affirmative action in university admissions. AFBR has also brought challenges against the board diversity measures in California. Another opponent is the National Center for Public Policy Research (NCPPR), a think tank that focuses on "free market solutions to today's public policy problems."

In August 2021, AFBR filed a Petition for Review of the SEC's approval of the rule in the Fifth Circuit. In its supporting brief, AFBR argues that the rule violates equal protection and the First Amendment's free speech clause, is an unconstitutional exercise of legislative powers reserved to Congress, is not supported by substantial evidence, and is not designed to

[103] Elizabeth King, *The Importance of the NYSE's Market-Driven Approach to Board Diversity*, NYSE Bd. Advisory Council (June 16, 2022), https://www.nyse.com/boardadvisory/the-importance-of-the-nyse-s-market-driven-approach-to-board-diversity.

accomplish statutorily required objectives.[104] AFBR further asserted that the SEC exceeded its statutory authority by approving the Nasdaq rule that requires disclosure of non-material information on board diversity. NCPPR filed a similar Petition for Review in October 2021 in the U.S. Court of Appeals for the Third Circuit, which was transferred to the AFBR case in the Fifth Circuit that same month. Its supporting brief echoes AFBR's arguments.[105] AFBR also argued that the Nasdaq rule was state action subject to constitutional scrutiny because "the Rule required SEC approval, the SEC independently justified and made judgments about the Rule, and Nasdaq has an ongoing statutory obligation to enforce the Rule."[106]

In response, the SEC contended that it acted reasonably in concluding that the rule is consistent with the Exchange Act and that the rule did not involve state action because it was being implemented by a private actor.[107] The SEC further asserted that the rule falls within established standards for compelled speech under the First Amendment and that the rule does not violate the First Amendment because the rule requires only disclosure and does not dictate what a company may say or whom it may hire.[108]

Nasdaq filed a brief as an intervenor, arguing primarily that Nasdaq is a private company, and thus there is no state action to challenge.[109]

Several groups of amici filed briefs in support of the rule, asserting points that fall generally into two categories: (1) that the rule is good for companies and investors; and (2) that the rule is good for transparency. In addition, FINRA filed an amicus brief in support of the rule narrowly focused on the state action issue.[110] The briefs arguing that the rule benefits companies and investors were filed by an "Ad Hoc Coalition of Nasdaq-Listed Companies"[111] and a group of "Investors and Investment Advisers."[112]

The "Nasdaq-Listed Companies" brief also argues that diverse boards further the public interest and that the rule is not burdensome because it provides significant flexibility and autonomy.[113] The "Investors and Investment Advisers" brief makes the additional point that investors and advisors consider board diversity when making investment decisions and

---

[104] Opening Brief for Petitioner Alliance for Fair Board Recruitment, Alliance for Fair Board Recruitment v. SEC, No. 21-60626 (5th Cir. Nov. 22, 2021), ECF No. 103.

[105] Opening Brief for Petitioner National Center for Public Policy Research, Alliance for Fair Board Recruitment v. SEC, No. 21-60626 (5th Cir. Dec. 20, 2021), ECF No. 113.

[106] Reply Brief for Petitioner Alliance for Fair Board Recruitment at 16, Alliance for Fair Board Recruitment v. SEC, No. 21-60626 (5th Cir. Apr. 1, 2022), ECF No. 186.

[107] Brief for Respondent Securities and Exchange Commission, Alliance for Fair Board Recruitment v. SEC, No. 21-60626 (5th Cir. Feb. 18, 2022), ECF No. 127.

[108] *Id.*

[109] Brief of Intervenor the Nasdaq Stock Market LLC, Alliance for Fair Board Recruitment v. SEC, No. 21-60626 (5th Cir. Feb. 25, 2022), ECF No. 152.

[110] Brief of Financial Industry Regulatory Authority, Inc. as Amicus Curiae in Support of Respondent and Intervenor on the State-action Issue, Alliance for Fair Board Recruitment v. SEC, No. 21-60626 (5th Cir. Feb. 25, 2022), ECF No. 145.

[111] Brief of Ad Hoc Coalition of Nasdaq-Listed Companies as Amicus Curiae in Support of Respondent, Alliance for Fair Board Recruitment v. SEC, No. 21-60626 (5th Cir. Feb. 25, 2022), ECF No. 141.

[112] Brief of Investors and Investment Advisers as Amici Curiae in Support of Respondent Securities and Exchange Commission, Alliance for Fair Board Recruitment v. SEC, No. 21-60626 (5th Cir. Feb. 24, 2022), ECF No. 140.

[113] *See* Brief of Ad Hoc Coalition of Nasdaq-Listed Companies, *supra* note 111.

therefore want the information that the rule requires listed companies to disclose.[114] The briefs praising increased "transparency" resulting from the rule include one filed by the ACLU[115] and one by a group of "Academic Experts in the Fields of Business, Management, and Economics."[116] These briefs emphasize the public's interest in receiving corporate board diversity information. The ACLU brief specifically notes that the public has a First Amendment interest in receiving this information and that Nasdaq has a First Amendment interest in requiring its disclosure.[117]

On the other hand, 17 states, through their attorneys general, together filed an amicus brief in support of the NCPPR.[118] The 17 amici are Arizona, Alabama, Alaska, Arkansas, Florida, Indiana, Kansas, Kentucky, Louisiana, Mississippi, Missouri, Montana, Nebraska, Oklahoma, South Carolina, Texas, and Utah.

According to the 17 states, the rule exceeds the SEC's authority under the Securities Exchange Act because corporate board composition is "a traditional state concern," noting that several states have already enacted or adopted policies related to board diversity. They assert that "the choice to have such laws—or not to have them—is a matter for the states, subject to constitutional and statutory limitations."[119] They also argue that the rule would require listed companies to violate civil rights laws in several of the amici states, including Arizona's prohibition against classifying employees or applicants based on race, color, religion, sex, age, or national origin.[120]

California's statute, discussed below, goes a step beyond the Nasdaq disclosure rule by requiring all publicly traded companies headquartered in California to include at least one director from an underrepresented community on its board (by December 2021) or face fines. The statute also requires the state to report on compliance by affected companies.

2. *California's Board Diversity Requirements*

In 2018 and 2020, California enacted two statutes mandating diversification of boards of publicly traded companies with "principal executive offices" in California. These statutes authorized the state to track the composition of those boards and to issue fines for noncompliance. Senate Bill 826 (S.B. 826), enacted in 2018 and codified as Corporations Code section 301.3, required publicly traded companies headquartered in California to appoint a

---

[114] *See* Brief of Investors and Investment Advisers, *supra* note 112.

[115] Brief of Amicus Curiae American Civil Liberties Union, Inc. in Support of Respondent Securities and Exchange Commission and Intervenor the Nasdaq Stock Market LLC, Alliance for Fair Board Recruitment v. SEC, No. 21-60626 (5th Cir. Feb. 25, 2022), ECF No. 146.

[116] Brief of Academic Experts in the Fields of Business, Management, and Economics as Amici Curiae in Support of Respondent Securities and Exchange Commission, Alliance for Fair Board Recruitment v. SEC, No. 21-60626 (5th Cir. Feb. 25, 2022), ECF No. 150.

[117] *See* Brief of Amicus Curiae American Civil Liberties Union, *supra* note 115.

[118] Amicus Brief of the States of Arizona, Alabama, Alaska, Arkansas, Florida, Indiana, Kansas, Kentucky, Louisiana, Mississippi, Missouri, Montana, Nebraska, Oklahoma, South Carolina, Texas, and Utah in Support of Petitioner National Center for Public Policy Research, Alliance for Fair Board Recruitment v. SEC, No. 21-60626 (5th Cir. Dec. 27, 2021), ECF No. 119.

[119] *Id.* at 12–13.

[120] *Id.* at 13.

minimum number of female directors. Two years later, Assembly Bill 979 (A.B. 979), codified as Corporations Code section 301.4, imposed a similar regime for directors from "underrepresented communities," defined in the statute to include members of racial minorities and the LGBTQ+ community.

Champions of both initiatives emphasized that legislative action was necessary to correct discrepancies in the composition of boards, which were disproportionately white, cisgender, and male. Supporters emphasized that diversification of boards would not only address and remedy discrimination but also improve corporate performance, thereby enriching California and benefiting the public.

Legal challenges were swift. Opponents of the statutes filed suits both in state and federal courts asserting that the statutes employed unconstitutional classifications of board candidates, based on gender and race, that did not serve a compelling government interest. And, as noted above, in two state cases the California courts agreed.[121] The federal case is pending and being held in abeyance until any appeal of either state court decision becomes final.

On April 1, 2022, in *Crest v. Padilla* (*Crest - A.B. 979*), Judge Green—of the Los Angeles Superior Court—held that Section 301.4, which mandated appointment of directors from underrepresented communities, violated the California Constitution's Equal Protection Clause.[122] The court concluded that the law resulted in disparate treatment of similarly situated qualified candidates for corporate boards on the basis of their race, sexual orientation, or gender identity, triggering strict scrutiny.[123] The court concluded there was no compelling government interest to treat candidates from underrepresented communities differently from others, in part, because it found no "convincing evidence" of discrimination against those candidates.[124]

However, the state did not submit evidence of such a statistical discrepancy between directors and qualified candidates. To the contrary, the state explained that the pipeline of candidates were C-suite executives who, like the directors themselves, were largely white, cisgender males.[125]

In rejecting the state's purported compelling interest in remediating this discrepancy at the corporate board level, the court distinguished between evidence suggesting discrimination in the *formation* of the candidate pool and discrimination in the *choice* of candidates from that pool for director seats. It observed that while the statistics might constitute "evidence of discrimination in selection of C-suite executives," that issue was not before the court.[126]

The court was unwilling to assume that this discrepancy in the pipeline was the result of past, overt discrimination. Instead, in a footnote, it postulated that "any robust notion of cultural pluralism requires a factfinder to at least consider the possibility that the presence

---

[121] *See* Crest v. Padilla (*Crest - A.B. 979*), No. 20-STCV-37513, 2022 WL 1073294, at 1 (Cal. Sup. Ct. L.A. Cnty. Apr. 1, 2022); Crest v. Padilla (*Crest - S.B. 826*), No. 19-STCV-27561, slip op. at 23 (Cal. Sup. Ct. L.A. Cnty. May 13, 2022).

[122] *Crest - A.B.* 979, 2022 WL 1073294, at 1.

[123] *Id.* at 17.

[124] *Id.* at 19.

[125] *Id.* at 14.

[126] *Id.* (recognizing that although the issue was not before the court, "perhaps it should be").

or absence of a given group in a given industry is the product of benign cultural preferences."[127] The court also rejected arguments by the state that the statute furthered a compelling government interest because diverse boards employ more inclusive workplace standards and strengthen corporate performance. While the court did not question these benefits, it held that a "state's generic interest in healthy businesses is not sufficiently specific or immediate to permit the use of suspect classifications."[128]

On May 13, 2022, Judge Duffy-Lewis—also of the Los Angeles Superior Court—reached a similar conclusion in a second action also titled *Crest v. Padilla* (*Crest - S.B. 826*).[129] The court abrogated Section 301.3, which mandated the appointment of a minimum number of females to boards, concluding that the statute violated the Equal Protection Clause of the California Constitution. Judge Duffy-Lewis reasoned that, because the statute afforded disparate treatment to qualified candidates for corporate board positions on the basis of gender, without furthering a compelling government interest, it violated equal protection.[130] Echoing *Crest - A.B. 979*, the court reasoned that while discrepancies may exist in how individuals come under consideration as board candidates, the board selection process did not differentiate between men and women.[131] The *Crest - S.B. 826* court also ruled that the state failed to put forward "strong" evidence to show that including women on boards served a compelling state interest. Like the *Crest - A.B. 979* court, the *Crest - S.B. 826* court was not persuaded by claims concerning the economic benefits of diversification and found that adding women to boards was not necessary to "boost California's economy."[132]

The *Crest - S.B. 826* court concluded that the state's empirical evidence of the economic benefits associated with corporations having more female board members was unpersuasive, stating "the studies [the state] cited failed to sufficiently show a causal connection between women on corporate boards and [improved] corporate governance and did not otherwise provide reliable conclusions."[133] The court further opined that the state's purported interest in "gender-balancing" did not further a state interest in "remedying discrimination."[134]

Implicit in this conclusion is the idea that the disparity between men and women on boards may be attributable to some factor other than discrimination, perhaps the same "benign cultural differences" cited, but not explained, by Judge Green in *Crest - A.B. 979*.

It remains to be seen how the statutes will fare in the appellate courts. Appeals of both *Crest - A.B. 979* and *Crest - S.B. 826* are pending.[135]

On appeal, the state can be expected to raise again a variety of points made in the trial court actions, including the following: (1) Contrary to the challengers' arguments, these statutes do

[127] *Id.* at 14 n.21.

[128] *Id.* at 16.

[129] *See Crest - S.B. 826*, slip op. at 23.

[130] *Id.*

[131] *Id.* at 12–13, 19.

[132] *Id.* at 10–11.

[133] *Id.* at 11.

[134] *Id.* at 15.

[135] *See* Crest v. Padilla, No. B321726 (Cal. App. 2d); Crest v. Padilla, No. B322276 (Cal. App. 2d).

not impose a "quota" that excludes some candidates but instead require only that each board have a critical mass of diverse board members; (2) A company can choose to increase the total number of board seats such that the diverse board members are merely additive; and (3) A critical mass of diverse board members furthers the state's interest in allowing diverse members true participation on a board, given that a lone diverse member, for instance, is not as likely to be truly heard and bring the full benefits of diverse perspectives into the boardroom.

In addition, the state will likely argue again that the nature of board recruitment and appointments make it impossible to prove individualized discrimination, as both *Crest - A.B. 979* and *Crest - S.B. 826* concluded was necessary, because pursuing remedies for generalized discrimination is not a sufficiently compelling interest. Board appointments are not made through a public or even systematized process; one does not apply to be a board member. Rather, board members and sometimes recruiters identify candidates who are then approached, but the pool of candidates is mostly drawn from the board members' or recruiters' informal networks. That system tends to replicate existing demographics of board members. It is impossible, given this network-driven system, to prove that any particular woman or member of an underrepresented community has been discriminated against. The appeals will most likely, at the earliest, be decided in 2023.

The rulings, if not overturned on appeal, spell an end to California's board diversity requirements as currently framed. Both courts rejected arguments by the state that remediating discrimination against women and members of underrepresented communities, and enhancing corporate performance through board diversity, constitutes compelling state interests justifying the statutes' diversity requirements. These rulings come even as many institutional investors and activist shareholders apply mounting pressure to diversify corporate boards.

Key Takeaways

The backlash against ESG is broad-based and increasingly vocal. Key takeaways about this trend include:

- Many critics would likely not consider themselves to be part of *any* backlash and would certainly not see themselves as critics of environmental protection, measures to benefit historically marginalized groups, or good corporate governance. Many are opposed to the means, not the ends.
- State governments have been some of the loudest critics of ESG disclosure requirements and other mandates.
- ESG requirements raise significant issues under state corporate law, including challenges to traditional corporate governance under the guise of stakeholder capitalism.
- The SEC's proposed ESG disclosure rules should be expected to face significant challenges in the courts, strengthened by the U.S. Supreme Court's recent decision in *West Virginia v. EPA*.
- Human capital management aspects of ESG have generally survived challenges when they have had the backing of federal law and seek to add disclosure regarding executive pay.
- While initial adverse court rulings are being appealed, board diversification efforts seem to face an uphill battle in the courts.

4

ESG in the United Kingdom and European Union

Simon Firth, Niels Ersbøll, Kardia Leung, and Lazarinka Naydenova

I. Introduction

A. The United Kingdom

The United Kingdom (UK) has in recent years experienced a legislative push towards ESG accountability driven in part by investor and consumer demand as well as other significant regulatory developments. For example, in June 2019, the UK became the first major economy to pass legislation that commits the country to net-zero emissions by 2050.[1] It has also incrementally developed regulations to align with the principles of the Task Force on Climate-related Financial Disclosures (TCFD), such as introducing mandatory ESG reporting by certain large private and listed companies, as discussed in Section III.A.1 below.

B. The European Union

ESG has been high up in the European Union's (EU) agenda in recent years. Two of the six priorities that the European Commission (EC) set for itself to execute in the period 2019 to 2024 are (1) ensuring the European Green Deal and (2) building an economy that works for people, which includes by promoting human rights.

[1] HM Gov't, Net Zero Strategy: Build Back Greener (2021), https://assets.publishing.service.gov.uk/government/uploads/system/uploads/attachment_data/file/1033990/net-zero-strategy-beis.pdf. Net zero means that the UK's total greenhouse gas emissions would be equal to or less than the emissions the UK removed from the environment. This can be achieved by a combination of emission reduction and emission removal.

The European Green Deal aims to make Europe the first climate-neutral continent by 2050 by reducing net emissions of greenhouse gases in a cost-effective, fair, and competitive way; safeguarding biodiversity; establishing a circular economy; and eliminating pollution.[2] The EU has committed to reduce its emissions by at least 55 percent by 2030 and to take action to limit global warming to well below 2°C. With these goals in mind, in the last years the EC has been reshaping the existing legal framework for Member States, companies, and individuals. The scope of the reforms is broad, and it spreads to clean energy supply across the economy, industry, production and consumption, large-scale infrastructure, transport, food and agriculture, construction, taxation, social benefits, and others.

Some legislative initiatives are far-reaching and require businesses to regulate not only their own behavior and accountability, but also that of their entire supply chain. Notable examples of EU recent action are the following:

- In 2020, the EU Taxonomy Regulation[3] was published. This legislative act creates a system that classifies the economic activities considered to be environmentally sustainable by the EU. The idea behind the EU taxonomy is to help companies navigate their business in a more climate-friendly direction, to give certainty to investors and protect them from greenwashing (as described further in Section III.A.2 below), and to allow investments to flow when they are most needed. The EU Taxonomy Regulation contains reporting obligations for companies to disclose whether and how their activities pursue sustainable goals.
- Companies face disclosure obligations under the Sustainable Finance Disclosure Regulation (SFDR)[4] and the new Corporate Sustainability Reporting Directive (CSRD), which came into force on January 5, 2023. The former applies to financial market participants and advisors, and contains several levels of disclosure duties asking to identify adverse sustainability impacts as well as the actions planned or undertaken to counter them, and asking to provide detailed entity and product information. The latter extends the scope of the existing EU Non-Financial Reporting Directive (NFRD) by including more reporting requirements and additional categories of companies that are subject to them. As discussed in Section II.B below, the CSRD applies to all listed companies (except for micro-enterprises) and other large companies that meet certain criteria of size.[5] The first companies are expected to apply the new CSRD rules for the first time in the financial year 2024, for reports published in 2025.

---

[2] This objective is laid down in the European Climate Law (ECL). The ECL itself is aimed at ensuring that all EU policies contribute and play their part toward reaching this objective.

[3] Regulation (EU) 2020/852 of the European Parliament and of the Council of 18 June 2020 on the Establishment of a Framework to Facilitate Sustainable Investment, and Amending Regulation (EU) 2019/2088, 2020 O.J. (L 198). More initiatives on sustainable finance are available at https://ec.europa.eu/info/business-economy-euro/banking-and-finance/sustainable-finance_en.

[4] Regulation (EU) 2019/2088 of the European Parliament and of the Council of 27 November 2019 on Sustainability-related Disclosures in the Financial Services Sector, 2019 O.J. (L 317) 1.

[5] The criteria include any two of the following three conditions: (i) a balance sheet total of €20 million or more; (ii) net turnover of €40 million or more; and (iii) 250 employees on average during the last financial year.

- Finally, under the draft EU Corporate Sustainability Directive published by the EC in February 2022,[6] businesses active in the EU may also need to conduct ESG-related due diligence of their entire supply chain.[7] (Note that the EU Taxonomy Regulation and the SFDR are discussed in Section III.B below.)

In December 2021, the EC published a proposed revision of the Directive on Environmental Crime[8] in which it proposes to criminalize additional environmental offenses such as illegal timber trade, ship recycling and abstraction of water, and serious breaches of certain legislation, which may cause adverse environmental impact. The main envisaged sanctions include imprisonment and fines, but additional types of penalties are foreseen, including withdrawal of permits, disqualifications, and exclusion from access to public funding.

The EC also increasingly uses EU competition law as a tool to expedite the achievement of its ESG objectives. It is in the process of updating both its horizontal and its vertical guidelines for the assessment of agreements between economic operators, where it will provide guidance on how initiatives pursuing sustainability objectives will be assessed. The EC is also reframing its state aid toolbox[9] and taking a closer look at mergers with a connection to sustainability.

These are just a few of many projects running at the EU level with relevance for ESG. As it would be difficult to discuss all of them in the present contribution, we focus on the three key areas for businesses: corporate finance and governance, sustainable finance, and antitrust.

II. Corporate Finance and Governance

A. The United Kingdom

1. Listed Companies

The Financial Conduct Authority (FCA), the principal UK financial regulator, is responsible for overseeing compliance by listed companies with the TCFD.

Most publicly traded companies are required by the FCA to state whether their financial announcements are in line with certain climate change-related criteria and provide an explanation for any areas where they are not. Guidance on these rules is set out in the FCA's Environmental, Social and Governance Sourcebook.[10] As the UK moves towards its goal of net-zero greenhouse gas emissions by 2050, we expect to see the FCA take a more stringent approach with enforcing these reporting requirements.

---

[6] *Proposal for a Directive of the European Parliament and of the Council Amending Directive 2013/34/EU, Directive 2004/109/EC, Directive 2006/43/EC and Regulation (EU) No. 537/2014, as Regards Corporate Sustainability Reporting*, COM (2021) 189 final (Apr. 21, 2021).

[7] Regulation (EU) 2019/2089 of the European Parliament and of the Council of 27 November 2019 Amending Regulation (EU) 2016/1011 as Regards EU Climate Transition Benchmarks, EU Paris-aligned Benchmarks and Sustainability-related Disclosures for Benchmarks, 2019 O.J. (L 317) 17.

[8] *Proposal for a Directive of the European Parliament and of the Council on the Protection of the Environment Through Criminal Law and Replacing Directive 2008/99/EC*, COM (2021) 851 final (Dec. 15, 2021).

[9] Including through the revised Guidelines on State Aid for Climate, Environmental Protection and Energy 2022, 2022 O.J. (C 80) 1–89.

[10] *See* Financial Conduct Authority (FCA), ENVIRONMENTAL, SOCIAL AND GOVERNANCE SOURCEBOOK (2023), https://www.handbook.fca.org.uk/handbook/ESG.pdf.

2. *Key ESG Legislation and Regulations*

As noted earlier, there is no single, overarching piece of ESG legislation or regulation in the UK. We have set out below the key legislation and regulations that businesses, regardless of size, should be aware of and comply with.

a. Companies Act 2006

Under the Companies Act 2006 (the "Companies Act"), section 172 ("Section 172"), directors of a UK company are under a primary duty to promote the success of the company for the benefit of its shareholders as a whole. This duty requires directors to take into consideration the wider need to foster business relationships; the impact of the company's operations on the community and the environment; and its reputation for high standards of business conduct.

In this respect, a key regulation for UK ESG disclosures is the annual reporting requirements under the Companies Act. All companies (except the smallest) must prepare an annual directors' report.[11] However, large companies that are either listed, exceed £500 million in annual turnover, or have more than 500 employees are required to include a separate statement in their annual report explaining (a) how the directors fulfilled their duties under Section 172 in the relevant fiscal year; (b) how the directors fostered the company's business relationships with suppliers, customers, and others; and (c) how they engaged with more than 250 UK employees in the year.

In addition, large and medium-sized UK companies are legally required to publish a separate annual strategic report (such reporting obligations are separate to and distinct from any other reporting obligations that may be imposed by other regulatory authorities).[12] The strategic reports must include certain nonfinancial information on ESG-related items, such as the business's environmental impact; employee disclosures; social, community, and human rights issues; and the company's policies on each.

b. Companies (Strategic Report) (Climate-related Financial Disclosure) Regulations 2022 (Regulations) and the Limited Liability Partnerships (Climate-related Financial Disclosure) Regulations 2022

On April 6, 2022, the Companies (Strategic Report) (Climate-related Financial Disclosure) Regulations 2022 (Regulations)[13] and the Limited Liability Partnerships (Climate-related

[11] Small companies are exempt from the requirement to file a directors' report. To qualify as a small company, a company must meet at least two of the following conditions: (1) annual turnover must be not more than £10.2 million; and/or (2) the balance sheet total must be not more than £5.1 million; and/or (3) the average number of employees must be not more than 50.

[12] Small companies are exempt from the requirement to prepare a strategic report. If a company meets two out of the three following criteria, the company is not small and therefore will have to prepare a strategic report: (1) the average number of employees is greater than 50; and/or (2) annual turnover is greater than £6.5 million; and/or (3) gross assets are greater than £3.26 million.

[13] The Companies (Strategic Report) (Climate-related Financial Disclosure) Regulations 2022, SI 2022/31, https://www.legislation.gov.uk/uksi/2022/31/made/data.pdf.

Financial Disclosure) Regulations 2022[14] came into force, making climate-related financial disclosures mandatory for certain limited liability partnerships (LLPs), publicly quoted companies, banks, insurance companies, and large private companies. The new legislation also adds environmental reporting to all UK Public Interest Entities[15] required to produce "non-financial information statements" under existing reporting regulations. Consequently, ESG-related reporting has become (if not already so) the hot topic of discussion for most organizations that are subject to the mandatory reporting requirements.

c. The Large and Medium-sized Companies and Groups (Accounts and Reports) Regulations 2008

Emissions reporting forms a core part of evidencing how climate risks and opportunities are being managed over time. As set out in the UK government's non-binding guidance on mandatory climate-related financial disclosures in February 2022,[16] the principal regulatory regime for the disclosure of emissions in the UK was set out in the Streamlined Energy and Carbon Report (SECR). These regulations complement, and do not duplicate, existing SECR requirements for quoted companies to report on their global energy use and for large businesses to report their UK annual energy use and greenhouse gas emissions. For the relevant companies, the requirements are set out in the Large and Medium-sized Companies and Groups (Accounts and Reports) Regulations 2008.[17]

d. The Climate Change Act 2008

The Climate Change Act 2008 (CCA 2008) is the UK's main climate change law. It calls for a 100 percent reduction in net greenhouse gas emissions by 2050 relative to 1990 levels in the UK.[18] We note that the CCA 2008 places most of the obligations on the UK government, not individual organizations, and it allows carbon trading for larger organizations.

---

[14] The Limited Liability Partnerships (Climate-related Financial Disclosure) Regulations 2022, SI 2022/46, https://www.legislation.gov.uk/uksi/2022/46/made/data.pdf.

[15] The UK definition of Public Interest Entity (PIE) has the meaning given in regulation 2 of Statutory Auditors and Third Country Auditors Regulations 2016 and is currently broadly defined as entities whose transferable securities are admitted to trading on a regulated market; credit institutions; or insurance undertakings. SI 2016/649 § 2. Note, however, that as of the time of writing, the UK is set to reform its corporate reporting and audit regime. One of the planned reforms is to expand the definition of PIE to include private companies, AIM-listed companies, and third sector companies that have 750 or more employees and £750m turnover, bringing as many as 600 new companies under the new classification.

[16] UK Dep't for Bus., Energy & Indus. Strategy, Mandatory Climate-related Financial Disclosures by Publicly Quoted Companies, Large Private Companies and LLPs: Non-binding Guidance (2022), https://assets.publishing.service.gov.uk/government/uploads/system/uploads/attachment_data/file/1056085/mandatory-climate-related-financial-disclosures-publicly-quoted-private-cos-llps.pdf.

[17] The Large and Medium-sized Companies and Groups (Accounts and Reports) Regulations 2008, SI 2008/410, https://www.legislation.gov.uk/uksi/2008/410/contents/made.

[18] The CCA 2008 introduced carbon budgets that put legally binding limits on the amount of greenhouse gases the UK can emit over a five-year period with the intention of setting out a cost-effective path to achieving longer-term climate targets. So far, six carbon budgets have been put into law; the latest (sixth) budget, imposed by the Carbon Budget Order 2021 (June 23, 2021), covers the years 2033 to 2037. Each budgetary five-year period is calculated with the aim of achieving an average annual reduction of carbon dioxide emissions against 1990 levels.

e. The UK Corporate Governance Code 2018 and Stewardship Code 2020

The UK Corporate Governance Code 2018 (UKCGC) issued by the FRC consists of principles of good governance to ensure that a company operates effectively, complies with legal requirements, and reports reliably.

The UKCGC applies to all companies with a premium listing of equity shares on the Main Market of the London Stock Exchange, whether incorporated in the UK or elsewhere. The UKCGC is a "comply or explain" code. The Listing Rules (described in further detail in this section at subsection f below) require UK-listed companies to include in their annual corporate reports and accounts a disclosure statement setting out how they have applied the principles, whether they have complied with the UKCGC's provisions, and explaining and justifying any noncompliance.

Other publicly traded companies (such as those listed on AIM [London Stock Exchange's market for small and medium-size growth companies] are not subject to the Listing Rules, but the exchange to which they are admitted may impose reporting requirements against a corporate governance code. Large non-publicly traded companies (measured by turnover, balance sheet total, and employee count) must include a similar "corporate governance statement" in their annual report.

In October 2019, the FRC published the UK Stewardship Code 2020 (UKSC), which introduced ESG expectations as the new normal for investors. In essence, the UKSC sets out principles that apply to asset owners and asset managers to ensure they are meeting expectations on how they are managing money on behalf of savers and pensioners and how this leads to sustainable benefits for the economy, the environment, and society. It also sets out good practice for institutional investors on engagement with investee companies.

Accordingly, corporate governance has become increasingly crucial for all stakeholders and represents the highest behavioral standards and thresholds that companies should be striving to attain. As such, the UKCGC and UKSC are considered fundamental developments in the UK for regulating listed companies and institutional investors, respectively, in respect of ESG-related issues.

f. New listing rules for listed companies

The UK government published its Green Finance Strategy in July 2019,[19] outlining its commitment to reaching net-zero greenhouse gas emissions by 2050 through supporting investment in green and low-carbon technologies, services, and infrastructure. In response to this, the FCA made a number of proposals to amend the Listing Rules to encourage certain listed companies to include climate-related disclosures in their annual financial reports as recommended by the TCFD.

The Listing Rules now require UK-incorporated and overseas commercial companies with a premium listing to include climate-related disclosures in their annual reports that

[19] HM Gov't, Green Finance Strategy: Transforming Finance for a Greener Future (2019), https://assets.publishing.service.gov.uk/government/uploads/system/uploads/attachment_data/file/820284/190716_BEIS_Green_Finance_Strategy_Accessible_Final.pdf.

follow the TCFD recommendations.[20] Furthermore, for accounting periods beginning on or after January 1, 2022, companies with a standard listing of equity shares, companies with standard listed shares other than equity shares, or standard listed issuers of global depositary receipts representing equity shares (in each case, other than investment entities or shell companies [such as special purpose acquisition companies]) are now required to include a statement in their annual financial report setting out climate-related financial disclosures consistent with the TCFD.[21]

The new Listing Rules encourage companies to consider the following when determining whether its climate-related financial disclosures are consistent with TCFD guidance:

- whether a company's disclosures provide sufficient detail to enable investors and other users to assess the company's exposure to, and approach to, addressing climate-related issues; and
- whether the company should carry out its own assessment to ascertain the appropriate level of detail to be included in its climate-related financial disclosures, taking into account factors such as (a) the level of its exposure to climate-related risks and opportunities, and (b) the scope and objectives of its climate-related strategy (depending on the nature, size, and complexity of the listed company's business).

The FCA believes the increased transparency of how listed companies are affected by climate-related factors will improve market efficiency and allow investors to allocate capital in a way that supports the transition to a greener economy and is ultimately aligned with the UK government's net-zero economy goals.

3. *ESG Considerations in United Kingdom Corporate Finance*

As the UK's ESG legal landscape continues to unfold, it is clear that key stakeholders, such as investors, customers, and business partners, expect to see a defined ESG strategy from the companies they engage with in order to satisfy their own agenda in relation to ESG matters such as climate risk, decarbonization, and "S" (i.e., Social) factors such as diversity and inclusion. Subsequently, company boards and management teams have become increasingly conscious of ESG considerations in corporate transactions. These considerations are explored further below.

a. ESG considerations in private merger and acquisition deals

In a recent publication by Deloitte,[22] it reported that ESG is a key new driver in mergers and acquisitions (M&A). In particular, having a favorable ESG profile can give companies reputational and financial advantages in a number of ways, including attracting capital from

---

[20] FCA, FCA Handbook, Listing Rule 9.8.6 (2022), https://www.handbook.fca.org.uk/handbook/LR/9/8.html.

[21] FCA, Enhancing Climate-related Disclosures by Standard Listed Companies, Policy Statement PS21/23 (2021).

[22] Deloitte, ESG: A New Driver in M&A, (2022), https://www2.deloitte.com/content/dam/Deloitte/uk/Documents/financial-advisory/deloitte-uk-esg-a-new-driver-in-mergers-and-acquisitions.pdf.

ESG-focused investors, promoting positive stakeholder engagement, including with customers and suppliers, and assisting with the recruitment and retention of employees.

In addition, buyers are increasingly assessing the ESG strategy and culture of an acquisition target and whether they are compatible with and aligned to its own ESG goals. Buyers are now actively conscious about the ESG benefits and opportunities that may arise through M&A, as well as mitigating potential risks. The UK's appetite for making available more green financing options and the focus on ESG reporting discussed earlier in this chapter are also having an impact on M&A transactions. As such, companies should be considering how M&A can assist them in achieving their ESG-related objectives, and determining how the right acquisitions can be used to improve their own ESG credentials.

B. The European Union

1. *Overview of ESG Due Diligence in the European Union*

In February 2022, the EC published its proposed Directive on Corporate Sustainability Due Diligence[23] (CSDDD), which proposed to require EU Member States to transpose into national law the following mandatory obligations on businesses operating in the single market:[24]

a. establish a corporate due diligence duty for companies to identify, bring to an end, prevent, mitigate, and account for adverse human rights and environmental impacts in their own operations and value chains; and
b. introduce duties for directors of EU companies to set up and oversee the implementation of the due diligence process and integrate due diligence into the corporate strategy.

In November 2022, the European Council (the "Council") adopted its negotiating position on the CSDDD, and subsequently on June 1, 2023, the European Parliament agreed on its position on it. The CSDDD will require large EU companies or non-EU companies active in the EU to undertake due diligence on their own activities and that of their suppliers, and to identify, mitigate, or avoid any actual or potential adverse impacts of their business operations.[25] Small and medium-sized enterprises (SME), including micro-enterprises, are not in scope of the CSDDD but may be impacted as contractors or subcontractors to companies

[23] Press Release, EC, Just and Sustainable Economy: Commission Lays Down Rules for Companies to Respect Human Rights and Environment in Global Value Chains (Feb. 23, 2022), https://single-market-economy.ec.europa.eu/news/just-and-sustainable-economy-commission-lays-down-rules-companies-respect-human-rights-and-2022-02-23_en.

[24] *Proposal for a Directive of the European Parliament and of the Council on Corporate Sustainability Due Diligence and Amending Directive (EU) 2019/1937*, COM (2022) 71 final (Feb. 23, 2021).

[25] The new CSDDD rules will apply to the following companies and sectors: (1) EU companies that are either (a) limited liability companies of substantial size and economic power (with 500 or more employees and EUR 150 million or more in net turnover worldwide) ("Group 1"); or (b) limited liability companies operating in defined high-impact sectors, which do not meet both Group 1 thresholds but have more than 250 employees and a net turnover of EUR 40 million worldwide and more ("Group 2") (for Group 2 companies, rules will start to apply two years later than for Group 1); and (2) non-EU companies active in the EU with turnover threshold aligned with Groups 1 and 2, generated in the EU.

in scope. Companies that have an SME business partner will also be required to support them to comply with the due diligence measures.

In anticipation of the new CSDDD rules, we expect to see an increasing number of EU companies developing or enhancing their policies and procedures to address adverse human rights and environmental impacts. From an M&A deal perspective, we also expect to see potential buyers of target companies that fall within the scope of the CSDDD rules to carry out more diligent review of a target company's value supply chain and commercial arrangements to ensure that any relevant third-party contractors captured by the new rules also have satisfactory ESG measures in place.

The CSDDD is intended to complement the existing reporting regime under the NFRD. However, as noted in the introduction of this chapter, the CSRD revises and extends the scope of the sustainability reporting[26] requirements introduced by the NFRD, and therefore companies required to report under the NFRD and CSRD will not have a separate reporting requirement under the CSDDD. It should be noted that the rules introduced by the NFRD remain in force until companies have to apply the new rules of the CSRD. In addition, the CSDDD and CSRD are expected to be applied in tandem by corporate entities. While the CSDDD sets out mandatory due diligence that companies must comply with throughout their supply chains with regard to human rights and environmental impacts, the CSRD serves as the overarching reporting vehicle by which companies will report their relevant sustainability activities.

III. Sustainable Finance

A. The United Kingdom

1. *Climate-related Disclosures*

Since January 1, 2022, the FCA has required certain UK asset managers, life insurers, and FCA-regulated pension providers to make climate-related disclosures consistent with the recommendations of the TCFD. The rules relate to a firm's role as a fiduciary—that is, how it takes climate-related matters into account in its management or administration of assets.

The type of firms in scope of the rules are:

a. asset managers, namely investment portfolio managers, management companies of UK Undertakings for Collective Investment in Transferable Securities (UCITS), and UK alternative investment fund managers (AIFMs). The products and portfolios within the scope for asset managers include UK-authorized funds, unauthorized alternative investment funds (AIFs) managed by a UK AIFM, and portfolio management services; and

[26] The reporting and disclosure requirements set out by the CSRD principally relate to sustainability issues, ranging from a company's plan to ensure compliance with net-zero targets to the role of the board and management in sustainability matters. The CSRD aims to improve the existing NFRD regime by reformulating the reporting obligations from a "collection of non-financial topics for reporting" to a mandate to report on "sustainability matters" and their "principal impacts."

b. life insurers and FCA-regulated pension providers (collectively referred to as "asset owners") in relation to insurance-based or noninsurance-based investment products, depending on the entity.

The above activities constitute "TCFD in-scope business" and the products in scope as "TCFD products."

a. The ESG Sourcebook

The FCA's rules on climate-related disclosures are contained in the FCA's Environmental, Social and Governance Sourcebook (the "ESG Rules").[27] These rules require in-scope firms to make disclosures on an annual basis at entity and product level.

At entity level, an annual TCFD entity report must be published in a prominent place on the main website of the firm's business, setting out how it takes climate-related matters into account in managing or administering investments on behalf of clients and consumers.[28]

At product level, disclosures (including a core set of climate-related metrics) on the firm's products and portfolios must be made publicly in a prominent place on the main website of the firm's business and included or cross-referenced in an appropriate client communication, or made upon request to certain eligible institutional clients.[29]

The ESG Rules are accompanied by guidance to help firms determine whether their disclosures are consistent with the TCFD's recommendations and recommended disclosures, and/or other requirements.[30] A firm is exempt from the disclosure requirements if and for as long as the assets under administration or management in relation to its TCFD in-scope business amount to less than £5 billion calculated as a three-year rolling average on an annual assessment.[31]

The FCA has implemented the ESG Rules in two phases. From January 1, 2022, those rules have applied to asset managers with assets under management (AUM) of more than £50 billion and asset owners with £25 billion or more in AUM or administration relating to in-scope business.[32] From January 1, 2023, the ESG Rules have applied to the remaining in-scope firms listed above who do not fall within the exemption. The first public disclosures had to be made by June 30, 2023, for the first wave of firms and from June 30, 2024, for the second.[33]

The ESG Rules apply to TCFD in-scope business carried out from an establishment maintained by an in-scope firm in the UK, irrespective of where its clients, products, or portfolio are domiciled. The rules do not apply to third-country branches in the UK.

---

[27] FCA, *supra* note 10.

[28] *Id.* at 2/2.

[29] *Id.*

[30] *Id.* at 2/3.

[31] *Id.* at 1/4.

[32] *Id.* at TP 1/1.

[33] *Id.* at TP 1/3.

b. Task Force on Climate-related Financial Disclosures entity reports

A firm's TCFD entity report needs to be consistent with TCFD recommendations and include:

- climate-related financial disclosures regarding the overall assets managed or administered by the firm in relation to its TCFD in-scope business;
- an explanation where its approach to a particular investment strategy, asset class, or product is materially different to its overall entity-level approach to governance, strategy, or risk management under the TCFD recommendations; and
- an explanation of how the firm's strategy under the TCFD recommendations has influenced the decision-making and process by which it delegates functions, selects delegates, and relies on services, strategies, or products offered or employed by third parties, including delegates.[34]

Further disclosures include the firm's approach to climate-related scenario analysis, how it applies climate-related scenario analysis in its investment and risk decision-making process, and quantitative examples to demonstrate the firm's approach to climate-related scenario analysis, where reasonably practicable.[35]

c. Product level reports

A firm has to include its TCFD product report, or an adequately contextualized and prominent cross-reference and hyperlink to where the report can be found, in client communications that follow the annual reporting deadline of June 30.[36] Client communications include annual fund reports, periodic client reports, annual reports to with-profits policyholders, and annual pension benefit statements. (There are limited exceptions to this requirement.) The report must be provided at a given calculation date.

The ESG Rules address the content of the report and include disclosures according to the following metrics: (a) scope 1 and 2 greenhouse gas emissions; (b) scope 3 greenhouse gas emissions; (c) total carbon emissions; (d) total carbon footprint; and (e) weighted average carbon intensity.[37] Firms must also set out contextual information to explain how metrics should be interpreted, and metrics need to be accompanied by a historical time series for comparison.[38]

The ESG Rules also contain requirements on scenario analysis (that is, the consideration of various plausible future scenarios under a set of assumptions and constraints to arrive at a range of hypothetical outcomes). For portfolios with concentrated exposures or higher exposures to more carbon-intensive sectors, firms need to describe these and make certain specific disclosures in relation to them.[39]

---

[34] *Id.* at 2/6.

[35] *Id.* at 2/6–2/7.

[36] *Id.* at 2/9.

[37] *Id.* at 2/10.

[38] *Id.*

[39] *Id.* at 2/11.

2. *Sustainability Disclosure Requirements and Investment Labels*

In October 2022, the FCA published a consultation paper (CP)[40] on Sustainability Disclosure Requirements (SDR) and investment labels, setting out proposals building on their earlier views set out in its Discussion Paper on the same subject matter published in November 2021.[41]

The CP addresses concerns that firms may be making exaggerated, misleading, or unsubstantiated sustainability-related claims about their products that do not stand up to closer scrutiny ("greenwashing"). To this end, in the CP, the FCA proposes new rules to help consumers (or "retail investors") navigate complex investment products and to protect them from greenwashing. The proposals capture the core elements of the TCFD regime: sustainable investment labels; qualifying criteria that firms must meet to use a label; product- and entity-level disclosures; and naming and marketing rules.

a. Scope

The core elements of the SDR regime (labeling and classification, disclosure and naming, and marketing rules) are directed at investment funds (primarily those marketed to retail investors in the UK) and the firms that manage or distribute those products. However, the FCA seeks views on expanding the regime to FCA-regulated asset owners in respect of their investment products and also proposes targeted rules for the distributors of investment products to retail investors in the UK.

b. The Financial Conduct Authority's proposals

The FCA's proposals cover the following main areas:

a. Sustainable investment labels. The labeling regime will assess products based on the sustainability objective they are seeking to achieve. The three proposed labels are:
   i. sustainable focus—investment in assets that are environmentally and/or socially sustainable;
   ii. sustainable improvers—investment products designed to improve the environmental and/or social sustainability of assets over time, including in response to the stewardship influence of the firm; and
   iii. sustainable impact—products designed to provide solutions to environmental or social problems to achieve positive, real-world impact.[42]

There is no hierarchy between the proposed labels, each being designed to deliver a different profile of assets and consumer preferences. Firms will be able to choose whether or not to label their products but will nevertheless need to meet the proposed qualifying criteria if they choose to do so.

b. Consumer-facing disclosures. Firms must provide easily accessible product-level information to consumers, including their sustainability objective, investment

---

[40] FCA, Sustainability Disclosure Requirements (SDR) and Investment Labels, Consultation Paper CP22/20 (2022), https://www.fca.org.uk/publication/consultation/cp22-20.pdf.

[41] FCA, Sustainability Disclosure Requirements (SDR) and Investment Labels, Discussion Paper DP 21/4 (2021), https://www.fca.org.uk/publication/discussion/dp21-4.pdf.

[42] FCA, *supra* note 40, at 17.

approach, and performance against the objective. These must be produced for products with or without a sustainable investment label.

c. **Detailed disclosures.** These are targeted at a wider audience (e.g., institutional investors and consumers seeking more information) and are:
   i. Pre-contractual disclosures (e.g., in the fund prospectus) setting out the sustainability-related features of an investment product. Sustainability-related information must be disclosed both for products that use a label and for products that do not use a label but that have sustainability-related features that are integral to their investment strategy.
   ii. Ongoing sustainability-related performance information in a sustainability product report, including key sustainability-related performance indicators and metrics, to be produced for products that use a label.
   iii. A sustainability entity report covering how firms are managing sustainability-related risks and opportunities. These disclosures must be made regardless of whether an in-scope firm uses a label.
d. **Naming and marketing rules** to include a general anti-greenwashing rule clarifying that sustainability-related claims must be clear, fair, and not misleading, and restricting the use of certain sustainability-related terms such as "ESG," "green," or "sustainable" in product names and marketing materials unless the product uses a sustainable investment label.
e. **Requirements for distributors** to ensure that product-level information (including the labels) is made available to retail investors.

c. Timing

The FCA recognizes that firms will need time to apply the new rules and proposes that the labeling, naming, marketing, and initial disclosure requirements will not come into effect until at least June 30, 2024. The anti-greenwashing rule will come into effect immediately on publication of the FCA's final SDR and investment labeling rules.

d. Overlap with other jurisdictions

The FCA has sought, as far as possible, to achieve international coherence with other regimes, notably the SFDR in the EU and proposals by the U.S. Securities and Exchange Commission (SEC) in the United States. In Annex 1 of the CP, the FCA maps its proposals to the SFDR requirements and the SEC's proposals.[43] Since the UK framework is designed as a labeling regime, with detailed criteria to determine eligibility, its starting point is different from both the SFDR and the SEC's proposals. Products that do not meet the qualifying criteria under the FCA's proposals will not be able to use any of the sustainable investment labels under its proposed regime. Therefore in Annex 1, the FCA details steps firms will need to consider when determining how a product categorized under the SFDR or SEC's proposals would be treated under the FCA's proposals.

[43] *Id.* at 82.

B. The European Union

1. The Sustainable Finance Disclosure Regulation

The SFDR (defined in the introduction to this chapter), which came into force in 2021, requires EU financial market participants to make policy decisions pertaining to the integration of sustainability principles in their businesses.[44] In-scope firms are required to make certain disclosures on their websites and to clients and investors on a pre-contractual and periodic basis about their financial products, and to varying degrees depending upon whether the AIF has an ESG focus.

The SFDR requires consideration and disclosure of how ESG factors are adopted in decision-making processes in a consistent and harmonized manner. It aims to harmonize disclosure standards across EU Member States so that comparisons of different financial products and services can be made.

a. To whom does the Sustainable Finance Disclosure Regulation apply?

SFDR applies, among others, to "financial market participants" (also referred to as "in-scope firms") and, from the perspective of investing, such participants include an investment firm that provides portfolio management, an AIFM, a manufacturer of a pension product, and a UCITS management company.

The SFDR applies regardless of whether or not these entities have an express sustainability or ESG focus, although there are additional disclosure requirements for such focused providers or advisors.

The SFDR defines certain key terms, including:[45]

- "financial product," which includes a portfolio managed by an investment firm, an AIF, a UCITS, pension scheme, and pension product.
- "sustainability risk," which means an ESG "event or condition that, if it occurs, could cause an actual or a potential material negative impact on the value of the investment."
- "sustainable investment," which means "an investment in an economic activity that contributes to an environmental objective, as measured, for example, by key resource efficiency indicators on the use of energy, renewable energy, raw materials, water and land, on the production of waste, and greenhouse gas emissions, or on its impact on biodiversity and the circular economy, or an investment in an economic activity that contributes to a social objective, in particular an investment that contributes to tackling inequality or that fosters social cohesion, social integration and labour relations, or an investment in human capital or economically or socially disadvantaged communities, provided that such investments do not significantly harm any of those objectives and that the investee companies follow good governance practices, in particular with respect to sound management structures, employee relations, remuneration of staff and tax compliance."
- "sustainability factors," which mean "environmental, social and employee matters, respect for human rights, anti-corruption and anti-bribery matters."

---

[44] Regulation (EU) 2019/2088, *supra* note 4.

[45] *Id.* at 8–9.

b. Entity-level disclosures

Financial market participants must publish and maintain on their websites:

a. where they consider principal adverse impacts of investment decisions on sustainability factors, a statement on due diligence policies with respect to those impacts, taking due account of their size, the nature and scale of their activities, and the types of financial products they make available; or
b. where they do not consider adverse impacts of investment decisions on sustainability factors, clear reasons for why they do not do so, including, where relevant, information as to whether and when they intend to consider such adverse impacts.[46]

Financial market participants must include in their remuneration policies information on how those policies are consistent with the integration of sustainability risks and must publish that information on their websites.

c. Pre-contractual disclosures

Under Article 6 of the SFDR, a financial market participant must include in pre-contractual disclosures descriptions of:

a. the manner in which sustainability risks are integrated into their investment decisions; and
b. the results of the assessment of the likely impacts of sustainability risks on the returns of the financial products they make available.[47]

Where financial market participants deem sustainability risks not to be relevant, the descriptions referred to in paragraph (a) shall include a clear and concise explanation of the reasons for that. The way that these disclosures are made depends on the financial product, so for example, a UCITS must include the disclosures in its prospectus.[48]

SFDR disclosure depends on the product offered based on the criteria in Articles 6, 8, and 9.

Article 6 products
An Article 6 financial product may include financial assets that do not integrate any kind of sustainability into the investment process, such as defense and certain energy businesses.

Article 8 products
An Article 8 financial product (an "Article 8 product," and often referred to as a "light green product") is one that promotes, among other characteristics, environmental or social characteristics, or a combination of those characteristics, but does not have sustainable investing as a core objective.

Article 9 products
An Article 9 financial product (an "Article 9 product," and often referred to as a "dark green product") is one that has sustainable investment as its objective.

---

[46] *Id.* at 9.

[47] *Id.* at 10.

[48] *Id.*

Article 9 products must be clearly categorized as financial products that make sustainable investments with an environmental objective and/or sustainable investments with a social objective, in each case identified by a percentage of such investments the product will or did make.

In-scope firms offering Article 8 and Article 9 products must disclose, among other things, sustainability indicators, binding elements of the investment strategy, good governance practices, sustainable investments, and principal adverse impacts (PAIs).

d. Overlap with the Markets in Financial Instruments Directive

EU investment firms are regulated under the Markets in Financial Instruments Directive (MiFID)[49] and related EU legislation. MiFID requires these firms to undertake suitability assessments as to whether a service or a product is either suitable or appropriate for a particular investor, taking into account such factors as the investor's knowledge and experience, financial situation, and investment objectives. Under new EU legislation affecting investment firms, they must now also assess a client's preferred minimum proportion of sustainable investment, preferred minimum proportion of taxonomy-aligned investment, and consideration of principal adverse impacts when investing.

e. Regulatory technical standards

The EC has supplemented the SFDR with regulatory technical standards (RTS),[50] which include prescribed form templates for pre-contractual disclosures and annual reports for Article 8 and Article 9 products as well as the PAI reporting template and indicators.

The RTS came into force on January 1, 2023, and together, the SFDR, the Taxonomy Regulation (see Section III.B.2 below), and the RTS constitute a single rulebook for sustainability disclosures for financial products deriving from or distributed in the EU.

f. Website disclosures

Financial market participants must publish and maintain on their websites the following information for each Article 8 and Article 9 product:

a. a description of the environmental or social characteristics or the sustainable investment objective;
b. information on the methodologies used to assess, measure, and monitor the environmental or social characteristics or the impact of the sustainable investments selected for the financial product, including its data sources, screening criteria for the underlying assets, and the relevant sustainability indicators used to measure the environmental or social characteristics or the overall sustainable impact of the financial product; and
c. certain other information referenced in Articles 8, 9, and 11, including, for example, regarding sustainability-related impacts for Article 9 products.[51]

---

[49] Directive 2014/65/EU of the European Parliament and of the Council of 15 May 2014 on Markets in Financial Instruments and Amending Directive 2002/92/EC and Directive 2011/61/EU, 2014 O.J. (L 173) 349.

[50] The RTS are contained in Commission Delegated Regulation (EU) 2022/1288 of 6 April 2022, 2022 O.J. (L 196) 1.

[51] Regulation (EU) 2019/2088, *supra* note 4, at 13.

The RTS prescribe how and where website disclosures should be presented and provide mandatory headings for Article 8 and Article 9 products. They also set out the information that should be included under each heading. Firms must keep the information published on their websites up to date in accordance with the RTS and clearly mention the date of publication of the information and the date of any update.[52]

That information must be published in a separate section of the website titled "Sustainability-related disclosures" and in the same part of the website as the other information relating to the financial products, including marketing communications.[53]

The RTS further require that firms clearly identify the financial product to which the information in the sustainability-related disclosure section relates and prominently display the environmental or social characteristics or the sustainable investment objective of that financial product.[54]

2. *The Taxonomy Regulation*

The EU Taxonomy Regulation (as referenced in the introduction to this chapter) provides a framework for financial market participants to classify environmentally sustainable economic activities, and among other things aims to prevent greenwashing.[55] It specifies six environmental objectives: (1) climate change mitigation; (2) climate change adaptation; (3) the sustainable use and protection of water and marine resources; (4) the transition to a circular economy; (5) pollution prevention and control; and (6) the protection and restoration of biodiversity and ecosystems.[56] The disclosure obligations under the Regulation came into force with respect to conditions (1) and (2) on January 1, 2022, and for the remaining four conditions on January 1, 2023.

In time, the intention is to extend the taxonomy beyond purely environmentally sustainable objectives to include social objectives.

The Regulation supplements the disclosure obligations that apply to financial market participants under the SFDR for Article 6, 8, and 9 products. For Article 6 products, pre-contractual and ongoing disclosures need to include a statement expressly stating that they do not take into account the EU criteria for environmentally sustainable economic activities.[57] For Article 8 and Article 9 products, which invest in an economic activity that contributes to an environmental objective, the pre-contractual and ongoing disclosures will need to contain certain additional information.[58]

---

[52] *See* Commission Delegated Regulation (EU) 2022/1288, *supra* note 50.

[53] *Id.* at 21.

[54] *Id.* at 22.

[55] Regulation (EU) 2020/852, *supra* note 3.

[56] *Id.* at 17.

[57] *Id.* at 28.

[58] *Id.* at 29.

a. Entity-level disclosures

In-scope firms must use technical screening criteria to assess a company's economic activities and determine whether each activity meets the taxonomy criteria. Then they must aggregate the percentage of taxonomy alignment at investment and product level.

Firms must disclose information on how and to what extent the corporation's activities are associated with economic activities that qualify as environmentally sustainable under the Taxonomy Regulation.

3. Impact on Non-European Union and Non-United Kingdom Firms

The SFDR impacts non-EU firms selling financial products and services to EU clients and investors where SFDR compliant pre-contractual disclosures must be made. Also where the non-EU firm is, for example, a delegate of an EU investment firm, that firm will impose SFDR-derived compliance obligations on the delegate. The non-EU firm may also be required to make periodic and website disclosures—for example, where there are EU investors in a fund managed by it.

IV. Antitrust

A. Introduction

Simply put, EU competition law and policy aim to protect the rivalry between companies that drives consumer benefit. Traditionally, that consumer benefit tended to be measured mainly in increased choice and lower prices.[59] Increasingly, however, companies are competing on innovation, and EU competition law is increasingly concerned with protecting the dynamic competition that drives innovation. This competition through innovation includes efforts to bring technology to the market that will help achieve, for example, a carbon-neutral society, such as renewable energy. Where successful, those companies will capture market share as demand shifts from fossil fuels towards renewable energy. But companies are also in a much broader sense increasingly competing on efforts to ensure that their offerings meet consumer demand in terms of sustainability, including through environmental, social, or corporate governance responsible behavior. Indeed, businesses in a variety of industries (transport, energy, agriculture, etc.) are under significant pressure from regulators to meet the EU's Green Deal objectives. As these features have become part of the competitive paradigm, so has the need to ensure competition law compliance as companies collaborate in ESG-related fields. The task that lies ahead for competition regulators is to identify those instances where companies—for example, under cover of purely technical cooperation on standards—collude to limit the rivalry between them in seeking better sustainability outcomes,[60] while ensuring

---

[59] For information on the antitrust assessment of ESG aspects of company collaborations in the United States, please see Chapter 24—Spotting and Navigating Antitrust Risk.

[60] For example, Case AT.39824—*Trucks* included allegations of collusion over timing for the introduction of emission technologies for trucks to comply with emissions standards and the passing on to customers the costs to meet those rules. In Case AT.40178—*Car Emissions* (the "Car emissions cartel"), several car manufacturers were found to have colluded on technical standards in relation to the cleaning of car exhaust. More recently, this year the EC together with the UK Competition and Markets Authority (CMA) conducted surprise inspections at premises of

that guidance is available on permitted forms of collaborations that is sufficiently clear so that companies will not shy away from working together in pursuit of those sustainability objectives. Indeed, there can be little doubt that efficient and lawful ESG collaboration has the potential to yield significant benefits for consumers.

Against this background, the EC is in the process of reforming its competition law toolbox to make it fit the Green Deal package. The reform covers antitrust as well as mergers and state aid.

In addition, national competition authorities (NCAs) in several Member States, such as the Netherlands, Greece, Austria, and Germany, are actively working on incorporating ESG considerations into their policies and enforcement efforts. The UK Competition and Markets Authority (CMA) has also recently published guidance on the application of competition law to sustainability agreements between competitors.[61]

As these new policies and guidelines are developed, businesses have the opportunity to use competition law to their benefit. Given the political importance of driving investment and innovation in achieving the EU's Green Deal objectives, regulators are keen to show the way for legally acceptable forms of collaboration. Some of the NCAs mentioned above, such as the Dutch Authority for Consumers and Markets (ACM), are well ahead of the EC in providing this type of positive guidance. However, as with any emerging area of antitrust law, there are many complexities, both in navigating the rules and in ensuring internal organizations are properly educated on the risks and guardrails. Indeed, regulators have already shown that they will condemn agreements among competitors that purport to be based on the pursuit of ESG objectives but in fact harm price or other avenues of competition.

B. Sustainability and Horizontal Cooperation

Article 101 of the Treaty on the Functioning of the European Union (TFEU) contains a general prohibition against companies entering into anti-competitive agreements[62] to fix prices, divide customers or territories, decrease production, or limit innovation. Not just explicit agreements are caught but also "concerted practices." Companies may run afoul of these rules simply by exchanging sensitive business information revealing their future strategy because doing so removes the uncertainty that otherwise would exist between them and drive the rivalry essential to effective competition.[63] Conduct that infringes Article 101(1) TFEU exposes companies to a risk of heavy fines of up to 10 percent of their annual turnover.

---

trade associations and member companies involved in recycling end-of-life vehicles on concerns they may have colluded in relation to the collection, treatment, and recovery of end-of-life cars and vans that are considered waste.

[61] *Guidance: Environmental Sustainability Agreements and Competition Law*, CMA, GOV.UK (Jan. 27, 2021), https://www.gov.uk/government/publications/environmental-sustainability-agreements-and-competition-law/sustainability-agreements-and-competition-law.

[62] The reference to sustainability agreements concerns cooperation agreements between businesses (including industry-wide initiatives and decisions of trade associations) for the attainment of sustainability goals, such as tackling climate change.

[63] Equivalent prohibitions exist in the national laws of all EU Member States. National competition authorities are bound to apply EU law in parallel with national law in their investigations.

Not all agreements and conduct entailing a limitation of competition are unlawful, however. Some restrictions are understood to be necessary in pursuit of effective collaboration. Subject to certain conditions, agreements that include restrictions can therefore be exempted under Article 101(3) TFEU.[64] That does not mean that all agreements that restrict competition escape the prohibition of Article 101(1) TFEU simply because they are necessary for the pursuit of a sustainability objective. For an exemption to be available, the negative effects of the restrictions must be balanced by allowing consumers a fair share of the resulting benefits.

1. *What Are the Main Concerns?*

One of the main competition law concerns in relation to collaboration that ostensibly pursues sustainability objectives is that instead of furthering better and more efficient solutions, the **behavior is a cover for a hardcore restriction of competition**. The best example is an agreement between competitors on how to translate increased costs resulting from a sustainability standard into increased sale prices. Another key example is an agreement to limit sustainability efforts to a common lower denominator—for example, agreeing to work towards a legal minimum standard but not go beyond that, even if technically possible. Importantly, these concerns can arise in the context of otherwise lawful collaboration, such as trade association technical working groups.[65] The other often-cited concern is that in the context of lawful collaboration—for example, to establish common standards—competitors **exchange competitively sensitive information** that is not necessary for the collaboration. That could happen bilaterally, as part of trade association discussions, or within technical working groups created for a specific ESG initiative. The concern is that if the information is sensitive enough—for example, information on costs or prices—it allows the companies to coordinate their conduct and not compete as aggressively. Depending on the circumstances, such information exchange may be sufficient for a finding of cartel conduct.

2. *Other Possible Concerns*

Outside those limited instances, a concern may arise despite the collaboration not having as its objective to restrict competition where the collaboration nevertheless causes anti-competitive

---

[64] Agreements should meet the following exemption criteria: (i) they produce objective, concrete, and verifiable efficiencies; (ii) they allow consumers a fair share of the benefits resulting from those efficiencies; (iii) all the restrictions are necessary for the benefits to materialize; and (iv) they do not result in complete elimination of competition. Detailed guidance on the assessment of those criteria is contained in the EC's draft Horizontal Guidelines.

[65] In the Car emissions cartel, companies discussed the introduction of new legal standards for nitrogen oxide in car exhaust, and various technical aspects, most of which were perfectly legal. However, according to the EC's findings, through these discussions, they also signaled to each other that they would not aim at cleaning the exhaust beyond the level required by the legal standard. The EC considered that they could do better but signaled to each other that they would not. It is the EC's first cartel decision to be based solely on a restriction of technical developments, as opposed to classic cartel behavior such as price-fixing or market-sharing. Previously, although EU rules prohibit competitors from restricting competition by limiting technical development, the EC had never found a violation of EU antitrust rules solely on the basis of technical development restriction.

effects. Under EU law, companies must, as a rule, undertake this analysis themselves rather than seek preclearance from the EC, a standard referred to as "self-assessment."[66] That is, companies must get comfortable (with the help of counsel) that they satisfy the requirements of Article 101(3) TFEU. This often involves a thorough analysis of the agreement or arrangement. Parties will need to:

- Substantiate efficiencies achieved through the agreement, which could be broad and varied, such as cleaner production or distribution technologies, less pollution, improved conditions of production and distribution, more resilient infrastructure or supply chains, better-quality products, etc.
- Clearly establish that any restrictions imposed are indispensable to the attainment of those benefits. That includes analysis of whether the agreement as such as well as each of the restrictions of competition it entails are reasonably necessary for the claimed sustainability benefits to materialize and that there are no other economically practicable and less restrictive means of achieving them. This analysis is complex and must take account of standards already imposed through regulation. Agreements that unnecessarily limit individual participants' freedom to pursue sustainability in the most effective way are not likely to pass muster.
- Show that a fair share of the benefits will be passed on to consumers. Here, a key question is the extent to which sustainability improvements that benefit society as a whole, as opposed to benefits accruing to customers in the relevant market, can be taken into account. There is detailed guidance in the EC Horizontal Guidelines (and in the NCA guidelines issued in, for example, the Netherlands and more recently in Austria). So far, the Dutch NCA has shown openness to novel theories that would allow consideration of broader benefits and is looking at the question on a case-by-case basis,[67] while the EC appears to be more conservative and focused on benefits that are substantial to consumers in the relevant market. The EC's analysis is expected to evolve as it builds case law on the matter.
- Show that the agreement does not allow the parties to eliminate competition in relation to substantial elements of the relevant product(s).

---

[66] Previously, companies could notify their agreements to the EC and request an individual clearance or exemption, confirming that the agreement complied with the conditions of Article 101 TFEU. The notification system was abolished in 2004 when it was left to the companies to self-assess. To assist companies in this regard, the option existed to seek informal guidance but only in exceptional cases that pose novel questions where there is no legal certainty.

[67] For example, in a recent case, the Dutch NCA cleared an agreement between garden centers covering 80 percent of the market that had decided to temporarily boycott and not supply products from plant growers that use illegal pesticides. The Dutch NCA applies an "illicit competition theory" according to which plant growers using pesticides may gain a competitive advantage over growers that do not use such pesticides because the plants of the former grow better and fewer plants die. The Dutch NCA found that an agreement aimed at curtailing illegal pesticides, such as the one in the case of the garden centers, does not violate competition rules. This was the case as long as the exclusion process was transparent and due process is in place before any plant grower can be excluded.

The guidelines published by the EC and NCAs are of significant help in the analysis.[68]

Several NCAs (e.g., the Netherlands, Germany, Austria) and the EC encourage parties to collaborate on efforts to use mechanisms for seeking individual guidance on whether specific agreements and planned initiatives comply with the antitrust rules. The EC has recently updated its Informal Guidance Notice[69] to loosen the criteria required for companies to seek such comfort from the EC. Companies are now entitled to do so if the agreement or initiative at stake raises "novel or unresolved questions" where there is "no sufficient clarity in the existing Union legal framework." Companies must still do their homework, as the application to the authorities must always be based on the businesses' own assessment of the situation. There are no strict deadlines for the EC (or national authorities) to issue a decision, and the time required to receive a response depends on the circumstances and complexities of each case.

At the end of the process, the EC issues guidance letters. Guidance letters do not create rights or obligations for the applicants or third parties, nor can they prejudge the assessment of the agreement by the EU courts, but the EC will normally not impose fines on companies that have complied in good faith with a guidance letter. The EC is not precluded from re-examining the same agreement again, and in such a case, it will take into account any subsequent changes in the facts, new aspects, and developments in the case law.

NCAs have similar procedures in place, and some NCAs appear willing to go further in blessing particular ESG collaboration efforts.[70] The practice of the Dutch NCA, which has

---

[68] EC, Guidelines on the Applicability of Article 101 of the Treaty on the Functioning of the European Union to Horizontal Co-operation Agreements (2023); *Guidelines on Sustainability Agreements Are Ready for Further European Coordination*, ACM (Jan. 26, 2021), https://www.acm.nl/en/publications/guidelines-sustainability-agreements-are-ready-further-european-coordination; Austrian Fed. Competition Auth., Guidelines on the Application of Sec. 2, Para. 1 Cartel Act to Sustainability Cooperations (Sustainability Guidelines) (2022), https://www.bwb.gv.at/fileadmin/user_upload/AFCA_Sustainability_Guidelines_English_final.pdf.

[69] Commission Notice on Informal Guidance Relating to Novel Questions Concerning Articles 101 and 102 of the Treaty on the Functioning of the European Union that Arise in Individual Cases, 2022 O.J. (C 381/07) 9.

[70] Most recently, the German NCA gave guidance to companies in the banana sector who joined forces to promote fair wages and a cooperation agreement on animal welfare standards; *see* Press Release, Bundeskartellamt, Achieving Sustainability in a Competitive Environment – Bundeskartellamt Concludes Examination of Sector Initiatives (Jan. 18, 2022), https://www.bundeskartellamt.de/SharedDocs/Meldung/EN/Pressemitteilungen/2022/18_01_2022_Nachhaltigkeit.html. But it refused to bless a proposed financing model by milk producers for payment for raw milk because the proposal meant agreeing on surcharges; *see* Press Release, Bundeskartellamt, Surcharges Without Improved Sustainability in the Milk Sector: Bundeskartellamt Points Out Limits of Competition Law (Jan. 25, 2022), https://www.bundeskartellamt.de/SharedDocs/Meldung/EN/Pressemitteilungen/2022/25_01_2022_Agrardialog.html. The Dutch NCA approved: (i) soft-drink suppliers to jointly abolish plastic handles on multipacks; *see ACM Is Favorable to Joint Agreement Between Soft-drink Suppliers About Discontinuation of Plastic Handles*, ACM (July 26, 2022), https://www.acm.nl/en/publications/acm-favorable-joint-agreement-between-soft-drink-suppliers-about-discontinuation-plastic-handles; (ii) major garden centers to limit the use of illegal pesticides by plant growers; *see ACM Agrees to Arrangements of Garden Centers to Curtail Use of Illegal Pesticides*, ACM (Sept. 2, 2022), https://www.acm.nl/en/publications/acm-agrees-arrangements-garden-centers-curtail-use-illegal-pesticides; (iii) Shell and TotalEnergies to cooperate in storage of carbon dioxide; *see ACM: Shell and TotalEnergies Can Collaborate in the Storage of CO2 in Empty North Sea Gas Fields*, ACM (June 27, 2022), https://www.acm.nl/en/publications/acm-shell-and-totalenergies-can-collaborate-storage-co2-empty-north-sea-gas-fields; and (iv) gas and electricity network operators to cooperate to reduce carbon dioxide emissions; *see System Operators Can Collaborate in Order to Reduce CO2 Emissions*, ACM (Feb. 28, 2022), https://www.acm.nl/en/publications/system-operators-can-collaborate-order-reduce-co2-emissions.

been leading the way, suggests a decision can be issued within one to three months, and in urgent cases (such as in the context of the COVID-19 pandemic) within weeks. Decisions are normally published online, allowing businesses more broadly to benefit from insights into regulators' approaches to specific issues.

3. *Safe Harbors*

Companies that self-assess will also find substantial guidance in guideline documents issued by regulators. The EC Horizontal Guidelines specifically address sustainability standardization agreements and create a so-called "soft safe harbour."[71] Sustainability standardization agreements are those whereby competitors may agree to adopt and comply with certain sustainability standards—for example, an agreement to replace nonsustainable products with sustainable ones—or to only purchase production inputs that are manufactured in a sustainable manner to qualify for specific labeling. These agreements can raise concerns, however, if they lead to price coordination, foreclose alternative standards, or exclude or discriminate against competitors. Absent those concerns, companies will be safe if they can demonstrate that the standard is (1) **transparently developed** in an open process, (2) the standard is **not imposed** on companies that do not wish to participate, (3) participants are **free to go beyond the standard,** (4) there is **no exchange of information** that is not necessary to develop, adopt, or modify the standard, (5) **access to requirements and conditions for achieving compliance** (e.g., labeling) is non-discriminatory, (6) the standard does not lead to substantially **higher prices or less choice,** and (7) there is a monitoring mechanism in place. Outside these conditions, it is necessary to assess the agreement case by case.

Special rules also apply to **the agricultural sector.** In December 2021, the EU adopted a derogation from the competition rules for the entire agri-food supply chain. This covers agreements between primary producers and other actors in the food value chain aimed at higher sustainability standards than those required by law in relation to environmental objectives, reduction in the use of and managing risks linked to pesticides, and animal health and welfare.

The EC is in the process of adopting guidance on how to assess these cases.

C. National Guidance

NCAs have also issued valuable guidance. The Dutch ACM published a draft guidance paper in 2020 on the assessment of sustainability agreements (the "Dutch Guidance").[72] A remarkable feature is that parties that follow the Dutch Guidance in good faith will not be exposed to fines, even if they get the assessment wrong. The Greek NCA is proposing to establish a "regulatory sandbox" for sustainability initiatives—a space for companies

[71] *Annex to the Communication from the Commission Approval of the Content of a Draft for a Communication from the Commission Guidelines on the Applicability of Article 101 of the Treaty on the Functioning of the European Union to Horizontal Co-operation Agreements*, C (2022) 1159 final (Mar. 1, 2022).

[72] ACM, Draft Guidelines: Sustainability Agreements, Opportunities Within Competition Law (2021), https://www.acm.nl/sites/default/files/documents/second-draft-version-guidelines-on-sustainability-agreements-oppurtunities-within-competition-law.pdf.

to run their sustainability initiative by the regulator before implementing it and seek comfort that the initiative is compliant.[73] The French and German NCAs have also announced informal guidance to come,[74] and the UK CMA has published guidelines on sustainability agreements.[75]

D. Sustainability and Merger Control

Environmental and sustainability aspects increasingly play a role in the EC's merger assessment. The EC has been exercising stricter scrutiny over mergers in sectors of the circular economy.[76] Recent merger precedents demonstrate how sustainability aspects fit into the merger control framework: they may affect market definition and the assessment of closeness of competition if sustainability aspects constitute differentiating factors in the eyes of customers,[77] or they may be the basis for substantive concerns.[78]

Sustainability as an efficiency defense is also on the enforcers' radar screen. The EC's chief competition economist, Pierre Régibeau, stated in early 2021 that "it would make a lot of sense to also consider out-of-market efficiencies," although he did "not expect de facto a large number of merger cases to be handled differently even if we take those benefits very seriously." At the end of 2020, his team of economists, which has only a consultative role, formed a group looking for ways to assess sustainability claims in actual cases.[79]

Finally, the EC has hinted that it may use Article 22 of the EU Merger Regulation[80] to address sustainability concerns. Article 22 allows NCAs to refer to the EC merger cases that fall below national notification thresholds if they raise significant competition concerns. The EC suggested that for acquisitions of nascent competitors that may lead to a loss of innovation in, for example, a sustainability context, the ability to refer to the EC may be a helpful tool.[81]

---

[73] *See Sustainability Sandbox*, HELLENIC COMPETITION COMM'N, https://www.epant.gr/en/enimerosi/sandbox.html (last visited Jan. 17, 2023).

[74] *See* Press Release, Bundeskartellamt, Achieving Sustainability in a Competitive Environment, *supra* note 70.

[75] *Guidance: Environmental Sustainability Agreements and Competition Law, supra* note 61.

[76] In 2021, three transactions were approved with remedies (Case M.10047 – *Schwarz Group/Suez Waste Management Companies*, Case M.9969—*Veolia/Suez*, and Case M.10249—*Derichebourg Environnement/Groupe Ecore Holding*), while one transaction (Case M.9938 – *Kingspan Group/Trimo*) was abandoned by the parties after the EC found concerns and initiated an in-depth review.

[77] *See* Case M.10047—*Schwarz Group/Suez Waster Management Companies* and Case M.9706—*Novelis/Aleris*.

[78] *See* Case M.9409—*Aurubis/Metallo*.

[79] Axel Gutermuth et al., *EU Merger Control—Recent Developments and Ongoing Trends*, ARNOLD & PORTER KAYE SCHOLER LLP (June 13, 2022), https://www.arnoldporter.com/en/perspectives/advisories/2022/06/eu-merger-control-recent-developments.

[80] Council Regulation (EC) No 139/2004 of 20 January 2004 on the Control of Concentrations Between Undertakings, 2004 O.J. (L 24) 1.

[81] EC, *Competition Policy in Support of Europe's Green Ambition, in* COMPETITION POLICY BRIEF 1, 6–7 (Sept. 2021).

E. Sustainability and State Aid

State aid is financial support provided by Member States to selected companies by which they grant them distortive advantage over their competitors. Such financial support is in principle prohibited unless notified by Member States and approved by the EC in advance. This is an area that is very specific to the EU due to its nature as a political and economic union comprising 27 independent states.

The EC is in the process of reviewing its state aid rules to meet the needs of the Green Deal. The changes are aimed at broadening the scope of application to new industry areas and technologies, and to additional categories of companies, including SMEs. The changes also seek to make it impossible or at least more difficult and less advantageous for projects involving polluting technologies (e.g., fossil fuels, energy-intensive users) to receive aid, while the granting of aid in areas important to the green transition (e.g., low-carbon recharging, improvement of energy efficiency of buildings and resource efficiency) will be facilitated by more favorable conditions or by removing the requirement for prior EC approval.

Key Takeaways

- Large and medium-sized private and public companies need to be alive to the evolving rules around disclosure and nonfinancial ESG reporting in the UK and the EU as both jurisdictions move toward the net-zero emissions goal by 2050.
- In an M&A context, potential buyers should be factoring ESG issues into their M&A strategy. ESG due diligence should be carried out on a target company, and buyers should be cognizant of the risk that supply chains and other commercial arrangements between a target company and third parties may fall within the scope of relevant ESG regulations.
- Although UK companies are generally no longer subject to EU laws, the new CSDDD reporting rules are expected to affect certain non-EU companies active in the EU.
- Firms within the scope of sustainable finance regulation face a deluge of new regulation and technical standards, requiring them to dedicate significant resources to comply. The complexity and level of detail involved raises issues around interpretation and implementation.
- The reach of regulations imposed in the UK and the EU is broad and catches U.S. and other third-country firms selling financial products and services in those jurisdictions.
- Companies are increasingly competing on ESG efforts, and there is a need to ensure competition law compliance as companies collaborate in ESG-related fields. At the same time, companies must ensure that their collaborative ESG efforts do not harm consumers through higher prices or reduced choice.
- The EC and NCAs in the EU and the UK are in the process of adopting new rules and tools to make sure that competition law contributes to the broader sustainability goals that governments have set for themselves.

- As these new policies and guidelines are developed, businesses have the opportunity to use competition law to their benefit, contribute to sustainability, have an impact on their supply chain, and attract more investment. However, as with any emerging area of antitrust law, there are many complexities, both in navigating the rules and in ensuring internal organizations are properly educated on the risks and guardrails, which companies should consider.

PART II

Environmental: Understanding Risks and Opportunities around Climate and Other Issues

5

Key Principles Related to Climate Risk

Jonathan S. Martel and Sandra Rizzo

I. Types of Climate Risk

A core element of a company's consideration of its interaction with the communities and world in which it operates is the risk posed to the company by climate change and the greenhouse gas emissions the business contributes to the environment. The focus of this chapter is the risk posed by climate change to the business itself, and thus to those who might invest in or depend on the business.[1] The disclosures at issue here are not primarily concerned with the risks posed by the business's operation to others or society at large.[2] Risks of climate change to a business can be significant and commonly have been classified into one of three broad types of risk: physical, transition, and liability risks.[3] We will discuss each in turn.

A. Climate Risk Type 1: Physical Risk

Physical risk means the risk imposed by physical events related to a changing climate, including a higher risk of severe and more frequent weather events such as hurricanes, floods, drought,

[1] Rick Lord et al., *Understanding Climate Risk at the Asset Level: The Interplay of Transition and Physical Risks*, S&P Global (Nov. 2019), https://www.spglobal.com/en/research-insights/featured/understanding-climate-risk-at-the-asset-level-the-interplay-of-transition-and-physical-risks.

[2] Emma Cox et al., *Time to Get Serious About the Realities of Climate Risk*, PwC (May 16, 2022), https://www.pwc.com/gx/en/services/sustainability/publications/risks-and-opportunities-of-climate-change-on-business.html.

[3] Andrew MacFarlane & Katie Lennon, *The Risks Associated with Climate Change*, AXA XL, Mar. 2021, https://axaxl.com/-/media/axaxl/files/pdfs/campaign/climate-risk/section-1/climate_2the-risks-associated-with-climate-change_axa-xl_re.pdf?sc_lang=en&hash=A510F73D7DE0F0FF4FD392E82B85F220.

and severe heat, as well as collateral events such as wildfires and the impacts of such events and trends on property, infrastructure, and business supply chains.[4] Physical risk is generally of three types, as elaborated further below: (1) risk to physical assets themselves; (2) risk attendant to the supply chain; and (3) the risk of changing demand for goods and services.[5]

1. *Physical Risk Type 1: Risk to Physical Assets*

Climate risks include risks to physical assets. Increased frequency and intensity of droughts, hurricanes, cyclones, floods, fires, and temperatures all will have a physical impact on assets and people where these events occur. These extraordinary events may eliminate the viability of continued business operations at certain locations—for example, if heat levels begin to scorch crops or eliminate healthy conditions for outdoor work in the area. Increasing temperatures also could make certain diseases more prevalent in people and crops. For example, Campbell Soup Company, in its 2022 10-K report, disclosed as risks that "[w]e may be subject to decreased availability or less favorable pricing for certain commodities that are necessary for our products"; "[a]dverse weather conditions and natural disasters can reduce crop size and crop quality, which in turn could reduce our supplies of raw materials, lower recoveries of usable raw materials"; and "[w]e may also be subjected to decreased availability or less favorable pricing for water."[6] On the other hand, increasing temperatures in some locations could improve growing conditions. Weather-related events such as floods and fires could damage or destroy physical assets. Glaciers, forests, and ocean ecosystems are forms of natural capital that climate change is expected to continue to deteriorate and change, impacting businesses that rely on the economic activity they foster.

2. *Physical Risk Type 2: Supply Chain Risk*

Supply chains can pose potential bottlenecks to the production of a myriad of products. Supply chain disruptions thus can have widespread impacts and have become a catchphrase in day-to-day life, as they in recent years have impacted everything from lumber prices and availability to the prices and lead times to obtain new automobiles that rely on semiconductors and microchips. The manufacture and transport of these inputs to production of other products have been disrupted by severe weather events that are expected to intensify and occur more often due to climate change.

Businesses rely upon many product components as necessary inputs to production that travel globally through a network of ports, rail lines, and highways along their route to their final destination. International freight travels predominantly by ship. Sea level increases may threaten coastal ports, many of which are not significantly higher than sea level.

While rising sea levels that affect transportation is a widespread example of a supply chain risk, discrete events will pose risks with less capacity to be predicted in time and place. For

---

[4] *The Rise of ESG in Third-Party Risk Management*, PROCESSUNITY, https://info.processunity.com/the-rise-of-esg-in-third-party-risk-management.html#goToForm.

[5] J. ROBERT BROWN, JR., THE REGULATION OF CORPORATE DISCLOSURE § 7.06 (Wolters Kluwer 4th ed. 2022).

[6] Campbell Soup Co., Annual Report (Form 10-K) (Sept. 22, 2022), http://edgar.secdatabase.com/735/1673222000093/filing-main.htm.

example, freezing temperatures in the winter of 2021 in Texas and its resulting power outages shuttered several major semiconductor plants, straining an industry already struggling from the effects of the pandemic.[7] The same event also disrupted rail transport, as Union Pacific shut down intermodal gates "as a result of weekend winter weather that impacted railroad crews" and "told customers to expect a delay of at least 72 hours for shipments moving through Texas and parts of the Gulf Coast."[8] In other examples, heavy rainfall has damaged infrastructure on major commercial waterways, halting shipping. Conversely, drought also has grounded cargo ships or reduced loads they can carry. In the face of need, trucks used for transport have been diverted to relief aid. Fires have halted rail car travel.[9] Floods have forced pipeline closures.[10] While some may have chalked up the disruption in the lumber market in recent years to the pandemic, in fact what has been described as a once-in-a-century rainfall severed critical railroad and highway links to Canada's largest port, which in turn prompted lumber companies to scale back their production, having subsequent impacts on everything from lumber, to paper pulp, to the wide array of assets built and manufactured using them.

3. *Physical Risk Type 3: Changing Demand for Products and Services*

As climate risks change, so too will demand for certain products and services as a direct result of a changing climate. Ski resorts may face challenges due to reduced snowfall in certain areas, with studies projecting a "decline in season length" that is expected to be most "pronounced at resorts closest to the North American coast."[11] Similarly, demand for recreational equipment may be impacted by reduced snowfall in the winter and extreme heat that makes certain summer activities less appealing. On the other side of the coin, services like flood remediation and forest fire suppression have seen demand upticks in areas more and more prone to these events.

B. Climate Risk Type 2: Transition Risk

Transition risk means the risk to businesses as societies and economies reduce greenhouse gas emissions to mitigate the physical risks of climate change. As PriceWaterhouseCoopers has explained: "Transition risks are risks inherent in the large-scale transformation

---

[7] Jacques Leslie, *How Climate Change Is Disrupting the Global Supply Chain*, YALE ENV'T 360 (Mar. 10, 2022), https://e360.yale.edu/features/how-climate-change-is-disrupting-the-global-supply-chain ("The Texas freeze last February caused the worst involuntary energy blackout in U.S. history.").

[8] Matt Leonard, *Winter Weather Disrupts Western Rail Service, Logistics Networks*, SUPPLY CHAIN DIVE (Feb. 16, 2021), https://www.supplychaindive.com/news/rail-intermodal-winter-weather-disrupts-western-fedex-ups-snow-ice/595119/.

[9] Marcy Nicholson & Natalie Obiko Pearson, *Supply Chain Crunch as B.C. Wildfires Halt Hundreds of Rail Cars, Slowing Exports*, BLOOMBERG NEWS (July 7, 2021), https://financialpost.com/news/economy/western-fires-halt-hundreds-of-canada-rail-cars-slowing-exports.

[10] *Trans Mountain Pipeline Shut Down After Severe Rain, Flooding in B.C.*, CBC NEWS (Nov. 15, 2021, 5:25 PM), https://www.cbc.ca/news/canada/calgary/trans-mountain-pipeline-shutdown-weather-1.6249982.

[11] Ethan Clark, The Impact of 21st Century Climate Change on Ski Season Length for Western North American Ski Resorts Under RCP4.5 and RCP8.5 Emission Scenarios (Dec. 9, 2020) (M.Sc. thesis, University of British Columbia), https://open.library.ubc.ca/collections/ubctheses/24/items/1.0395198.

required to shift to a low-carbon economy" and "also arise from changes in policy, such as carbon tax, or changes to markets, for example, changing consumer behavior."[12] These risks can include policy and regulatory risks, technological risks, market risks, reputational risks, and legal risks. The most direct transition risks include direct regulation requiring reduction in greenhouse gas emissions, such as regulations imposing limits on emissions from automobiles, with impacts on directly regulated manufacturers and indirect impacts on fuel suppliers. Transition risks can also include shifts based on investors' reluctance to deploy capital in greenhouse gas-intensive industries, making capital for such industries more expensive. Such transition risks may "strand" or accelerate depreciation of assets due to changes in investors' preferences, law, regulation, consumer sentiment, or the like. Transition risks can also create opportunities as new, sustainable technologies gain market adoption and market share, attract investment, or qualify for legal subsidies and regulatory benefits.

Various industries will face transition risks as efforts to cut greenhouse gas emissions will change the fuels that will be burned, the manufacturing techniques, and even the products that will be offered in many applications going forward. The coal-fired electric generation industry is a good example of an industry that has faced major transition risks.[13] Others include the automotive industry and the oil industry as the transition away from combustion engines and toward electrification takes hold.[14] Growing regulatory restrictions on natural gas heating and cooking appliances in some communities are another example. A company's perceived or real ability to adapt to transition risks will have impacts on its valuation. Capital markets will consider the reputational risk of investing, and the cost of capital will adapt based on investors' perceptions of this risk.[15]

On the other hand, transition will bring opportunities for some businesses, which may be considered a negative risk. For example, businesses focused on renewable energy, energy storage, or other greenhouse gas mitigation such as carbon capture and sequestration may see an increase in investment, demand, and valuation.[16] Just as regulations may burden fossil fuel electric generation, regulations, tax, and other government subsidies may encourage carbon capture and sequestration technologies, biofuels, and sustainable aviation fuel.[17]

---

[12] *Climate Risk Modeling: What You Need to Know to Get Started*, PwC, https://www.pwc.com/us/en/services/esg/library/climate-risk-modeling.html (last visited Jan. 15, 2023).

[13] *Coal-Fired Electricity*, Int'l Energy Agency (2022), https://www.iea.org/reports/coal-fired-electricity.

[14] Elisa Asmelash & Ricardo Gorini, Int'l Renewable Energy Agency, International Oil Companies and the Energy Transition (2021), https://irena.org/Technical-Papers/Oil-companies-and-the-energy-transition.

[15] Ben Cahill, *National Oil Companies Leaning into the Energy Transition*, Ctr. for Strategic & Int'l Stud. (Feb. 14, 2022), https://www.csis.org/analysis/national-oil-companies-leaning-energy-transition.

[16] Isabel Contreras & Christopher Helman, *Green Growth 50: Learning from Companies Boosting Profits While Cutting Emissions*, Forbes (Nov. 16, 2021, 6:00 AM), https://www.forbes.com/sites/isabelcontreras/2021/11/16/growing-green-50-companies-that-raised-profits-while-cutting-emissions/?sh=14ee1973e125.

[17] Michael Rodgers et al., *Inflation Reduction Act Offers Significant Tax Incentives Targeting Energy Transition and Renewables*, White & Case (Aug. 17, 2022), https://www.whitecase.com/insight-alert/inflation-reduction-act-offers-significant-tax-incentives-targeting-energy-transition.

C. Climate Risk Type 3: Liability Risk

Liability risk is the risk imposed on insurers or others who are perceived as having liability when lawsuits or insurance claims are brought or made by entities that have suffered climate change-related losses.[18] Liability risk can include regulatory fines and even exposure to criminal liability. For example, many lawsuits brought by state and local governmental entities are pending in the United States against oil companies for alleged contributions to causing climate change,[19] and oil companies have turned to insurers to cover such claims.[20] Related liability risks may include credit risk, when assets lose value due to a negative event and the company can no longer service its debt payments.

II. Types of Greenhouse Gas Emissions

In accounting for a business's climate impacts, greenhouse gas emissions are commonly categorized by type and are referred to as Scope 1, Scope 2, or Scope 3 emissions, depending on how the emissions arise.[21] Much guidance regarding the three categories of emissions is based on material gathered in The Greenhouse Gas Protocol's Corporate Accounting and Reporting Standard, which provides requirements and guidance for companies and other organizations preparing a corporate-level greenhouse gas emissions inventory.[22] The Greenhouse Gas Protocol is a joint endeavor of the World Resources Institute and World Business Council for Sustainable Development, and its Standard covers the accounting and reporting of seven greenhouse gases covered by the Kyoto Protocol—carbon dioxide, methane, nitrous oxide, hydrofluorocarbons, perfluorocarbons, sulfur hexafluoride, and nitrogen trifluoride.

This section will explain what comprises each of the three types.

Scope 1 emissions are greenhouse gas emissions from assets that a company directly owns and controls. Businesses with a physical footprint typically have Scope 1 emissions. These "direct emissions" primarily include fuel a business burns to heat or power buildings, operate vehicles, and run other equipment in industrial, manufacturing, or commercial processes, whether it be coal, oil, natural gas, gasoline, diesel fuel, propane, lubricants, vegetable oil, or biomass such as wood. Direct Scope 1 emissions also include what are known as "fugitive" emissions that cannot be captured, measured, or controlled through a vent. An example of these emissions includes leaking of refrigerants that are greenhouse gases from commercial cooling equipment like air conditioners and refrigerators, fire suppression systems, and

---

[18] Ben Zigterman, *Insurance Industry Groups Criticize Litigation, Regulations*, LAW360 (Aug. 30, 2022, 9:45 PM), https://www.law360.com/articles/1525775/insurance-industry-groups-criticize-litigation-regulations.

[19] *U.S. Climate Change Litigation Database*, COLUM. L. SCH., SABIN CTR. FOR CLIMATE CHANGE L. & ARNOLD & PORTER KAYE SCHOLER LLP, http://climatecasechart.com/us-climate-change-litigation/ (last visited Jan. 15, 2023).

[20] Hope Patti, *Hawaii Gas Co. Says Insurer Must Cover Climate Change Suits*, LAW360 (Aug. 11, 2022, 1:38 PM), https://www.law360.com/articles/1520086/hawaii-gas-co-says-insurer-must-cover-climate-change-suits.

[21] *Greenhouse Gases at EPA*, ENVIRONMENTAL PROTECTION AGENCY (EPA), https://www.epa.gov/greeningepa/greenhouse-gases-epa (July 18, 2022).

[22] WORLD RES. INST., WORLD BUS. COUNCIL FOR SUSTAINABLE DEV., THE GREENHOUSE GAS PROTOCOL: A CORPORATE ACCOUNTING AND REPORTING STANDARD, (2004), https://ghgprotocol.org/sites/default/files/standards/ghg-protocol-revised.pdf.

certain industrial chemicals and processes. Another example is leaks of methane from natural gas gathering, processing, and distribution systems and from equipment to burn natural gas, such as burners.

Notably, given that Scope 1 emissions include direct emissions only, they exclude emissions from assets that support a business that the business does not directly own and control.[23] For example, Scope 1 emissions do not include fuel burned by a contractor's vehicles, by equipment that is not the company's own, or by commercial airplanes on which the business's employees travel.[24] Scope 1 emissions also do not include emissions from assets that are divested, as those become the Scope 1 emissions of the acquirer. Therefore, divestment converting emitting assets to cash can reduce the seller's Scope 1 emissions, though of course those emissions are not eliminated.

Scope 2 emissions are indirect emissions that occur as a result of the company's consumption of energy purchased from a third-party supplier (as opposed to self-generated). These types of emissions are associated with purchases of electricity, steam for industrial purposes, or district heating and cooling (steam or heated or chilled water delivered through a network of insulated pipes). A company's utility bill typically will account for monthly usage, simplifying the process of quantifying usage of purchased energy. Scope 2 emissions are often not quantifiable on a per-unit-of-energy-used basis but may vary based on the fuel inputs of the energy provider to produce the energy. For example, the electricity provider's generation fuel mix as among coal, natural gas, biomass, wind, and solar over time will impact the Scope 2 emissions associated with usage of the generator's electricity.

Scope 3 emissions are those that a business indirectly generates by virtue of activities throughout its operation, including those that occur upstream in its supply chain and downstream in the use or consumption of its products. Scope 3 emissions frequently comprise the vast majority or a company's emissions, may be the most varied, and may also be the most difficult to quantify accurately. For example, DHL Express Nordic, among other things, is a worldwide package deliverer. It found that 98 percent of its emissions in Sweden related to transportation services provided by third parties. Its contracts with service providers now require the providers to track the vehicles used, miles traveled, fuel efficiency, and related data to allow DHL to calculate its Scope 3 emissions.[25]

The U.S. Environmental Protection Agency (EPA) has recognized a total of 15 categories of Scope 3 emissions based on the work of the Greenhouse Gas Protocol, discussed above.[26] Of the 15, 8 are associated with upstream activities, or those that occur early in the process of creating or providing the good or service, and another 7 are associated with downstream

---

[23] *Id.*

[24] *Scope 1 and Scope 2 Inventory Guidance*, EPA, https://www.epa.gov/climateleadership/scope-1-and-scope-2-inventory-guidance (Sept. 9, 2022).

[25] World Res. Inst., *supra* note 22.

[26] *Scope 3 Inventory Guidance*, EPA, https://www.epa.gov/climateleadership/scope-3-inventory-guidance (Feb. 14, 2023), referring to Greenhouse Gas Protocol, *Technical Guidance for Calculating Scope 3 Emissions (Version 1.0), Supplement to the Corporate Value Chain (Scope 3) Accounting & Reporting Standard* (2013), https://ghgprotocol.org/scope-3-technical-calculation-guidance.

activities, or those that occur later in the process of creating or providing the good or service. Depending on the entity that is accounting for these emissions, there can be overlaps among categories. For example, both the manufacturer of a lawnmower and the manufacturer of fuel that the lawnmower uses (whether gasoline or electricity) may account for downstream emissions from the use of the lawnmower. Likewise, a company that builds warehouses may account for emissions to build and operate those warehouses, while another company that leases the warehouses for use to distribute products may also account for those same emissions occurring downstream to store its goods.

A. Upstream Scope 3 Emissions

The eight types of Scope 3 emissions from upstream activities are:

1. Business Travel—This category includes emissions associated with travel for work purposes by air, railroad, bus, or vehicles for hire, excluding commuting to the workplace.[27]
2. Employee Commuting—This category includes emissions released during the daily commute to the workplace by private vehicle or public transportation.[28]
3. Waste Generation—This category encompasses emissions associated with waste the business disposes in landfills or that goes to wastewater treatment facilities.[29] For example, this would include the crates or boxes in which raw materials are shipped to a business that are placed in a dumpster.
4. Purchased Goods and Services—This category includes the emissions from the production of the goods and services that are used by the business, such as the manufacturing, transportation, and assembly of construction materials for the buildings a business occupies, and the paper, office supplies, furniture, and the like used by the business, as well as raw materials used for manufacturing products.[30]
5. Transportation and Distribution—This category includes the emissions from transportation of raw materials and goods to the business by suppliers or the transportation of goods from the business by customers whether by land, sea, or air, as well as third-party warehousing of goods.[31] For example, this category would include the emissions from UPS or FedEx deliveries of inputs the company uses.
6. Fuel and Energy-Related Activities—This category includes the energy associated with the production of fuel and energy that is purchased and consumed by the

[27] *Category 6: Business Travel*, *in* Greenhouse Gas Protocol, *supra* note 26, https://ghgprotocol.org/sites/default/files/standards_supporting/Chapter6.pdf.

[28] *Category 7: Employee Commuting*, *in* Greenhouse Gas Protocol, *supra* note 26, https://ghgprotocol.org/sites/default/files/standards_supporting/Chapter7.pdf.

[29] *Category 5: Waste Generated in Operations*, *in* Greenhouse Gas Protocol, *supra* note 26, https://ghgprotocol.org/sites/default/files/standards_supporting/Ch5_GHGP_Tech.pdf.

[30] *Category 1: Purchased Goods and Services*, *in* Greenhouse Gas Protocol, *supra* note 26, https://ghgprotocol.org/sites/default/files/standards_supporting/Chapter1.pdf.

[31] *Category 4: Upstream Transportation and Distribution*, *in* Greenhouse Gas Protocol, *supra* note 26, https://ghgprotocol.org/sites/default/files/standards_supporting/Chapter4.pdf.

company to the extent not otherwise captured in Scopes 1 and 2. (This is distinct from the direct Scope 1 emissions from the use of that fuel by the business.)[32]

7. Capital Goods—This category relates to the emissions associated with goods that are used to manufacture a product, to provide a service, or to store, sell, and deliver merchandise. This includes emissions associated with the production of machinery and process equipment for a manufacturing business.[33]
8. Upstream Leased Assets—This category captures the emissions from the operation of leased assets that are used to create the goods or provide the services that are not already captured in Scopes 1 and 2.[34]

B. Downstream Scope 3 Emissions

The following are types of Scope 3 emissions from downstream activities:

1. Investments—This category is primarily relevant to large financial institutions and others involved in investment opportunities. For such relevant entities, greenhouse gas accounting includes (a) equity investments, (b) debt investments, (c) project finance, (d) managed investment, and (e) client services.[35]
2. Downstream Distribution and Transportation—This category includes the emissions occurring due to the transportation and distribution of products the company sells that are transported by third parties, such as distribution of agricultural products.[36]
3. Processing of Sold Products—This category applies to intermediate products that require further processing before they can be used and includes the emissions associated with that further processing. For example, for a manufacturer of raw materials such as iron or steel, this includes emissions associated with manufacturing of products by customers using the raw materials.[37]
4. Franchises—A franchisee may report emissions associated with the franchisor's operations (the Scope 1 and 2 emissions of the franchisor).[38] For example, a

[32] *Category 3: Fuel- and Energy-Related Activities Not Included in Scope 1 or Scope 2*, *in* Greenhouse Gas Protocol, *supra* note 26, https://ghgprotocol.org/sites/default/files/standards_supporting/Chapter3.pdf.

[33] *Category 2: Capital Goods*, *in* Greenhouse Gas Protocol, *supra* note 26, https://ghgprotocol.org/sites/default/files/standards_supporting/Chapter2.pdf.

[34] *Category 8: Upstream Leased Assets*, *in* Greenhouse Gas Protocol, *supra* note 26, https://ghgprotocol.org/sites/default/files/standards_supporting/Chapter8.pdf.

[35] *Category 15: Investments*, *in* Greenhouse Gas Protocol, *supra* note 26, https://ghgprotocol.org/sites/default/files/standards_supporting/Chapter15.pdf.

[36] *Category 9: Downstream Transportation and Distribution*, *in* Greenhouse Gas Protocol, *supra* note 26, https://ghgprotocol.org/sites/default/files/standards_supporting/Chapter9.pdf.

[37] *Category 10: Processing of Sold Products*, *in* Greenhouse Gas Protocol, *supra* note 26, https://ghgprotocol.org/sites/default/files/standards_supporting/Chapter10.pdf.

[38] *Category 14: Franchises*, *in* Greenhouse Gas Protocol, *supra* note 26, https://ghgprotocol.org/sites/default/files/standards_supporting/Chapter14.pdf.

McDonald's restaurant owned by a franchisee may report McDonald's corporate-level emissions in this category.

5. Downstream Leased Assets—This covers emissions from the assets a company leases that are not otherwise captured in Scope 1 or 2.[39]
6. Use of Sold Products—These are the emissions associated with the use of the company's product by a consumer. For example, a gasoline manufacturer or an automobile manufacturer would account for emissions from the use of automobiles in this category.[40]
7. End-of-Life Retirement—This captures the impact of the disposal of the company's products by the consumer once they have reached the end of their useful lives. For example, this may include emissions associated with the transportation, disposal, or recycling of products ranging from packaging, to agricultural, to motor vehicles.[41]

III. ESG Climate Considerations

ESG climate considerations may affect a company's business risk, but they also provide businesses with the opportunity to disclose how they are handling climate risks and to build a desired image as to sustainability efforts. Various corporate policy options exist for businesses that wish to make voluntary disclosures above and beyond those frequently increasing disclosures that are required by law for certain companies. In addition, S&P Global calculates ESG scores for companies as a means to measure their "exposure to and performance on key ESG risks and opportunities, the quality and completeness of their public disclosures, and their awareness of emerging but underreported ESG issues."[42] The maximum/best score is 100; a low score can contribute to reputational risk. While S&P Global considers a myriad of factors in developing its scores, one of the activities it engages in to develop its scores is monitoring media reports relating to workplace "crime, corruption, fraud, illegal commercial practices, human rights abuses, labor disputes and workplace safety, catastrophic accidents, or environmental violations," all areas that contribute to reputational risk. This section will address the communities within which a business may face reputational risks, outline some of the forums for making disclosures, and discuss some of the main types of corporate policy options for addressing ESG climate considerations.

First off, we will discuss what a reputational risk is. Reputational risk is one that occurs when negative events impact a company, changing opinions and perceptions among the company's stakeholders, including investors, lenders, customers, government regulators, and the

[39] *Category 13: Downstream Leased Assets*, *in* Greenhouse Gas Protocol, *supra* note 26, https://ghgprotocol.org/sites/default/files/standards_supporting/Chapter13.pdf.

[40] *Category 11: Use of Sold Products*, *in* Greenhouse Gas Protocol, *supra* note 26, https://ghgprotocol.org/sites/default/files/standards_supporting/Chapter11.pdf.

[41] *Category 12: End-of-Life Treatment of Sold Products*, *in* Greenhouse Gas Protocol, *supra* note 26, https://ghgprotocol.org/sites/default/files/standards_supporting/Chapter12.pdf.

[42] S&P Global, S&P Global ESG Scores Methodology (2022), https://www.spglobal.com/esg/documents/sp-global-esg-scores-methodology-2022.pdf.

public at large, which then adversely impact the company's profits, brand value, and image in the public eye.[43]

Reputational risks can threaten the survival of even very prominent companies because of the rapid and significant decline in market capitalization a negative event and its associated loss of trust and goodwill toward the company can prompt. Volkswagen's focus on electrification and investment in electric charging infrastructure following publicity regarding its "Dieselgate"[44] scandal reflects an effort to repair reputational harm by demonstrating a commitment to addressing climate change.[45]

Equity investors, lenders, customers, governmental entities, and the public at large eventually will learn of and react to major negative events, leading to a reputational risk. Institutional investor Vanguard has explained that its funds vote on climate matters seeking to send important messages about actions it believes are consistent or inconsistent with the interests of investors.[46] Companies that already have made efforts to take ESG factors into account before a negative event occurs may be able to reduce the risk, as both the perception of leadership and actual leadership regarding a company's environmental and social performance may inure to the company's benefit.[47]

How do companies get ahead of the curve on these issues? More and more they are using polished reports of sustainability commitments and achievements, advertisements, and marketing campaigns to create ESG haloes. For example, Swedish brand Oatly, which has experienced rapid growth in the United States based on its sustainability efforts and the favorable environmental perception of its oat milk product, reported in its prospectus, "We have torn down the conventional corporate approach to brand building and have developed a voice that is human, compelling and honest."[48]

Publicly traded companies, of course, are subject to required disclosures relating to climate risks that are material to investors under securities laws, as elaborated in Chapter 23—Public Company Disclosures. Materiality is discussed further in Chapter 23. Materiality concepts may be relevant both based on the materiality of the financial risk to the company (sometimes called "single materiality") and with regard to the materiality of the impact on the environment and people caused by the company's action (sometimes called "double materiality"). Indeed, in the European Union, the Corporate Sustainability

[43] Jacob H. Hupart, *Public Criticism of Ratings Used for ESG Investing*, Nat'l L. Rev. (Sept. 29, 2022), https://www.natlawreview.com/article/public-criticism-ratings-used-esg-investing.

[44] Peter Campbell, *Carmakers Embrace Greener Vision in Wake of Dieselgate*, Fin. Times (May 4, 2022), https://www.ft.com/content/01ebf162-6556-4808-b23f-260b4498043e.

[45] Victoria Waldersee, *Volkswagen Targeting 20-30% Automation at New Electric Vehicle Plant,* Reuters, Oct. 11, 2022, 5:43 AM, https://www.reuters.com/business/autos-transportation/volkswagen-targeting-20-30-automation-new-electric-vehicle-plant-2022-10-11/.

[46] Vanguard, Vanguard Inv. Stewardship Insights: Why Climate Change Matters to Long-term Investors (2020), https://corporate.vanguard.com/content/dam/corp/advocate/investment-stewardship/pdf/perspectives-and-commentary/ISWHYC_062020.pdf.

[47] Amy Myers Jaffe, *This Was the Year Investors and Business Put Big Bets on Climate*, Wall St. J. (Dec. 13, 2021, 10:00 AM), https://www.wsj.com/articles/investors-climate-2021-11638372735.

[48] Grace Garwood, *Big Food Companies See ESG 'Halo' as Key to Building Brands,* The Food Inst. (Oct. 22, 2021), https://foodinstitute.com/focus/big-food-companies-see-esg-halo-as-key-to-building-their-brands/.

Reporting Directive incorporates the concept of "double materiality" to reflect both these inward- and outward-looking concepts, and some voluntary ESG disclosure frameworks are also based on materiality, such as the Global Reporting Initiative in which companies report based on material metrics.

But these mandatory reports and voluntary reporting frameworks are far from the only venues for addressing climate considerations. With increasing frequency, companies are opting voluntarily to present their climate-related data, goals, and progress in sustainability reports; in advertising and marketing materials, including on social media; in newspapers, television spots, and magazines; and beyond. Differentiated and consistent messaging and marketing can target investors, employees, and consumers of a company's brand. For example, Ben & Jerry's, as an ice-cream purveyor, is not peddling the healthiest of products but has strategically evoked a wholesome reputation through catchphrases like "Do the World a Flavor" and "If It's Melted, It's Ruined" combined with its public messaging regarding its fair trade and climate commitment policies.[49]

ESG reports are one of the specific ways to relay ESG climate messaging.[50] An ESG report can be tailored to a specific audience, whether that be consumers, investors, shareholders, or regulators.[51] While ESG issues may be covered in the company's annual report, some companies are moving toward also releasing ESG-specific reports to supplement the more limited information that a securities report typically would cover as material to investors. For example, Microsoft's 2021 Environmental Sustainability Report, from pledges to promises, contains more than 100 pages of content relating its experience in pursuing carbon negative, water positive, waste reduction, and ecosystem improvement.[52] As the Microsoft example shows, a stand-alone ESG report may relay the company's vision and approach to doing business in an environmentally conscious way, as well as provide details on the company's actual performance with real-life examples. Through these reports, a company may differentiate information that is relevant to various stakeholders, such as employees, the community in which the company operates, government regulators, and a company's customers, from information that is specifically material to investors.

ESG policy statements also have been used to convey ESG climate messaging. McDonald's, for example, has issued a policy document indicating its focus on "reducing emissions in our restaurant operations, engaging suppliers to reduce emissions in supply chains, strengthening the resilience of our business and using our voice to advocate for collective transformation." In addition to discussing its business, the statement allows the company to explain its commitment to incorporating sustainability as a core value, and its goals such as

---

[49] *If It's Melted, It's Ruined*, BEN & JERRY'S, https://www.benjerry.com/values/issues-we-care-about/climate-justice (last visited January 15, 2023).

[50] Fabrizio Tocchini & Grazia Cafagna, *The ABCs of ESG Reporting: What Are ESG and Sustainability Reports, Why Are They Important, and What Do CFOs Need to Know?*, WOLTERS KLUWER (Mar. 9, 2022), https://www.wolterskluwer.com/en/expert-insights/the-abcs-of-esg-reporting.

[51] CITI, 2021 ENVIRONMENTAL, SOCIAL & GOVERNANCE REPORT (2022), https://www.citigroup.com/citi/about/esg/download/2021/Global-ESG-Report-2021.pdf?ieNocache=992.

[52] MICROSOFT, 2021 ENVIRONMENTAL SUSTAINABILITY REPORT (2022), https://query.prod.cms.rt.microsoft.com/cms/api/am/binary/RE4RwfV.

dates for achieving carbon neutrality in various aspects of its operations or products.[53] An effective policy statement will contain specific action items the company is taking or outcomes it is targeting based upon its business activities. McDonald's statement, for example, explains that in 2021 it joined the United Nations Race to Zero campaign, committing to achieve net-zero emissions by 2050 but goes further in providing granular examples of its actions, indicating that it is investing in renewable energy, LED lighting, energy-management systems, and energy-efficient kitchen equipment for its restaurants.

Finally, companies can engage with government regarding ESG climate matters, letting the regulator proactively know what the company is doing to manage ESG risks to build its reputation and therefore attempt to minimize the reputational risk that a future event may cause. For example, in recent comments to the Federal Energy Regulatory Commission, Apple touted its status as an early proponent and purchaser of clean energy products and took the opportunity to tell the regulator that "Apple is committed to achieving carbon neutrality for our entire carbon footprint by 2030, including moving our supply chain to clean power, and have been carbon neutral in our own operations since 2020."[54]

Regardless of the type of publication or disclosure a company uses to espouse its climate messaging, the company will need to decide what that messaging will be. The choices run the gamut from policies that the company will achieve net-zero emissions by a certain date, such as Apple's commitment to do so by 2030, to targets and aspirational goals, such as Canon Global's "aim" to realize net-zero by 2050.[55] Once companies announce their policy, over time these reports may provide metrics to measure progress, announce milestones reached, and tout the implications of achieving the milestone or goal. Of course, adherence to such policies and progress toward a company's stated goals may be important metrics that sophisticated or probing audiences such as government regulators may consider. And failure to adhere to such policies may create its own risks of misrepresentations, as explained in Chapter 9—Green Marketing Claims and Communications: Charting a Course through Choppy Waters.

IV. Tools

Now that we have discussed the types of climate risks, have an understanding of the three types of greenhouse gas emissions, and are familiar with the concepts of reputational risk and how to manage it, we will cover the people and things that businesses rely on to develop and achieve their ESG goals.

While a company's C-suite usually consists of a Chief Executive Officer, Chief Financial Officer, Chief Operating Officer, Chief Information Officer, and General Counsel, there is

---

[53] *Climate Action*, McDonald's, https://corporate.mcdonalds.com/corpmcd/our-purpose-and-impact/our-planet/climate-action.html (last visited Aug. 15, 2023).

[54] Letter from Arvin Ganesan, Head of Glob. Env't & Energy Pol'y, Apple, to Chairman Glick, Fed. Energy Regul. Comm'n, at 1 (Oct. 13, 2022), https://elibrary.ferc.gov/eLibrary/filedownload?fileid=86026BDF-8AAB-CCE5-9262-83D32CB00000.

[55] *Environment Target and Achievement*, Canon Glob., https://global.canon/en/environment/target.html (last visited Jan. 15, 2023).

a new entrant being added to the top brass in some companies, with a particular focus on the company's ESG agenda. This new entrant can be called a Chief ESG Officer or a Chief Sustainability Officer.[56] In and of itself, having an appointed Chief ESG Officer or Chief Sustainability Officer will send a signal to the public about the company's prioritization of, and attention to, ESG issues, including climate change.[57] Beyond perceptions, however, substantively, that senior person can be of great benefit to companies seeking to advance their climate goals given the value added by a professional who understands the company's business and sustainability efforts and whose role also faces outward to disseminating information to stakeholders.

For companies without the size and wherewithal to appoint a full-time officer, or with needs that cannot readily be filled by in-house personnel, outside consultants increasingly are honing their resumes and touting their capabilities to serve as ESG ambassadors.[58] Such outside consultants may bring experience across multiple companies within an industry and across industries.[59]

Beyond people, standard-setting organizations, and their approvals and endorsements are tools that can be brought to bear in branding and achieving environmental targets. Sustainability standard-setting has gained wide attention, and international bodies have established standardized protocols.[60] One leading example is the Task Force on Climate-Related Financial Disclosure (TCFD), which has established a recommended framework for disclosures on financial risks and opportunities related to climate change that leading companies have adopted.[61] Other examples include CDP, a nonprofit that provides a voluntary environmental reporting framework; the International Sustainability Standards Board, which was established by the International Financial Report and Standards Foundation that more broadly sets financial accounting standards; and the Science-Based Targets Initiative, which is a partnership between CDP, the United National Global Compact, the World Resources Institute, and the World Wide Fund for Nature, and which reviews corporate greenhouse gas emission reduction targets against a science-based methodology to provide approval that they are aligned with the goals of the Paris Agreement.

---

[56] Laura Cohn et al., *Does Your Organization Need a Chief Sustainability Officer?*, GARTNER (Apr. 25, 2022), https://www.gartner.com/en/articles/does-your-organization-need-a-chief-sustainability-officer.

[57] Press Release, Mastercard, Mastercard Names Ellen Jackowski Chief Sustainability Officer (July 25, 2022), https://www.mastercard.com/news/press/2022/july/mastercard-names-ellen-jackowski-chief-sustainability-officer/.

[58] Michelle Winters, *The Rise of Sustainability Consulting*, CONSERVICE ESG BLOG (Apr. 21, 2021), https://www.gobyinc.com/the-rise-of-sustainability-consulting/.

[59] *Sustainability*, MAZARS, https://www.mazars.us/Home/Services/Sustainability?gclid=EAIaIQobChMIrf6mkvf7-gIVwdzICh0_qAulEAAYASAAEgIeqvD_BwE (last visited Jan. 15, 2023) ("Mazars has extensive experience helping clients navigate complexities, risks, and opportunities of sustainability and related regulations in a range of jurisdictions.").

[60] David Pace & Rachel Decelis, *Reporting on Climate Risk and Carbon Reduction: Early Adoption, Steadily Rising*, KPMG (Sept. 2022), https://home.kpmg/mt/en/home/insights/2022/10/survey-of-sustainability-reporting-2022/climate-risk.html.

[61] FORD, TCFD REPORT 2022 (2022), https://corporate.ford.com/content/dam/corporate/us/en-us/documents/reports/tcfd-report.pdf.

There are also standard-setting organizations for specific industries.[62] For example, in the building industry, construction so as to qualify for Leadership in Energy and Environmental Design (LEED) certification can be pursued. LEED is an internationally recognized environmental program with a presence in upwards of 30 countries that provides a means of verifying that a building or a group of buildings is designed and built so as to improve energy savings, water efficiency, indoor environmental quality, and carbon dioxide emissions reduction.[63]

Partnering with the EPA through the ENERGY STAR Program for which EPA holds a registered trademark is a similar mechanism.[64] ENERGY STAR, however, is an option applicable to even more entities, including builders and developers, manufacturers, commercial and industrial businesses, retailers, utilities, state and local governments, and nonprofit organizations. ENERGY STAR certifications cover everything from household appliances and products like refrigerators, washers and dryers, room air conditioning units, light bulbs, and smart thermostats to new residential construction and upgrades made to pre-existing buildings and plants.

Benchmarking may also be used hand in hand with tools like certifications or the adoption of voluntary standards. ESG benchmarking exercises involve a systematic effort to evaluate the performance of certifications and the adoption of voluntary standards in reducing environmental impacts.[65] In real estate, for example, GRESB,[66] formerly known as the Global Real Estate Sustainability Benchmark, is a common tool used to benchmark a company's ESG performance against the performance of peers to obtain rankings that can then be shared with investors and other stakeholders. Investors that include the world's largest pension funds and investment managers use GRESB data and analytics as they make financial and investment decisions.[67]

Another tool companies can bring to bear are risk management practices and guides. These are documented policies and procedures that the company requires its personnel to adhere to on a day-to-day basis to reduce the company's exposure to climate-related incidents and associated losses.

V. Sector-Specific Observations

While most of the discussion about climate risk we have covered thus far applies across industries, we will now present some observations specific to certain sectors as to which climate presents a particularly great opportunity or risk.

---

[62] *BREEAM: The World's Leading Science-based Suite of Validation and Certification Systems for a Sustainable Built Environment*, BRE, https://bregroup.com/products/breeam/ (last visited Jan. 15, 2023).

[63] *LEED Rating System*, U.S. GREEN BLDG. COUNCIL, https://www.usgbc.org/leed (last visited Jan. 15, 2023).

[64] ENERGY STAR has become a ubiquitous household term since the creation of the program in 1992, with a common perception of high efficiency and desirability. *See About ENERGY STAR*, ENERGY STAR, https://www.energystar.gov/about?s=mega (last visited Jan. 15, 2023).

[65] *About Us: Sustainable Real Asset Investment & Financial Consultancy and ESG Software*, EVORA GLOB., https://evoraglobal.com/about/ (last visited Jan. 15, 2023).

[66] *Welcome to GRESB: Actionable ESG Data and Benchmarks for Financial Markets*, GRESB, https://www.gresb.com/nl-en/ (last visited Jan. 15, 2023).

[67] *Sustainability Report Assurance*, DNV, https://www.dnv.com/services/sustainability-report-assurance-11176 (last visited Jan. 15, 2023).

A. Financial Services

Financial services firms, including banking and lending entities and other investment vehicles, find themselves in a unique "driver-seat" position in being able to catalyze the adoption of climate-friendly environmental change.[68] Among other things, financial services firms can facilitate investments as well as promote liquidity and recognize climate-related efforts in business valuations. They often also can engage in offering mechanisms for risk management.[69]

For example, financial entities may offer mutual funds that are screened for ESG criteria and only invest in companies deemed to have leading ESG practices. Financial entities may play a multifaceted role relating to ESG practices, including:

- Researching and advocating for strong corporate governance practices;
- Engaging with company management teams and boards of directors, and participating in proxy voting, to ensure that portfolio companies are taking the appropriate steps to address the risks that climate change poses to long-term investors;
- Communicating expectations as to board oversight as it relates to climate-related risks, including messaging that board members must have the requisite skill, perspective, and independence to exercise appropriate climate risk oversight;
- Requiring evidence that boards have robust strategies and mitigation measures in place to address climate risks; and
- Seeking transparency as to plans to remain resilient and successful in the face of changing regulatory and market conditions through clear, comprehensive, and comparable climate risk disclosures, including any specific climate change transition targets and progress toward achieving those targets over time.

Given the demand for climate-friendly investment options, the finance industry also faces risk in ensuring that assurances it may provide regarding its ESG and climate-related investment standards are substantiated and not misleading. Adherence to standard-setting bodies and careful explanations of assurances are critical in limiting exposure to claims by financial regulators and investors.

B. Energy Production

Given the status of energy production as one of the top contributors to greenhouse gas emissions and the widely acknowledged role of renewable energy sources in reducing those very same emissions, energy producers have a unique opportunity to accelerate greenhouse gas emissions reductions. They have been doing so by taking actions such as retiring higher emitting assets (or divesting such assets, though divestment of fossil fuel assets to others who will continue production does not itself reduce emissions); replacing them with increasing

[68] *Financial Institution Net-zero Transition Plans*, Glasgow Fin. All. for Net Zero, https://www.gfanzero.com/our-work/financial-institution-net-zero-transition-plans/#real-economy (last visited Jan. 15, 2023).

[69] Tracy McDermott, *COP27 and Beyond: An Open Letter from the NZBA Chair to Members*, UN Env't Programme Fin. Initiative (Oct. 17, 2022), https://www.unepfi.org/industries/banking/letter-from-chair/.

percentages of renewable generation resources; pursuing policies to advance carbon capture and sequestration; planning for an increasingly electrified future; advocating for prices on carbon; innovating with research and development and investments in new technologies; and publicizing their commitment to accelerating change through the adoption of policies and procedures.[70]

C. Energy-Intensive Heavy Industries

Energy-intensive heavy industries, such as steel manufacturers, are under increasing pressure to reduce their emissions. Many have joined the bandwagon in making commitments to achieve net-zero emissions by 2050 and are engaging in efforts to develop frameworks or guidance to adopt greener production practices. In order to achieve emissions reductions associated with energy-intensive heavy industries, various practices are being employed, from recycling to investing in the development of completely new manufacturing methods.

The steel industry,[71] where energy can be upwards of one-third of the cost of production, offers a prime case study.[72] While the industry has a high recycling rate, there is not nearly enough scrap metal to meet the world's demand. Thus, the industry is shifting toward processes that create steel with hydrogen, or that combine more traditional steelmaking processes with technologies that capture emissions. There are challenges associated with these changes, as hydrogen-based steelmaking may double or triple the cost per ton of steel produced, which in turn will increase the prices of untold numbers of downstream products, ultimately impacting the global economy. On top of this, steel companies that voluntarily pursue these expensive methods will face stiff price competition from rivals that do not, placing them in the position of advocating for the imposition of policies such as carbon border adjustments. Separate from using an entirely new fuel stock, using carbon capture and related technologies could allow steel companies to burn waste, create valuable byproducts during the process, and achieve not only carbon-neutral but carbon-negative steelmaking operations. Regulation to "level the playing field" also may advantage producers that are "ahead of the curve" in investing in lower-emitting production methods, and then relying on regulators to require competitors to keep up. Incentives in the Inflation Reduction Act and Bipartisan Infrastructure Act for carbon capture and hydrogen development may assist in defraying the costs of this transition.

D. Transportation

Transportation historically has been a top source of emissions, but unlike the steel industry, which is facing complex challenges in developing greener manufacturing methods, the transportation industry has a ready answer in electrification, which along with hydrogen-fueled

[70] Press Release, South Pole Team, Going Green, Then Going Dark—One in Four Companies Are Keeping Quiet on Science-based Targets (Oct. 18, 2022), https://www.southpole.com/news/going-green-then-going-dark.

[71] Am. Iron & Steel Inst., Facts About American Steel Sustainability, https://www.steel.org/wp-content/uploads/2021/11/AISI_FactSheet_SteelSustainability-11-3-21.pdf.

[72] Press Release, Am. Iron & Steel Inst., AISI Comments on CRU Steel Industry Study (May 26, 2021), https://www.steel.org/2021/05/aisi-comments-on-cru-steel-industry-study/.

vehicle development and adoption, are primed to become industry game-changers.[73] The speed with which consumers have adopted electrified vehicles has exceeded expectations in many circles, with supply chain issues and high costs limiting even more accelerated adoption. Certain parts of the transportation industry, such as rail, shipping, and aviation, face higher hurdles to electrification, and focus has turned to lower-emitting liquid fuels like green hydrogen and sustainable aviation fuel made from renewable biofuels.

E. Agriculture

Advancements in agriculture are being pursued in response to climate considerations to reduce usage of water, fertilizer, and fossil fuels.[74] For example, precision farming, also known as site-specific crop management or satellite farming, is being employed on some farms. It uses information technology to ensure optimum health and productivity of crops.[75] The precision farming technique largely depends on specialized equipment such as sensing devices, antennas and access points, and automation and control systems, and may employ technologies such as bioengineering, robotics and automation, imagery and sensors, and big data. For example, a farmer may employ these technologies to assess precisely when to plant certain crops and how to lay out their fields for maximum production, manage the application of fertilizers to be most efficient, and advise when and how much to water crops through drip rather than flood irrigation.

Efforts to reduce the levels of traditional inputs needed to grow crops such as land, water, fertilizer, herbicides, and insecticides are also at play in the agricultural area. There are enzymes being deployed to increase plant growth, feed additions being used to minimize greenhouse gases from animal byproducts, and satellites being used to improve soil administration.

Key Takeaways

- Climate-related risks include physical risks, transition risks, and liability risks.
  - Physical risks associated with climate change can generally be categorized in one of three ways: (1) risk to physical assets themselves; (2) risk attendant to the supply chain; and (3) the risk of changing demand for goods and services.
  - Transition risks are risks inherent in the large-scale transformation required to shift to a low-carbon economy.

---

[73] Skylar Woodhouse, *Amtrak Aims for Net-Zero Greenhouse Gas Emissions Goal by 2045*, Bloomberg (Sept. 9, 2022, 12:01 PM), https://www.bloomberg.com/news/articles/2022-09-22/amtrak-aims-for-net-zero-greenhouse-gas-emissions-goal-by-2045?leadSource=uverify%20wall.

[74] Ben Riensche & Ajay Vir Jakhar, *Here's How We Can Use Agriculture to Fight Climate Change*, World Econ. F. (Sept. 20, 2019), https://www.weforum.org/agenda/2019/09/here-s-how-we-can-use-agriculture-to-fight-climate-change/#:~:text=Reducing%20tillage%2C%20expanding%20crop%20rotations,carbon%20generated%20by%20other%20industries.

[75] *Climate-smart Agriculture,* The World Bank, https://www.worldbank.org/en/topic/climate-smart-agriculture (Apr. 5, 2021).

    - Liability risk is the risk imposed on insurers or others who are perceived as having liability when lawsuits or insurance claims are brought or made by entities that have suffered climate change-related losses.
- Emissions are categorized by their scope as either Scope 1, 2, or 3 emissions.
    - Scope 1 emissions are greenhouse gas emissions from assets that a company directly owns and controls.
    - Scope 2 emissions are indirect emissions that occur as a result of the company's consumption of energy purchased from a third-party supplier.
    - Scope 3 emissions are those that a business indirectly generates by virtue of activities throughout its operation, including those that occur upstream in its supply chain and downstream in the use of the consumption of its products. Scope 3 emissions frequently comprise the vast majority of a company's emissions, may be the most varied, and may also be the most difficult to quantify accurately.
- A company seeking to manage its climate risks from an ESG perspective must keep in mind management of its reputational risk, the handling of its climate messaging through written means, and the message itself.
- Various tools have been used to address climate risk. Some companies have added a Chief ESG Officer or a Chief Sustainability Officer to their executive teams, joined with standard-setting organizations, acceded to gaining their approvals and endorsements, have engaged in ESG benchmarking exercises, employed risk management practices and guides, or used a combination of tools.

6

Climate-Related Disclosure Obligations at the Federal and International Level

Therese M. Fox, Brian D. Israel, and Sarah Grey

I. Introduction

Climate-related disclosure grows increasingly relevant. Investors and other stakeholders are demanding it, with voices and numbers getting louder and bigger. This movement started to gain momentum in the United States in 2007, when the Environmental Defense Fund and Ceres petitioned the U.S. Securities and Exchange Commission (SEC) to issue climate disclosure rules,[1] and then-New York Attorney General Andrew Cuomo launched an investigation into the climate disclosures (or lack thereof) of several electric utility companies and Peabody Energy.[2] In 2010, the SEC issued guidance, requiring corporate disclosure of material climate change risks and opportunities.[3] Of more recent memory, shareholders of British Petroleum voted in favor of climate-related disclosure in 2019, and over the course of the next two years, similar proposals were adopted by other oil and gas companies, including

[1] Petition for Interpretive Guidance on Climate Risk Disclosure, Cal. Pub. Emps.' Ret. Sys. et al., Securities and Exchange Commission (SEC) (Sept. 18, 2007), https://www.sec.gov/rules/petitions/2007/petn4-547.pdf.

[2] *See, e.g.*, Nicholas Confessore, *Xcel to Disclose Global Warming Risks*, N.Y. Times (Aug. 27, 2008), https://www.nytimes.com/2008/08/28/business/28energy.html.

[3] Press Release, Env't Def. Fund, SEC Issues Ground-Breaking Guidance Requiring Corporate Disclosure of Material Climate Change Risks and Opportunities (Jan. 27, 2010), https://www.edf.org/news/sec-issues-ground-breaking-guidance-requiring-corporate-disclosure-material-climate-change-risk.

Exxon Mobil,[4] Occidental Petroleum,[5] and Valero Energy.[6] The push for increased transparency around climate risks has infiltrated other industries beyond oil and gas, as seen by shareholder and leadership action in companies such as Berkshire Hathaway,[7] BlackRock,[8] and Amazon.[9]

With increased appetite and pressure for climate-minded action, companies were responding (or are being forced to respond), at least verbally. Companies laid out climate action plans that included lofty goals and projections. This may be good in theory, but many question how much the words on paper translate to realistic and tangible action, pointing to the prevalence of green marketing. Mandatory disclosure attempts to circumvent this issue by forcing companies to ensure their actions mirror their words and guaranteeing access to reliable information. It also allows comparability across companies, benefiting investors and consumers.

Because of the evolving reporting landscape, companies should remain aware of developments in federal, state, and international climate disclosure requirements, which may apply differently to individual entities, require different methodologies to estimate emissions, or entail different reporting requirements. Compliance with these regimes will require companies to devote significant time and resources, and failure to comply will result in consequences.

At the federal level, the SEC has taken note, as seen through its sweeping proposal on climate-related disclosure. The proposed climate-related disclosure would require all public companies that are registrants to disclose emissions data; climate-related risks, targets, or goals; risk-management procedures; and financial statement metrics.[10] The SEC's proposed rule would also significantly expand the scope of existing federal obligatory disclosures required under the U.S. Environmental Protection Agency's (EPA's) Greenhouse Gas Reporting Program (GHGRP).[11] For context, the GHGRP requires certain large greenhouse gas (GHG) facilities that emit GHGs, suppliers of fossil fuels, and carbon dioxide injection sites in the United States to report on their annual emissions of carbon dioxide, methane, nitrous

---

[4] *See* Christopher Helman, *Shareholders Rebuke Exxon Mobil on Climate, In a Wake-Up Call for Big Oil*, FORBES (May 27, 2021, 10:00 AM), https://www.forbes.com/sites/christopherhelman/2021/05/27/shareholders-rebuke-exxonmobil-on-climate-in-a-wake-up-call-for-big-oil/?sh=3fe9a47f51e4.

[5] *See* Paul Takahashi, *Climate Votes Fought by Major Oil Companies Get Key Backing (1)*, BLOOMBERG L. (Apr. 25, 2022, 6:12 PM), https://news.bloomberglaw.com/esg/climate-votes-fought-by-major-oil-companies-get-key-backing.

[6] *Id. See also* Jason Halper et al., *Investors and Regulators Turning Up the Heat on Climate-Change Disclosures*, HARV. L. SCH. F. ON CORP. GOVERNANCE (Oct. 4, 2021), https://corpgov.law.harvard.edu/2021/10/04/investors-and-regulators-turning-up-the-heat-on-climate-change-disclosures/.

[7] *See* Peter Eavis, *Warren Buffet Faces Renewed Climate Change Challenge by Investors*, N.Y. TIMES (Apr. 25, 2022), https://www.nytimes.com/2022/04/25/business/energy-environment/warren-buffett-climate-change.html.

[8] *See* Cam Simpson & Saijel Kishan, *How BlackRock Made ESG the Hottest Ticket on Wall Street*, BLOOMBERG (Dec. 31, 2021, 5:53 PM), https://www.bloomberg.com/news/articles/2021-12-31/how-blackrock-s-invisible-hand-helped-make-esg-a-hot-ticket.

[9] *See* Ross Kerber et al., *Amazon's Socially-Focused Shareholder Proposals Fall Short at Annual Meeting*, REUTERS, May 25, 2022, 4:33 PM, https://www.reuters.com/business/sustainable-business/amazoncom-faces-record-challenges-shareholder-meeting-2022-05-25/.

[10] The Enhancement and Standardization of Climate-related Disclosures for Investors, Securities Act Release No. 11,042, Exchange Act Release No. 94,478, 87 Fed. Reg. 21334 (proposed Apr. 11, 2022) (to be codified at 17 C.F.R. pts. 210, 229, 232, 239, 249), https://www.sec.gov/rules/proposed/2022/33-11042.pdf [hereinafter Proposed Rule].

[11] 40 C.F.R. § 98 (2022).

oxide, sulfur hexafluoride, hydrofluorocarbons, perfluorocarbons, and other fluorinated gases.[12] The comment period for the SEC's Proposed Rule originally closed October 6, 2022, but was reopened with the deadline extended to 14 days following publication of the reopening release in the Federal Register.[13] If finalized, the Proposed Rule would begin a phased rollout, with timing depending on the size and nature of the filer.[14]

Development of climate disclosure in the United States at the state level has not caught up with progress made at the federal level, and for this reason, this chapter focuses on the federal and international developments. The existing state-level disclosure rules currently in effect primarily focus on either the insurance industry or statewide GHG reporting[15]—it is not nearly as developed or comprehensive as the federal proposal. Many believed California would be the first state to fall into step with the SEC with California State Senate Bill (S.B.) 260, a climate reporting bill that, if passed, would have required U.S.-based companies with annual revenue over $1 billion that do business in California to report their Scope 1, 2, and 3 emissions to the California Secretary of State.[16] The bill had previously passed in the state Senate 23–7. If enacted, S.B. 260 would have gone beyond the requirements in the proposed SEC rule. Depending on the outcome of the proposed SEC rule, as well as its fate after any legal challenges, S.B. 260 could be given new life. S.B. 260 does show that there is support for climate action, and more widespread climate-related disclosure at the state level in the future is likely. The question is one of timing.

International sovereignties are further along than the United States in that other countries and international governing regimes have mandatory climate-related disclosure requirements in place. This chapter focuses primarily on the United Kingdom (UK) with commentary on the European Union (EU), where relevant.[17] In 2021, the UK's Financial Conduct Authority (FCA) expanded its Task Force on Climate-Related Financial Disclosures (TCFD) requirements to include standard issuers and to incorporate TCFD's updated guidance relating to metrics, targets, and transition plans.[18] The TCFD framework provides guidance to companies that disclose climate-related financial risks to investors, lenders, and insurers through providing recommendations on the types of information that companies should

[12] Environmental Protection Agency (EPA), General Provisions Information Sheet (2018), https://www.epa.gov/sites/default/files/2018-02/documents/generalprovisions_infosheet.pdf; *Greenhouse Gas Reporting Program (GHGRP)*, EPA, https://www.epa.gov/ghgreporting (Mar. 3, 2023). Disclosure Requirements are also discussed below under Scope 1 and Scope 2.

[13] The SEC reopened the public comment periods for 11 rulemaking releases due to a technological error; the Proposed Rule was one of the 11 affected releases.

[14] Proposed Rule, *supra* note 10, at 45–46.

[15] States that have adopted some form of climate-related reporting policy for insurance companies include Washington, Oregon, California, New Mexico, Minnesota, Maryland, Delaware, Connecticut, Rhode Island, Massachusetts, Maine, Vermont, New York, and the District of Columbia. Influence Map, The US Insurance Sector and Climate-Related Financial Regulation: How the Sector Is Delaying and Diluting Emerging Key Regulations 11 (2022), https://influencemap.org/site/data/000/018/InfluenceMap_US_Insurance_Report_May_2022.pdf. Statewide GHG reporting has been adopted in California, Oregon, and Washington.

[16] S. 260, 2021-2022 Reg. Sess. (Cal. 2022). The California legislature shot down S.B. 260 on September 1, 2022.

[17] There are other international jurisdictions advancing climate disclosure. This chapter focuses on the UK and EU regimes, as they are more developed.

[18] Financial Conduct Authority, Enhancing Climate-related Disclosures by Standard Listed Companies, Policy Statement PS 21/23 (2021), https://www.fca.org.uk/publication/policy/ps21-23.pdf.

disclose.[19] It was created in 2015 in response to the 2015 global financial crisis that resulted from fiscal events in Switzerland and Greece, a drop in crude oil, a devaluation of the yuan, and a quick sell-off of Chinese equities.[20] The framework provides recommendations in the areas of governance, strategy, risk management, and metrics and targets.[21]

The UK also adopted the enhanced TCFD-aligned climate-related disclosure requirements for asset managers and certain asset owners.[22] Around the same time and also based on the TCFD framework, the EU passed a proposal, the Corporate Sustainability Reporting Directive (CSRD), to expand the scope of the Non-Financial Reporting Directive (NFRD),[23] which was passed on November 10, 2022, and as of January 2023 has entered into force in EU law.[24] The CSRD introduces more detailed reporting requirements and applies to major companies, finance firms, and small and midsize enterprises (SME).[25]

This chapter proceeds by first providing a brief overview of the federal (the proposed SEC rule) and international (UK and EU) climate-related disclosure policies. It then compares and contrasts the two, where applicable, across five key areas: (1) climate risk; (2) transition risk; (3) Scope 1 and Scope 2; (4) Scope 3; and (5) carbon offsets. This chapter concludes by providing takeaways to aid practitioners going forward.

A. U.S. Federal Overview

On March 21, 2022, the SEC voted to approve a 490-page proposal on climate-related disclosures, which would be contained in proposed Article 14 to Regulation S-X and proposed Subpart 1500 in Regulation S-K (the "Proposed Rule"). The comment period originally closed October 6, 2022, but was reopened with the deadline extended to 14 days following publication of the reopening release in the Federal Register. As of publication, the SEC has taken no future action.

If finalized, the Proposed Rule would represent the first time public companies in the United States (and foreign private issuers reporting in the United States) would be subject to

---

[19] *See* Task Force on Climate Related Financial Disclosures (TCFD), https://www.fsb-tcfd.org/about/ (last visited Mar. 4, 2023).

[20] Anora Mahmudova, *The Events that Rocked Financial Markets in 2015*, MarketWatch (Dec. 22, 2015, 7:24 AM), https://www.marketwatch.com/story/the-events-that-rocked-financial-markets-in-2015-2015-12-22.

[21] TCFD, *supra* note 19.

[22] FCA, Enhancing Climate-Related Disclosures by Asset Managers, Life Insurers and FCA-Regulated Pension Providers (2021), https://www.fca.org.uk/publication/policy/ps21-24.pdf.

[23] Press Release, Council of the EU, New Rules on Corporate Sustainability Reporting: Provisional Political Agreement Between the Council and the European Parliament (June 30, 2022, 11:15 PM), https://www.consilium.europa.eu/en/press/press-releases/2022/06/21/new-rules-on-sustainability-disclosure-provisional-agreement-between-council-and-european-parliament/.

[24] Press Release, Council of the EU, Council Gives Final Green Light to Corporate Sustainability Reporting Directive (Nov. 28, 2022, 10:30 AM), https://www.consilium.europa.eu/en/press/press-releases/2022/11/28/council-gives-final-green-light-to-corporate-sustainability-reporting-directive/; Directive (EU) 2022/2464 of the European Parliament and of the Council of 14 December 2022 amending Regulation (EU) No 537/2014, Directive 2004/109/EC, Directive 2006/43/EC and Directive 2013/34/EU, as regards corporate sustainability reporting, 2022 O.J. (L 322) 15 [hereinafter Directive (EU) 2022/2464].

[25] Avery Ellfeldt, *U.K. Takes 'Major Step' to Curb Corporate Green Washing*, Politico Pro (Oct. 19, 2021, 7:10 AM), https://subscriber.politicopro.com/article/eenews/2021/10/19/uk-takes-major-step-to-curb-corporate-green-washing-282099.

such detailed reporting requirements, though, as discussed below, multinational companies already face similar requirements in Europe and elsewhere. The Proposed Rule would add (1) a new subpart to Regulation S-K that requires registrants to disclose certain climate-related information in a separate section of their registration statements and annual reports, and (2) a new article to Regulation S-X that requires registrants to include certain climate-related financial statement metrics and related disclosure in a note to their consolidated financial statements. Many of the features of the proposed disclosure requirements are modeled on the TCFD framework, which is the same framework guiding the UK's policy.

Both the SEC's authority to issue a rule of this nature as well as the very detailed requirements of the Proposed Rule are highly controversial, resulting in a likelihood that, if finalized in similar form to the proposal, the rule will be litigated. The number of public comments received by the SEC during the comment period—over 14,500—highlights the controversy. A majority of the comments support the proposal, although even some of those in support note concerns. The two most common opposing arguments include (1) the SEC lacks authority to issue a rule of this nature,[26] and (2) compliance with the Proposed Rule would be unduly burdensome, imposing significant costs on companies. The second argument primarily focuses on the inclusion of Scope 3 GHG emissions. The form of the final rule will reflect whether the SEC heeded any of the constructive comments received.

If passed, the Proposed Rule would include a phase-in period for all registrants, with the timing determined by the registrant's filer status, with a later phase-in period for Scope 3 emissions disclosures. The list below reflects the phase-in schedule based on a December 2022 final rule, which was the original, expected passage date.[27] Although this date is now obsolete, it is instructive of what the timing and intervals might look like should the Proposed Rule be implemented.

- **Registrant Type:** Large Accelerated Filer
  - Disclosure Commencement (Fiscal Year)*: 2023, with filing done in 2024
  - GHG Emissions Metrics (Fiscal Year)**: 2024, with filing in 2025
- **Registrant Type:** Accelerated Filer and Non-Accelerated Filer
  - Disclosure Commencement (Fiscal Year)*: 2024, with filing done in 2025
  - GHG Emissions Metrics (Fiscal Year)**: 2025, with filing in 2026
- **Registrant Type:** Smaller Reporting Company
  - Disclosure Commencement (Fiscal Year)*: 2025, with filing done in 2026
  - GHG Emissions Metrics (Fiscal Year)**: Exempt

**All proposed disclosures, including GHG emissions metrics: Scope 1, Scope 2, and associated intensity metric, but excluding Scope 3.*
***GHG emissions metrics: Scope 3 and associated intensity metric.*

[26] This argument, if litigated, may prove successful, based on recent Supreme Court decisions. *See* West Virginia v. EPA, 142 S. Ct. 2587 (2022). Writing for the majority, Chief Justice Roberts relied on the major questions doctrine and concluded that it was "not plausible" Congress gave the EPA authority to adopt a regulatory scheme that would force a nationwide transition away from coal-generated electricity and that a "decision of such magnitude and consequence rests with Congress itself, or an agency acting pursuant to a clear delegation from that representative body." Following this decision, some have speculated the Supreme Court's reliance on the major questions doctrine could indicate a legal hurdle for other agencies with significant climate-related agenda items, such as the SEC and its proposal for mandatory climate-related disclosures.

[27] Information in the list is pulled from SEC, Fact Sheet: Enhancement and Standardization of Climate-Related Disclosures 3 (2022), https://www.sec.gov/files/33-11042-fact-sheet.pdf.

B. International Overview

The UK holds the distinction of being the first Group of Twenty (G20) country[28] to legally require companies to disclose their climate-related risks and opportunities, where material.[29] The disclosure should include how climate change is addressed in corporate governance, the impacts on strategy, how climate-related risks and opportunities are managed, and the performance measures and targets applied in managing the foregoing.[30] Made through amendments to the Companies Act 2006 Regulations 2013 (the "2013 Regulations") and the Limited Liability Partnerships Regulations 2008 (the "2018 Regulations"), certain publicly quoted companies, large private companies, and limited liability partnerships (LLPs) (collectively referred to as "UK Subject Parties") will be required to incorporate TCFD-aligned climate disclosures in their annual reports or reporting.[31] These amendments expanded the scope of climate-related disclosures in the UK. UK Subject Parties must adhere to these requirements beginning with accounting periods that start on or after April 6, 2022, with non-LLPs including such disclosures in the new Non-Financial and Sustainability Statement in the Strategic Report and LLPs including it in either the Energy and Carbon Report, the Directors' Report, or the Strategic Report.[32]

Other than the amended provisions, the terms of the 2013 Regulations and 2018 Regulations remain in effect. These regulations are the enactment of the UK's Streamlined Energy and Carbon Reporting (SECR), the original policy that required "large businesses" in the UK to make climate-related disclosures beginning in 2019.[33] "Large businesses" include registered and unregistered companies that are required to prepare company accounts and reports and LLPs that meet two or more of the following requirements in a single year: (1) turnover of at least £36 million; (2) balance sheet total of £18 million or more; and (3) at least 250 employees.[34]

The EU followed on the heels of the UK: on June 30, 2022, the European Parliament and the Council of the European Union (the "Council") agreed upon the language of the CSRD

[28] The members of the G20 include Argentina, Australia, Brazil, Canada, China, France, Germany, India, Indonesia, Italy, Japan, Republic of Korea, Mexico, Russia, Saudi Arabia, South Africa, Turkey, the United Kingdom, the United States, and the European Union, with Spain listed as a permanent guest. *About G20*, G20, https://www.g20.org/en/about-g20/#overview (last visited Jan. 16, 2023).

[29] Press Release, UK Dep't for Bus., Energy & Indus. Strategy et al., UK to Enshrine Mandatory Climate Disclosures for Largest Companies in Law (Oct. 29, 2021), https://www.gov.uk/government/news/uk-to-enshrine-mandatory-climate-disclosures-for-largest-companies-in-law.

[30] UK Dep't for Bus., Energy & Indus. Strategy, Mandatory Climate-related Financial Disclosures by Publicly Quoted Companies, Large Private Companies and LLPs: Non-binding Guidance (2022), https://assets.publishing.service.gov.uk/government/uploads/system/uploads/attachment_data/file/1056085/mandatory-climate-related-financial-disclosures-publicly-quoted-private-cos-llps.pdf [hereinafter UK Mandatory Climate-related Disclosures].

[31] The Companies (Strategic Report) (Climate-Related Financial Disclosure) Regulations 2022, https://www.legislation.gov.uk/uksi/2022/31/contents/made; The Limited Liability Partnerships (Accounts and Audit) (Application of Companies Act 2006) Regulations 2008, https://www.legislation.gov.uk/uksi/2008/1911/contents; *see also*, UK Mandatory Climate-related Disclosures, *supra* note 30.

[32] UK Mandatory Climate-related Disclosures, *supra* note 30.

[33] HM Gov't, Environmental Reporting Guidelines: Including Streamlined Energy and Carbon Reporting Guidance (2019), https://assets.publishing.service.gov.uk/government/uploads/system/uploads/attachment_data/file/850130/Env-reporting-guidance_inc_SECR_31March.pdf [hereinafter UK Env't Reporting Guidelines].

[34] *Id.* at 29.

(sometimes referred to as the "CSRD Agreement"),[35] which amends the current NFRD.[36] The EU regime entered into force on January 5, 2023. It requires all "large EU companies" and all listed companies (except listed micro-enterprises) to report out on how environmental issues threaten their bottom lines, how their own operations threaten the planet, and the detailed steps companies will take to reach zero emissions by 2050.[37] A company, regardless if it is public or private, qualifies as a "large EU company" if it meets at least two of the following criteria: (1) employs more than 350 employees; (2) has a turnover of over €40 million; or (3) has total assets of at least €20 million. This also applies to EU subsidiaries of non-EU companies.[38] For companies operating in the EU-regulated markets, only non-European companies with net turnover of at least €150 million in the EU (at a consolidated level) and that have one or more large or listed subsidiaries in the EU, or a branch in the EU with net turnover of at least €40 million, will be subject to the CSRD requirements.[39] Similar to the U.S.'s Proposed Rule, the CSRD will begin a phased rollout in 2025, depending on the size and nature of the entity as follows: (1) reporting in 2025 on the fiscal year 2024 for companies already subject to the NFRD; (2) reporting in 2026 on the fiscal year 2025 for large companies not presently subject to the NFRD; (3) reporting in 2027 on the fiscal year 2026 for listed SMEs (except micro undertakings), small and non-complex credit institutions, and captive insurance undertakings; and (4) reporting in 2029 on the fiscal year 2028 for third-country undertakings with net turnover above €150 million if they have at least one subsidiary or branch in the EU exceeding certain thresholds.[40]

Now that the CSRD is in effect, it is expected that each of the 27 EU Member States must pass the CSRD into local law within 18 months of January 5, 2023.[41]

The European Financial Reporting Advisory Group (EFRAG) is responsible for drafting the sustainability reporting standards that subject companies will have to comply with under the CSRD Agreement.[42] Although the EU has agreed on the language to guide EFRAG in developing the corresponding reporting standards, the specific standards are still in the process of being developed, with a projected deadline of June 2023. In light of this, analysis specific to the EU's CSRD Agreement in the sections that follow is, at times, informed

---

[35] Directive (EU) 2022/2464, *supra* note 24.

[36] Peter Wollmert and Andrew Hobbs, *How the EU's New Sustainability Directive Is Becoming a Game Changer*, EY (Aug. 1, 2022), https://www.ey.com/en_gl/assurance/how-the-eu-s-new-sustainability-directive-is-becoming-a-game-changer.

[37] Ellfeldt, *supra* note 25. *See also*, Corporate Sustainability Reporting, EUR. COMM'N, https://finance.ec.europa.eu/capital-markets-union-and-financial-markets/company-reporting-and-auditing/company-reporting/corporate-sustainability-reporting_en (last visited Mar. 4, 2023) [hereinafter CSR].

[38] Directive 2013/34/EU of the European Parliament and of the Council of 26 June 2013 on the annual financial statements, consolidated financial statements and related reports of certain types of undertakings, amending Directive 2006/43/EC of the European Parliament and of the Council and repealing Council Directives 78/660/EEC and 83/349/EEC, 2013 (L 182) 19.

[39] Wollmert & Hobbs, *supra* note 36.

[40] Press Release, Council of the EU, *supra* note 24.

[41] Wollmert & Hobbs, *supra* note 36.

[42] *Id.*

speculation, since some of the guidance provided in the CSRD to EFRAG is framed more as a suggestion for consideration than a directive for inclusion in the final rules.

EFRAG is also responsible for a second set of standards that specify disclosure requirements by sector as well as standards for listed SMEs and for non-EU companies, which is expected in June 2024.[43] This sector-specific approach would be unique to the EU. Although other sovereignties, such as the United States, do have certain industry requirements (for insurance companies, for example), it is not as individualized as the EU standards.

A second aspect of the CSRD Agreement that makes it unique is the directionality of impact when it comes to materiality. The U.S.'s Proposed Rule focuses on the impact of climate change on a company: how do climate-specific, external factors impact the company (the "outside-in" perspective)?[44] The CSRD Agreement, conversely, incorporates a double-materiality standard: companies will be required to disclose the outside-in perspective as well as the "inside-out."[45] The inside-out perspective evaluates how a company's activities impact external factors.[46] An additional and important distinction between the CSRD Agreement and the U.S.'s Proposed Rule is the scope of those external factors. The SEC focuses on the inside-out perspective and specifically as it relates to climate-related events and environmental circumstances. Not only does the CSRD Agreement emphasize a double-materiality standard, it also requires companies to look beyond environmental stimuli in its inside-out assessment to assess the impact of the company's activities on "social and employee matters, respect for human rights, anti-corruption and bribery matters."[47] The reporting requirements will require companies to disclose information that is material from (1) each of the materiality perspectives (outside-in and inside-out) individually and (2) each of the materiality perspectives jointly.[48]

With the U.S. federal and international contexts in place, this chapter proceeds by assessing each, where applicable, under five key areas: Physical Risk, Transition Risk, Scopes 1 and 2, Scope 3, and Carbon Offsets.

II. Physical Risk

"Physical Risks" are defined as "both acute risks and chronic risks to the registrant's business operations or the operations of those with whom it desires to do business."[49] Acute risks are event-driven and may relate to shorter-term, extreme weather events, such as hurricanes, floods, and tornadoes, among others.[50] Chronic risks are related to longer-term weather

[43] *Id.*

[44] Donato Calace, Conducting Double Materiality Assessments: A 5-Step Process (Part 1), PRACTICAL ESG (Aug. 10, 2021), https://practicalesg.com/2021/08/conducting-double-materiality-assessments-a-5-step-process-part-1/.

[45] Directive (EU) 2022/2464, *supra* note 24, at 24.

[46] Calace, *supra* note 44.

[47] Directive (EU) 2022/2464, *supra* note 24, at 24.

[48] *Id.*

[49] Proposed Rule, *supra* note 10, at 457.

[50] *Id.* at 458.

patterns and related effects, such as sea level rise, drought, increased wildfires, decreased arability of farmland, decreased habitability of land, and decreased availability of fresh water.[51]

A. Federal—Proposed Rule

The new S-K regulations would require a registrant to disclose any climate-related risks reasonably likely to have a material impact on the registrant's business or consolidated financial statements.[52] These risks encompass both physical and transition risks, although a company would be required to differentiate between the two (transition risks are discussed in Section III below). A company would also have to describe whether the risk is acute or chronic and identify material risks that may manifest over the short, medium, and long term.[53] In this context, the SEC articulates a concept of materiality that includes both magnitude and probability of occurrence.[54] For physical risks specifically, the registrant must identify the physical location(s) of the assets subject to the risk.[55] Registrants may also, but are not required to, disclose climate-related opportunities (e.g., cost savings associated with reduced energy usage, new product/service demands that may benefit the filer).[56] Following disclosure of the physical risks, registrants must disclose the potential impacts those risks have on the filer's strategy, business model, and outlook.[57] Requirements related to adoption of a transition plan are discussed in Section III below.

B. International

The UK requires disclosure of similar information as the United States requires but with less tedious and more open-ended requirements. In the UK, UK Subject Parties must include a description of the principal climate-related risks and opportunities arising in connection with the company's operations and the relevant time periods.[58] Line-item detail is not required; rather, in determining the level of detail that is necessary, UK Subject Parties are directed to "consider the range of geographical locations in which it operates [and] the extent to which those geographical locations may be subject to both acute and chronic physical risks. Where elements of a supply chain or items of critical infrastructure are likely to be exposed to increased physical risks, it may be important to consider mitigating actions."[59] Unlike the U.S.'s Proposed Rule, the UK law does not require a company to distinguish between acute

---

[51] *Id.*

[52] *Id.* at 56.

[53] *Id.* at 59, 63.

[54] *Id.* at 65.

[55] *Id.* at 59.

[56] *Id.* at 63.

[57] *Id.* at 72–76.

[58] UK Mandatory Climate-related Disclosures, *supra* note 30.

[59] *Id.*

and physical risks, and companies are directed to *consider* locations in which it operates that may be impacted, rather than specifically *identify* the physical location of impacted assets.

The EU's CSRD Agreement notes the importance of physical and transition risks and suggests that this should be considered as EFRAG develops the reporting requirements. The CSRD notes that "users"[60] are interested in understanding companies' physical and transition risks and how companies plan to adapt to different climate scenarios as well as the EU's climate neutrality goal.

III. Transition Risk

"Transition Risks" are the risks inherent in changing strategies, policies, or investments as society and industry work to reduce their reliance on carbon and impact on the climate. As defined in the U.S.'s Proposed Rule, transition risk means

> the actual or potential negative impacts on a registrant's consolidated financial statements, business operations, or value chains attributable to regulatory, technological, and market changes to address the mitigation of, or adaptation to, climate-related risks, such as increased costs attributable to changes in law or policy, reduced market demand for carbon-intensive products leading to decreased prices or profits for such products, the devaluation or abandonment of assets, risk of legal liability and litigation defense costs, competitive pressures associated with the adoption of new technologies, reputational impacts (including those stemming from a registrant's customers or business counterparties) that might trigger changes to market behavior, consumer preferences or behavior, and registrant behavior.[61]

A. Federal—Proposed Rule

Related to transition risks, a registrant may adopt a transition plan (i.e., a strategy to reduce physical and transition risks)[62] as part of its climate-related risk-management strategy. If a registrant does adopt a transition plan, it must "describe the plan, including the relevant metrics and targets used to identify and manage any physical and transition risks."[63] The registrant should discuss, as applicable, how it plans to mitigate or adapt to physical risks, including those concerns with "energy, land, or water use and management."[64] For example, "a company operating in areas subject to severe storms might have a transition plan that

[60] The CSRD defines "users" as individuals falling under two primary groups. The first group consists of "investors, including asset managers, who want to better understand the risks and opportunities that sustainability issues pose for their investments and the impacts of those investments on people and the environment. The second group . . . consists of civil society actors, including non-governmental organisations and social partners, that wish to better hold [companies] to account for their impacts on people and the environment." Directive (EU) 2022/2464, *supra* note 24, at 18.

[61] Proposed Rule, *supra* note 10, at 458.

[62] *Id.* at 461.

[63] *Id.* at 468.

[64] *Id.*

includes reinforcing its physical facilities to better withstand such weather events, or a plan to relocate those facilities."[65] The registrant should also discuss, as applicable, how it plans to mitigate or adapt to transition risks, including "[l]aws, regulations, or policies that . . . restrict GHG emissions or products with high GHG footprints," "[i]mposition of a carbon price," and "[c]hanging demands or preference of consumers, investors, employees, and business counterparties."[66] The registrant may also describe how it plans to achieve any identified climate-related opportunities, such as "the production of products that may facilitate the transition to a lower carbon economy" or "the generation or use of renewable power."[67]

If a registrant has adopted a transition plan, it must update its disclosure about its transition plan each fiscal year.[68] Also, because transition planning "inherently requires judgments and predictions about the future," discussion of a transition plan and updates thereto would be eligible for the Private Securities Litigation Reform Act of 1995 (PSLRA) forward-looking statement safe harbors, assuming all other statutory requirements for those safe harbors are satisfied.[69]

B. International

The United Kingdom mandate directs UK Subject Parties to identify transition risks and opportunities under four categories: technology, policy, market, and legal and reputational.[70] Like the U.S.'s Proposed Rule, this should include those risks associated with mitigating and adapting to climate change, with a similar focus on those that would have the greatest impact on the company and that have the greatest likelihood of occurring (a materiality assessment).[71] Impact can be both positive and negative. The disclosure should be sufficiently detailed to allow an individual not associated with the company to easily understand, as relevant, (1) the actual (present) and potential (future) impacts; (2) how instrumental the impacted asset is to the company; (3) what areas or operations of the company the risk impacts; and (4) what the company's mitigation and/or adaptation plan is specific to that risk.[72]

IV. Scope 1 and Scope 2

Scope 1 emissions include direct GHG emissions from operations owned or controlled by the registrant. Examples of Scope 1 emissions include emissions from combustion in owned or controlled boilers, furnaces, and vehicles and emissions from chemical production in owned or controlled process equipment.[73] Scope 2 emissions include indirect GHG emissions from

---

[65] *Id.* at 104.

[66] *Id.* at 468.

[67] *Id.* at 468–69.

[68] *Id.* at 468.

[69] *Id.* at 103.

[70] UK Mandatory Climate-related Disclosures, *supra* note 30.

[71] *Id.*

[72] *Id.*

[73] UK Env't Reporting Guidelines, *supra* note 33, at 50.

generation of purchased or acquired electricity used by the registrant's owned or controlled operations. As defined under the SECR, these include "emissions released into the atmosphere associated with [a company's] consumption of purchased electricity, heat, steam and cooling . . . [that] are a consequence of [a company's] activities, but which occur at sources [it] does not own or control."[74]

A. Federal—Proposed Rule

Under the Proposed Rule, both Scope 1 emissions and Scope 2 emissions must be disclosed even if not material. Companies must disclose methodology, significant inputs, and significant assumptions used to calculate GHG emissions metrics under each. Disclosure of total Scope 1 emissions must be separate from total Scope 2 emissions, and all scope of emissions must be disaggregated as between constituent GHGs (e.g., carbon dioxide [CO_2], methane, hydrofluorocarbons).[75] Significantly, the Proposed Rule requires reporting of emissions in *gross* terms, excluding any offsets purchased.[76]

For Scope 1 and Scope 2 emissions, certain registrants would also be required to include an attestation report and disclose information regarding the attestation service provider.[77] In years two and three after the Scope 1 and Scope 2 emissions requirements take effect, filers must provide limited assurance (e.g., equivalent to the review of a registrant's interim financial statement); in years four and beyond, filers must provide reasonable assurance (e.g., the audit rigor applied to a registrant's 10-K). The final rule would specify minimum attestation report requirements and minimum standards for acceptable attestation frameworks, and would require an attestation service provider to meet certain minimum qualifications. Requirements for the attestation provider include that it is "an expert in GHG emissions by virtue of having significant experience in measuring, analyzing, reporting, or attesting to GHG emissions" and independent of the registrant.[78] Registrants subject to the foregoing requirement include accelerated and large accelerated filers.[79] Filers other than accelerated or large accelerated filers must disclose whether any of their GHG emissions disclosures were subject to voluntary third-party attestation or verification and certain information regarding the third-party attestation, if applicable.

Under the GHGRP, the EPA requires subject facilities that emit GHGs to disclose annual facility emissions aggregated for all source categories; an indication of whether the facility has been assigned a plant code;[80] annual emissions for each source category located at the facility;

---

[74] *Id.*

[75] Proposed Rule, *supra* note 10, at 151.

[76] *Id.* at 152.

[77] *Id.* at 215.

[78] *Id.* at 239–40.

[79] An "accelerated filer" is a filer with a public float of $75 million or more but less than $700 million. A "large accelerated filer" is a filer with a public float of $700 million or more.

[80] Plant code is defined in 40 CFR § 98.6 and would be assigned by either the Department of Energy's Information Administration or by the EPA's Clean Air Markets Division.

and other relevant information, such as unit- or process-level emissions, activity data (i.e., fuel use, feedstock inputs), or quality assurance and quality control data.[81] Subject suppliers must disclose the annual quantity of GHG supplied, aggregated for all GHGs from all applicable supplier categories, and annual quantity of each GHG supplied from each supplier category.[82]

B. International

Scope 1 and Scope 2 emissions disclosures are addressed under the UK's SECR. Quoted companies must report out on their global Scope 1 and Scope 2 emissions; unquoted companies and LLPs must report out on their UK Scope 1 and Scope 2 emissions, but only as such emissions relate to the entity's UK energy use.[83]

The EU's CSRD Agreement does not get granular on Scope 1 or Scope 2. It just notes that users want to understand how companies are reducing or plan to reduce GHG emissions as part of their climate mitigation and adaptation strategies, including Scope 1, Scope 2, and, where relevant, Scope 3 emissions,[84] and as such, EFRAG should consider this as it develops the reporting requirements.

V. Scope 3

Scope 3 emissions are indirect GHG emissions that occur in upstream and downstream activities in a company's value chain that are not Scope 2 emissions.[85] Upstream activities generally relate to those steps early in the manufacturing process and the parties involved, such as suppliers and providers of raw materials used by the registrant in making its product(s). Downstream activities generally relate to those steps post-manufacturing and the parties involved in such activities, which may include transportation and distribution, selling and processing of the registrant's product(s), waste generated in operations, end-of-life treatment of sold products, and investments.

A. Federal—Proposed Rule

A company must disclose Scope 3 emissions if material or if the company has set an emissions reduction target that includes these emissions. A company's assessment of materiality should consider whether there is "a substantial likelihood that a reasonable investor would consider [it] important when making an investment or voting decision."[86] For financial institutions, Scope 3 emissions include the GHG emissions they lend to or invest in. Smaller reporting companies are exempt from Scope 3 disclosure requirements.

---

[81] EPA, General Provisions Information Sheet, *supra* note 12.

[82] *Id.*

[83] UK Env't Reporting Guidelines, *supra* note 33, at 50.

[84] Directive (EU) 2022/2464, *supra* note 24, at 30.

[85] Proposed Rule, *supra* note 10, at 150.

[86] *Id.* at 162.

To explain and justify the SEC's inclusion of this disclosure requirement, the Proposed Rule provides a series of examples of when Scope 3 emissions disclosures would be material. The Proposed Rule specifically notes oil and gas product manufacturers as companies for whom "Scope 3 emissions are likely to be material and thus necessary to an understanding of a registrant's climate-related risks."[87] The Proposed Rule notes that a registrant's assessment of the materiality of Scope 3 emissions should consider whether those emissions make up a large portion of the company's overall GHG impact. It does not require use of a specific quantitative threshold, but notes that some companies use 40 percent as a benchmark for determining whether Scope 3 emissions are material.[88] For many companies, this may not be an appropriate analytical tool: for example, if a company has a very small GHG footprint to begin with, and its Scope 3 emissions are 90 percent of its overall emissions, it may be justified in concluding its Scope 3 emissions do not necessitate inclusion in filings as material. The SEC notes that investors may be interested in *why* a company elected not to disclose Scope 3 emissions, but it did not include a mandatory requirement that a company explain this in the filings.

Scope 3 is a more controversial aspect of the Proposed Rule—as the SEC acknowledges, because registrants do not directly control Scope 3 emissions, it may be more difficult to collect data to accurately calculate these emissions than Scopes 1 and 2; however, registrants have the ability to "influence" parties in their value chain to reduce climate risks.[89] Unlike Scopes 1 and 2, the Proposed Rule does not require attestation and assurances for Scope 3 emissions, to the extent Scope 3 emissions must be disclosed.[90] Additionally, the Proposed Rule provides a safe harbor for Scope 3 emissions disclosures, under which Scope 3 emissions will not be deemed fraudulent statements unless made without a reasonable basis or disclosed other than in good faith. There will also be a longer phase-in period for Scope 3 emissions disclosure.

B. International

The UK's SECR addresses Scope 3 emissions disclosure. Scope 3 emissions disclosure is strongly encouraged but ultimately voluntary for quoted companies. Unquoted companies and LLPs must disclose certain Scope 3 emissions, such as energy use and related emissions from business travel in rental cars or employee-owned vehicles where the company is responsible for purchasing the fuel; disclosure of other Scope 3 emissions is strongly encouraged but ultimately voluntary.[91] Similar to the U.S.'s Proposed Rule, Scope 3 emissions disclosure is subject to materiality.[92]

---

[87] *Id.* at 165.

[88] *Id.*

[89] *Id.* at 161.

[90] *Id.* at 232.

[91] UK Env't Reporting Guidelines, *supra* note 33, at 50.

[92] TCFD, Implementing the Recommendations of the Task Force on Climate-Related Financial Disclosures 3 (2021), https://assets.bbhub.io/company/sites/60/2021/07/2021-TCFD-Implementing_Guidance.pdf.

As addressed above under Scope 1 and Scope 2, the EU's CSRD Agreement recognizes that users want to understand how companies are reducing or plan to reduce GHG emissions, including Scope 3 emissions.[93] The CSRD provides additional guidance, noting that "a priority for users is to receive information about which Scope 3 categories are significant in the case of the [company], and about the emissions in each of those Scope 3 categories. The sustainability reporting standards should therefore specify the information [companies] should report with regard to such matters."[94]

Value chains are an important part of Scope 3, and the EU's CSRD Agreement makes clear there should be increased emphasis on value chain impacts. The CSRD stipulates that companies should include greater granularity around due diligence requirements.[95] The CSRD defines due diligence as "the process that [companies] carry out to identify, monitor, prevent, mitigate, remediate or bring an end to the principal actual and potential adverse impacts connected with their activities and identifies how [companies] address those adverse impacts."[96] Similar to the U.S.'s Proposed Rule, the CSRD incorporates a materiality standard, focusing on the actual or potential adverse impacts that "ranks among the greatest impacts connected with the [company's] activities. . . ."[97] The CSRD also provides a form of a safe harbor whereby, for the first three years post-implementation, if companies are unable to locate all information regarding the value chain that would be necessary to sufficiently meet the reporting requirement, rather than make the disclosure, companies can opt to "explain the efforts made to obtain the information about its value chain, the reasons why that information could not be obtained," and the company's plans to obtain the information in the future.[98]

VI. Carbon Offsets

A carbon offset is any activity that "compensates for the emission of carbon dioxide (CO_2) or other [GHGs] (measured in carbon dioxide equivalents [CO_{2e}]) by providing for an emission reduction elsewhere."[99] If carbon reductions are equal to the carbon emissions (also referred to as a "carbon footprint"), the activity is "carbon neutral."[100]

A. Federal—Proposed Rule

Registrants must disclose use of carbon offsets or renewable energy credits (RECs) in implementing a net emission reduction strategy.[101] As explained in the Proposed Rule, use of RECs

[93] Directive (EU) 2022/2464, *supra* note 24, at 30.

[94] *Id.*

[95] *Id.* at 24.

[96] *Id.* at 24–25.

[97] *Id.* at 25.

[98] *Id.*

[99] *Carbon offset*, Britannica Online, https://www.britannica.com/technology/carbon-offset (last visited Aug. 14, 2023).

[100] *Id.*

[101] Proposed Rule, *supra* note 10, at 77.

or offsets may be significant to understanding the financial implications of a company's climate mitigation and GHG reduction strategy in that offsets and RECs may be expensive if scarce, an offset may need to be written off or may decrease substantially in value (e.g., if "protected forest land that burns in a wildfire no longer represents a reduction in GHG emissions" for that filer), and the timeframe over which such a company must incur these expenses.[102]

If a registrant has set climate-related targets or goals and it uses carbon offsets or RECs as part of that, it must also disclose data to indicate whether and how much progress it is making toward achieving those targets. This disclosure must include the amount of carbon reduction represented by the offsets or the amount of generated renewable energy that is represented by the credits; the source of the offsets or credits; a description and location of the underlying projects; any registries or other authentication of the offsets or credits; and the cost of the offsets or credits. This disclosure must be updated annually, and the PSLRA forward-looking safe harbor may apply.

In addition, registrants must disclose, if used, its internal carbon price(s) and the rationale for selecting the carbon price used, as well as, if used, a description of analytical tools, such as scenario analyses, to assess the impact of climate-related risks.[103] The SEC views these additional disclosures as necessary to inform stakeholders regarding "how a registrant is planning for and managing climate-related risks"; however, there is no substantive requirement for registrants to use internal carbon prices or implement scenario analyses.[104]

B. International

The UK does not currently have carbon offsets as part of its required disclosures. It is not clear whether the required disclosures stemming from the CSRD Agreement in the EU will include carbon offsets, although the CSRD does highlight for EFRAG's consideration that users are interested in the level and scope of GHG emissions and "removals attributed to the [company], including the extent to which the [company] uses offsets and the source of those offsets."[105] The guidance continues on to highlight the importance of access to reliable information relating to offsets to alleviate concerns around double-counting and overestimations.[106]

Key Takeaways

Soon, companies will no longer have the option of whether they want to make climate-related disclosures. U.S. federal, international, and state laws continue to evolve, with increased and more detailed requirements and an expanding scope encompassing an increasing number of

[102] *Id.* at 78–79.

[103] *Id.* at 79–83.

[104] *Id.* at 81.

[105] Directive (EU) 2022/2464, *supra* note 24, at 30.

[106] *Id.*

companies. Because of the evolving reporting landscape, companies must remain aware of developments across regimes. The following are intended as quick takeaways that companies should keep in mind as they operate in this environment:

1. **Start Now.** Compliance will take time.
2. **Stay Apprised.** This is an ever-changing landscape and companies, regulators, standard-setters, and auditors need to stay apprised of developments at the federal, state, and international levels.
3. **Know Your Company.** Companies must be aware of their own specific situation, facts, and data—this is not a copy/paste from a comparable company.
4. **Walk the Talk.** Regimes are cracking down on green marketing. Companies must show they are following through on what they promise.

7

Considerations in Setting Voluntary Greenhouse Gas Emissions Reduction Targets

Ethan G. Shenkman and Erin Grubbs Peña

I. Introduction and Aims of This Chapter

An increasing number of companies have announced voluntary greenhouse gas (GHG) emissions reduction goals. According to the Net Zero Tracker database maintained by the United Nation's (UN's) Energy & Climate Intelligence Unit, for example, 40 percent (or 799) of the world's largest publicly traded corporations have net-zero targets as of the end of 2022, up from 617 the previous year.[1] This chapter reviews some of the main factors that companies typically consider in establishing voluntary commitments. This chapter may also be helpful to attorneys, advisors, or investors seeking to understand existing commitments of corporate entities.

Voluntary decarbonization goals have come under increased scrutiny as regulatory bodies, nongovernmental organizations (NGOs), and other stakeholders have attempted to evaluate and standardize voluntary GHG emissions reduction goals.[2] For example, UN Secretary General António Guterres recently launched a High-Level Expert Group to "develop stronger and clearer standards" for net-zero emissions pledges by non-state actors,

[1] *Recommendations and Current Realities*, NET ZERO TRACKER (Nov. 15, 2022), https://zerotracker.net/analysis/recommendations-and-current-realities.

[2] Joeri Rogelj et al., *Net-zero Emissions Targets Are Vague: Three Ways to Fix*, NATURE (Mar. 16, 2021), https://www.nature.com/articles/d41586-021-00662-3.

including businesses, investors, cities, and regions.[3] The UN Expert Group issued its report and recommendations during the lead-up to the 27th Conference of the Parties to the UN Framework (COP27),[4] suggesting that net-zero pledges from non-state actors should be in line with the Intergovernmental Panel on Climate Change (IPCC) scenarios limiting warming to 1.5°C (i.e., where global emissions decline by at least 45 percent by 2030—and reach net zero by 2050); should have interim targets every five years starting in 2025; and should cover all GHG emissions and scopes of emissions.[5] The international standards-setting body, the International Organization for Standardization (ISO), also used the gathering at COP27 to launch a series of "Guidelines" for non-state actors on net-zero commitments in order to address "the fragmented net zero governance landscape."[6]

Catherine McKenna, former Canadian Minister of Environment and Climate Change, who leads the UN's High-Level Expert Group, explained why this issue has attracted so much attention: "The recent avalanche of net-zero pledges by businesses, investors, cities and regions will be vital to keep 1.5°C alive and to build towards a safe and healthy planet, but only if all pledges have transparent plans, robust near-term action, and are implemented in full[.]"[7]

Because there is no single standard, set of definitions, or oversight body to govern voluntary GHG emissions reduction goals, companies will need to approach the goal-setting process thoughtfully and with sufficient resources, expertise, and internal governance systems in place. Companies may face encouragement, as well as questions and criticisms, from a wide variety of stakeholders, including consumers, shareholders, institutional investors, government regulators, international bodies, and NGOs.[8] Many companies are therefore being advised to carefully define their voluntary goals in a transparent manner, with a clear plan for how they will be implemented and progress tracked over time. Companies are also being advised to consider the increased regulatory and litigation risk associated with announcing such goals, given developments discussed elsewhere in this book.[9]

---

[3] *Expert Group on the Net-zero Emissions Commitments of Non-state Entities*, UN Sec'y-Gen. (Mar. 31, 2022), https://www.un.org/sg/en/content/sg/personnel-appointments/2022-03-31/expert-group-the-net-zero-emissions-commitments-of-non-state-entities%C2%A0.

[4] *COP27: Delivering for People and the Planet*, UN, https://www.un.org/en/climatechange/cop27 (last visited Apr. 1, 2023).

[5] UN High-level Expert Grp. on the Net Zero Emissions Commitments of Non-state Entities, Integrity Matters: Net Zero Commitments by Businesses, Financial Institutions, Cities and Regions (2022), http://www.un.org/sites/un2.un.org/files/high-level_expert_group_n7b.pdf.

[6] *Net Zero Guidelines*, ISO, https://www.iso.org/netzero (last visited Apr. 1, 2023). ISO is an independent, non-governmental international organization with a membership of 167 national standards bodies.

[7] *Expert Group on the Net-zero Emissions Commitments of Non-state Entities*, *supra* note 3.

[8] Joeri Rogelj et al., *supra* note 2.

[9] This chapter is focused on voluntary, non-binding commitments and does not address legal or regulatory requirements that mandate GHG emissions reductions and/or reporting; nor does it address issues surrounding litigation risk or potential liability for false or misleading claims. The legal implications of setting voluntary decarbonization goals—for example, compliance with U.S. Securities and Exchange Commission (SEC) climate disclosure requirements—are addressed elsewhere in this book. *See, e.g.*, Chapter 6—Climate-related Disclosure Obligations at the Federal and International Level, and Chapter 23—Public Company Disclosures. Sector-specific strategies for meeting decarbonizations goals are addressed in Chapter 5—Key Principles Related to Climate Risk.

This chapter offers an introduction to key concepts relevant to voluntary GHG emissions reduction goals, but it is not intended to provide legal advice or to endorse any particular approach or set of definitions or standards. Companies should consult with experts in the field and trusted legal advisors when embarking down this path. Additional resources relating to voluntary, private-sector decarbonization goals are listed at the end of this chapter.

II. History and Current Trends

In 2006, the ice cream maker Ben & Jerry's released a "Global Warming Social Footprint," which asked the following question: "Exactly *how much* should we be reducing our greenhouse gas emissions each year" in order to "successfully meet the challenge of global warming as a world community?"[10] Ben & Jerry's thus became one of the first companies seeking to establish voluntary GHG emissions reduction targets consistent with what the world needs to do to avoid the worst impacts of climate change.[11] (It also spawned a new flavor, "Save our Swirled."[12]) Not many companies followed suit during the early 2000s, which may not be surprising given that the U.S. Environmental Protection Agency (EPA), at the time, was still unwilling to regulate GHGs as air pollution.

Much changed by the time the Paris Climate Agreement was signed in 2015. A total of 196 nations agreed to limit global warming to "well-below" 2°C above pre-industrial levels and to "pursue efforts" to limit warming to 1.5°C. However, the Agreement's decentralized approach—and the apparent insufficiency of nationally determined pledges to meet the stated temperature goals—led to calls for increased leadership from the private sector. A growing number of companies made voluntary commitments to reduce their carbon footprints after 2015.

Around this same time, the UN and several NGO collaborators formed the Science-Based Targets initiative (SBTi). The SBTi introduced the concept of "science-based" climate targets—which SBTi defines as a GHG reduction pathway "in line with what the latest climate science deems necessary to meet the goals of the Paris Agreement"—while offering companies industry-specific methods, tools, and guidelines for setting such targets.[13]

The number and breadth of voluntary GHG emissions goals accelerated around the time of COP26, the UN Climate Change Conference that took place in Glasgow in late 2021. By the time the summit concluded, many of the world's largest companies and financial institutions had announced significant new plans aimed at mitigating global warming. More than

[10] *2006 Social & Environmental Assessment Report*, Ben & Jerry's (2006), https://www.benjerry.com/about-us/sear-reports/2006-sear-report#globwarmsocfootprint. In 2002, Ben & Jerry's had set a goal to reduce its carbon dioxide (CO_2) emissions from its manufacturing process by 10 percent over 5 years. *Id.* But the 2006 commitment would try to "identify an annual level of carbon emissions that our Company's manufacturing operations could emit (in the form of carbon dioxide) that would represent our proportionate share of" certain global climate goals. *Id.*

[11] Anders Bjørn et al., *Can Science-based Targets Make the Private Sector Paris-aligned? A Review of the Emerging Evidence*, 8 Current Climate Change Reps. 53, 54 n.10 (2022), https://www.ncbi.nlm.nih.gov/pmc/articles/PMC9287239/.

[12] *United Nations Climate Change Secretariat Joins Forces with Ben & Jerry's to Unveil a 'Sweet' Way to Take Action on Climate Change*, UN Climate Change (Sept. 3, 2015), https://unfccc.int/news/ben-jerry-s-save-our-swirled-initiative.

[13] *How It Works*, SBTi, https://sciencebasedtargets.org/how-it-works#i-already-have-an-emissions-reduction-target-how-i-can-join-the-sbti (last visited Apr. 1, 2023).

"5,200 businesses pledged to meet net-zero carbon targets by 2050, and some 450 banks, insurers, and investors—collectively representing $130 trillion in assets and 40 percent of the world's private capital—committed to making their portfolios climate neutral during the same period."[14] According to SBTi, by the end of 2021, "2,253 companies across 70 countries and 15 industries, representing more than one third ($38 trillion USD) of global market capitalization, had approved emissions reductions targets or commitments" through the organization's programs.[15]

III. Ambition Loop between Public and Private Sectors

An increasing number of governments at the national, state/provincial, and municipal levels have also set aspirational GHG emissions reduction and net-zero targets. Under President Biden, for example, the United States set "an economy-wide target of reducing its net zero greenhouse gas emissions by 50-52 percent below 2005 levels in 2030."[16] In its nationally determined contribution (NDC) for purposes of the Paris Climate Agreement, the United States stated that its 2030 NDC "is expected to put the United States on a path to achieve net-zero emissions, economy-wide, by no later than 2050. . . ."[17]

Worldwide, the number of national net-zero targets set in legislation or policies has surged to 65 percent of total GHG emissions coverage, from just 10 percent in December 2020, according to the UN's Net Zero Stocktake 2022 report. Moreover,

- "91% of global GDP is now captured by national government net zero targets, up from 68% in December 2020";
- "National government targets represent at least 83% of global GHG emissions (up from 61% in December 2020)"; and
- "80% of the global population (up from 52%) is represented by national net zero targets."[18]

---

[14] Kassia Yanosek & David G. Victor, *How Big Business Is Taking the Lead on Climate Change*, McKinsey Sustainability (Mar. 7, 2022) https://www.mckinsey.com/capabilities/sustainability/our-insights/sustainability-blog/how-big-business-is-taking-the-lead-on-climate-change.

[15] *Companies Committed to Cut Emissions in Line with Climate Science Now Represent $38 Trillion of Global Economy*, SBTi (May 12, 2022), https://sciencebasedtargets.org/news/companies-committed-to-cut-emissions-in-line-with-climate-science-now-represent-38-trillion-of-global-economy. As another example, 4,100 companies and other organizations have disclosed through CDP that they have developed a 1.5°C aligned climate transition plan. CDP P'ships Team, *Developing and Delivering a Credible Climate Transition Plan: How Our Accredited Solutions Providers Can Support You*, CDP (Feb. 28, 2023), https://www.cdp.net/en/articles/climate/developing-a-transition-plan-how-our-accredited-solutions-providers-can-support.

[16] The United States of America Nationally Determined Contribution, Reducing Greenhouse Gases in the United States: A 2030 Emissions Target 6, https://unfccc.int/sites/default/files/NDC/2022-06/United%20States%20NDC%20April%2021%202021%20Final.pdf.

[17] *Id.* at 23.

[18] *Net Zero Stocktake 2022*, Net Zero Tracker (June 13, 2022), https://zerotracker.net/insights/pr-net-zero-stocktake-2022.

Commentators have observed an "ambition feedback loop," as voluntary private-sector commitments have encouraged greater levels of ambition by governmental bodies, and increased governmental ambitions have spurred more voluntary goal-setting by companies.[19]

As in the private sector, public-sector decarbonization goals have come under increased scrutiny and demands for accountability. Debates over the meaning of net zero, multifarious attempts at standard setting, and the evolution of monitoring and verification protocols are as relevant to governmental bodies as they are to companies, and stakeholders in the private sector should follow these parallel developments closely.

IV. Types of Voluntary Commitments and Motivations

The literature cites many different examples of voluntary GHG emissions targets across all economic sectors. Companies have used a variety of different terms, along a number of different parameters, to describe their goals. The Voluntary Carbon Markets Integrity Initiative (VCMI), for example, cited the following companies (in a 2022 publication) to illustrate just a few of the many ways that companies have framed their climate goals:

- Dalmia Cement: *carbon negative* by 2040.
- Danone: *carbon neutral* across its entire global value chain by 2050.
- Google: operating 24/7 *carbon free* by 2030.
- IKEA: *climate positive* by 2030 by reducing more [GHG] emissions than the IKEA value chain emits.
- Mahindra & Mahindra Ltd.: *carbon neutral* as a group by 2040.
- Microsoft: *carbon negative* by 2030 and removal of all historic emissions.
- Netflix: *net-zero* [GHG] emissions by the close of 2022.
- Unilever: *net-zero* emissions for products by 2039.[20]

Commentators have noted that voluntary corporate GHG reduction goals are often motivated by a combination of "efficiency, resource supply, competition, and reputational goals." Many companies are seeking to achieve a synergy between "profit maximization" and "altruistic preferences or norms."[21]

Some companies have expressed the view that voluntary GHG commitments can "yield more energy-efficient operations, boost employee morale, burnish a company's reputation, and respond to pressure from customers, investors, and lenders"; they can also be used to

---

[19] *The Ambition Loop*, World Res. Inst., https://www.wri.org/initiatives/ambition-loop (last visited Apr. 1, 2023).

[20] VCMI, Provisional Claims Code of Practice 12 (2022), https://vcmintegrity.org/wp-content/uploads/2022/06/VCMI-Provisional-Claims-Code-of-Practice.pdf. VCMI is a multistakeholder platform, backed by the United Kingdom government, that is developing guidance on how carbon credits can be voluntarily used and claims by businesses as part of credible, net-zero decarbonization strategies. *Id.* For other examples, *see* VCMI, Use Cases and Case Studies of Company Climate Commitments (2021), https://vcmintegrity.org/wp-content/uploads/2021/07/Case-Studies.pdf.

[21] Albert C. Lin, *Making Net Zero Matter*, 79 Wash & Lee L. Rev. 679, 704 (2022) (citations omitted), https://scholarlycommons.law.wlu.edu/cgi/viewcontent.cgi?article=4771&context=wlulr.

"express corporate values and improve a company's strategic position" vis-à-vis competitors in the marketplace.[22]

According to a study by McKinsey & Company, the "argument for global companies to reduce their [GHG] emissions" is based on the following propositions:

- Business operations around the world are now subject to greater climate and transition risks.
- Consumers are clamoring for eco-friendly products and responsible corporate behaviors.
- Investors are increasingly embracing capital-allocation strategies that take [ESG] issues into account.
- Policymakers and government organizations are exploring the potential regulation of carbon emissions.[23]

It was also found that the very exercise of setting carbon-reduction targets can "be an important step for organizations."[24] Among other things, the study indicated that businesses that set "bold" targets were more likely to demonstrate early progress in meeting those goals; early success in hitting emission-reduction targets was a good predictor that subsequent targets would also be met; and setting shorter-term targets for 2025 and 2030 were critical for mobilizing organizations to take action.[25]

V. Specific Considerations in Setting Voluntary Greenhouse Gas Reduction Commitments

For companies considering whether to announce voluntary GHG emissions reduction goals, or to supplement or update existing commitments, there is a lot to consider. This chapter briefly highlights eight key considerations in setting such goals:

1. **Scope:** Which scopes and types of GHG emissions will be covered?
2. **Boundaries:** What are the corporate and geographic limitations of the commitment?
3. **Measurement and Reporting:** How will emissions and reductions be measured? Where and how will the company report its goals and progress?
4. **Baseline, Level of Ambition, and Pace of Reductions:** What is the level of reductions sought to be achieved, from what baseline, and on what timeline?
5. **Net Zero:** Will the commitment include a net-zero pledge? How will net zero be defined?

---

[22] *Id.*

[23] Leonardo Banchik et al., *On Target: How to Succeed with Carbon-reduction Initiatives*, McKinsey & Co. (May 3, 2021), https://www.mckinsey.com/capabilities/strategy-and-corporate-finance/our-insights/on-target-how-to-succeed-with-carbon-reduction-initiatives.

[24] *Id.*

[25] *Id.*

6. **Comparisons with Paris-Consistent Scenarios:** Will the company seek to align its voluntary GHG emissions targets with scenarios that are consistent with the Paris Agreement's temperature goals?
7. **Carbon Credits and Offsets:** To what extent will negative emissions technologies and other forms of carbon offsets be counted and under what conditions?
8. **Transparency, Verification, Accountability:** What type of oversight exists for these commitments (e.g., government, frameworks for disclosure)?

A. Consideration #1: Scope

As a threshold matter, companies interested in developing net-zero or GHG emissions reduction commitments will want to ensure that they have a firm handle on the scope of their own GHG emissions and understand how those emissions are being measured and reported. One of the first steps, then, in defining voluntary goals is to decide what the scope of their commitments will be.

1. What scope of greenhouse gas emissions is covered?

In determining the scope of emissions covered, an essential resource is the GHG Protocol, which provides widely used GHG accounting standards for companies. This includes both measuring and reporting GHG emissions along with classifying these emissions into three different scopes:[26]

- **Scope 1** emissions are the direct emissions from a company's owned or controlled operations.[27]
- **Scope 2** emissions are indirect emissions from the generation of purchased energy (e.g., electricity, steam, heating, or cooling).[28]
- **Scope 3** emissions are all other indirect emissions that occur upstream (i.e., from a company's suppliers) and downstream (i.e., from a company's customers).[29]

The GHG Protocol divides Scope 3 emissions further into 15 distinct categories.[30]

- **Upstream Scope 3** emissions include: (1) purchased goods and services; (2) capital goods; (3) fuel- and energy-related services (not included in Scope 1 or Scope 2); (4) upstream transportation and distribution; (5) waste generated in operations; (6) business travel; (7) employee commuting; and (8) upstream leased assets.[31]

[26] *Companies and Organizations*, GREENHOUSE GAS PROTOCOL, https://ghgprotocAol.org/companies-and-organizations (last visited Apr. 1, 2023).

[27] GREENHOUSE GAS PROTOCOL, CORPORATE VALUE CHAIN (SCOPE 3) ACCOUNTING AND REPORTING STANDARD: SUPPLEMENT TO THE GHG PROTOCOL CORPORATE ACCOUNTING AND REPORTING STANDARD 28 (2011), https://ghgprotocol.org/sites/default/files/standards/Corporate-Value-Chain-Accounting-Reporing-Standard_041613_2.pdf.

[28] *Id.*

[29] *Id.*

[30] *Id.* at 31–32.

[31] *Id.* at 32.

- **Downstream Scope 3** emissions include: (9) downstream transportation and distribution; (10) processing of sold products; (11) use of sold products; (12) end-of-life treatment of sold products; (13) downstream leased assets; (14) franchises; and (15) investments.[32]

For more in-depth descriptions of Scopes 1, 2, and 3 emissions, *see* CHAPTER 5—KEY PRINCIPLES RELATED TO CLIMATE RISK.

According to a 2021 study by McKinsey, about 74 percent of disclosed corporate GHG emissions reduction targets are limited to Scopes 1 and 2 emissions.[33] Only 26 percent of disclosed targets are aimed at reducing Scope 3 emissions, or those emissions that are not directly owned or controlled by the company.[34]

Scope 3 emissions are notoriously more difficult for a company to identify, define, track, and control than a company's Scope 1 and 2 emissions.[35] A key difficulty with Scope 3 emissions is the number of partners in the upstream and downstream value chain for which a company needs to account.[36] These partners can span the globe and for larger companies can be in the thousands or tens of thousands.[37] In the context of the U.S. Securities and Exchange Commission's (SEC's) proposed climate disclosure regulations, a significant controversy has arisen concerning the definition of Scope 3 emissions, and how and whether they should be reported and in what contexts.[38]

In addition, some advocates have suggested the development of a new category of emissions reductions: Scope 4 emissions, also known as "avoided emissions." Scope 4 refers to GHG "emission reductions that occur outside of a product's life cycle or value chain, but as a result of the use of that product."[39] Although not a new concept,[40] Scope 4 emissions are becoming a popular discussion topic as more and more companies are committing to net zero and trying to capture the full range of indirect GHG benefits that their products and services produce and enable. In the view of some commentators, "[w]hile not a perfect solution, the concept of

---

32 *Id.*

33 Leonardo Banchik et al., *supra* note 23.

34 *Id.*

35 Jim Wetekamp, *Are You Prepared to Report on Scope 3 Emissions?*, FORBES (June 21, 2022), https://www.forbes.com/sites/forbestechcouncil/2022/06/21/are-you-prepared-to-report-on-scope-3-emissions/?sh=3b699fd158ef.

36 *Id.*

37 *Id.*

38 Andrew Ramonas & Clara Hudson, *SEC's Gensler Weighs Concern About Indirect Emissions Reporting*, BLOOMBERG L. (Sept. 12, 2022, 6:47 PM), https://news.bgov.com/esg/secs-gensler-weighs-concern-about-indirect-emissions-reporting. The controversy over Scope 3 emissions is addressed in more detail in the chapters on SEC climate disclosure requirements (*see* CHAPTER 6—CLIMATE-RELATED DISCLOSURE OBLIGATIONS AT THE FEDERAL AND INTERNATIONAL LEVEL, and CHAPTER 23—PUBLIC COMPANY DISCLOSURES). *See also Breaking Down Corporate Net-Zero Climate Targets*, MSCI (May 24, 2021), https://www.msci.com/www/research-report/breaking-down-corporate-net/02516231792; *Index Innovation for Net Zero*, S&P GLOBAL, https://www.spglobal.com/esg/insights/it-s-all-within-scope-with-sp-global-scope-3-data (last visited Apr. 1, 2023).

39 Laura Draucker, *Do We Need a Standard to Calculate "Avoided Emissions"?*, GREENHOUSE GAS PROTOCOL (Nov. 5, 2013), https://ghgprotocol.org/blog/do-we-need-standard-calculate-%E2%80%9Cavoided-emissions%E2%80%9D.

40 Greenhouse Gas Protocol published a blog post on "Avoided Emissions" using the term Scope 4 in 2013. *Id.*

scope 4 (or avoided) emissions does reconcile the GHG Protocol principles with decisions that are actually being taken by company Boards, with the actions that are expected from companies to reduce CO_2 emissions."[41] The idea of Scope 4 emissions as a meaningful category has also come under criticism from a variety of stakeholders, however, and companies are being advised to proceed cautiously in exploring this relatively new and undefined concept.

2. *Which types of greenhouse gas emissions are covered?*

Companies will also need to decide which of the six major GHGs (carbon dioxide [CO_2], methane, nitrous oxide, hydrofluorocarbons, perfluorocarbons, and sulfur hexafluoride) will be covered by their target.[42] Which gases a company chooses to include in its commitments will be based on the nature of its business and industrial processes and will have different implications for climate change. CO_2 accumulates and lasts for hundreds to thousands of years in the atmosphere, so decreasing CO_2 emissions is critical, but the impact of already-existing CO_2 in the atmosphere will remain for centuries.[43] On the other hand, shorter-lived GHGs, like methane, last for a shorter period of time in the atmosphere, so reducing these types of emissions will lessen contributions to global warming relatively quickly.[44]

B. Consideration #2: Boundaries

Companies will need to determine the geographic and corporate boundaries of their commitments.

1. *What are the corporate and geographic limitations of the commitment?*

- **Enterprise vs. Product-Specific Commitments.** Companies have announced commitments that cover all corporate activities, while others have focused on particular products or product lines. Some companies have done both.[45]
- **Corporate control.** Another target boundary consideration is the organizational boundary. Companies can choose to report based on equity share, financial control, or operational control.[46] Under an equity share approach, "a company accounts for GHG emissions from operations according to its share of equity in the operation."[47] This type of approach reflects a company's economic interest and the extent

---

[41] Jarlath Molloy, *Scope 4: Do We Need a New Category of Emissions to Better Address Corporate Climate Action?*, Climate Disclosure Standards Bd. (Jan. 31, 2020), https://www.cdsb.net/blog/corporate-reporting/1005/scope-4-do-we-need-new-category-emissions-better-address-corporate.

[42] Greenhouse Gas Protocol, A Corporate Accounting and Reporting Standard 78 (2004), https://ghgprotocol.org/sites/default/files/standards/ghg-protocol-revised.pdf.

[43] Joeri Rogelj et al., *supra* note 2.

[44] *Id.*

[45] According to VCMI, "Enterprise-Wide Claims" represent "achievement at the enterprise level." By contrast, "Brand-, Product-, and Service-Level Claims represent achievement across the full value chain of a specific brand (line of products or services), product, or service." VCMI, Provisional Claims Code of Practice, *supra* note 20, at 21.

[46] Greenhouse Gas Protocol, Corporate Value Chain (Scope 3), *supra* note 27, at 29.

[47] *Id.*

it has "risk and rewards flowing from an operation."[48] Under the financial control approach, "a company accounts for 100 percent of the GHG emissions over which it has financial control," so a company would not account for operations that it has an interest in but does not financially control.[49] Lastly, under the operational control approach, "a company accounts for 100 percent of the GHG emissions over which it has operational control," so a company would not account for operations that it has a financial interest in but does not operationally control.[50]

- **Geography.** Companies will also need to decide what geographical operations are covered by their target.[51] A company may choose to include all operations or just certain operations depending on the GHG inventory reliability of certain geographic areas. For example, a company may choose to include only country or regional operations with reliable GHG inventory data.[52]

It is important for companies to be thoughtful and transparent in defining the boundaries of voluntary GHG emissions reduction goals. Some commentators, for example, have raised concerns about net-zero leakage. "Leakage occurs when efforts to reduce emissions in one place shift emissions to another place where they are uncontrolled or uncounted. For example, 'protecting' an acre of forest in Brazil from logging through a carbon offset program may result in the logging of an acre of forest in Borneo."[53]

C. Consideration #3: Measurement and Reporting

As a threshold matter, in order to measure and report on the success of a company's GHG emissions reduction goals, a company will want to have a clear understanding of what its emissions are. A company should also consider what purposes its GHG inventory will serve. For example, a company's GHG emissions inventory may serve business goals like managing GHG risks and identifying reduction opportunities, reporting publicly, participating in voluntary GHG programs, participating in mandatory reporting programs, participating in GHG markets, and being recognized for early voluntary action.[54] By developing a comprehensive GHG emissions inventory, a company can understand its emissions profile and potential GHG-related exposure.[55]

---

[48] *Id.*

[49] *Id.*

[50] *Id.*

[51] Greenhouse Gas Protocol, A Corporate Accounting and Reporting Standard, *supra* note 42, at 78.

[52] *Id.*

[53] Martin Reeves et al., *Will Net-zero Get Us to Net Zero Emissions*, BCG Henderson Inst. (Jan. 31, 2022), https://bcghendersoninstitute.com/will-net-zero-get-us-to-net-zero-emissions-c9ae50a6e014 (discussing multiple concerns with corporate net-zero pledges, including additional concerns not reviewed here); *see also* Kelly Levin et al., *What Does "Net-Zero Emissions" Mean? 8 Common Questions, Answered*, World Res. Inst. (Mar. 20, 2023), https://www.wri.org/insights/net-zero-ghg-emissions-questions-answered.

[54] Greenhouse Gas Protocol, A Corporate Accounting and Reporting Standard, *supra* note 42, at 11.

[55] *Id.*

1. *How will greenhouse gas emissions reductions be measured?*

Measuring GHG emissions is a technical question that is mostly beyond the scope of this chapter. At a high level, companies will need to determine a calculation or measurement approach for their GHG emissions. In some cases, direct measurement of GHG emissions may be feasible for certain kinds of industrial processes through monitoring concentrations and flow rates directly at the point of release, such as an exhaust stack. More commonly, companies calculate GHG emissions based on different types of emissions factors.[56] Emission factors are calculated ratios that provide an estimate of GHG emissions compared to an activity at the emissions source,[57] such as the pounds of CO_2 emissions for every megawatt hour of electricity.[58]

According to the GHG Protocol, most small- to medium-sized companies and many larger companies calculate Scope 1 emissions based on purchased quantities of commercial fuel and emission factors.[59] Companies mainly calculate Scope 2 emissions from "metered electricity consumption and supplier-specific, local grid, or other published emission factors."[60] Finally, companies commonly calculate Scope 3 emissions from third-party emission factors and activity data like fuel use or passenger miles.[61] As discussed above, calculating Scope 3 emissions can be a complex and uncertain exercise because of the number of entities in the upstream and downstream value chain that the analysis may need to account for.[62]

2. *Where/how to report?*

The GHG Protocol suggests reporting information should be "relevant, complete, consistent, transparent and accurate."[63] Where feasible, the protocol also suggests that companies disclose:

- the scope and boundary of emissions covered and the reporting period;
- emissions data separately for each scope;
- emissions data separately for all six GHGs;
- the year chosen as a base year;
- the appropriate context for any significant emissions;

[56] *Id.* at 42.

[57] *Id.*

[58] EPA Ctr. for Corp. Climate Leadership, Emission Factors for Greenhouse Gas Inventories (2022), https://www.epa.gov/system/files/documents/2022-04/ghg_emission_factors_hub.pdf.

[59] Greenhouse Gas Protocol, A Corporate Accounting and Reporting Standard, *supra* note 42, at 42.

[60] *Id.*

[61] *Id.*

[62] Jim Wetekamp, *supra* note 35.

[63] Greenhouse Gas Protocol, A Corporate Accounting and Reporting Standard, *supra* note 42, at 63.

- the emissions data for "CO_2 emissions from biologically sequestered carbon (e.g., CO_2 from burning biomass/biofuels)"; and
- the methodology for calculating or measuring emissions, and any specific sources, facilities, or operations excluded.[64]

Companies often report information on their GHG emissions, and on progress in meeting their voluntary reduction goals, through public reports such as a sustainability report, an ESG report, and/or an annual report.

D. Consideration #4: Baseline, Level of Ambition, and Pace of Reductions

Once a company determines the scope and boundaries of its voluntary commitment, it will need to decide how to frame and define its GHG reductions target, how quickly it will reach its target, and what the interim targets and milestones will be.

1. *What is the level of greenhouse gas emissions reductions?*

Companies frequently state their reduction targets either as an absolute emissions target or as an intensity-based target.[65]

Absolute emissions targets reduce the total magnitude of GHG emissions over time. Companies state these targets as a specific percentage or quantity of GHG emissions that will be reduced, and the unit is normally carbon dioxide equivalent, or "CO_2e" (e.g., reduce CO_2e emissions by X percent by 2030).[66] Setting an absolute emissions target provides a specific quantity of GHG reductions to the atmosphere, but it may be difficult to achieve if a company's business or the demand for its products grows unexpectedly.[67]

Emissions intensity targets reduce emissions relative to a business metric over time. Companies state these targets as CO_2e compared to a business metric (e.g., reduce CO_2e by X percent per ton or units of product produced by 2030).[68] Emissions intensity targets can increase the comparability of GHG performance among companies.[69] They also tend to incentivize efficiency improvements in industrial processes and the increased production of products with lower carbon intensities.

2. *What is the baseline?*

Companies need to choose a baseline year against which their reduction targets will be measured. Companies may choose a fixed target base year, meaning the GHG reduction goals

[64] *Id.*

[65] *Id.* at 77.

[66] *Id.* at 76.

[67] *Id.*

[68] *Id.*

[69] *Id.*

stated relative to a specific fixed target year in the past.[70] For example, a company's target might be to emit X percent less in year B than in year A, where year A is a specific fixed year.[71] Alternatively, companies may choose a rolling target base year if it may be challenging to obtain "reliable and verifiable data for a fixed target base year."[72] For example, a company's target might be "over the next X years we will reduce emissions every year by Y percent compared to the previous year."[73]

3. *How quickly will the reductions be achieved?*

Companies must determine the target completion date for the emissions reductions. Companies may set short-, medium-, and/or long-term targets. There is not a clear definition of short-, medium-, and long-term targets, but generally short-term targets are set for completion within the next 1–5 years, medium-term targets are set for completion within the next 5–15 years, and long-term targets are set for completion within the next 15–30 years.[74]

According to a 2021 study by McKinsey, 44 percent of organizations that are disclosing their GHG emissions targets have short-term targets, or targets that will achieve certain reductions by 2025.[75] Twenty-seven percent of companies that are disclosing their targets have medium-term targets, or targets that will achieve certain reductions by 2026 to 2040.[76] Two percent of companies are disclosing long-term targets, or targets that will achieve certain reductions by 2031 to 2050 or later.[77] The final 27 percent of companies have targets across short-, medium-, and long-term time horizons.[78] Some commentators believe that targets are more credible when they include near- and midterm goals.[79]

E. Consideration #5: Net Zero

Whereas many companies previously focused their voluntary GHG emissions reduction goals on percentage emissions reduction targets, corporate climate ambitions are increasingly expressed in terms of reaching net-zero emissions by a certain target date.[80] The concept of net-zero emissions is central to implementation of the Paris Climate Agreement: the UN has stated that the world's GHG emissions must be reduced by 45 percent by 2030, and must

---

[70] *Id.* at 79.

[71] *Id.*

[72] *Id.*

[73] *Id.*

[74] Climate Action 100+, Climate Action 100+ Net Zero Company Benchmark 1–2 (2022), https://www.climateaction100.org/wp-content/uploads/2021/10/Climate-Action-100-v1.1-Benchmark-Indicators-Oct21.pdf.

[75] Leonardo Banchik et al., *supra* note 23.

[76] *Id.*

[77] *Id.*

[78] *Id.*

[79] Kelly Levin et al, *supra* note 53.

[80] Sam Fankhauser et al., *The Meaning of Net Zero and How to Get It Right*, 12 Nat. Climate Change 15-21 (2022), https://www.nature.com/articles/s41558-021-01245-w#citeas.

achieve a net-zero state by 2050, in order to realize the Agreement's global temperature goals.[81] "Net zero is important because—for CO_2 at least—this is the state at which global warming stops."[82]

What it means to achieve a global state of net-zero GHG emissions is defined somewhat differently by various organizations, but, in essence, net zero refers to "a state in which the [GHGs] going into the atmosphere are balanced by removal out of the atmosphere."[83] The UN, for example, defines net zero as "cutting [GHG] emissions to as close to zero as possible, with any remaining emissions re-absorbed from the atmosphere, by oceans and forests for instance."[84] According to the World Resources Institute, "[n]et-zero emissions . . . will be achieved when all emissions released by human activities are counterbalanced by removing carbon from the atmosphere in a process known as carbon removal."[85]

Translating the concept of net-zero global GHG emissions to the level of individual corporations or businesses can be challenging, but a number of organizations have attempted to provide general guidance. VCMI, for example, defines a corporate "long-term net zero commitment" as a "company commitment to aggressively reduce emissions across its value chain (Scopes 1, 2, 3) to zero—or to a residual level aligned with global net zero—no later than mid-century."[86] It opines that, for purposes of such a commitment, "residual emissions are balanced out by permanent removals (including high-quality removal carbon credits). To achieve this goal, most companies will need to reduce emissions by at least 90 to 95 percent across all emissions scopes no later than 2050."[87]

One of the most significant recent developments is the Race to Zero Campaign, which was created in 2019 by the UN Framework Convention on Climate Change (UNFCCC) sponsored Climate Change Champions for Climate Action.[88] The Race to Zero Campaign considers an individual actor having reached a net-zero state when "[a]n actor reduces its emissions following science-based pathways, with any remaining GHG emissions attributable to that actor being fully neutralized by like-for-like removals (e.g., permanent removals for fossil carbon emissions) exclusively claimed by that actor, either within the value chain or through purchase of valid offset credits."[89] The Race to Zero Campaign claims to include 52 regions,

---

[81] *See For a Livable Climate: Net-zero Commitments Must Be Backed by Credible Action*, UN, https://www.un.org/en/climatechange/net-zero-coalition (last visited Apr. 1, 2023); *see also* Paris Agreement to the United Nations Framework Convention on Climate Change art. 4.1 (2015), https://unfccc.int/sites/default/files/english_paris_agreement.pdf (emphasizing need for states to "achieve a balance between anthropogenic emissions by sources and removals by sinks of greenhouse gases in the second half of this century.").

[82] *Shifting the Dial on Money's Climate Impact*, Oxford Martin Sch., Univ. of Oxford, https://www.oxfordmartin.ox.ac.uk/long-read/moneys-climate-impact/ (last visited Apr. 14, 2023).

[83] *What Is Net Zero?*, Univ. of Oxford, https://netzeroclimate.org/what-is-net-zero/ (last visited Sept. 14, 2022).

[84] *For a Livable Climate: Net-zero Commitments Must Be Backed by Credible Action*, *supra* note 81.

[85] Kelly Levin et al., *supra* note 53.

[86] VCMI, Provisional Claims Code of Practice, *supra* note 20, at 18.

[87] *Id.*

[88] *Race to Zero Campaign*, UNFCCC, https://unfccc.int/climate-action/race-to-zero-campaign (last visited Apr. 1, 2023).

[89] UNFCCC, Race to Zero, Race to Zero Lexicon, https://racetozero.unfccc.int/wp-content/uploads/2021/04/Race-to-Zero-Lexicon.pdf.

1,103 cities, 7,126 companies, 1,103 educational institutions, 541 financial institutions, over 3,000 hospitals from 60 healthcare institutions, and 24 "other" institutions.[90]

F. Consideration #6: Comparison with Paris-Consistent Global Emissions Scenarios

Closely related to the concept of net zero is whether a company will attempt to align its voluntary GHG emissions goals with science-based scenarios of what the world will look like in 2050 if the Paris Agreement's temperature goals are realized.

As noted above, the Paris Agreement aims to "[hold] the increase in the global average temperature to well below 2°C above pre-industrial levels and [pursue] efforts to limit the temperature increase to 1.5°C above pre-industrial levels."[91] The Agreement, however, does not identify any particular pathway to reaching these global goals. Indeed, there are hundreds of Paris-consistent scenarios that multiple organizations have identified, with different degrees of overshoot, speed of reductions, and reliance on removals and negative emissions technologies. The International Energy Agency (IEA), for example, has identified a wide variety of possible scenarios.[92] The IPCC provided its own overview of Paris-compliant scenarios in Chapter 3 of the Working Group III contribution to its Sixth Assessment Report.[93]

What it means for an *individual company's* GHG emissions pledges to be "aligned" with Paris-consistent global scenarios is not straightforward. The Paris Agreement sets goals at the level of nation-states, not individuals. Moreover, the Agreement leaves it to member states to define their own emissions pathways, or "nationally determined contributions," to achieve a global net-zero state. "There is no official yardstick against which the adequacy, ambition or fairness of nationally determined contributions is measured."[94] Furthermore, it is up to each member state to determine how these contributions will be achieved among the different economic sectors and individual entities operating within its borders.

Nonetheless, several organizations have been encouraging companies to ensure that their individual climate commitments are consistent with science-based, Paris-compliant scenarios. And an increasing number of companies are undertaking this analysis for their own emissions targets.

For example, VCMI defines a "science-aligned" decarbonization pathway or trajectory as the "sequence of emission reduction milestones over time in line with what the latest

[90] *Race to Zero*, UNFCCC, https://climatechampions.unfccc.int/join-the-race/ (last visited Apr. 1, 2023). Non-state actors join the Race to Zero Campaign through other initiatives and networks, such as Business Ambition for 1.5C, Business Declares, CBN Expert Community, Certified B Corporation, The Climate Pledge, Exponential Roadmap Initiative, Planet Mark, and the SME Climate Hub.

[91] Paris Agreement to the United Nations Framework Convention on Climate Change, *supra* note 81, at art. 2.1(a).

[92] *See, e.g.*, IEA, Net Zero by 2050: A Roadmap for the Global Energy Sector (2021), https://iea.blob.core.windows.net/assets/deebef5d-0c34-4539-9d0c-10b13d840027/NetZeroby2050-ARoadmapfortheGlobalEnergySector_CORR.pdf.

[93] IPCC Working Group III, Climate Change 2022: Mitigation of Climate Change (2022), https://www.ipcc.ch/report/sixth-assessment-report-working-group-3/.

[94] Sam Fankhauser et al., *supra* note 80.

climate science deems necessary to meet the goals of the Paris Agreement: to limit global warming to well below 2 degrees Celsius above pre-industrial levels and to pursue efforts to limit warming to 1.5 degrees Celsius above pre-industrial levels by mid-century."[95] It further defines a science-based "decarbonization pathway" as the "sequence of milestones in a company's plan to achieve long-term net zero emissions, including interim targets . . . verified by a credible, independent third party."[96]

As another example, the UN Race to Zero and the University of Oxford define the term "1.5°C aligned" to mean that a company's GHG emissions reduction target is aligned with scenarios that result in a "long-term warming outcome of below 1.5°C with some probability (e.g., 50%, 66%) and some amount of overshoot (e.g., no, low), both of which should be explicitly stated."[97]

SBTi is frequently cited as an organization that has offered to identify "science-based targets" in order to "provide a clearly-defined pathway for companies to reduce greenhouse gas (GHG) emissions, helping prevent the worst impacts of climate change and future-proof business growth."[98] Among other principles, SBTi recommends that long-term net-zero targets "should be supported by *interim* science-based emission reduction targets to drive action within timeframes that are aligned with corporate planning and investment cycles and to ensure emission reductions that are consistent with Paris-aligned mitigation pathways."[99]

G. Consideration #7: Reliance on Carbon Credits and Offsets

Another consideration in setting voluntary GHG emissions reduction targets is whether and to what extent these targets will include measures that are based not on reductions in the company's own emissions, but on reductions achieved and credited by third parties or with carbon-removal technologies (i.e., negative emissions). Companies will need to consider what their policy will be with respect to carbon credits and offsets.

1. *What are the relevant definitions?*

A carbon credit is an "emissions unit that is issued by a carbon crediting program and represents an emission reduction or removal of greenhouse gases."[100] An "offset" refers to the "use of a carbon credit as a substitute for within value chain emissions abatement and counted as reductions toward an emissions reductions target."[101] Carbon removal refers to the "[w]ithdrawal of [GHGs] from the atmosphere as a result of biologic processes or deliberate

95 VCMI, Provisional Claims Code of Practice, *supra* note 20, at 40.

96 *Id.* at 22, 18.

97 UNFCCC, Race to Zero, Race to Zero Lexicon, *supra* note 89 (note: the quoted text is from the University of Oxford's website; the Race to Zero uses an almost identical definition).

98 *How It Works*, SBTi, *supra* note 13.

99 SBTi, Foundations for Science-based Net-zero Target Setting in the Corporate Sector 10 (2020), https://sciencebasedtargets.org/resources/files/foundations-for-net-zero-full-paper.pdf.

100 VCMI, Provisional Claims Code of Practice, *supra* note 20, at 37.

101 *Id.* at 39.

human activities."[102] These include enhancing existing biological sinks of CO_2 (such as the forests or oceans) and using chemical engineering or other technologies to remove CO_2 from the atmosphere and permanently sequester it, for example, in deep underground geologic formations (a process known as "direct air capture").[103]

2. *To what extent will negative emissions technologies and other forms of carbon offsets be counted and under what conditions?*

On the one hand, the use of high-quality carbon credits by companies has been recognized as an important means of accelerating climate change mitigation and driving additional climate-related financing into low- and middle-income countries. It is also thought that keeping warming to between 1.5°C and 2°C will now be possible only with significant negative emissions achieved by solutions that remove carbon from the atmosphere and permanently sequester it.

On the other hand, concerns have been raised about potential overreliance on offsets to meet GHG emissions reduction targets. Some stakeholders have voiced concerns that the use of carbon credits could hinder, delay, or replace the GHG abatement action within companies and their supply chains. In addition, perceived shortcomings in standards, accounting mechanisms, and verification protocols have resulted in concerns about the validity of emissions reduction claims, especially those associated with certain kinds of offsets. Companies making climate-related claims when using carbon credits could face significant legal risks if the credits are determined to be unreliable. Moreover, without clear and transparent guidance about the use of carbon credits, investors and consumers are not able to efficiently allocate capital.

A number of organizations and initiatives offer guidance on what constitutes a "high quality" carbon credit. They include the Integrity Council on Voluntary Carbon Markets; the International Civil Aviation Organization's Carbon Offsetting and Reduction Scheme for International Aviation; the GHG Protocol's Carbon Removals and Land Sector Initiative; relevant guidance developed under Article 6 of the Paris Agreement; and VCMI.[104]

For example, VCMI posits that, to meet the basic criteria for high-quality credits that may be used for a corporate climate commitment, the credits must, among other factors:

- Be "[a]ssociated with a recognized and credibly governed standard-setting body that provides transparent, independent, and robust processes for quantification, validation, registration, monitoring, verification, approval, and retirement tracking."

[102] *Id.* at 40.

[103] There are a wide range of negative emission solutions. "Natural" climate solutions, such as reforestation, take advantage of biological mechanisms. "Engineered" removals, such as bioenergy with carbon capture and storage and direct air capture and storage sequester CO_2 geologically in deep underground formations. Negative emissions technologies may be necessary for offsetting difficult-to abate emissions in industries such as cement, chemicals, and steel. They also allow the removal of historical emissions from the atmosphere if needed to meet global temperature goals.

[104] As noted above, this chapter is not intended to provide legal advice or to endorse any particular approach or set of definitions or standards, including for what constitutes a valid or high-quality carbon offset. The organizations listed here are for illustrative purposes only.

- "[M]eet robust requirements for global and local stakeholder consultation, including with Indigenous Peoples and local communities."
- Be of "[h]igh environmental quality," which means they "(a) reflect reductions and/or removals that go beyond those that would occur in the absence of demand for carbon credits; (b) are monitored, measured, robustly quantified, and independently verified by a credible, independent third party; and (c) are generated from activities that have measures in place to address material risks of nonpermanence and leakage."[105]

Due to the uncertainties that currently exist in voluntary carbon credit markets, several organizations have recommended that companies limit their reliance on credits and offsets in establishing voluntary GHG emissions reduction goals; utilize only high-value credits and offsets; and avoid relying on credits and offsets as additional to, rather than substituting for, mitigation of the companies' own emissions where feasible. At a minimum, companies will want to be transparent regarding their use of credits and offsets in connection with any voluntary climate commitments.

H. Consideration #8: Transparency, Verification, and Accountability

Transparency and verification are important to understand voluntary commitments. With more and more companies, countries, and subnational entities making net-zero pledges, there is concern that these voluntary commitments may allow "too much discretion in the design of net-zero pathways and may therefore not be consistent with global net zero, or with ambitious climate action more generally."[106]

1. *What type of government oversight exists for these commitments?*

Governments can and do play a concrete role in transparency, verification, and accountability. For example, the SEC's proposed rule on "Enhancement and Standardization of Climate-Related Disclosures for Investors" requires registrants that have set any climate-related targets or goals (e.g., reduction of GHG emissions) to disclose those targets and goals and how they intend to meet them.[107] The SEC's proposal requires the registrant to disclose the scope of emissions included in the target, the unit of measurement (e.g., absolute or intensity), the time horizon for the target, the baseline time period, any interim targets, and how the registrant intends to meet the targets or goals (e.g., will the registrant increase energy

---

[105] VCMI, Provisional Claims Code of Practice, *supra* note 20, at 30. Similarly, the Taskforce on Scaling Voluntary Carbon Markets (TSVCM) has produced a set of core carbon principles that carbon credits should meet in order to be considered high quality—they must be: (1) real; (2) additional; (3) based on realistic and credible baselines; (4) monitored, reported, and verified in a transparent manner; (5) permanent; (6) have any carbon leakage accounted for and minimized; (7) counted once (i.e., no double counting); and (8) structured to avoid net environmental harms. TSVCM, Taskforce on Scaling Voluntary Carbon Markets, Final Report (2021), https://www.iif.com/Portals/1/Files/TSVCM_Report.pdf.

[106] Sam Fankhauser et al., *supra* note 80.

[107] The Enhancement and Standardization of Climate-related Disclosures for Investors, Securities Act Release No. 11,042, Exchange Act Release No. 94,478, 87 Fed. Reg. 21334, 21471 (proposed Apr. 11, 2022) (to be codified at 17 C.F.R. pts. 210, 229, 232, 239, 249) [hereinafter SEC Proposed Rule].

efficiency, transition to less carbon-intensive products, or purchase offsets or renewable energy credits?).[108] The SEC proposes this disclosure to provide "more comparable, consistent and reliable metrics" of climate-related targets or goals.[109] It acknowledges that this may disincentivize companies from making such commitments, and that the risk of litigation or enforcement actions "could result in registrants being more cautious in their decision to set climate-related targets."[110] However, it believes there is a benefit for companies to signal "credible value-enhancing commitments to investors" and will help investors understand progress with the climate-related targets or goals.[111] For a further discussion on the SEC's proposed rule, see CHAPTER 6—CLIMATE-RELATED DISCLOSURE OBLIGATIONS AT THE FEDERAL AND INTERNATIONAL LEVEL, and CHAPTER 23—PUBLIC COMPANY DISCLOSURES.

Another example is the EPA, which received funding from Congress through the Inflation Reduction Act to support "enhanced standardization and transparency of corporate climate action commitments and plans to reduce greenhouse gas emissions," "enhanced transparency regarding progress toward meeting such commitments and implementing such plans," and "progress toward meeting such commitments and implementing such plans."[112]

A related issue is whether regulators will require corporate disclosures to be attested to or verified by a third party. Existing federal obligatory disclosures regarding GHG emissions is largely limited to EPA's Greenhouse Gas Reporting Program (GHGRP).[113] The GHGRP requires certain large GHG facilities that emit GHGs, suppliers of fossil fuels, and CO_2 injection sites in the United States to annually report their GHG emissions, but the GHGRP does not require third-party verification. In contrast, the SEC's proposed rule would require companies to include an attestation report and disclose information regarding the attestation service provider with respect to Scope 1 and Scope 2 emissions.[114] The trend in other GHG reduction programs (e.g., Low Carbon Fuel Standards, cap-and-trade) is to require some sort of third-party verification. Many companies already use third-party verification in their ESG reports, through auditing by a consulting company, but companies should be careful of actors that purport to be experts in this field.

2. *What frameworks for disclosure exist for these commitments?*

In addition to government organizations, there is a role for voluntary disclosure frameworks to assist companies. For example:

- **Task Force on Climate-related Financial Disclosures** (TCFD) provides recommendations on the type of information that companies should disclose to assist investors, lenders, and insurance underwriters with assessing risks related to climate change.

---

[108] *Id.*

[109] *Id.* at 21438.

[110] *Id.* at 21448.

[111] *Id.*

[112] Inflation Reduction Act, H.R. 5376, sec. 60111(a) 117th Cong. (2022) (enacted), https://www.congress.gov/117/bills/hr5376/BILLS-117hr5376enr.pdf.

[113] 40 C.F.R. pt. 98.

[114] SEC Proposed Rule, *supra* note 107, at 21346.

TCFD states that climate-related targets should include certain characteristics to ensure the targets are "specific and complete" to align with TCFD's fundamental principles for effective disclosure.[115] Considerations include whether the targets are aligned with strategy and risk management goals; linked to relevant metrics; quantified and measurable; clearly specified over time (including a clearly defined baseline, time horizon, and interim targets); understandable and contextualized; periodically reviewed and updated; and reported annually.[116]

- **Sustainability Accounting Standards Board** provides reporting guidance mainly focused on reporting of financially material sustainability information, which includes guidance for reporting entities that wish to disclose Scope 1, 2, or 3 emissions.[117]
- **Global Reporting Initiative** provides standards for large or small, private or public, organizations "to understand and report on their impacts on the economy, environment and people in a comparable and credible way, thereby increasing transparency on their contribution to sustainable development."[118]
- **CDP** "runs the global disclosure system for investors, companies, cities, states and regions to manage their environmental impacts."[119] Companies can disclose through CDP by completing CDP's annual questionnaires on climate change, forests, and water security.[120]

Appendix

Additional Resources for Voluntary GHG Emissions Reduction Goals

- **Greenhouse Gas Protocol**
    - GHG Protocol Corporate Accounting and Reporting Standard (2004) provides guidance and requirements when preparing a GHG emissions inventory.[121]
    - GHG Protocol Corporate Value Chain (Scope 3) Accounting and Reporting Standard (2011) provides a methodology to account for and report Scope 3 emissions.[122]

---

[115] TCFD, TASK FORCE ON CLIMATE-RELATED FINANCIAL DISCLOSURES, GUIDANCE ON METRICS, TARGETS, AND TRANSITION PLANS 31 (2021), https://assets.bbhub.io/company/sites/60/2021/07/2021-Metrics_Targets_Guidance-1.pdf.

[116] *Id.* at 31–35.

[117] *SASB Implementation Supplement – Greenhouse Gas Emissions and SASB Standards*, SASB STANDARDS (Oct. 11, 2020), https://www.sasb.org/knowledge-hub/sasb-implementation-supplement-greenhouse-gas-emissions-and-sasb-standards/.

[118] *The Global Standards for Sustainability Impacts*, GLOB. REPORTING INITIATIVE, https://www.globalreporting.org/standards/ (last visited Apr. 2, 2023).

[119] CDP, https://www.cdp.net/en (last visited Apr. 2, 2023).

[120] *How to Disclose as a Company*, CDP, https://www.cdp.net/en/companies-discloser/how-to-disclose-as-a-company (last visited Apr. 2, 2023).

[121] GREENHOUSE GAS PROTOCOL, A CORPORATE ACCOUNTING AND REPORTING STANDARD (2004), https://ghgprotocol.org/sites/default/files/standards/ghg-protocol-revised.pdf.

[122] GREENHOUSE GAS PROTOCOL, CORPORATE VALUE CHAIN (SCOPE 3) ACCOUNTING AND REPORTING STANDARD: SUPPLEMENT TO THE GHG PROTOCOL CORPORATE ACCOUNTING AND REPORTING STANDARD (2011), https://ghgprotocol.org/sites/default/files/standards/Corporate-Value-Chain-Accounting-Reporing-Standard_041613_2.pdf.

  - GHG Protocol Product Life Cycle Accounting and Reporting Standard (2011) provides a methodology to account for and report product lifecycle emissions.[123]
- **UN Race to Zero Campaign**
  - Lexicon attempts to clarify key terms often used when discussing GHG reduction targets.[124]
  - Interpretation Guide provides guidance on the Race to Zero application and review process.[125]
- **U.S. EPA**
  - *EPA Center for Corporate Climate Leadership, Target Setting*, EPA (Sept. 30, 2022).[126]
  - Corporate GHG Inventorying and Target Setting Self-Assessment (Apr. 2020) is designed for companies to use the self-assessment as "an internal communication and management resource, a proxy benchmarking assessment, and an educational tool."[127]
  - Annual GHG Inventory Summary and Tracking Form (2021) provides a format for companies to track GHG emissions over time against their GHG reduction target.[128]
- **SBTi—SBTi offers resources for companies at all stages of target setting.[129] A few of those resources include:**
  - Foundations of Science-based Target Setting in the Corporate Sector (Sept. 2020), which "lays out the conceptual foundations for credible, science-based net-zero targets for the corporate sector."[130]
  - Value Change in the Value Chain: Best Practices in Scope 3 Greenhouse Gas Management (Nov. 2018), which "summarizes the latest best practices

---

[123] Greenhouse Gas Protocol, Product Life Cycle Accounting and Reporting Standard (2011), https://ghgprotocol.org/sites/default/files/standards/Product-Life-Cycle-Accounting-Reporting-Standard_041613.pdf.

[124] UNFCCC, Race to Zero, Race to Zero Lexicon, https://racetozero.unfccc.int/wp-content/uploads/2021/04/Race-to-Zero-Lexicon.pdf.

[125] UNFCCC, Race to Zero, Interpretation Guide (2021), https://racetozero.unfccc.int/wp-content/uploads/2021/04/Race-to-Zero-EPRG-Criteria-Interpretation-Guide.pdf.

[126] *EPA Center for Corporate Climate Leadership, Target Setting*, EPA, https://www.epa.gov/climateleadership/target-setting (Sept. 30, 2022).

[127] EPA Ctr. for Corp. Climate Leadership, Corporate GHG Inventorying and Target Setting Self-Assessment: V1.0 (2020), https://www.epa.gov/sites/default/files/2020-04/documents/corporate-ghg-inventorying-and-target-setting-self-assessment.pdf.

[128] EPA Ctr. for Corp. Climate Leadership, Annual GHG Inventory Summary and Target Tracking Form (2021), https://www.epa.gov/sites/default/files/2015-07/summaryform_0.xls.

[129] *Resources*, SBTi, https://sciencebasedtargets.org/resources/?tab=background#resource (last visited Apr. 2, 2023).

[130] SBTi, Foundations for Science-based Net-zero Target Setting in the Corporate Sector (2020), https://sciencebasedtargets.org/resources/files/foundations-for-net-zero-full-paper.pdf.

in reducing scope 3 GHG emissions by describing different emissions reduction levers companies can employ."[131]
    - Pathways to Net-Zero (Oct. 2021), which "provides more information on pathways used by the SBTi."[132]
- **Other resources:**
    - **VCMI's** Provisional Claims Code of Practice (or Claims Code) on credible voluntary use of carbon credits by companies and other non-state actors and associated public claims.[133]
    - **Carbon Pricing Leadership Coalition's** Report of the Task Force on Net Zero Goals and Carbon Pricing.[134]
    - **Gold Standard's** Scope 3 Value Chain Interventions Guidance.[135]
    - **University of Oxford's** The Oxford Principles for Net Zero Aligned Carbon Offsetting.[136]

---

131 SBTi, Value Change in the Value Chain: Best Practices in Scope 3 Greenhouse Gas Management (2018), https://sciencebasedtargets.org/resources/files/SBT_Value_Chain_Report-1.pdf.

132 SBTi, Pathways to Net-zero, SBTi Technical Summary (2021), https://sciencebasedtargets.org/resources/files/Pathway-to-Net-Zero.pdf.

133 VCMI, Provisional Claims Code of Practice (2022), https://vcmintegrity.org/wp-content/uploads/2022/06/VCMI-Provisional-Claims-Code-of-Practice.pdf

134 Carbon Pricing Leadership Coal., Report of the Task Force on Net Zero Goals & Carbon Pricing (2021), https://www.carbonpricingleadership.org/s/CPLC-_NetZero_Report.pdf.

135 Gold Standard, Value Chain (Scope 3) Interventions – Greenhouse Gas Accounting & Reporting Guidance (2021), https://www.goldstandard.org/sites/default/files/value_change_scope3_guidance-v.1.1.pdf.

136 Univ. of Oxford, The Oxford Principles for Net Zero Aligned Carbon Offsetting (2020), https://www.smithschool.ox.ac.uk/sites/default/files/2022-01/Oxford-Offsetting-Principles-2020.pdf.

8

Other Emerging Environmental Issues from Biodiversity to Animal Welfare

Tyler L. Burgess and Brian D. Israel

I. Introduction

According to the World Economic Forum, over half of the global gross domestic product is moderately or highly dependent on natural resources such as air, water, land, forests, and minerals.[1] Commonly referred to as "natural capital," the earth's resources provide benefits and economic value by purifying air and water; serving as the source of food, fuels, and medicines; moderating the impacts of climate change; and providing cultural benefits through recreation and tourism, among many other benefits—these benefits are collectively referred to as "ecosystem services."

Many natural resources, however, are under threat from a myriad of human activities, such as deforestation, overfishing, nonsustainable agricultural and livestock practices, and over-exploitation of other natural resources. Investors and activists, recognizing the resulting business risks, have begun pressuring companies to reduce their impacts to natural resources and accelerate the transition to sustainable business practices. While investor focus has largely been on climate change, there is an increasing focus on other emerging environmental issues, such as biodiversity, animal welfare, plastic use and disposal, water use, and the rights of nature.

[1] World Econ. F., Nature Risk Rising: Why the Crisis Engulfing Nature Matters for Business and the Economy 13 (2020), https://www3.weforum.org/docs/WEF_New_Nature_Economy_Report_2020.pdf; BlackRock, BlackRock Investment Stewardship: Engagement Principles 2 (2022), https://www.blackrock.com/corporate/literature/publication/blk-stewardship-priorities-final.pdf.

While somewhat less developed than disclosure metrics for climate change risk,[2] there are existing and developing frameworks that ESG practitioners should consider when evaluating the business's natural capital-related risks and opportunities.[3] Of particular interest is the Task Force on Nature-related Financial Disclosures (TNFD),[4] which is preparing a framework that will guide companies on disclosing their nature-related risks similar to the framework for climate risk presented by the Task Force on Climate-related Financial Disclosures (TCFD).[5]

Meanwhile, shareholder proposals on environmental issues have more than doubled in recent years, and the support for those proposals has increased as well.[6] In 2021, BlackRock supported 44 out of 130 environmental shareholder proposals (34 percent),[7] up from 7 out of 111 (6.3 percent) in 2019-2020.[8] Many of those proposals are climate-related, but around a quarter of them cover other emerging environmental topics.[9]

This chapter will go into more detail about these emerging issues, including a discussion of the pressures companies are seeing and responses they can implement.

II. Biodiversity

According to the United Nations, biodiversity—the variability within species, between species, and of ecosystems[10] —is declining at the fastest rate in human history.[11] This decline is driven by changes in land and sea use, direct exploitation of organisms, climate change,

[2] *See, e.g.*, United Nations Principles for Responsible Investment (UN PRI), Climate Metrics, https://www.unpri.org/download?ac=16427.

[3] *See also* Nat. Cap. Coal., Natural Capital Protocol (2016), https://naturalcapitalcoalition.org/wp-content/uploads/2018/05/NCC_Protocol_WEB_2016-07-12-1.pdf (framework for incorporating natural capital into decision-making); *Natural Capital Accounting and Valuation of Ecosystem Services Project*, UN Sys. of Env't Econ. Acct., https://seea.un.org/home/Natural-Capital-Accounting-Project (last visited Jan. 5, 2023) (Natural Capital Accounting and Valuation of Ecosystem Services is an accounting framework addressing natural capital issues).

[4] *Welcome to the TNFD Nature-related Risk & Opportunity Management and Disclosure Framework*, Task Force on Nature-related Financial Disclosures, https://framework.tnfd.global/ (last visited Jan. 5, 2023).

[5] Also note the European Commission's Align Project, which "is a three-year project aiming at providing businesses and financial institutions with principles and criteria for biodiversity measurement and valuation." European Comm'n, Recommendations for a Standard on Corporate Biodiversity Measurement and Valuation, Aligning Accounting Approaches for Nature (2022), https://capitalscoalition.org/wp-content/uploads/2021/03/330300786-Align-Report_v4-301122.pdf.

[6] Marc Treviño, Melissa Sawyer & June Hu, Sullivan & Cromwell, Lessons from the 2021 Proxy Season 5 (2021), https://www.sullcrom.com/files/upload/Lessons-from-the-2021-Proxy-Season.pdf; Jackie Cook & Lauren Solberg, *The 2021 Proxy Voting Season in 7 Charts*, Morningstar (Aug. 5, 2021), https://www.morningstar.com/articles/1052234/the-2021-proxy-voting-season-in-7-charts.

[7] BlackRock, Investment Stewardship Annual Report 126 (2021), https://www.blackrock.com/corporate/literature/publication/annual-stewardship-report-2021.pdf.

[8] BlackRock, Investment Stewardship Annual Report 17 (2020), https://www.blackrock.com/corporate/literature/publication/blk-annual-stewardship-report-2020.pdf.

[9] *Id.*

[10] Convention on Biological Diversity, *Article 2. Use of Terms* (2006), https://www.cbd.int/convention/articles/?a=cbd-02.

[11] Intergovernmental Sci.-Pol'y Platform on Biodiversity & Ecosystem Servs., The Global Assessment Report on Biodiversity and Ecosystem Services 10 (2019), https://ipbes.net/sites/default/files/inline/files/ipbes_global_assessment_report_summary_for_policymakers.pdf; World Econ. F., The Global Risks Report 2020 46 (2020), https://www3.weforum.org/docs/WEF_Global_Risk_Report_2020.pdf.

pollution, and invasive alien species.[12] The World Economic Forum Global Risks Perception Survey ranked biodiversity loss as the third most severe risk facing the planet over the next 10 years, behind climate action failure and extreme weather.[13] In response to these increasing concerns, the parties at the 15th Conference of Parties (COP15) to the United Nations Convention on Biological Diversity adopted the Kunming-Montreal Global Biodiversity Framework, which sets goals and targets to address the global loss of biodiversity by 2030.[14]

Investors recognize that impacts on biodiversity can, in some instances, have material impacts on the companies they invest in. For example, pharmaceutical companies often benefit from robust biodiversity in searching for new medicines.[15] As such, investors have begun pressuring companies to address biodiversity, and ESG practitioners evaluating a company's risks and opportunities may consider reporting standards such as the Global Reporting Initiative (GRI) Biodiversity Standards[16] and the Global Biodiversity Score[17] to ensure adequate disclosure.

Given the broad range on causes of biodiversity loss, it is frequently impossible to directly quantify an individual company's impact on biodiversity. It is especially difficult to aggregate biodiversity impacts for large global companies.[18] Many investors focus instead on companies' impacts on the principal *drivers* of biodiversity loss by considering, for example, whether a business engages in deforestation practices. Some companies are now initiating action and making specific commitments to address biodiversity concerns. For example, BNP Paribas committed to supporting global efforts to halve forest loss by 2020 and end it by 2030.[19] It plans to do so by having companies in its portfolios comply with No Deforestation, No Peat and No Exploitation (NDPE) standards.[20] Aviva, a multinational insurance company based in the United Kingdom, has focused on agriculture on the topic of pollinators

[12] *Models of Drivers of Biodiversity and Ecosystem Change*, Intergovernmental Sci.-Pol'y Platform on Biodiversity & Ecosystem Servs., https://ipbes.net/models-drivers-biodiversity-ecosystem-change (last visited Jan. 8, 2023).

[13] World Econ. F., The Global Risks Report 2022 7 (2022), https://www3.weforum.org/docs/WEF_The_Global_Risks_Report_2022.pdf.

[14] *COP15: Nations Adopt Four Goals, 23 Targets for 2030 in Landmark UN Biodiversity Agreement*, Convention on Biological Diversity (Dec. 19, 2022), https://www.cbd.int/article/cop15-cbd-press-release-final-19dec2022.

[15] Vidushi Neergheen-Bhujun et al., *Biodiversity, Drug Discovery, and the Future of Global Health: Introducing the Biodiversity to Biomedicine Consortium, A Call to Action*, 7 J. Glob. Health 1 (2017), https://www.ncbi.nlm.nih.gov/pmc/articles/PMC5735771/.

[16] Global Reporting Initiative (GRI), Standards (2021) and GRI 304: Biodiversity (2016), https://www.globalreporting.org/how-to-use-the-gri-standards/gri-standards-english-language/ (last visited Jan. 8, 2023).

[17] Centers for Disease Control and Prevention Biodiversité, Measuring the Contributions of Business and Finance Towards the Post-2020 Global Biodiversity Framework: 2019 Technical Update (2020), http://www.mission-economie-biodiversite.com/wp-content/uploads/2020/07/N15-TRAVAUX-DU-CLUB-B4B-GBS-UK-MD-WEB.pdf.

[18] United Nations Principles for Responsible Investment (UN PRI), Investor Action on Biodiversity: Discussion Paper 6 (2020), https://www.unpri.org/download?ac=11357.

[19] BNP Paribas, Global Sustainability Strategy 29 (2019), https://docfinder.bnpparibas-am.com/api/files/1FC9FC6C-0DA8-468E-90B3-016DDB5CD270.

[20] *Id.*

and how they affect crop yields and prices.[21] And AXA IM engaged with 33 companies, focusing on having board and management expertise, biodiversity policies in place, reporting progress, and maintaining engagement.[22]

Below is a nonexhaustive list of topic areas interested practitioners and investors may wish to consider in evaluating a company's biodiversity risks and opportunities (adapted from BlackRock's recommendations on evaluating natural capital):[23]

- Policies and practices to assess a company's biodiversity-related risks and opportunities, including whether the company maintains metrics and targets;
- Initiatives that encourage innovation in sustainable business practices;
- Sustainable agricultural practices that focus on land-use efficiencies and preserving natural habitat, minimizing greenhouse gas (GHG) emissions and the adverse impacts of climate change;
- Sustainable agricultural and livestock practices that limit the contamination of soil and water, including minimizing the use of fertilizers, pesticides, chemicals, or wide-spectrum antibiotics;
- Conducting wildlife presence/absence surveys with a particular focus on threatened and endangered species;
- Initiatives to limit the introduction of, or reduce the presence of, invasive species;
- Initiatives to evaluate supply chains and sources of raw materials and components for sustainable business practices, including energy use; and
- Commitment to engagement with indigenous peoples on issues that may impact their communities.

Recently, two corporate commitment programs related to biodiversity have been gaining traction: No Net Loss (NNL) and Net Positive Impact (NPI) goals.[24] NNL is "a target for a development project in which the impacts on biodiversity caused by the project are balanced or outweighed by measures taken to avoid and minimize the project's impacts to undertake on-site rehabilitation/restoration, and finally to offset the residual impacts, so that no overall biodiversity loss results." Meanwhile, NPI or "net gain" exists where the gain exceeds the loss.[25] And the European Union agreed to a provisional regulation that provides for deforestation-free supply chains in an effort to minimize forest degradation.[26]

---

[21] Steve Waygood et al., Aviva, Frontiers in Sustainable Agriculture: Putting Your Money Where Your Mouth Is 14 (2018), https://www.longfinance.net/documents/1720/frontiers-in-sustainable-agriculture_jXOR7v9.pdf.

[22] UN PRI, *supra* note 18, at 25–26.

[23] BlackRock, Our Approach to Engagement on Natural Capital 2 (2022), https://www.blackrock.com/corporate/literature/publication/blk-commentary-engagement-on-natural-capital.pdf [hereinafter BlackRock, Our Approach].

[24] Hugo J. Rainey et al., *A Review of Corporate Goals of No Net Loss and Net Positive Impact on Biodiversity*, 49 Oryx 1 (2014), https://www.researchgate.net/profile/John-Pilgrim/publication/271934685_A_review_of_corporate_goals_of_No_Net_Loss_and_Net_Positive_Impact_on_biodiversity/links/561643e408ae0f2140067f39/A-review-of-corporate-goals-of-No-Net-Loss-and-Net-Positive-Impact-on-biodiversity.pdf.

[25] *Id.*

[26] European Commission Press Release, Green Deal: EU Agrees Law to Fight Global Deforestation and Forest Degradation Driven by EU Production and Consumption (Dec. 6, 2022), https://ec.europa.eu/commission/presscorner/detail/en/ip_22_7444.

Additionally, a number of oil and gas and mining companies committed to avoid developing in World Heritage Sites, which are particularly critical biodiversity centers.[27] One example is Soco International's announcement that it dropped plans to explore the Virunga National Park in the Democratic Republic of Congo after investor and nongovernmental organization backlash.[28]

III. Animal Welfare

A second major area of nonclimate ESG focus is animal welfare.[29] Activists have advocated for principles like the Five Freedoms of animal welfare and dolphin-safe tuna for decades.[30] The Five Freedoms of animal welfare are generally considered to be the following: freedom from hunger and thirst; freedom from discomfort; freedom from pain, injury, and disease; freedom to express normal and natural behavior; and freedom from fear and distress.[31]

Institutional shareholders are becoming increasingly attuned to animal welfare issues when making investment decisions. At Coller Capital, "[o]ne area we believe has historically been under-represented in ESG analysis is farm animal welfare."[32] They consider the International Finance Corporation Good Practice Note on Animal Welfare in Livestock Operations, and the Business Benchmark on Farm Animal Welfare, or Freedom Food, among other guidance.[33] Coller Capital notes that in making investment decisions, "we generally recommend approval only where we are satisfied that one of the following conditions is met: Appropriate animal welfare standards are being followed; a plan for a transition to appropriate animal welfare standards is being implemented; the investment will facilitate a transition to appropriate animal welfare standards."[34] Similarly, "Glass Lewis believes that it is prudent for management to assess potential exposure to regulatory, legal and reputational risks associated with all business practices, including those related to animal welfare."[35]

Companies considering implementing animal welfare metrics into their business model should be aware of certain practical considerations. Disclosure of animal testing could be a double-edged sword; investors may appreciate the disclosure but may also give nondisclosing companies the benefit of the doubt. To counter that phenomenon, Institutional Shareholder Services (ISS) ESG suggests that investors use proxy indicators instead to avoid punishing

---

[27] UN PRI, *supra* note 18, at 20.

[28] *Id.*

[29] *See* Ian Woods, *Animal Welfare: An Emerging Investor Issue*, AMP Capital (June 20, 2019), https://www.ampcapital.com/au/en/insights-hub/articles/2019/june/animal-welfare-an-emerging-investor-issue.

[30] Melissa Elischer, *The Five Freedoms: A History Lesson in Animal Care and Welfare*, Mich. State Univ. Expansion (Sept. 6, 2019), https://www.canr.msu.edu/news/an_animal_welfare_history_lesson_on_the_five_freedoms.

[31] *Five Freedoms: The Gold Standard of Animal Welfare*, Am. Humane Soc'y (Oct. 17, 2016), https://www.americanhumane.org/blog/five-freedoms-the-gold-standard-of-animal-welfare/.

[32] Coller Capital, Responsible Investment: ESG Policy 5 (2016), https://www.collercapital.com/sites/default/files/Coller_Capital%27s_ESG_Policy__%202.pdf.

[33] *Id.*

[34] *Id.*

[35] Glass Lewis, Shareholder Initiatives: 2020 Proxy Paper Guidelines 4 (2019), https://www.glasslewis.com/wp-content/uploads/2016/11/Guidelines_Shareholder_Initiatives.pdf.

companies that do disclose.[36] For companies that choose to disclose animal welfare information, a commonly used metric is the Business Benchmark on Farm Animal Welfare.[37] It is used by food companies to measure farm animal welfare management, policy commitment, and performance and disclosure.[38]

The following examples discuss specific issues related to animal welfare—namely, the use of gestating pig crates, transitioning to cage-free egg supplies, and avoiding animal testing.

A. Gestation Pig Crates

In terms of more specific animal welfare issues, perhaps one of the most prominent is the use of gestation pig crates—small metal enclosures where breeding sows are put during pregnancy. Critics point out that they restrict movement and lead to several negative health outcomes.[39] Defenders of the practice claim that it reduces aggression between the pigs.[40] Using gestation crates is currently banned in nine U.S. states (as well as the United Kingdom, Switzerland, and Sweden), but the vast majority of pigs in the United States are not located in those jurisdictions.[41]

Many companies have undertaken initiatives to phase out these practices in response to shareholder pressures. Major restaurant chains McDonald's, Burger King, and Wendy's and grocery stores Kroger, Safeway, and Costco have promised to avoid pork from sources using gestation crates.[42] Notably, investor Carl Icahn spearheaded a recent shareholder initiative requesting that McDonald's eliminate the use of gestation pig crates by the end of 2022, but the proposal failed.[43] BlackRock recommended voting against the proposal because it felt

---

[36] Dominika Dobielewska et al., ISS ESG, Cruelty-Free Portfolios: How To Approach Animal Testing In Investments? 9 (2021), https://www.issgovernance.com/file/publications/iss-esg-cruelty-free-portfolios.pdf.

[37] Nicky Amos et al., Bus. Benchmark on Farm Animal Welfare, The Business Benchmark on Farm Animal Welfare Report 2021 (2021), https://www.bbfaw.com/media/2126/bbfaw-report-2021_final.pdf.

[38] *Id.*

[39] The Humane Soc'y of the U.S., An HSUS Report: Welfare Issues with Gestation Crates for Pregnant Sows 1 (2013), https://www.humanesociety.org/sites/default/files/docs/hsus-report-gestation-crates-for-pregnant-sows.pdf.

[40] Jeremy N. Marchant-Forde, *Housing and Welfare of Sows During Gestation*, *in* Sow Welfare Fact Sheet (2010), https://www.ars.usda.gov/ARSUserFiles/50201500/Sow%20Housing%20Fact%20Sheet.pdf; David Jackson & Gary Marx, *Pork Producers Defend Gestation Crates, but Consumers Demand Change*, Chi. Trib. (Aug. 3, 2016), https://www.chicagotribune.com/investigations/ct-pig-farms-gestation-crates-met-20160802-story.html.

[41] *Hog Welfare Laws Cover 9 States and 3 Percent of the National Herd in 2022*, USDA Econ. Rsch. Serv., https://www.ers.usda.gov/data-products/chart-gallery/gallery/chart-detail/?chartId=103505 (Mar. 16, 2022).

[42] *Animal Health & Welfare*, McDonald's, https://corporate.mcdonalds.com/corpmcd/our-purpose-and-impact/food-quality-and-sourcing/animal-health-and-welfare.html (last visited Jan. 8, 2023); P.J. Huffstutter, *McDonald's To End Pork Gestation Crate Use by 2022*, Reuters, May 31, 2012, https://www.reuters.com/article/us-mcdonalds-pig-crates/mcdonalds-to-end-pork-gestation-crate-use-by-2022-idUSBRE84U1FR20120531; Lynne Curry, *After a Decade of Promises, Has the Food Industry Made Progress on Gestation Crates?*, Civil Eats (Mar. 21, 2018), https://civileats.com/2018/03/21/after-a-decade-of-promises-has-the-food-industry-made-progress-on-gestation-crates/.

[43] Amelia Lucas, *Carl Icahn Loses Proxy Fight with McDonald's over Animal Welfare*, CNBC (May 26, 2022, 12:16 PM), https://www.cnbc.com/2022/05/26/carl-icahn-loses-proxy-fight-with-mcdonalds-over-animal-welfare.html#:~:text=Activist%20investor%20Carl%20Icahn%20lost,the%20treatment%20of%20pregnant%20pigs; Lauren Hirsch, *Carl Icahn Gets Only 1 Percent of McDonald's Investors to Support His Campaign on Pigs*, N.Y. Times (May 26, 2022), https://www.nytimes.com/2022/05/26/business/carl-icahn-mcdonalds-pigs.html.

that McDonald's disclosures on animal welfare were sufficiently detailed and that its plan to source 100 percent of its pork from suppliers not using gestation crates by the end of 2024 represented adequate progress.[44]

On the other hand, Glass Lewis encouraged Tyson Foods to stop using gestation crates because of the economic disadvantage it would experience if it failed to do so because of a significant number of major restaurant chains committing to sourcing pork from suppliers that have phased out gestation crates or were in the process of doing so.[45]

B. Cage-Free Eggs

Many companies now have a goal of transitioning their egg supply to be entirely cage-free by 2025 or earlier.[46] Nationwide, the number of hens in cage-free environments rose from 4 percent in 2010 to 28 percent in 2020.[47] Walmart has made some progress in recent years but has only increased its cage-free supply to 20 percent, up from 17 percent in 2020.[48] McDonald's has been more successful and reports that 74 percent of its eggs are from cage-free sources, up from 33 percent in 2019.[49]

C. Animal Testing

Another focus area within the animal welfare sector is animal testing. This issue implicates ethical questions that complicate the picture of investor preferences. Some believe that animal testing is categorically wrong, while others credit it for saving countless human lives.[50]

What is clear is that there is a fundamental distinction between pharmaceutical and non-pharmaceutical testing, with the former getting far more deference than the latter. The "general trend is to move away from animal testing in the cosmetics industry."[51] ISS ESG screens for companies involved in animal testing and considers whether they have a public policy based on the Replace, Reduce, Refine (3R) model.[52] MSCI ESG Research LLC (MSCI), an ESG data provider for companies like Fidelity, "identifies companies involved in testing

---

[44] BLACKROCK, INVESTMENT STEWARDSHIP, VOTE BULLETIN: MCDONALD'S CORPORATION 3 (2022), https://www.blackrock.com/corporate/literature/press-release/vote-bulletin-mcdonalds-may-2022.pdf.

[45] GREEN CENTURY, SHAREHOLDER PROPOSAL REGARDING GESTATION CRATES (2016), https://www.greencentury.com/wp-content/uploads/2018/06/Glass-Lews_Tyson-_Report.pdf.

[46] EGGTRACK, https://www.eggtrack.com/en/ (last visited Jan. 8, 2023).

[47] Scott McFetridge, *Why Cage-free Eggs Becoming Norm: It's What People Want*, ASSOCIATED PRESS, Feb. 11, 2022, https://apnews.com/article/business-iowa-des-moines-animals-animal-welfare-1a611490e5af70a9b9d7b9f8b903bb6f.

[48] *Id.*

[49] MCDONALD'S, *supra* note 42; Huffstutter, *supra* note 42; Curry, *supra* note 42.

[50] *See* Karen Wallace, *Against Animal Testing? Check Out These Funds*, MORNINGSTAR (Mar. 4, 2020), https://www.morningstar.com/articles/969879/against-animal-testing-check-out-these-funds.

[51] DOBIELEWSKA ET AL., ISS ESG, *supra* note 36, at 4.

[52] *Id.* at 6.

products or product ingredients of any sort on animals, breeding animals for animal testing purposes, exhibiting animals and operating factory farms."[53]

Many cosmetics companies have responded to shareholder and customer pressure to stop or reduce their animal testing. Unilever, a multinational consumer goods company, announced that it backs a global ban on animal testing for cosmetics.[54] Procter & Gamble, Avon, and Estée Lauder have followed suit.[55] Food companies, which often test health attributes on animals, have responded as well. In 2015, Barilla committed to immediately ban animal testing throughout its supply chain. And Pepsi and Coke agreed in 2007 to stop financing research that uses animals to test or develop their products.[56]

IV. Plastics

Investor engagement on plastics pollution is an increasingly important topic. Marine plastic pollution has increased tenfold since 1980 and is projected to triple by 2040.[57] This presents climate, environmental, policy, reputational, and health risks to companies with exposure; companies may face ESG pressures on either the production side or the pollution side.

Around 40 percent of global plastics produced are used in packaging.[58] In general, "[p]lastic pollution presents risks to companies and consumers as it threatens food safety and quality, human health, coastal tourism, and contributes to climate change."[59] In the plastic packaging space, there are three main entity types: those that make the raw materials, those that create the packaging to hold products, and those that put the products on the shelves. Investors are interested in seeing companies in each of these categories move toward a "circular economy" model, which is touted for its waste reduction and value recouping potential.[60]

---

[53] MSCI, Business Involvement Methodology Overview 8 (2020), https://www.msci.com/documents/1296102/14524248/MSCI+ESG+Research+BISR+Methodology+Overview.pdf.

[54] *Supporting a Future Global Ban on Animal Testing for Cosmetics*, Unilever (May 3, 2022), https://www.unilever.com/news/news-search/2022/supporting-a-future-global-ban-on-animal-testing-for-cosmetics/.

[55] *Our Commitment to #BeCrueltyFree*, Procter & Gamble, https://us.pg.com/cruelty-free/ (last visited Jan. 8, 2023); *Avon For Animals*, Avon, https://www.avonworldwide.com/about-us/our-values/policies-positions/animal-welfare (last visited Jan. 8, 2023); *Animal Testing*, Estée Lauder Cos., https://www.elcompanies.com/en/our-commitments/viewpoints/animal-testing (last visited Jan. 8, 2023).

[56] Brenda Goodman, *Pepsi and Coke Agree to Stop Financing Research That Uses Animals*, N.Y. Times (May 31, 2007), https://www.nytimes.com/2007/05/31/business/31testing-web.html?_r=1&.

[57] World Econ. F., The Global Risks Report 2020, *supra* note 11, at 46; The Pew Charitable Trusts, Breaking the Plastic Wave 9 (2020), https://www.pewtrusts.org/-/media/assets/2020/07/breakingtheplasticwave_report.pdf.

[58] Rory Sullivan & Rebecca Chapman, UN PRI, A Guide to Investor Engagement on Plastic Packaging: Containers and Packaging Producers 5 (2021), https://www.unpri.org/download?ac=14017; The Pew Charitable Trusts, *supra* note 57, at 17; WBCSD, Upcoming UN Treaty on Plastic Pollution 4 (2022), https://www.wbcsd.org/contentwbc/download/14029/202484/1.

[59] BlackRock, Our Approach, *supra* note 23, at 8.

[60] The Pew Charitable Trusts, *supra* note 57.

One common commitment that companies make is to join the Ellen MacArthur Foundation's Global Commitment, with the following expectations:[61]

- Take action to eliminate problematic or unnecessary plastic packaging by 2025;
- Take action to move from single-use packaging towards reuse models where relevant by 2025;
- Ensure 100 percent of plastic packaging is reusable, recyclable, or compostable by 2025;
- Set an ambitious 2025 post-consumer recycled content target across all plastic packaging used;
- Report annually and publicly on progress; and
- Commit to collaborate towards increasing reuse/recycling/composting rates for plastic.

The Ellen MacArthur Foundation's Global Commitment initiative has commitments from many large companies, including Apple, PepsiCo, and Walmart.[62] Other commitment programs such as the U.S. Plastics Pact[63] and the New Plastics Economy Global Commitment[64] are seeing growth in their rosters. A study of the 50 largest consumer-facing and publicly traded corporations with operations in North America found that 18 of them have a virgin plastic packaging reduction goal, up from just two in 2019.[65] And 29 of those companies have set goals for 100 percent of their packaging to be recyclable, compostable, or reusable, up from 19 in 2019.[66] A leader in this effort is Unilever, which set a goal to reduce virgin plastic by 50 percent by 2025, including absolute elimination of 100,000 tons of plastic.[67] And a coalition of companies, including PepsiCo and the Coca-Cola Company, endorsed a report on Building a Circular Economy for Packaging[68] that addresses plastics

[61] *Id.* at 16. In addition, some jurisdictions, such as the European Union, have issued mandatory regulations intended to reduce single-use plastics and move towards a circular economy. *See, e.g.*, Directive (EU) 2019/904 of the European Parliament and of the Council of 5 June 2019 on the reduction of the impact of certain plastic products on the environment, 2019 O.J. (L 155) 1.

[62] *Signatory Reports*, Ellen MacArthur Found., https://ellenmacarthurfoundation.org/global-commitment/signatory-reports (last visited Jan. 9, 2023).

[63] Press Release, U.S. Plastics Pact, U.S. Plastics Pact Unveils National Strategy to Achieve 2025 Circular Economy Goals (June 15, 2021), https://usplasticspact.org/u-s-plastics-pact-unveils-national-strategy-to-achieve-2025-circular-economy-goals/.

[64] *New Plastics Economy, A Vision of a Circular Economy for Plastic*, Ellen MacArthur Found., https://emf.thirdlight.com/link/86tanzqdbppx-8rdpns/@/preview/1?o (last visited Jan. 9, 2023).

[65] As You Sow, Corporate Plastic Pollution Scorecard 6 (2021), https://static1.squarespace.com/static/59a706d4f5e2319b70240ef9/t/6154c623609b283fdc013b6c/1632945709916/AsYouSow2021_PlasticsScorecard_fin-v2_20210927.pdf.

[66] *Id.* at 7.

[67] *Id.* at 6.

[68] The Consumer Goods F. Coal. of Action on Plastic Waste, Building a Circular Economy for Packaging: A View from the Consumer Goods Industry on Optimal Extended Producer Responsibility (2020), https://www.theconsumergoodsforum.com/wp-content/uploads/Building-a-Circular-Economy-for-Packaging-Dec-2022.pdf.

waste and committed to Extended Producer Responsibility programs that shift responsibility for recycling back to the manufacturer (as opposed to the consumer).

Not surprisingly, the number of companies annually reporting their plastic recycled content use doubled in 2021.[69] For example, the Coca-Cola Company reports 9 out of 10 As You Sow's data transparency pillars, including the number of plastic units and overall packaging units it produces and sells.[70]

However, where investors view companies as failing in their steps to reduce plastics pollution, or where a company is perceived as not disclosing information relevant to assessing associated business risks, investors have taken to shareholder proposals to force action. Specifically, investors have signaled interest in having companies follow the guidelines set forth in the 2020 Pew Report, *Breaking the Plastic Wave*,[71] which provides a roadmap for an 80 percent reduction of plastic pollution by 2040.[72]

At Amazon, BlackRock supported a shareholder proposal requesting that the Board "issue a report 'describing how the company could reduce its plastics use in alignment with the 1/3 reduction findings of the Pew Report, or other authoritative sources, to reduce the majority of ocean pollution.'"[73] While the proposal only got 48.9 percent shareholder support, BlackRock supported this proposal because it claims that Amazon does not explicitly disclose the total amount of plastic used in its packaging, something that impedes shareholders' ability to assess the company's progress.[74] In response, Amazon noted that a report the shareholder proposal relied upon significantly overestimated the company's plastics use and highlighted the company's efforts to increase recycled plastic content in its packaging and reduce single-use plastics.[75]

At McDonald's, BlackRock voted against a similar proposal because it felt the company's existing disclosure was sufficient in that it outlined clear policies and targets to reduce the use of plastics.[76] In contrast, BlackRock supported a shareholder proposal at Kroger requesting a board report on "plastic packaging, estimating the amount of plastics released to the environment by [Kroger's] use of plastic packaging, from the manufacture of plastic source materials, through disposal or recycling, and describing any company strategies or goals to reduce the use of plastic packaging to reduce these impacts."[77] BlackRock supported this proposal because Kroger had yet to finalize the details of its 2030 strategy (regarding sustainable

[69] As You Sow, *supra* note 65, at 14.

[70] *Id.* at 6.

[71] The Pew Charitable Trusts, *supra* note 57.

[72] *Id.* at 15.

[73] BlackRock, Investment Stewardship, Vote Bulletin: Amazon.com, Inc. 3 (2022), https://www.blackrock.com/corporate/literature/press-release/blk-vote-bulletin-amazon-may-2022.pdf.

[74] *Id.*

[75] Amazon, Notice of 2022 Annual Meeting of Shareholders & Proxy Statement 42 (2022), https://s2.q4cdn.com/299287126/files/doc_financials/2022/ar/Amazon-2022-Proxy-Statement.pdf.

[76] *Id.*

[77] BlackRock, Investment Stewardship Annual Report 108 (2022), https://www.blackrock.com/corporate/literature/publication/annual-stewardship-report-2021.pdf.

packaging) and lagged some of its peers that had made more robust commitments to reduce the overall use of plastic in both their operations and supply chain.[78]

As You Sow[79] has been much more aggressive in the plastics realm, a position embodied in its Investor Declaration on Plastic Pollution.[80] Its 2025 goal is to engage companies on waste reduction through responsible production and recycling or composting of consumer products and packaging to preserve Earth's limited natural resources. Its most successful proposal was the 2021 proposal for DuPont to report on spills of plastic pellets released into the environment, which passed with 81 percent support.[81] That same proposal received only 7 percent support in 2019.[82]

There are a few practical considerations that ESG practitioners should consider with respect to plastics:

- Companies with a credible path towards achieving set goals and targets will likely be better positioned to respond to and potentially avoid confrontation with activist shareholders.
- Proactively engaging with all stakeholders, including with respect to plastics, will help a company foresee and get ahead of any press releases, shareholder initiatives, or other actions that could overshadow a company's ESG progress.
- Companies and ESG practitioners should be mindful when making claims that a product is compostable or recyclable to avoid liability with respect to green marketing.
- Definitions and standards around what is compostable or recyclable vary in each jurisdiction. As such, proactively engaging with regulators and industry groups can help large companies navigate these regulatory complexities.

V. Water

Companies can face physical, regulatory, and reputational risks from agricultural operations or supply chains that are heavily water-dependent.[83] Physical risks may include locations in flood zones, water use in areas experiencing water stress, and others.[84] Operating costs will likely rise as companies work to meet more stringent water conservation regulations, as

---

[78] *Id.*

[79] As You Sow, 2020 Strategic Plan (2020), https://static1.squarespace.com/static/59a706d4f5e2319b70240ef9/t/5e62c5190e519e04ec5c753c/1583531311567/2020AYSStrategicPlanReport_FIN.pdf.

[80] *Plastic Solutions Investor Alliance, Investor Declaration on Plastic Pollution*, As You Sow, https://www.asyousow.org/our-work/waste/ocean-plastics/declaration-on-plastic-pollution-citing-plastic-pollution (last visited Jan. 9, 2023).

[81] Press Release, As You Sow, Record-Setting 81% of DuPont Shareholders Approve Proposal Calling for Plastic Pellet Pollution Reporting (May 3, 2021), https://www.asyousow.org/press-releases/2021/5/3/dupont-shareholders-approve-plastic-pellet-pollution-reporting.

[82] *DowDupont: Disclosure of Plastic Pellet Spills and Cleanup Actions*, As You Sow (Nov. 28, 2018), https://www.asyousow.org/resolutions/2018/11/28/dowdupont-report-on-consumer-packaging.

[83] *Id.*; *What Is Agricultural Supply Chain Water Risk?*, UN PRI (Mar. 6, 2018), https://www.unpri.org/environmental-issues/what-is-agricultural-supply-chain-water-risk/2795.article.

[84] TCFD, Guidance on Metrics, Targets, and Transition Plans (2021), https://assets.bbhub.io/company/sites/60/2021/07/2021-Metrics_Targets_Guidance-1.pdf.

will insurance premiums in response to uncertainty.[85] This is especially true for data center operations and companies in the food and beverage, apparel, electric power, and agricultural sectors.[86] For example, agriculture is the world's largest user of water, representing 70 percent of the world's fresh water use, and supply chains dependent on it.[87] Because of that and other water-related risks, investors started pressuring companies to act.

In evaluating a company's disclosures on water issues, ESG practitioners should consider, among other factors, the company's water use and plans for water efficiency, reduction, or recycling both in their operations and through their supply chains, policies, and targets to ensure sustainable business practices leading to water security both for the business and the community within which it operates (particularly in areas of high water stress or demand), and management of waste disposal and pollution-related risks.[88] Water risks frequently overlap with climate risks. Accordingly, investors and companies may look to the TCFD for guidance on water issues.[89]

Many companies are responding to shareholder pressures by increasing their disclosures on water risks.[90] The United Nations Principles for Responsible Investment (UN PRI) encourages companies to match the performance of their peers, take collective action, and improve disclosure on water risks in agricultural supply chains.[91] PRI coordinated a collaborative engagement on water risks in agricultural supply chains starting in 2014; 84 percent of those companies improved their disclosure of water risks by 2017.[92] PRI has praised several companies for their disclosure and operations in the water space.[93] For example, PRI cited Nestle and its stated commitments to achieve water efficiency and sustainability, advocate effective water policies and stewardship, treat discharged water, engage with suppliers, raise awareness on water conservation, and improve access to water and sanitation across the value chain.[94] PRI also praised Diageo for taking action once it identified its water risks. Diageo ensures sustainable water stewardship practices where it has operational control of agricultural land and encourages suppliers to disclose water-related information.[95]

---

[85] BlackRock, Troubled Waters: Water Stress Risks to Portfolios (2020), https://www.blackrock.com/us/individual/literature/whitepaper/bii-water-risks-july-2020.pdf.

[86] *What Is Agricultural Supply Chain Water Risk?*, *supra* note 83; BlackRock, Troubled Waters: Water Stress Risks to Portfolios, *supra* note 85.

[87] *Environmental Issues, Executive Summary: Global Investor Portfolios Are Increasingly Exposed to Water-related Risk*, UN PRI (Mar. 5, 2018), https://www.unpri.org/environmental-issues/growing-water-risk-resilience-an-investor-guide-on-agricultural-supply-chains/2793.article; UN PRI, Growing Water Risk Resilience: An Investor Guide on Agricultural Supply Chains 7 (2018), https://www.unpri.org/download?ac=4195 [hereinafter UN PRI, Growing Water Risk Resilience].

[88] BlackRock, Our Approach, *supra* note 23, at 5.

[89] TCFD, *supra* note 84.

[90] UN PRI, Growing Water Risk Resilience, *supra* note 87.

[91] *Id.* at 5.

[92] *Id.* at 12.

[93] *Id.* at 17.

[94] *Id.*

[95] *Id.* at 20.

Investors are aware, however, that water management and associated risk is not equal across the globe. In China, for example, 90 percent of the country depends on polluted groundwater supplies, according to the United Nations.[96] Massachusetts Financial Services Investment Management became concerned that supply issues and protests posed a material risk to a beverage company operating there.[97]

Despite the increasing steps companies have taken to address water concerns in recent years, further efforts may be needed both in terms of identifying and addressing the issues. To illustrate this, BlackRock supported a shareholder proposal on water use at Alphabet because the company "does not explicitly disclose annual water use or other risk metrics by location; therefore, it is difficult for stakeholders to determine the company's regional approach, localized water stress trends and risks, as well as possible progress year over year."[98] As with other proposals, BlackRock supported this in part because Alphabet's peers had already disclosed such information. On the other hand, Vanguard did not support a shareholder proposal relating to Origin Energy's fracking activities because the company "had taken appropriate and sufficient action to manage related risks and impacts and was providing adequate reporting to the public."[99]

VI. Rights of Nature

One of the most recent emerging ESG issues is the so-called rights of nature—a movement to recognize legal status for nature, which would grant ecosystems the right to exist, flourish, and even have standing in courts to defend themselves.[100] While law has traditionally treated nature as property,[101] under an alternate model, outlined in Christopher Stone's 1972 book *Should Trees Have Standing?*, natural entities should have lawyers to speak for them, just like corporations, states, infants, and others do. For example, the Earth Law Center's Universal Declaration of the Rights of Rivers establishes that rivers should have (1) the right to flow, (2) the right to perform essential functions within its ecosystem, (3) the right to be free from pollution, (4) the right to feed and be fed by sustainable aquifers, (5) the right to native biodiversity, (6) the right to restoration, and (7) the right to maintain lateral and longitudinal connectivity.[102]

---

[96] *Id.* at 34.

[97] *Id.*

[98] BLACKROCK, INVESTMENT STEWARDSHIP, VOTE BULLETIN: ALPHABET, INC. 2 (2022), https://www.blackrock.com/corporate/literature/press-release/blk-vote-bulletin-alphabet-jun-2022.pdf.

[99] VANGUARD, VANGUARD INVESTMENT STEWARDSHIP INSIGHTS, VOTING INSIGHTS: ENVIRONMENTAL AND SOCIAL PROPOSALS AT ORIGIN ENERGY 3 (2021), https://corporate.vanguard.com/content/dam/corp/advocate/investment-stewardship/pdf/perspectives-and-commentary/Insights_Origin_1908018.pdf.

[100] Tiffany Challe, *The Rights of Nature — Can an Ecosystem Bear Legal Rights?* COLUM. CLIMATE SCH. (Apr. 22, 2021), https://news.climate.columbia.edu/2021/04/22/rights-of-nature-lawsuits/.

[101] *Rights of Nature: FAQs*, CMTY. ENV'T LEGAL DEF. FUND, https://celdf.org/rights-of-nature/faqs/ (last visited Jan. 9, 2023).

[102] EARTH L. CTR. & INT'L RIVERS, UNIVERSAL DECLARATION OF THE RIGHTS OF RIVERS 5 (2020), https://static1.squarespace.com/static/55914fd1e4b01fb0b851a814/t/5fb2a147e72ae95178 67f45e/1605542218936/UDRR_Nov+2020+Final.pdf.

This movement is in a nascent stage but is not unprecedented. In 2008, Ecuador became the first country to formally recognize and implement the rights of nature; Ecuador's constitution states: "Nature . . . where life is reproduced and occurs, has the right to integral respect for its existence and for the maintenance and regeneration of its life cycles, structure, functions and evolutionary processes. All persons, communities, peoples, and nations can call upon public authorities to enforce the Rights of Nature." And in 2017, the New Zealand Parliament recognized the personhood of the Whanganui River, the culmination of a decades-long conflict with native tribes.[103] The Maori people consider the river sacred, but it had suffered water quality degradation from farming and hydropower operations.[104] The act in question appointed two guardians of the river, one to represent the native Māori people and the other to represent the government. [105]

Parts of the United States have responded as well. In 2010, Pittsburgh, Pennsylvania, passed an ordinance recognizing the rights of nature as part of a ban on shale gas drilling and fracking. In 2019, Toledo, Ohio, adopted the Lake Erie Bill of Rights (giving lake rights of its own) in response to toxic algae blooms that shut down city water.[106] However, the bill was declared invalid a year later after a farmer challenged the law on grounds that it made him vulnerable to "massive liability" for fertilizing his fields because he couldn't be sure how much would run off into the lake. The state of Ohio joined the suit, claiming that the city infringed on its environmental regulatory authority.[107]

Legal actions based on the rights of nature have been largely symbolic.[108] In Ecuador, the Vilcabamba River won a lawsuit against a construction company for dumping construction rubble into the river.[109] Yet there was no enforcement of the judgment, and the practice continued.[110] In the United States, the Colorado River filed suit against the state of Colorado, seeking recognition of its legal personhood and rights; plaintiffs voluntarily dismissed the action after the state moved to dismiss on jurisdictional grounds.[111]

In Colombia, plaintiffs sued the Ministry of the Environment, saying that their fundamental rights to a healthy environment, life, health, food, and water were threatened by

---

[103] Julia Hollingsworth, *This River in New Zealand Is Legally a Person. Here's How It Happened*, CNN (Dec. 11, 2020, 9:43 PM), https://www.cnn.com/2020/12/11/asia/whanganui-river-new-zealand-intl-hnk-dst/index.html.

[104] Jeremy Lurgio, *Saving the Whanganui: Can Personhood Rescue a River?*, GUARDIAN (Nov. 29, 2019, 2:00 PM), https://www.theguardian.com/world/2019/nov/30/saving-the-whanganui-can-personhood-rescue-a-river.

[105] *Id.*; Te Awa Tupua (Whanganui River Claims Settlement) Act 2017, Mar. 20, 2017, https://www.legislation.govt.nz/act/public/2017/0007/latest/whole.html#DLM6830861.

[106] LAKE ERIE BILL OF RIGHTS, https://www.utoledo.edu/law/academics/ligl/pdf/2019/Lake-Erie-Bill-of-Rights-GLWC-2019.pdf; Sigal Samuel, *Lake Erie Now Has Legal Rights, Just Like You*, Vox (Feb. 26, 2019, 11:00 PM), https://www.vox.com/future-perfect/2019/2/26/18241904/lake-erie-legal-rights-personhood-nature-environment-toledo-ohio.

[107] Nicole Pallotta, *Federal Judge Strikes Down 'Lake Erie Bill of Rights,'* ANIMAL LEGAL DEF. FUND (May 4, 2020), https://aldf.org/article/federal-judge-strikes-down-lake-erie-bill-of-rights/.

[108] Tiffany Challe, *supra* note 100.

[109] *Id.*

[110] *Id.*

[111] Colo. River Ecosystem v. Colorado, No. 1:17-cv-02316 (D. Colo.).

climate change and the government's failure to reduce deforestation in the Amazon.[112] The Colombian Supreme Court recognized rights of the Amazon and ordered the government to develop and implement action plans to halt deforestation.[113] A similar suit was filed in Peru, and a decision is pending.[114]

While this is an interesting area of emerging concern, there remain many questions about whether and how the rights of nature movement will gain a toehold. For example, how will courts measure damages? And could a river's guardian be responsible if it floods and causes damage?[115] These questions and more will need answers in the coming years.

Key Takeaways

- This is a rapidly evolving and important area.
- Investors and shareholders are increasingly focused on environmental issues that extend beyond climate risk—including biodiversity, animal welfare, plastics, and water issues.
- Companies may want to consider their policies and practices, set goals and advance initiatives that encourage innovation in sustainable business practices, and utilize metrics and targets to evaluate their progress.
- Companies with a credible path towards achieving set goals will likely be better positioned to respond to, and potentially avoid, confrontation with activist shareholders.
- There are existing and developing frameworks that ESG practitioners should consider when evaluating a business's disclosure obligations and natural capital-related risks and opportunities, including, among others, the anticipated TNFD.

[112] Tiffany Challe, *supra* note 100.

[113] *Id.*

[114] *Id.*

[115] *Id.*

9

Green Marketing Claims and Communications: Charting a Course through Choppy Waters

Sarah Grey and Brian D. Israel

I. Introduction

Given the increased interest in ESG in recent years, focus has intensified on how companies present "green" or environmentally friendly marketing claims and communications. This chapter summarizes the United States and select international regulatory authorities related to environmental marketing claims and provides suggestions on how to mitigate risks of false or misleading environmental marketing claims. First, in the United States, the Federal Trade Commission (FTC) regulates environmental marketing claims pursuant to Section 5(a) of the Federal Trade Commission Act (the "FTC Act"). The FTC promulgates the Green Guides, a nonbinding administrative guidance, that applies to environmental marketing claims generally as well as particular types of claims, such as those related to carbon offsets and renewable energy. As discussed in greater detail below, the FTC has enforced the Green Guides sporadically depending on the administration; however, it has consistently targeted "degradability," "ozone-safe and ozone-friendly," "recyclable," and general "environmentally friendly" claims. Below, we address the FTC's views on how marketers must substantiate environmental marketing claims to avoid committing deceptive practices.

Second, the chapter addresses a variety of international laws and regulatory authorities relevant to environmental marketing claims, including those in the European Union, the Netherlands, and the United Kingdom. In general, international authorities suggest a high degree of caution when making claims about a product's lifecycle emissions, carbon neutrality, and company-wide commitments to sustainability and/or "climate-friendliness."

In light of interest from regulators and other stakeholders in ensuring the public is not misled by green marketing claims, companies should thoroughly vet any such claims and communications and proceed cautiously, taking into account the laws, regulations, and precedents (both court and administrative) in relevant jurisdictions. We discuss several practical guidelines for consideration in Section III below.

II. U.S. Authority: Focus on the Federal Trade Commission's Regulation of Environmental Marketing Claims

Section 5(a) of the FTC Act prohibits "unfair or deceptive acts or practices in or affecting commerce."[1] An act or practice is unfair if it causes or is likely to cause "substantial injury" to consumers which is not reasonably avoided by consumers and is not outweighed by countervailing benefits to consumers or to competition.[2] An act or practice is deceptive if it involves a material representation, omission, or practice that is likely to mislead a consumer acting reasonably in the circumstances.[3]

A. The Green Guides

In 1992, the FTC issued its Use of Environmental Marketing Claims ("Green Guides") as an industry guide for environmental marketing.[4] Revised most recently in 2012, the Green Guides provide both general principles and specific illustrations to help marketers avoid unfair or deceptive environmental claims under Section 5(a).[5] The FTC intends to refresh the Green Guides in coming months.[6]

In terms of scope, the Green Guides apply broadly to "claims about the environmental attributes of a product, package, or service in connection with the marketing, offering for sale, or sale of such item or service to individuals."[7] In addition, the Green Guides "apply to environmental claims in labeling, advertising, promotional materials, and all other forms of marketing in any medium, whether asserted directly or by implication, through words, symbols, logos, depictions, product brand names, or any other means."[8] Establishing compliance

---

[1] 15 U.S.C. § 45(a).

[2] 15 U.S.C. § 45(n).

[3] *See* Policy Statement on Deception, 103 F.T.C. 174, 175 (1984) (appended to Cliffdale Assocs. Inc., 103 F.T.C. 110 (1984)) (hereinafter Deception Statement).

[4] *See* Guides for the Use of Environmental Marketing Claims, 77 Fed. Reg. 62122, 62122 (Oct. 11, 2012) (to be codified at 16 C.F.R. pt. 260).

[5] 16 C.F.R. § 260.2.

[6] *See* Regulatory Review Schedule, 86 Fed. Reg. 35239 (July 2, 2021).

[7] 16 C.F.R. § 260.1(c).

[8] 16 C.F.R. § 260.1(d).

with the Green Guides can be difficult given that much of the guidance is general. Some of the guidance, however, is more specific, such as the guidance regarding offsets.

The Green Guides do not carry the force of law, nor do they preempt federal, state, or local laws.[9] As such, while compliance with the Green Guides may provide a safe harbor from FTC prosecution, compliance will not preclude prosecution under certain state or local regulations for deceptive marketing practices.[10]

California, for instance, generally maintains that compliance with the Green Guides is a defense to a charge of deceptive environmental marketing.[11] However, California has also promulgated its own more rigorous standards applicable to marketers who make general "environmentally friendly" claims.[12] Among other requirements, marketers must maintain written records supporting the validity of such representations,[13] and this information must be furnished to any member of the public if requested.[14] Additionally, advertisers must comply with California's specific provisions related to "compostable," "biodegradable," or "decomposable" claims.[15]

B. The Federal Trade Commission's Enforcement and Adjudication Process

The FTC may challenge unfair or deceptive practices through administrative adjudication, initiated by filing a complaint against the marketer or by filing an action in federal court, as addressed below.[16] Once the FTC has issued its complaint, the marketer can elect to settle the charges. If the marketer agrees to settle, it may then sign a consent agreement, consent to entry of a final order, and waive all right to judicial review.[17] If, however, the marketer contests the charges, then the complaint is adjudicated before an administrative law judge pursuant to the FTC's Rules of Practice.[18] Where the FTC finds through adjudication that a practice violates Section 5(a) of the FTC Act, it must rely on a federal district court to obtain civil penalties and injunctive relief and to secure consumer redress for violations.[19] Stipulated final orders have the force of law when approved and signed by a district court judge.[20]

---

[9] 16 C.F.R. § 260.1(b).

[10] *See id.*

[11] Cal. Bus. & Prof. Code § 17580(a)(5).

[12] Cal. Bus. & Prof. Code § 17580.

[13] Cal. Bus. & Prof. Code § 17580(a).

[14] Cal. Bus. & Prof. Code § 17580(b).

[15] Cal. Pub. Res. Code § 42357.

[16] 15 U.S.C. § 43.

[17] *See A Brief Overview of the Federal Trade Commission's Investigative, Law Enforcement, and Rulemaking Authority*, Federal Trade Comission (FTC) (May 2021), www.ftc.gov/about-ftc/what-we-do/enforcement-authority.

[18] *Id.*

[19] *Id.*

[20] *Id.*

In the environmental context, the FTC often reaches consent agreements or settlements rather than proceeding with adjudication.[21] In these circumstances, the FTC issues press releases and Federal Register notices containing analysis to aid public comment. While helpful to understand the types of environmental claims that the FTC finds deceptive, these press releases and Federal Register notices provide scant insights into the legal analysis that the FTC applies in determining when to pursue, and how to resolve, enforcement actions.

C. Enforcement Trends

The FTC's enforcement of the Green Guides historically has been sporadic and dependent on changes in administration.[22] When it first issued the Green Guides in 1992, the FTC pursued claims aggressively.[23] However, under the George W. Bush administration, the FTC did not initiate a single action under the Green Guides.[24] In 2009, the FTC recommitted to enforcing the Green Guides.[25]

To date, most FTC enforcement actions have concerned "biodegradability," "recyclability," "ozone-safe or ozone-friendly," and general "environmentally friendly" claims made in product advertisements.[26]

FTC enforcement has historically not focused on general business-wide green marketing theories. In March 2021, three environmental groups—Global Witness, Greenpeace USA, and Earthworks—filed a complaint with the FTC against Chevron for allegedly misleading consumers about the "green" nature of its operations.[27]

The environmental groups contend that Chevron's media campaigns—including its "ever-cleaner energy" pledge and "higher returns, lower carbon" strategy—represent deceptive green marketing in light of Chevron's significant contribution to petroleum production.[28]

---

[21] *See, e.g.*, Decision and Order, ICP Construction, Inc., FTC Docket No. C-4648 (April 27, 2018) www.ftc.gov/system/files/documents/cases/1623081_c-4648_icp_decision_and_order.pdf.

[22] *See* Perrin Cooke, *Green Guide Gaps: Expanding FTC Authority over Low-Carbon Marketing Claims*, 39 Colum. J. Env't L. 105, 125 (2014).

[23] *Id.*

[24] *Id.* at 126.

[25] *Id.*

[26] *See e.g.*, *In re* First Brands Corp., No. 902 3113, 1991 WL 639959 (F.T.C. Sept. 10, 1991) (FTC targeted a trash bag manufacturer for misrepresenting that its plastic trash bags were degradable when the product was only degradable in specialized composting environments rather than traditional landfills); *In re* AJM Packaging Corp., 118 F.T.C. 56 (1994) (manufacturer of plastic products agreed to cease representing products as "recyclable" given the lack of qualifying recycling facilities available to consumers); Proposed Agreement Containing Consent Order, *In re* Am. Plastic Lumber, Inc., FTC File No. 1323200 (June 19, 2014), https://www.ftc.gov/system/files/documents/cases/140619aplorder.pdf (lumber company agreed to consent order where it overstated the percentage of recycled materials in its plastic products); Press Release, FTC, Paint Companies Settle FTC Charges that They Misled Consumers; Claimed Products Are Emission- and VOC-free and Safe for Babies and Other Sensitive Populations (July 11, 2017), www.ftc.gov/news-events/press-releases/2017/07/paint-companies-settle-ftc-charges-they-misled-consumers-claimed.

[27] *See* Press Release, Earthworks, Accountability Groups File First of Its Kind FTC Complaint Against Chevron for Misleading Consumers on Climate Action (Mar. 16, 2021), https://earthworks.org/media-releases/accountability-groups-file-first-of-its-kind-ftc-complaint-against-chevron-for-misleading-consumers-on-climate-action.

[28] *See* Press Release, Greenpeace, Greenpeace Jointly Files FTC Complaint Against Chevron (Mar. 16, 2021), www.greenpeace.org/usa/news/greenpeace-jointly-files-ftc-complaint-against-chevron.

The complaint alleges that Chevron's social media promotions, television advertisements, and digital ads violated the Green Guides in the following ways:

1. Statements implied that Chevron's business operations do not harm, or even help, the environment despite Chevron's role in oil spills and natural disasters;
2. Chevron asserted that they produce "ever-cleaner" or "clean" energy while spending less than 0.2 percent of capital expenditures on renewable energy sources;
3. Chevron misrepresented the benefits of "biomethane" as a "renewable natural gas;" and
4. Chevron misled consumers with "deceptive jargon" such as "reducing emissions intensity" while they nonetheless continued to increase its oil and gas production.[29]

Finally, because complaints, like the one filed against Chevron, and any corresponding FTC investigation are usually confidential, the contours governing acceptable company-wide sustainability marketing practices in this context are uncertain. Moreover, the complaint against Chevron is just one example of how parties, including state actors, have pursued these types of claims, with litigation under a variety of state and federal theories (nuisance, tort, etc.) another avenue.[30] However, companies can still rely on general principles, guidelines for particular environmental marketing claims, and FTC enforcement actions under the Green Guides as guidance for best practices for product marketing.

D. The "Green Guides": General and Particular Compliance Principles

The Green Guides provide both general principles applicable to all environmental marketing and specialized guidance tailored to particular types of environmental claims. In terms of general principles, the Green Guides outline four standards that apply to all environmental claims. Specifically, environmental claims should:

1. Be clear, prominent, and understandable;
2. Distinguish between benefits of the product, packaging, or service;
3. Not overstate, either directly or by implication, negligible environmental benefits; and
4. Substantiate the basis of a comparison, in the case of comparative claims.[31]

In addition to these general principles, the Green Guides also include specific guidance for general environmental benefit claims and 13 particular environmental marketing claims, namely (1) carbon offsets; (2) certifications and seals of approval; (3) compostable; (4) degradable; (5) free of; (6) non-toxic; (7) ozone-safe and ozone-friendly; (8) recyclable;

---

[29] *Id.*

[30] *See, e.g.*, District of Columbia v. Exxon Mobil Corp., No. 22-7163 (D.C. Cir.).

[31] 16 C.F.R. §§ 260.3(a)–(d).

(9) recycled content; (10) refillable; (11) made with renewable energy; (12) made with renewable materials; and (13) source reduction claims.[32]

In the sections that follow, we discuss the guidance for general environmental claims as well as the specific guidance for claims related to carbon offsets and renewable energy.

1. *General Environmental Benefit Claims*

The "general environmental benefit claims" section of the Green Guides addresses broad marketing claims, such as a product being "eco-friendly" or "green."[33] Under this section, it is "deceptive to misrepresent, directly or by implication, that a package, product, or service offers a general environmental benefit."[34] This section warns against making broad, unqualified claims because they are difficult—if not impossible—to substantiate.[35]

Instead, marketers should "use clear and prominent qualifying language that limits the claim to its specific benefit."[36] If a qualified claim still conveys that a product has an overall environmental benefit, then marketers should also analyze the "trade-offs resulting from the benefit(s) to determine if they can substantiate this claim."[37] Moreover, even if a marketer qualifies and substantiates a general environmental claim, the claim is still problematic if the context of the advertisement nonetheless implies a deceptive environmental claim.[38]

The FTC has consistently challenged general "environmentally friendly" or "environmentally safe" claims.[39]

More recently, in 2016, Volkswagen settled charges with the FTC, the U.S. Department of Justice, and the State of California for its "Clean Diesel" advertising campaign.[40] In a complaint filed in the Northern District of California, the FTC alleged that Volkswagen's seven-year "Clean Diesel" ad campaign violated Section 5(a) of the FTC Act because it falsely marketed its diesel vehicles as environmentally friendly.[41] In truth, the cars had illegal defeat devices designed to mask elevated emissions during testing.[42]

---

[32] *See* 16 C.F.R. §§ 260.4–260.17.

[33] 16 C.F.R. § 260.4.

[34] 16 C.F.R. § 260.4(a).

[35] 16 C.F.R. § 260.4(b).

[36] 16 C.F.R. § 260.4(c).

[37] *Id.*

[38] 16 C.F.R. § 260.4(d).

[39] *See, e.g.*, In re Mr. Coffee, Inc., 117 F.T.C. 156, 158 (1994) (coffee filter manufacturer disseminated false and misleading claims that coffee filters were chlorine-free when, in truth, filters still contained elemental chlorine and generated harmful byproducts).

[40] *See* Partial Stipulated Order for Permanent Injunction and Monetary Judgment, FTC v. Volkswagen Grp. of Am., Inc., No. 3:16-01534 (N.D. Cal. Oct. 25, 2016), https://www.ftc.gov/system/files/documents/cases/2104_-_final_signed_ftc_order.pdf.

[41] *See* Press Release, FTC, FTC Charges Volkswagen Deceived Consumers with Its "Clean Diesel" Campaign (Mar. 29, 2016), www.ftc.gov/news-events/press-releases/2016/03/ftc-charges-volkswagen-deceived-consumers-its-clean-diesel.

[42] *Id.*

The FTC complaint outlined that Volkswagen marketed its diesel vehicles as low-emission, environmentally friendly, emissions-compliant, and likely to maintain a high resale value.[43] In addition, Volkswagen purposefully targeted eco-conscious consumers.[44] Volkswagen promoted these "clean" vehicles through high-profile marketing campaigns, including "Super Bowl ads, online social media campaigns, and print advertising."[45] Specifically, Volkswagen's promotional materials represented that the vehicles reduce nitrogen oxides (NO_x) emissions by 90 percent and have fewer NO_x emissions than gasoline-powered cars.[46] In reality, however, the FTC found (based on the investigations conducted by the EPA and the California Air Resources Board) that these vehicles emitted up to 4,000 percent *more* than the legal limit of NO_x.[47]

In two related settlements (involving marketing but also several other substantive claims by the United States and California), Volkswagen agreed to spend up to $14.7 billion by offering consumers buyback and lease termination options.[48] The company also agreed to spend $4.7 billion to mitigate pollution caused by these vehicles and to invest in green technology.[49]

2. *Carbon Offsets Claims*

FTC enforcement actions have not yet focused directly on claims related to carbon offsets. As such, the illustrations from the Green Guides represent the best authority on the subject. The Green Guides establish three principles governing carbon offsets claims.[50]

First, "given the complexities of carbon offsets, sellers should employ competent and reliable scientific accounting methods to properly quantify claimed emission reductions and to ensure they do not sell the same reduction more than one time."[51]

Second, according to the FTC, "it is deceptive to misrepresent, directly or by implication, that a carbon offset represents emission reductions that have already occurred or will occur in the immediate future."[52] Instead, to avoid deception, marketers should "clearly and prominently disclose if the carbon offset represents emission reductions that will not occur for two years or longer."[53] As an example of a deceptive claim, the Green Guides describe website content inviting consumers to purchase offsets to "neutralize the carbon emissions from your

---

[43] *Id.*

[44] *Id.*

[45] *Id.*

[46] *Id.*

[47] *Id.*

[48] *See* Press Release, FTC, Volkswagen to Spend up to $14.7 Billion to Settle Allegations of Cheating Emissions Tests and Deceiving Customers on 2.0 Liter Diesel Vehicles (June 28, 2016), www.ftc.gov/news-events/press-releases/2016/06/volkswagen-spend-147-billion-settle-allegations-cheating.

[49] *Id.*

[50] 16 C.F.R. § 260.5.

[51] 16 C.F.R. § 260.5(a).

[52] 16 C.F.R. § 260.5(b).

[53] *Id.*

flight."[54] In reality, the proceeds would fund projects that would not reduce greenhouse gas emissions for at least two years.[55] Accordingly, the language is deceptive.[56] However, the language would be permissible if it added a qualification stating that the projects would begin to reduce emissions in two years.[57]

Third, according to the FTC, "it is deceptive to claim, directly or by implication, that a carbon offset represents an emission reduction if the reduction, or the activity that caused the reduction, was required by law."[58] For example, it would be deceptive to claim that a product will "offset 'dirty' driving habits" where the offset involves methane capture at a landfill and state law already requires such methane capture.[59]

3. *Renewable Energy Claims*

Like with carbon offsets claims, FTC enforcement actions have not yet addressed renewable energy claims. Instead, the Green Guides offer four principles and examples for permissive renewable energy claims.[60]

First, marketers should not misrepresent that a product or package is made with renewable energy or that a service uses renewable energy.[61] Specifically, marketers should not make unqualified renewable energy claims, either directly or by implication, if fossil fuels or electricity derived from fossil fuels are used to manufacture *any* part of the advertised item or used to power *any* part of the advertised service—unless the marketer has matched nonrenewable energy use with renewable energy certificates.[62] For example, it is deceptive for an advertiser to promote a clothing line as "made with wind power" when the marketer buys wind energy for only 50 percent of the energy it uses to make the clothing.[63] This claim would be permissible if the marketer qualified that "we purchase wind energy for half of our manufacturing facilities."[64]

Second, the Green Guides emphasize that marketers should have substantiation for all express and reasonably implied claims involving renewable energy because consumers tend to interpret these claims differently than intended.[65] Primarily, a marketer should specify the sources of its renewable energy (e.g., wind, solar, or a mix) to minimize the risk of deception.[66]

---

[54] 16 C.F.R. § 260.5.

[55] *Id.*

[56] *Id.*

[57] *Id.*

[58] 16 C.F.R. § 260.5(c).

[59] 16 C.F.R. § 260.5.

[60] *See* 16 C.F.R. § 260.15.

[61] 16 C.F.R. § 260.15(a).

[62] *Id.*

[63] 16 C.F.R. § 260.15.

[64] *Id.*

[65] 16 C.F.R. § 260.15(b).

[66] *Id.*

Third, according to the FTC, it is deceptive for a marketer to make unqualified "made with renewable energy" claims unless virtually all of the significant manufacturing processes involved in making the product are powered with renewable energy (or nonrenewable energy matched by renewable energy certificates).[67] If not, the marketer should "clearly and prominently specify the percentage of renewable energy" that powered the significant manufacturing processes involved.[68] For example, it is not deceptive for a company to advertise that a product is "assembled using renewable energy" if it powers the assembly line process entirely with renewable energy.[69]

Fourth, if a marketer generates renewable electricity but sells the electricity as renewable energy certificates, it is deceptive for the marketer to represent that it uses renewable energy.[70] For an advertisement to be permitted in these circumstances, it would need to specify that the entity generates renewable energy but sells all of it to others.[71]

In conclusion, while compliance with the Green Guides is not a guaranteed safe harbor defense, the Green Guides provide several principles for environmental marketers to minimize the risk of FTC enforcement actions.

E. "Substantiation" of Environmental Claims

As discussed above, the Green Guides define a deceptive environmental marketing claim as "a representation, omission, or practice" that is "likely to mislead consumers acting reasonably under the circumstances and is material to the consumers' decision."[72] To determine whether an advertisement is deceptive, the FTC conducts a three-step inquiry considering (1) what claims, express and implied, the advertisement conveys; (2) whether those claims are false, misleading, or unsubstantiated; and (3) whether the claims are material to prospective consumers.[73] This section addresses the second prong of the inquiry.

1. *Marketers must substantiate all environmental claims, express and implied, that an advertisement conveys to reasonable consumers*

The Green Guides require environmental marketers to substantiate all claims.[74] Proper substantiation means that an advertiser ensures that all reasonable interpretations of claims are truthful, not misleading, and supported by a reasonable basis before they make such claims.[75] While advertisers must substantiate express and implied claims, they do not need to

[67] 16 C.F.R. § 260.15(c).

[68] *Id.*

[69] *Id.*

[70] 16 C.F.R. § 260.15(d).

[71] *Id.*

[72] 16 C.F.R. § 260.2; *see* Deception Statement, *supra* note 3, at 175.

[73] POM Wonderful v. FTC, 777 F.3d 478, 490 (D.C. Cir. 2015).

[74] 16 C.F.R. § 260.2.

[75] *Id.*; *see* FTC Policy Statement Regarding Advertising Substantiation, appended to Thompson Med. Co., 104 F.T.C. 648, 839 (1984).

substantiate purely subjective "puffing"—or "claims not capable of measurement or which consumers would not take seriously."[76]

The FTC engages in a two-step inquiry to determine whether a challenged environmental claim lacks substantiation and is thus false or misleading: (1) it determines the required level of substantiation needed to support the claim; and (2) it asks whether the defendant possessed that level of substantiation.[77] Extrinsic evidence, such as expert testimony, may be useful to determine the required level and adequacy of substantiation a marketer possesses.[78] In *ECM BioFilms*, the FTC issued a final order finding that a plastics manufacturing company committed unlawful deceptive marketing practices by disseminating false, misleading, and unsubstantiated claims related to the biodegradability properties of its plastics additive.[79] The key selling point of the plastics additive was its putative ability to accelerate the biodegradation of plastics.[80] On its website and through promotional materials, the company represented its products as "biodegradable," "biodegradable in a landfill," and "biodegradable in some period greater than a year."[81] The FTC concluded that ECM disseminated the following problematic claims: ECM plastics are fully biodegradable in landfills in nine months to five years; they will completely decompose within a reasonably short period of time (e.g., within five years, including in a landfill); and that scientific tests prove ECM's efficacy claims.[82]

Similarly, the FTC's 2019 action, *Lights of America, Inc.*, discusses inadequate substantiation.[83] In *Lights of America*, the FTC sued a lightbulb manufacturing company for misrepresenting the light output and life expectancy of its LED lightbulbs.[84] Because the company made claims using specific facts and figures, a "high level of substantiation, such as scientific or engineering tests" was required.[85] There, the company did not meet this substantiation burden because none of the LED testing data it offered supported its lifetime claims.[86] In fact, its own internal testing corroborated that its lifetime claims were false.[87] Moreover, even if a test had supported the lifetime claims for one type of lamp, the court reasoned this

---

[76] *In re* Bristol-Myers Co., 102 F.T.C. 21, 321 (1983).

[77] Opinion at 40, ECM BioFilms, Inc., FTC Docket No. 9358 (Oct. 19, 2015), www.ftc.gov/system/files/documents/public_statements/819651/151019ecmbiofilmsopinioncomm.pdf.

[78] *See id.* at 39.

[79] *Id.* at 1–2.

[80] *Id.* at 3.

[81] *Id.* at 1.

[82] *Id.* at 37.

[83] *See* Findings of Fact and Conclusions of Law, FTC v. Lights of Am., Inc., No. 8:10-cv-01333-JVS-MLG (C.D. Cal. Sept. 17, 2013), www.ftc.gov/system/files/documents/cases/130917lightsfindings.pdf.

[84] *Id.* at 2.

[85] *Id.* at 93.

[86] *Id.* at 94.

[87] *Id.* at 99.

test would not represent proper substantiation for other types of lamps.[88] For disseminating false and unsubstantiated claims, the company was ordered to pay $21 million to the FTC for consumer redress.

The Green Guides state that environmental marketing claims usually require "competent and reliable scientific evidence."[89] The Green Guides define this standard as "tests, analyses, research, or studies that have been conducted and evaluated in an objective manner by qualified persons and are generally accepted in the profession to yield accurate and reliable results."[90] Furthermore, "such evidence should be sufficient in quality and quantity based on standards generally accepted in the relevant scientific field, when considered in light of the entire body of relevant and reliable scientific evidence, to substantiate that each of its marketing claims is true."[91] Competent and reliable scientific evidence does *not* include anecdotal evidence from customers, newspaper or magazine articles, sales materials from the manufacturer, nor low return rate or money-back guarantees.[92]

2. *The FTC determines adequacy of substantiation on a claim-by-claim basis*

Once the required level of substantiation is determined, the FTC next assesses whether the marketer possesses those levels of substantiation.[93] The marketer "must have had some recognizable substantiation for the representation *prior* to making it in the advertisement."[94] Defendants have the burden of establishing what substantiation they relied on for their product claims.[95] The FTC engages in a detailed analysis of extrinsic evidence, including scientific studies and expert testimony, to determine whether the marketer possessed adequate substantiation.[96]

F. Beyond the Regulatory Context: Litigation

Outside of the regulatory context, governmental entities are bringing green marketing claims under state consumer protection statutes.[97]

[88] *Id.* at 98.

[89] 16 C.F.R. § 260.2.

[90] *Id.*

[91] *Id.*

[92] *See* FTC, ADVERTISING SUBSTANTIATION PRINCIPLES, www.ftc.gov/sites/default/files/attachments/training-materials/substantiation.pdf.

[93] *Id.* at 43.

[94] FTC v. Direct Mktg. Concepts, Inc., 569 F. Supp. 2d 285, 298 (D. Mass. 2009) (emphasis added).

[95] *Id.*

[96] *See ECM BioFilms*, *supra* note 77, at 44–49.

[97] *See e.g.*, Complaint, City of New York v. Exxon Mobil Corp., No. 1:21-cv-04807 (S.D.N.Y. May 28, 2021); Complaint, Commonwealth v. Exxon Mobil Corp., No. 19-cv-03333 (Mass. Super. Ct. Oct. 24, 2019).

In addition to this litigation, California public officials have a history of enforcing green marketing claims under that state's laws that incorporate the Green Guides as well as additional, more recent green marketing claim laws such as Senate Bill 243 enacted in October 2021. That law prohibits the use of symbols or other claims suggesting recyclability, including the "chasing arrows symbol," on any product or packaging failing to meet California's recyclability criteria, which are set forth in the statute.[98] The display of the chasing arrows symbol or other symbol or statement on a product that is not recyclable is deemed a deceptive or misleading claim under the Environmental Marketing Claims Act.

In recent years, California district attorneys have brought actions and achieved settlements from a variety of companies. In 2021, the Sonoma County District Attorney along with 22 other district attorneys' offices in California, resolved green marketing cases with Chewy, Inc., PetSmart, LLC, Petco Animal Supplies, Inc., and Target Corporation based on allegations the companies sold dog waste bags and other plastic products such as bowls and brushes to California residents that were labeled as "eco-friendly" and "biodegradable" but did not meet those standards.[99] In addition, in 2018, the Monterey County District Attorney, with 22 other district attorneys, announced a $1.512 million settlement in a case against Amazon, alleging Amazon deceived consumers by advertising plastic products as "biodegradable" and "compostable."[100]

California has been a predominant venue for consumer claims regarding alleged ESG misrepresentations due to the perception that its laws are consumer-friendly.[101] Traditionally, actions brought under the state's consumer protection statutes focused on false or misleading statements such as "100% natural" or "organic."[102] In recent years, however, California consumer class actions have focused on a variety of other marketing terms, such as "sustainably sourced" (chocolate products),[103] "recyclable" (single-serve plastic coffee pods),[104] "100%

---

[98] *See* Cal. Pub. Res. Code § 42355.51.

[99] Press Release, Sonoma Cnty. Dist. Att'y, District Attorney Jill Ravitch Announces Greenwashing Settlements with Chewy, Petco, PetSmart, and Target (Aug. 11, 2021), https://da.sonomacounty.ca.gov/da-announces-greenwashing-settlements-with-chewy-petco-petsmart-and-target.

[100] Meegan Brooks & Anthony Anscombe, *Navigating FTC Guidance and Green Marketing Litigation*, Bloomberg L. (Oct. 2019), https://www.steptoe.com/a/web/195909/NavigatingFTCGuidance.pdf.

[101] David Hackett et al., *Growing ESG Risks: The Rise of Litigation*, 50 Env't L. Rep. (Env't L. Inst.) 10849, 10850 (2020).

[102] *Id.* at 10851.

[103] *See* Walker v. Nestle USA, Inc., No. 3:19-cv-723-L-BGS, 2020 WL3317194, at *1 (S.D. Cal. June 17, 2020). In this case, the plaintiff has alleged the labels of "UTZ Certified" and "Sustainably Sourced" on the defendant's chocolate product packaging are misrepresentations along with claims that the products "[s]upport farmers" and "help improve the lives of cocoa farmers." The plaintiff alleged she bought the product in reliance on the social and environmental benefits and such labels are deceptive since the defendant allegedly sources its cocoa from West African cocoa plantations that rely on child labor and child slave labor, contribute to deforestation, and use other practices harmful to the environment.

[104] *See* Smith v. Keurig Green Mountain, Inc., 393 F. Supp. 3d 837, 841 (N.D. Cal. 2019).

recyclable" (single-use water bottles),[105] and "reef friendly" (sunscreen),[106] to name a few.[107] The cases have sometimes been successful. For example, in *Smith v. Keurig Green Mountain, Inc.*, the court in 2019 denied a motion to dismiss the putative class action alleging that "recyclable" single-serve plastic coffee pods were mislabeled.[108] In February 2022, Keurig agreed to pay $10 million and update labeling on its single-serve coffee pod to end the class action.[109] (The "sustainably sourced" chocolate products, "100% recyclable" water bottles, and "reef friendly" sunscreen cases are still ongoing.[110])

III. International Authorities

Below we briefly summarize a variety of authorities in international jurisdictions that address deceptive marketing claims that may be applied in the environmental context, and certain international authorities that directly address such claims, similar to the Green Guides in the United States. We address authorities first in the European Union (EU), followed by the Netherlands, and then the United Kingdom (UK), and learnings to be gleaned from enforcement of environmental marketing laws in those jurisdictions, where available.

A. European Union

The overarching EU authority prohibiting unfair commercial practices, including misleading actions and omissions of commercial claims, is Directive 2005/29/EC, the Unfair Commercial Practices Directive (UCPD). Guidance issued by the European Commission pursuant to this directive directly addresses environmental marketing claims (the "UCPD Guidance").[111]

---

[105] *See* Complaint, Sierra Club v. Coca-Cola Co., No. 4:21-cv-04644, 2021 WL 2459172 (N.D. Cal. June 16, 2021). In *Sierra Club v. Coca-Cola Co.*, Sierra Club sued Coca-Cola Company and Blue-Triton Brands, Inc. (formerly known as Nestle Waters North America, Inc.) for allegedly unlawful, unfair, and deceptive business practices under California state law with respect to the advertising, marketing, and sale of water bottled in single-use plastic bottles labeled "100% Recyclable."

[106] *See* White v. Kroger Co., No. 21-cv-08004-RS, 2022 WL 888657, at *2 (N.D. Cal. Mar. 25, 2022). In *White v. Kroger Co.*, the court denied a motion to dismiss a putative class action where plaintiff alleged sunscreen products sold by defendant Kroger Co. under its "house brand" are misleadingly labeled "reef friendly" when they contain ingredients with the potential to damage reefs. The court noted that while California statutes and FTC's Green Guides do not specifically list "reef friendly" as a prohibited term, the statutes expressly extend to "environmentally friendly" and "any other like term." The plaintiff brought claims under California Unfair Competition Law, California False Advertising Law, and California Consumers Legal Remedies Act, as well as breach of implied warranty and unjust enrichment.

[107] *White v. Kroger Co.*, 2022 WL 888657, at *2.

[108] *Keurig Green Mountain, Inc.*, 393 F. Supp. 3d at 841.

[109] Morgan Conley, *Keurig to Pay $10M, Edit K-Cup Labels to End False Ad Row*, Law360 (Feb. 25, 2022, 5:13 PM).

[110] Walker v. Nestle USA, Inc., No. 3:19-cv-723-L-DEB, 2022 U.S. Dist. LEXIS 56178 (S.D. Cal. Mar. 28, 2022); Walker v. Nestle USA, Inc., No. 3:19-cv-723-L-BGS, 2020 WL 3317194 at *1 (S.D. Cal. June 17, 2020); *White v. Kroger Co.*, 2022 WL 888657, at *2; *Sierra Club v. Coca-Cola Co.*, 2021 WL 2459172. *But see* White v. Kroger Co., No. 21-cv-08004-RS, 2022 U.S. Dist. LEXIS 104231 (N.D. Cal. June 10, 2022) (granting manufacturer's motion for summary judgment because the manufacturer was not the manufacturer of the products purchased by the plaintiff).

[111] *See Commission Staff Working Document on Guidance on the Implementation/Application of Directive 2005/29/EC on Unfair Commercial Practices*, at 1, COM (2016) 320 final (May 25, 2016).

Specifically, the guidance suggests two main principles: First, "traders must present their green claims in a clear, specific, accurate and unambiguous manner, to ensure that consumers are not misle[d]."[112] Second, "traders must have the evidence to support their claims and be ready to provide it to competent enforcement authorities in an understandable way if the claim is challenged."[113] As a general matter, "[e]nvironmental claims can be misleading if they are based on vague and general statements of environmental benefits such as 'environmentally friendly', 'green', 'nature's friend', 'ecological', 'sustainable', 'environmentally correct', 'climate friendly', or 'gentle on the environment'."[114] General statements are less likely to be misleading when paired with prominent specifications or explanatory statements on the product's environmental impact.[115] Such claims are potentially deceptive if they would lead an average consumer to make a transaction decision she otherwise would not have made.[116] The UCPD Guidance provides as an example of a misleading claim one that highlights only an aspect of a product's lifecycle impacts, rather than a holistic approach that explains the product's overall environmental impact.[117]

The European Commission recently focused specifically on green marketing in its screening of websites to identify breaches of EU consumer laws.[118] The 2021 analysis studied environmental claims from various industries and found that "in 42% of cases authorities had reason to believe that the claim may be false or deceptive and could therefore potentially amount to an unfair commercial practice under the Unfair Commercial Practices Directive (UCPD)."[119] Marketers may accordingly expect increased scrutiny of environmental claims moving forward.

B. The Netherlands

The Netherlands Authority for Consumers and Markets (ACM)—which is tasked with competition oversight, enforcement of consumer protection laws, and regulation of the telecommunication, postal services, transport, healthcare, and energy industries—recently promulgated specific guidelines relevant to environmental marketing claims regarding carbon neutrality as well as sustainability more broadly (the "Sustainability Guidelines" or "Guidelines"). As such, the ACM provides more specific guidance than many international jurisdictions.[120] Given

---

[112] *Id.* at 97 (emphasis omitted).

[113] *Id.*

[114] *Id.* at 99 (emphasis omitted).

[115] *Id.* at 101.

[116] *Id.*

[117] *Id.* at 100.

[118] *See* European Commission Press Release IP/21/269, Screening of Websites for 'Greenwashing': Half of Green Claims Lack Evidence (Jan. 28, 2021), https://ec.europa.eu/commission/presscorner/detail/en/ip_21_269.

[119] *Id.*

[120] *See* Autoriteit Consument & Markt, Guidelines Sustainability Claims (2021), www.acm.nl/sites/default/files/documents/guidelines-suistainability-claims.pdf.

the Sustainability Guidelines' recent (2021) promulgation, we are not aware of enforcement actions involving alleged violations.

The Sustainability Guidelines specify that marketers must make sustainability benefits of their products clear and substantiate those claims with up-to-date facts.[121] For example, the Guidelines state that the claim "carbon neutral" can only be made if a calculation has been made of the total emissions of greenhouse gases produced by the product, and the total emissions are zero.[122] Marketers must disclose where offsets are used to achieve carbon neutrality, including the "key aspects of the CO_2-compensation scheme."[123]

Additionally, the Sustainability Guidelines draw distinctions between product-specific sustainability claims and those of a company or brand.[124] It instructs companies to "distinguish between information about the sustainability efforts of the company (or parts thereof) and the specific information about the benefits of a product." The Guidelines go on to state that "[y]ou cannot use any claims about the company to make a product seem sustainable or the other way around."[125]

Further, according to the Sustainability Guidelines, claims about the sustainability efforts of the entire company must be "proportional to the actual sustainability efforts and impact on human rights, animal rights and the environment," and companies should be careful not to "exaggerate" such efforts.[126]

C. The United Kingdom

Similar to the Netherlands, the UK has guidance specific to environmental claims (the "UK Guidance").[127] The UK Guidance requires that carbon neutrality claims must be clear regarding the nature of offsets involved in achieving neutrality: the business "should provide information about the scheme (which should be based on recognised standards and measurements, capable of objective verification). If not, consumers are liable to be misled into thinking the products or processes themselves generate no (or few) emissions, when this is unlikely to be the case."[128] Further, companies must provide an explanation of claims related to how, as a company, it is going green in order to avoid misleading consumers. For example, a company should provide "an explanation of the steps the company takes to buy or invest in renewable energy, or what it does to off-set its carbon footprint."[129]

---

121 *Id.* at 2.

122 *Id.* at 13.

123 *Id.* at 14.

124 *Id.* at 16.

125 *Id.*

126 *Id.*

127 *See* UK Competition and Markets Authority, CMA Guidance on Environmental Claims on Goods and Services: Helping Businesses Comply with Their Consumer Protection Law Obligations (2021) https://assets.publishing.service.gov.uk/government/uploads/system/uploads/attachment_data/file/1018820/Guidance_for_businesses_on_making_environmental_claims_.pdf.

128 *Id.* at § 3.73.

129 *Id.* at 43.

Beyond the UK Guidance, the UK's Advertising Standards Authority (ASA) has codified rules regarding nonbroadcast advertising, sales, and direct and promotional marketing that may be relevant.[130] For example, with respect to claims related to products' lifecycle, marketers "must base environmental claims on the full life cycle of the advertised product, unless the marketing communication states otherwise, and must make clear the limits of the life cycle. . . . Marketers must ensure claims that are based on only part of the advertised product's life cycle do not mislead consumers about the product's total environmental impact."[131]

Environmental organizations may bring claims related to violations of the ASA's rules, or the agency may initiate action independently. In a recent action, an organization called Biofuelwatch challenged whether certain claims made by Haven Power were misleading, including the claim that the majority of the electricity it supplies "produces 86% less carbon than coal-generated energy."[132] Biofuelwatch alleged this claim was misleading because the calculation methodology was disputed by some within the scientific community; however, the ASA found that the methodology used "was consistent with the UK's existing methodology for accounting for carbon emissions in the energy sector and . . . therefore considered it was legitimate for the claim to be made on that basis."[133] Further, given the specialized knowledge of those who likely engaged with the ad, e.g., "business users, either energy managers, specialist energy brokers or energy analysts," the ASA determined that "much of its audience would have a specialist knowledge of the energy sector and were likely to understand the methodology which underpinned the claim."[134] Finally, environmental organizations may also bring complaints before the UK's National Contact Point related to deceptive advertising.

Key Takeaways

The regulatory enforcement and litigation trends around green marketing claims in recent years show no signs of abating, particularly (as addressed in other chapters) as ESG continues to be a focal point within companies, and among legislators and regulators. Companies should carefully consider the following questions to minimize risk of green marketing or deceptive practices claims:

- ***Ambiguity is not necessarily helpful***—General or vague statements of environmental benefits are frequently viewed by government authorities as more likely to be deceptive or misleading.
- ***Substantiation is critical***—With regard to climate-related claims in particular, the government is likely to require robust scientific proof of the accuracy of any claims, including reliable accounting methodologies for any GHG assertions. A company

[130] *See generally Rule 11, Environmental Claims*, UK Advertising Standards Authority (ASA), www.asa.org.uk/type/non_broadcast/code_section/11.html (last visited Apr. 17, 2023).

[131] *Id.* at Rule 11.4.

[132] *See ASA Ruling on Haven Power Ltd*, ASA (Feb. 24, 2021), www.asa.org.uk/rulings/haven-power-ltd-a19-569987-haven-power-ltd.html.

[133] *Id.*

[134] *Id.*

would be well-served to address several questions related to substantiation, including the following: What is the nature of the evidence supporting this claim? Is the audience appropriately understanding the context of the claim and any limitations on the evidence supporting it? Will the evidence supporting the claim go stale, or will the claim need to be updated as facts change? As a general matter, the more technical the claim, the more detailed the evidence supporting it must be.

- ***Legalistic precision is not sufficient***—Truthfulness and substantiation requirements will increasingly be applied to any reasonable *inferences* of environmental marketing claims, even if those inferences are beyond the express statements made.
- ***Omissions can also be deceptive***—Failure to include important context (such as a separate legal requirement) can trigger an assertion that an environmental claim is misleading.
- ***Attention to business-wide activities***—While government enforcement to date has focused on claims related to specific products, it may be worth evaluating methods of articulating claims to ensure congruence with the company's overall business.
- ***Understand the jurisdiction***—As discussed above, there are varying requirements, case precedents, and guidance documents depending on the jurisdiction. Companies need to know the precise laws, regulations, guidance, and precedents that are potentially applicable to the claims.
- ***Ensure consistency***—Across similar communications, companies will want to ensure that the environmental attributes of its products or services, or of the company in general, are appropriately consistent. For example, does an advertisement discuss a particular product one way and the ESG report explains its environmental attributes in a different way?

With thoughtful inquiry and consideration—as well as precise awareness of the applicable regulations or guidance—companies may mitigate risks of deceptive environmental marketing claims.

PART III

Social: Finding a Path for Complex Social Issues

10

Key Principles Related to Diversity, Equity, and Inclusion

Amber Hay, Janice Bashford, Ebony Slaughter-Johnson, Vincent Brown, and Jocelyn Porter

I. Introduction

Diversity, Equity, and Inclusion (DE&I) may be regarded as a concept that has become part of the lexicon utilized by corporations and human resources professionals intent on reshaping workplace culture, but DE&I is rooted in the civil rights movement of the 1960s.[1] According to the Greenlining Institute, DE&I principles have gone through several iterations. In the early years, efforts to integrate workplaces, schools, and communities pursuant to the civil rights laws led to an emphasis on tolerance.[2] From the mid-1970s into the 1990s, the focus shifted to championing diversity to ensure that leadership in both the public and private sectors captured the diversity of the nation.[3]

This chapter defines "diversity" as differences among people with respect to race, gender, sexual orientation, and other identities.[4] "Equity" practices acknowledge the existence of institutionalized disparities and seek to correct these disparities through the intentional distribution of resources.[5] "Inclusion" refers to the practice of welcoming and

---

[1] Danielle Beavers, The Greenlining Inst., Diversity, Equity and Inclusion Framework: Reclaiming Diversity, Equity and Inclusion for Racial Justice 4 (2018), http://greenlining.org/wp-content/uploads/2018/03/DEI-Framework.pdf.

[2] *Id.*

[3] *Id.*

[4] *See, e.g.*, Exec. Order No. 14035, 86 C.F.R. 34593 (2021).

[5] *Id.*

valuing those with diverse identities.[6] It is important to note that the precise definition may vary depending on the context and the authority. In order to precisely advise your client, please be mindful of how the jurisdiction in which they operate defines these terms.[7]

As the activism of the original civil rights movement was defined by bus boycotts and sit-ins, so too has economic pressure served as a crucial tool in this more modern movement in support of corporate consciousness. Consumers are leveraging their purchasing power to pressure companies into building a diverse workforce and embracing inclusive practices.[8] The success of this tactic is perhaps best illustrated by the public response in the wake of the tragic murder of George Floyd.

The murder of George Floyd,[9] which was recorded by a pedestrian on a smartphone and soon circulated among millions via social media, gave rise to the largest mass protest movement in American history.[10] Millions across the country, and millions more around the world, called for reforms to American policing.[11] As these calls were directed towards policymakers at the local, state, and federal level, they were heard by corporate America.[12] As the public demanded police accountability,[13] corporations sought to hold themselves accountable.

II. Corporate Diversity, Equity, and Inclusion Practices

Many of the world's most high-profile corporations across a variety of industries have adopted DE&I practices. In the "Black Lives Matter" era, corporations have promised to promote wealth attainment within communities of color, advance small-business initiatives led by entrepreneurs of color, and increase financial investment in low-resourced communities and communities of color.[14] Introspection has also inspired corporations to train employees on the importance of diversity and equity and construct career pipelines for diverse talent within their ranks.

---

[6] *Id.*

[7] No state statutory definition of "diversity" appeared in our research. However, as the legal landscape is frequently changing, it is important to perform due diligence.

[8] Tamara Charm et al., *Rise of the Inclusive, Sustainable Consumers*, McKinsey & Co. (Apr. 28, 2022), https://www.mckinsey.com/featured-insights/sustainable-inclusive-growth/future-of-america/rise-of-the-inclusive-sustainable-consumers.

[9] Derrick Bryson Taylor, *George Floyd Protests: A Timeline*, N.Y. Times (Nov. 5, 2021), https://www.nytimes.com/article/george-floyd-protests-timeline.html.

[10] Larry Buchanan et al., *Black Lives Matter May Be the Largest Movement in U.S. History*, N.Y. Times (July 3, 2020), https://www.nytimes.com/interactive/2020/07/03/us/george-floyd-protests-crowd-size.html.

[11] *Protests Across the Globe After George Floyd's Death*, CNN (June 13, 2020), https://www.cnn.com/2020/06/06/world/gallery/intl-george-floyd-protests/index.html.

[12] Tracy Jan et al., *As Big Corporations Say 'Black Lives Matter,' Their Track Records Raise Skepticism*, Wash. Post (June 13, 2020), https://www.washingtonpost.com/business/2020/06/13/after-years-marginalizing-black-employees-customers-corporate-america-says-black-lives-matter/.

[13] Buchanan, *supra* note 10.

[14] Tracy Jan et al., *Corporate America's $50 Billion Promise*, Wash. Post (Aug. 23, 2021), https://www.washingtonpost.com/business/interactive/2021/george-floyd-corporate-america-racial-justice/.

Apple has created a career pipeline to bring students of color that graduate from historically Black colleges and universities into its ranks by offering an internship program.[15] The technology giant also purports to train its hiring professionals "in inclusive hiring practices" and to "buil[d] inclusion and diversity measures into [its] candidate assessment framework."[16] The Walt Disney Company, a power player in the global entertainment industry, supports the Black Talent Network, the Women's Talent Network for Asian American Pacific Islanders, and the Women's Talent Network for Latina Talent "[t]o attract and retain diverse talent at the executive level."[17] An assortment of affinity groups and "Business Employee Resource Groups" are designed to advance the corporation's efforts to foster a "culture of belonging."[18]

Where two of the banks that would come to comprise JPMorgan Chase & Co. once contributed to the slave trade,[19] the global financial services provider has now committed itself to investing $30 billion in the financial health and prosperity of communities of color.[20] That financial investment has been coupled with initiatives to empower entrepreneurs from historically marginalized communities with information and skills to foster success.[21] Offices within JPMorgan Chase & Co., like the Office of Asian & Pacific Islander Affairs and the Office of LGBTQ+ Affairs, endeavor to advocate for stakeholders and partners from these communities.[22] Elsewhere in the financial services industry, BlackRock, Inc., has made a series of tangible commitments to promote its workforce diversity.[23] For example, the company has pledged to increase the representation of women among its senior leadership to 32.5 percent by 2024.[24]

III. Legal and Political Challenges to Diversity, Equity, and Inclusion Efforts

A California law that required publicly-traded corporations to fill at least one seat on their boards of directors with a member of an underrepresented community was struck down in

[15] *Inclusion & Diversity: Partnering to Challenge Systemic Bias*, APPLE, https://www.apple.com/diversity/ (last visited Jan. 11, 2023).

[16] *Inclusion & Diversity: Hiring Practices with Shared Goals in Mind*, APPLE, https://www.apple.com/diversity/ (last visited Jan. 11, 2023).

[17] *People: Talent Development*, THE WALT DISNEY CO., https://impact.disney.com/diversity-inclusion/people/ (last visited Jan. 11, 2023).

[18] *Culture: Our Commitment to a Culture of Belonging*, THE WALT DISNEY CO., https://impact.disney.com/diversity-inclusion/culture/ (last visited Jan. 11, 2023).

[19] *JPMorgan: Predecessors Linked to Slavery*, NBC NEWS (Jan. 21, 2005), https://www.nbcnews.com/id/wbna6851727.

[20] *Racial Equity Commitment*, JPMORGAN CHASE & CO., https://www.jpmorganchase.com/impact/racialequity (last visited Jan. 11, 2023).

[21] *Id.*

[22] *People: Centers of Excellence*, JPMORGAN CHASE & CO., https://www.jpmorganchase.com/impact/people (last visited Jan. 11, 2023).

[23] *Diversity, Equity and Inclusion*, BLACKROCK, INC., https://www.blackrock.com/corporate/about-us/diversity-equity-and-inclusion (last visited Jan. 11, 2023).

[24] *Id.*

April 2022.[25] The California Superior Court agreed with the plaintiff, the conservative nonprofit Judicial Watch,[26] that the law attempted to implement an impermissible quota system in violation of the California constitution.[27]

Other states require companies to make board diversity disclosures without entering into the constitutionally thorny territory of mandated diversity quotas.[28] Washington requires public companies incorporated in the state to maintain "a gender-diverse board of directors," or a board in which women represent at least 25 percent of seated directors "for at least two hundred seventy days of the fiscal year preceding the applicable annual meeting of shareholders."[29] Publicly-traded companies with "principal executive office[s] located in Illinois" must clarify the demographic diversity of directors and executive officers, describe their efforts to "promot[e] diversity, equity, and inclusion" within their leadership structure, and detail their processes for selecting directors and executive officers.[30] The latter disclosure must include an explanation of how demographic diversity is considered in the selection processes.[31] The University of Illinois Systems will subsequently analyze this information in a public report.[32] New York requires "domestic corporation[s]" and "foreign corporation[s] authorized to do business" in New York to disclose the gender diversity of their boards of directors.[33] Maryland similarly instructs publicly-traded companies and nonprofits incorporated in the state with operating budgets of more than $5 million to disclose the number of women that sit on their boards of directors.[34]

While some states are working to entrench DE&I principles, and other ESG principles, into corporate governance, other Republican-led states are working to dismantle them. Missouri Attorney General Eric Schmitt and Louisiana Attorney General Jeff Landry are leading more than a dozen other states' attorneys general in investigating Morningstar, Inc.[35] The coalition has accused the financial services firm, which guides investors in understanding the

---

[25] Assemb. 979, 2019-2020 Reg. Sess. (Cal. 2020), https://leginfo.legislature.ca.gov/faces/billTextClient.xhtml?bill_id=201920200AB979 (the enacted legislation was invalidated by *Crest v. Padilla*, No. 20 STCV 37513, 2022 WL 1073294 (Cal. Super. Ct. Apr. 1, 2022)).

[26] Valerie Richardson, *California Judge Strikes Down Law Requiring Racial, LGBTQ Diversity on Corporate Boards*, WASH. TIMES (Apr. 4, 2022), https://www.washingtontimes.com/news/2022/apr/4/california-judge-strikes-down-law-requiring-racial/.

[27] *Crest v. Padilla*, 2022 WL 1073294.

[28] *Id.*

[29] WASH. REV. CODE § 23B.08.120(1).

[30] 805 ILL. COMP. STAT. § 5/8.12(c).

[31] 805 ILL. COMP. STAT. § 5/8.12(c)(7)–(8).

[32] 805 ILL. COMP. STAT. § 5/8.12(d).

[33] N.Y. BUS. CORP. LAW § 408(1)(d).

[34] MD. CODE ANN., TAX-PROP. § 11-101(c)(2).

[35] Ross Kerber, *Exclusive: Missouri Attorney General Investigates Morningstar Over ESG Ratings*, REUTERS, Aug. 3, 2022, https://www.reuters.com/business/sustainable-business/exclusive-missouri-attorney-general-investigates-morningstar-over-esg-ratings-2022-08-03/; *see also 18 States Join Missouri Attorney General Investigation Over Morningstar ESG (2022)*, BALLOTPEDIA, https://ballotpedia.org/18_states_join_Missouri_Attorney_General_investigation_over_Morningstar_ESG_(2022).

ESG landscape, of violating consumer protection laws, including the Missouri Merchandising Practices Act.[36] Attorney General Schmitt additionally alleges the firm violated a Missouri law meant to shield Israel from critiques regarding its historic relationship with Palestine.[37] Eighteen Attorneys General separately charged BlackRock with improperly prioritizing promoting ESG principles ahead of client interests like generating profits.[38]

Attorney General Jeff Landry has doubled down on his hostility to ESG principles, issuing a legal guidance to Louisiana financial officials about the tendency of investment firms "to use money from public and state employee pension plans to push their own political agendas and force social change through use of ESG criteria."[39] BlackRock, Vanguard, and State Street are specifically alleged to have made ESG-conscious investments in violation of their duty of loyalty to their clients to disclose all material facts that guide their investment decision.[40] While Attorney General Landry affirmed that ESG-conscious investments are not inherently unlawful, he concluded the guidance with a warning: investment firms that pursue such investments "without full disclosure to their investor-clients" are in violation of Louisiana law, a promise of aggressive litigiousness on the part of the state.[41]

Some states have gone so far as to boycott financial services firms that embrace ESG principles. As of July 2022, West Virginia maintains a Restricted Financial Institutions List that identifies firms with which the state will not transact.[42] Goldman Sachs Group Inc., JPMorgan Chase & Co, Morgan Stanley, Wells Fargo & Co, and BlackRock are the first to be blacklisted for pursuing "written environmental or social policies categorically limiting commercial relations with energy companies engaged in certain coal mining, extraction or utilization activities, rather than considering the financial or risk profile for each company," in the words of West Virginia State Treasurer Riley Moore.[43] Texas took a similar approach, passing a law blacklisting financial services firms that "refus[e] to deal with . . . compan[ies] because the company . . . engages in the exploration, production, utilization, transportation, sale, or manufacturing of fossil fuel-based energy."[44] Texas Comptroller Glenn Hegar, whose office will maintain the blacklist of financial services firms that boycott the fossil fuel industry,

---

[36] Kerber, *supra* note 35.

[37] *Id.*

[38] Press Release, Off. of La. Att'y Gen., ESG Practices Conflicting with Louisiana Law, Attorney General Jeff Landry Issues Legal Guidance to State Retirement Systems, http://www.ag.state.la.us/Article/13066.

[39] Memorandum from Jeff Landry, Att'y Gen., La. to Hon. John M. Schroder, Treasurer, et al., at 1 (Aug. 30, 2022), http://www.ag.state.la.us/Files/Article/13066/Documents/2022.08.30-AGGuidanceonESG_Final.pdf.

[40] *Id.* at 2–4.

[41] *Id.* at 4.

[42] Jacob H. Hupart, *West Virginia Penalizes Major Companies for Embracing ESG Principles*, MINTZ (July 29, 2022), https://insights.mintz.com/post/102hty2/west-virginia-penalizes-major-companies-for-embracing-esg-principles.

[43] Press Release, W. Va. State Treasurer's Off., Treasurer Moore Publishes Restricted Financial Institution List (July 28, 2022), https://wvtreasury.com/About-The-Office/Press-Releases/ID/452/Treasurer-Moore-Publishes-Restricted Financial Institution List.

[44] Jacob H. Hupart, *Texas Identifies Financial Companies Targeted for Divestment Due to "Energy Boycott,"* MINTZ (Aug. 29, 2022), https://insights.mintz.com/post/102hvxz/texas-identifies-financial-companies-targeted-for-divestment-due-to-energy-boyco.

announced the first 10 designees in August 2022.[45] His announcement accompanied a denunciation of ESG-consciousness as having "produced an opaque and perverse system in which some financial companies no longer make decisions in the best interest of their shareholders or their clients, but instead use their financial clout to push a social and political agenda shrouded in secrecy."[46]

At the federal level, the U.S. Securities and Exchange Commission (SEC) has approved a rule by Nasdaq that would require impacted companies to make board diversity disclosures and "to have, or explain why they do not have, at least two diverse directors, including one who self-identifies as female and one who self-identifies as either an underrepresented minority[] or LGBTQ+."[47] The rule is scheduled to take effect within one year of the SEC's approval, but it faces an existential threat in the meantime.[48] Complaints from two conservative activist groups, the National Center for Public Policy Research and the Alliance for Fair Board Recruitment, have culminated in a case before the U.S. Court of Appeals for the Fifth Circuit that will determine the legality of the Nasdaq rule and set a precedent for other companies that may follow suit.[49]

Approval of the Nasdaq rule coincided with the release of a report by the SEC Asset Management Advisory Committee (AMAC) in July 2021 that scrutinized the diversity and inclusivity of the asset management industry.[50] Premised on what it described as the significant lack of diversity across the industry, the committee offered a series of recommendations to facilitate the level of transparency necessary to address these oversights.[51] These include imposing "enhanced" diversity disclosures on investment advisors and investment companies that mandate reporting their internal diversity data to the SEC.[52] Investment companies should be additionally required "to include disclosure on whether and to what extent the registrant's policies include diverse asset management firms in the pool of those considered and/or selected," according to AMAC.[53] Concern regarding the restrictive tendencies sometimes displayed by investment advisors prompted the committee to recommend the SEC to release

---

[45] Press Release, Tex. Comptroller of Pub. Accts., Texas Comptroller Glenn Hegar Announces List of Financial Companies that Boycott Energy Companies (Aug. 24, 2022), https://comptroller.texas.gov/about/media-center/news/20220824-texas-comptroller-glenn-hegar-announces-list-of-financial-companies-that-boycott-energy-companies-1661267815099.

[46] *Id.*

[47] *Nasdaq to Advance Diversity Through New Proposed Listing Requirements*, NASDAQ (Dec. 1, 2020), https://www.nasdaq.com/press-release/nasdaq-to-advance-diversity-through-new-proposed-listing-requirements-2020-12-01; *see also Statement on Nasdaq's Diversity Proposals – A Positive First Step for Investors*, U.S. Securities and Exchange Commission (SEC) (Aug. 6, 2021), https://www.sec.gov/news/public-statement/statement-nasdaq-diversity-080621.

[48] NASDAQ, *supra* note 47.

[49] Andrew Ramonas, *SEC's Board Diversity Drive Runs Risk of More Legal Challenges*, BLOOMBERG L. (Oct. 22, 2021), https://news.bloombergtax.com/securities-law/secs-board-diversity-drive-runs-risk-of-more-legal-challenges.

[50] SEC ASSET MGMT. ADVISORY COMM., REPORT AND RECOMMENDATIONS ON DIVERSITY AND INCLUSION IN THE ASSET MANAGEMENT INDUSTRY (2021), https://www.sec.gov/files/spotlight/amac/amac-report-recommendations-diversity-inclusion-asset-management-industry.pdf.

[51] *Id.* at 10–13.

[52] *Id.* at 10.

[53] *Id.*

guidance as to how fulfillment of fiduciary duties could be compatible with engaging asset management firms.[54] That guidance materialized in October 2022 when the SEC affirmed that investment advisors could offer counsel based on DE&I principles, provided that counsel also advances the "best interest of the client based on the client's objectives."[55]

According to its "Fall 2022 Unified Agenda of Regulatory and Deregulatory Actions,"[56] the SEC plans to follow AMAC's recommendation regarding diversity disclosures. A pending proposed rulemaking would "enhance registrant disclosures about the diversity of board members and nominees."[57] SEC Chair Gary Gensler described DE&I principles as essential to the SEC's mission to "protect investors" and nurture "fair markets," suggesting that the SEC may pursue additional rulemakings and actions to promote diversity in the financial services industry.[58]

Conservative politicians largely tend to disagree with Chair Gensler. Many argue that DE&I principles, and other ESG principles, create financial harm by distracting corporations from their obligations to their shareholders. Florida Governor Ron DeSantis is one of the more vocal opponents of DE&I and ESG principles. He championed the Stop the Wrongs to Our Kids and Employees (WOKE) Act,[59] which seeks to chill trainings and discussions related to DE&I in workplaces on the premise that these ideas have led to a "perversion of financial investment priorities."[60] Workplace activities that discuss the privileges that come with holding certain identities, engender feelings of "distress" and "guilt" for holding certain identities, and propose that American foundational "virtues" are tools of oppression, among other "concepts," constitute prohibited discrimination.[61]

A legal challenge mounted by a small coalition of Florida-based businesses has temporarily blocked the enforcement of the law as it pertains to the aforementioned workplace prohibitions.[62] Chief District Judge Mark Walker of the U.S. District Court for the Northern District of Florida agreed with the coalition, justifying his decision to impose a temporary injunction on the grounds that the law worked an unconstitutional burden on their First Amendment rights.[63] Moreover, he characterized several of the prohibited "concepts"

---

[54] *Id.* at 11–12.

[55] *Staff FAQ Relating to Investment Adviser Consideration of DEI Factors*, SEC, https://www.sec.gov/tm/staff-faq-relating-investment-adviser-consideration-dei-factors (Oct. 13, 2022).

[56] *Fall 2022 Unified Agenda of Regulatory and Deregulatory Actions*, Off. of Info. & Regul. Affs., Off. of Mgmt. & Budget, Exec. Off. of the President, https://www.reginfo.gov/public/do/eAgendaMain (last visited Jan. 12, 2023).

[57] *Securities and Exchange Commission (SEC): Corporate Board Diversity Proposed Rule*, Off. of Info. & Regul. Affs., Off. of Mgmt. & Budget, Exec. Off. of the President, https://www.reginfo.gov/public/do/eAgendaViewRule?pubId=202210&RIN=3235-AL91 (last visited Jan. 12, 2023).

[58] *A Mission for Inclusion: In Conversation with Gary Gensler*, SEC (Nov. 10, 2022), https://www.sec.gov/sec-stories/mission-inclusion-conversation-gary-gensler#bubble-1.

[59] 2022 Fla. Laws 72, http://laws.flrules.org/2022/72. The law is also known as the "Individual Freedom Act."

[60] Press Release, Fla. Governor Ron DeSantis, Governor Ron DeSantis Eliminates ESG Considerations from State Pension Investments (Aug. 23, 2022), https://flgov.com/2022/08/23/governor-ron-desantis-eliminates-esg-considerations-from-state-pension-investments/.

[61] Honeyfund.com, Inc. v. DeSantis, No. 4:22-cv-227, 2022 WL 3486962 (N.D. Fla. Aug. 18, 2022).

[62] *Id.*

[63] *Id.* at *15.

as "mired in obscurity" and "unintelligible."[64] The fate of this portion of the law rests in the hands of the U.S. Court of Appeals for the Eleventh Circuit now that Florida has filed a Notice of Appeal challenging the injunction.[65]

Although it represents an unprecedented attempt to regulate private workplaces, the "Stop WOKE Act" is part and parcel with other state-led efforts to limit discussions of DE&I principles in public forums. Texas, Oklahoma, Tennessee, Iowa, and Idaho have recently passed laws that prevent public schools from teaching critical race theory (CRT), a pedagogy most commonly taught in law schools that explores the ways in which the law reflects and perpetuates racism.[66] The aforementioned federal decision will likely give states pause before passing laws that mirror the "Stop WOKE Act," but the enthusiasm of states for anti-CRT laws suggests that efforts to regulate DE&I practices will continue.

Congressional Republicans took their cues from their state colleagues during the 117th Congress. Representative Chip Roy (R-TX) introduced the No ESG at TSP Act (H.R. 7896) to prevent the spread of ESG principles that "advance . . . woke racial and gender ideologies intent on dividing the republic," among other outrages.[67] Senator Pat Toomey (R-PA) used his powers as the ranking member of the Senate Committee on Banking, Housing, and Urban Affairs to quell federal efforts to promote DE&I initiatives, going so far as to launch an investigation into several of the Federal Reserve Banks for conducting DE&I research.[68] He and his colleague, House Committee on Financial Services Ranking Member Patrick McHenry (R-NC), decried efforts by federal regulators to promote corporate diversity as "mission creep" into the realm of social policy.[69]

Meanwhile, Democratic members of Congress largely supported DE&I initiatives throughout the 117th Congress. Democrats introduced the Improving Corporate Governance Through Diversity Act of 2021 (H.R. 1277/S. 374) and the Promoting Diversity and Inclusion in Banking Act of 2021 (H.R. 2516). Under their leadership, the House passed the Corporate Governance Improvement and Investor Protection Act (H.R. 1187).[70] House Committee on Financial Services Chairwoman Maxine Waters (D-CA) and Senate Committee on Banking, Housing, and Urban Affairs Chairman Sherrod Brown (D-OH) separately

---

[64] *Id.* at *12–13.

[65] Andrew Atterbury, *DeSantis Appeals Injunction Over Anti-'woke' Law*, PoliticoPRO (Sept. 19, 2022), https://subscriber.politicopro.com/article/2022/09/desantis-appeals-injunction-over-anti-woke-law-00057513.

[66] Char Adams et al., *Map: See Which States Have Passed Critical Race Theory Bills*, NBC News (June 17, 2021), https://www.nbcnews.com/news/nbcblk/map-see-which-states-have-passed-critical-race-theory-bills-n1271215.

[67] Press Release, Congressman Chip Roy, Rep. Roy Introduces Bill to Stop Taxpayer Dollars in Woke ESG Funds (May 27, 2022), https://roy.house.gov/media/press-releases/rep-roy-introduces-bill-stop-taxpayer-dollars-woke-esg-funds.

[68] Press Release, U.S. Senate Comm. on Banking, Hous., & Urb. Affs.-Minority, Toomey Launches Review of Mission Creep by Regional Federal Reserve Banks (Mar. 29, 2021), https://www.banking.senate.gov/newsroom/minority/toomey-launches-review-of-mission-creep-by-regional-federal-reserve-banks.

[69] *Id.*; *see* Press Release, U.S. House Fin. Servs. Comm.-Republicans, McHenry Statement on Updated SEC Guidance on Shareholder Proposals Regarding Social Issues (Nov. 3, 2021), https://republicans-financialservices.house.gov/news/documentsingle.aspx?DocumentID=408186.

[70] Corporate Governance Improvement and Investor Protection Act, H.R. 1187, 117th Cong. (2021).

cheered the SEC's approval of the aforementioned Nasdaq rule,[71] then joined forces in a May 2022 letter to Chair Gensler urging him to spearhead additional diversity reporting.[72] Seventeen Democratic Attorneys General issued a joint defense of the materiality of ESG factors to the investment decision-making process in a November 2022 letter to the leadership of the House Committee on Financial Services and the Senate Committee on Banking, Housing, and Urban Affairs.[73]

The debate surrounding the propriety of corporate activism generally shows no signs of abating. Only days into 2023, newly elected Speaker Kevin McCarthy (R-CA) used his first speech in the position during the 118th Congress to blast "woke indoctrination in our schools" to enthusiastic applause from the House Republican caucus, suggesting that scrutiny of all efforts to promote diversity and inclusivity will be a core component of the House Republican majority mission.[74] Kentucky State Treasurer Allison Ball similarly used the early days of the new year to place 11 corporations, including JPMorgan Chase & Co and BlackRock, on a blacklist for potential state divestment for allegedly eschewing investments in the fossil fuels industry.[75] Despite hostile rhetoric and threats from policymakers, corporate interest in DE&I principles is ongoing. AMC Entertainment Holdings, Inc., tapped two women, Denise "Dee" Clark and Keri Putnam, to serve on its board of directors.[76] Their terms began on January 1, 2023.[77]

Key Takeaways

Lawyers advising corporations that engage in DE&I practices should be aware that their clients may attract scrutiny because of such engagement, particularly from leaders in Republican-controlled states. Much of the scrutiny will be rhetorical in the form of disparaging letters or reproving statements during media appearances. Other actions by state leaders may be more impactful. Some may follow Florida's lead in passing laws designed to restrict the extent to

---

[71] Press Release, U.S. Senate Comm. on Banking, Hous., & Urb. Affs.-Majority, Brown Applauds SEC for Approving New Diversity Standards (Aug. 6, 2021), https://www.banking.senate.gov/newsroom/majority/brown-applauds-sec-for-approving-new-diversity-standards; *Waters Applauds SEC's Approval of a National Stock Exchange Rule to Require Diversity Data Reporting*, Just the Real News (Aug. 11, 2021), https://www.justtherealnews.com/congress/waters-applauds-secs-approval-of-a-national-stock-exchange-rule-to-require-diversity-data-reporting/.

[72] *Waters and Brown Urge SEC Chair Gensler to Require Data Reporting to Improve Future Rulemakings on Human Capital and Diversity Disclosure*, Just the Real News (May 24, 2022), https://www.justtherealnews.com/congress/waters-and-brown-urge-sec-chair-gensler-to-require-data-reporting-to-improve-future-rulemakings-on-human-capital-and-diversity-disclosure/.

[73] Letter from Seventeen Attorneys General to Congress (Nov. 21, 2022), https://oag.dc.gov/sites/default/files/2022-11/ESG%20Letter_Final_11.18.22.pdf.

[74] *California Republican Kevin McCarthy Delivers His Victory Speech After Being Elected as Speaker of the House* CSPAN (Jan. 7, 2023), https://www.c-span.org/video/?c5050186/california-republican-kevin-mccarthy-delivers-victory-speech-elected-speaker-house.

[75] Lauren Sforza, *Kentucky Treasurer Says 11 Banks Subject to Divestment Due to Energy Company 'Boycotts,'* Yahoo (Jan. 3, 2023), https://www.yahoo.com/entertainment/kentucky-treasurer-says-11-banks-200615315.html.

[76] *AMC Entertainment Holdings, Inc. Board of Directors Elects Denise "Dee" Clark and Keri Putnam to Serve as Directors of the Company, Effective January 1, 2023*, Yahoo (Dec. 29, 2022), https://finance.yahoo.com/news/amc-entertainment-holdings-inc-board-211000047.html.

[77] *Id.*

which corporations may engage in DE&I practices. Others may follow Kentucky's lead in imposing financial punishment on corporations with DE&I objectives.

Activities at the federal level may protect corporations on the receiving end of state backlash from some of the most adverse consequences. A law that cabins the First Amendment rights of corporations or employees will not pass constitutional muster. Federal regulators have seemingly endorsed the economic benefits of corporate DE&I practices and the legality of investments based on DE&I principles by recognizing their financial value to investors.

Congressional Republicans will join their state counterparts in scrutinizing corporations that engage in DE&I practices. Lawyers advising these clients should understand that the more high-profile they are, the more likely their senior leaders are to find themselves answering written requests for information from House Republicans and appearing before House committees. Lawyers should prepare their clients for the latter by ensuring they can speak to the corporation's diversity data, methods of incorporating DE&I principles into investment decisions, and the financial consequences of such methods. These hearings will presumably form the basis of anti-DE&I legislation, but lawyers should understand that this legislation has no political future. Democratic control of the Senate means that any hostile legislation that emerges from the House of Representatives will die in the upper chamber. By the same token, however, divided control of Congress means that any pro-DE&I legislations will similarly fail.

Despite the backlash, lawyers should recall several key points. First, their corporate clients are not outliers in adopting DE&I practices, as they join many of the profitable multinational corporations highlighted toward the beginning of this chapter. To attack your client's practices would undoubtedly require a politician to wage war on industry giants, which is antithetical to their political interests. Second, although state and federal case law with respect to impermissible DE&I practices is limited, precedent offers some analogous situations that lend insight as to how courts may regard certain efforts. Years before *Crest v. Padilla*, the Supreme Court suggested that the use of diversity quotas is constitutionally problematic in *Regents University of California v. Bakke*.[78] The Court held that the University of California's special admissions program, which set aside a certain number of seats in the medical school class for members of "disadvantaged" applicants, including those who were members of a minority group, violated the Equal Protection Clause.[79]

The Court's decision in *United Steelworkers of America, AFL-CIO-CLC v. Weber* somewhat nuances *Bakke* to suggest that quotas may be used to correct specific instances of institutionalized inequity. In *United Steelworkers of America, AFL-CIO-CLC v. Weber*, the Supreme Court upheld an affirmative action plan that reserved 50 percent of the positions in a craft-workers training program for Black workers.[80] As part of its analysis, the Court initially clarified that because the employer's plan was not "state action," the case did not present a violation of the Equal Protection Clause of the Fourteenth Amendment.[81] The court also

---

[78] *See, e.g.*, Regents of the Univ. of Cal. v. Bakke, 438 U.S. 265 (1978).

[79] *Id.* at 274-75, 319.

[80] United Steelworkers of America, AFL-CIO-CLC v. Weber, 443 U.S. 193 (1979).

[81] *Id.* at 200.

recognized that Congress did not intend to wholly prohibit private and voluntary affirmative action efforts as a method for resolving racial discrimination in employment when it passed the Civil Rights Act of 1964.[82] In affirming the affirmative action plan, the court emphasized that the plan was created to address historic discrimination that had shut out Black employees from the craft-workers position and did not "unnecessarily trammel the interests of the white employees."[83] The plan also was a temporary measure that would only be in place until the racial imbalance was remedied.[84]

Finally, even the Republican staff of the Senate Committee on Banking, Housing, and Urban Affairs had to admit that "[t]here is nothing wrong with activist investing,"[85] which is perhaps one of the most aggressive ways of promoting corporate activism. The greatest challenge to corporate clients that engage in DE&I practices is political interest at the state and federal level.

---

[82] *Id.* at 203-05.

[83] *Id.* at 208.

[84] *Id.* at 199.

[85] Minority Staff of the U.S. Senate Comm. on Banking, Hous., & Urb. Affs., The New Emperors: Responding to the Growing Influence of the Big Three Asset Managers 17 (2022), https://www.banking.senate.gov/imo/media/doc/the_new_emperors_responding_to_the_growing_influence_of_the_big_three_asset_managers.pdf.

11

Key Principles Related to Workforce Well-Being

Kathryn Geoffroy and Kaitlin Robinson

I. Human Capital Management

While much of the focus on ESG has been centered around climate risk and corporate diversity, human capital management (HCM) is rapidly becoming an important ESG issue. HCM refers generally to the view that workers are "assets" that are crucial to business performance and, accordingly, should be managed as carefully as physical and financial assets.[1] HCM is a broad concept that has been used to refer to elements of workforce well-being, including compensation and benefits, physical and mental health, and employee input (through labor organizations and otherwise).

HCM has taken on a more significant role in how investors view companies in recent years. In 2017, BlackRock CEO Larry Fink raised issues related to HCM in his open letter, asserting that companies "must improve their capacity for internal training and education to compete for talent in today's economy and fulfill their responsibilities to their employees" and "lend their voice to developing a more secure retirement system for all workers, including the millions of workers at smaller companies who are not covered by employer-provided plans."[2] More recently, as discussed below, the U.S. Department of Labor (DOL) and the U.S. Securities and Exchange Commission (SEC), have set forth important disclosure requirements related to human capital resources, including compensation and other benefits. This

[1] George S. Georgiev, *The Human Capital Management Movement in U.S. Corporate Law*, 95 TULANE L. REV. 639 (2021).

[2] Larry Fink, *Larry Fink's 2017 Letter to CEOs*, BLACKROCK, https://www.blackrock.com/corporate/investor-relations/2017-larry-fink-ceo-letter (last visited Mar. 20, 2023).

captures the broad array of issues affected by HCM, including mandatory disclosure and fair employment regimes, standard practices of companies regarding compensation practices, and voluntary ESG well-being activities and disclosures.

This chapter provides a summary of some primary elements of workforce well-being, including compensation and benefits, labor organizations, and mental and physical health. In addition, this chapter provides several practical considerations to help companies and other stakeholders navigate the rapidly evolving landscape related to human capital management.

II. The U.S. Securities and Exchange Commission's Human Capital Disclosure

For businesses required to make disclosures to the SEC, HCM is officially more than just a buzzword. In November 2020, the SEC changed its disclosure requirements to require registrants to provide "a description of the registrant's human capital resources, including in such description any human capital measures or objectives that management focuses on in managing the business, to the extent such disclosures would be material to an understanding of the registrant's business taken as a whole."[3] In enacting these disclosure requirements, the SEC noted that "in many cases, human capital disclosure is important information for investors" and that "[h]uman capital is a material resource for many companies and often is a focus of management, in varying ways, and an important driver of performance."[4] The current applicable rule requires, specifically, that registrants disclose the following:

> A description of the registrant's human capital resources, including the number of persons employed by the registrant, and any human capital measures or objectives that the registrant focuses on in managing the business (such as, depending on the nature of the registrant's business and workforce, measures or objectives that address the development, attraction and retention of personnel.[5]

This requirement underscores the significance of HCM in the current corporate landscape. In June 2022, the Working Group on Human Capital Accounting Disclosure submitted a petition for public rulemaking around HCM disclosures, specifically requesting that the SEC develop rules to require public companies to disclose "sufficient information to allow investors to assess the extent to which firms invest in their workforce."[6] This signals that the SEC may revisit the issue in 2023.

---

[3] Modernization of Regulation S-K Items 101, 103, and 105, Securities Release Act No. 10,825, Exchange Act Release No. 89,670, 85 Fed. Reg. 63726, 63737 (Oct. 8, 2020) (to be codified at 17 C.F.R. pts. 229, 239, 240); with the requirements set forth in 17 C.F.R. § 229.101(c)(2)(ii).

[4] *Id.* at 63739.

[5] 17 C.F.R. § 229.101(c)(2)(ii).

[6] Letter from the Working Grp. on Hum. Cap. Acct. Disclosure to Vanessa A. Countryman, Sec'y, SEC (June 7, 2022), https://www.sec.gov/rules/petitions/2022/petn4-787.pdf.

III. Compensation Issues

A. Compensation Considerations Generally

One key part of the HCM discussion is how employees are compensated. Compensation can serve many important functions for an employer, including helping an employer to recruit and retain key employees, incentivizing employees to meet financial and individual performance goals, and maintaining company culture and morale. Compensation packages for executives, in particular, are often also designed to align the management team's interests with those of shareholders.

Common forms of compensation include base salary or wages; bonuses, commissions, and other cash incentive compensation; and equity awards. The forms of compensation an employer elects to use vary based on many factors, such as market norms in the employer's industry, the developmental stage and size of the company, and the role of the employee within the employer's organization. For example, technology industry start-ups are much more likely to rely on stock option grants as a significant portion of incentive compensation for the employee population broadly because they provide a way for early-stage companies that are sometimes low on cash to incentivize early employees who are dedicated to the growth of the company.

In addition, the types of compensation vary in importance among different types of employees. Base salary or hourly wages are very important to hiring and retention for entry-level or lower-wage employees, while for more senior and management-level employees, equity awards or incentive bonuses may be a significantly larger percentage of total compensation. Individuals in sales roles often have lower base compensation, and a significant portion of their compensation is comprised of commissions that are based on the amount of business and sales that they bring in or retain. As discussed later in this chapter, with respect to benefits, employees increasingly consider whether employers offer medical benefits and match of 401(k) contributions when selecting an employer, while fewer employers provide traditional pension benefits.

Compensation packages are often designed to allow an employer to remain competitive, while also being tailored to issues specific to their employee population. However, as discussed below, the increasing focus on ESG has also elevated conversations about the incentives that compensation creates and has brought increased scrutiny on factors such as the disparity between executive and nonexecutive compensation. In addition, these concerns regarding income inequality have led to political movements pushing for employers to offer a "living wage," and bills in state and federal legislatures have proposed or adopted a $15 minimum wage.[7]

[7] The "Raise the Wage Act of 2021" was introduced and stalled in Congress. California and Washington, D.C., have a minimum wage that is $15 or higher (with exceptions), while Connecticut, Delaware, Florida, Hawaii, Illinois, Maryland, Massachusetts, New Jersey, Rhode Island, and Virginia are increasing minimum wages on an indexed basis and will reach $15 per hour or higher over the next few years.

B. Compensation for Executive Officers

When offering employment to executive officers, companies have historically focused on creating compensation structures that are competitive enough to attract and retain an executive while incentivizing the executive to focus on the growth and performance of the company. Typical executive compensation arrangements include larger base salary than nonexecutive employees, annual bonuses targeted to a percentage of base salary (tied to the achievement of performance metrics), equity grants (which may be time-based or may vest based on the achievement of performance metrics), or perquisites such as housing or car stipends or reimbursements. Executives may also participate in nonqualified deferred compensation plans, which provide deferred compensation to a select group of management or highly compensated employees.

Executive compensation packages are more likely to include severance and change in control arrangements. While companies may have standalone severance plans that cover the employee population generally, there are often unique arrangements for the chief executive officer and other executives. Severance arrangements are typically payable on a "good leaver" termination (a termination by the company without "cause" or a resignation by the executive for "good reason") and may include continuing base salary payments for a period of time that commonly ranges from six months to two years; payment of the employer portion of COBRA premiums; unpaid but earned bonus payments for the prior year; and prorated bonus payments for the portion of the year prior to termination. Executives may receive larger "double-trigger" severance payments or acceleration of vesting for equity if an executive's employment is terminated within a period following a change in control.

In recent years, there has been an increased focus on disparities between the compensation of executive officers and other employees. For public companies, that has resulted in a mandatory "pay ratio" disclosure,[8] which requires a tabular disclosure in proxy statements and other public filings with the SEC that calculates the ratio of the median of the annual total compensation of employees of the company (excluding the principal executive officer [usually the chief executive officer]) to the annual total compensation of the principal executive officer of the company. This allows a direct comparison between compensation for public company principal executive officers and their other employees, which may raise questions from employees, unions, or other stakeholders of the company. While higher executive packages are considered part of the cost of hiring and retaining a qualified executive, employees may see the disproportionate differences in these compensation packages as part of a broader issue regarding corporate priorities and income inequality.

There are also ongoing discussions about the incentives created by executive compensation. Companies are increasingly considering whether to incorporate ESG factors into the performance metrics for incentive compensation. Common arguments for including ESG-related considerations, especially HCM-related considerations such as diversity, equity, and inclusion metrics, include that they incentivize executives to consider the longer-term benefits associated with focusing on workforce well-being and sustainability, and that including the

[8] 17 C.F.R. § 229.402.

factors demonstrates a greater dedication to championing social issues that may be of concern to employees, consumers, shareholders, and investors. An August 2021 article from Aon plc. indicated that the use of these metrics in executive compensation is much more common in larger public companies, and that in fiscal year 2020, 57 percent of the S&P 500 companies had incorporated some ESG metrics in either short-term or long-term incentive plans, 40 percent of which "involve human capital management-related measurements, with the most prevalent in that group being diversity, equity and inclusion, followed by talent/development and turnover/retention."[9] This trend does not appear to be as prominent in smaller public companies or private companies.

C. General Public Company Compensation Considerations

Public companies have additional considerations in designing compensation structures because they are required to make disclosures regarding compensation practices in their annual public filings with the SEC, which provides investors, employees, and other stakeholders with the opportunity to review the company's practices. Private companies that go public, either through an initial public offering or through transactions with special purpose acquisition corporations (SPACs),[10] typically adjust their compensation practices in connection with going public, including adopting new equity incentive plans and formalizing some compensation practices.

Institutional investors and third-party proxy advisory services, such as Institutional Shareholder Services (ISS) and Glass Lewis, provide an extra layer of scrutiny regarding executive compensation arrangements, especially with respect to equity incentive plans and on "Say-on-Pay" issues discussed below.[11] Both entities have equity plan scorecards, which they have released publicly and which they use to assess a public company's equity incentive plans to advise investors regarding whether they should vote in favor of or against the approval of new plans or amendments to existing plans.

Public companies and their compensation committees should be aware that decisions they make regarding compensation, especially with respect to their executive officers, may need to be disclosed publicly. For that and other reasons, it is common for public companies

[9] Richard Harris et al., *As More Firms Add ESG Metrics to Executive Pay, Best Practices Are Emerging*, Aon plc (Aug. 2021), https://humancapital.aon.com/insights/articles/2021/as-more-firms-add-esg-metrics-to-executive-pay,-best-practices-are-emerging.

[10] Special purpose acquisition corporations (SPACs) are "blank check" companies that are established to acquire companies to take them public (known as "de-SPAC" deals) within a certain period of time following the establishment of the SPAC. Although transactions with SPACs have slowed recently, a June 2022 article in Bloomberg Law News reported a total of 373 de-SPAC deals that have closed since 2016, and additional 119 SPACs with pending announced deals. Grace Maral Burnett, *Analysis: Time Pressure Builds on De-SPAC Deals*, Bloomberg L. (June 10, 2022, 5:00 AM), https://news.bloomberglaw.com/bloomberg-law-analysis/analysis-time-pressure-builds-on-de-spac-deals.

[11] Copies of current ISS voting guidelines, which include guidelines that they use to assess compensation practices, can be found here: https://www.issgovernance.com/policy-gateway/2021-voting-policies/. Copies of current ISS U.S. voting guidelines and supplemental policies with respect to equity compensation and other executive compensation issues can be found here: https://www.glasslewis.com/wp-content/uploads/2021/11/US-Voting-Guidelines-US-GL-2022.pdf?hsCtaTracking=257fcf1c-f11e-4835-81a3-d13fbc7b1f4c%7C1dad2378-213f-45f6-8509-788274627609 and https://www.glasslewis.com/supplementary-guidance/.

to hire outside compensation consultants to advise the company's compensation committee in designing compensation structures and to assist with benchmarking compensation against the company's peers to ensure that they are consistent with market norms.

D. U.S. Securities and Exchange Commission Disclosures Regarding Compensation

SEC rules set forth the requirements for executive compensation disclosures for public companies.[12] The compensation disclosures typically are a significant portion of annual proxy statements (or other SEC filings requiring executive compensation disclosures).

Generally, the Summary Compensation Table requires a summary of the compensation received by the company's named executive officers in the prior three fiscal years, which includes base salary, bonuses, stock option awards, stock awards, nonequity incentive plan compensation, the change in pension value and nonqualified deferred compensation earnings, and all other compensation.[13] SEC rules also require disclosures for the grant of plan-based awards, outstanding equity awards at the fiscal year-end, options exercised and stock vested, pension benefits, nonqualified deferred compensation, and potential payments on a termination or change in control, as well as other narrative disclosures. Public companies that are not emerging growth companies, smaller reporting companies, or foreign private issuers are required to provide a narrative description in the Compensation Discussion and Analysis section of the material elements of the company's compensation for its named executive officers, including the objectives of compensation programs, what each element of compensation is designed to reward, and how the elements of the compensation structure fit into overall compensation objectives.[14]

Companies are required to conduct Say-on-Pay votes, which are nonbinding votes in which companies ask that shareholders approve the compensation for their executive officers.[15] This provides shareholders with the opportunity to express perspectives on how reasonable compensation packages are directly to the company. Shareholders vote on how frequently to hold Say-on-Pay votes, which must be held at least every three years. While Say-on-Pay votes are not binding, a public company that has failed a Say-on-Pay vote usually adjusts compensation packages, modifies performance metrics, or expands future compensation disclosures.

In August 2022, the SEC also adopted final rules that require new pay-versus-performance disclosures.[16] These disclosures must be included in applicable filings in fiscal years ending on or after December 16, 2022. The new disclosures are intended to show the

[12] 17 C.F.R. § 229.402.

[13] Emerging growth companies and smaller reporting companies have more limited disclosure requirements, in accordance with 17 C.F.R. § 229.402(l).

[14] 17 C.F.R. § 229.402(b).

[15] 15 U.S.C. § 78n–1.

[16] Pay Versus Performance, Exchange Act Release No. 95,607, 87 Fed. Reg. 55134 (Sept. 8, 2022) (to be codified at 17 C.F.R. pts. 229, 232, 240).

relationship between the compensation actually paid to the company's principal executive officer and the company's other named executive officers and the financial performance of the company, considering metrics such as the total shareholder return of the company, the total shareholder return of the company's peer group, the company's net income, and another company-selected measure. These new disclosures will be key for compensation committees to understand and to consider in deciding on compensation structures for the 2023 fiscal year and beyond.

IV. Welfare and Benefits Issues

A. Benefit Plans Generally

Another key consideration related to workplace well-being for employees is benefit plan offerings for employees. Which benefits an employer offers depends on the size of the employer, the number of employees, and the costs of coverage. Benefit plans generally fall within one of two categories: retirement benefits and health and welfare benefits. Benefit plans may be subject to various levels of regulation under laws such as the Employee Retirement Income Act of 1974 (ERISA), the Internal Revenue Code of 1986, and the Patient Protection and Affordable Care Act. Benefit plan structures are important to consider not only as recruitment and retention methods but also as ways to promote the well-being of employees.

Welfare benefits may either be fully insured (with an insurance company processing and paying claims, and the employer and employee paying premiums) or self-insured (with the employer providing health insurance coverage, and often purchasing stop-loss insurance coverage to cover some costs). Larger employers are more likely to have fully insured coverage for employees. Some smaller employers instead utilize the services of a professional employer organization (PEO) in order to provide welfare benefits to their employees without the administrative and compliance burden of providing welfare benefits on its own. PEOs are co-employers of the company's employees and often provide payroll services and sponsor benefit plans in which employers may participate.

Some common welfare benefit plans that an employer may provide to employees include medical insurance, dental insurance, vision insurance, life insurance, accidental death and dismemberment coverage, short-term disability, and long-term disability. Employers may also provide tax-incentivized arrangements such as health savings accounts paired with high-deductible health plans, health reimbursement arrangements, or flexible spending accounts.

Retirement plans are typically either "defined contribution" plans or "defined benefit" plans. Defined contribution plans are plans such as 401(k) plans or profit sharing plans, in which specified amounts are contributed to the plan on behalf of a participant—often including a "match" to employee contributions to encourage employees to save for their retirement—but no specific distributions are guaranteed in retirement. Defined benefit plans are plans such as traditional pension plans, in which specified amounts are expected to be received by participants in retirement. While some larger employers and public companies still sponsor and maintain defined benefit plans, in recent years they have become less common because defined contribution plans impose fewer obligations on employers with respect to the ongoing funding of the plans and plan administration.[17]

Employers who have union employees may also have obligations to contribute to "multiemployer pension plans." Multiemployer pension plans are plans in which all employers who have employees in the union and who have contribution obligations under the collective bargaining agreement contribute. Due to long-standing issues related to multiemployer pension plan funding, the American Rescue Plan Act of 2021 contained provisions that would allow certain financially troubled multiemployer pension plans to apply for financial assistance from the Pension Benefit Guaranty Corporation.

B. Retirement Plan Investments and ESG

As employees and other stakeholders become increasingly concerned about ESG issues, there has been much more focus on its impact in retirement plan investments. One issue that has arisen in the retirement plan context is whether plan fiduciaries, when selecting investment options for both self-directed and defined benefit retirement plans, should be permitted to select ESG-focused funds. Plan fiduciaries are subject to higher standards of fiduciary duty under ERISA.

DOL guidance has gone back and forth on this issue in recent years. In 2020, the DOL released final regulations which, among other things, required plan fiduciaries to select investments based solely on considerations of "pecuniary factors," or factors that are expected to have a material effect on risk and/or return of an investment.[18] The Biden administration then announced that it would not enforce these regulations, which it viewed as limiting the ability of plan fiduciaries to invest plan assets in ESG-focused funds.[19] In December 2022, the DOL released final regulations that would permit plan fiduciaries to consider ESG factors and select ESG-focused investment alternatives when discharging their duties of prudence and loyalty.[20] Among other changes, the regulations explicitly permit a prudent fiduciary to consider any factor material to the risk-return analysis, including ESG-related factors. However, fiduciaries would still not be permitted to sacrifice investment returns or take additional investment risk to promote benefits or goals unrelated to the interests of the participants and beneficiaries in their retirement income. These regulations continue to be a source of political

[17] The U.S. Bureau of Labor Statistics released data stating that in March 2019, only 12 percent of private industry employees participate in defined benefit pension plans, with only 62 percent of those plans being open plans to which ongoing contributions are made. In March 2009, 20 percent of private industry employees participated in defined benefit pension plans. *Employee Benefits Survey: What Statistics Does the BLS Provide on Frozen Defined Benefit Plans*, U.S. Bureau of Labor Stat., https://www.bls.gov/ebs/factsheets/defined-benefit-frozen-plans.htm (last visited Apr. 2, 2023).

[18] Financial Factors in Selecting Plan Investments, 85 Fed. Reg. 72846 (Nov. 13, 2020) (to be codified at 29 C.F.R. pts. 2509, 2550).

[19] Press Release, U.S. Department of Labor (DOL), US Department of Labor Releases Statement on Enforcement of Its Final Rules on ESG Investments, Proxy Voting by Employee Benefit Plans (Mar. 10, 2021), https://www.dol.gov/newsroom/releases/ebsa/ebsa20210310.

[20] Prudence and Loyalty in Selecting Plan Investments and Exercising Shareholder Rights, 87 Fed. Reg. 73822 (Dec. 1, 2022) (to be codified at 29 C.F.R. pt. 2550).

controversy; on January 26, 2022, a coalition of 24 states sued the DOL, seeking to stop the new 2022 final regulations from taking effect.[21]

C. Welfare Benefit Plans and Social Issues

Employees also increasingly expect employers to make decisions regarding which benefits they offer to employees in response to ongoing political and social changes. One key area relates to mental health and wellness benefits. In recent years, many employers have highlighted the benefits they provide with respect to mental health and employee wellness as a recruiting tool in an increasingly competitive labor market. Wellness programs and incentives for healthy choices can be an important benefit to employees, while also benefitting an employer financially by lowering health plan costs. Some employers considered or implemented increases to these benefits during the COVID-19 pandemic due to a combination of factors that include the transition for some employees to working remotely and broader mental health challenges caused by the pandemic. A survey performed by the Society for Human Resource Management (SHRM) in March 2021 of 578 employees found that 58 percent of workers felt exhausted when leaving work, 48 percent of workers felt depleted at the end of their workday, and 41 percent felt burned out from their work.[22]

The Kaiser Family Foundation 2021 Employer Health Benefits Survey, which surveyed 1,686 firms (including both public and private firms) and which was published November 10, 2021,[23] found that employers made changes as a result of the COVID-19 pandemic to increase access and support for the mental health of their employees. Sixteen percent of employers surveyed developed new resources, such as employee assistance programs, to support the mental health of their employees, and 31 percent of employers surveyed expanded the ways in which enrollees could get mental health or substance abuse services, such as through telemedicine. The survey also reported that 38 percent of smaller firms and 58 percent of larger firms provided or expanded online counseling services for emotional or financial distress, relationship issues, or other stressful situations.

In 2022, the U.S. Supreme Court ruled in *Dobbs v. Jackson Women's Health Organization*[24] to overturn *Roe v. Wade*, which allows states to prohibit or restrict abortion care. The public reaction from employers provides an example of how employers are increasingly expected, by employees and other stakeholders, to take positions that affect the health and welfare of portions of the employee population. Following the ruling, some employers announced travel reimbursement policies and other plan changes for employees and their dependents who travel to access abortion care in a state in which it would not be illegal or

[21] Complaint for Declaratory and Injunctive Relief, Utah v. Walsh, No. 2:23-cv-00016 (N.D. Tex. Jan. 26, 2022).

[22] Alexander Alonso, *Employers Expand Mental Wellness Support*, Society Human Resource Management (May 31, 2022), https://www.shrm.org/hr-today/news/hr-magazine/summer2022/pages/employers-expand-mental-wellness-support.aspx.

[23] *2021 Employer Health Benefits Survey*, Kaiser Fam. Found. (Nov. 10, 2021), https://www.kff.org/health-costs/report/2021-employer-health-benefits-survey/.

[24] Dobbs v. Jackson Women's Health Org., 142 S. Ct. 2228 (2022).

restricted, dealing with many complex legal and logistical issues. A Bloomberg Law article[25] mentioned that shareholders are "already asking for reports on the risks that the state-specific framework for reproductive health care may have on the company" and emphasized that this would be the subject of proxy shareholder proposals for public companies. While private companies do not have the same level of external pressure from third-party shareholders, and many have accordingly not made public statements regarding providing such benefits, there may still be internal pressure from employees to take a stance or offer benefits. Other benefits which are receiving similar attention in light of the *Dobbs* ruling include infertility benefits and benefits for transgender employees seeking gender reassignment treatment or hormone therapy.

V. Role of Compensation Committees

Typically, board-level compensation committees have been involved in executive compensation and retirement and equity compensation plans, but not as involved in welfare and medical benefit issues. As navigating issues related to employee welfare becomes more complex, there have also been discussions regarding board-level involvement in these issues. Many of these discussions focus on expanding the role and authority of compensation committees to focus on employee well-being, as compensation committees may have greater insight into the bigger picture regarding compensation fairness and how compensation incentives affect employees.[26] A 2019 study by Willis Towers Watson of the largest 100 public companies by revenue found that 58 percent of the companies studied require compensation committees to maintain oversight of broad-based compensation programs and benefits, 33 percent have given the committee diversity and inclusion program oversight, and 15 percent have given the committee oversight of employee culture, relations, and engagement.[27] For public companies, the addition of a human capital disclosure discussed above[28] has also focused compensation committees on HCM issues. The role of the compensation committee in a time of increasing focus on ESG considerations will likely be a topic of ongoing discussion.

VI. Unions

Unions and other kinds of labor organizations have traditionally provided a mechanism for advocating for and promoting workforce wellness. Based on a survey conducted in 2019, nearly half of nonunion workers say they would vote for a union, compared to approximately

[25] Abigail Gampher, *Analysis: Corps Face Stakeholder Benefit Inquiries After Dobbs*, Bloomberg L. (Aug. 17, 2022, 5:00 AM), https://news.bloomberglaw.com/bloomberg-law-analysis/analysis-corps-face-stakeholder-benefit-inquiries-after-dobbs.

[26] Leo E. Strine, Jr. & Kirby Smith, *Toward Fair Gainsharing and a Quality Workplace for Employees: How a Reconceived Compensation Committee Might Help Make Corporations More Responsible and Restore Faith in American Capitalism*, 76 The Bus. Law. 31 (June 4, 2020), https://papers.ssrn.com/sol3/papers.cfm?abstract_id=3619273.

[27] Robert Newbury et al., *Compensation Committees & Human Capital Management*, Harv. L. Sch. F. on Corp. Governance (Aug. 27, 2019), https://corpgov.law.harvard.edu/2019/08/27/compensation-committees-human-capital-management./.

[28] Modernization of Regulation S-K Items 101, 203, and 105, *supra* note 3.

one-third in national surveys conducted in 1977 and 1995.[29] Unions have come to the forefront in recent years, with highly publicized unionization efforts underway at corporate behemoths like Starbucks and Amazon. The Biden administration has indicated its support for these efforts, including hosting union organizers at the White House in May 2022.[30] Social media has been an effective tool for publicizing allegations of worker mistreatment at these companies. Social media has also served to publicize perceived "union-busting" activities by companies in an effort to weaponize public opinion.[31] While the online drama and politicization of the issue seems to be dominating the national discussion, it is important for employers to remember that there are federal rules governing treatment of unions and efforts to unionize that must be followed.

The National Labor Relations Act forbids employers from interfering with, restraining, or coercing employees in the exercise of rights relating to organizing, forming, joining, or assisting a labor organization for collective bargaining purposes, or from working together to improve the terms and conditions of their employment.[32] Employers may not discriminate in hiring, promotion, or any other term or condition of employment in order to encourage or discourage membership in any labor organization.[33] By the same token, a labor organization may not restrain or coerce employees in the exercise of their rights to unionize (or not).[34] And in "right-to-work" states,[35] employees cannot be forced as a condition of employment to join or pay dues or fees to a labor union.

VII. Employee Health

A. Physical Health

Workforce physical and mental well-being is an important aspect of the emphasis on HCM. In 2020, a World Economic Forum report revealed that "[s]takeholders increasingly expect organizations to care for the health of employees and their families and to uphold their rights to adequate physical and mental well-being."[36]

---

[29] Thomas A. Kochan et al., *Worker Voice in America: Is There a Gap Between What Workers Expect and What They Experience?*, 72 ILR Rev. 3 (Jan. 2019).

[30] Juliana Kaplan, *President Biden Says Amazon Union Organizer Christian Smalls Is His 'Kind of Trouble' and 'Let's Not Stop,'* Bus. Insider (May 11, 2022), https://www.businessinsider.com/biden-christian-smalls-trouble-amazon-labor-union-dont-stop-organizing-2022-5.

[31] *See, e.g.*, Rani Molla, *Starbucks Is Not Playing Nice With Its New Union*, Vox (Aug. 25, 2022), https://www.vox.com/recode/2022/8/25/23309517/starbucks-union-contract-bargaining-strikes.

[32] 29 U.S.C. § 158(a) (2012).

[33] *Id.*

[34] 29 U.S.C. § 158(b) (2012).

[35] 27 states currently have "right to work" laws: Arizona, Alabama, Arkansas, Florida, Idaho, Georgia, Indiana, Kansas, Iowa, Kentucky, Michigan, Louisiana, Mississippi, Nebraska, Missouri, Nevada, North Dakota, North Carolina, Oklahoma, South Dakota, South Carolina, Tennessee, Utah, Virginia, Texas, Wisconsin, and Wyoming.

[36] World Econ. F., Measuring Stakeholder Capitalism: Towards Common Metrics and Consistent Reporting of Sustainable Value Creation 32 (2020), https://www3.weforum.org/docs/WEF_IBC_Measuring_Stakeholder_Capitalism_Report_2020.pdf.

The coronavirus pandemic amplified these concerns, especially for so-called "essential" businesses whose employees could not do their jobs from home. For example, in March 2020, Amazon workers in New York went on strike over alleged coronavirus concerns, including inadequate cleaning, multiple outbreaks, a lack of protective gear, and hazard pay.[37] The crossover between the coronavirus pandemic and HCM was made explicit by Senator Mark R. Warner (D-VA.), who wrote to the SEC on May 19, 2020, asserting that "[n]ow, more than ever, investors and the public should have access to comprehensive, timely, and comparable information related to companies' human capital management practices."[38] The pandemic shone a spotlight on the importance to investors and the public of safeguarding employee health in the workplace.

Companies should keep in mind that—in addition to practical concerns about protecting the health of their workforces—they must also conform to the laws around employee health. For example, the Occupational Safety and Health Administration (OSHA) imposes regulations intended to create a safe working environment. These regulations require—among other things—that employees receive workplace safety and health training in a language they understand, work on machines that are safe, receive required safety equipment, and be protected from toxic chemicals.[39] Employees have the right to request an OSHA inspection and speak to the inspector and report illness and injury without fear of retaliation.[40]

This also includes the critical requirement that information gathered about an employee's health must always be kept separate from their general employment file and treated as a confidential medical record.[41]

B. Vaccines

Vaccines continue to be a challenging human resource issue, particularly for businesses questioning whether to require vaccination for their employees. The Equal Employment Opportunity Commission (EEOC) has indicated in its guidance that employers can require employees to be vaccinated before returning to the physical workplace. But employers should make sure that their vaccination policies and plans are consistent with all applicable laws, including the Americans with Disabilities Act (ADA) and Title VII.

The ADA allows employers to have qualification standards for work that include "a requirement that an individual shall not pose a direct threat to the health or safety of individuals in the workplace."[42] As a result, employers may require employees to be vaccinated

[37] Kenya Evelyn, *Amazon Fires New York Worker Who Led Strike Over Coronavirus Concerns*, The Guardian (Mar. 31, 2020), https://www.theguardian.com/us-news/2020/mar/31/amazon-strike-worker-fired-organizing-walkout-chris-smallls.

[38] Letter from Mark R. Warner, U.S. Sen., & Cynthia Axne, U.S. Rep., to Jay Clayton, Chairman, SEC (May 19, 2020), https://www.warner.senate.gov/public/_cache/files/4/a/4aba539c-5143-4fb7-beee-bced48a6e5c6/E0A663AA106A171F1404DFDF66B7A675.5.19.20-letter-to-sec-on-human-capital-disclosure-and-covid-19-final.pdf.

[39] *OSHA Worker Rights and Protections*, DOL, https://www.osha.gov/workers (last visited on Jan. 27, 2023).

[40] *Id.*

[41] 42 U.S.C. § 12112(d)(3)(B) (2008).

[42] 29 C.F.R. § 1630.10 (2021).

before returning to the physical workplace because COVID-19 presents a direct threat to health and safety. Some employees may not be able to receive the vaccine for medical reasons, or may object to receiving the vaccine because of a sincerely held religious belief. The ADA requires employers to reasonably accommodate employees' covered disabilities, and Title VII requires that employers reasonably accommodate employees' religious beliefs. Both of these requirements are potentially implicated by requiring that employees get the COVID-19 vaccine. Regarding the latter (which are likely less familiar to employers than traditional medical accommodation requests), accommodation requests based on a sincerely held religious belief must be taken into account, provided the accommodation would not pose an "undue hardship" upon the employer.[43] While the EEOC does allow an employer to require employees to provide proof of the "sincerity" of its employees' alleged religious beliefs in the event the employer has a bona fide doubt regarding either the religious nature or the sincerity of a particular belief/practice, the agency has cautioned that the employer can only make a "limited inquiry" and that employees can make the requisite showing in a variety of means, including a written or oral explanation from the employee or others who are aware of the employee's religious belief.[44]

If an employee requests an exemption from a mandatory vaccination policy because of a disability or sincerely held religious belief, the employer should engage in the interactive process to determine whether a reasonable accommodation that does not impose an undue hardship on the employer can be made. If an employer cannot exempt or provide a reasonable accommodation to an employee who cannot be vaccinated, the employer may exclude the employee from the workplace.

C. Mental Health

In addition to physical health concerns, as discussed in the discussion of employee benefits above, concerns about employees' mental health are at the forefront of discussions around HCM and ESG more broadly. According to 2018 data, one in four adults experience mental illness each year, and an estimated 18 percent of the adult U.S. population have an anxiety disorder.[45] Accordingly, mental health is a significant factor in hiring and retention. According to hiring site Monster's 2020 "State of the Candidate" survey, the top factors driving candidates to seek different jobs (besides compensation) were "job dissatisfaction" and "improved flexibility and lifestyle."[46]

---

[43] *What You Should Know About COVID-19 and the ADA, the Rehabilitation Act, and Other EEO Laws: K. Vaccinations—Overview, ADA, Title VII, and GINA*, Equal Employment Opportunity Commission (EEOC), at § K.6,https://www.eeoc.gov/wysk/what-you-should-know-about-covid-19-and-ada-rehabilitation-act-and-other-eeo-laws#K (last visited Apr. 3, 2023).

[44] *Questions and Answers: Religious Discrimination in the Workplace*, EEOC https://www.eeoc.gov/laws/guidance/questions-and-answers-religious-discrimination-workplace (last visited Apr. 3, 2022).

[45] Morra Aarons-Mele, *We Need to Talk More About Mental Health at Work*, Harv. Bus. Rev. (Nov. 1, 2018), https://hbr.org/2018/11/we-need-to-talk-more-about-mental-health-at-work.

[46] *Make the Mental Health of Employees Central to Your Recruitment Strategy*, Monster, https://hiring.monster.com/resources/workforce-management/company-culture/mental-health-and-wellness-recruitment-strategy/ (last visited Aug. 23, 2023).

This emphasis may be driven in part by the fact that organizations that maintain high standards in mental health for their employees have seen increases in productivity and efficiency.[47] Indeed, a study published in *The Lancet* in 2016 found that for every $1 invested in mental health programs, employers could save $2 to $4 on other expenses.[48] The study concluded that an investment of $147 billion between 2016 and 2030 to scale up effective treatment coverage for depression and anxiety would yield an estimated return of $310 billion.[49]

Key Takeaways

HCM and workforce well-being are becoming crucial issues for employers in light of the need to attract and retain an increasingly sophisticated workforce and heightened scrutiny from regulators and other stakeholders.

- Companies should design compensation structures that allow them to remain competitive, while also understanding that individual employees' roles and seniority level often inform key compensation considerations for recruitment and retention.
- Companies should consider carefully what incentives executive compensation provides and should consider whether adding ESG metrics to performance-based compensation would be beneficial and consistent with market norms in their industries.
- Public companies and compensation committees should be aware of disclosures with respect to compensation decisions, pay equity, and pay versus performance when crafting and implementing compensation policies for executives.
- Companies should create employee benefit structures that seek to meet the needs of the employee population and promote workplace well-being within the companies' cost and other constraints.
- With growing focus on ESG considerations and other related issues, companies should be increasingly prepared for both internal and external pressures from employees and other stakeholders to respond to social issues relating to compensation and employee benefits.
- Companies should consider the roles of their compensation committees in relation to broader employee compensation and employee well-being initiatives.

[47] Garen Staglin, *Why ESG Metrics & Strategies Should Include Mental Health*, Forbes (Oct. 14, 2021, 1:32 PM), https://www.forbes.com/sites/onemind/2021/10/14/why-esg-metrics–strategies-should-include-mental-health/?sh=430c1264403d.

[48] Dan Chisolm et al., *Scaling-up Treatment of Depression and Anxiety: A Global Return on Investment Analysis*, 3 The Lancet 415 (2016), https://www.thelancet.com/journals/lanpsy/article/PIIS2215-0366(16)30024-4/fulltext.

[49] *Id.*

12

Tools for ESG across Borders

E. Whitney Debevoise

I. Introduction

Long before anyone coined the phrase ESG, multinational companies learned that good citizenship can mean good business and better returns. This chapter discusses a set of voluntary international standards that companies can use to guide their ESG efforts globally—the Organisation for Economic Co-operation and Development's (OECD's) Guidelines for Multinational Enterprises (the "Guidelines").[1] The Guidelines also provide useful due diligence guidance for companies engaged in cross-border activity.

Starting with Harvard Business School Professor Raymond Vernon's seminal work *Sovereignty at Bay*[2] in 1971, academics and policymakers debated whether the nation-state had become irrelevant and multinational enterprises (MNEs) had too much power. Out of this debate, OECD produced the Guidelines for Multinational Enterprises in 1976. The Guidelines have since been updated, most significantly in 2011, by adding a chapter addressing human rights to existing guidance on such topics as the environment, labor, anti-bribery, corporate governance, disclosure, supply chain management, and taxation. That update essentially incorporated The United Nations (UN) Guiding Principles on Business and Human Rights (the "Principles"),[3] adopted by the UN Human Rights Council in 2011. The Principles offer a set of guidelines for states and companies to prevent and address human rights abuses committed in business operations and supply chains.

---

[1] Organisation for Economic Co-operation Development (OECD), OECD Guidelines for Multinational Enterprises (2011), http://dx.doi.org/10.1787/9789264115415-en.

[2] Raymond Vernon, Sovereignty at Bay: The Multinational Spread of U.S. Enterprises (1971).

[3] UN Office of the High Comm'r for Human Rights, Guiding Principles on Business and Human Rights: Implementing the United Nations "Protect, Respect and Remedy" Framework, UN Doc. HR/PUB/11/04 (2011), https://www.ohchr.org/documents/publications/guidingprinciplesbusinesshr_en.pdf.

The Guidelines, as supplemented by the Principles, have helped to develop and improve corporate social responsibility in the last 12 years. Both instruments provide companies an international standard of behavior consistent with good corporate practices and respect for human rights. Usefully, each offers due diligence standards that help companies in their efforts to identify and address the risks associated with adverse impacts across the ESG space.

The instruments are useful not only for MNEs but also for investors and countries. Investors now have a tool for assessing the level of a company's corporate governance and respect for human rights, which is relevant for an investor trying to evaluate potential negative reputational, financial, and even criminal consequences of certain corporate activity. The instruments also offer governments an international standard to require of foreign companies operating in their territory.

This chapter briefly describes the Guidelines, their characteristics, their legal nature, and how they can be useful for many parties.

II. Organisation for Economic Co-operation and Development's Guidelines for Multinational Enterprises

A. The Guidelines: Their Genesis and Evolution

In light of broad criticism of MNEs in the 1970s, the OECD initiated one of the first formal efforts to develop corporate social responsibility and corporate governance standards. In 1976, the OECD adopted a "Declaration on International Investment and Multinational Enterprises," which included the Guidelines as an annex. The OECD has continued to develop and refine the Guidelines and has since adopted due diligence standards for a series of industries.

The Guidelines began as soft (i.e., voluntary) law for both the OECD countries and the companies operating or based in them. The first set of Guidelines contained a set of general principles and standards to which OECD member countries and companies could refer when developing their approach to corporate social responsibility and good corporate governance.

The original Guidelines focused on compliance with national laws, the making of positive contributions to economic and social progress in the countries of operation (host countries), the contribution to technology transfer (when feasible), a first set of general principles regarding environmental protection, and respect for freedom of association and collective bargaining, rights previously recognized by International Labour Organization (ILO) conventions.[4]

The second key development related to the OECD Guidelines came in 1984 with the adoption of the National Contact Point (NCP) system. NCPs are offices established in all OECD member states to promote the Guidelines and to resolve differences that arise in the application of the Guidelines.

The next big step in the evolution of the Guidelines came with the OECD Council Decision of June 27, 2000 (2000 Decision), which changed the nature of the Guidelines. Although they remained voluntary for companies, they became mandatory (hard law) for OECD member states. Based on Article 5 of the OECD charter, the organization is entitled

[4] John Gerard Ruggie & Tamaryn Nelson, *Human Rights and the OECD Guidelines for Multinational Enterprises: Normative Innovations and Implementation Challenges*, 22 Brown J. World Affs. 99, 101 (2015).

to take decisions that are legally binding on all its members, and the OECD's Directorate for Legal Affairs concluded that Council Decisions are

> legally binding on all those Members who do not abstain when the Act (Decision) is adopted. While they are not treaties, they do entail, for Member countries, the same kind of legal obligations as those subscribed to under international treaties. Members are obliged to implement Decisions and they must take the measures necessary for such implementation.[5]

In other words, the Guidelines become legally binding obligations under public international law for OECD member countries.[6]

The 2000 Decision stimulated multinationals incorporated in an OECD country to follow the Guidelines in all countries in which they were operating, including non-OECD member countries, and encouraged non-member countries and countries in the process of admission to OECD membership to start the process of full implementation of the Guidelines in their territory. The 2000 Decision also expanded the coverage of the Guidelines to include respect for human rights (not limited only to labor-related rights as in the original Guidelines). The 2000 Decision also encouraged the disclosure of information regarding companies' activities, finances, and performance; emphasized the complete elimination of forced child labor; set forth basic principles of environmental management; and included principles against corruption, anti-competitive practices, and tax evasion.[7]

The 2000 Decision strengthened the NCP system by providing procedural guidance that must be taken into account by members when establishing an NCP and by entitling communities, nonmember countries, individuals, and nongovernmental organizations (NGOs) to file complaints against a company before an NCP. Following the 2000 Decision, it was clear that NCPs were to function as a nonjudicial conflict resolution resource, using mediation and conciliation to try to resolve conflicts.[8]

The NGO community has taken up the invitation, and NCPs have requested NCP reviews in 450 cases.[9] These cases are treated confidentially during their pendency, but companies may be under home country legal obligations to disclose the existence of such complaints under domestic securities law and/or legislation regarding supply chains.[10] Disclosure, even if it comes at the end of a mediation process, can cause reputational harm of interest both to companies and to investors.

---

[5] Scott Robinson, *International Obligations, State Responsibility and Judicial Review Under the OECD Guidelines for Multinational Enterprises Regime*, 30 Utrecht J. Int'l & Eur. L. 68, 70 (2014).

[6] Notwithstanding, there is still an open debate about the effective international responsibility of a member for non-compliance with the Guidelines or the NCP system. For further information on the subject, please refer to *id.* at 75.

[7] Ruggie & Nelson, *supra* note 4, at 102.

[8] Robinson, *supra* note 5, at 71.

[9] OECD, Annual Report on the OECD Guidelines for Multinational Enterprises 2020: Update on National Contact Point Activity 9–43 (2021), http://mneguidelines.oecd.org/2020-Annual-Report-MNE-Guidelines-EN.pdf.

[10] The California Transparency in Supply Chains Act of 2010 (CTSCA), codified at Cal. Civ. Code §1714.43, was one of the first pieces of legislation focused on modern slavery and human trafficking in supply chains. U.S. Securities & Exchange Commission (SEC) reporting rules, as well as the UK Modern Slavery Act, https://www.legislation.gov.uk/ukpga/2015/30/contents/enacted, might also require disclosure.

Finally, the 2011 revision of the Guidelines included a new chapter on human rights. This effort brought the Guidelines into harmony with the then-recently approved UN Guiding Principles on Business and Human Rights, incorporating their "protect, respect and remedy" framework. The 2011 revision also brought a more comprehensive approach to corporate due diligence, responsible supply chain management, and a reinforced procedural guide for NCPs.[11]

B. Due Diligence Guidance for Responsible Business Conduct

To ensure the effectiveness and adequate measurement of company adherence to the Guidelines, which the OECD has equated with "Responsible Business Conduct" (RBC), the OECD has developed a follow-up instrument called "OECD Due Diligence Guidance for Responsible Business Conduct" ("the "Guide").[12] Companies use the Guide to implement their own due diligence processes to identify the risks that they could face in their operations and to adopt proper measures to cease, reduce, repair, or mitigate any adverse impact.

Although the Guide received its impetus from G-7 Leaders' Declarations in 2015 and 2017, it emerged from a multi-stakeholder process with OECD and non-OECD countries and representatives from business, trade unions, and civil society. The Guide is a practical tool for use by any type of MNE and includes descriptions, scopes, and a detailed procedure for RBC due diligence as well as Annexes with questions and examples regarding the process itself. The pragmatic approach of the Guide makes it a valuable and efficient tool for managements, audit committees, or external auditors conducting RBC due diligence. Moreover, as it proposes a single framework applicable to almost any type of company, its results may allow investors to compare the level of compliance across companies.[13]

The OECD has also developed specialized, sector-specific due diligence guidance for industries with a history of supply chain-related issues, such as conflict minerals, garments and footwear, and agriculture.[14]

1. *Scope of the Due Diligence: Types of Business Relationships Covered*

The Guide covers any type of business relationship, including, but not limited to, suppliers, franchisees, licensees, joint ventures, investors, clients, contractors, and costumers. It thus covers complete supply chains.

2. *The Due Diligence Process*

The Guide contemplates a six-step due diligence process.[15] The first step seeks to embed RBC into policies and management systems.[16] It does so by employing three procedures. The first

[11] Robinson, *supra* note 5, at 70.

[12] OECD, OECD Due Diligence Guidance for Responsible Business Conduct (2018), http://mneguidelines.oecd.org/OECD-Due-Diligence-Guidance-for-Responsible-Business-Conduct.pdf.

[13] *Id* at 9.

[14] *Id* at 3.

[15] *Id.* at 21.

[16] *Id.* at 22.

procedure involves reviewing and updating existing policies on issues of RBC to align them with the Guidelines.[17] If no policy exists, the MNE must devise and develop a specific policy addressing the most significant risks. Further, applying a consistent ESG value of transparency, the enterprise must make its policies publicly available, using, for example, its corporate website, investor relations office, and communications to employees. Updating of existing policies should respond to a risk analysis undertaken by the company.

The second procedure involves embedding the updated policies into company oversight bodies and management systems so that they are implemented as part of the company's regular business processes.[18] Oversight and responsibility must be assigned to a senior management member, and board-level responsibility must also be assigned (e.g., to an audit committee). There should also be department-level responsibilities taking into account risk exposure.

The third procedure involves incorporation of RBC expectations and policies into engagements with suppliers and other business relationships.[19]

In order to engage other stakeholders and business partners, the MNE should communicate key aspects of its policies and expectations to relevant business relationships and include terms and conditions that reflect its expectations in contracts and other types of agreements. Also, when feasible, establishing a prequalification process or due diligence for suppliers is a recommended practical action.

The second step of the due diligence process involves identifying and assessing actual and potential adverse impacts associated with the MNE's operations, products, or services.[20] Here the enterprise proceeds on four fronts. First, it carries out a broad scoping exercise to identify all areas of the business where risks are most likely to be present and most significant.[21]

Second, starting with the significant risk areas identified, the company carries out iterative and in-depth assessments of prioritized operations and business relationships.[22] This work could include mapping the MNE's operations and business relationships, cataloging specific Guideline standards associated with the risks being assessed, assessing the nature and extent of actual and potential impacts linked to prioritized operations, and reassessing at regular intervals.

Third, the enterprise should assess its involvement with the actual or potential adverse impacts identified in order to determine the appropriate responses.[23] Specifically, the company can assess whether the MNE caused or contributed to the adverse impact.

Finally, drawing on the information obtained on actual and potential adverse impacts, the company can prioritize the most significant risks for action based on severity and

[17] *Id.*

[18] *Id.* at 23.

[19] *Id.* at 24.

[20] *Id.* at 25.

[21] *Id.*

[22] *Id.* at 26–27.

[23] *Id.* at 27.

likelihood.[24] This action will be relevant where it is not possible to assess all the identified risks simultaneously.

The third step in the due diligence process is to cease, prevent, and mitigate adverse impacts.[25] Thus, once a risk has been identified (see step 2), the company should evaluate activities that are causing or contributing to adverse impacts.

Assigning responsibilities in the senior levels of management would be helpful in this step. If a total cessation of activities is not possible due to contractual or legal obligations, draft a roadmap for the winding down of damaging activities. After cessation, update the MNE policies to prevent or mitigate future adverse impacts. Furthermore, based on the previous prioritization, companies can develop and implement plans to prevent or mitigate actual or potential adverse impacts that are linked to the MNE's operations, products, or services by business relationships (providers, joint ventures, partners, clients, etc.).[26]

The fourth step is to track implementation and results by examining the implementation and effectiveness of the MNE's due diligence activities.[27] In turn, the lessons learned can be used to improve the process in the future.

The fifth step calls for communication of how impacts are addressed.[28] This involves communicating externally relevant information on due diligence policies and processes conducted to identify and address actual or potential adverse impacts, including the findings and outcomes. It also involves development of a communication strategy to inform stakeholders and all relevant third parties about the activities performed, the results obtained, and the actions taken. The MNE's annual sustainability or corporate responsibility reports or other appropriate forms of disclosure could be used. Disseminating the information in a way that is easily accessible and appropriate for individuals and affected communities (e.g., the corporate website, at the MNE's premises) and in accessible languages is highly recommended.

For human rights impacts, a company needs to be prepared to communicate with the impacted or potentially impacted rightsholders in a timely and culturally sensitive and accessible manner.

Finally, step six involves providing for or cooperating in remediation when appropriate.[29] When the MNE determines that it has caused or contributed to actual adverse impacts, it should address such impacts by providing for or cooperating in their remediation. This step may require some difficult choices out of concern for the liability of the MNE, but if the MNE feels obliged under the terms of the Guidelines, it may want to be forward-leaning about remediation.

Remediation could mean restoring the affected person or persons to the situation they would be in had the adverse impact not occurred. It should be proportionate to the

[24] *Id.* at 28.

[25] *Id.* at 29.

[26] *Id.* at 30–31.

[27] *Id.* at 32.

[28] *Id.* at 33.

[29] *Id.* at 34.

significance and scale of the adverse impact. For human rights impacts, consult with experts and engage with affected rightsholders and their representatives to determine the remedy.

It can also be important to assess the level of satisfaction of those who have raised complaints with the process and its outcome.

When appropriate, companies can also provide for or cooperate with legitimate remediation mechanisms through which impacted stakeholders and rightsholders can raise complaints and seek to have them addressed by the MNE. Referral of an alleged impact to a legitimate remediation mechanism may be particularly helpful in situations where there are disagreements about whether the MNE caused or contributed to adverse impacts, or on the nature and extent of the remediation to be provided.

C. Guidelines Issues and Responsible Business Conduct Diligence: Summary[30]

The Guidelines are an evolving body of principles and recommendations for companies and specific obligations for OECD members regarding corporate social responsibility, good corporate governance, and in general high standards of corporate behavior according to international law and international instruments about human rights. But not all of the principles and recommendations set forth in the Guidelines are evaluated in the due diligence process.

A brief summary of the recommendations that form part of the due diligence process for assessing RBC follows:

1. *Disclosure*

- Enterprises should ensure that timely and accurate information is disclosed on all material matters regarding their activities, structure, financial situation, performance, ownership, and governance.
- Disclosure policies of enterprises should include, but should not be limited to, material information on (a) financial and operating results; (b) enterprise objectives; (c) major share ownership and voting rights; (d) remuneration policy for members of the board and key executives, and information about board members; (e) related party transactions; (f) foreseeable risk factors; (g) issues regarding workers and other stakeholders; and (h) governance structures and policies.
- Enterprises are encouraged to communicate additional information that could include (a) value statements or statements of business conduct intended for public disclosure; (b) policies and other codes of conduct to which the enterprise subscribes; (c) its performance in relation to these statements and codes; (d) information on internal audit, risk management, and legal compliance systems; and (e) information on relationships with workers and other stakeholders.

[30] The following description presents a general overview of the principles, recommendations, and obligations included in the Guidelines, and it is not an exhaustive description of its content. Numbering used here is not necessarily consistent with the numbering in the Guidelines.

- Enterprises should apply high-quality standards for accounting, and for financial as well as nonfinancial disclosure, including environmental and social reporting where they exist. An annual audit should be conducted by an independent, competent, and qualified auditor.

2. *Human Rights*

MNEs should:

- Respect human rights, which means MNEs should avoid infringing on the human rights of others and should address adverse human rights impacts with which they are involved.
- Within the context of their own activities, avoid causing or contributing to adverse human rights impacts and address such impacts when they occur.
- Seek ways to prevent or mitigate adverse human rights impacts that are directly linked to the enterprise's business operations, products, or services by a business relationship, even if the enterprise does not contribute to those impacts but, for example, a supplier does.
- Have a policy commitment to respect human rights.
- Carry out human rights due diligence as appropriate to the size, nature, and context of operations and the severity of the risks of adverse human rights impacts.
- Provide for or cooperate through legitimate processes in the remediation of adverse human rights impacts where the MNE recognizes that it has caused or contributed to negative impacts.

3. *Employment and Industrial Relations*

MNEs should:

- (a) Respect the right of workers to establish or join and be represented by trade unions; (b) contribute to the abolition of child labor; (c) contribute to the elimination of all forms of forced or compulsory labor; and (d) be guided throughout their operations by the principle of equality of opportunity and treatment in employment and non-discrimination against their workers.
- (a) Provide such facilities to workers' representatives as may be necessary to assist in the development of effective collective bargaining agreements; (b) provide information to workers' representatives that is needed for meaningful negotiations on conditions of employment; and (c) provide information to workers and their representatives that enables them to obtain a true and fair view of the performance of the entity.
- Promote consultation and cooperation between employers and workers and their representatives on matters of mutual concern.
- (a) Observe standards of employment and industrial relations no less favorable than those observed by comparable employers in the host country; (b) when operating in developing countries, provide the best possible wages, benefits, and conditions of work within the framework of government policies; and (c) take adequate steps to ensure occupational health and safety in operations.

- In their operations, employ local workers and provide training with a view to improving skill levels.
- In considering changes in their operations which would have major employment effects, in particular in the case of the closure of an entity involving collective layoffs or dismissals, provide reasonable notice of such changes to representatives of the workers in their place of employment and their organizations, and, where appropriate, to the relevant governmental authorities, and cooperate with the worker representatives and appropriate governmental authorities so as to mitigate adverse effects to the maximum extent practicable.
- In the context of bona fide negotiations with workers' representatives on conditions of employment, or while workers are exercising a right to organize, not threaten to transfer the whole or part of an operating unit from the country concerned or to transfer workers from the enterprise's component entities in other countries in order to unfairly influence those negotiations or to hinder the exercise of a right to organize.
- Enable authorized representatives of the workers in their employment to negotiate on collective bargaining or labor-management relations issues and allow the parties to consult on matters of mutual concern with representatives of management who are authorized to make decisions on these matters.

4. Environment

Enterprises should take due account of the need to protect the environment, public health, and safety. In particular, enterprises should:

- Establish and maintain a system of environmental management appropriate to the enterprise, including such items as (a) collection and evaluation of information regarding the environmental, health, and safety impacts of their activities; (b) establishment of measurable objectives and targets for improved environmental performance; and (c) regular monitoring and verification of progress toward environmental, health, and safety objectives or targets.
- (a) provide the public and workers with adequate, measurable, and verifiable information on the potential environment, health, and safety impacts of the activities of the enterprise and (b) engage in adequate communication and consultation with the communities directly affected by the enterprise.
- Assess, and address in decision-making, the foreseeable environmental, health, and safety-related impacts associated with the processes, goods, and services of the enterprise over their full lifecycle.
- Maintain contingency plans for preventing, mitigating, and controlling serious environmental and health damage from the company's operations and mechanisms for immediate reporting to the competent authorities.
- Continually seek to improve corporate environmental performance by encouraging such activities as (a) adopting technologies and procedures that reflect standards concerning environmental performance; (b) developing and providing products or services that have no undue environmental impacts; (c) promoting higher levels of

awareness among customers of the environmental implications of using the products and services of the enterprise; and (d) exploring and assessing ways of improving the environmental performance of the enterprise.
- Provide appropriate education and training to workers in environmental, health, and safety matters.
- Contribute to the development of environmentally meaningful and economically efficient public policy.

5. Anticorruption Practices

Enterprises should not, directly or indirectly, offer, promise, give, or demand a bribe or other undue advantage to obtain or retain business or other improper advantage. Enterprises should also resist the solicitation of bribes and extortion. In particular, enterprises should:

- Not offer, promise, or give undue pecuniary or other advantage to public officials or the employees of business partners.
- Develop and adopt adequate internal controls, ethics, and compliance programs.
- Prohibit or discourage—in internal company controls, ethics, and compliance programs or measures—the use of small facilitation payments, which are generally illegal in the countries where they are made, and when such payments are made, accurately record them in books and financial records.
- Ensure properly documented due diligence pertaining to the hiring, as well as the appropriate and regular oversight of agents, and ensure that remuneration of agents is appropriate and for legitimate services only.
- Enhance the transparency of their activities in the fight against bribery, bribe solicitation, and extortion.
- Promote employee awareness of and compliance with company policies and internal controls, ethics, and compliance programs or measures against corrupt practices.
- Not make illegal contributions to candidates for public office or to political parties or to other political organizations.

6. Consumer Interest

When dealing with consumers, enterprises should:

- Ensure that the goods and services they provide meet all agreed or legally required standards for consumer health and safety.
- Provide accurate, verifiable, and clear information that is sufficient to enable consumers to make informed decisions.
- Provide consumers with access to fair, easy-to-use, timely, and effective nonjudicial dispute resolution and redress mechanisms, without unnecessary cost or burden.
- Not make representations or omissions, or engage in any other practices that are deceptive, misleading, fraudulent, or unfair.
- Support efforts to promote consumer education in areas that relate to their business activities.

- Respect consumer privacy and take reasonable measures to ensure the security of personal data that they collect, store, process, or disseminate.
- Cooperate fully with public authorities to prevent and combat deceptive marketing practices.

D. The National Contact Points

The NCP system plays an important role in the promotion and development of the Guidelines. Today, there are 50 NCPs (one in each OECD member state) promoting and applying the Guidelines to resolve complaints through mediation and conciliation. While there is no prescribed structure for an NCP, they must operate in accordance with "core criteria," namely visibility, accessibility, transparency, and accountability. In addition, NCPs must handle cases in a way that is impartial, predictable, equitable, and compatible with the Guidelines.[31]

The NCPs perform an important informational and promotional role, and they:

1. Make the Guidelines known and available by appropriate means, including through online information, and in national languages. Prospective investors (inward and outward) should be informed about the Guidelines, as appropriate.
2. Raise awareness of the Guidelines and their implementation procedures, including through cooperation, as appropriate, with the business community, worker organizations, other NGOs, and the interested public.
3. Respond to inquiries about the Guidelines from:
    a. other NCPs;
    b. the business community, worker organizations, other NGOs, and the public; and
    c. governments of non-adhering countries.

The NCP also provides a nonjudicial conflict resolution tool, participating in a predictable, impartial, and equitable manner to solve any issues that may arise in relation with the application of or adherence to the Guidelines.

In this regard, the NCP will:

1. Make an initial assessment of whether the issues raised in a particular matter merit further examination and respond to the parties involved.
2. Where the issues raised merit further examination, offer good offices to help the parties involved to resolve the issues. For this purpose, the NCP will consult with these parties and where relevant:
    a. Seek advice from relevant authorities and/or representatives of parties involved in the application of the Guidelines (business community, worker organizations, other NGOs, and relevant experts).
    b. Consult the NCP in the other country or countries concerned.

[31] For further information about the current state of NCPs, refer to OECD, National Contact Points for Responsible Business Conduct—Providing Access to Remedy: 20 Years and the Road Ahead (2020), http://mneguidelines.oecd.org/NCPs-for-RBC-providing-access-to-remedy-20-years-and-the-road-ahead.pdf.

c. Seek the guidance of the OECD Investment Committee if it has any doubt about the interpretation of the Guidelines in particular circumstances.
d. Offer and, with the agreement of the parties involved, facilitate access to consensual and non-adversarial means, such as conciliation or mediation, to assist the parties in dealing with the issues.

3. At the conclusion of the procedures and after consultation with the parties involved, make the results of the procedures publicly available, taking into account the need to protect sensitive business and other stakeholder information. Importantly, the NCP is bound to maintain the confidentiality of the proceedings during the course of evaluating a complaint and any subsequent conciliation or mediation process.

E. Investor Concerns

The main concern of investors will be to know whether a company is in compliance with the Guidelines (and what level of compliance it has) and if it has been (or is) part of a proceeding with an NCP.

In keeping with the Guidelines, MNEs are required to report their adherence to the public in the most accessible manner possible. This disclosure can be made in any or all of the following: (a) sustainability reports, (b) corporate website, (c) office of investor relations, and (d) MNE premises. An investor could refer to any of these sources to confirm whether a particular enterprise has adhered to the Guidelines.

Publicity concerning the involvement of a company in an NCP case is limited until the case is closed. On the other hand, the final outcome of an NCP case can be made public, and MNEs involved in NCP proceedings may want to plan for the publicity that may follow. The OECD maintains for consultation a database listing more than 450 cases.[32]

The NCP process can involve mediation and conciliation and possible remediation payments if thought appropriate. Although a company could decide to accept a mediation outcome, it is not obliged to do so.

III. Conclusion

At bottom, ESG initiatives are all designed to improve the returns of business by promoting good corporate citizenship. This involves the application of basic principles of transparency, respect for workers, human rights, and the environment, as well as basic ethical practices and fair treatment of consumers. The OECD Guidelines incorporate all of these concerns and have through an evolutionary process stood the test of time as an instrument for achieving today's ESG goals, even if the term ESG appears nowhere in the Guidelines. Management and investors would do well to become familiar with the Guidelines and measure companies by their adherence to, and observance of, the Guidelines. Although the Guidelines are not hard law for companies, they capture the spirit of ESG in today's marketplace.

---

[32] *See Database of Specific Instances*, OECD Responsible Bus. Conduct: OECD Guidelines for Multinat'l Enters., https://mneguidelines.oecd.org/database/ (last visited Jan. 19, 2023).

13

Dealing with Highly Politicized Social Issues

Peter Gioello

I. Introduction

Companies are facing increasing pressure from various stakeholders to respond to certain politicized social issues (e.g., reproductive rights, racial equality, gender equality, gun manufacturing, LGBTQ+ rights, voting rights). However, it is essential that company leaders devote an adequate amount of time and resources before responding to a particular social issue. In doing so, business leaders must carefully balance the competing needs of stakeholders, sometimes in the spur of the moment. A company's legal advisor may be called upon to advise a company regarding if, when, and how to respond to such issues, given the high stakes at play, including whether the company has or can timely develop the requisite subject-matter expertise to inform decision-making. This chapter provides attorneys with both practical guidance and factors to consider when helping clients, especially public-facing clients, respond to these hot-button issues.[1]

[1] See Chapter 20—Internal Investigations for key principles about maintaining privilege and other considerations when conducting an internal investigation with potential legal ramifications.

A. Factors to Consider before Responding to a Highly Politicized Social Issue

Step 1	Understand the social issue and motives.
Step 2	Review relevant company positions on the issue.
Step 3	Conduct a stakeholder analysis.
Step 4	Consider the potential legal and reputational risks.
Step 5	Conduct a peer analysis to see if and how competitors have responded.
Step 6	Determine appropriate form if taking a position on the issue.

II. Step 1: Understand the Social Issue and Motives

While companies may wish instantly to respond when confronted with a highly politicized social issue, it is often important to take adequate time to understand the issue and the various risks before taking action. Here are some suggestions to get a better understanding of the issue:

- Unless an isolated event, take time to look at and understand the history and events leading up to a particular social issue
- Consider whether there is an underlying motive behind any stakeholder request for the company to take a position that could lead to potential backlash or other conflicts
- Consult industry and peer groups to see if they have any insight or information about the particular issue or event
- Review press coverage of the issue from multiple angles

III. Step 2: Review Relevant Company Positions on the Issue

Before responding to a highly politicized issue, a company should first obtain and consider all previous *public* positions or statements it has taken related to the social issue to avoid conflicting or untruthful statements. Doing this work may also help companies decide whether to speak at all regarding the issue, as reporters, politicians, and competitors may question inconsistent positions.

Public positions or statements may include the following:

- Statements made in public filings, the company website, or ESG reports
- Mission statements, codes of conduct, or similar creeds
- Public commitments, donations, or involvement in actions relating to the issue
- Social media posts by the company, its senior leadership, or board members
- Speeches or comments made in seminars, educational settings, industry groups, or in the media

Companies should also consider any internal positions or policies on a particular issue that may bolster or defend the company in responding to the specific issue, as well as to ensure consistency or prepare to explain any discrepancies.

Nonpublic positions or statements may include the following:

- Employee training and internal communication
- Direct communication with stakeholders, including shareholders
- Advisory reports prepared by external consultants
- Internal policies, company intranet, or any internal newsletters
- Nonpublic board information including any presentations or reports

IV. Step 3: Conduct a Stakeholder Analysis

Even when time is of the essence, one of the most critical factors to consider when deciding whether and how to respond to a highly politicized issue is how a particular decision or social issue might impact company stakeholders. Key stakeholders include employees, community, suppliers, customers, shareholders, and government. An analysis of each stakeholder (as shown in the following table) may help companies avoid stakeholder conflicts or backlash as a result of a particular action.

Stakeholder	Potential Issues That Could Arise Due to a Company's Failure to Consider Key Stakeholders
Employees	Employee retention, lack of diversity, poor innovation, reduced productivity, and limited engagement
Customers	Reduced loyalty, harm to brand premium, and reduced patronage
Community	Poor public image, protests, local political or regulatory issues, nuisance, and lawsuits
Suppliers	Lack of trust, reduced interdependency, supply chain disruptions, higher costs, and failure to meet contractual obligations
Shareholders	Shareholder suits, shareholder pressure, shareholder divestment, and other shareholder resolution
Government	Backlash, legislation, political pressure, and increased regulatory pressure

Companies may assign different values at different times to each of its key stakeholders depending on their needs and values but also the social issue in question. Due to the rapid advance of technology and social media, employees and other stakeholders now have ample opportunity to meaningfully express their positions and garner support from peers and the public. As such, it is essential to look at all key stakeholders when responding to politicized social issues.

A. Employee Stakeholders

Evaluation of employee satisfaction goes beyond employee compensation and benefits. A study has found that when employees believe in their organization, they are more likely to stay with that organization.[2] The 2022 so-called "Great Resignation" has highlighted how much of an impact employee stakeholders can exert on a corporation.[3] Social issues related to employees as stakeholders may come from numerous sources, including, but not limited to, corporate public positions (or lack thereof) on social, legal, and political issues; work/life balance in the age of hybrid workplaces; and employee satisfaction and support. More illustrative examples may include remote work policies; diversity, equity, and inclusion policies; and employee empowerment policies.

To better understand the unique needs and intricacies of employee stakeholders, decision-makers may choose to:

- Have conversations with human resources and other employee-facing teams, including those who have direct and honest communication with employees,
- Review positions and guidance from professional or other organizations that serve their employees,
- Analyze employee satisfaction through existing human resources reports, and
- Talk directly to employees at all levels.

Once the company understands its employees' wants and values, the company is in a better position to consider how a particular decision or action may impact its workforce.

B. Community Stakeholders

The community stakeholder category includes the public at large, but also organizations and groups that may have an interest in the company or the particular issue at hand. The community makeup and needs for each company look different and will also depend on the particular social issue in question. In order to analyze and consider the community stakeholder, companies should consider both its broader impact on society and issues caused by its physical presence or footprint.

Company leadership may use the following tools and resources to identify and consider its broader impact on society:

- Search the public domain for any negative news articles about the organization
- Provide reputable polling showing public opinion of the social issue in question
- Collaborate with public relations specialists to identify business risks that may not be apparent

Companies may also wish to engage with community stakeholders proactively. Over time, companies will develop a relationship with certain community stakeholders that may also help inform the company on whether and how to respond to a highly politicized social issue.

---

[2] Asha Binu Raj, *Impact of Employee Value Proposition on Employees' Intention to Stay: Moderating Role of Psychological Contract and Social Identity*, 10 S. Asian J. Bus. Stud. 203 (Sept. 14, 2020), https://www.emerald.com/insight/content/doi/10.1108/SAJBS-10-2019-0183/full/html.

[3] Sarah Green-Vieux, *Trending Topics in ESG: The Great Resignation*, Novata (Feb. 22, 2022), https://www.novata.com/breaking-down-the-hottest-trends-in-esg-the-great-resignation/.

In some circumstances, certain physical facilities may be the incubator to social issues (e.g., a labor strike or unionization in a particular location). Further, most multinational corporations have key areas in which they are established, operate, and conduct business, and these areas may be very different geopolitically. Companies may consider the following list of factors to help identify and understand relevant micro-community stakeholders and related considerations:

- Facilities that may operate in geopolitically diverse or politically active communities;
- Headquarters, regional offices, flagships, and other facilities that hold a prominent place in a micro-community;
- Facilities that have any potential adverse impact on air, noise, or water pollution;
- Facilities that have an adverse impact on localities and quality of life through disruption of traffic flow, heavy consumption of natural resources or energy, smaller commerce competition (i.e., mom-and-pop shops), and consumption of public safety resources;
- Facilities perceived by the public as ugly or nonconforming to the local community feel;
- Facilities that had significant pushback from the local community at inception;
- Facilities that are abandoned or utilized for different purposes than originally planned;
- Facilities that may hold historical or cultural significance; and
- Facilities taken by eminent domain.

The community also includes nongovernmental organizations (NGOs), communities of faith, or other community groups that may have an interest in a particular facility or business for various reasons. Here are some suggestions to identify NGOs or other community groups to consider in a stakeholder analysis:

- Interviewing the organization's public relations and legal departments to identify NGOs who are focused on the organization
- Identifying if the social issue in question has a broad impact (i.e., impact across all organizational properties)
- Completing peer reviews to identify best practices related to community engagement for the organization related to the social issue of concern

C. Suppliers

When responding to a particular social issue, companies should look beyond their operations and assets and consider how their supply chain partners may react to a specific action and vice versa. Through this review, companies may identify whether the social issue in question has the potential to interfere with supplier arrangements or cause supply chain delays. Depending on the scope of the social issue, the company's size, and other factors, the company may find itself with limited supplier options or incur additional costs that it may have to pass on to its customers. Further, as discussed under legal implications below, there may also be potential legal liability.

D. Consumers and Customers

A 2021 PricewaterhouseCoopers study found that 83 percent of consumers believe that corporations should be "actively shaping ESG best practices."[4] As corporations make critical social decisions in the context of ESG, it is vital to consider consumer sentiment as it relates to a particular politicized social issue.

Companies might utilize the following resources when determining the unique consumer makeup of an organization:

- Analyze consumer surveys and market trends;
- Interview marketing and product development teams within the corporation to get a better idea of demographics and any conflicting interests;
- Compare reputable polling data to determine ideological sentiment among various demographics as it relates to the social issue in question;
- Review competitors to see what policies they may have adopted about the social issue in question; and
- Identify consumer advocacy groups to identify various positions on the social issue.

E. Shareholders

Of course, companies must also consider their shareholders in the analysis. It is helpful to consult with the organization's investor relations team to identify any potential activist investors. It is also beneficial to find out if there has been any nonpublic engagement or interaction with shareholders that could give rise to a conflict with a particular decision or action. Companies that ignore shareholders entirely may face shareholder suits or be subject to onerous shareholder resolutions or divestment. Given the ultimate authority and influence shareholders possess, coupled with the volume of shareholder ESG resolutions that may be social in nature, a company should consult with its attorney to discuss the importance of considering shareholder views when making decisions about how to address important politically divisive social issues.

F. Government

Government should be understood to include local, state, federal, and foreign laws and regulations and public positions held by politicians and governmental entities. Given the government's authority (e.g., permitting the charter of a public company, levying fines, and other sanctions), an attorney should advise the organization on whether a company may face legal repercussions as a result of its response to a particular social issue.

Companies addressing politically divisive social issues should also consider potential backlash from politicians stemming from the company's public opinion on social issues. This backlash may present itself as a general protest by a politician or targeted legislation. It

[4] *2021 Consumer Intelligence Series Survey on ESG*, PwC (2021), https://www.pwc.com/us/en/services/consulting/library/consumer-intelligence-series/consumer-and-employee-esg-expectations.html.

could also directly affect a company's reputation, goodwill, and brand if made a caricature by public figures.

An organization can consider the following additional factors to develop a thorough analysis of government stakeholder implications:

- Identify local, state, national, and foreign laws and regulations related to the social issue in question;
- Analyze the political environment of an organization's headquarters, or where it has a sizeable operational presence to identify potential backlash from the local government as it relates to the social issue in question; and
- Identify how other like-sized organizations operating within the same jurisdiction have responded to the same or similar social issues.

V. Step 4: Consider the Potential Legal and Reputational Risks

As attorneys, we must outline potential legal risks when advising clients on how to respond to a particular situation, including highly politicized social issues. In some situations, companies may have to weigh the social impact versus the legal impact of failing to respond to a social issue, and how each may affect the company's bottom line. There are also direct and indirect legal consequences a company should consider when a company decides how to act.

Direct legal consequences, such as a violation of applicable law, subject the company to potential litigation or regulatory enforcement. Indirect legal consequences come in various forms and can include backlash by state legislative bodies or politicians, canceled contracts, lawsuits, or shareholder suits.

VI. Step 5: Conduct a Peer Analysis to See If and How Competitors Have Responded

One benefit of modern technology is the ability to quickly see if and how competitors publicly respond to a particular issue.[5] Competitors who respond first may gain the benefit and praise for being the first to react but also are the first to receive the backlash from those who oppose the particular social issue and may make judgment errors based on an incomplete understanding of the facts and circumstances. Those who choose to remain silent or wait it out are sometimes criticized for not responding soon enough but may gain additional insight to help them consider the potential impact of taking a position on the issue. At the very least, companies should look at the range of public corporate responses to a particular social issue, which may provide additional insight on the potential outcome of an action or decision in response to a politicized social issue. Industry groups are also useful forums where companies can gain additional insight and communicate with one another on how to respond to a particular issue.

[5] *See* Chapter 23—Public Company Disclosures.

VII. Step 6: Determine Appropriate Form If Taking a Position on This Issue

Many companies have become accustomed to using social media to make a statement or take an official position when a social issue arises. While instant, posting on social media sometimes invites a response from the opposition that can create a more significant issue. In some circumstances, social media posting might be the best response, but it is not the only choice. The form of how to respond is not universal, and again, companies should consider its various stakeholders, potential impacts, and any legal implications when deciding how to speak. Here are some alternative forums and methods for responding to a highly politicized social issue:

- Proactively contact the media and schedule a press conference with established parameters;
- Donate to a specific cause or issue;
- Empower employees or provide incentives as it relates to a particular issue;
- Make public pledges or set appropriate goals; and
- Modify or issue new policy statements or codes of conduct on a particular issue.

After thoroughly analyzing the various stakeholder interests, legal implications, and potential financial impact, a company may wish to stay silent on a particular issue. Employees and activists may view this "silence" as taking a position one way or the other.[6] On the other hand, staying silent may provide the company time to analyze the issue further and consider the best time to take a position. The decision to speak or not is a balancing act, and there may not be a right or wrong answer. It is important to consider the pros and cons of each scenario and make an informed decision.

VIII. Examples and Analysis

The following section applies the above steps and factors to a historical example to illustrate the various considerations and factors to consider before responding to a highly politicized social issue.

A. Woolworth and the Greensboro Sit-Ins

On February 1, 1960, four Black students protested after they were refused service at an F.W. Woolworth store because of its discriminatory policies.[7] Each day that followed, more and more students joined the protest, with around 300 at one point blocking the lunch counter business.[8] Woolworth at first did not concede, and the City of Greensboro, where the store was located, enacted tighter segregation laws, leading to the arrest of 45 students.[9]

---

[6] William Arruda, *Playing It Safe on Social Issues? Here's Why Neutral Is Not the Way to Go*, FORBES (Sept. 8, 2022), https://www.forbes.com/sites/williamarruda/2022/09/08/playing-it-safe-on-social-issues-heres-why-neutral-is-not-the-way-to-go/?sh=1091bf7d52ca.

[7] *Greensboro Sit-in*, HIST. (Jan. 25, 2022), https://www.history.com/topics/black-history/the-greensboro-sit-in.

[8] *Id.*

[9] *Greensboro Lunch Counter Sit-in*, LIBR. OF CONG., https://www.loc.gov/exhibits/odyssey/educate/lunch.html (Dec. 9, 1998).

B. Analysis

Step 1	Understand the social issue and motives.	• Deep-seated racism in the southeastern United States.[10] • The Civil Rights movement began in the 1950s.[11]
Step 2	Review relevant company positions on the issue.	• Segregated lunch counters with policies to refuse service to Black customers.
Step 3	Conduct a stakeholder analysis.	• Consumer-base opinion is divided based on consumer identity and consumer geopolitical affiliation. Possible supplier issues if the civil rights movement progresses. • Shareholders' main focus is likely on profit. • Community includes both the local community holding the sit-ins and the broader public perception during this time period. • Employees (which included persons of color) worked at Woolworth and likely had varying opinions on the matter. • Government: Segregation was legally permissible throughout the southern United States.
Step 4	Consider the potential legal and reputational risks.	• Financial impact of possible boycotts from either side.
Step 5	Conduct a peer analysis to see if and how competitors have responded.	• Hochschild, Kohn & Company (Baltimore) integrated their dining room after several large protests.[12] • Rich's (Knoxville) desegregated their dining area, later deciding to segregate again, but ultimately decided to sell rather than deal with the issue.[13]
Step 6	Determine appropriate form if taking a position on the issue.	• Woolworth eventually desegregated the counter in July 1960.[14]

C. Additional Information

Following the incident, the students organized boycotts of the store and Woolworth's profits decreased by one-third, ultimately leading them to retract the discriminatory policy.[15] By 1964, the Civil Rights Act abolished discrimination across the nation.[16] While this historical example is informative, companies today should consider the influence of social media technology that further accelerates the need for a diligent review when responding to a highly politicized social issue.

[10] *Greensboro Sit-in*, *supra* note 7.

[11] *Id.*

[12] Michael Lisicky, *Racial Injustice Outlived the American Department Store*, FORBES (June 6, 2020, 9:00 AM), https://www.forbes.com/sites/michaellisicky/2020/06/06/racial-injustice-outlived-the-american-department-store/?sh=98864776233b.

[13] *Id.*

[14] Sascha Cohen, *Why the Woolworth's Sit-in Worked*, TIME (Feb. 2, 2015, 11:00 AM), https://time.com/3691383/woolworths-sit-in-history/.

[15] *Greensboro Sit-in*, *supra* note 7.

[16] Civil Rights Act of 1964, Pub. L. No. 88-352 (Title VII), 42 U.S.C. § 2000e *et seq.* (1964).

IX. Conclusion

The ultimate decision on whether to address and subsequently when and how to respond to a highly politicized social issue will depend on several factors, and attorneys advising companies should exercise caution and weigh all the variables and considerations unique to their client. Each situation is unique and will require careful attention to the particular social issue in question as it relates to your client's particular needs. Attorneys should think reactively but also proactively when advising clients on dealing with such matters because the wrong decision could have significant legal ramifications as well as impact on a company's reputation for decades, if not forever.

Key Takeaways

- Corporate leaders face increasing pressure from competing stakeholders when it comes to highly politicized social issues.
- It is important to pause before responding and take an ample amount of time to consider the risks and potential outcomes of taking a position.
- The six steps outlined above are one resource attorneys may wish to consult when advising companies on how to respond to politicized social issues.
- A stakeholder analysis is a necessary component of understanding the potential implications and risks associated with a particular position.
- Staying neutral might be seen as taking a position to some stakeholders.

14

Environmental Justice

Brian D. Israel, Elise Henry, and Adam Masurovsky

I. Introduction

The U.S. Environmental Protection Agency (EPA) describes environmental justice as "the fair treatment and meaningful involvement of all people regardless of race, color, national origin, or income, with respect to the development, implementation, and enforcement of environmental laws, regulations, and policies."[1] Broadly, the goal of the environmental justice movement has included (1) addressing the disproportionate impact of environmental harms (traditionally focused on industrial practices and waste management) on low-income and historically marginalized communities, (2) engendering greater involvement of communities with environmental justice concerns as stakeholders in environmental decision-making (e.g., facility siting, environmental review, and permitting processes), and (3) preventing or mitigating the harms to those communities and investing in their environmental and economic resiliency.

While not always applicable, some companies are paying close attention to environmental justice trends as potentially "material" risks in recent filings, and some have developed environmental justice policies, sometimes expressly as a component of their overall ESG approach. One company noted, for example, that its board has a "longstanding commitment to ESG," including "with respect to environmental justice, along with other risks and opportunities related to the four elements of our sustainability program: safety, talent,

[1] *Environmental Justice*, U.S. Environmental Protection Agency (EPA), https://www.epa.gov/environmentaljustice (last visited Jan. 9, 2023).

climate leadership and communities."[2] Others have noted that environmental justice policies, such as the state legislative initiatives discussed further below, "could materially affect our business and prospects."[3] And discussions of environmental justice as an ESG criterion are likely to grow with rising awareness of environmental justice issues as the Biden administration reinvigorates the government's focus on environmental justice, as discussed below. Moreover, there is a growing perspective that climate change will result in greater consequences for vulnerable groups. As a result, environmental justice concerns will likely factor into climate change considerations that are already discussed under the umbrella of ESG.

This chapter briefly discusses environmental justice initiatives at the federal, state, and local levels, as well as some of the tools available to companies who are navigating these issues.

II. Brief History of Environmental Justice

Environmental justice concerns are not new. Early sparks of the environmental justice movement began in the 1960s during the civil rights movement, when historically disadvantaged groups began fighting against environmental threats affecting their communities. In the following decades, the movement as we recognize it today formed as a result of the growing recognition of the disproportionate impacts of environmental concerns on low-income communities and, in particular, communities of color.[4]

In 1983, following a protest against the siting of a hazardous waste site in Warren County, North Carolina—a predominantly minority county—the U.S. General Accounting Office (now the Government Accountability Office, or GAO) undertook a landmark study that found that hazardous waste sites in three southeastern states were disproportionately located near black communities.[5] As a result of this study and other initiatives that followed, the EPA established an Office of Environmental Equity and the National Environmental Justice Advisory Council, and set new guidelines and standards for incorporating environmental justice considerations into federal agency decision-making.[6]

[2] Republic Services, Inc., Proxy Statement (Schedule 14A) 4 (Apr. 21, 2022), https://investor.republicservices.com/static-files/067e2e30-a5f9-4918-9a87-68442403c7dc; *see also* Citigroup Inc., Annual Report (Form 10-K) 60–61 (Feb. 28, 2022), https://www.citigroup.com/citi/investor/data/q2104c.pdf (noting the importance of environmental justice in its plan to support a transition to net-zero emissions by 2050); Xcel Energy Inc., Proxy Statement (Schedule 14A) 22 (Apr. 5, 2022), https://d18rn0p25nwr6d.cloudfront.net/CIK-0000072903/feac0773-f421-472b-9b45-3b8601c23b2d.html (explaining that a component of its ESG strategy is working to address "energy and policy issues, such as climate change, environmental justice, social equity, and the responsible transition from coal").

[3] Covanta Holding Corp., Annual Report (Form 10-K) 34 (Feb. 21, 2021), https://www.sec.gov/Archives/edgar/data/225648/000022564821000008/cva-20201231.htm.

[4] *See also*, Brian D. Israel, *An Environmental Justice Critique of Risk Assessment*, 3 N.Y.U. Env'T L. J. 469 (1995) (exploring ways in which environmental risk assessments may fail to detect risks in overburdened communities).

[5] Government Accountability Office (GAO), Siting of Hazardous Waste Landfills and Their Correlation with Racial and Economic Status of Surrounding Communities (1983), http://archive.gao.gov/d48t13/121648.pdf.

[6] *Environmental Justice Timeline*, EPA, https://www.epa.gov/environmentaljustice/environmental-justice-timeline (last visited Jan. 9, 2023).

In February 1994, former President Bill Clinton signed Executive Order No. 12898 on federal efforts focusing on environmental justice in minority and low-income populations. Pursuant to the executive order, "each Federal agency shall make achieving environmental justice part of its mission." The order further established an Interagency Working Group on Environmental Justice (EJ IWG) to coordinate environmental justice strategies across the federal agencies. One of these strategies included explicit incorporation of environmental justice concerns into National Environmental Policy Act (NEPA) analyses, which the EPA adopted through published guidance in 1998.[7] These early efforts were later furthered by the Obama administration, which reconvened the EJ IWG and in 2011 adopted an interagency memorandum of understanding to "declare the continued importance of identifying and addressing environmental justice considerations in agency programs, policies, and activities" and "renew the process under Executive Order 12898 for agencies to provide environmental justice strategies and implementation progress reports."[8]

Despite decades of awareness of environmental justice issues, both federal and state governments have struggled to take concrete actions to address the reality of persistent disproportionate impacts from environmental stressors.

A heightened focus in recent years on issues of racial justice and the disparate treatment of communities of color that emerged out of discourse on policing practices and the Black Lives Matter movement has catalyzed a renewed emphasis in environmental policy on issues of environmental justice. In addition to reinvigorating governments' focus on environmental justice policymaking, this movement has led to heightened scrutiny of private-sector practices on issues of race and social justice, making those issues critical components of corporate policies. The combined emphasis in recent years on both environmental (and particularly climate) policy and on racial equity could promote environmental justice considerations within ESG analyses.

As discussed further below, the links among environmental justice, climate justice, and social justice are becoming more and more apparent to policymakers. In March 2021, for example, in a speech on "Meeting Investor Demand for Climate and ESG Information at the SEC," then acting chair of the U.S. Securities and Exchange Commission (SEC), Allison Herren Lee, linked issues of racial justice and the need for climate policy. Lee noted that "[p]rotests in the wake of the senseless killings of George Floyd and others have driven focus on racial justice. In both of these narratives [racial justice and COVID impacts] we can also see connections to climate risk. . . . We know climate presents heightened risks for marginalized communities, linking it to racial justice concerns."[9]

---

[7] EPA, Final Guidance for Incorporating Environmental Justice Concerns in EPA's NEPA Compliance Analyses (1998), https://www.epa.gov/sites/default/files/2015-04/documents/ej-guidance-nepa-compliance-analyses.pdf.

[8] Memorandum of Understanding on Environmental Justice and Executive Order 12898, https://www.epa.gov/sites/default/files/2015-02/documents/ej-mou-2011-08.pdf.

[9] Allison Herren Lee, Acting Chair, U.S. Securities and Exchange Commission (SEC), A Climate for Change: Meeting Investor Demand for Climate and ESG Information at the SEC (Mar. 15, 2021), https://www.sec.gov/news/speech/lee-climate-change.

III. The Rise of Environmental Justice Initiatives under the Biden Administration

The federal government's focus on environmental justice issues and climate justice issues has been reinvigorated by the Biden administration. The following excerpt from the White House's web page on environmental justice encapsulates this administration's approach to environmental justice issues:

> For far too long, communities across our country have faced environmental injustices, bearing the brunt of toxic pollution, enduring underinvestment in infrastructure and critical services, and suffering disproportionate impacts from climate change.
>
> President Biden and Vice President Harris campaigned on confronting longstanding environmental injustices and inequities, and they have delivered with actions that make a positive difference in people's lives.[10]

Since taking office, President Biden has issued a number of executive orders and memoranda that bring environmental justice concerns to the forefront on a national level.

On January 27, 2021, the White House issued Executive Order No. 14008 on tackling the climate crisis. The Order initiated a "government-wide approach" to addressing climate change and environmental justice and established several new environmental justice initiatives, including:

- The White House Environmental Justice Interagency Council (IAC), an intergovernmental body that seeks to advance environmental justice and develop strategies to address current and historic environmental injustice;[11]
- The White House Environmental Justice Advisory Council, a committee that advises the IAC and the Chair of the Council on Environmental Quality on ways to increase the federal efforts to address environmental justice;
- The Justice40 Initiative, which aims to provide 40 percent of the overall benefits of federal investments relating to climate change, clean energy, and other areas to overburdened communities;
- The development of a Climate and Economic Justice Screening Tool to help identify communities for the purposes of the Justice40 Initiative; and
- The establishment of an Environmental Justice Scorecard to track the performance of federal agencies from an environmental justice perspective, including on the Justice40 Initiative.

The Biden administration issued two more recent executive orders reaffirming its commitment to its "whole-of-government" approach to environmental justice. In its Executive

---

[10] *Environmental Justice*, The White House, https://www.whitehouse.gov/environmentaljustice/ (last visited Jan. 9, 2023).

[11] *White House Environmental Justice Interagency Council*, The White House, https://www.whitehouse.gov/environmentaljustice/white-house-environmental-justice-interagency-council/ (last visited Jan. 9, 2023).

Order on "Further Advancing Racial Equity and Support for Underserved Communities Through the Federal Government," issued on February 16, 2023, the administration directed federal agencies to establish teams specifically devoted to coordinating and advancing equity initiatives, such as those geared specifically toward environmental justice.[12] Subsequently, in its Executive Order on "Revitalizing Our Nation's Commitment to Environmental Justice for All," issued on April 21, 2023, the administration established the White House Office of Environmental Justice and directed agencies to use the legal tools available to them to focus on environmental justice issues.[13] In particular, the Executive Order highlighted environmental review under NEPA and tribal consultation requirements for permit as opportunities to incorporate input from environmental justice communities and advance environmental justice priorities.

The EPA also reinforced its commitment to environmental justice after the Biden administration took office. For example, in 2021, the EPA issued two memoranda concerning environmental justice:

1. on April 30, 2021, the EPA Office of Enforcement and Compliance Assurance (OECA) issued a memorandum titled "Strengthening Enforcement in Communities with Environmental Justice Concerns,"[14] calling for an increase in facility inspections in overburdened communities, the implementation of remedies that benefit overburdened communities, and increased engagement with communities about enforcement cases that affect them; and
2. on June 21, 2021, OECA issued another memorandum titled "Strengthening Environmental Justice Through Criminal Enforcement,"[15] calling for increased outreach to crime victims in overburdened communities and enhanced remedies, including restitution to redress harms to these victims.

In early 2022, following his "Journey to Justice" tour, EPA Administrator Michael S. Regan announced several actions the EPA will take to respond to the concerns of overburdened communities, including, *inter alia,* conducting unannounced inspections of suspected noncompliant facilities and expanding air-monitoring tools and technologies to enhance enforcement. The announcement also described several agency-wide and community-specific

[12] *Executive Order on Further Advancing Racial Equity and Support for Underserved Communities Through the Federal Government*, The White House (Feb. 16, 2023), https://www.whitehouse.gov/briefing-room/presidential-actions/2023/02/16/executive-order-on-further-advancing-racial-equity-and-support-for-underserved-communities-through-the-federal-government/.

[13] *Executive Order on Revitalizing Our Nation's Commitment to Environmental Justice for All*, The White House (Apr. 21, 2023), https://www.whitehouse.gov/briefing-room/presidential-actions/2023/04/21/executive-order-on-revitalizing-our-nations-commitment-to-environmental-justice-for-all/.

[14] Memorandum from Lawrence E. Starfield, Acting Assistant Adm'r, Office of Enforcement and Compliance Assurance (OECA), EPA, to OECA Office Directors and Deputies, Enforcement and Compliance Assurance Directors and Deputies & Regional Counsels and Deputies (Apr. 30, 2021), https://www.epa.gov/sites/default/files/2021-04/documents/strengtheningenforcementincommunitieswithejconcerns.pdf.

[15] Memorandum from Lawrence E. Starfield, Acting Assistant Adm'r, OECA, EPA, to Senior Managers and Special Agents, Off. of Crim. Enf't, Forensics and Training, & Regional Criminal Enforcement Counsels, Off. of Reg'l Couns. (June 21, 2021), https://www.epa.gov/system/files/documents/2021-07/strengtheningejthroughcriminal062121.pdf.

actions that the EPA plans to undertake to address environmental justice issues in communities that are "marginalized, underserved, and overburdened by pollution."[16]

In March 2022, the EPA released its strategic plan for fiscal years 2022–2026, which includes several environmental justice initiatives and specific goals—including, for example, ensuring that 55 percent of all the EPA's annual inspections relate to communities with potential environmental justice concerns by September 30, 2026.

On September 24, 2022, the EPA announced the launching of a new national office called the Office of Environmental Justice and External Civil Rights.[17] The new office was formed to:

- Improve and enhance the agency's ability to infuse equity, civil rights, and environmental justice principles and priorities into all EPA practices, policies, and programs.
- Support the fair treatment and meaningful involvement of all people with respect to the development, implementation, and enforcement of environmental laws, regulations, and policies regardless of race, color, national origin, or income.
- Engage communities with environmental justice concerns and increase support for community-led action through grants and technical assistance.
- Enforce federal civil rights laws that, together, prohibit discrimination on the basis of race, color, or national origin (including on the basis of limited-English proficiency); sex; disability; or age by applicants for and recipients of federal financial assistance from the EPA.
- Provide services and expertise in alternative dispute resolution, environmental conflict resolution, consensus-building, and collaborative problem-solving.[18]

Then on September 30, 2022, the EPA's Office of Land and Emergency Management released the EPA's "EJ Action Plan: Building Up Environmental Justice in EPA's Land Protection and Cleanup Programs," focusing on strategies to strengthen compliance and enforcement, incorporate environmental justice considerations in the agency, increase community engagement, and advance the Biden administration's Justice40 Initiative.[19] The EPA also recently published a proposed new rule on regulating greenhouse gas emission from fossil-fuel-fired power plants.[20] Along with this proposed rulemaking, the EPA published a "Fact Sheet for

[16] *Journey to Justice*, EPA, https://www.epa.gov/environmentaljustice/journey-justice (last visited Jan. 9, 2023).

[17] EPA merged three existing programs to create the new Office: the Office of Environmental Justice, External Civil Rights Compliance Office, and Conflict Prevention and Resolution Center.

[18] Press Release, EPA, EPA Launches New National Office Dedicated to Advancing Environmental Justice and Civil Rights (Sept. 24, 2022), https://www.epa.gov/newsreleases/epa-launches-new-national-office-dedicated-advancing-environmental-justice-and-civil.

[19] Press Release, EPA, EPA Finalizes Environmental Justice Action Plan for Land Protection and Cleanup Programs (Sept. 30, 2022), https://www.epa.gov/newsreleases/epa-finalizes-environmental-justice-action-plan-land-protection-and-cleanup-programs.

[20] New Source Performance Standards for Greenhouse Gas Emissions from New, Modified, and Reconstructed Fossil Fuel-Fired Electric Generating Units; Emission Guidelines for Greenhouse Gas Emissions from Existing Fossil Fuel-Fired Electric Generating Units; and Repeal of the Affordable Clean Energy Rule, 88 Fed. Reg. 33240 (May 23, 2023) (to be codified at 40 C.F.R. pt. 60).

Communities with Environmental Justice Concerns."[21] The fact sheet discusses the environmental justice analysis that the EPA performed in developing the proposed rule, including how many communities overburdened by pollution live near fossil-fuel-fired power plants. It further discusses the estimated reductions in concentrations of pollutants that affect such communities (such as ozone and PM2.5) as a result of the rule, and the requirement that individual states in establishing their greenhouse gas emissions standards under the proposed rule conduct "meaningful engagement" with environmental justice communities.

Other federal agencies have incorporated environmental justice into their policies and procedures. In 2019, the U.S. Department of Energy (DOE), for example, published its Second Five-Year Implementation Plan on Environmental Justice.[22] The plan focuses on increasing community engagement with the DOE on agency actions, further incorporating environmental justice principles into the NEPA process, and complying with Title VI of the Civil Rights Act with respect to DOE funding recipients. Similarly, the Federal Energy Regulatory Commission (FERC), in April 2022, released an Equity Action Plan, which focuses on enhancing public participation by underserved communities, strengthening tribal engagement and consultation, and further incorporating environmental justice considerations into energy infrastructure permitting decisions.[23]

The Biden administration has also interwoven environmental justice into federal permitting and environmental reviews. Recent guidance on NEPA analyses—which have included analysis of the socioeconomic impacts of certain federal actions for over two decades—emphasizes the importance of accurately measuring environmental justice impacts and meaningfully engaging with impacted communities.[24] The administration's Permitting Action Plan, released in May 2022, incorporates early and meaningful public outreach with disadvantaged communities as a "key element" in implementation of the Infrastructure Investment and Jobs Act (IIJA).[25] And in January 2023, the EPA began requiring states seeking IIJA funding for carbon capture, use, and storage permitting programs to develop environmental justice plans.[26]

Congress has also taken notice of environmental justice concerns. Notably, the Inflation Reduction Act, passed in August 2022, has been touted by the Biden administration as the

---

[21] EPA, Fact Sheet for Communities With Environmental Justice Concerns, Greenhouse Gas Standards and Guidelines for Fossil Fuel-Fired Power Plants, Proposed Rule (May 23, 2023), https://www.epa.gov/system/files/documents/2023-05/FS-EJ-GHG-for%20Power%20Plants%20-%20FINAL%205-10-23.pdf.

[22] U.S. Department of Energy (DOE), Department of Energy 2019 Environmental Justice Second Five-Year Implementation Plan (2019), https://www.energy.gov/sites/default/files/2019/05/f62/2019FiveYearImplementationPlan_ONLINE.pdf.

[23] *Equity Action Plan*, FERC, https://www.ferc.gov/equity (April 15, 2022).

[24] National Environmental Policy Act Guidance on Consideration of Greenhouse Gas Emissions and Climate Change, 88 Fed. Reg. 1196 (Jan. 9, 2023).

[25] The Biden-Harris Permitting Action Plan to Rebuild America's Infrastructure, Accelerate the Clean Energy Transition, Revitalize Communities, and Create Jobs (2022) https://www.whitehouse.gov/wp-content/uploads/2022/05/Biden-Harris-Permitting-Action-Plan.pdf.

[26] Letter from Michael S. Regan, Adm'r, EPA, to State Governors (Jan. 18, 2023), https://www.epa.gov/system/files/documents/2023-01/Class%20VI%20LOI%20-%20Governors%201-18-23.pdf; *see also* Letter from Michael S. Regan, Adm'r, EPA, to State Governors, at 2 (Dec. 9, 2022), https://www.epa.gov/system/files/documents/2022-12/AD.Regan_.GOVS_.Sig_.Class%20VI.12-9-22.pdf (noting that "States should include environmental justice as a core element in implementing their Class VI programs.").

"single largest and most ambitious investment in the ability of the United States to advance clean energy, cut consumer energy costs, confront the climate crisis, promote environmental justice, and strengthen energy security. . . ."[27] The law commits over $60 billion in spending on environmental justice initiatives.[28] That funding, much of which will go through the EPA and the Federal Housing Administration,[29] will support initiatives such as improving climate change resiliency, decreasing air pollution, and mitigating other environmental impacts in low-income and minority communities.[30] For example, the law commits funding to the EPA to support a transition to clean heavy-duty vehicles (e.g., school buses, garbage trucks) in Clean Air Act nonattainment areas.[31] The law also creates significant tax incentives for investments in renewable energy projects located in low-income communities or on Tribal land,[32] and establishes a "Greenhouse Gas Reduction Fund" targeting investments in clean energy and climate projects, particularly those that would benefit disadvantaged communities.[33]

IV. State and Local Government Environmental Justice Initiatives

State and local governments have also begun to prioritize environmental justice issues in ways that intersect with ESG. Similar to initiatives at the federal level, state and local actions have focused on mitigating the burdens of climate change and pollution on historically underserved areas, such as low-income and minority communities, as well as ensuring equitable investments in clean energy technologies that serve those communities as well.

For example, California has long seen itself as a leader regarding environmental justice issues. California law defines environmental justice as "the fair treatment and meaningful involvement of people of all races, cultures, incomes, and national origins, with respect to the development, adoption, implementation, and enforcement of environmental laws, regulations, and policies."[34] The law further describes environmental justice as including a healthy environment for all people, the reduction or elimination of pollution burdens for populations and communities experiencing the adverse effects of that pollution, the provision of technical assistance to communities most impacted by pollution, and the promotion of meaningful participation of such communities in environmental and land-use decision-making processes.

---

[27] *Executive Order on the Implementation of the Energy and Infrastructure Provisions of the Inflation Reduction Act of 2022*, THE WHITE HOUSE (Sept. 12, 2022), https://www.whitehouse.gov/briefing-room/presidential-actions/2022/09/12/executive-order-on-the-implementation-of-the-energy-and-infrastructure-provisions-of-the-inflation-reduction-act-of-2022/.

[28] *See Inflation Reduction Act (IRA) Summary: Energy and Climate Provisions*, BIPARTISAN POL'Y CTR. (Aug. 4, 2022), https://bipartisanpolicy.org/blog/inflation-reduction-act-summary-energy-climate-provisions/.

[29] *See* Inflation Reduction Act, Pub. L. No. 117-169, § 60201, 136 Stat. 1818, 2078 (2022).

[30] *See id.*

[31] *Id.* § 60101, 136 Stat. at 2063.

[32] *Id.* § 13103, 136 Stat. at 1921.

[33] *Id.* § 60103, 136 Stat. at 2065.

[34] CAL. GOV'T CODE § 65040.12(e).

The law requires at a minimum that government entities consider the recommendations from communities most impacted by pollution when making environmental and land-use decisions.

Assembly Bill (AB) 617, signed into law in 2017, focuses on implementing policies to improve air quality and public health in communities that experience disproportionate burdens from exposure to air pollutants. The bill directs the California Air Resources Board (CARB) and local air districts to protect overburdened communities and requires the implementation of community-level air-monitoring and emission-reduction plans, expedited best available retrofit control technology, enhanced emission-reporting requirements, and increased penalty provisions. CARB also may direct grant funding to communities determined to have the highest air pollution burden. In response to AB 617, CARB established the Community Air Protection Program to reduce exposure in communities most impacted by air pollution. Air monitoring and emission reduction programs have already been implemented in a number of communities. These efforts can be monitored via CARB's CommunityHub dashboard.[35]

Also in California, in 2018, the California Attorney General's office founded a Bureau of Environmental Justice, with the mission of "protect[ing] people and communities that endure a disproportionate share of environmental pollution and public health hazards." The California Bureau of Environmental Justice has taken numerous enforcement actions, including a 2021 lawsuit against the City of Fontana challenging the approval of a warehouse project located close to a polluted community.[36] The lawsuit alleges, among other things, that the city's environmental review of the project failed to adequately consider the project's environmental impacts in violation of the California Environmental Quality Act. The proposed project would be located in a low-income neighborhood that is allegedly already exposed to especially high levels of air pollution.

More recently, California implemented a requirement that a certain amount of proceeds from the state's cap-and-trade program for greenhouse gases be directed toward disadvantaged communities.[37]

California is not alone. For example, in 2020, New Jersey passed an environmental justice law with what are considered some of the most stringent requirements of its kind. The New Jersey law requires permit applications for new or expanded industrial facilities to consider the environmental and public health impacts on historically overburdened communities, and the denial of such permits if the facility will have a disproportionately negative impact on such communities.[38] Some companies in New Jersey have tied in this law and environmental justice in general with their broader sustainability and ESG commitments.[39]

---

[35] *Community Air Protection Program Communities, CommunityHub*, CARB, https://ww2.arb.ca.gov/capp-communities (last visited Apr. 17, 2023).

[36] California v. City of Fontana, No. CIVSB2121829 (Cal. Super. Ct. July 23, 2021).

[37] *California Climate Investments to Benefit Disadvantaged Communities*, Cal. Env't Prot. Agency, https://calepa.ca.gov/envjustice/ghginvest/ (last visited Jan. 9, 2023).

[38] Act of Sept. 18, 2020, Ch. 92, https://dep.nj.gov/wp-content/uploads/ej/docs/ej-law.pdf.

[39] *See, e.g.*, Press Release, Covanta, Covanta Shares New Jersey's Commitment to Environmental Justice (Sept. 18, 2020), https://www.covanta.com/news/press-releases/covanta-shares-new-jerseys-commitment-to-environmental-justice.

Other state initiatives on environmental justice and ESG include a law passed in 2021 in Massachusetts that requires environmental impact reports for projects that have an impact on air quality and are located near certain communities.[40]

In addition to statewide initiatives, local governments are also implementing ESG policies that incorporate environmental justice principles. The City of Denver recently launched a taxpayer-funded Climate Protection Fund that is required to invest a certain percentage toward directly benefitting under-resourced and vulnerable communities, specifically naming environmental and climate justice programs as eligible.[41] Similarly, the City of Miami developed its Miami Forever Carbon Neutral Plan, which is focused in part on creating economic opportunities through the "green economy" for vulnerable climate justice communities.[42]

V. ESG Policies and Environmental Justice

While environmental justice and ESG have generally been treated as distinct concepts in policymaking and corporate practice, there are natural overlaps between the two concepts. Environmental justice has historically called on governments and the private sector to both understand and mitigate the disproportionate environmental harms of industrial processes and sites on our most vulnerable and marginalized communities. ESG has emerged as a call on the private sector to both understand and mitigate environmental and social harms more generally. As both environmental justice and ESG have moved into the spotlight, there are signs that policymaking and corporate practice are beginning to incorporate environmental justice into ESG initiatives.

A. Climate Action and Environmental Justice

Actions to address climate change have emerged as a natural bridge in both policymaking and corporate practice between environmental justice and ESG concepts. "Climate justice"—a variation on the concept of environmental justice that has gained prominence in recent years in advocacy for climate action—is based on the well-established understanding that the impacts of climate change will disproportionately be felt by low-income and marginalized communities.[43] Similar to environmental justice, climate justice frames the need for climate action in the context of those disproportionate impacts and calls for an emphasis on mitigation and adaptation for those communities.

While ESG climate initiatives, as discussed in Chapter 5—Key Principles Related to Climate Risk, Chapter 6—Climate-Related Disclosure Obligations at the Federal

[40] *See* Act of Mar. 26, 2021, Ch. 8, https://malegislature.gov/bills/192/S9.

[41] Alliance for a Sustainable Future, Cities Advancing Climate Action: Leveraging Federal Funds for Local Impact, A Resource Guide 25–29 (2022), https://www.usmayors.org/wp-content/uploads/2022/03/Alliance-for-a-Sustainable-Future-WEB.pdf.

[42] *Id.* at 40–43.

[43] Press Release, EPA, EPA Report Shows Disproportionate Impacts of Climate Change on Socially Vulnerable Populations in the United States (Sept. 2, 2021), https://www.epa.gov/newsreleases/epa-report-shows-disproportionate-impacts-climate-change-socially-vulnerable; Allison Herren Lee, *supra* note 9.

AND INTERNATIONAL LEVEL, and CHAPTER 23—PUBLIC COMPANY DISCLOSURES, have typically focused on the disclosure of climate-related risks, efforts to decarbonize or achieve net-zero emissions, and investments in climate adaptation and resiliency, there is growing recognition in policymaking and corporate practice of the overlap between ESG climate initiatives and environmental justice. In May 2021, for example, the Biden administration issued an Executive Order on Climate-Related Financial Risk, which directs the development of a government-wide climate risk strategy to identify and disclose climate-related financial risks to government programs.[44] The Executive Order notes the administration's policy of advancing "accurate disclosure of climate-related financial risk" and "mitigat[ing] that risk and its drivers while accounting for and addressing disparate impacts on disadvantaged communities and communities of color."[45]

Additionally, as noted above, the recently passed Inflation Reduction Act includes significant funding and incentives for environmental justice initiatives. Much of this funding is directed toward projects related to climate change initiatives such as emissions reductions, extreme heat risk mitigation, resiliency and adaptation, and investments in clean energy technologies in low-income communities or on Tribal land.[46]

B. Shareholder Advocacy

Shareholder advocacy groups are also paying attention to environmental justice as a serious consideration when evaluating corporate responsibility. For example, a nonprofit organization called As You Sow, founded in 1992 and whose mission is "to promote environmental and social corporate responsibility through shareholder advocacy, coalition building, and innovative legal strategies" releases a "Racial Justice S&P 500 Scorecard" that applies certain metrics to analyze each company's environmental impact of operations on communities of color. As You Sow has undertaken significant activity in shareholder advocacy initiatives pushing for corporate net-zero greenhouse gas emissions.[47]

Similar shareholder initiatives from unions and ESG investment funds have called on companies to conduct independent environmental justice and civil rights audits,[48] or to incorporate environmental justice concepts into their financing decisions.[49]

---

[44] *Executive Order on Climate-related Financial Risk*, THE WHITE HOUSE (May 20, 2021), https://www.whitehouse.gov/briefing-room/presidential-actions/2021/05/20/executive-order-on-climate-related-financial-risk/.

[45] *Id.*

[46] *See* Inflation Reduction Act, Pub. L. No. 117-169, § 60201, 136 Stat. 1818, 2078 (2022).

[47] *See, e.g.*, Press Release, As You Sow, General Electric Agrees to Ambitious Net-Zero-by-2050 Target (July 15, 2021), https://www.asyousow.org/press-releases/2021/7/15/general-electric-net-zero-by-2050-target.

[48] Megan Quinn, *Stericycle Shareholders Pass Civil Rights Proposal, Similar Proposals Pass at WM, Fail at Republic*, WASTE DIVE (June 2, 2022), https://www.wastedive.com/news/teamsters-parnassus-civil-rights-environmental-justice-wm-republic-stericycle/622527/.

[49] TRILLIUM ASSET MGMT., CLIMATE ADVOCACY, 2021-2022 CORPORATE ENGAGEMENT UPDATE (2022), https://assets-global.website-files.com/5ecd0982c9d00e2865ce6691/6304f7860cc27297483e0b00_Climate%20Work%20Advocacy%20INS009-082022.pdf.

VI. Environmental Justice and Key Considerations for Companies

As federal and state governing bodies begin taking environmental justice issues more seriously, investors' awareness of environmental justice issues may grow, and there may be increased demand for incorporation of environmental justice into corporate ESG policies and expectations. Such demands are already occurring, as noted above, with shareholders asking companies to assess their environmental impacts through a social justice lens, and incorporate those considerations into their sustainability practices. More concrete policy and legislative actions are being taken by both the federal government and state and local governments to address both environmental and climate justice issues. Climate justice is itself a growing component of climate policy actions and ESG initiatives.

As such, companies should prepare for the further inclusion of environmental justice and climate justice as explicit concerns by governments and other stakeholders, and understand the policy and legislative trends that create both opportunities and risks for companies. Such policy and legislative actions may range from assessing and disclosing environmental justice and climate justice impacts to incorporating environmental justice criteria in environmental permitting reviews, and providing financial incentives for companies to invest in environmental justice and climate-vulnerable communities.

In some cases, companies may seek to investigate whether communities surrounding a proposed or existing facility are considered overburdened. Companies may consider performing environmental justice analyses when selecting sites for new projects or when considering expanding operations at existing facilities. At a minimum, a facility located in an environmental justice or overburdened community is likely to experience a higher level of agency scrutiny when it comes to permitting, inspections, and enforcement. Fortunately, there are several tools available that companies can utilize to better understand and minimize the environmental justice impacts of their operations. Such tools include EPA's EJScreen, which combines environmental and socioeconomic data to provide a map of potential environmental justice indicators in a given community.[50] There are several state-based equivalents available as well (e.g., for California,[51] Washington,[52] and New York[53]). Additionally—given that a key component of environmental justice principles is to enhance stakeholder engagement with communities, and particularly with historically marginalized groups, in which companies are operating or have facilities—companies can seek out ways to enhance community

[50] *EJScreen: Environmental Justice Screening and Mapping Tool*, EPA, https://www.epa.gov/ejscreen (last visited Jan. 10, 2023).

[51] *CalEnviroScreen*, Cal. Off. of Env't Health Hazard Assessment, https://oehha.ca.gov/calenviroscreen (last visited Jan. 10, 2023).

[52] *Washington Environmental Health Disparities Map*, Wash. State Dep't of Health, https://doh.wa.gov/data-and-statistical-reports/washington-tracking-network-wtn/washington-environmental-health-disparities-map (last visited Jan. 10, 2023).

[53] *Maps & Geospatial Information System (GIS) Tools for Environmental Justice*, N.Y. Dep't of Env't Conservation, https://www.dec.ny.gov/public/911.html (last visited Jan 10, 2023).

engagement on issues of environmental management to better understand any potential concerns and how to mitigate those in an inclusive manner.

In addition to mitigating risks, companies may consider opportunities to proactively incorporate environmental justice practices into their ESG policies and decision-making. Not only are there significant incentives at the federal level, as is increasingly the case at the state and local levels, such practices may also attract ESG-driven investment while avoiding or minimizing environmental justice risks and impacts.

Finally, companies with facilities located (or that may be located) in an overburdened community should work together and form relationships with representatives of the surrounding community to understand community concerns and get ahead of potential issues. Among other actions, companies may consider implementing additional air-monitoring programs to maintain transparency with agencies and the community. Companies managing legacy contamination issues at environmental justice sites should consider similar actions.

Key Takeaways

- Environmental justice is a major (and growing) focus in federal, state, and local policymaking and legislative agendas. At the federal level, the Biden administration has increasingly made environmental justice objectives concrete and comprehensive.
- Climate justice is a growing component of climate change discussions.
- Environmental justice and climate justice considerations fit squarely within ESG.
- Companies should prepare for the likely inclusion of environmental justice and climate justice considerations by governments and other stakeholders.
- Companies can use the tools available to assess and minimize the environmental justice impacts of their operations.
- In some cases, companies may consider developing an environmental justice policy to help guide internal decision-making.

PART IV

Governance: Practical Advice for Getting Governance Right

15

Governance: Role of the Board

Teresa L. Johnson, Nicholas O'Keefe, Jyoti Gill, Arthur Luk, and William C. Perdue

I. Introduction

Delaware law provides that the business and affairs of Delaware corporations are managed by or under the direction of the corporation's board of directors.[1] In discharging their duty to manage or oversee the management of the corporation, directors are subject to the fiduciary duties of loyalty and care. Consistent with these duties, the board is responsible for overseeing the corporation's risk management, which includes ESG risks. With the wide range of issues and corporate functions that ESG cuts across, the growing number of regulations and lawsuits related to ESG issues, and the increasing attention from investors and other key stakeholders, board members are under considerable pressure to focus on ESG issues.

II. Corporate Governance

While there is no legal definition, corporate governance can be seen as the system of controls and procedures by which individual corporations are managed, and as a key element of overall corporate strategy and performance. A corporation's governance system is influenced by several stakeholder groups, whose interests may diverge or conflict. The primary stakeholder groups of a corporation consist of shareholders, creditors, managers and employees, the board of directors, customers, suppliers, and government/regulators. The board of directors is the central pillar of the governance structure, serves as the link between shareholders and managers, and acts as the shareholders' internal monitoring tool within the company.

[1] Del. Code Ann. tit. 8, § 141(a).

In the context of ESG, the "G" represents the processes and practices relating to corporate governance. By way of example, it encompasses issues related to the structure and composition of the board of directors and board committees, including board diversity, director expertise in relevant topics, and director overboarding; policies and practices such as those relating to executive compensation, risk management, legal compliance, business practices and ethics, financial and nonfinancial reporting and disclosures, and interactions with stakeholders; shareholder rights; and oversight over business strategy.

III. Role of the Board and Duties of Board Members

Section 141(a) of the Delaware General Corporation Law provides that the business and affairs of Delaware corporations are managed by, or under the direction of, the corporation's board of directors. The board discharges this responsibility by making major decisions for the corporation and by appointing and supervising officers who run the day-to-day operations of the corporation, propose strategies and objectives, and implement the corporation's business plan. Pursuant to these responsibilities, directors owe the core fiduciary duties of loyalty and care to the corporation and its shareholders. Courts and practitioners sometimes also refer to other duties, such as the duty of good faith, the duty of disclosure, and the duty of oversight, but courts generally treat these as obligations that stem from the core fiduciary duties of care and loyalty.[2]

A. Duties of Care and Loyalty

The duty of care requires directors to inform themselves, "prior to making a business decision, of all material information reasonably available to them"[3] and not to simply rubber stamp management's recommendations. In ascertaining whether directors have complied with their duty of care, courts have looked to factors such as whether directors have been informed of relevant internal and external developments, engaged in discussion with relevant advisors, reviewed relevant documents, and made a reasonable inquiry of relevant issues.[4] Note, however, that while the board is required to be reasonably informed, it is not required to be informed of every fact.[5]

The duty of loyalty requires directors to act and make decisions in the good-faith belief that the decisions are in the best interests of the corporation and its shareholders, without favoring their own personal interests, and to refrain from conduct that would injure the corporation and its shareholders.[6]

Delaware law presumes that in making business decisions, the directors of a corporation were disinterested and acted on an informed basis, in good faith, and in the honest belief that

[2] Stone v. Ritter, 911 A.2d 362 (Del. 2006); Stroud v. Grace, 606 A.2d 75, 84 (Del. 1992).

[3] Aronson v. Lewis, 473 A.2d 805, 812 (Del. 1988).

[4] *See, e.g.*, Metro. Life Ins. Co. v. Aramark Corp., 1998 Del. Ch. LEXIS 70 (Feb. 5, 1998).

[5] *See In re* Walt Disney Co. Derivative Litig., 731 A.2d 342 (Del. Ch. 1988).

[6] *The Delaware Way: Deference to the Business Judgment of Directors Who Act Loyally and Carefully*, DEL. CORP. L., https://corplaw.delaware.gov/delaware-way-business-judgment/ (last visited Oct. 6, 2022).

the actions taken were in the best interests of the corporation.[7] This presumption is known as the "business judgment rule." It protects directors from personal liability from decisions made in their capacities as directors where the presumption applies. The business judgment rule is a judicially created rule to protect good faith decisions of directors from judicial second-guessing. A party challenging the propriety of director action bears the burden of rebutting the applicability of this presumption. Where the rule applies, directors will not be subject to liability for decisions that satisfy a rational business purpose.[8] Where the presumption is rebutted through a requisite showing of lack of loyalty or due care, the board has the burden of proving the "entire fairness" of the decision.[9]

B. Duty of Oversight

Delaware courts have interpreted directors' fiduciary duties as encompassing a duty of oversight.[10] Under the seminal *Caremark* decision,[11] the "board of a Delaware corporation has a fiduciary obligation to adopt internal information and reporting systems that are reasonably designed to provide to senior management and to the board itself timely, accurate information sufficient to allow management and the board, each within its scope, to reach informed judgments concerning both the corporation's compliance with law and its business performance."[12] The *Caremark* standard for oversight liability "draws heavily upon the concept of director failure to act in good faith," which itself implicates the duty of loyalty.[13] The basis for director liability under *Caremark* is "(a) the directors utterly failed to implement any reporting or information system or controls; or (b) having implemented such a system or controls, consciously failed to monitor or oversee its operations thus disabling themselves from being informed of risks or problems requiring their attention. In either case, imposition of liability requires a showing that the directors knew that they were not discharging their fiduciary obligations."[14] Only "a sustained or systematic failure of the board to exercise oversight—such as an utter failure to attempt to assure a reasonable information and reporting system exists—will establish the lack of good faith that is a necessary condition to liability."[15]

Caremark encompasses two elements: (a) a duty to make a good faith effort to implement a board-level system of risk monitoring and reporting and (b) a duty to actually monitor. Courts have differentiated between the monitoring of ordinary course business risks, on the one hand, and monitoring of fraudulent or criminal conduct, or other legal compliance,

---

[7] *Aronson*, 473 A.2d at 812.

[8] Brehm v. Eisner, 746 A.2d 244, 264 n.66 (Del. 2000).

[9] *In re* Trados Inc. Shareholder Litig., 2009 WL 2225958, at *6 (Del. Ch. July 24, 2009).

[10] *In re* Caremark Int'l Inc. Derivative Litig., 698 A.2d 959 (Del. Ch. 1996).

[11] *Id.*

[12] *In re* China Agritech, Inc. S'holder Derivative Litig., No. 7163-VCL, 2013 WL 2181514, at *18 (Del. Ch. May 21, 2013) (quoting *Caremark*, 698 A.2d at 970).

[13] *Stone*, 911 A.2d 362; *Stroud*, 606 A.2d at 84.

[14] *Id.*

[15] *In re* Citigroup Inc. S'holder Derivative Litig., 964 A.2d 106 (Del. Ch. 2009).

on the other hand.[16] Monitoring of ordinary course business risks will typically fall within the presumptions of the business judgment rule. A failure to implement systems to monitor fraud, criminal conduct, workplace harassment, or other legal compliance is the type of failure that has been recognized by courts as giving rise to *Caremark* liability.

Courts have looked at the following factors as evidence of a lack of good-faith implementation of risk-monitoring systems:

- The lack of any board committee assigned with responsibility for overseeing the applicable risk issue;
- Where a committee has been assigned to oversee the risk, the committee having completely failed to perform the role assigned to it;
- The lack of any whistleblower system that would permit whistleblowers to report concerns directly to the board;
- The lack of any regularly scheduled board discussions of the risk at issue;
- The lack of any regular process or protocols requiring management to keep the board apprised of the risks at issue;
- The fact that management received information that could be described as yellow flag or red flag, but failed to pass it on to the board;
- Management giving the board selective information that was intended to minimize the significance of the risk; and
- The lack of any mention in board minutes of a discussion regarding the risk at issue.[17]

Courts have held that the monitoring system has to be implemented in good faith, but it does not have to be perfect.[18] The *Marchand* case, decided in 2019, has been followed by an uptick in successful *Caremark* claims, including the expansion of *Caremark* duties to executives by a Delaware Chancery Court in the 2023 *McDonald's* case.[19]

IV. Board Oversight of ESG Risks

As indicated elsewhere in this guide, boards are confronted with ESG considerations in a multitude of contexts, including business decisions, legal compliance, and interactions with the government, investors, and other stakeholders. Boards need to be proactive, consistent

---

[16] *See, e.g., In re* Facebook, Inc. Section 220 Litig., No. 2018-0661-JRS, 2019 WL 2320842 (Del. Ch. May 31, 2019).

[17] *In re* The Boeing Co. Derivative Litig., No. 2019-0907-MTZ, 2021 WL 4059934 (Del. Ch. Sept. 7, 2021); Marchand v. Barnhill, 212 A.3d 805 (Del. 2019).

[18] Hughes v. Xiaoming Hu, No. 2019-0112-JTL, 2020 WL 1987029 (Del. Ch. Apr. 27, 2020) (differentiating *In re* Gen. Motors Co. Derivative Litig., No. 9627-VCG, 2015 WL 3958724 (Del. Ch. June 26, 2015), where a reporting system existed but the argument was that it should have been better).

[19] *In re* McDonald's Corp. S'holder Derivative Litig., 289 A.3d 343 (Del. Ch. 2023). Notably, though the January *McDonald's* decision allowed the plaintiffs' breach of duty of oversight claim against McDonald's former Chief People Officer (arising out of the failure to exercise oversight over workplace harassment claims) to survive a motion to dismiss, the same Delaware Chancery Court judge dismissed the related case against the board of McDonald's Corporation arising out of the same circumstances, noting that the plaintiffs failed to adequately show that the board acted in bad faith. *In re* McDonald's Corp. S'holder Derivative Litig., No. 2021-0324-JTL, 2023 WL 2293575 (Del. Ch. Mar. 1, 2023).

with their duties regarding long-term value creation and their *Caremark* oversight duties, in monitoring ESG-related risks.

A. Types of ESG Risk

The following are some of the broad categories of risks that are implicated by ESG considerations:

- Litigation risks—This includes a wide range of matters, including (1) supply chain issues focused on matters such as human rights and child labor, (2) claims under consumer protection laws based on environmental misrepresentations, (3) claims based on diversity, equity, and inclusion initiatives focused on boards and management, and (4) a broad range of climate-related litigation, which has been increasing and is expected to continue to increase in the future.[20] This last category includes matters specific to the litigants, such as the construction of buildings in areas vulnerable to rising sea levels; litigation intended to advance climate policies that target not just fossil fuel companies but other companies with a high carbon footprint, such as meat and dairy companies; cases targeting financial market actors with respect to matters such as inadequate disclosure, greenwashing, and management of climate change risk; and claims invoking constitutional and human rights theories.
- Regulatory risks—As indicated elsewhere in this book, there are multiple regulatory regimes that are implicated by ESG. The Supreme Court's recent *West Virginia v. EPA*[21] decision is likely to increase regulatory uncertainty and heighten the need for effective corporate monitoring.
- Disclosure risk—Failure to include materially complete and accurate disclosure about ESG-related occurrences and trends can create securities law exposure for U.S. public companies. On March 4, 2021, the U.S. Securities and Exchange Commission (SEC) announced the creation of a Climate and ESG Task Force in the Division of Enforcement.[22] According to the SEC's release, an initial focus of the initiative is "to identify any material gaps or misstatements in issuers' disclosure of climate risks under existing rules." The SEC has also proposed new climate change rules ("SEC Proposed Climate Rules") that, if adopted as proposed, will require extensive disclosure by public companies regarding climate-related risks and greenhouse gas emissions.[23]
- Human capital risks—Human capital management has emerged as a key component of ESG analysis and is widely recognized as a potential source of both financial

[20] *See, e.g.*, Joana Setzer & Catherine Higham, Grantham Rsch. Inst. on Climate Change & the Env't, Global Trends in Climate Change Litigation: 2021 Snapshot (2021), https://www.lse.ac.uk/granthaminstitute/publication/global-trends-in-climate-litigation-2021-snapshot/.

[21] West Virginia v. EPA, 142 S. Ct. 2587 (2022).

[22] Press Release, U.S. Securities and Exchange Commission (SEC), SEC Announces Enforcement Task Force Focused on Climate and ESG Issues (Mar. 4, 2021), https://www.sec.gov/news/press-release/2021-42.

[23] The SEC Proposed Climate Rules were issued on March 21, 2022. The final rules have not been published as of the publication date of this book. *See* Chapter 6—Climate-Related Disclosure Obligations at the Federal and International Level for more detail.

and reputational risk for organizations. Human capital management encompasses issues such as compensation and benefits and pay equity; employee engagement; talent development and management; diversity, equity, and inclusion; and health and safety, including working conditions, anti-harassment policies, and structured safety protocols such as disaster planning and pandemic measures. The SEC and the Delaware courts have shown an increasing focus on workplace harassment claims as a source of ESG-related liability, as evidenced by the Delaware Chancery Court's decision in the January 2023 *McDonald's* case, the related SEC cease-and-desist order against McDonald's Corporation and its former chief executive officer, and the SEC cease-and-desist order against Activision Blizzard, Inc., for disclosure control failures arising out of widespread employee complaints of workplace misconduct.[24]

- Climate-related physical risks—Business harm caused by climate-related disasters, including short-term harm such as tornadoes, floods, heat waves, hurricanes, and wildfires, and longer-term phenomena such as droughts, sea-level rises, and temperature increases (an example of this is Pacific Gas and Electric's 2019 bankruptcy filing after destruction caused by the 2018 Camp Fire).
- Climate-related transition risks—Regulatory, technological, and market changes arising from mitigating or adapting to climate-related risks. This includes factors such as increased costs and decreasing profits, asset devaluations, the cost of adopting new technologies, and changes in consumer preferences.
- Reputational risks—Social media and other electronic information-sharing platforms have increased visibility and scrutiny of corporate activity. For example, images of oil spills, employee claims of harassment and abuse, allegations of ecosystems and indigenous communities impacted by extractive industry projects, cybersecurity breaches that expose customer data, or stories of child labor can be shared around the globe in hours. Such scrutiny not only engenders reputational risk but can also jeopardize supply agreements and consumer loyalty, and amplify risk of government investigations, enforcement, and litigation.
- Data privacy and data security breach risks—Data collection and storage implicates each of the "E," "S," and "G" elements of ESG. The framework within which data is stored and protected can be seen as a data governance framework. An ineffective data governance framework has implications for the soundness of a corporation's overall corporate governance. Social issues are implicated through protection of employee data. For corporations, such as social media companies, social issues also arise from the potential perception that their platforms engender harm to minors and minorities.

[24] *See In re McDonald's*, 289 A.3d 343; *see also* Stephen J. Easterbrook, Securities Act Release No. 11144, Exchange Act Release No. 96610, 2023 WL 143292 (Jan. 9, 2023); Activision Blizzard, Inc., Exchange Act Release No. 96796, 2023 WL 1765354 (Feb. 3, 2023). The Delaware Chancery Court found that corporate officers have a duty of oversight in denying the defendant officers' motion to dismiss in the January 2023 *McDonald's* case—notably, a parallel suit brought against the McDonald's board, arising out of the same facts, was dismissed by the same court in March 2023, citing the protections of the business judgment rule and concluding that the directors had acted in good faith to address the observed "red flags" in conduct. Though the case against the McDonald's directors was dismissed, the court noted that *Caremark* duties of a board extend beyond "mission critical" risks to broader central compliance risks.

Environmental issues are implicated through factors such as the energy-intensive nature of generating and storing data, and the requirement to ensure that data is stored in locations that are less vulnerable to climate risks.

- Risks based on lobbying—There is increased focus from governments, investors, and nongovernmental organizations on the lobbying positions of trade associations and how those positions align with the statements of member companies. For example, Congress has questioned some companies on their interactions with trade associations and the groups' positions on climate change. From the investor perspective, BlackRock explained that "we expect companies to monitor the positions taken by trade associations of which they are active members on such issues for consistency on major policy positions and to provide an explanation where inconsistencies exist."[25]
- Risks associated with lost opportunities—ESG is not just about managing risks but also about seizing opportunities (as discussed in the next section below). Managing ESG issues well can enhance corporate value and performance and create competitive advantages against industry peers that could otherwise go uncaptured.

B. Oversight of ESG Risks

The business judgment rule affords boards flexibility in how they implement their oversight systems and controls. There are several publicly available frameworks that can be used for reference. For example, the Committee of Sponsoring Organizations of the Treadway Commission (COSO) has published a framework[26] for enterprise risk management (ERM), which it defines as "the culture, capabilities, and practices, integrated with strategy-setting and performance, that organizations rely on to manage risk in creating, preserving, and realizing value." The COSO framework includes five elements:

- Governance and Culture (including exercise of board risk oversight, establishment of operating structures, defining a culture, demonstrating commitment to values, and involvement of capable individuals);
- Strategy and Objective-setting (including analysis of business context, definition of risk appetite, evaluation of alternative strategies, and formulation of business objectives);
- Performance (including identification, assessment, and prioritization of risk; implementation of risk responses; and development of portfolio view);
- Review and Revision; and
- Information, Communication, and Reporting.

COSO and the World Business Council for Sustainable Development (WBCSD) have developed a variation of the COSO framework that is focused on ERM for ESG-related

[25] BlackRock, Our 2021 Stewardship Expectations: Global Principles and Market-level Voting Guidelines 8 (2020), https://www.blackrock.com/corporate/literature/publication/our-2021-stewardship-expectations.pdf.

[26] Committee of Sponsoring Organizations of the Treadway Commission (COSO), Enterprise Risk Management—Integrating with Strategy and Performance (2017), https://www.coso.org/SitePages/Enterprise-Risk-Management-Integrating-with-Strategy-and-Performance-2017.aspx?web=1.

risks.[27] Ceres, a sustainability nonprofit organization, further refined the COSO approach to come up with a number of recommendations to boards that focus on risk identification, risk assessment, and risk mitigation.[28] The Task Force on Climate-related Financial Disclosures (TCFD) has promulgated recommendations for climate-related financial disclosures to assist public companies and other organizations to "more effectively disclose climate-related risks and opportunities."[29] The TCFD framework was heavily relied on by the SEC when promulgating the SEC Proposed Climate Rules.

C. Board Committees

An effective ESG oversight program will typically entail use of one or more board committees. Under Delaware law, a duly appointed board committee holds all powers delegated to it by the full board (or as otherwise provided for in the certificate of incorporation or bylaws).[30] Directors are protected from liability when they rely in good faith on reports from committees, officers, or employees, or from experts selected with reasonable care where the directors reasonably believe the reports are within the experts' professional or expert competence, when making decisions for the corporation.[31] There are variations in approach as to which board committees address ESG risks. Deliberations on ESG risks should be coordinated across committees—the board should establish systems for committees to work with each other on ESG risk oversight. Committee charters should be updated to address newly added ESG responsibilities. Below are examples of board committees and types of ESG risk oversight that each might undertake:

- Audit Committee—The audit committee, which public company boards are required to have, sometimes oversees the organizational risk management process to ensure ESG risks are adequately identified, processed, and assessed. The audit committee may oversee disclosure of ESG risks; it can ensure ESG issues are identified and prioritized as part of an ERM process.
- Risk Committee—Some boards choose to allocate general ESG oversight to the board's general risk committee, with the audit committee retaining oversight of ESG-related financial risk.

[27] COSO & World Business Council for Sustainable Development (WBCSD), Enterprise Risk Management: Applying Enterprise Risk Management to Environmental, Social and Governance-related Risks (2018), https://www.wbcsd.org/Programs/Redefining-Value/Making-stakeholder-capitalism-actionable/Enterprise-Risk-Management/Resources/Applying-Enterprise-Risk-Management-to-Environmental-Social-and-Governance-related-Risks.

[28] Veena Ramani & Hannah Saltman, Ceres, Running the Risk: How Corporate Boards Can Oversee Environmental, Social and Governance (ESG) Issues (2019), https://www.ceres.org/sites/default/files/reports/2020-01/Running%20the%20Risk_Ceres_2020.pdf.

[29] Task Force on Climate-related Financial Disclosures (TCFD), Final Report: Recommendations of the Task Force on Climate-related Financial Disclosures (2017), https://assets.bbhub.io/company/sites/60/2021/10/FINAL-2017-TCFD-Report.pdf.

[30] Del. Code Ann. tit. 8, § 141(c)(2).

[31] Del. Code Ann. tit. 8, § 141(e).

- Sustainability/Corporate Social Responsibility (CSR) Committee—Other boards allocate ESG-related risks to a separate sustainability/CSR committee, with non-ESG risks allocated to a separate risk committee, the audit committee, or the nominating and governance committee.
- Nominating and Governance Committee—The nominating and governance committee may integrate ESG within board training and board performance evaluations and consider ESG or sustainability experience in director qualifications and board composition. Diversity of a board's composition, in terms of gender, underrepresented communities, or similar factors is also in the purview of the nominating and governance committee.
- Compensation/Human Resources Committee—This committee may take ESG issues into account by incentivizing executives to mitigate ESG-related risks; overseeing the effect of the corporation's public corporate strategy on ESG issues on the corporation's ability to recruit and retain talent; and overseeing policies and procedures on workforce development, including pay equity and diversity.

D. Board ESG Expert

During the Keynote Address at the 2021 Society for Corporate Governance National Conference, SEC Commissioner Allison Herren Lee said,

> To effectively address climate and ESG risks, boards need adequate expertise on these subjects. Yet research shows that, while boards have made strides in recent years, directors may still fall short in terms of ESG credentials. Companies should consider ways to enhance the ESG competence of their boards. These efforts could include integrating ESG considerations into their nominating processes in order to recruit directors that will bring ESG expertise to the board; training and education efforts to enhance board members' expertise on ESG matters; and considering engagement with outside experts to provide advice and guidance to boards.[32]

This underscores the decision that boards must make in the context of ESG governance: whether to have an expert on a specific ESG topic on the board or address the knowledge gap by educating the current directors, drawing from their collective experience and supplementing with outside expertise as needed. There are several pros and cons to consider with respect to this topic.

Pros:

- An ESG expert would be a key leader in satisfying the board's oversight of an ESG-compliant growth strategy and would be positioned to support the board in

[32] Allison Herren Lee, Comm'r, SEC, Climate, ESG, and the Board of Directors: "You Cannot Direct the Wind, But You Can Adjust Your Sails" (June 28, 2021), https://www.sec.gov/news/speech/lee-climate-esg-board-of-directors.

mitigating risks of industry-relevant ESG factors, such as carbon emissions, worker safety, and fair compensation practices. By adding expert ESG competence, boards can better support management in ESG strategy and enhance corporate governance for all stakeholders.[33]

- A knowledgeable director can influence the board's discussions and decisions to a greater degree than an outside consultant. And having such expertise on the board shows external stakeholders that the company takes ESG seriously.[34]
- Institutional investors are increasingly emphasizing their expectation that boards have adequate expertise on climate and ESG subjects to effectively address such risks. For instance, Vanguard, in a comment letter to the SEC on climate change disclosures, expressed its view that corporate disclosure should allow investors "to assess the climate competency of a company's board."[35]

Cons:

- If a board decides an ESG expert is needed on the board, that suggests the board should do the same for other important topics and subject matters. But having single-subject expert directors for separate areas does not maximize efficiency for the board or the company. Ideally, directors bring an array of core skills to the table (not just one subject area) and have the ability to raise informed questions on a variety of topics and to absorb and analyze large amounts of complex information (even in areas in which they are not experts). In turn, these directors can build the necessary ESG understanding through academics and access to outside expertise.[36]
- Relying on consultants for outside expertise, as opposed to board candidates, allows boards to select consultants with deep subject-matter expertise on specific ESG topics, as opposed to board candidates who would need both the knowledge of those specific topics and the broad experience that makes them suitable to serve as a director. Accordingly, the pool of such consultants is likely to be a lot bigger than the pool of such board candidates.[37]
- The ESG director could be treated as an expert and thus have greater exposure to liability under federal securities laws (there is a safe harbor for audit

[33] Nasdaq, *The Value of ESG Experts on Future Corporate Boards* (May 25, 2022, 8:52 AM), https://www.nasdaq.com/articles/the-value-of-esg-experts-on-future-corporate-boards.

[34] BCG & INSEAD Corp. Governance Ctr., Directors Can Up Their Game on Environmental, Social, and Governance Issues: The BCG-INSEAD Board ESG Pulse Check (2022) https://www.insead.edu/sites/default/files/assets/dept/centres/icgc/docs/directors-can-up-their-game-on-environmental-social-and-governance-issues-march2022.pdf.

[35] *See* Letter from John Galloway, Principal & Inv. Stewardship Officer, The Vanguard Grp., Inc., to Vanessa A. Countryman, Sec'y, SEC (June 11, 2021), https://www.sec.gov/comments/climate-disclosure/cll12-8906800-244148.pdf.

[36] Ernst & Young, How Can Boards Strengthen Governance to Accelerate Their ESG journeys? EY Long-term Value and Corporate Governance Survey (2022), https://assets.ey.com/content/dam/ey-sites/ey-com/en_gl/topics/attractiveness/ey-long-term-value-and-corporate-governance-survey-february-2022-v2.pdf.

[37] BCG & INSEAD Corp. Governance Ctr., *supra* note 34.

committee financial experts under Reg S-K, but the SEC did not propose one under the ESG rules).[38]

- "Cognitive entrenchment"—Studies have shown that as people gain deeper expertise in an area, they acquire more accurate and detailed knowledge but also become less flexible in their thinking and less likely to change their perspective. So expert-dominated boards might be less effective in responding to new information or unfamiliar situations.[39]
- Single-subject experts can negatively impact the level of "task conflict"—the extent to which board members have different viewpoints, ideas, and opinions about the decisions they face. Some amount of task conflict is essential because it allows the board to explore and discuss more alternatives. But research suggests that a high proportion of subject-matter experts can suppress task conflict because nonexpert directors may defer too much to the judgment of experts.[40] This can also have a negative effect on collegiality.

E. Disclosure of ESG Issues

Given the importance of ESG issues to many stakeholders, companies may wish to share information with the market about their commitment to ESG matters, management of ESG risks, and progress towards ESG goals. In addition, the SEC disclosure rules, both those in effect as of the publication date of this book and the SEC's Proposed Climate Rules that may be adopted, may require issuers to include disclosures in their periodic reports about ESG matters and risks. The board should be guiding the strategy about how, when, and what to say in ESG disclosures. These ESG disclosures may be in response to pressure from investors and other stakeholders, or to comply with SEC disclosure requirements, as described below. ESG disclosures may be qualitative or quantitative. Qualitative ESG disclosures and public statements should reinforce the company's purpose statement, while quantitative metrics help companies measure their progress toward goals and help investors compare companies across industries. Once a company has decided on its purpose, messaging, metrics, and which standards and frameworks to use, it will have to consider where to disclose the information. Among the most common platforms are proxy statements, CSR/sustainability reports, company websites, SEC periodic reports, and social media platforms. These choices should be informed by regulatory requirements, stakeholder preferences, and

[38] Section 11 under the Securities Act creates liability for directors and certain others for material misstatements and omissions in registration statements. There is a due diligence defense available to directors, where a director "had, after reasonable investigation, reasonable ground to believe and did believe, at the time such part of the registration statement became effective, that the statements therein were true . . . ." Case law indicates that this standard will be harder to satisfy where the director is deemed to be an expert in the topic to which the defective disclosure relates. Section 10(b) under the Securities Exchange Act of 1934 also creates a liability regime for material misstatements or omissions, but not just in registration statements, and with an additional "scienter" element required for liability. Case law indicates that the scienter requirement is also easier to satisfy for directors who are experts in the topic to which the defective disclosure relates.

[39] András Tilcsik & Juan Almandoz, *When Having Too Many Experts on the Board Backfires*, Harv. Bus. Rev. (Aug. 29, 2016), https://hbr.org/2016/08/when-having-too-many-experts-on-the-board-backfires.

[40] *Id.*

peer practices, as well as the liability risk associated with SEC and other public disclosures. Regardless of where it is presented, the measuring and reporting of information should be developed under established policies and procedures to help ensure the information is complete, accurate, and reliable.

1. SEC Regulations and Board Oversight of SEC Reports

Disclosure issues are critically important for public companies. Failure to make required disclosures, or making materially inaccurate disclosures, can trigger liability to the SEC and to shareholders. Rules 10b-5 and 12b-20 under the Securities Exchange Act of 1934, and Sections 11 and 12(a) under the Securities Act of 1933, obligate public companies to ensure their disclosures are materially complete and accurate. Information is material if there is a substantial likelihood that a reasonable investor would consider it important in determining whether or not to make an investment.[41] To the extent ESG issues are material, they may be required to be disclosed in the Annual Report on Form 10-K and in other periodic reports filed with the SEC. (For details about SEC regulations and guidance related to climate-related disclosures, refer to CHAPTER 6—CLIMATE-RELATED DISCLOSURE OBLIGATIONS AT THE FEDERAL AND INTERNATIONAL LEVEL.) Determining whether those ESG risks and opportunities will have a material impact on a company's strategy, messaging, risk assessment, and reporting is critical as companies compete for capital. Determining materiality for ESG purposes creates its own challenge, and boards have a key oversight role to play.

"Reporting up" processes identifying material financial, operational, and other risks affecting the company should address ESG risks. It is the board's job to oversee that process and ensure that management has designed these processes in such a way to help ensure that material ESG risks are identified, verified, and then brought to the board's attention. Management's judgment about which of the issues to bring to the board should be informed by a materiality analysis, and the board should understand management's process for identifying the ESG issues relevant to the company, assessing those issues for materiality, and deciding what to disclose and where. In their oversight role, boards are concerned with ensuring the accuracy of the information disclosed, including internal processes and controls for both qualitative information and quantitative metrics which confirm and support that ESG disclosures are materially accurate and contain no material omissions. Over the past several years, strong investor interest has shifted the analysis of how both climate- and diversity-related actions must be assessed for materiality. As such, the assessment of financial and non-financial impacts of ESG issues should not be static, and it is incumbent on the board to ensure that the company has a robust process for regularly reviewing its ESG materiality assessments, the factors covered in those assessments (including the applicable regulatory requirements), and decisions about what to disclose and where.

---

[41] TSC Indus. v. Northway, Inc., 426 U.S. 438 (1976).

2. *Corporate Sustainability Reports*

Many companies (including the vast majority of the largest U.S. publicly traded companies) publish sustainability or CSR reports detailing their ESG goals and the ESG metrics and risks of their business operations. CSRs have become the principal channel for many companies to communicate with their stakeholders and the market about the company's sustainability performance and impact. They are not mandatory in the United States[42] but are becoming relatively common, and in 2021, 96 percent of companies in the S&P 500[43] published sustainability or CSR reports even though not required by law to do so.

If a company decides to publish a CSR report, it is critical that the sustainability disclosures in the CSR report align with the company's periodic SEC filings to avoid inconsistencies, misstatements, and overstatements of sustainability performance that could lead to liability under securities law. Importantly, SEC Rule 10b-5 applies to any information released to the public by a company, and accordingly, liability under Rule 10b-5 applies to sustainability disclosures in voluntary sustainability reports. Therefore, a reporting company's internal review process for its sustainability report requires the same amount of rigor as is applied to disclosures in a company's SEC filings. The SEC has become increasingly focused on CSR disclosures. Notably, the SEC included a question in its 2021 sample climate-related disclosure comment letter about providing ESG disclosures in a company's CSR that were broader than those included in the periodic reports filed with the SEC.[44] The board should ensure that the CSR has been prepared with appropriate "reporting up" and quality assurance processes, just as it would for preparing SEC periodic reports. The board should also ensure that management, in consultation with the company's securities counsel, has reviewed the CSR to confirm that it does not contain disclosures of any material information that has not been previously disclosed in the company's periodic reports, and that information disclosed in the CSR is consistent with disclosures in the periodic reports.[45]

F. ESG Opportunities

ESG also presents opportunities for companies that boards should consider in structuring and guiding the company's strategy. According to Ocean Tomo, 90 percent of the S&P

[42] Mandatory ESG disclosures are required in certain other jurisdictions. For example, in the United Kingdom, listed companies are mandated to provide a report disclosing annual greenhouse gas emissions and diversity under the Companies Act 2006. Additionally, in April 2021, the European Union adopted the Corporate Sustainability Reporting Directive proposal that will require entities that meet two of the three following criteria: a net turnover of more than €40 million, balance sheet assets greater than €20 million, and/or more than 250 employees to disclose environmental, social, and employee-related matters, such as antibribery, corruption, and human rights performance, effective January 2023.

[43] *S&P 500® + Russell 1000® 2022 Sustainability Reporting in Focus*, GOVERNANCE & ACCOUNTABILITY INST., INC., https://www.ga-institute.com/research/ga-research-directory/sustainability-reporting-trends/2022-sustainability-reporting-in-focus.html (last visited July 10, 2023).

[44] *Sample Letter to Companies Regarding Climate Change Disclosures*, SEC, https://www.sec.gov/corpfin/sample-letter-climate-change-disclosures (Sept. 22, 2021).

[45] Some issuers are including disclaimer language in their CSRs noting that the inclusion of information in the CSR does not signify that such information is "material" for SEC purposes. *See, e.g.*, AMAZON, DELIVERING PROGRESS EVERY DAY: AMAZON'S 2021 SUSTAINABILITY REPORT (2022), https://sustainability.aboutamazon.com/2021-sustainability-report.pdf.

500's market value today is comprised of intangible assets, such as human capital, customer loyalty, and brand identification, and such assets can be substantially affected by a company's ESG position.[46] ESG opportunities can lead to increased revenue, lower operating expenses, reduced regulatory enforcement and legal costs, increased resilience, improved reputation, and/or higher levels of employee engagement and productivity. Therefore, ESG can be viewed not only as a way to avoid risks but also as a way for companies to gauge and identify future opportunities to seize unrealized value, set themselves apart from their peers, and gain a competitive advantage in attracting and retaining talent and driving future corporate growth.

The TCFD[47] identified the following areas of climate-related opportunity:

- Resource efficiency—Companies can successfully reduce operating costs by improving energy efficiency in their production and distribution processes, buildings, machinery, appliances, and transportation equipment. Companies may also reduce operating costs by improving efficiency in their water usage and waste management.
- Energy sources—Companies may also find opportunities in shifting to clean energy sources. Clean energy costs are rapidly declining, and storage capabilities are improving.[48] Companies that shift their energy usage toward low-emission energy sources could potentially save on annual energy costs.
- Products and services—Companies that innovate and develop new low-emission products and services may improve their competitive advantage and capitalize on shifting consumer and producer preferences. Examples include consumer goods and services that place a greater emphasis on a product's carbon footprint in its marketing and labeling, and producer goods that place emphasis on reducing emissions.
- Developing new markets[49]—Companies that proactively seek opportunities in new markets may better position themselves for the transition to a lower-carbon economy. New market opportunities can be created through collaboration with governments, development banks, small-scale local entrepreneurs, and community groups seeking to shift to a lower-carbon economy.
- Climate resilience—ESG also presents opportunities for companies to increase their climate resilience (e.g., their adaptive capacity to respond to climate change to better manage the associated risks and seize opportunities, including the ability to respond to transition risks and physical risks). By improving efficiency, designing new production processes, and developing new products, a company may position itself to weather climate changes more effectively and efficiently.

---

[46] *Intangible Asset Market Value Study*, Ocean Tomo, https://www.oceantomo.com/intangible-asset-market-value-study/ (last visited Apr. 11, 2023).

[47] TCFD, *supra* note 29.

[48] *Power Forward 3.0: How the Largest U.S. Companies Are Capturing Business Value While Addressing Climate Change*, Ceres (Apr. 25, 2017), https://www.ceres.org/resources/reports/power-forward-3.

[49] Per the TCFD Final Report, this is meant to capture both opportunities in new markets and new types of assets. It also includes opportunities that may be captured through underwriting or financing green bonds and infrastructure (i.e., low-emission energy production, energy efficiency, grid connectivity, or transport networks).

V. Constituents Focused on ESG

A. Institutional Investors

HSBC's 2021 sustainable financing and investing survey, which polled around 2,000 issuers and institutional investors, found that 59 percent of investors have a general ESG policy in place and that 85 percent of large investors (those with more than $25 billion in assets) have implemented a company-wide ESG approach. BlackRock, State Street, and Vanguard have all announced ESG voting policies and priorities, and in 2021, they all signed on to the Net Zero Asset Managers Initiative, a commitment to push the companies in which they invest toward cutting their net greenhouse gas emissions completely by 2050.[50] They also have adopted voting policies focused on various ESG issues, including the achievement of board diversity in gender and members of underrepresented communities, and on providing adequate disclosure and oversight of material ESG risk factors.[51]

Some examples of ESG policies in BlackRock's 2023 Proxy Voting guidelines for U.S. securities include (1) an expectation that boards be diverse, stating that boards should aspire to 30 percent diversity, with at least two directors who identify as female and at least one who identifies as a member of an underrepresented group; (2) support for incentive plans that foster the sustainable achievement of results—both financial and non-financial, including ESG; and (3) a request for companies to disclose a business plan for how they intend to deliver long-term financial performance through the transition to global net zero and the considerations related to having a reliable energy supply and just transition affect their plans.[52]

Additionally, pension funds are becoming more focused on ESG issues. The California State Teachers' Retirement System (CalSTRS), the second-largest pension fund in the United States with more than $300 billion in assets, announced recently that beginning with the 2022 proxy season, it will oppose directors who are moving too slowly on diversity and climate change and support shareholder proposals that seek to reduce carbon emissions. CalSTRS is also pushing the companies in which it invests to diversify their boards and to provide more information about diversity of board members, as well as more climate-related disclosures.[53] However, as noted in more detail below, other states are taking the opposite approach and pushing back on ESG considerations and limiting their pension funds' ability to invest in ESG-focused funds.

---

[50] Vanguard withdrew from the Net Zero Asset Managers Initiative in December 2022, citing concerns about the role of index funds and its independence, *see* https://corporate.vanguard.com/content/corporatesite/us/en/corp/articles/update-on-nzam-engagement.html.

[51] BLACKROCK, BLACKROCK INVESTMENT STEWARDSHIP: PROXY VOTING GUIDELINES FOR U.S. SECURITIES (2023), https://www.blackrock.com/corporate/literature/fact-sheet/blk-responsible-investment-guidelines-us.pdf; STATE STREET GLOBAL ADVISORS, SUMMARY OF MATERIAL CHANGES TO STATE STREET GLOBAL ADVISORS' 2023 PROXY VOTING AND ENGAGEMENT GUIDELINES (2023), https://www.ssga.com/lu/fr/institutional/etfs/library-content/pdfs/asr-library/summary-material-changes-ssga-proxy-voting-and-engagement.pdf; VANGUARD, INVESTMENT STEWARDSHIP: 2022 SEMIANNUAL REPORT (2022), https://corporate.vanguard.com/content/dam/corp/advocate/investment-stewardship/pdf/policies-and-reports/investment_stewardship_semiannual_report_2022.pdf.

[52] BLACKROCK, *supra* note 50.

[53] Press Release, Karen Doron, CalSTRS, CalSTRS Will Escalate Proxy Votes to Achieve Board Diversity, Net Zero Progress and Climate Change Action (Mar. 30, 2022), https://www.calstrs.com/calstrs-will-escalate-proxy-votes-to-achieve-board-diversity-net-zero-progress-and-climate-change-action.

B. Proxy Advisors

Many investors look to proxy advisors—particularly Institutional Shareholder Services Inc. (ISS) and Glass Lewis, which as of 2022 controlled 97 percent of the proxy advisory market[54] —for advice regarding how to vote on shareholder proposals. The proxy advisors accordingly play an important role because ESG matters are often the subject of shareholder proposals, particularly under proxy rule 14a-8.[55] ESG proposals received a record level of support in 2021, including about 70 environmental proposals (with those that went to a vote averaging 51 percent support) and 130 social proposals (with those that went to a vote averaging 42 percent support); however, investor support for ESG proposals declined in the 2023 proxy season, which in part could be ascribed to the backlash against ESG as described below.[56] Many shareholders who vote on such proposals are institutional investors that follow the recommendations from ISS and Glass Lewis, with studies indicating that ISS and Glass Lewis can sway shareholder votes in the range of 13 percent to 30 percent for various corporate governance issues.[57] Therefore, the still high degree of support for ESG proposals arguably stems from ISS and Glass Lewis's proxy voting guidelines on climate, board, and workforce diversity and "responsiveness." These guidelines continue to lend support to ESG-related shareholder proposals, such as ISS issuing vote recommendations on the basis of a lack of board gender and racial/ethnic diversity and Glass Lewis's use of environmental and social metrics in the analysis of its advisory vote on executive compensation.[58]

Failure to adequately address ESG-related issues can also lead to a recommendation by the proxy advisory firms against specific directors. For example, in the 2023 updates to its voting policies, ISS included the following policy:

> For companies that are significant greenhouse gas (GHG) emitters, through their operations or value chain, generally vote against or withhold from the incumbent chair of the responsible committee (or other directors on a case-by-case basis) in cases where ISS determines that the company is not taking the minimum steps needed to understand, assess, and mitigate risks related to climate change to the company and the larger economy.[59]

---

[54] Wayne Winegarden, *Proxy Advisory Firms and the ESG Risk*, Forbes (July 25, 2022, 9:04 AM), https://www.forbes.com/sites/waynewinegarden/2022/07/25/proxy-advisory-firms-and-the-esg-risk/?sh=798e7a9212d1.

[55] *See* Chapter 18—Responding to Shareholder Initiatives.

[56] Jeff Green & Saijel Kishan, *Support for ESG Shareholder Proposals Plummets Amid GOP Backlash*, Bloomberg (June 9, 2023, 7:53 AM), https://www.bloomberg.com/news/articles/2023-06-09/support-for-esg-shareholder-proposals-plummets-amid-gop-backlash.

[57] Kevin Chua et. al., ShareAction, Another Link in the Chain: Uncovering the Role of Proxy Advisors in Investor Voting (2020), https://cdn2.assets-servd.host/shareaction-api/production/resources/reports/Another-Link-in-the-Chain_Uncovering-the-role-of-proxy-advisors-in-investor-voting.pdf.

[58] Institutional Shareholder Services (ISS), United States Proxy Voting Guidelines Benchmark Policy Recommendations (effective 2023), https://www.issgovernance.com/file/policy/active/americas/US-Voting-Guidelines.pdf?v=1; Glass Lewis, 2023 Proxy Guidelines (2022), https://www.glasslewis.com/wp-content/uploads/2022/11/US-Voting-Guidelines-2023-GL.pdf?hsCtaTracking=45ff0e63-7af7-4e28-ba3c-7985d01e390a%7C74c0265a-20b3-478c-846b-69784730ccbd.

[59] ISS, *supra* note 58, at 17.

In Glass Lewis's 2023 voting guidelines, Glass Lewis indicated it will "generally recommend voting against the governance committee chair of a company in the Russell 1000 index that fails to provide explicit disclosure concerning the board's role in overseeing environmental and social issues."[60]

C. Activist Investors

Activist investors seek to influence a company's strategy and actions through shareholder engagement, voting and collaboration with other investors, and pressuring for board representation, sometimes through proxy contests. Activist investors have had great success in advancing ESG initiatives and changes in the companies in which they have invested, and boards should be mindful of the influence and power that activist investors can wield. One of the most notable recent examples was the successful proxy contest waged by Engine No. 1, an activist that uses sustainability data to drive long-term value,[61] in 2021, to install three directors on the board of Exxon Mobil, aiming to push the company to act on the emerging global energy transition to clean and renewable sources of energy and reduce its carbon footprint. This also illustrates the importance of institutional investors, as Engine No. 1 only held 0.02 percent of Exxon's shares, but Engine No. 1's campaign was supported by some of Exxon's biggest institutional investors. BlackRock, Vanguard, and State Street (which collectively held nearly 20 percent of the voting shares of the company) voted against Exxon's leadership and gave Engine No. 1 powerful support, as did the California Public Employees' Retirement System, CalSTRS, and the New York State Common Retirement Fund.

Other activist funds also apply pressure to advance ESG concerns. Governance is a frequent target of hedge fund activists because it gives them a platform to pressure for both governance and non-governance related changes. Social issues can also serve as a basis for activism. In 2018, two activist funds, Jana Partners and CalSTRS, issued an open letter to Apple, asking Apple to explore software tools to limit harm to young users of iPhones. Apple subsequently introduced a "wellness feature" on its iPhones. Jana Partners now advertises on its website that it "applies an ESG lens to potential investments." Other established activists, including ValueAct and Trian Partners, have also started to focus on ESG-related issues. New activist funds with an ESG focus, such as Impactive Capital, are being formed. The increase in the number of funds that engage in ESG activism is likely to result in an increase in ESG-related campaigns in the future.

Boards and the companies that they lead are also under increasing pressure by various stakeholders to respond to highly politicized social issues, such as the Black Lives Matter movement, or the 2022 *Dobbs* ruling overturning *Roe V. Wade*. Please see Chapter 13—Dealing with Highly Politicized Social Issues for a deep dive into those considerations.

[60] Glass Lewis, *supra* note 58, at 8.

[61] *See Thinking*, Engine No. 1, https://engine1.com/thinking/ (last visited Apr. 11, 2023).

D. Backlash

The push by institutional investors, proxy advisors, and other stakeholders towards ESG has triggered some backlash among investors and stakeholders who ascribe to shareholder capitalism or have concerns with companies setting their corporate policies in furtherance of social goals. This creates challenges for boards in balancing concerns of different stakeholders and constituents while also seeking to act in the best interests of the company. State legislatures in a number of conservative-leaning states have passed legislation limiting investments by state pensions and other funds in ESG-focused investment funds or entities that boycott certain industries, such as fossil fuels or gun manufacturers. Texas passed a law on June 14, 2021, that prohibits Texas public pension plans from investing in or contracting with companies that boycott certain energy companies. On August 24, 2022, the Texas Comptroller announced a list of financial companies and products that allegedly "boycott energy companies"—among the top 10 financial firms named are BlackRock, Credit Suisse, and UBS, and the products the state blacklisted include nearly 350 open-end U.S. mutual funds and exchange-traded funds from numerous other managers, many of which are labeled as sustainable, responsible, impact, or ESG funds. Additionally, Florida's governor proposed legislation in July 2022 that directs the state's fund managers to invest state funds in a manner that prioritizes the highest return on investment, clearly defines the factors to consider in investment decisions, and states that ESG considerations will not be included in Florida's pension investment management practice. Boards will want to navigate these competing considerations carefully, keeping in mind the corporation's overall strategy and corporate purpose and the long-term interests of the corporation.

Board diversity also has been the subject of resistance from conservative activists and state officials. Nasdaq's rule requiring boards of listed companies to either meet membership diversity standards or explain the lack of diversity has been the subject of litigation by conservative activists raising equal protection and First Amendment claims.[62] A coalition of 17 state attorneys general, including Texas, Arizona, and Florida, filed an amicus brief supporting the challenge to the Nasdaq rule, claiming that the SEC exceeded its authority to regulate board composition, which, the amici claimed, is a matter for state law. The California laws on board diversity (which, unlike Nasdaq's diversify or disclose rule, are mandates requiring minimum numbers of women or members of underrepresented communities) were similarly challenged in state courts and overturned at the trial court level on equal protection grounds.[63] That said, institutional investors and other stakeholders continue to push for greater board diversity, and the movement towards more diverse boards, whether required or not, appears here to stay. Boards, and in particular, nominating and governance committees, should be mindful of the concerns of their shareholders and other stakeholders regarding board diversity as they consider new board members to fill vacancies.

---

[62] Nasdaq, Nasdaq's Board Diversity Rule: What Companies Should Know (2022), https://listingcenter.nasdaq.com/assets/Board%20Diversity%20Disclosure%20Five%20Things.pdf; see filings in Alliance for Fair Board Recruitment v. SEC, No. 21-60626, which is currently before the U.S. Court of Appeals for the Fifth Circuit.

[63] Crest v. Padilla, No. 20-STCV-37513, 2022 WL 1073294, at *1 (Cal. Super. Ct. Apr. 1, 2022); Crest v. Padilla, No. 19-STCV-27561, slip op. at 23 (Cal. Super. Ct. May 13, 2022).

VI. Effects of ESG-Related Concerns on Directors and Officers Liability Insurance

The rise of litigation and regulatory activity relating to ESG matters has increased legal exposure for companies and their officers and directors. As noted above, the SEC launched an ESG Task Force in 2021 to focus on ESG-related disclosure and enforcement, and in 2022, the Task Force cracked down on alleged misstatements and omissions regarding ESG-related statements by investment advisors and issuers, announcing significant settlements of enforcement actions.[64] In May 2022, the SEC also proposed expanded disclosure requirements regarding the naming of funds and investment advisors to combat "greenwashing."[65] Private plaintiffs have also brought litigation seeking to hold companies and their directors accountable for alleged greenwashing misrepresentations.[66] Various other types of litigation risk are described in Section IV.A (Types of ESG Risk) above.

Directors & Officers (D&O) liability insurance can be a tool to mitigate some of the potential ESG-related exposures companies and directors and officers face, but the coverage availability depends on—and can vary by—the terms of a given D&O liability insurance policy. Policyholders should carefully and proactively evaluate what risks may be covered under their existing D&O policies and, if needed, modify existing coverage or consider new coverage specific to ESG-related risks. Corporate policyholders, including individual directors and officers, who are concerned about ESG-related risks, should maximize their available D&O coverage at the time of underwriting, including by understanding, and limiting, the scope of potential ESG-related policy exclusions.

Directors and officers should be aware of policy provisions that may limit or preclude coverage for ESG claims, for example:

- Conduct exclusions—D&O policies frequently contain exclusions that preclude coverage for criminal or deliberately fraudulent wrongdoing, and the excluded conduct is established by a final adjudication.[67]

[64] Press Release, SEC, SEC Announces Enforcement Task Force Focused on Climate and ESG Issues (Mar. 4, 2021), https://www.sec.gov/news/press-release/2021-42; Press Release, SEC, SEC Charges Brazilian Mining Company with Misleading Investors About Safety Prior to Deadly Dam Collapse (Apr. 28, 2022), https://www.sec.gov/news/press-release/2022-72; Press Release, SEC, SEC Charges BNY Mellon Investment Adviser for Misstatements and Omissions Concerning ESG Considerations (May 23, 2022), https://www.sec.gov/news/press-release/2022-86.

[65] Enhanced Disclosures by Certain Investment Advisers and Investment Companies About Environmental, Social, and Governance Investment Practices, Securities Act Release No. 11,068, Exchange Act Release No. 94,985, Investment Advisers Act Release No. 6034, Investment Company Act Release No. 34,594, 87 Fed. Reg. 36654 (proposed June 17, 2022) (to be codified at 17 C.F.R. pts. 200, 230, 232, 239, 249, 274, 279).

[66] *See* Shawn Collins & Lisa M. Northrup, *The Legal Risks of Greenwashing Are Real*, Bloomberg L. (July 25, 2022, 4:00 AM), https://news.bloomberglaw.com/environment-and-energy/the-legal-risks-of-greenwashing-are-real.

[67] As an example of "moral reprehensibility," in the United Kingdom (UK), there was a record fine of 90 million pounds against a company for illegal sewage discharges into waterways in breach of UK environmental laws. This fine was against the company so it would not be covered by a D&O policy, but the Judge called out the "flagrant disregard for . . . the law by the Defendant's board of directors, and/or a deliberate failure by the board of directors" to prevent the offenses. This shows the importance of directors needing to ensure that their company policies are effective. Env't Agency v. S. Water Servs. Ltd., Sentencing Remarks of Mr. Justice Johnson, 9 July 2021, https://www.judiciary.uk/wp-content/uploads/2022/07/Southern-Water-Sentencing-Remarks.pdf.

- Pollution exclusion—D&O policies typically contain exclusions relating to pollution. Some pollution exclusions purport to apply to all claims arising out of or attributable to "pollution," broadly defined. Other pollution exclusions are drafted more narrowly and specifically allow coverage for securities claims relating to pollution, such as lawsuits alleging public misstatements regarding pollution-related liabilities. While there may be strong arguments against application of pollution exclusions to many ESG claims (e.g., that contemporary climate change litigation does not implicate exclusions aimed at traditional "pollution"), policyholders would benefit from narrowing the scope of the exclusion during underwriting, focusing in particular on seeking a carve-out for securities-related claims.
- Misrepresentation/rescission provisions—In some instances, insurers may respond to ESG claims by seeking to rescind a D&O insurance policy, or otherwise avoid coverage, based upon alleged misrepresentations made in underwriting submissions. Management should ensure that their company's underwriting submission does not include false or misleading statements, including with respect to ESG. Beyond that, a "severability clause" in the D&O policy can provide that the knowledge or intent of any one individual insured shall not be imputed to others.
- Definition of "Securities Claim"—Typical public company D&O policies afford coverage for (a) losses of directors and officers arising from a claim against directors or officers, (b) losses of the company to the extent the company indemnifies directors or officers, and (c) losses of the company arising from a "Securities Claim" asserted against the company. ESG claims often may be asserted against the company rather than against individual directors and officers, and thus coverage may hinge on the definition of "Securities Claim" under the policy. Securities Claim definitions can vary, with some limited to claims for a violation of a law regulating securities, but others more broadly encompassing claims brought by security holders of the company in their capacity as such. Policyholders should evaluate Securities Claim definitions in their policies to ensure that they encompass potential ESG-related claims.
- Definition of "Loss"—Typical D&O policies limit coverage to "Loss" as defined in the policy, and insurers may seek to use carve-outs within the definition of "Loss" to limit coverage. For example, some policies may provide that "Loss" does not include civil fines and penalties asserted in a government action. Even where such civil fines and penalties are not included in the definition of covered "Loss," however, D&O policies may nevertheless provide for reimbursement of defense costs incurred in connection with defending claims seeking civil fines and penalties.
- Bodily injury/property damage exclusion—D&O policies typically contain exclusions applicable to bodily injury and property damage. If an ESG claim bears any relation to bodily injury or property damage, there is a risk that coverage may be excluded. In this regard, it is generally preferable for these exclusions to be worded as exclusions "for" bodily injury or property damage, rather than "arising out of" because "for" tends to support a narrower interpretation of the exclusion.

Key Takeaways

- A board's consideration of ESG risks and opportunities must be grounded in the directors' fiduciary duties of care, loyalty, and oversight.
- In fulfilling their obligation to exercise oversight, directors should be mindful of the *Caremark* duties to (a) make a good-faith effort to implement a board-level system of risk monitoring and reporting and (b) actually monitor risk.
- ESG risks range widely, from litigation, regulatory, and disclosure, to reputational and climate-related risks.
- Boards may wish to follow one of the publicly available ESG risk oversight methodologies, such as COSO, Ceres, or TCFD.
- ESG risks may fall under the purview of various board committees, including Audit, Risk, Sustainability, Nominating and Governance, and Compensation. Boards should be mindful to make clear delineations in committee charters regarding responsibility for assessing specified ESG risks.
- It is critical for boards to closely supervise disclosure of ESG risks, particularly in periodic reports submitted to the SEC, and to be mindful of discrepancies between the company's periodic reports and CSRs. There should be a well-thought-out rationale for any information included in a CSR that is not included in periodic reports.
- ESG may have a silver lining: directors should keep in mind that companies may have the opportunity to benefit from ESG matters, such as climate-friendly innovations and improved workforce productivity and morale, in addition to overseeing ESG risk management.
- Boards should take into account the ESG concerns of the company's stakeholders, including institutional investors, proxy advisors, and activist investors.
- ESG may also pose a balancing act for boards, as some investors and state pension funds are pushing back on making ESG a priority over monetary returns.
- Directors should take a close look at their D&O insurance coverage to assess its protection against ESG-related risks.

16

Role of Management

Erik C. Walsh, Teresa L. Johnson, and Xixi Chen

I. Introduction

Although the focus on corporate ESG strategy and risk management might feel like a new phenomenon given recent high-profile corporate ESG initiatives, regulatory developments, and political debate, the practice of good corporate governance—or the "G" in ESG—has long been a foundational principle for well-run companies.[1] Stated broadly, corporate governance is the set of rules, practices, and processes by which an entity operates; it provides the framework, oversight, and culture required to meet the company's goals. This chapter will cover management's role in an effective corporate governance framework, with a focus on good governance considerations surrounding a company's evaluation and decision-making about environmental and social issues. We also will discuss how management can implement the company's ESG-related values into its culture, a foundational component of corporate governance. Because governance itself is a stand-alone prong of ESG, this chapter also covers substantive governance of critical issues such as human capital management, codes of ethics, whistleblower policies, corporate transparency, and data privacy policies.

In implementing the company's ESG-related strategies and risk management procedures, management should be mindful of its responsibilities to the company and its fiduciary obligations to company shareholders and regulatory requirements, especially given the heightened scrutiny and rigorous requirements under which public companies operate. Therefore, we begin with a summary of management's fiduciary obligations under state law and certain

[1] While this chapter focuses on the responsibilities of public company management, many of the concepts we discuss apply equally to management of other entities, such as private companies, limited liability companies, and partnerships.

U.S. Securities and Exchange Commission (SEC) regulations and guidance that may impact ESG-related disclosures for which management is responsible.

II. Management Responsibilities under State Corporate Law and U.S. Securities and Exchange Commission Regulations

Management should focus on its fiduciary duties when implementing the company's ESG strategy and risk management procedures. Under Delaware law, corporate officers owe the same fiduciary duties of loyalty and care that the directors owe to the corporation and its shareholders.[2] In January 2023, a Delaware Court of Chancery expressly held that the policies underlying a director's "Caremark"[3] fiduciary duty of oversight "apply equally, if not to a greater degree, to officers."[4] The duty of care requires fiduciaries, including corporate officers, to be informed of all reasonably available material information before making business decisions.[5] This includes ESG-related issues that are material to the company's strategies, operations, and risks. The duty of loyalty requires officers to act in good faith and to place the interests of the corporation and its shareholders above their own interests.[6]

SEC reporting rules require management to make certain disclosures and certifications in SEC filings. For example, reporting company chief executive officers (CEOs) and chief financial officers are required to certify the accuracy of financial and certain other information contained in the annual reports on Form 10-K and quarterly reports on Form 10-Q.[7] (A company must also file current reports on Form 8-K to report certain specified events, typically within four business days after occurrence of the event.)[8] Further, 10-Ks must include a report from management on the company's internal control over financial reporting (ICFR).[9] The purpose of the ICFR requirement is to provide reasonable assurances that the company's financial statements are prepared in accordance with generally accepted accounting

[2] Gantler v. Stephens, 965 A.2d 695, 708-09 (Del. 2009).

[3] *In re Caremark International Inc. Derivative Litigation* holds that there is a fiduciary mandate to ensure that "information and reporting systems exist in the organization that are reasonably designed to provide to senior management and to the board itself timely, accurate information sufficient to allow management and the board, each within its scope, to reach informed judgment concerning both the corporation's compliance with law and its business performance." 698 A.2d 959, 970 (Del. Ch. 1996).

[4] *In re* McDonald's Corp. S'holder Derivative Litig., 289 A.3d 343, 349 (Del. Ch. 2023) (citing *In re Caremark*, 698 A.2d at 959). Notably, though the January *McDonald's* decision allowed the plaintiffs' breach of duty of oversight claim against McDonald's former Chief People Officer (arising out of the failure to exercise oversight over workplace harassment claims) to survive a motion to dismiss, the same Delaware Chancery Court judge dismissed the related case against the board of McDonald's Corporation arising out of the same circumstances, noting that the plaintiffs failed to adequately show that the Board acted in bad faith. *In re* McDonald's Corp. S'holder Derivative Litig., No. 2021-0324-JTL, 2023 WL 2293575, at *1 (Del. Ch. Mar. 1, 2023).

[5] Smith v. Van Gorkom, 488 A.2d 858, 872 (Del. 1985).

[6] Ivanhoe Partners v. Newmont Mining Corp., 535 A.2d 1334, 1345 (Del. 1987).

[7] 15 U.S.C. § 7241.

[8] 17 C.F.R. § 240.13a-11.

[9] 17 C.F.R. § 229.308. If the company is an accelerated filer or large accelerated filer, the 10-K must also include the public accounting firm's attestation report on the company's ICFR. 17 C.F.R. § 229.308(b).

principles (GAAP) and are reliable. Management also is required to evaluate any change in the company's ICFR that occurred during a fiscal quarter that has materially affected, or is reasonably likely to materially affect, the company's ICFR.[10]

For many companies, it is likely that ESG-related matters—for example, climate-related risks—must be disclosed under existing SEC guidance as material in 10-Ks, 10-Qs, and possibly 8-Ks, depending on the event.[11] If the SEC's proposed rule, The Enhancement and Standardization of Climate-Related Disclosures for Investors (the "Proposed Climate-Related Disclosure Rule"), is adopted, many public companies will be required to make significantly enhanced climate-related disclosures. Further information about such climate-related disclosures can be found in Chapter 6—Climate-Related Disclosure Obligations at the Federal and International Level.

III. ESG-Related Corporate Governance Considerations for Management

To ensure they are well-informed on ESG-related matters affecting their company's strategic, operational, and risk management plans—and thereby ensure they are satisfying their fiduciary obligations and that the company is meeting its SEC reporting and disclosure requirements—corporate officers with ESG-related responsibilities should consider the following:

- **Establish a management-level ESG committee.** The size, and even the existence of, the ESG committee will depend on the size and nature of the company. The growing trend has been to establish an ESG committee comprised of cross-functional leadership—for example (to the extent the company has such positions), the chief human resources officer, chief sustainability officer, the general counsel, head of Diversity, Equity, and Inclusion (DE&I), chief financial officer, chief technology officer, head of vendor management, head of government relations, and the chief marketing officer (or others with public-facing responsibilities). The head of each of the foregoing functions may opt to delegate their seat to their respective management. Whether or not to delegate seats on the ESG committee will depend on how responsibility for ESG-related issues is allocated and how executive management prioritizes ESG-related issues. The ESG committee's work will benefit significantly from participation by those members of management who are most knowledgeable about the company's ESG considerations and actions, ideally with sufficient seniority to implement change.

---

[10] 17 C.F.R. § 229.308(c).

[11] In 2010, the SEC published interpretive guidance for public companies regarding disclosure requirements relating to climate change matters (the "2010 Guidance"). The 2010 Guidance recommended disclosure, where material to the company, of: (i) the impact of pending or existing climate change-related legislation, regulations, and international accords; (ii) the indirect consequences of regulation or business trends; and (iii) the physical impacts of climate change. Commission Guidance Regarding Disclosure Related to Climate Change, Securities Act Release No. 9106, Exchange Act Release No. 61,469, 75 Fed. Reg. 6290 (Feb. 8, 2010) (to be codified at 17 C.F.R. pts. 211, 231, 241). The 2010 Guidance did not create specific disclosure requirements related to climate change. As of the date of publication of this book, such specific disclosures are pending in the SEC's Proposed Climate-related Disclosure Rule.

- **Define the ESG committee's responsibilities.** Companies should consider formalizing the management ESG committee by creating a committee charter that states the committee's purpose and primary responsibilities. Responsibilities could include:
  - assisting the board in setting the company's overall ESG strategy by recommending policies and business objectives, and assessing and managing ESG risks and opportunities;
  - overseeing both required and voluntary ESG disclosures to ensure all disclosures are consistent, accurate, and not misleading; and
  - overseeing internal and external communications to increase investor and other stakeholder awareness of ESG-related issues within the company. The management ESG committee should work closely with the board committees tasked with handling ESG matters, as described in CHAPTER 15—GOVERNANCE: ROLE OF THE BOARD.
- **Track ESG-related data.** Ensure that the ESG-related information being tracked, analyzed, and reported to the board aligns with the types of ESG-related information the company will disclose in its public filings. *This is imperative.* For example, the company may wish—or, depending on the materiality of the information, be required—to disclose information concerning its ESG-related risks, risk mitigation controls, or business strategies. Management should know well in advance what the company intends to disclose about ESG-related matters so that the company has gathered the necessary and accurate information to support the disclosures. As discussed in CHAPTER 9—GREEN MARKETING CLAIMS AND COMMUNICATIONS: CHARTING A COURSE THROUGH CHOPPY WATERS, CHAPTER 23—PUBLIC COMPANY DISCLOSURES, and CHAPTER 24—SPOTTING AND NAVIGATING ANTITRUST RISK, the SEC has become increasingly aggressive in scrutinizing public company filings for material misstatements and omissions on ESG-related matters and has been pursuing investigations and enforcement actions against companies for overstating the ESG *bona fides* of their company or investment products.

  Where reporting standards are not required by law, data collection, analysis, and reporting efforts should be based on the company's selection of a voluntary reporting standard, such as the widely-adopted frameworks recommended by the Task Force on Climate-related Financial Disclosures (TCFD), Global Reporting Initiative, or Sustainability Accounting Standards Board. Adoption of such widely used and reputable reporting standards removes a lot (but not all) of the uncertainty in determining what ESG-related data to collect, analyze, and disclose. It also provides a degree of comfort knowing that your company is handling ESG disclosures in a way similar to many other companies; in fact, consistency in reporting across companies and even across countries is one of the goals of such disclosure frameworks. The SEC's proposed rules regarding climate-related disclosures are based on the TCFD framework, so that has the benefit of the imprimatur of U.S. securities regulators.
- **Create an ESG compliance dashboard.** Establish a dashboard that defines the company's ESG-related requirements and goals, identifies the ESG-related "risk owners,"

identifies the individuals or committees responsible for ensuring compliance with the requirements and goals, and tracks implementation and compliance with relevant policies. Management should keep in mind that the company's requirements and goals may arise from law or regulation, company policy, or voluntary commitments the company has made on matters such as greenhouse gas (GHG) emission reductions, sustainability plans, human rights issues, or privacy concerns.

- **Track regulatory and political developments.** Establish a tracker of ESG-related regulatory developments in all jurisdictions in which the company operates. The ESG-related regulatory landscape is rapidly evolving, yet not always in the same direction. Management should be aware of recent ESG-related backlash, typically in states with conservative governors, attorneys general, and comptrollers. Some such states recently have blacklisted and withdrawn state investments from certain financial institutions for allegedly giving undue consideration to ESG factors in making investment decisions or for having publicized carbon emission reduction goals for their own operations and portfolios.[12] And in October 2022, 19 Republican state attorneys general (AGs) launched a coordinated investigation by issuing civil investigative demands (essentially, subpoenas) to six major U.S. banks, seeking information related to their membership in the United Nations' Net-Zero Banking Alliance (NZBA) and other climate-related initiatives.[13] The AGs also sought information about the banks'

[12] On August 23, 2022, Florida Governor Ron DeSantis issued a resolution directing the state's fund managers to make investment decisions without considering ESG factors, and in January 2023, the State's Chief Financial Officer prohibited the Florida Deferred Compensation Plan for state employees from investing in ESG strategies. Press Release, Fla. Governor Ron DeSantis, Governor Ron DeSantis Eliminates ESG Considerations from State Pension Investments (Aug. 23, 2022), https://www.flgov.com/2022/08/23/governor-ron-desantis-eliminates-esg-considerations-from-state-pension-investments/; Press Release, MyFloridaCFO, CFO Patronis Issues Directive Prohibiting ESG Fund Participation for Employee Retirement Program (Jan. 23, 2023), https://www.myfloridacfo.com/news/pressreleases/details/2023/01/23/cfo-patronis-issues-directive-prohibiting-esg-fund-participation-for-employee-retirement-program. In August 2022, the Texas Comptroller announced that state pension funds and other entities must divest from 10 major financial firms that he claims "boycott" energy companies. Press Release, Tex. Comptroller of Pub. Accts., Texas Comptroller Glenn Hegar Announces List of Financial Companies that Boycott Energy Companies (Aug. 24, 2022), https://comptroller.texas.gov/about/media-center/news/20220824-texas-comptroller-glenn-hegar-announces-list-of-financial-companies-that-boycott-energy-companies-1661267815099. West Virginia also has declared certain banks ineligible for state banking contracts for allegedly boycotting fossil fuel industries. David Gelles, *West Virginia Punishes Banks that It Says Don't Support Coal*, N.Y. Times (June 28, 2022), https://www.nytimes.com/2022/07/28/business/west-virginia-fossil-fuel-banks.html. Indiana Attorney General Todd Rokita issued an advisory opinion in September 2022 stating that Indiana law prohibits the state's public retirement system from choosing investments or investment strategies to further general ESG goals. Letter from Todd Rokita, Att'y Gen., Ind., to The Honorable Eric Koch, Ind. S. (Sept. 1, 2022), https://content.govdelivery.com/attachments/INAG/2022/09/01/file_attachments/2259125/Official Opinion 2022-3.pdf.

[13] According to the NZBA commitment statement, member banks commit to transitioning their own operational GHG emissions and GHG emissions attributable to their lending and investment portfolios to align with pathways to net-zero emissions by 2050 or earlier, as well as interim reduction targets by 2030. UN Env't Programme Fin. Initiative, Net-zero Banking Alliance, Industry-led, UN-convened, https://www.unepfi.org/wordpress/wp-content/uploads/2021/04/UNEP-FI-NZBA-Commitment-Statement.pdf. The NZBA has publicly asserted that there are no binding reduction targets on its members. *See* Tracey McDermott, *COP27 and Beyond: An Open Letter from the NZBA Chair to Members*, UN Env't Programme Fin. Initiative (Oct. 17, 2022), https://www.unepfi.org/industries/banking/letter-from-chair/ (reiterating that NZBA members "must continue to set their own individual targets and make independent decisions as to how to meet those targets.").

decisions to decline or stop providing banking services to customers because of net-zero or other ESG-related reasons.[14]

- **Conduct an ESG-related risk assessment.** Companies should consider conducting a separate ESG-related risk assessment—or incorporating risk assessments on ESG factors into existing risk assessments—to identify new risks or risks that need to be reconsidered in light of recent regulatory developments, company policy and strategy changes, shareholder concerns, and shifting popular and political sentiments. As with any effective risk assessment, an ESG-related risk assessment must be dynamic and updated regularly to account for new regulations, corporate strategy, products offered, and geographies in which the company operates. Management should strive to implement or enhance relevant controls in response to such periodic risk assessments. Management's approach to ESG-related risk assessment should be reviewed and coordinated with the board committee(s) responsible for addressing ESG-related risk.
- **Work with experts.** Management should confer with internal and, if necessary, external consultants to understand complex ESG-related issues such as the measurement and analysis of Scope 1, Scope 2, and Scope 3 GHG emissions. As discussed below, for this example in particular, management of public companies soon may be responsible for disclosing data on the company's GHG emissions to the SEC and therefore will need to understand exactly what it is they are disclosing.
- **Establish a methodology for determining materiality.** All public company disclosures, including ESG-related disclosures, are governed by the materiality standard set forth by the U.S. Supreme Court in *Basic v. Levinson*,[15] as interpreted and applied in subsequent case law and in SEC regulations. Under that standard, information is material and therefore must be disclosed if "there is a substantial likelihood that a reasonable shareholder would consider it important" in making an investment or voting decision, or if it would have "significantly altered the total mix of information made available."[16] In the absence of specific ESG-related disclosure requirements, such as those that would be mandated if the SEC's Proposed Climate-Related Disclosure Rule is adopted, management should bear this standard in mind in determining whether or not it must disclose ESG-related data. (Of course, even if not "material," under the *Basic* definition, management still may wish to disclose certain ESG-related information that may be beneficial to the company.) On highly technical, difficult-to-measure data such as GHG emissions, management should document its materiality standards and determinations carefully to respond to potential investor and regulator questions. This materiality review of ESG-related disclosures should be integrated with

[14] *See* Press Release, Ken Paxton, Att'y Gen. of Tex., Paxton Launches Investigation into Six Major Banks for Collusion-in-Lending Practices that Potentially Violate Consumer Protection Laws (Oct. 19, 2022), https://www.texasattorneygeneral.gov/news/releases/paxton-launches-investigation-six-major-banks-collusion-lending-practices-potentially-violate.

[15] 485 U.S. 224, 231–32 (1988).

[16] *Id.*

the company's regular "reporting-up" process for validating disclosures for securities law purposes.

- **Management Reporting.** As discussed in CHAPTER 15—GOVERNANCE: ROLE OF THE BOARD, the board of directors sets the strategic direction of the company on ESG-related matters and is responsible for overseeing management's implementation of the board's strategy. Like corporate officers, the board must be informed of all reasonably available material information to make well-informed business decisions.[17] This includes information that allows the board to adequately assess enterprise-wide risk, determine an appropriate risk management framework, assess reputational concerns, and investigate red flags of potential misconduct or potentially deficient systems and controls. In addition to the board's fiduciary obligations, investors are increasingly insisting on greater disclosure and transparency of the board's ESG-related business strategies, corporate governance, and oversight. In order for the board to satisfy its fiduciary obligations and respond to investor inquiries on ESG-related matters, management therefore must ensure it reports necessary ESG-related information to the board (or the board committee(s) charged with ESG-related matters).

As to the type of ESG-related information to report to the board, this will vary depending on the company. One guiding principle should be to avoid inundating the board with reams of paper on technical ESG matters that present raw data without benefit of appropriate board-level synthesis and analysis—for example, complex climate analytics. Management should make the effort to tailor board reports to include the key ESG-related information in a concise and accessible manner. Consider charts, trends, peer comparisons, benchmarks, and brief narratives when presenting ESG-related metrics.

As to the regularity of such reporting to the board, again, this will vary depending on the company. If a board does not have a standing ESG discussion item on the agenda for every board meeting, and instead addresses ESG issues on a quarterly or even less frequent basis, management should consider the type of ESG-related information that it should affirmatively bring to the board's attention out of cycle, and whether to advise the board to consider ESG issues at each meeting, especially considering the rapidly evolving regulatory and political landscapes and popular sentiment on ESG-related issues.

A. Integrating ESG into Corporate Culture

Some studies have found that integrating ESG factors into corporate culture adds value, not just in an intangible sense but also to the bottom line and shareholder value. For example, according to a 2021 study, between 1984 and 2020, "on average, an equal-weighted portfolio of public companies" appearing on *Fortune*'s annual "100 Best Companies to Work For" list, which suggests a commitment to employee satisfaction (an ESG factor), "earned an excess return of 2% to 2.7% a year." Remarkably, "[e]xcess returns were even higher during times of financial crisis, with the portfolio producing 1.4% in excess returns a month,

[17] *Smith*, 488 A.2d at 872.

or up to 16.8% a year."[18] The management consulting group McKinsey & Co. also reports that a company's strong ESG culture correlates positively with equity return, and further concludes that better ESG performance correlates with a reduction in downside risk "as evidenced, among other ways, by lower loan and credit default swap spreads and higher credit ratings."[19] A recent study of more than 3,000 firms' stock performance between late February and late March 2020, at the onset of the pandemic when markets were in free-fall, found that the companies perceived by the public as behaving more responsibly had higher stock prices than competitors. Based in part on these results, the study predicted that companies will face increasing pressure to improve performance on ESG dimensions in the future.[20] Generally speaking, implementing ESG considerations into corporate culture also has a positive impact on attracting, retaining, and motivating high-quality employees; when employees work for a company whose visions are aligned with their own, employees tend to perform better and are happier, which in turn fosters a healthier corporate culture and better company performance.

What is "corporate culture" and how can management seek to implement ESG factors into it? Corporate culture is, by nature, a somewhat amorphous concept. One broad definition describes it as the "attitudes, behaviors and understanding about risk, both positive and negative, that influence the decisions of management and personnel and reflect the mission, vision and core values of the organization."[21]

While the guiding principles of a company's culture should be set by the board, robust management leadership behavior and communications are indispensable for successfully integrating the desired culture with the workforce and into the business operations. As Harvard Business School Professor George Serafeim put it: "Many executives incorrectly believe that simple actions will suffice: improving ESG disclosures, releasing a sustainability report, or holding a sustainability-focused investor relations event. Some companies take those actions, fail to see a benefit, and grow disappointed or frustrated. In some cases they face criticism and negative reaction from investors."[22]

Executives therefore should ensure they are delivering a convincing ESG narrative that is sustainable, inclusive, and consistent; it should serve the dual purpose of encouraging

---

[18] Sabrina Escobar, *The 100 Best Companies to Work for Are Great Stocks to Buy in a Crisis*, BARRONS (July 6, 2022, 1:17 PM), https://www.barrons.com/articles/100-best-companies-to-work-for-stocks-51657127674 (citing a study by Hamid Boustanifar and Young Dae Kim).

[19] Witold Henisz et al., *Five Ways that ESG Creates Value*, MCKINSEY Q. (Nov. 2019), https://www.mckinsey.com/capabilities/strategy-and-corporate-finance/our-insights/five-ways-that-esg-creates-value. *See also* George Serafeim, *Social-impact Efforts that Create Real Value*, HARV. BUS. REV. (Sept.-Oct. 2020), https://hbr.org/2020/09/social-impact-efforts-that-create-real-value (author's study of more than 3,000 firms between late February and late March 2020, at the onset of the pandemic when markets were in free fall, found that the companies the public perceived as behaving more responsibly had less negative stock returns than competitors and predicting that companies will face increasing pressure to improve performance on ESG dimensions in the future).

[20] George Serafeim, *supra* note 19.

[21] COMM. OF SPONSORING ORGS. OF THE TREADWAY COMM'N & WORLD BUS. COUNCIL FOR SUSTAINABLE DEV., ENTERPRISE RISK MANAGEMENT: APPLYING ENTERPRISE RISK MANAGEMENT TO ENVIRONMENTAL, SOCIAL AND GOVERNANCE-RELATED RISKS 16, (2018), https://www.wlrk.com/docs/2018COSOEnterprisingRiskManagementGuide_3566090_1.PDF.

[22] George Serafeim, *supra* note 19.

employees to embrace the company's ESG commitments and conveying to investors and other stakeholders the company's ESG vision. Management should consider whether:

- Its tone conveys support for the company's ESG-related goals, including ESG-related goals pertaining to the company's business objectives as well as to the work environment.
- Communications with staff, both in substance and tone (e.g., in meetings, town halls, informal interactions), reinforce the company's ESG-related values.
- Hiring and promoting decisions take into account whether an individual's skills and principles are aligned with the company's ESG-related objectives.
- Compensation decisions incorporate metrics that advance the company's key ESG values.

An increasing number of CEOs have been explicit that the above considerations factor into their management styles and priorities. In his 2022 CEO ESG letter, Equifax's CEO Mark W. Begor stated that the company is "making a strong investment in [ESG] priorities in a way that is aligned with [the] company purpose—to help people live their financial best," and that purpose is what "drives [its] 13,000 global employees every day."[23] The Chair and CEO of Eli Lilly, David Ricks, conveyed in the company's ESG report that achieving ESG goals "starts from the top" and that the company expects "all [its] employees to treat ESG objectives no differently than other vital business challenges."[24]

B. Focal Points of Corporate Governance

Like the environmental and social components of ESG, corporate governance is an umbrella term which incorporates many aspects of the day-to-day management and operation of a company. In this section, we will examine several corporate governance topics that have garnered significant recent attention.

1. Human Capital Management

One prominent trend has been an increase in public companies making disclosures related to human capital management (HCM), the process of strategic hiring, workforce management, and workforce productivity. The increase results in large part from the 2020 SEC rule mandating public companies to include disclosure in their 10-Ks about their human capital resources, including the number of persons employed, and, if material, any human capital measures or objectives that the company focuses on in managing the business (e.g., measures or objectives that address the development, attraction, and retention of personnel).[25]

---

[23] Mark W. Begor, Equifax, Inc., ESG @ Equifax, CEO Message (2022), https://assets.equifax.com/marketing/US/assets/2022-ceo-esg-letter.pdf.

[24] David A. Ricks, *A Message from Our CEO*, Eli Lilly & Co. (2022), https://esg.lilly.com/ceo-letter.

[25] 17 C.F.R. § 229.101(c)(2)(ii).

Even if not required to be disclosed under SEC rules, many companies have taken it upon themselves to implement DE&I principles into their HCM function. These principles are often reflected in new or enhanced hiring and employment practices. Below is a sampling of recent corporate DE&I initiatives that typify the approaches more companies have been implementing in this area.

An increasing number of companies have created the role of chief diversity officer (or diversity director or other similar title). In 2020 and 2021, at least 60 companies reported appointing for the first time a chief diversity officer[26] who is responsible for, among other things, designing and evaluating DE&I initiatives in hiring and promotion, allocating resources to DE&I initiatives, and advancing the company's DE&I agenda. Another increasingly popular hiring practice is for the company to adopt a policy requiring that a diverse slate of applicants be interviewed before extending an offer for an open position. As a specific example (outside the realm of public companies), over 115 major law firms have committed to following the Mansfield Rule in an effort to increase and sustain more diverse and inclusive workforces.[27] The latest iteration of the Mansfield Rule requires that women, minority attorneys, LGBTQ+ attorneys, and lawyers with disabilities make up 30 percent of the candidate pool for recruitment, governance roles, equity partner promotions, and inclusion in formal pitch presentations to clients.

In addition to hiring practices, a growing number of companies are implementing initiatives that focus on strengthening equity and inclusion within the company. For example, Mastercard has implemented an annual pay practice assessment framework that reviews compensation decisions for potential gender pay gaps and addresses pay disparities that are not well accounted for.[28] Mastercard employees can also voice pay disparity concerns through various internal channels.[29] Intuit has committed to prioritizing equity in its DE&I efforts and has been harnessing its various affinity groups to better understand the experience of its minority employees and integrate their voices into the company's DE&I strategy.[30] In response to the rise of anti-Asian violence during COVID-19, Morgan Stanley provided a series of programs that were designed to help employees cope and alleviate the consequences of racial trauma.[31] Many companies now have employee resource groups (ERGs), which can take the form of business resource groups, employee networks, team member networks, or affinity groups. These ERGs help create an organic and welcoming workplace through a

---

[26] Gena Cox & David Lancefield, *5 Strategies to Infuse D&I into Your Organization*, HARV. BUS. REV. (May 19, 2021), https://hbr.org/2021/05/5-strategies-to-infuse-di-into-your-organization.

[27] Law Firm Chairs & Managing Partners on Behalf of the Mansfield Rule 4.0 Participating Firms, *An Open Letter from the 2020-2021 Mansfield Law Firms' Chairs & Managing Partners*, DIVERSITY LAB (2021), https://www.diversitylab.com/mansfield-rule-4-0/.

[28] *Diversity Equity Inclusion, Creating Limitless Possibilities for Everyone*, MASTERCARD, https://www.mastercard.us/en-us/vision/who-we-are/diversity-inclusion.html (last visited Apr. 12, 2023).

[29] *Id.*

[30] INTUIT, DIVERSITY, EQUITY AND INCLUSION (2021), https://www.intuit.com/oidam/intuit/ic/en_us/content/intuit-dei-report-2021-icom.pdf.

[31] MORGAN STANLEY, 2021 DIVERSITY AND INCLUSION REPORT (2021), https://www.morganstanley.com/assets/pdfs/2021-diversity-and-inclusion-report.pdf.

community-based approach. They also serve as valuable strategic resources to the company and help them give back to society.[32] Delta's Latin and Hispanic ERG, ADELANTE, has long contributed to the growth of the Latin and Hispanic community within the company by offering professional and networking support to employees,[33] and Hilton's various ERGs have focused on community outreach, such as counseling local high school students who were interested in a career in hospitality and offering workshops to staff at the local health center.[34]

In the process of structuring and implementing DE&I initiatives, it is imperative that management be mindful of federal, state, and local anti-discrimination laws while conducting recruiting and hiring activities. Companies should ensure that their interviewers are trained on appropriate interview process techniques and that they do not make hiring decisions based on any legally protected characteristic.

Management's role in preventing workplace harassment is an HCM topic that has recently become the focus of civil litigation and regulatory agency enforcement action, as demonstrated by the Delaware Chancery Court's decision in the January 2023 *McDonald's* case (see Section II above), the related SEC cease-and-desist order against McDonald's and its former CEO, and the February 2023 SEC cease-and-desist order against Activision Blizzard, Inc., for disclosure control failures arising out of widespread employee complaints of workplace misconduct. These matters underscore not just the importance of maintaining *effective* anti-harassment policies but also demonstrate an increasing possibility of individual liability for responsible management who fail to appropriately address workplace harassment concerns.[35]

2. *Code of Ethics and Whistleblower Policies*

The Sarbanes-Oxley Act, the SEC's rules and regulations, and exchanges like the New York Stock Exchange and Nasdaq impose on certain public companies, investment companies, and executive officers an obligation to comply with certain corporate governance standards relating to codes of ethics. Even if a company is not subject to a statutory or regulatory requirement to adopt a code of ethics, it is still best practice for most companies to adopt a code of ethics to guide employees, uphold corporate integrity, and ensure compliance with the law. There is no one right approach for writing a code, and relevant provisions will vary depending on the size and nature of business, among other factors. Below, however, are some

---

[32] Benjamin Colton et al., *Human Capital Management and Diversity Disclosures and Practices*, Harv. L. Sch. F. on Corp. Governance (Feb. 14, 2022), https://corpgov.law.harvard.edu/2022/02/14/human-capital-management-and-diversity-disclosures-and-practices/.

[33] *Celebrating Culture During Latin and Hispanic Heritage Month and Beyond*, Delta (Oct. 15, 2021, 2:45 PM), https://news.delta.com/celebrating-culture-during-latin-and-hispanic-heritage-month-and-beyond.

[34] Diversity & Inclusion at Hilton: We Are Diverse by Nature and Inclusive by Choice, Hilton (2019), https://www.hilton.com/en/corporate/wp-content/uploads/2019/11/20190225_External-Diversity-Brochure.pdf.

[35] *See In re McDonald's*, 289 A.3d at 343; *see also* Stephen J. Easterbrook, Securities Act Release No. 11144, Exchange Act Release No. 96610, 2023 WL 143292 (Jan. 9, 2023); Activision Blizzard, Inc., Exchange Act Release No. 96796, 2023 WL 1765354 (Feb. 3, 2023).

basic principles that may be helpful for companies to keep in mind when drafting or revising their company's code of ethics:

- The code should be concise and written in a way that is easy to understand. Instead of using legalese, it should outline expected and prohibited behavior. Consider illustrative hypotheticals to facilitate understanding of the code.
- Input from various departments, including the legal, compliance, risk management, and human resources departments, should be sought to ensure that the code sufficiently addresses the compliance requirements and operational needs across the company.
- The code should apply to all employees, all the way up to the CEO.
- New hires and lateral employees should be educated about the existence and role of the code during the employment onboarding process.
- Mandatory, periodic training sessions for all employees should be considered to enhance and reinforce employee understanding of the code.
- The code should be easily accessible (e.g., published on the company website).
- The code should embody the company's core values, objectives, and strategies. It should be tailored towards the industry and region that the company is situated in, and adapt to the changing corporate and social needs.
- The code should be consistent and align with other corporate policy documents, such as the employee handbook and data collection policy.
- The code should be reviewed periodically and updated if necessary to incorporate regulatory developments and changing business needs.

Against the ESG backdrop, recommended topics to be covered in the code may include bribery (and policies on making and receipt of gifts); data collection and handling of personal identifiable information; discrimination; diversity and inclusion; environmental concerns; harassment (sexual and otherwise); honesty with customers, counterparties, fellow employees, and regulators; privacy; and social responsibility (what the company perceives its role in society to be and how it intends to fulfill its social responsibilities—for instance, through advancing social causes, building awareness of socially responsible products and processes, or contributing to sustainable development).

Relatedly, a prominent dimension of corporate ethics that has attracted increased regulatory scrutiny is the company's whistleblower program. The Sarbanes-Oxley Act imposes on public companies an obligation to implement whistleblower protections within the company. Recent laws have been enhancing whistleblower protections as well as increasing whistleblower incentives to encourage more reporting. For example, under the 2021 Anti-Money Laundering Act, whistleblowers who voluntarily provide original information about money laundering to their employer, U.S. Treasury Department, or U.S. Department of Justice are now entitled to up to 30 percent of amounts collected by the government in cases where sanctions exceed $1 million (the award cap under the old law was $150,000).

Having a well-functioning internal reporting channel may not only be necessary to satisfying legal requirements, it is also indispensable for effective corporate governance.

By enabling employees to reveal misconduct and voice concerns without fear of retaliation, a quality whistleblower program will act as a pillar of a company's culture and go a long way toward maintaining shareholder and investor trust. The key, however, is that it must be a "quality" whistleblower program. A whistleblower program will fail if employees do not feel encouraged to report, if they fear retaliation for reporting, or if they believe that their report will fall on deaf ears. Management (and in some cases the board) must respond timely and appropriately to whistleblower reports and conduct appropriate inquiries. In creating or revising a whistleblower program, management should consider the following:

- Communicate clearly to employees the channels through which they can submit their reports. Ensure that a variety of channels are available (e.g., a whistleblower hotline staffed by a third party, a secure web form, and speaking directly to management).
- Ensure that employees know they may always report information to the company's regulators and law enforcement agencies.
- Establish mechanisms to ensure that once whistleblower reports are received, an investigation process will be initiated and the reports will be handled in a timely and appropriate manner. Communicate, if possible, with the whistleblower to let them know that management has heard their concern, is reviewing it, and will take it seriously.
- Provide anonymity and confidentiality protection so that employees will be encouraged to speak up. Management, all the way up to the CEO, should promote the whistleblower reporting channel.
- Build employee confidence that no retaliatory actions will be taken against a whistleblower. Have an anti-retaliation provision and enforce it.

3. *Corporate Transparency*

Another key corporate governance theme is corporate transparency, which concerns the extent to which corporate ownership and corporate behavior are visible to outsiders. Governments around the globe have sought to enhance regulatory requirements in this field and shine a light on companies with anonymous ownership and opaque business activities. For instance, on September 30, 2022, U.S. Treasury's Financial Crimes Enforcement Network (FinCEN) published its final rule on beneficial ownership information filing requirements (BOI Rule), a key aspect of the 2021 Corporate Transparency Act (CTA). Under the BOI Rule, starting in January 2024, certain entities will be obligated to disclose to FinCEN two categories of individuals: (1) the beneficial owners of the entity and (2) individuals who have filed an application with specified governmental authorities to create the entity or register it to do business in the United States.[36]

Although a large number of companies are exempt from the BOI Rule—which is intended to increase transparency of shell companies—it is recommended that all companies review

[36] Beneficial Ownership Information Reporting Requirements, 87 Fed. Reg. 59498 (Sept. 30, 2022) (to be codified at 31 C.F.R. pt. 1010).

the "reporting companies" definition in the BOI Rule carefully to determine if they will be subject to the reporting requirement.

Another emerging trend in connection with corporate transparency is sustainability reporting (e.g., the disclosure of material nonfinancial information that incorporates a company's ESG concerns). According to the Governance & Accountability Institute, in 2011, only 20 percent of S&P 500 companies published corporate sustainability reports (CSRs). In 2020, 92 percent of such companies published CSRs.[37] As discussed in CHAPTER 15—GOVERNANCE: ROLE OF THE BOARD and CHAPTER 23—PUBLIC COMPANY DISCLOSURES, it is important that management responsible for publishing CSRs ensures the reports are consistent with the company's SEC filings. ESG-related disclosures contained in SEC filings that are materially inconsistent with statements in CSRs can present an easy case for an SEC enforcement action. Disclosure related to DE&I goals—even when not required by the SEC human capital disclosure rule discussed above—is also on the rise. For example, in 2021, all the big four accounting firms (Deloitte, EY, KPMG, and PricewaterhouseCoopers [PwC]) published a DE&I transparency report, in which they set goals to increase female and minority representations in the U.S. workforce and among U.S. partners, principals, and managing directors.[38]

4. Data Protection

The pursuit of ESG initiatives often involves the collection, analysis, and reporting of ESG metrics. Often, these metrics consist of highly sensitive data and personal information. This in turn may intensify existing data privacy and security obligations that companies already have to comply with, such as those imposed by the California Consumer Privacy Act or General Data Privacy Regulation in Europe. Data security and privacy issues are a central dimension of the "G" component in ESG, both in the sense that they present an ongoing operational risk, and that consumers demand assurance that their information will be handled properly and protected against potential breaches. Overall, regulatory bodies and ESG rating agencies are increasingly scrutinizing data security, and there is a trend among companies to categorize disclosure related to data security as falling under the ESG disclosure umbrella.

As with any type of operational risk confronting a company, an effective data protection framework should include mechanisms that can timely identify and manage security

---

[37] GOVERNANCE & ACCOUNTABILITY INST., INC., S&P 500® + RUSSELL 1000® 2021 SUSTAINABILITY REPORTING IN FOCUS: EXAMINING 2020 SUSTAINABILITY REPORTING TRENDS OF THE LARGEST PUBLICLY-TRADED COMPANIES IN THE U.S. (2021), https://www.ga-institute.com/fileadmin/ga_institute/images/FlashReports/2021/Russell-1000/G&A-Russell-Report-2021-Final.pdf?vgo_ee=%2Blm3dBsAbRsxtrJH1Y4F2IAAtfIZi8WrdeVEU9apdpM%3D.

[38] DELOITTE, 2021 DIVERSITY, EQUITY, AND INCLUSION (DEI) TRANSPARENCY REPORT (2021), https://www2.deloitte.com/content/dam/Deloitte/us/Documents/about-deloitte/dei-transparency-report.pdf; PwC, BUILDING ON A CULTURE OF BELONGING: 2020 PwC DIVERSITY & INCLUSION TRANSPARENCY REPORT (2020), https://www.pwc.com/us/en/about-us/diversity/assets/diversity-inclusion-transparency-report.pdf; KPMG, DIVERSITY, EQUITY AND INCLUSION: 2021 U.S. DEI TRANSPARENCY REPORT (2021), https://www.kpmg.us/content/dam/global/pdfs/2021/kpmg-us-2021-dei-report.pdf; EY, EY DEI TRANSPARENCY REPORT: PATHWAYS TO PROGRESS (2021), https://assets.ey.com/content/dam/ey-sites/ey-com/en_us/topics/diversity/ey-transparency-report-d-i-v1.pdf.

risks. Security audits should be conducted on a regular basis, and employees should be educated on compliance requirements to increase their awareness about cyber threats. There should be robust protocols for handling data breaches and data recovery, and communicating and reporting security incidents to relevant stakeholders. The overarching framework should be regularly revisited to adapt to rapid changes in the digital and regulatory spheres.

Even if not statutorily required to do so, management should consider disclosing how it handles ESG data. Doing so can earn customer and investor trust by demonstrating that the company is capable of protecting the confidentiality of customer data and is resilient to data breaches and cyberattacks. Again, this is a balancing exercise, in that the company will be subject to liability for any information that is disclosed (even voluntarily) and will, to some degree, be setting a precedent to continue disclosing that information (even if unfavorable), so it is critical that the company is confident in the accuracy of any disclosed information and an undertaking to continuing to disclose it.

Key Takeaways

- The foundation for ESG considerations arises from management's fiduciary duties under state law. In addition, ESG analysis and disclosure may be required by SEC disclosure regulations (even in the absence of specific climate-related disclosure requirements, as proposed in 2022), and management therefore should carefully review SEC requirements.
- Management should consider establishing a cross-functional ESG committee comprised of the heads of internal functions that are key to ESG matters, such as the general counsel, chief human resources officer, chief sustainability officer, and others—or their delegees. The management ESG committee should have clearly defined responsibilities, including tracking ESG-related data—as well as political and regulatory developments—creating an ESG compliance dashboard, and conducting an ESG-related risk assessment. It is critical for the management ESG committee to integrate with the board-level committee(s) responsible for ESG issues, including providing appropriately tailored and properly validated ESG information to the board.
- ESG should be integrated into corporate culture, including through top-down leadership from the CEO and senior management.
- Human capital management is an important element of ESG values, specifically key initiatives around DEI, such as enhanced consideration of DE&I in hiring practices, creating a chief diversity officer role, and employee affinity groups.
- Company codes of ethics (which many companies are required to have under applicable laws, regulations, and listing rules) should embody a company's ESG values. Whistleblower programs should be well-structured to protect against retaliation and establish processes for prompt and thorough evaluation of whistleblower claims.

- Transparency in a company's ownership helps illustrate its open-minded approach to governance.
- Corporate sustainability reports have become increasingly common and offer companies a way to speak publicly about ESG commitments. Companies should be careful to ensure that disclosures in CSRs are coordinated and consistent with SEC reports and other public disclosures.
- Because the collection of ESG metrics may involve gathering information that is protected under applicable privacy laws or otherwise sensitive, it is critical for companies to maintain strong data privacy protections and to build trust and credibility by disclosing their approach to handling ESG data.

17

ESG Management Systems: Creating the Foundation for Success[1]

Paul Nabhan

I. Introduction

While other chapters of this book address the bona fide underlying ESG issues, the role of the board and management as part of corporate governance, and required disclosures, this chapter addresses ESG management systems. ESG management systems are comprised of the systems, controls, and processes thereunder ("Systems"), and they bridge the gap between a company's ESG strategy and disclosures and inform a company's board and management of its progress toward its strategic goals. Systems also contribute to information integrity and to risk management of ESG metrics.

The scope of this chapter is to provide legal and conceptual parameters for consideration. This chapter begins by laying out the legal foundation under corporate law and securities regulation with respect to the duty to implement Systems and remain informed, and by fulfilling such duties, companies will have a reasonable basis upon which to make ESG disclosures and mitigate the risk of anti-fraud liability. Companies may find that the most efficient path to designing high-quality Systems for ESG metrics is relying on the expertise of their financial functions and leveraging their established disclosure controls, procedures, and internal control over financial reporting principles and procedures, particularly if such satisfy an accepted internal control framework. After establishing the legal foundation, this

[1] Thank you to Bryan Benjamin, Kendall Lynch, and Brian McKeown for additional guidance, insight, and support in preparing this chapter.

chapter discusses the contexts in which reliable ESG metrics add value, such as investor or creditor demand, strategy implementation, or enhanced information sets. However, with such potential benefits, companies must also implement corresponding risk management policies and safeguards to curtail the risk of fraud by directors, management, or employees.

This chapter does not advocate for or endorse any specific product or risk management framework. Systems continue to be an evolving field, and market trends or accepted market approaches may change.

II. Underlying Legal Requirements

A. Legal Liability under Corporate Law and Securities Regulation

Let's start with general principles. Under corporate law, directors of a corporation owe fiduciary duties of care, loyalty, and good faith to shareholders to be able to use the business judgment rule to shield themselves from personal liability. Embedded within these fiduciary duties are the duty of attention and the duty of monitoring.[2] Under the landmark *Caremark* decision, a "director's obligation includes a duty to attempt in good faith to assure that a corporate information and reporting system, which the board concludes is adequate, exists, and that failure to do so under some circumstances may, in theory at least, render a director liable for losses caused by non-compliance with applicable legal standards," upon which the court earlier noted that "relevant and timely information is an essential predicate for satisfaction of the board's supervisory and monitoring role" under Delaware General Corporation Law Section 141.[3] The court clarified that the appropriate level of detail is a question of business judgment but that it was important that the board nonetheless exercise a good-faith judgment that the corporation's information and reporting system is, in concept and design, adequate to satisfy the board's responsibilities.[4]

The recent *Marchand* decision elaborated upon *Caremark*. In *Marchand*, the court permitted the plaintiffs' *Caremark* claim to proceed where the board itself had not implemented a system to monitor food safety at the board level and where prior to the lawsuit (a) no board committee addressing food safety existed; (b) no regular process or protocols that required management to keep the board apprised of food safety compliance practices, risks, or reports existed; (c) no schedule for the board to consider on a regular basis any key food safety risks existed; (d) management received reports that contained what could be considered red flags, but the board minutes do not show that such were disclosed to the board; (e) the board was only given favorable information about food safety by management but not important reports that presented otherwise; and (f) the board meetings were devoid of any suggestion that food safety issues were regularly discussed.[5] To the court, the sum of the foregoing facts supported

---

[2] The *Caremark* and *Marchand* cases described in the following paragraphs separately attribute these duties to the duty of care and the duty of loyalty; parsing out which is more appropriate is beyond the scope of this chapter.

[3] *See In re* Caremark Int'l Inc. Derivative Litig., 698 A.2d 959, 970 (Del. Ch. 1996).

[4] *Id.*

[5] *See* Marchand v. Barnhill, 212 A.3d 805, 822 (Del. 2019).

the inference that no system of board-level compliance monitoring and reporting existed at the corporation, and that when a plaintiff can plead an inference that a board has undertaken no efforts to make sure it is informed of a compliance issue intrinsically critical to the company's business operation, such also supports an inference that the board has not made the good-faith effort required under *Caremark*. Further, the court distinguished the fact that just because a corporation nominally complies with such regulations, such does not imply that the board of directors implemented a system to monitor food safety at the board level.[6]

It follows that as companies start disclosing ESG information, tracking it for strategic purposes, and especially if such becomes statutorily required, companies (at the direction of the board of directors) must implement certain Systems such that their boards remain timely informed about ESG issues. Such should include, at a minimum, designated members of the board addressing ESG issues under a regular process in conjunction with management, bona fide discussion by the board of ESG issues arising from such regular communication with management and occurring on a regular basis, and ensuring management provides the board with complete and unbiased information concerning ESG issues. Indeed, the foregoing factors resemble the corporate governance disclosures contemplated by the SEC's Proposed Rule on Climate Change Disclosures (the "Proposed Rule") with respect to how climate-related information is generated and disseminated within an organization. By implementing such in good faith, directors of companies may rely on the business judgment rule to shield themselves from legal liability in a derivative action.

For public companies, such legal risk is compounded by general anti-fraud principles from securities regulation. Under Exchange Act Rule 10b-5:

> It shall be unlawful for any person, directly or indirectly, by the use of any means or instrumentality of interstate commerce, or of the mails or of any facility of any national securities exchange,
>
> (a) To employ any device, scheme, or artifice to defraud,
>
> (b) To make any untrue statement of a material fact or to omit to state a material fact necessary in order to make the statements made, in the light of the circumstances under which they were made, not misleading, or
>
> (c) To engage in any act, practice, or course of business which operates or would operate as a fraud or deceit upon any person, in connection with the purchase or sale of any security.[7]

Provisions similar to Rule 10b-5 appear in different areas of securities regulation, with Congress and the SEC reweighing the legal elements to match the legal liability with the type of offering or transaction at hand (and, if applicable, the corresponding gatekeeper function thereto). For example, regarding a company's initial public offering, Securities Act Section 11(e) permits stockholders to seek damages equal to the decrease in value from the price paid, rather than the amount of damages caused by such untrue statement under Rule

---

[6] *Id.* at 822–23.

[7] 17 C.F.R. § 240.10b-5.

10b-5, heightening the risk of legal liability by nixing the causation element of the traditional anti-fraud test.

However, in making disclosures with respect to securities, courts have noted that in providing information to stockholders, companies must also have a reasonable basis for statements made. Notably, the court in *Merck* stated:

> In [Omnicare, Inc. v. Laborers Dist. Council Constr. Indus. Pension Fund, 575 U.S. 175 (2015)], the corporate defendants filed a registration statement with the SEC . . . in which the defendants . . . made two statements giving their opinion about the company's legal compliance. [The Court] found that a statement of opinion . . . may give rise to liability if the expressed belief is at odds with information known to the speaker. The Court reasoned that "a reasonable investor may, depending on the circumstances, understand the opinion statement to convey facts about the speaker's basis for holding that view." It concluded: "if a registration statement omits material facts about the issuer's inquiry into or knowledge concerning a statement of opinion, and if those facts conflict with what a reasonable investor would take from the statement itself, then § 11's omissions clause creates liability." The Omnicare Court, moreover, noted that these principles concerning the manner in which a reasonable person understands statements of opinion and, thus, how opinions could be considered fraudulent are "not unique to § 11." Rather, they are fundamental to the common law of misrepresentation, which recognizes the implied assertion of knowledge that an opinion carries. . . . [Thus,] the Omnicare Court's analysis squares with earlier holdings in this case [that an opinion] may constitute securities fraud if defendants either subjectively disbelieved the opinion they asserted or lacked a reasonable basis for their expressed belief.[8]

On the other hand, for other statements made, the plaintiffs were unable to demonstrate that the defendants "knowingly or recklessly deceived the public[.]"[9]

Hence, in making public disclosures, without a reasonable basis for statements made, companies may be subject to legal liability for damages caused by such statements. It follows that the corporate information and reporting system implemented by a company's board under corporate law principles should be designed to be sufficient to provide a foundation of information flow within an organization that could create the support needed to formulate a reasonable basis for public disclosures made pursuant to securities regulation. Therefore, companies should aim to design their information and reporting systems to be strong enough to shield themselves from legal liability under both corporate law and securities regulation.

B. Reporting Requirements under the Sarbanes-Oxley Act

Under the Sarbanes-Oxley Act (SOX), which was enacted in response to the Enron scandal, public companies must receive an audit opinion as to their internal control over financial

[8] *See In re* Merck & Co., Inc. Sec., Derivative & ERISA Litig., Nos. 05-1151, 05-2367 (SRC), 2015 WL 2250472, at *20-23 (D.N.J. May 13, 2015).

[9] *Id.* at *14.

reporting (ICFR), as well as for its management to assess their ICFR and their disclosure controls and procedures (DCP).[10] SOX requires each periodic report containing financial statements filed by an issuer with the U.S. Securities and Exchange Commission (SEC) under Exchange Act Section 13(a) or 15(d) (e.g., Form 10-K or Form 10-Q) to be accompanied by a written statement of the issuer's chief executive officer (CEO) and chief financial officer (CFO) that certifies that the public report containing the financial statements fully complies with the requirements of Section 13(a) or 15(d) and that information contained in the periodic report fairly presents, in all material respects, the financial conditions and results of operations of the issuer.[11] Rule 13a-15 defines ICFR and DCP as follows:

> **ICFR** is a process designed by, or under the supervision of, an issuer's principal executive and principal financial officers, or persons performing similar functions, and effected by such issuer's board of directors, management, and other personnel to provide reasonable assurance regarding the reliability of financial reporting and the preparation of financial statements for external purposes in accordance with generally accepted accounting principles and includes those policies and procedures that: (1) pertain to the maintenance of records that in reasonable detail accurately and fairly reflect the transactions and dispositions of the assets of such issuer; (2) provide reasonable assurance that transactions are recorded as necessary to permit preparation of financial statements in accordance with generally accepted accounting principles, and that receipts and expenditures of such issuer are being made only in accordance with authorizations of management and directors of such issuer; and (3) provide reasonable assurance regarding prevention or timely detection of unauthorized acquisition, use or disposition of such issuer's assets that could have a material effect on the financial statements.
>
> **DCP** means controls and other procedures of an issuer that are designed to ensure that information required to be disclosed by such issuer in the reports that it files or submits under the Exchange Act is recorded, processed, summarized, and reported within the time periods specified in the SEC's rules and forms; they include, without limitation, controls and procedures designed to ensure that information required to be disclosed by such issuer in the reports filed or submitted under the Exchange Act is accumulated and communicated to such issuer's management, including its principal executive and principal financial officers, or persons performing similar functions, as appropriate to allow timely decisions regarding required disclosure.

As a result of the implementation of SOX requirements and relevant to the management of ESG metrics, most companies receiving financial statement audits already have ICFR and DCP in place, which companies can leverage to design internal controls around ESG metrics and the disclosure thereof.

---

[10] *See* Reg. S-K Item 307, 17 C.F.R. § 229.307, and Item 308, 17 C.F.R. § 229.308.

[11] *See* 18 C.F.R. §§ 1350(a)-(b).

Critically, with ESG information to be disclosed within companies' Form 10-Ks and Form 10-Qs, companies' CEOs and CFOs' certifications will also cover ESG metrics and disclosures. To that end, SOX § 304 also adds clawback provisions, which state that if a company has to restate its financial statements because of material noncompliance, as a result of misconduct, with any financial reporting requirement under the securities laws, the CEO and CFO of such company must reimburse the company for any bonus or other incentive-based or equity-based compensation received during the 12-month period following the first public issuance or filing with the SEC of such document *and* any profits realized from the sale of such company's securities during that 12-month period.[12] Though the common perception is that the SEC is reluctant to enforce clawbacks under SOX § 304, the SEC did so recently;[13] it is unknown whether this enforcement is a one-time event or a signal of increased willingness by the SEC's Division of Enforcement to seek clawbacks from CEOs and CFOs whose certifications fail because of material noncompliance with financial reporting requirements, which may plausibly occur as a result of ESG information in the financial statements. [14]

Indeed, looking ahead toward the Proposed Rule, companies' ICFR and DCP will have to consider ESG metrics and required disclosures, given that most of the proposed disclosures will appear in publicly traded companies' Form 10-Ks or Form 10-Qs. Specifically, the Proposed Rule would amend Regulations S-K and S-X, inherently implicating both ICFR and DCP, though the final version of the Proposed Rule is expected to scale back some of the proposed disclosures, particularly with respect to those that would appear in an issuer's financial statements.[15] As a result, companies should expect to have at least some aspects of their ESG reporting run through their financial functions, and at the most, companies should contemplate relying on the expertise of their financial functions for the purpose of designing internal controls around the collection of ESG data for the complete, accurate, and reliable reporting of such.

C. The Committee of Sponsoring Organizations of the Treadway Commission Framework

SOX and its implementing regulations require for certain public companies that management assess ICFR and DCP and for such companies to receive an audit opinion as to their

[12] *See* 15 U.S.C. § 7243(a). In addition, the SEC's new Exchange Act Rule 10D-1 will further subject executive officers (defined more broadly therein) to potential clawbacks over a three-year lookback period if a company must restate its financial statements because of material noncompliance with any financial reporting requirement under securities laws. *See* 17 C.F.R. § 240.10D-1.

[13] *See* Joseph Jackson and Colm Callan, Securities Act Release No. 10925, Exchange Act Release No. 91042, 2021 WL 396761 (Feb. 2, 2021).

[14] *See, e.g.*, SEC v. Baker, No. A-12-CA-285-SS, 2012 WL 5499497, at *3 (W.D. Tex. Nov. 13, 2012) ("[The SEC] has been historically reluctant to utilize § 302 in the ten years since Sarbanes-Oxley was enacted. . . . However, a sword does not cease to be a sword, even though it may languish in the scabbard, and likewise, federal agencies have discretion in when and how to carry out regulatory enforcement actions.").

[15] *See* Jean Eaglesham & Paul Kiernan, *SEC Considers Easing Climate-disclosure Rules After Investor Pushback*, Wall St. J. (Feb. 3, 2023, 7:30 AM) https://www.wsj.com/articles/sec-considers-easing-climate-disclosure-rules-after-investor-pushback-11675416111. *See also infra* note 25 regarding scaling back the disclosures of an issuer's value chain's emissions from the Proposed Rule.

ICFR, which begs the question of which framework management and auditors should use to evaluate (and design, if management) ICFR and DCP. The SEC does not prescribe a specific framework for public companies. Rather, the SEC only required that management base its evaluation of the effectiveness of a company's ICFR on a suitable, recognized control framework established by a body or group that has followed due-process procedures, including the broad distribution of the framework for public comment. The SEC added that a suitable framework must be free from bias, permit reasonably consistent qualitative and quantitative measurements of a company's internal control, be sufficiently complete so that those relevant factors that would alter a conclusion about the effectiveness of a company's internal controls are not omitted, and be relevant to an evaluation of ICFR.[16]

In practice, public companies predominantly employ the framework created by the Committee of Sponsoring Organizations of the Treadway Commission (COSO)—COSO's *Internal Control—Integrated Framework* (2013) (the "2013 COSO Framework").[17] While the SEC does not require public companies to utilize the 2013 COSO Framework, the SEC acknowledged that the 2013 COSO Framework satisfied its criteria for management's annual internal control evaluation and disclosure requirements.[18] Indeed, by fiscal year 2017, over 99 percent of publicly traded companies with audited opinions over their ICFR reported using the 2013 COSO Framework.[19] As a result, this author posits that it is appropriate to view the 2013 COSO Framework as the market standard for an internal control framework, though there may be other relevant frameworks for practitioners to consider.

COSO was organized in 1985 to sponsor the National Commission on Fraudulent Financial Reporting. This National Commission was sponsored jointly by the American Accounting Association, the American Institute of Certified Public Accountants, Financial Executives International, the Institute of Internal Auditors, and the Institute of Management Accountants (formerly the National Association of Accountants). COSO's stated goal is to provide thought leadership dealing with what they consider three interrelated subjects: enterprise risk management (ERM), internal control, and fraud deterrence. To that end, COSO first published a framework regarding internal control in 1992, which was refreshed over 20 years later with the 2013 COSO Framework. The 2013 COSO Framework, which was refreshed with SOX requirements in mind, offers guidance pertaining to an entity's control environment, risk assessment, control activities, information and communication, and monitoring activities. These attributes should be analyzed across an entity's operations, reporting, and compliance functions, and again within an entity at the entry level, division, operating

---

[16] *See* Management's Report on Internal Control over Financial Reporting and Certification of Disclosure in Exchange Act Periodic Reports, Securities Act Release No. 8238, Exchange Act Release No. 47,986, Investment Company Act Release No. 26,068, 68 Fed. Reg. 36636 (June 18, 2003) (to be codified at 17 C.F.R. pts. 210, 228, 229, 240, 249, 270, 274).

[17] For a high-level overview of the 2013 COSO Framework, *see* Committee of Sponsoring Organizations of the Treadway Commission (COSO), Internal Control – Integrated Framework, Executive Summary (2013), https://www.coso.org/Shared%20Documents/Framework-Executive-Summary.pdf.

[18] *Id.*

[19] *See* Kristyn Plante, *Adopting the 2013 COSO Framework: Fiscal 2017 Update*, Audit Analytics (Nov. 28, 2018), https://blog.auditanalytics.com/adopting-the-2013-coso-framework-fiscal-2017-update/.

unit, and function area. In addition, COSO also published a framework regarding ERM in 2004 titled *Enterprise Risk Management—Integrated Framework*, which was refreshed in 2017 with a release titled *Enterprise Risk Management—Integrating with Strategy and Performance.*[20]

By virtue of COSO being sponsored by five prominent accounting industry groups, the accounting industry has effectively adopted COSO's pieces in its approach to designing Systems for companies. This is critical because, notwithstanding the SOX requirement for publicly traded companies to receive an opinion as to their ICFR, external auditors still must examine companies' ICFR and DCP as part of their own preliminary risk assessment in conjunction with an audit of financial statements. Such examination occurs in conjunction with every financial statement audit, which may be required not only by the SEC but also contractually (such as by vendors, investors, or creditors), and in conjunction with such, auditors and accountants would be utilizing the 2013 COSO Framework in assessing and/or designing their ICFR and DCP.

The 2013 COSO Framework is not limited to solely financial reporting and is, in fact, intended to be applied to any aspect of an organization. In March 2023, COSO published *Achieving Effective Internal Control Over Sustainability Reporting (ICSR): Building Trust and Confidence through the COSO Internal Control—Integrated Framework*, a supplement to the 2013 COSO Framework that addresses its application to sustainability reporting.[21] By applying the foregoing principles to the reporting of ESG metrics, companies can design and integrate ICFR and DCP for ESG metrics and disclosures in conjunction with those already in existence for financial reporting with a bona fide expectation that in doing so the Systems around ESG metrics and disclosures will be at the same caliber as those required for financial reporting under SOX.

This chapter does not seek to prescribe or specifically design Systems around ESG metrics or disclosures. Companies should seek the advice of their accountants, consultants, or legal counsel with respect to the design of internal controls tailored to their organization's needs.

III. Capturing ESG Metrics and Informing Strategy

Companies generally need to capture ESG metrics for three reasons: regulatory-mandated disclosures, augmented disclosures desired by investors and creditors, and internal decision-making with respect to a company's strategy.

Public companies in particular currently have certain regulatory-mandated disclosures, and the Proposed Rule would substantially increase the scope of ESG disclosures (even if scaled back prior to finalization). Notwithstanding, investors and creditors may demand additional ESG disclosures, such as those posited under a framework by the former Sustainability

---

[20] For a high-level overview of the 2017 ERM framework, *see* COSO, Enterprise Risk Management—Integrating with Strategy and Performance, Executive Summary (2017), https://www.coso.org/Shared%20Documents/2017-COSO-ERM-Integrating-with-Strategy-and-Performance-Executive-Summary.pdf.

[21] *See* COSO, Achieving Effective Internal Control Over Sustainability Reporting (ICSR): Building Trust and Confidence Through the COSO Internal Control—Integrated Framework (2023), https://www.coso.org/Shared%20Documents/COSO-ICSR-Report.pdf.

Accounting Standards Board (SASB) or the Sustainability Disclosure Standards recently issues by the International Sustainability Standards Board (ISSB) in June 2023, the latter of which deliberates and issues standards that guide the disclosure of sustainability information by companies to investors by industry.[22] At the time of the writing of this chapter, widespread market acceptance of any specific voluntary ESG disclosure frameworks remains in flux and may change.

Companies may also have ESG strategic goals. For example, the Proposed Rule would require disclosure of how climate change is integrated into strategy, climate expertise on the board of directors, and how information regarding climate change is flowing between the board of directors and management, which would inherently result in ESG initiatives being woven into a company's strategy. As another example, prompted by Nasdaq's diversity rule, a company may choose to set a goal to have 50 percent of its board members be women by 2025. Indeed, ESG goals and metrics seem to fit neatly into commonly used strategic frameworks used by management,[23] so the integration of ESG activities and goals into a company's strategy would be a natural evolution given any new mandatory or market-desired disclosures.

Effective management of ESG starts with the defining and capturing of ESG metrics. As with financial information, capturing data is easy, but ensuring that that data is ultimately complete, accurate, and reliable from the point of capture to the ultimate publication is the key challenge for management. Indeed, Systems are essential to a company's management and board of directors' ability to have confidence that data was accurately captured and remained accurate as that data was shared among different persons, departments, and committees.[24] Further, if a company is subject to SOX, its CEO and CFO must certify that any public report containing financial statements fully complies with the requirements of Section 13(a) or 15(d). As such, designing and implementing such Systems around ESG metrics—similar to that of financial information—is critical to companies having high-quality information on hand.

This goal is further complicated by the fact that certain ESG metrics may be objective but difficult to obtain (such as greenhouse gas emissions),[25] while other ESG metrics may be

[22] In August 2022, the SASB became subject to the oversight of and was consolidated into the ISSB, which was established by the IFRS Foundation.

[23] For example, the "Balanced Scorecard" framework, which balances the use of financial and nonfinancial performance metrics to evaluate performance. *See* Robert S. Kaplan & David P. Norton, *The Balanced Scorecard—Measures that Drive Performance*, Harv. Bus. Rev. (Jan.-Feb. 1992), https://hbr.org/1992/01/the-balanced-scorecard-measures-that-drive-performance-2.

[24] Further, as described below in Section IV—Risk Management Around ESG Information, as incentives continue to be weaved into a company's strategy, analysts' expectations, and compensation, the need to mitigate fraud risk also arises.

[25] Further to this point, U.S. Securities and Exchange Commission (SEC) Chair Gensler reportedly hedged in a recent interview regarding certain disclosures of an issuer's value chain's emissions in the Proposed Rule, noting that the calculations of such emissions were not as "well developed" as those emissions disclosures for just the issuer's emissions; however, several lawmakers have expressed their concern that softening such requirement would enable issuers to hide the total emissions of their activities, effectively frustrating the purpose of the disclosure requirement. *See* Chelsey Cox, *SEC Chair Gensler Says 'Scope 3' Emissions Disclosures Aren't 'Well Developed,' Hinting They Could Be Scaled Back in Climate Rule* (Mar. 7, 2023, 1:58 PM), https://www.cnbc.com/amp/2023/03/06/sec-chairman-gensler-hints-that-agency-could-scale-back-scope-3-emissions-disclosure.html; Letter from Elizabeth Warren, U.S. Sen., et al. to The Honorable Gary Gensler, Chair, SEC (Mar. 5, 2023), https://www.warren.senate.gov/imo/media/doc/2023.03.05%20

easy to obtain but subjective. Though often associated with climate change, ESG also encompasses goals related to diversity, such as race, ethnicity, religion, or sexual orientation, as well as corporate governance itself. With respect to diversity or demographic metrics, individuals traditionally self-identify their characteristics without a corresponding check or verification of individuals' responses by the company. Although companies must report certain demographic metrics to the U.S. Equal Employment Opportunity Commission (or voluntarily in their own corporate social responsibility reports), companies should consider whether existing Systems for capturing such data are strong enough to offset the risk of legal liability under securities regulation. Thus, management should consider how to design and implement controls around such self-identified characteristics to ensure the completeness, accuracy, and reliability of such without inadvertently violating any employment or civil rights statutes.[26] Further, governance-related metrics, by themselves, may be insufficient for portraying the full picture of an organization's governance, as the key issue with governance typically falls on its quality and/or design, which is subjective, rather than the number of meetings, length of discussion, or any other quantifiable data points. It is difficult to capture any metrics that could reveal what could go wrong, and it is difficult to ascertain governance issues until an actual problem arises.[27]

That being said, it is this author's observation that many companies are likely already engaging in initiatives that would be considered ESG-forward (and potentially meriting disclosure as an ESG initiative under a voluntary framework), which means management may already be incorporating and analyzing ESG information into their strategic decisions, albeit informally and/or intuitively. Indeed, we are unaware of any company housing its backup servers in Death Valley, California, irrespective of climate change. We expect that one of the more challenging endeavors for companies will be to take these formerly intuitive considerations and build them out into formal criteria that will reflect the taxonomy that will be used in the ESG reporting regime. Among other things, this may entail disaggregating climate change risk from other categories of risk, such as operating risk or credit risk; adopting and honing definitions and policies surrounding ESG vocabulary to the extent not statutorily defined; and designing and implementing the appropriate Systems around the formal analysis of the newly identified attributes and consistent application of the foregoing definitions and policies from the employee level to the board level and, if applicable, doing such in a way that adheres to SOX and provides a reasonable basis for public disclosures. For example, in the event of a hurricane, management would need to accurately and consistently determine whether the hurricane was a climate change-related event or simply a climate-related event,

---

Letter%20to%20SEC%20re%20Climate%20Risk%20Disclosure%20Rule.pdf. *See also supra* note 15 regarding scaling back the required disclosures in an issuer's audited financial statements from the Proposed Rule.

[26] For example, in certain situations, under the Civil Rights Act of 1964, an employer may not be able to ask an employee about sexual orientation. Likewise, in certain situations, under the Americans with Disabilities Act of 1990, an employer may not be able to ask if an employee is disabled. Knowing when and how these parameters apply is critical to establishing proper Systems around ESG information for the purpose of disclosure. Companies should seek specialized legal counsel when designing such controls to avoid legal liability.

[27] *See, e.g.*, William R. Kinney, Jr., Roger D. Martin & Marcy L. Shepardson, *Some Observations About SOX 404(b) Control Process Audits*, SSRN, Sept. 24, 2012, https://papers.ssrn.com/sol3/papers.cfm?abstract_id=2155144.

identify which ensuing expenses are truly a result of the hurricane, facilitate the established process between the relevant departments in tagging such financial information as ESG, and consider whether to relocate out of the hurricane-affected area and the associated costs thereto. Thus, as management perform their gap analyses for ESG metrics, first identifying what the company is already naturally doing may reveal a smaller gap than expected and minimize the number of action items needed for implementation.

This author also observes that not only will companies need to capture additional ESG metrics, but that another nuanced area of implementation will be determining who will capture data and when. We expect that, to some extent, Systems will be designed and implemented akin to and that will run through a company's financial function; however, ESG metrics are *not* (by themselves) financial information and will likely need to be captured by a nonfinancial function. Indeed, another challenge that management should expect in designing and implementing Systems is change management among employees, including new cross-functional teams, resistance to change, and the use of existing skills (and the current sentiments behind them) for new and different purposes, particularly as operating functions become intertwined with regulatory functions.[28] Thus, in addition to the additional training needed for a company's financial function, a company must train employees in operations functions that are relevant to the ESG metrics being captured so that such metrics can be completely, accurately, and reliably captured from the outset. Further to this point, in addition to training, depending on the industry and how a particular company is affected by or attempts to address ESG objectives, expertise with respect to the relevant issues will be necessary. ESG issues have not traditionally been part of the education and training for lawyers, accountants, or other consultants until recently. ESG expertise is a new skill set, and companies should consider how such will affect their training and hiring practices accordingly.

In aiming to capture complete, accurate, and reliable ESG metrics, companies and practitioners should consider the following:

- Differentiate between which ESG metrics will be for internal use and which will be for public disclosure, and within ESG metrics for public disclosure, which will impact or be reported in the financial statements; public disclosures will require greater scrutiny and warrant stronger internal controls (and possibly ICFR) to respond to and compensate for the increased legal liability associated therewith.
- Consider where and how it may be possible to leverage and rely on existing internal controls to simply augment controls for new ESG metrics.

[28] The initial interactions between new ESG cross-functional teammates may be quite awkward. Management will need to utilize change management methods to implement the interpersonal aspects of their Systems successfully. For example, management should consider employing microchange techniques to assist employees in successfully navigating the mindset shifts needed to effect large-scale enterprise transformation. *See* Jeff Kavanaugh & Rafee Tarafdar, *Break Down Change Management into Small Steps*, Harv. Bus. Rev. (May 3, 2021), https://hbr.org/2021/05/break-down-change-management-into-small-steps; Erika Andersen, *Change Is Hard. Here's How to Make It Less Painful.*, Harv. Bus. Rev. (Apr. 7, 2022), https://hbr.org/2022/04/change-is-hard-heres-how-to-make-it-less-painful. *See also* Andy Rugeroni, *Developing ESG Strategy Is Hard, but Executing It Is Even Harder*, Harv. Bus. Rev. (June 29, 2022), https://hbr.org/sponsored/2022/06/developing-esg-strategy-is-hard-but-executing-it-is-even-harder.

- For those ESG metrics that focus on social and diversity issues, consider consulting specialists for the design and implementation of Systems and for the relevant legal limitations with respect to collecting such data to enhance the quality of ESG metrics captured while avoiding any inadvertent legal liability.
- Consider the role and utility of software, automation, and artificial intelligence in facilitating the capture of ESG metrics. We expect additional software options to become available once the Proposed Rule is finalized and mandatory disclosures are known. For financial institutions, this would also include any requirements for climate scenario stress testing, which at the time of this writing will enter a pilot program with six major banks beginning in 2023.[29]

While some ESG metrics must be captured for the purpose of public disclosure, others must be captured for the purpose of strategic management. Ensuring that the ESG metrics are complete, accurate, and reliable is crucial for both business and legal reasons. Indeed, corporate law principles and existing SEC disclosure requirements, especially those under the Proposed Rule,[30] contemplate that ESG considerations will need to be intertwined and holistically integrated into a company's strategy. And, in fact, academics have long advocated a framework for integrating nonfinancial goals into a company's strategy.[31] A company's board and management cannot make strategic decisions based on unreliable data and may be subject to legal liability if they have not established corporate information and reporting systems in good faith. Investors and creditors cannot make investing or lending decisions with inaccurate disclosures and would likely have a cause of action under corporate and securities law for any damages caused thereby if so. And in the ESG context, ESG goals cannot be achieved if the data relied upon to achieve them is bad. Succinctly, as the saying goes, "garbage in, garbage out."

The accurate capture of ESG metrics with respect to strategy serves two purposes. The first is that such will help the company track and achieve its ESG goals. By establishing the proper Systems around ESG metrics, employees, management, and board members can rely and act upon such metrics. Crucially, from a legal perspective, as boards incorporate ESG

[29] *See* Press Release, Bd. of Governors of the Fed. Rsrv. Sys., Federal Reserve Board Announces that Six of the Nation's Largest Banks Will Participate in a Pilot Climate Scenario Analysis Exercise Designed to Enhance the Ability of Supervisors and Firms to Measure and Manage Climate-related Financial Risks (Sept. 29, 2022), https://www.federalreserve.gov/newsevents/pressreleases/other20220929a.htm.

[30] Under the Proposed Rule, public companies would have to discuss a board's oversight of climate-related risks and management's role in assessing and managing those risks. Specifically, with respect to the board's oversight, companies would need to disclose board members or committees that oversee climate-related risks, the process and frequency of doing such, and the process in which the board establishes and monitors climate-related goals; with respect to management's oversight, companies would need to disclose which positions or committees assess and manage climate-related risks, including the processes by which such are informed about and monitor such risks, and how they report such to the board of directors.

[31] The popular "Balanced Scorecard" is an example. A key aspect to the utility of the Balanced Scorecard is incorporating measurable goals into a company's performance plan that lead to the maximization of financial performance. *See* Kaplan & Norton, *supra* note 23. Although also used in the context of "days without an accident" or "average wait time," this author posits that a framework like the Balance Scorecard's approach would also be an appropriate framework through which to manage ESG risks and/or achieve ESG goals through the internal and strategic management of certain ESG metrics.

considerations into their strategies, this decreases the probability of legal liability in the event of a derivative action (if boards review the board packages received and take steps to ensure their completeness, accuracy, and reliability).[32]

The second involves SEC enforcement over false, unsubstantiated, or exaggerated disclosures regarding a company's ESG initiatives or activities. As companies make certain public disclosures with respect to their ESG initiatives, whether it be with respect to a specific ESG pledge or a general description of activities, companies must have a reasonable basis for statements made and expressed beliefs,[33] or else they run the risk of committing an anti-fraud violation. By establishing the appropriate Systems, companies create the support necessary to make public disclosures about their ESG activities and strategic initiatives. Further, with respect to ESG pledges, the Proposed Rule requires companies that have made a climate-related pledge not only to disclose the pledge but also the company's progress towards that goal and how the company is tracking such. By aligning strategic goals with publicly disclosed pledges and employing the Systems implemented to manage ESG metrics related thereto under corporate law and securities regulation, companies also mitigate the risk of legal liability.

Finally, companies should consider how ESG metrics inform patterns or trends in financial information. For example, should the Proposed Rule be finalized, the impact of certain climate-related conditions and events and transition activities would be disclosed in a company's financial statements. In addition to the Proposed Rule's baseline requirements, further information and greater insight may be gleaned from the relationship between the pattern or trend of the financial impact with the underlying ESG activity, which may be material. Designing and implementing the Systems to not only capture raw ESG metrics but also to prepare and present such in a way that conveys meaningful information from a strategic perspective may yield better decision-making internally and externally and higher-quality disclosures, and, as a result, mitigate the risk of legal liability.

IV. Risk Management around ESG Information

Maintaining the integrity of ESG information is where the rubber meets the road. This section will discuss the risk management considerations expected with integrating ESG metrics into a company's strategy and public disclosures.

At the outset, should the Proposed Rule go final, accelerated filers and large accelerated filers would be required to include an attestation report over its reported greenhouse gas emissions. Under the Proposed Rule, similar to the SEC's criteria around frameworks for internal controls, the standards to be applied in such an attestation would need to be publicly available at no cost and established by an organization that has followed due process procedures, including the broad distribution of such framework for public comment. Although the SEC noted it would not definitively prescribe an attestation standard to use, the SEC noted that relevant Public Company Accounting Oversight Board (PCAOB), American Institute of

[32] *See Marchand*, 212 A.3d at 805; *In re Caremark*, 698 A.2d at 959.

[33] *See In re Merck*, 2015 WL 2250472, at *1.

Certified Public Accountants (AICPA), and International Auditing and Assurance Standards Board (IAASB) standards meet its requirements. We clarify that while the Proposed Rule would require an attestation report over the greenhouse gas emissions, it would not require an attestation report over the *effectiveness* of internal control over greenhouse gas emissions disclosures. However, as with any assurance engagement, the attestation provider would likely begin with a risk assessment of the company's internal controls over greenhouse gas emissions in determining the extent of the procedures necessary given the risk of misstatement arising from such internal controls. Thus, the stronger the Systems established from the outset, the more the company will benefit from the reduced fees associated with attestations. Further, although the Proposed Rule would not require the attestation provider to be a public accounting firm, the fact that the SEC lists three organizations in the accounting industry as examples for attestation standards hints that the SEC may believe that expertise already exists there, even though the SEC has left the door open to other organizations. To that end, it is this author's observation that while at the time of the writing only about half of companies that report environmental metrics employ an accounting firm to perform attestation procedures, more companies are expected to employ accounting firms to do the same if the Proposed Rule is finalized because the Proposed Rule requires disclosure of the firm performing such attestation procedures and the established reputation of accounting firms' assurance services presents less risk for investors and creditors.

In addition, companies will be facing a massive learning curve in designing and implementing the Systems related to ESG metrics. However, it is this author's observation that companies are waiting to see the final form of the Proposed Rule before proceeding with augmenting their current Systems. As a result, companies will essentially be designing and implementing their Systems concurrently and presumably testing the waters with respect to the ensuing disclosures during the period required; as such, it is possible that companies will provide varying levels of detail in this first period before benchmarking and normalizing disclosures in subsequent periods.[34] As a result, there may be some legal or business risk in connection with companies' decisions to disclose too much or too little in the inaugural period of disclosure.

Hence, the entire reporting process is affected by the disclosure of ESG metrics. And consistent with the SEC's nod toward the attestations standards of the PCAOB, AICPA, and ISAAB, companies should consider utilizing the 2013 COSO Framework for designing and implementing appropriate Systems around ESG metrics and disclosures to produce information that will pass such attestation engagement.

Companies should consider the following in designing and implementing Systems around ESG metrics:

- Build upon existing Systems, as the external disclosure of such information to investors and creditors must follow a similar pathway as other financial information, and internal disclosure of such information to management and the board of directors

[34] A similar exercise occurred with respect to the recent requirement to disclose of human capital resources under Reg. S-K Item 105.

must follow a similar pathway as existing board package information; for example, consider adding an ESG expert to your existing disclosure committee.

- Consider the use of technology, automation, and artificial intelligence, as applicable, in designing such Systems, as such technology is less prone to manual error (effectively acting as its own control).
- Check with existing vendors to see if they offer any ESG packages or add-ons; for example, SAP, Workiva, and Diligent offer a form of ESG reporting.
- Start by performing a gap analysis—determine which ESG data and information will be relevant for complying with external reporting and internal strategic management, and design and implement the relevant Systems from there.
- Seek the advice of experts from cross-functional teams in designing and implementing necessary Systems, as the additional expertise and consensus will enhance the effectiveness of such and result in more complete, accurate, and reliable ESG data and information.
- Recall and implement the fundamental tenets of internal control design to ESG data and information, including segregation of duties, audit trails, and other preventive, detective, and corrective controls.

As ESG considerations become more intertwined with strategy—especially for public companies, which we expect to accelerate given the Proposed Rule's governance disclosures—it follows that companies may provide incentives to management or employees to achieve certain ESG objectives measured by ESG metrics. Having appropriate Systems around ESG metrics will be critical to preventing and mitigating the risk of fraud.

Indeed, former Treasury Secretary Tim Geithner noted (among other things) with respect to executive compensation that compensation should be tied to performance to link the incentives of executives and other employees with long-term value creation, which should be done by making performance-based pay conditioned on a wide range of internal and external metrics; compensation should be tightly aligned with the long-term value and soundness of a company; and risk assessments of compensation packages should be conducted and published to discourage imprudent risk-taking.[35] Although the context of Mr. Geithner's address related to the 2008 financial crisis, the principles he lays out certainly apply in the context of ESG considerations, especially in light of the Proposed Rule and Nasdaq's rule on board diversity. For example, an executive may receive a bonus for reducing greenhouse gas emissions at a faster pace than set forth in the company's publicly announced climate change pledge; further, such bonus may be contingent upon a longer-term objective, such as sustaining the reduction of greenhouse gas emissions after achieving the target threshold or successfully championing the re-election of diverse directors.

The implementation of incentives to achieve ESG goals is commendable. However, as has always been the case, with the aligning of strategy and financial incentives comes the

[35] *See* Press Release, U.S. Department of the Treasury, Statement by Treasury Secretary Tim Geithner on Compensation (June 10, 2009), https://home.treasury.gov/news/press-releases/tg163.

increased risk of fraud: just as how the finance department may "cook the books" to meet or exceed analyst expectations, the environmental team may paint a rosier picture of a company's ESG efforts if a financial reward is at stake.

In addition to compensation, there is fraud risk in connection with false, unsubstantiated, or exaggerated disclosures regarding a company's ESG initiatives or activities for the purpose of raising capital. Indeed, given the push for ESG disclosures from *investors*, it follows that at least an allotment of capital will be reserved for entities pursuing (and achieving) ESG initiatives alongside their primary business operations. If investors ever become willing to pay a premium for interests in ESG-forward companies—though note that we have not seen this yet—then such may incentivize management to mislead prospective investors with respect to their ESG activities in exchange for an enlarged investment.

Such fraud risk creates concern for several angles of legal liability. First is general anti-fraud liability. Particularly if the company is raising capital for a to-be-registered security, Section 11 of the Securities Act may be implicated, whereby legal liability would not be limited to just damages, unlike other anti-fraud provisions.[36] Second, if the company is a public company, the clawback provisions under SOX Section 304 and the new Exchange Act Rule 10D-1 would apply.

Companies should also be wary of the impact of fraud risk by *other* companies on its decisions to invest in Systems, or other infrastructure, related to ESG activities. As companies begin benchmarking against and competing with their industry peers with respect to ESG initiatives, as would occur with any opportunity, such companies must be alert to the fact that a competitor reporting figures "too good to be true" *could* be misreporting its activities, and the company should not necessarily follow such competitor's lead in terms of matching its operations. Indeed, data suggests that companies have over-invested resources (without ensuing returns) in response to competitors thought to be industry-leading but who were just committing accounting fraud,[37] and a similar phenomenon could be possible for ESG initiatives and incentive compensation. Further intensifying this issue are the potential ramifications the foregoing may have from a macroeconomic perspective as companies try to assess their contributions to industry-wide ESG objectives; should a competitor misreport its ESG activities, it may cause other companies to over-compensate or lowball their responses, not only affecting those companies financially but also incurring real-world consequences related to the underlying ESG issues.

The design and implementation of appropriate Systems is critical to the mitigation of fraud risk. By implementing Systems, it will be more difficult for bad actors to commit the aforementioned offenses. In doing such, companies should consider the following:

- Incorporate the evaluation of fraud with respect to ESG initiatives as part of the overall risk management system.

---

[36] *See* 15 U.S.C. § 77k.

[37] *See* Anne Beatty et al., *The Spillover Effect of Fraudulent Financial Reporting on Peer Firms' Investments*, 55 J. Acct. & Econ. 183 (2013).

- Design internal controls around ESG information similar to that of traditional financial information; such would include, among other things, designing and implementing strong preventive, detective, and corrective controls; inserting segregation of duties, where applicable; creating an audit trail for ESG metrics; and adding or placing people with the appropriate expertise onto the relevant board or management committees.
- Strengthen the alignment of incentives with strategy. In the context of compensation particularly, match the time horizons between the company's ESG objectives and incentives, and implement safeguards that prevent the need for a SOX clawback.
- Identify which ESG metrics related to strategy may also implicate ICFR, and consider the appropriate consequences and ramifications under SOX, including management's (and auditors', if applicable) assessment of ICFR and DCP.

Key Takeaways

ESG management systems bridge the gap between a company's strategy around ESG and disclosures and inform a company's board and management of its progress toward its strategic goals. Systems also contribute to information integrity and to the risk management of ESG metrics.

Systems need not necessarily be confined to software or other "tech" tools. Rather, Systems will likely be a combination of automated and manual activities, which should also be integrated into a company's existing internal controls and addressed by a company's existing risk management framework. As companies seek to design and implement Systems into their existing Systems, they should consider the following key takeaways:

- Start with a gap analysis to determine which ESG metrics are needed and/or desired by the board of directors and management for both internal and external purposes.
- Design and implement Systems around the ESG metrics identified to enhance the completeness, accuracy, and reliability of ESG metrics from capture to reporting.
- Recall and rely upon established concepts around the design of Systems for financial data when designing the same for ESG metrics.
- Consider how your Systems can be integrated or synced with existing Systems, particularly financial reporting systems, to benefit from economies of scale.
- Recall that the design and implementation of appropriate Systems around the capture and reporting of ESG metrics protects a company and its board of directors from legal liability under corporate law, as both may rely on the internal reporting of such ESG metrics when engaging in strategic decision-making.
- Recall that the design and implementation of appropriate Systems around the capture and reporting of ESG metrics also protects a company from legal liability under securities regulation, as the company will enhance its ability to rely on such information for the purpose of providing a reasonable basis for its ESG disclosures in its relevant filings.

- Recall that as ESG information becomes tied to financial metrics, SOX and legal liability thereunder will be implicated, meaning that the Systems around such ESG information in particular will be assessed as ICFR, not merely DCP.
- Be mindful that as ESG initiatives become further intertwined with a company's strategy, incentives for a company's board of directors and management will follow, posing risks that should be addressed and mitigated as part of the design of ESG Systems and pursuant to the company's risk management framework.

18

Responding to Shareholder Initiatives

Jennifer McLellan and Teresa L. Johnson

I. Introduction

Shareholder proposals have, over the past decades, transformed the corporate landscape, and many of those have urged companies to adopt governance best practices. Governance practices that are now commonplace, such as shareholder approval for poison pills, majority vote rules for director elections, and proxy access bylaws, are the product of shareholder proposal campaigns. Shareholder proponents have used shareholder proposals submitted in proxy materials to break down barriers for meaningful shareholder voice, pushing directors and management to confront investors' calls for transparency and accountability head-on. Shareholder proposals have proven to be a cost-effective, useful mechanism for investors to collectively give their views to management.

In the era of ESG, it should come as no surprise that shareholders are increasingly speaking up on environmental, ethical, political, and social issues. There is a surge of environmental and social-related shareholder proposals across various industries.

And while shareholder proposals are an important mechanism for investors to provide feedback to companies, convey their views, and influence company management with respect to ESG matters, they are not the only means. Shareholders are also making their voices heard through activist campaigns, direct engagement, independent proxy campaigns, and policy announcements. In recent years, for example, certain large investment funds, such as Vanguard, BlackRock, and State Street, as well as a number of big investment banks, have announced policies stating that they will cast their votes to influence ESG-related changes, such as the levels of diversity on a company's board.[1] Moreover, activist investors are using campaigns to force a veritable tidal wave of investor concerns on ESG issues to the forefront. For example, in May 2021, Engine No. 1 LLC (Engine No. 1), a sustainability-focused hedge fund, successfully battled ExxonMobil Corporation (Exxon) to install three new ESG-focused directors on to Exxon's board with the goal of pushing Exxon to reduce its carbon footprint.[2] At the time, Engine No. 1 held only a 0.02 percent stake in Exxon but was backed by some of Exxon's biggest institutional investors, including BlackRock and Vanguard.[3]

With ESG issues in the mainstream, companies need to think strategically in responding to shareholder initiatives, including by taking into account the varying viewpoints of their shareholders, maneuvering geopolitical challenges, and anticipating what future proxy seasons may bring. Support for ESG-related proposals has dropped recently, possibly in response to pressure in the economic environment. Accordingly, companies will need to balance the needs of different stakeholders, including shareholders, amid dynamic market forces.

This chapter provides an overview of shareholder proposal basics, including Exchange Act Rule 14a-8 and the U.S. Securities and Exchange Commission's (SEC's) 2022 proposed amendments thereto, discusses recent trends in ESG-related shareholder proposals, provides an overview of some of the challenges companies face in responding to shareholder initiatives, and offers some key takeaways for consideration in the context of shareholder initiatives.

---

[1] *See* Vanguard, Investment Stewardship 2022 Semiannual Report (2022), https://corporate.vanguard.com/content/dam/corp/advocate/investment-stewardship/pdf/policies-and-reports/investment_stewardship_semiannual_report_2022.pdf; BlackRock, Investment Stewardship Proxy Voting Guidelines for U.S. Securities (2023), https://www.blackrock.com/corporate/literature/fact-sheet/blk-responsible-investment-guidelines-us.pdf; State Street Global Advisors, Guidance on Diversity Disclosures and Practices (2022), https://www.ssga.com/library-content/pdfs/asset-stewardship/racial-diversity-guidance-article.pdf; Credit Suisse, Sustainability Report 2021 (2022), https://www.credit-suisse.com/media/assets/corporate/docs/about-us/investor-relations/financial-disclosures/financial-reports/csg-sr-2021-en.pdf; JPMorgan Chase & Co., 2021 Environmental Social & Governance Report (2022), https://www.jpmorgan.com/content/dam/jpmc/jpmorgan-chase-and-co/documents/jpmc-esg-report-2021.pdf; *Board Diversity Initiative*, Goldman Sachs, https://www.goldmansachs.com/our-commitments/diversity-and-inclusion/board-diversity/index.html (last visited Jan. 10, 2023).

[2] *See* Alastair Marsh & Saijel Kishan, *Engine No. 1's Exxon Win Provides Boost for ESG Advocates*, Bloomberg (May 27, 2021, 9:16 AM), https://www.bloomberg.com/news/articles/2021-05-27/engine-no-1-s-exxon-win-signals-turning-point-for-esg-investors?leadSource=uverify%20wall; *see also* Matt Phillips, *Exxon's Board Defeat Signals the Rise of Social-Good Activists*, N.Y. Times (June 9, 2021), https://www.nytimes.com/2021/06/09/business/exxon-mobil-engine-no1-activist.html.

[3] *See* BlackRock, Investment Stewardship, Vote Bulletin: ExxonMobil Corporation (2021), https://www.blackrock.com/corporate/literature/press-release/blk-vote-bulletin-exxon-may-2021.pdf. In a statement explaining its rationale for supporting Engine No. 1's appointees, BlackRock stated that while Exxon had taken steps to enhance its climate commitments and disclosures following its 2020 annual meeting, the company needed to take more urgent action. BlackRock explained, "those companies that proactively consider their operational footprint in the context of a low-carbon transition will be better positioned to avoid major disruptions and deliver long-term value to their shareholders." *Id.*

II. Shareholder Proposal Basics

A. Overview

Shareholders of a public company can advocate that the company and/or its board of directors take a specific course of action at an annual or special meeting by submitting a written shareholder proposal for inclusion in the annual proxy statement. Generally speaking, a shareholder proposal enables the shareholder to bring matters before other shareholders for a vote. Proposals consist of recommendations on a variety of topics, and most commonly consists of proposals on corporate governance matters—such as voting standards or director independence—and requests for disclosures to investors on various matters. Shareholder proposals must not be ambiguous or merely express an opinion; they must articulate a specific course of action.

To be eligible to submit a proposal, a shareholder must have continually held a certain amount of the company's stock for a certain time period.[4] A shareholder may submit no more than one proposal to a company for a particular shareholders' meeting.[5] The proposal must include an accompanying supporting statement,[6] may not exceed 500 words,[7] and must be timely submitted.[8]

The foregoing eligibility and procedural requirements are not the only limitations on proposals. Shareholder proposals are also limited to the scope of authority held by shareholders—when shareholders invest in a company, they are agreeing to a structure in which nearly all corporate decision-making authority is vested with the board of directors, which in turn delegates day-to-day managerial authority to officers. State corporate law gives shareholders certain governance rights, such as the right to elect directors and approve major corporate transactions, but those rights are not unfettered. Typically, shareholders do not have the power to require the company's board to take action on the basis that it would interfere with the board's ability to govern the affairs of the company. Instead, shareholder proposals are framed as recommendations from shareholders, which the board or management may decide to adopt or not. However, if the board chooses *not* to implement a shareholder proposal that gets broad shareholder support, that may harm the board's prospects for re-election at the next annual meeting.

---

[4] A shareholder must have continuously held (a) at least $2,000 in market value of the company's securities entitled to vote on the proposal for at least three years; (b) at least $15,000 in market value of the company's securities entitled to vote on the proposal for at least two years; or (c) at least $25,000 in market value of the company's securities entitled to vote on the proposal for at least one year. *See* 17 C.F.R. § 240.14a-8(b).

[5] *See* 17 C.F.R. § 240.14a-8(c).

[6] *See* 17 C.F.R. § 240.14a-8(b).

[7] *See* 17 C.F.R. § 240.14a-8(d). *See also* Daniel Hamilton, *Limits on Word Limit Under Rule 14A-8*, 96 Denv. L. Rev. F. (2018), https://digitalcommons.du.edu/cgi/viewcontent.cgi?article=1005&context=dlrforum (discussing the U.S. Securities and Exchange Commission's (SEC's) rigorous enforcement of the 500-word restriction).

[8] *See* 17 C.F.R. § 240.14a-8(e). Typically, proposals must be submitted by the deadline disclosed in the previous year's proxy statement (at least 120 days before the date of the company's proxy statement for the previous year's annual meeting). *Id.*

B. Rule 14a-8—the "Shareholder Proposal Rule"

Upon receiving a shareholder proposal, a company must confirm the proponent's eligibility and procedural compliance with the proxy rules. Shareholder proposals are governed by Exchange Act Rule 14a-8 (the "Shareholder Proposal Rule" or the "Rule").[9] According to the SEC, the Shareholder Proposal Rule is intended to facilitate "shareholders' traditional ability under state law to present their own proposals for consideration at a company's annual or special meeting, and . . . the ability of all shareholders to consider and vote on such proposals."[10] Under the Shareholder Proposal Rule, companies that are subject to the federal proxy rules generally must include shareholder proposals in their proxy statements unless a proposal is eligible for exclusion under the Rule.

As noted above, shareholder proposals may be excluded for eligibility or procedural deficiencies. The Shareholder Proposal Rule also includes 13 substantive bases for excluding shareholder proposals, which include matters deemed inappropriate for shareholder consideration through the proposal proposed, such as "materially false or misleading" proposals and those relating to "ordinary business"[11] matters. The purpose of the ordinary business exception is "to confine the resolution of ordinary business problems to management and the board of directors, since it is impracticable for shareholders to decide how to solve such problems at an annual shareholders meeting."[12] Companies may also exclude shareholder proposals that have already been substantially implemented, or that substantially duplicate or represent a resubmission of another shareholder proposal, though the SEC has proposed narrowing these exceptions as described below.[13]

If a company wishes to omit a proposal from its proxy statement, it has three options: (1) if the proposal falls within one of the 13 substantive exclusions, the company can assert its right to exclude the proposal and file its reasons for doing so with the SEC Division of Corporation Finance, which is generally in the form of a no-action request; (2) notify the SEC Division of Corporation Finance of its decision to drop the proposal on the basis of an exclusion and take the chance that neither the SEC nor the shareholders will litigate and ultimately prevail in a case for breach of Rule 14a-8; or (3) negotiate with the shareholder proposal proponent to have the proposal withdrawn. If the company files a no-action request asserting that the proposal falls within one of the substantive exclusions, and the SEC grants the request, the

---

[9] *See* 17 C.F.R. § 240.14a-8.

[10] Procedural Requirements and Resubmission Thresholds Under Exchange Act Rule 14a-8, Exchange Act Release No. 87,458, 84 Fed. Reg. 66458, 66459 (proposed Dec. 4, 2019) (to be codified at 17 C.F.R. pt. 240).

[11] *See* 17 C.F.R. § 240.14a-8(i)(7).

[12] Amendments to Rules on Shareholder Proposals, Exchange Act Release No. 40,018, Investment Company Act Release No. 23,200, 63 Fed. Reg. 29106, 29108 (May 28, 1998) (to be codified at 17 C.F.R. pt. 240). The SEC has explained that "[t]he 'ordinary business' exclusion is based in part on state corporate law establishing spheres of authority for the board of directors on the one hand, and the company's shareholders on the other." Amendments to Rules on Shareholder Proposals, Exchange Act Release No. 39,093, Investment Company Act Release No. 22,828, 62 Fed. Reg. 50682, 50683 (proposed Sept. 26, 1997) (to be codified at 17 C.F.R. pt. 240).

[13] *See* 17 C.F.R. § 240.14a-8(i)(10)–(12).

company will typically exclude the shareholder proposal from its proxy materials.[14] Alternatively, the company may engage in negotiations with the proposing shareholder for purposes of encouraging the shareholder to withdraw its proposal either during or after the no-action process, and may offer concessions that address the proponent's concerns in return. In most cases, in the absence of SEC no-action relief or withdrawal of the shareholder proposal by its proponent, the proposal will be included in the annual proxy statement and placed on the ballot for a shareholder vote. The annual proxy statement will include a statement by the shareholder proponent advocating for its proposal, and management will also include a statement regarding its position on the proposal (usually opposing the proposal).

In determining what steps to take after a shareholder proposal is received, it is imperative that companies consider their goals with respect to shareholder engagement. For example, the company may be focused on discouraging future proposals on similar topics, or on minimizing disruption to board processes, and decide to directly confront the issue at hand by revising its voting policies on the subject. A company might also use the proposal as an opportunity to advance its position on the subject issue. Identifying goals for shareholder engagement will enable the company to respond to shareholder proposals in strategic and thoughtful ways.

C. Proposed Amendments to the Shareholder Proposal Rule

In July 2022, the SEC proposed amendments to the Shareholder Proposal Rule, which would amend three of the 13 substantive bases for exclusion of shareholder proposals under the rule.[15] In its proposal, the SEC stated that the proposed amendments would "enhance the ability of shareholders to express diverse objectives and various ways to achieve those objectives through the shareholder proposal process."[16] The proposed amendments to the Shareholder Proposal Rule would revise the following bases[17] for exclusion:

1. **Substantial implementation**—The proposed amendments would amend the substantial implementation exclusion (which is currently framed as implementation of most, but not necessarily all, of a proposal's elements) to specify that a proposal may be excluded if the company has already implemented the essential elements of the proposal.

[14] The staff's no-action position is not legally binding, and the matter ultimately may be resolved by a federal district court. With respect to approximately 0.1 percent of proposals submitted for annual meetings from 2017 through 2021, companies who were granted no-action requests for exclusion of the proposal nonetheless included the shareholder proposal in its proxy. *See* Substantial Implementation, Duplication, and Resubmission of Shareholder Proposals Under Exchange Act Rule 14a-8, Exchange Act Release No. 95,267, Investment Company Act Release No. 34,647, at 36 (July 13, 2022), 87 Fed. Reg. 45052, 45062 (proposed July 27, 2022) (to be codified at 17 C.F.R. pt. 240), https://www.sec.gov/rules/proposed/2022/34-95267.pdf [hereinafter Proposing Release].

[15] *See generally* Proposing Release, *supra* note 14; *see also* SEC, Fact Sheet: Shareholder Proposals Under Rule 14a-8: Proposed Rules, https://www.sec.gov/files/34-95267-fact-sheet.pdf.

[16] Proposing Release, *supra* note 14, at 7.

[17] Of note, the SEC has stated that almost half of the no-action requests the staff received in 2021 under the Shareholder Proposal Rule were based on these three exclusions.

2. **Duplication**—The proposed amendments would clarify the duplication exclusion, which has been interpreted subjectively to exclude proposals with the same "principal focus" and has been viewed to incentivize shareholders to occupy the field by being the first to submit a proposal on a particular topic in the relevant proxy season. If the amendments are adopted, a proposal would only substantially duplicate another proposal if it addressed the same subject matter and sought the same objective by the same means.
3. **Resubmission**—The proposed amendments would narrow the resubmission exclusion (which currently allows exclusion of proposals sharing "substantially the same subject matter"[18]) to provide that a proposal constitutes a resubmission only if it substantially duplicates another proposal.

Proponents of the amendments have stated that the changes "would reduce costs and uncertainties to proponents and issuers alike" and would make the proposal process "more efficient, objective and predictable."[19] Conclusions would be more certain, and the amendments would reduce staff discretion. Further, the amendments would be "to the benefit of investors seeking clearer disclosure and analysis of the companies' responses to climate transition risks."[20]

From an ESG perspective, the proposed amendments are particularly important given the substantial increase in ESG-related shareholder proposals in the 2022 proxy season, as discussed in further detail below. If adopted as proposed, companies will likely see a further increase in voted proposals, as well as more submissions, granular and multiple proposals on the same topics.[21] Further, companies will likely face greater difficulty in successfully excluding shareholder proposals, which means that management will have to take a public stance on more shareholder proposals, potentially drawing criticism if they oppose proposals that have popular support.

III. ESG-Related Shareholder Proposals

Categorizing shareholder proposals can be inherently subjective, including when determining whether proposals focus on environmental, social, or governance matters, given the influence and overlap these topics have on one another. For purposes of providing some initial

[18] Rule 14a-8(i)(12) permits excluding duplicative shareholder proposals that address substantially the same subject matter as proposals included in the company's proxy materials in the preceding five years, if the proposal was voted on at least once in the past three years and did not reach specified voting thresholds.

[19] Letter from Sanford Lewis, Dir., S'holder Rts. Grp., to Vanessa A. Countryman, Sec'y, SEC, at 1 (July 25, 2022) [hereinafter Shareholder Rights Group Comment Letter]. *See also* Letter from Brandon J. Rees, Deputy Dir., Corps. & Cap. Mkts., Am. Fed'n of Lab. & Cong. of Indus. Orgs., to Vanessa A. Countryman, Sec'y, SEC, at 4 (Sept. 9, 2022) ("These needed clarifications will increase certainty for both companies and investors by providing more consistent and predictable determinations regarding the Rule 14a-8 exclusions, and thereby reduce costs of the shareholder proposal process for all parties."); Letter from Lisa Woll, CEO, US SIF: The F. for Sustainable and Responsible Investment, to Vanessa A. Countryman, Sec'y, SEC, at 2 (Sept. 16, 2022) ("The proposed amendments to Rule 14a-8 will give more clarity to shareholders submitting proposals and companies weighing whether to challenge a proposal by submitting a no-action request to the SEC staff.").

[20] Shareholder Rights Group Comment Letter, *supra* note 19, at 2.

[21] *See* June Hu et al., *2022 Proxy Season Review: Rule 14a-8 Shareholder Proposals*, Harv. L. Sch. F. on Corp. Governance (Aug. 25, 2022), https://corpgov.law.harvard.edu/2022/08/25/2022-proxy-season-review-rule-14a-8-shareholder-proposals/.

goalposts, we point to the proposed amendments to the Shareholder Proposal Rule, where the SEC generally categorized ESG-related proposals to include, among others:[22]

> ***Environmental*** proposals relate to sustainability, greenhouse gas emissions, climate change, community/environmental impact, and renewable energy.
> ***Social*** proposals relate to political contributions and lobbying disclosure, labor and health issues, human rights, and board diversity.
> ***Governance*** proposals relate to shareholder rights and takeover defenses, board structure and independence, and executive compensation.

While ESG-related proposals have a multitude of objectives, ESG-related proposals generally aim to elicit information from companies about particular issues, as well as change the way companies operate with respect to those issues. This can be accomplished through a few different channels, including by requiring companies to disclose information which could, once publicly known, trigger criticism and pressure to make operational changes (e.g., disclosure of pay inequities might prompt action to remedy any such inequities).[23]

IV. Recent ESG-Related Shareholder Proposal Trends

For the last decade or so, the majority of proposals submitted under the Shareholder Proposal Rule have been related to governance, director elections and compensation, takeover defenses, and other internal organizational decisions.[24] However, recent years have seen an uptick in shareholder proposals concerning the interests of consumers, employees, citizens, the environment, and society at large.[25]

A. Significant Increase in Environmental and Social Proposals; Decrease in Support

The 2022 proxy season was a roller-coaster ride for environmental and social (E&S) shareholder proposals—S&P Composite 1500 companies (which cover approximately 90 percent of U.S. market capitalization) faced over 500 E&S shareholder proposals (up from 408 in 2021).[26] Proposals on environmental and social/political topics "now represent a much larger portion of total submissions, surging to 63% of submissions after reaching a majority of submitted proposals for the first time in the 2021 proxy season, driven by a 38% year-over-year

[22] *See* Proposing Release, *supra* note 14, at 40.

[23] *See, e.g.*, Roberto Tallarita, *Stockholder Politics*, 73 Hastings L.J. 1617 (2022) (reporting empirical evidence on environmental and social proposals from 2010 to 2021).

[24] *Id.*

[25] *Id.* ("These 'social proposals' include not only big picture problems such as climate change, corporate lobbying, and employee diversity, but also a variety of narrower issues, such as smoke-free areas in the company's premises, energy efficiency in retail stores, the adverse effects of specific drugs, the sale of weapons to foreign governments, the effect of bank overdraft policies on low-income customers, employee ideological diversity, the use of cage-free eggs, or the acceptance of censorship policies in foreign countries.").

[26] *The 2022 Proxy Season: Forces Collide*, Sustainable Governance Partners (July 28, 2022), https://sgpgovernance.com/the-2022-proxy-season-forces-collide/.

(H1 2021 vs. H1 2022) increase in environmental proposals."[27] According to Glass Lewis, the increase "was largely as a result of proposals submitted by advocacy groups, such as NGOs and think tanks."[28]

Nonetheless, those proposals received less support than in prior years. According to Glass Lewis, average shareholder support for E&S resolutions dropped from 36 percent in 2020 to 31 percent in 2022.[29] For example, in 2022, shareholders of Chevron Corporation (Chevron, along with shareholders of other oil giants like ConocoPhillips Co. and Occidental Petroleum Corp.) voted against shareholder proposals calling for the company to disclose climate-related risks and set more rigorous climate-related targets to cut pollution. Specifically, Chevron's shareholders voted against four of five ESG-related proposals,[30] which included rejection of proposals regarding adoption of medium- and long-term greenhouse gas reduction targets, reviewing Chevron's business with conflict-complicit governments, and undertaking an internal racial equity audit.[31] Chevron's shareholders also voted against a shareholder proposal to report on impacts of the International Energy Agency's (IEA's) Net Zero scenario.[32] This proposal requested that Chevron's board of directors "provide an audited report addressing how application of the assumptions of the IEA's Net Zero by 2050 pathway would affect the assumptions and estimates underlying its financial statements, including its long-term commodity and carbon prices, remaining asset lives, existing and future asset retirement obligations, capital expenditures, and asset valuations (impairments). The report should be produced at reasonable cost and omitting proprietary information."[33] This was hardly novel—Chevron received a similar proposal in 2021,[34] which requested that Chevron's board "issue an audited report to shareholders on whether and how a significant reduction in fossil fuel demand, envisioned in the IEA Net Zero by 2050 scenario, would affect its financial position and

[27] Hu et al., *supra* note 21. According to the source, year-over-year changes were assessed by comparing H1 2022 and H1 2021 data for consistency, which included proposals submitted to and/or voted on at annual meetings of the U.S. members of the S&P Composite 1500 at meetings held on or before June 30, 2022 (the source estimates that 90 percent of U.S. public companies held their 2022 annual meetings by that date).

[28] Glass Lewis, Proxy Season 2022 Briefing: United States 4 (2022).

[29] *Id.*

[30] *See* Chevron Corp., 2022 Shareholder Proposal Voting Results (Form 8-K) (May 27, 2022), https://www.chevron.com/-/media/chevron/investors/documents/chevron-shareholder-proposal-voting-results.pdf. Shareholders overwhelmingly supported a proposal regarding a report on reliability of methane emission disclosures.

[31] *Id.*

[32] *Id.* The International Energy Agency (IEA) Net Zero scenario (NZE 2050) describes an energy sector pathway to achieve net zero emissions—meaning, net zero global greenhouse gas emissions. In October 2021, Chevon joined a list of energy companies taking steps to reduce their carbon footprint and set a target to cut operational emissions to net zero by 2050. *See Chevron Commits to Net Zero Operational Emissions by 2050*, Reuters, Oct. 11, 2021, https://www.reuters.com/business/sustainable-business/chevron-commits-net-zero-emissions-by-2050-2021-10-11/.

[33] Chevron Corp., 2022 Proxy Statement 92 (2022), https://www.chevron.com/-/media/shared-media/documents/chevron-proxy-statement-2022.pdf.

[34] Chevron's 2021 proxy statement also included an approved proposal regarding reducing Scope 3 emissions. *See* Chevron Corp., 2021 Proxy Statement 81 (2021), https://www.chevron.com/-/media/shared-media/documents/chevron-proxy-statement-2021.pdf.

underlying assumptions."[35] Notably, support for a report on impacts of the Net Zero 2050 scenario dropped from 47.8 percent in 2021 to 38.7 percent in 2022.[36]

The decline in support for environmental-related proposals was not limited to the oil and gas industry. Within the financial services industry, several environmental-related shareholder proposals urging companies to cease financing fossil fuel projects failed to achieve sufficient shareholder support. The "2022 Early Proxy Season Review" published by proxy solicitation firm Georgeson, Inc. (Georgeson) stated that such fossil fuel defunding proposals were rejected by companies' shareholders in every instance, with none receiving above 12.8 percent support.[37]

B. Prescriptive Proposals

One of the reasons for the decline in support was that many ESG-related shareholder proposals in the 2022 proxy season were viewed as overly "prescriptive," seeking specific strategic action rather than additional disclosure.[38] Large institutional investors like BlackRock were unwilling to support proposals that were "unduly prescriptive and constraining on the decision-making of the board or management, call for changes to a company's strategy or business model, or address matters that are not material to how a company delivers long-term shareholder value."[39] Given that the large institutional investors carry considerable voting power for publicly traded companies,[40] a shareholder proposal without institutional investor support would face steep odds to pass.

---

[35] *Id.* at 83. In recommending against the proposal, Chevron's board argued that the requested report was unnecessary given "Chevron's current disclosures and robust strategy, planning, and risk management processes." *Id.* at 84. Chevron's board had requested no-action relief with respect to this proposal on the basis of Rule 14a-8(i)(3) (as materially false and misleading), Rule 14a-8(i)(10) (substantial implementation through its published report), or, alternatively, Rule 14a-8(i)(11) (substantial duplication). *See* Letter from Elizabeth A. Ising, Gibson, Gunn & Crutcher LLP, to Off. of Chief Counsel, Div. of Corp. Fin., SEC (Jan. 18, 2021), https://www.sec.gov/divisions/corpfin/cf-noaction/14a-8/2021/beharchevron011821-14a8-incoming.pdf. In response, the SEC stated it was unable to concur with exclusion on any of the bases asserted. *See Shareholder Proposal No-action Responses*, SEC https://www.sec.gov/divisions/corpfin/cf-noaction/14a-8/shareholder-proposal-no-action-responses-2020-2021.htm (Oct. 22, 2021).

[36] *See* Chevron Corp., 2021 Shareholder Proposal Voting Results (Form 8-K) 3 (May 28, 2021), https://chevroncorp.gcs-web.com/static-files/d2f31ab5-ff7e-4100-bf52-b2cf7527e09c; Chevron Corp., 2022 Shareholder Proposal Voting Results, *supra* note 30, at 3.

[37] Georgeson, An Early Look at the 2022 Proxy Season 13 (2022), https://www.georgeson.com/us/insights/2022-early-proxy-season-review.

[38] *See The 2022 Proxy Season: Forces Collide, supra* note 26. *See also* BlackRock, 2022 Voting Spotlight Summary, BlackRock Investment Stewardship: A Look Into the 2021-2022 Proxy Voting Year 14 (2022), https://www.blackrock.com/corporate/literature/publication/2022-investment-stewardship-voting-spotlight-summary.pdf (observing that many of the proposals in the 2022 proxy season "were overly prescriptive as to information sought or timeframes").

[39] BlackRock, 2022 Climate-related Shareholder Proposals More Prescriptive than 2021, Investment Stewardship 2 (2022), https://www.blackrock.com/corporate/literature/publication/commentary-bis-approach-shareholder-proposals.pdf.

[40] BlackRock, Vanguard, and State Street "collectively manage approximately US$20 trillion in assets, hold on average more than 20 percent of any given S&P 500 company and cast approximately 25 percent of all votes at the annual meetings of US public companies." Thomas W. Christopher et al., *The INDEX Act: A Challenge to the Voting Influence of Institutional Investors that May Yield Unintended Consequences*, White & Case LLP (Nov. 3, 2022), https://www.whitecase.com/insight-our-thinking/index-act-challenge-voting-influence-institutional-investors-may-yield.

C. Decrease in U.S. Securities and Exchange Commission No-Action Relief

Based on the 2022 proxy season, the SEC granted fewer no-action letter requests to exclude shareholder proposals.[41] According to one study, no-action requests related to social/political shareholder proposals accounted for 81 percent of all no-action requests for annual meetings in the first half of 2022, up from 47 percent for the same period in the previous year.[42] This study found that the SEC granted relief to 17 percent of requests related to environmental proposals, 26 percent of requests related to social proposals, and 59 percent of requests related to governance proposals, compared to 47 percent, 74 percent, and 72 percent, respectively, for the same period in 2021.[43] And with the SEC's proposed amendments to the Shareholder Proposal Rule, this is a trend that may continue.

D. Emergence of Anti-ESG Proposals

"Anti-ESG" shareholder proposals were on the rise in the 2022 proxy season. According to Georgeson's "2022 Early Proxy Season Review," proposals from three proponents typically associated with conservative ESG views (The National Legal and Policy Center, the National Center for Public Policy Research, and Steven Milloy) submitted twice as many proposals in the 2022 versus 2021 proxy seasons that were critical of the evolving ESG landscape.[44] That said, these anti-ESG shareholder proposals fared poorly, averaging less than 3 percent support.[45]

According to Sustainable Governance Partners, an ESG consulting firm, it should come as "no surprise that 2022 proxy voting results created mixed messages and left room for interpretation" because the 2022 proxy season was framed against a backdrop of two colliding forces: "momentum from the record-breaking, ESG-driven shareholder revolts during the 2021 proxy season, running up against an energy crisis, rates of inflation not seen since 1981 and a global economic slowdown. In casting their votes at this year's shareholder meetings, investors were left to grapple with whether short-term pressures should take preceden[ce] over long-term systemic risks."[46] Looking ahead, there is some evidence

---

[41] *See, e.g.*, Ben Maiden, *Proxy Season 2022: The Story Behind Falling Support for ESG Proposals*, CORP. SEC'Y (Sept. 27, 2022), https://www.corporatesecretary.com/articles/esg/33171/proxy-season-2022-story-behind-falling-support-esg-proposals. *See also The 2022 Proxy Season: Forces Collide*, *supra* note 26.

[42] *See* SULLIVAN & CROMWELL LLP, 2022 PROXY SEASON REVIEW: PART 1, RULE 14A-8 SHAREHOLDER PROPOSALS 34–35 (2022), https://www.sullcrom.com/files/upload/sc-publication-2022-Proxy-Season-Part-1-Rule-14a-8.pdf.

[43] *Id.* at 33.

[44] GEORGESON, *supra* note 37, https://www.georgeson.com/us/insights/2022-early-proxy-season-review (indicating 52 in 2022 compared to 26 in 2021).

[45] Martha Carter et al., *What's ESG Got to Do with It?*, HARV. L. SCH. F. ON CORP. GOVERNANCE (Oct. 13, 2022), https://corpgov.law.harvard.edu/2022/10/13/whats-esg-got-to-do-with-it/#more-150617.

[46] *The 2022 Proxy Season: Forces Collide*, *supra* note 26. *See also* Ross Kerber and Simon Jessop, *Analysis: Big Oil Gets Investor Reprieve as Energy Worries Trump Climate Concerns*, REUTERS (May 16, 2022), https://www.reuters.com/business/energy/big-oil-gets-investor-reprieve-energy-worries-trump-climate-concerns-2022-05-13/ ("Investors' more supportive stance coincides with a surge in energy prices in the wake of Russia's invasion of Ukraine and follows the efforts of many companies to speed up plans to transition to a low-carbon economy after years of pressure.").

that ESG proposals—particularly in the environmental arena—are likely to increase. That said, it is difficult to predict how ESG-related shareholder proposals will fare, and there may be an ebb and flow to their success that ties to broader economic forces and immediate market drivers.

V. Factors to Consider in Responding to Shareholder Initiatives

Public companies have a delicate task in advising the market about their commitment to ESG-related matters, while not setting themselves up for liability. Moreover, there is no uniform view of "good" ESG practice, and companies may accordingly have challenges in balancing the needs of all of their stakeholders, including employees, the community, and shareholders.

As noted above, shareholders have taken both "pro-" and "anti-" ESG standpoints. For shareholders who support ESG, a company may find itself in a jurisdiction that could be hostile to this position. Alternatively, the opposite may be true—a company that has adopted a conservative approach to ESG issues might find itself the subject of an ESG-focused campaign by liberal stakeholders. State officials may put pressure on companies when it comes to climate change or worker diversity, which may upset those companies' shareholders.[47] As such, companies must balance the positions favored by their shareholders with positions favored by the governments of states in which they do business and by other stakeholders, such as employees or customers.

When confronting an ESG landscape with widely divergent views, it is imperative that companies devote time and resources to crafting a thoughtful decision-making framework to determine whether or not to speak out on a particular ESG issue. Companies need to develop talking points and a consistent message regarding the company and its goals in the ESG space. Companies should also designate individuals who will execute the communications plan. CHAPTER 13—DEALING WITH HIGHLY POLITICIZED SOCIAL ISSUES provides further detail on this.

Companies should not wait until proxy season to engage with their shareholders on ESG-related issues. Engaging with shareholders on a regular basis puts companies in a better position to explain nuanced ESG dilemmas. Moreover, consistently maintaining an open line of communication with significant shareholders (i.e., annual/quarterly meetings/calls) enables companies to better understand shareholders' views on the company's ESG strategy and performance, and sheds light on the rationales behind their votes.

Finally, companies should stay on top of trends. This includes keeping apprised of how other industry participants are responding to shareholder initiatives and analyzing their ESG-related disclosures and goals. Companies should also monitor the positions of their significant or influential shareholders in terms of ESG-related matters. Companies should review the voting policies of significant shareholders with a history of activism. Moreover, companies should pay attention to what activist advocates are focused on. By continually monitoring reports from activist groups, companies will be in a better position to revise and

---

[47] *See* CHAPTER 13—DEALING WITH HIGHLY POLITICIZED SOCIAL ISSUES for further discussion.

supplement their proxy statements to address identified deficient disclosures, and may be able to avoid being confronted with shareholder proposals calling for increased transparency. Companies should consider implementing internal programs for monitoring disclosures in order to keep up with market practices.

Key Takeaways

- In light of the SEC's proposed amendments to Rule 14a-8, companies should anticipate that it will become more difficult to exclude ESG-related shareholder proposals from their proxy statements.
- Companies should consider their goals with respect to shareholder engagement. For example, a company might use an ESG-related shareholder proposal as an opportunity to advance its position on a particular issue, to foster shareholder trust, or to collaborate with significant or otherwise important stakeholders on the proposed matter.
- Commenting publicly on ESG-related proposals comes with many risks, including the possibility of upsetting shareholders with widely divergent views on the same issue. Companies should keep in mind that the geopolitical landscape in which they are operating could have an effect on shareholder proposals and initiatives. Companies should be cautious not to let the ESG debate in the public square distract them from devoting sufficient time and resources to developing thoughtful decision-making frameworks to determine when and how to respond to those proposals and initiatives.
- Companies should make certain that their public statements related to ESG are consistent with their internal information to avoid potential fraud allegations.
- Companies should not limit their engagement with investors to the confines of proxy season but should be proactive about engaging with investors throughout the year to better understand investors' views on the company's ESG strategy and performance, in order to better understand the rationales behind their votes.
- Companies should consider implementing internal programs for monitoring disclosures in order to keep up with market practices.
- As companies navigate shareholder proposals and try to anticipate what proposals might come up in the proxy, it is imperative to stay on top of trends. For example, companies should:
    - Consider what other issuers in the industry are doing.
    - Pay attention to whether certain significant or other particular shareholders are repeatedly submitting proposals every year.
    - Keep apprised of what activist advocates are focused on and how this might affect next year's proxy season.
- By continually monitoring reports from activist groups, companies will be in a better position to revise and supplement their proxy statements to address identified deficient disclosures, and they may be able to avoid being confronted with shareholder proposals calling for increased transparency.

PART V

The Role of the Lawyer: Helping Companies Navigate Uncharted Waters

19

Due Diligence and ESG

Peter Gioello and Tyler L. Burgess

I. Introduction

As discussed throughout this book, many investors, corporations, and other stakeholders understand the important role ESG plays in our global economy. It is therefore no surprise that ESG considerations have become a routine part of the due diligence review on many deals, including as part of mergers and acquisitions (M&A) and finance transactions. This chapter will provide the reader with a broad overview of ESG due diligence, including practical guidance, as well as specific examples based on experience.

Before diving into the mechanics and process of ESG due diligence, it is important to first identify and understand specific environmental, social, and governance factors as they relate to deal work.

II. The "E" in ESG Due Diligence

Given the threat of climate change, inadequate supplies of natural resources, and pressure from environmentalists, it is common for clients and law firms to call on traditional environmental lawyers when faced with an ESG question. As a result, many environmental lawyers have either incorporated (or have endeavored to incorporate) ESG into their existing practice or have started standalone ESG practices. Challenges arise, however, when an environmental lawyer does not have a good understanding of the often-nuanced differences between traditional environmental law and environmental issues arising in the ESG context.

Traditional environmental due diligence typically covers topics such as environmental compliance, regulatory considerations, contamination liabilities, litigation and toxic torts, legacy liabilities, and oftentimes worker health and safety. Related but distinct, the "E" factors in ESG due diligence reviews often include these traditional topics but also focus on climate change risk and mitigation, air quality, natural resource management, biodiversity and ecological impacts, environmental impacts from overpopulation, food scarcity, and renewable energy, among other factors.[1]

ESG lawyers may wish to consult external resources such as the Sustainability Accounting Standard Board's (SASB's) Materiality Map and industry-specific guidelines to get a better understanding of specific ESG topics that may arise in due diligence.[2] In addition, it is important to consider environmental issues from an impact perspective—in other words, how a company's operations and footprint impact the environment and society at large. As an example, food scarcity is tied to environmental impacts due to the fact that the global food supply may be compromised by climate change, deforestation, or contamination.[3]

We have created the following sample list of "E" topics to cover in ESG due diligence reviews with deal-specific examples:

Environmental Due Diligence Topics	
Climate Change Impact	Considering target's physical locations to ensure business continuity of the combined entities in the event of extreme weather events.
Climate Change Regulations	Southeast buyer of West Coast assets must consider compliance with California climate change regulations such as A.B. 32, which may be unfamiliar.
Biodiversity	If there is planned expansion of target assets, ensure development budgets consider whether there are resulting impacts to protected species or habitats.
Air Quality	Despite compliance with air regulations, consider location of facilities near underserved communities, as contaminants could give rise to environmental justice issues.
Natural Resources	Buyer bottling entity purchasing distilleries must ensure adequate availability of water and other natural resources.
Energy	Review regulatory and litigation risks associated with use of offsets, and also ensure no "green marketing" issues arise when using terms such as "clean energy" in an offering document.
Waste and Hazardous Materials Management	Buyer should review target's waste streams and consider ways to build on existing initiatives and targets to minimize use.

---

[1] *See, e.g., infra* Chapters 5–9.

[2] *Exploring Materiality*, Sustainability and Accounting Standard Board (SASB) Standards, https://www.sasb.org/standards/materiality-map/ (last visited Apr. 14, 2023).

[3] *Sustainable Development Goals*, United Nations (UN), https://www.un.org/sustainabledevelopment/hunger/ (last visited Apr. 14, 2023).

III. The "S" and "G" in ESG Due Diligence

One pitfall to avoid is spending too much time on the "E" topics of ESG and missing important social and governance issues. Another challenge is the difficulty in understanding the interplay (and often overlap) between ESG due diligence topics and those items covered in other specialist areas. For example, non-ESG specialists often cover anti-corruption, tax, and cybersecurity as separate diligence topics on deals. Each of those areas also include governance issues to consider as part of ESG due diligence. At the very least, ESG lawyers should collaborate with other specialists and possibly consultants to ensure there is adequate coverage of each topic from both the traditional and ESG-related viewpoints. Practitioners should also consider each subject area in the overall ESG assessment as it relates to potential public reporting and disclosure requirements and stakeholder engagement. For example, a non-ESG practitioner covering information-technology/information-security (IT/IS) diligence might not think to review and verify IT/IS-related information contained in an ESG report. Employment lawyers may ask about work stoppages or harassment suits but may not evaluate the adequacy and effectiveness of corporate policies in these areas. Failure to consider these issues from a social and governance perspective could result in unassessed ESG risks and liabilities.

Below is a chart of "S" and "G" topics to consider with deal-specific considerations and general tips:

Social Due Diligence Topics	
Human Rights	Review target's supply chain to ensure adherence to child labor laws and ensure controls are in place to minimize reputational harm, including codes of conduct, audits, and adherence to supplier termination policies.
Data Security/Customer Privacy	Review disclosure of data privacy claims in sustainability report in light of recent data breaches. Consider information security risk management practices in light of industry norms. Consider the integration risks from a reputational standpoint.
Environmental Justice	Review press coverage and initiatives of activist groups in underserved communities to find out whether company or industry has been or is likely to be targeted. Consider whether combined entities pose a larger risk if there are operations in similar regions.
Product Stewardship	Ensure target's product labels comply with consumer safety regulations such as California's Proposition 65.
Consumer Welfare and Safety	Consider the number of recalls, frequency of product liability lawsuits, and potential reputational harm.
Labor Practices	Analyze hiring and pay inequities and potential backlash of employees and other stakeholders.
Worker Health and Safety	Ensure appropriate budgeting to be proactive in implementing appropriate industry standards and applicable worker safety regulations (e.g., Occupational Safety and Health Administration [OSHA]).
Employee Engagement, Diversity, and Inclusion	Ensure that Diversity, Equity, and Inclusion (DE&I) policies go beyond "checking the box" to ensure meaningful hiring and advancement of underrepresented workers.

Governance Due Diligence Topics	
Business Ethics	Identify any excessive instances of noncompliance with law or company codes of conduct that conflict with public statements around business ethics.
Anti-Corruption	Even if target's policies are robust and there is a lack of recent enforcement issues, consider operating jurisdictions and understand key risks (e.g., bribery) to evaluate the potential for liability and ensure adequate controls are in place.
Stakeholder Engagement	Identify all stakeholders and ensure appropriate engagement to proactively identify issues prior to business combination.
Board Structure	Review applicable laws for publicly listed companies, and ensure adequate board diversity.
Executive Compensation	Consider potential reputational harm to the extent executive compensation is prioritized over other stakeholder issues, including employee pay.

IV. ESG Due Diligence in Mergers and Acquisitions Transactions

The scope and depth of buyer due diligence in an M&A transaction depends on a variety of factors, including deal timing, risk tolerance, the structure of the transaction, and the nature and industry of the underlying entities. While no transaction is the same, deal teams traditionally focus on general business and legal risks and may also conduct targeted due diligence in a variety of specialty areas, which has traditionally included tax, litigation, bankruptcy, environmental, health and safety, labor/employee benefits, and regulatory compliance. As ESG has become mainstream, many deal teams include ESG as an additional specialty topic in due diligence reviews.

Those who do not regularly consider ESG risks and liabilities in M&A transactions should carefully weigh the potential material legal, reputational, and business risks of such a decision, including identifying costs associated with implementing voluntary ESG commitments and assessing the future climate-related costs for maintaining physical assets. For example, ignoring human rights issues or worker safety issues in a target's supply chain could lead to material supply chain disruptions, negative press attention, or legal liability depending on the circumstances and jurisdiction.[4] Similarly, poor Diversity, Equity, and Inclusion (DE&I) programs and initiatives can lead to harassment lawsuits (e.g., the "Me Too"

[4] As an example, grocery retailers and distributors had to consider the potential reputational harm that might arise as a result of an ESG-related article that suggested that some shrimp sourced from Thailand may have been peeled by slaves. Margie Mason et al., *Shrimp Sold by Global Supermarkets Is Peeled by Slave Labourers in Thailand*, The Guardian (Dec. 14, 2015, 1:16 PM), https://www.theguardian.com/global-development/2015/dec/14/shrimp-sold-by-global-supermarkets-is-peeled-by-slave-labourers-in-thailand.

movement) or worker retention issues, both of which can impact productivity and create reputational and business risks.

A. Where to Start?

As with every specialty area, ESG lawyers must understand the transaction, the underlying entities, and the parties in order to appropriately allocate time and resources. Practitioners should gather information on the deal context and company background before diving into due diligence. It is important to spend time reviewing background materials on the target, such as a company's website, available sustainability and related reports (including previous reports), public filings, recent press coverage, and any other pertinent resources. Buyer's counsel must also understand its client, the buyer, to consider both synergies and risks based on the combination of the two entities.

Once the ESG lawyer has a thorough understanding of the transaction and the related entities, it is vital to identify relevant ESG factors to consider on a particular transaction, guided by the sector of the target business and likely ESG topics at issue. It is also important to consider indirect ESG impacts that may arise as a result of the particular industry, operating location, key stakeholders, or any regulatory developments. For example, ESG issues to review may arise from a particular entity's physical location (e.g., within a coastal or flood zone), vulnerability to extreme weather events, or political instability in the host country, even if the entity is environmentally conscious and well run from a social and governance perspective. Again, SASB's Materiality Map is a good starting place, but there are also tools available, such as Landmark's Risk Horizon tool,[5] that consider multiple ESG risks and liabilities based on the jurisdiction, industry, and the company's global footprint.

Aside from identifying the target's specific ESG risks and liabilities, an experienced ESG lawyer can help the buyer consider opportunities as a result of the combined entities. For example, the target may have newer facilities in similar regions that emit less greenhouse gases (GHGs). If the buyer is struggling with DE&I, can the target's diversity metrics offer some relief? In some instances, the ESG opportunities are a "lever for value creation" and the driving force behind a transaction.[6]

Practically speaking, it is essential to understand the ESG profile of the company and the goals of the buyer in order to assess the ESG data of the combined entities. In addition, a proper ESG analysis will help lenders get comfortable with the acquisition from multiple perspectives, including financial risk, reputational risk, and whether the transaction conflicts with the lenders' own ESG programs and initiatives.

---

[5] *ESG Risk Management Made Simple*, RiskHorizon, https://go.landmark.co.uk/risk-horizon-esg-management (last visited Apr. 14, 2023).

[6] Andrew R. Brownstein & Carmen X.W. Lu, *ESG and M&A in 2022: From Risk Mitigation to Value Creation*, Harv. L. Sch. F. on Corp. Governance (Jan. 24, 2022), https://corpgov.law.harvard.edu/2022/01/24/esg-and-ma-in-2022-from-risk-mitigation-to-value-creation/.

The following table outlines suggested topics for practitioners to consider in their ESG due diligence reviews for M&A deals:

ESG Due Diligence Considerations in M&A	
Start of the Deal/Background Research	Review company websites, public filings, sustainability reports, industry data, press coverage, and other pertinent information to understand the key parties in a transaction.
Communication Between Parties/Letter of Intent	Ensure there are no limitations in the scope of due diligence that would prevent the buyer from digging in on ESG topics.
Due Diligence Requests	Do not rely solely on a company's sustainability report. Consider asking for policies, the structure of ESG governance, internal metrics, ESG committee board minutes, relevant claims or litigation, and documents or data that back up all public statements concerning ESG.
Deal Trackers	Consider a specific "ESG" category, but also review non-ESG sections and potential areas of overlap.
Diligence Calls	Create targeted ESG question lists that will ensure the proper individuals are on the call.
News and Database Searches	Conduct news, litigation, and regulatory database searches to identify issues that could give rise to liability or speak to inadequacies in ESG oversight, including reputational screening databases such as RepRisk and social media searches.
Consultants	Consider whether there are limitations in the ESG legal review, and engage ESG consultants for technical reviews, including with respect to accuracy and verification of GHG reporting. Consider engaging consultants under privilege with the ESG legal team.
Client Summary	Highlight ESG risks and issues, but lead with significant risks and issues rather than positive ESG attributes and reporting metrics to ensure they are given the proper weight in the analysis.
Purchase Agreements	After identifying ESG risks and issues, ensure adequate coverage in representations and warranties, or consider modifications to the agreements.
Financing	Consider what a particular lender or underwriter may request from an ESG standpoint, such as bank reputational concerns. Lenders and underwriters are increasingly conducting their own ESG due diligence; early coordination to ensure coverage of their key ESG focus areas is important.

B. Representations and Warranties

Prior to the focus on ESG factors in M&A, deal lawyers looking to cover ESG-related topics looked to traditional representations and warranties, both to identify issues and to mitigate risk. For example, environmental compliance representations cover compliance with applicable environmental laws, including climate change reporting requirements; labor representations shed light on worker grievances; and anti-bribery representations identify unethical corporate behavior. At this time, the market has not developed a standard ESG representation, but it is something a buyer may wish to consider, including in its agreements, if the traditional set of representations and warranties provides limited coverage. A standalone ESG representation or modifications to existing representations may be warranted for specific ESG risks, such as:

- Obtaining, compliance with, and renewal of ESG certifications;
- GHG emissions reporting and use of offsets;
- Product stewardship-related issues such as labeling, filings, certifications;
- "Me Too," harassment, or other workplace culture issues; and
- ESG issues in the supply chain (e.g., compliance with company codes of conduct, supply chain audits, proper termination of suppliers failing to meet ESG requirements).

C. Special Considerations for the Seller

ESG lawyers representing the seller should be thoughtful when responding to an ESG diligence request, especially if the company has publicly shared its sustainability information. It is important to set appropriate parameters and ensure that recent ESG data, if shared, has been analyzed by senior leadership and the legal team. ESG data is (or should be) refreshed regularly, but there may be a lag time between the availability of data and its release.

In addition, it is helpful to understand the ESG profile of the buyer and understand its stakeholders in order to appropriately respond to diligence requests and make the ESG due diligence process as seamless as possible. Having a team ready to respond would be useful, particularly if the seller is early in its ESG journey and has not published the relevant supporting data and documentation.

D. Public vs. Private Company Considerations

In M&A, the scope of ESG due diligence may depend on whether the buyer and/or seller is a public company. In the sale of a private company to a public company, sellers should be aware of any mandatory disclosure rules such as the Conflicts Minerals Rule.[7] As an example, if a seller in the jewelry or electronics business has a limited understanding of its supply chain, it should be prepared to answer questions and respond to diligence requests by the public company since the public company already has to report such information.

V. ESG Due Diligence in Financing Transactions

ESG due diligence in finance and capital markets deals builds upon many of the same due diligence concepts in M&A, but there are of course differences and additional risks to consider. For instance, capital markets deals are subject to federal securities regulations, including the

[7] *Fact Sheet - Disclosing the Use of Conflict Minerals*, SEC, https://www.sec.gov/opa/Article/2012-2012-163htm---related-materials.html (Mar. 14, 2017). In addition, the U.S. Securities and Exchange Commission (SEC) issued a proposed rule that would also require disclosure of certain climate-related information. *See* The Enhancement and Standardization of Climate-related Disclosures for Investors, Securities Act Release No. 11,042, Exchange Act Release No. 94,478, 87 Fed. Reg. 21334 (proposed Apr. 11, 2022) (to be codified at 17 C.F.R. pts. 210, 229, 232, 239, 249).

disclosure of material[8] information to investors along with several other prescribed disclosure requirements. As a result, the scope of ESG due diligence is less subjective to the parties' interests and must also focus on what is required under applicable law.

For finance deals such as loans, ESG factors may impact a borrower's credit worthiness or may result in reputational harm to the lender. This portion of this chapter will go into more detail about these considerations and lay out the steps to conduct ESG due diligence on capital markets deals and general considerations for other finance transactions such as loans.

A. Capital Markets

As discussed in CHAPTER 2—STAKEHOLDERS IN THE ESG ECOSYSTEM, investors and other stakeholders routinely request information in order to analyze ESG risks and liabilities when making investment decisions. In response, companies routinely disclose their sustainability metrics and efforts to the public and investors irrespective of regulatory requirements. Similar to M&A, ESG lawyers who focus on capital markets transactions should consider the underwriters' ESG profile before diving into ESG due diligence to ensure their key topic areas are addressed in the review. In addition, ESG lawyers must consider what diligence and disclosure may be required under applicable securities regulations in a capital markets transaction.

Prior to the launch of a capital markets transaction, investors receive disclosure in the form of a prospectus or offering memoranda. Similar to periodic filings, the offering document must comply with federal securities regulations, including the disclosure of material information to investors, as well as specific prescribed disclosures such as the Conflicts Minerals Rule.[9] As such, deal counsel must conduct due diligence to ensure the offering document complies with SEC requirements, including Rule 10b-5.[10] In many instances, the company's periodic filings are incorporated by reference into the offering document and should also be reviewed from an ESG standpoint in order to identify potential inconsistencies or violations of federal securities regulations.

The scope of ESG due diligence on each deal will depend on a number of factors, including deal timing, the structure of the transaction, and the parties involved. For ESG, it is important to request relevant ESG diligence materials and ask targeted ESG due diligence questions as part of the diligence process. Material ESG issues or risks may not be evident at the start of a deal process but may be discovered later in response to targeted ESG due diligence questions. As an example, if a deal team elects not to conduct ESG supply chain due diligence, the financing issuer may fail to identify material business issues that may require disclosure, such as major supply chain disruptions resulting from safety or child-labor issues.

---

[8] Basic, Inc. v. Levinson, 485 U.S. 224, 231–32 (1988) ("[T]o fulfill the materiality requirement there must be a substantial likelihood that the disclosure of the omitted fact would have been viewed by the reasonable investor as having significantly altered the total mix of information made available." (internal quotation marks and citations omitted)).

[9] *See Fact Sheet - Disclosing the Use of Conflict Minerals*, *supra* note 7.

[10] 117 C.F.R. § 240.10b-5; *see also* Janus Cap. Grp., Inc. v. First Derivative Traders, 564 U.S. 135, 137–38 (2011) ("Rule 10b–5 prohibits making any untrue statement of a material fact in connection with the purchase or sale of securities." (internal quotation marks and alterations omitted)).

The following list outlines ESG due diligence steps in a capital markets transaction:

ESG Due Diligence Considerations in Capital Markets Deals	
Background Research	Review Confidential Information Memoranda, any public filings, sustainability reports, or relevant industry data to understand ESG risk profile of financing issuer.
Due Diligence Request	List specific ESG documents to review, including reports and data to back up public sustainability reporting, consultant reports, board minutes, internal presentations, or other pertinent ESG information. Coordinate with financing issuers early in the process to ensure their diligence request lists are included in the review process.
Due Diligence Call	Separate ESG due diligence from other specialty areas, and make a concise list of questions relevant to the issuer or industry.
Diligence Memo/Downloads	Highlight key issues in terms appropriate in non-legal language, and consider both financial and reputational impact of key diligence findings because bankers will use in models and committee meetings.
Review of Offering Document	Review offering document in light of SEC requirements, and consider potential regulatory or litigation which may arise from ESG language (e.g., green marketing).

B. Loans

Since ordinary loans are not typically subject to federal securities regulations, the general due diligence process is typically truncated or limited to representations and warranties in the finance agreement. It is ultimately up to the borrower to decide whether additional ESG due diligence is required to satisfy its own internal due diligence procedures or to consider in its financial modeling. As banks and other financial institutions realize the value of ESG information to risk, impact, and valuation, ESG lawyers may increasingly receive standalone requests to conduct ESG due diligence in support of the loan.[11]

Banks and financial institutions must also ensure its lending practices do not conflict with the bank's internal ESG policy and goals. For example, if a bank has set aggressive climate change investment goals or commitments to reduce investment in fossil fuels as part of the transition to a carbon-free economy, the bank should exercise caution when loaning to carbon-intense industries.

[11] Many financial institutions implement the Equator Principles as a means of evaluating ESG risk when issuing loans. *See About the Equator Principles, A Financial Industry Benchmark for Determining, Assessing and Managing Environmental and Social Risk in Projects*, Equator Principles, https://equator-principles.com/about-the-equator-principles/ (last visited Apr. 14, 2023).

C. Credit Agreements

ESG-deal lawyers should also ensure there is adequate coverage of key ESG risks and liabilities in finance agreements such as credit agreements. Since the relationship between the parties is continuing after the deal closes, lawyers may also wish to consider ESG language in the affirmative covenant provisions to ensure there are adequate requirements to comply with applicable laws, including as it relates to climate change reporting and mitigation (e.g., offsets). These post-closing covenants are customary, and increasingly, there is a trend towards including material voluntary commitments (e.g., maintaining ESG ratings or voluntary certifications) in the covenants.

D. Timing and Scope

Distinct from M&A, financing and capital markets transactions typically run on a quicker timeframe. As such, ESG lawyers may be limited in the time they have to conduct their review and should plan accordingly. In addition, the creditworthiness of a borrower or issuer dictates the scope of due diligence, including ESG due diligence. For example, the time spent on due diligence in an investment-grade deal versus a high-yield transaction will differ. However, reputational risks, which may arise from a proper ESG due diligence analysis, can impact all parties. In all deals, it is important to conduct an appropriate level of ESG due diligence beyond merely "checking the box" in order to ensure adequate disclosure, limit investor scrutiny, and avoid litigation. As discussed in CHAPTER 20—INTERNAL INVESTIGATIONS, regulators, including the SEC, are bringing enforcement actions against issuers for failing to disclose or misrepresenting ESG risks and liabilities.

E. Sustainable Finance

Companies are also issuing "sustainable" finance instruments both in response to investor interest and to enhance existing programs and initiatives. ESG due diligence for sustainable finance deals requires a few extra steps beyond what we discussed above for M&A and financing transactions. For example, most sustainable finance deals follow prescribed standards such as the Green Bond Principles, set forth by the International Capital Market Association (ICMA).[12] The parties typically engage an external consultant or third-party reviewer who issues a secondary opinion that the particular sustainable finance deal complies with a specified framework that is tailored to the particular deal and issuer. It is also advisable to have an ESG lawyer ensure that there is adequate disclosure in the offering document that highlights any relevant risks associated with the sustainable finance deal.

ESG lawyers must also supplement the ESG due diligence question lists to account for the sustainable feature in the instrument. For example, in a "sustainability-linked bond"

---

[12] *Green Bond Principles (GBP)*, ICMA, https://www.icmagroup.org/sustainable-finance/the-principles-guidelines-and-handbooks/green-bond-principles-gbp/ (last visited Apr. 14, 2023).

that incentivizes the issuer for its ESG performance using Key Performance Indicators as qualifiers,[13] the ESG-deal lawyer may ask questions about policies, personnel, and resources available as it relates to the set goal or initiative.

VI. ESG Due Diligence—Other Considerations

A. Structure of the Deal Team

Practitioners have had to grapple with the proper way to structure deal teams and ESG practice groups to ensure proper coverage of ESG in due diligence reviews. No one way is correct, but at the very least, clients and law firms should ensure that the lawyer or team of lawyers covering ESG issues on a deal have a good understanding of each topic area, the structure and goals of a particular entity, and the transactional considerations when performing ESG due diligence. Pay particular attention to any teams marketing themselves as ESG experts but who have little experience in one or more ESG topic areas. For example, having a corporate governance attorney is a great addition to the deal team, but you also want someone on the team who is knowledgeable about environmental and social issues such as climate change, environmental justice, and contamination issues.

B. International Considerations

In both M&A and financing transactions, ESG lawyers must understand applicable ESG rules and regulations across the globe. It is important to look not only at specific ESG regulations but also at general ESG risks based on the industry and jurisdiction, including geopolitical concerns, availability of natural resources, politics, age/demographics, and quality of infrastructure, among other considerations.

For entities with assets or operations in the United Kingdom or European Union, it is important to look at mandatory reporting and disclosure requirements, climate change regulations, and consumer safety regulations as part of ESG due diligence. We have included a short (but not exhaustive) list of enacted and proposed ESG rules and regulations in the United Kingdom and European Union to consider when conducting ESG due diligence:

- Enacted:
  - Climate Benchmarks Regulation (EU 2019/2089)
  - Corporate Sustainability Reporting Directive (CSRD)
  - Sustainable Finance Disclosure Regulation (EU 2019/2088)
  - Taxonomy Regulation (EU 2020/852)
  - EU Emissions Trading System (EU ETS)
  - EU Registration, Evaluation, Authorisation and Restriction of Chemicals (EU REACH)

[13] *Sustainability-linked Bond Principles (SLBP)*, ICMA, https://www.icmagroup.org/sustainable-finance/the-principles-guidelines-and-handbooks/sustainability-linked-bond-principles-slbp/ (last visited Apr. 14, 2023).

  - The Companies (Strategic Report) (Climate-related Financial Disclosure) Regulations 2022
  - The Limited Liability Partnerships (Climate-related Financial Disclosure) Regulations 2022
- Proposed as of March 2023:
  - EU Green Bonds Regulation (EUGBR)
  - Corporate Sustainability Due Diligence Directive (CSDDD)

In certain regions of Latin America, Africa, and Asia, specifically in developing nations, it is important to spend additional time considering atypical social and political issues that may give rise to unforeseen social issues, including human rights violations and safety or labor issues. For example, retailers and food manufacturing entities have specific resources devoted to identification and mitigation of potential ESG risks and issues connected with the cocoa supply chain, including in parts of Africa.[14]

The scope and resources utilized for ESG due diligence for developing nations can vary, and ESG lawyers should consider both traditional and nontraditional sources of information, including human intelligence, local media searches, review by local counsel of court dockets, and regulatory databases. Also, ESG lawyers should identify local activist groups that may not have the appropriate resources to publicize their mission on the internet. Despite the fact that environmental and other regulators in these regions may not strictly enforce regulatory requirements, consider the potential impact that may arise as a result of activists and journalists who highlight certain ESG-related practices in the media.

Key Takeaways

- ESG practitioners should carefully consider background information, including public filings, sustainability reports, news, litigation, regulatory databases, and other sources to identify and evaluate the key ESG topic areas in their due diligence reviews.
- Early coordination with corporate and specialist teams as well as financing partners is essential to ensure that the ESG due diligence process covers all topic areas the parties need to review in order to be comfortable moving forward with the transaction.
- M&A and financing transactions have nuanced differences that require ESG practitioners to consider the context and deal dynamics in their review process.
- ESG disclosure and regulatory obligations are rapidly changing, and practitioners should stay abreast of the developments that may impact ESG due diligence reviews.
- Law firms should ensure ESG practice groups consist of lawyers with expertise in and knowledge of ESG topics.

[14] Mark Segal, *Nestlé Targets Child Labor in Cocoa Supply Chain, Paying Farmers to Enroll Children in School*, ESG Today (Jan. 27, 2022), https://www.esgtoday.com/nestle-targets-child-labor-in-cocoa-supply-chain-paying-farmers-to-enroll-children-in-school/.

20

Internal Investigations

Jane Norberg, Christian Schultz, Daniel M. Hawke, Andrew Johnson, and Sasha Zheng

I. Introduction

The well-publicized interest in ESG issues has been accompanied by internal investigations into alleged ESG-related misconduct. Some of these investigations concern novel categories of allegations; for example, companies have implemented new climate policies or reconsidered their social and diversity policies, which has generated concerns about implementation and accuracy of related disclosures. Many other investigations concern allegations that predate the interest in ESG as a category (for example, those that touch on more "social" issues such as workplace sexual harassment allegations and related workforce retention and satisfaction and the increased focus on the disclosures surrounding them).[1] Because ESG can mean different things to different people, and because the law is still evolving in this area, the spotlight on ESG has created increased scrutiny on all internal investigations, as many allegation categories may cross over into ESG considerations for regulators.

Internal investigations on ESG issues may arise in a variety of contexts, whether through whistleblower complaints, government civil or criminal inquiries, or in response to litigation. Some of the impetus toward an increase in internal investigations on ESG issues will likely be in response to growing government scrutiny. For example, in March 2021, the U.S. Securities and Exchange Commission (SEC) created a Climate and ESG Task Force, which has since

[1] *See, e.g.*, Activision Blizzard, Inc., Exchange Act Release No. 96796, 2023 WL 1765354 (Feb. 3, 2023).

brought several actions relating to misstatements and omissions regarding ESG issues. Since its inception, the Climate and ESG Task Force has investigated alleged misconduct ranging from green marketing claims to false and misleading statements regarding environmental safety considerations and workplace diversity or culture.[2] It is no surprise that companies have become more aware of the potential for liability related to their ESG policies and disclosures and statements related to these policies.

Existing principles and best practices for conducting internal investigations apply to an internal investigation focused on ESG. However, counsel should proceed especially carefully given the rapidly evolving laws and regulations applicable to ESG issues and the heightened awareness and public discourse surrounding ESG. A significant part of the law in this area remains unsettled, and legal and compliance personnel, as well as personnel from other departments within the company, may be encountering these issues for the first time. For these reasons, and others, it is important for counsel to lead—and be point person for—the investigation. This chapter provides considerations and guidelines for counsel to consider both generally for internal investigations and in particular when conducting an ESG-related internal investigation.

A special note on whistleblowers—internal whistleblowers may provide a wealth of information to the company during an internal investigation, but if handled improperly, the investigation can cause increased risk to the company of an SEC or other regulatory inquiry. Because whistleblowers are playing a prominent role in connection with internal investigations, and because of the heightened risks associated with whistleblowers, we devote a section to best practices related to whistleblowers in Section X of this chapter. We also make note throughout the chapter when there is a need for special considerations if there is an internal whistleblower.

II. Scope of Investigation

Determining the proper scope of an investigation into potential ESG-related misconduct raises unique implications regarding the individuals that may need to be interviewed in connection with the investigation. Due to the nature of the issues implicated in an ESG-related misconduct investigation, a wide range of individuals with highly specialized knowledge may need to be interviewed or consulted as part of the investigation (e.g., director of sustainability, environmental specialist, human resources, external communications). Due care should be given to the interview and subsequent sharing of information among the investigatory team, as well as other stakeholders (e.g., board of directors and outside auditors), to help ensure the protection of privileged/protected communications as well as confidential business information. The following sections in this chapter discuss, in part, best practices for preserving privileged/protected communications as well as confidential business information.

---

[2] BNY Mellon Inv. Adviser, Inc., Investment Advisers Act Release No. 6032, Investment Company Act Release No. 34591, 2022 WL 1631168 (May 23, 2022); Complaint, SEC v. Vale S.A., No. 22-cv-2405 (S.D.N.Y. Apr. 28, 2022); *see also* Erin Woo, *The S.E.C. Has Opened an Investigation into Activision Blizzard*, N.Y. Times (Oct. 28, 2021), https://www.nytimes.com/2021/09/20/business/activision-blizzard-sec-investigation.html.

III. Attorney–Client Privilege and Attorney Work-Product Protection

At the outset of any investigation, especially ESG investigations that may be highly sensitive, counsel should think carefully about how to best preserve attorney–client privileged communications and attorney work product from disclosure.[3] Not only does preserving potentially privileged documents and work product protect the company's public image, maintaining privilege and work product has significant implications for future follow-on litigation and government enforcement actions relating to the allegations in the investigation. Indeed, some of the first documents requested in any government subpoena or opposing parties in litigation are those produced in a company's internal investigation.

Attorney–client privilege in the United States applies to communications made in confidence between an attorney and client for the purpose of obtaining or providing legal advice.[4] Attorney–client privilege applies to outside counsel as well as in-house counsel who work in a legal capacity. The import of this is that whether an internal investigation is considered privileged depends on the purpose of the investigation. If the purpose of the investigation is predominantly legal in nature and is directed by counsel, courts are more likely to find that the investigation is privileged.[5] However, if the investigation involves routine business issues—for example, a routine inquiry into whether supply chain audits are being conducted in accordance with policy—courts are less likely to find that the investigation is privileged even if it is being conducted in part by an in-house counsel.[6] The work-product doctrine may also apply if the investigation was initiated in anticipation of litigation[7]—for example, an internal investigation triggered by a government subpoena or employee lawsuit. Similar to assertions of attorney–client privilege, courts may find that work-product protection does not apply in internal investigations where the investigation is not predominantly legal in nature.[8]

---

[3] *See, e.g.*, McGowan v. JPMorgan Bank, N.A., No. 18 Civ. 8680 (PAC) (GWG), 2020 WL 1974109 (S.D.N.Y. Apr. 24, 2020) (discussing privilege issues in the context of an unlawful discrimination suit).

[4] United States v. Chen, 99 F.3d 1495, 1501 (9th Cir. 1996).

[5] *See, e.g.*, Upjohn Co. v. United States, 449 U.S. 383, 392 (1981) (finding that attorney–client privilege did apply to the internal investigation and the privilege covered the communications between company employees and company attorneys); *In re* Kellogg Brown & Root, Inc., 756 F.3d 754, 760 (D.C. Cir. 2014) ("In the context of an organization's internal investigation, if one of the significant purposes of the internal investigation was to obtain or provide legal advice, the privilege will apply.").

[6] *See* Colton v. United States, 306 F.2d 633, 638 (2d Cir. 1962) ("Attorneys frequently give to their clients business or other advice which, at least insofar as it can be separated from their essentially professional legal services, give rise to no privilege whatever."); W. Sur. Co. v. United States, No. CV-16-00761-TUC-CKJ, 2018 WL 6788665, at *3 (D. Ariz. Dec. 21, 2018) ("Corporations may not conduct their business affairs in private simply by staffing a transaction with attorneys.") (internal quotation marks omitted); Complex Sys., Inc. v. ABN AMRO Bank N.V., 279 F.R.D. 140, 150 (S.D.N.Y. 2011) ("Moreover, even if a business decision can be viewed as both business and legal evaluations, the business aspects of the decision are not protected simply because legal considerations are also involved.") (internal quotation marks omitted).

[7] Hickman v. Taylor, 329 U.S. 495, 509–11 (1947); Cicel (Beijing) Sci. & Tech. Co. v. Misonix, Inc., 331 F.R.D. 218, 232 (E.D.N.Y. 2019).

[8] *See In re* Capital One Consumer Data Sec. Breach Litig., No. 1:19md2915 (AJT/JFA), 2020 WL 3470261, at *7 (E.D. Va. June 25, 2020) (holding that an internal investigation report, when conducted primarily for business purposes, is not considered attorney work-product and, therefore, must be disclosed).

Even if the investigation is privileged, however, underlying facts would not be privileged if discoverable from a source other than the attorney–client communication. As a result, in most cases, the ultimate resolution of the investigation will not be privileged. For example, the fact that an employee was disciplined or was terminated, or that a certain policy or practice no longer operated on a certain date, would be not privileged. Moreover, documents maintained by a company's compliance department that track metrics about the initiation and close-out of investigations may not be privileged. The dividing line between factual documents and privileged documents can be thin, but communications made for the purposes of enabling the company's lawyers to advise the company, or that reflect the substance of the attorney's legal advice, will generally be found to be privileged.

IV. Retaining Counsel

An initial issue for any internal investigation is the decision as to whether outside counsel should be retained. Frequently, in-house counsel can conduct an investigation faster and more efficiently than outside attorneys, as in-house counsel is already familiar with the company's policies and procedures, operations, and employees. In many instances, however, the company may wish to retain outside counsel, or may be expected to retain outside counsel for a variety of reasons. Outside counsel are sometimes considered to be more objective; in some investigations, in-house counsel or other high level, C-suite executives may be implicated by the allegations, and in-house counsel may be incentivized or pressured into improperly influencing the investigation. Other instances where companies should consider obtaining outside counsel are, for example, when the investigation may result in SEC reporting obligations if the allegations being investigated may be material to the company. Where there is a high risk of subsequent government investigation, the company should consider retaining outside counsel, as it is often expected by government regulators. When the allegations stem from an internal whistleblower reporter, the likelihood of the government being tipped off is high. Also, outside counsel often have subject-matter expertise in substantive and procedural aspects of the relevant law and have more capacity to conduct a thorough investigation than overburdened in-house counsel.

Finally, as discussed above, one major reason to retain outside counsel is the greater likelihood that attorney–client privilege and work-product protection will be preserved. There is greater risk that an investigation conducted by in-house counsel will be viewed as having a business purpose instead of a legal purpose and would not be protected by the attorney–client privilege or the work-product doctrine. Should a company decide to proceed with in-house counsel, in-house counsel should carefully and clearly document the legal nature of the investigation. This is particularly important if in-house counsel delegates the investigation to non-legal employees, such as those working in audit or compliance roles.[9] In such instances, to preserve the privilege, counsel should document that the compliance personnel are acting at the direction of legal counsel to assist in providing legal advice.

[9] *See, e.g.*, United States v. Kovel, 296 F.2d 918, 922 (2d Cir. 1961); United States v. Adlman, 68 F.3d 1495, 1500 (2d Cir. 1995).

As part of the decision to determine whether in-house counsel or outside counsel should conduct the investigation, the company should also consider who should supervise the investigation. For example, if the investigation concerns the conduct of members of the company's board of directors, the board of directors may be required to form a committee of independent directors to oversee the investigation. Similarly, an investigation into the conduct of high-level executive officers may be overseen by the company's audit committee or other independent members of the board of directors. Other investigations are generally overseen by the company's general counsel, or another member of the legal department, who can help coordinate document retention and collection, interviews, and monitor the costs of the investigation.

V. Document Hold Notices, Collection, and Review

After deciding to begin an internal investigation, counsel should take immediate action to preserve all potentially relevant documents, which is necessary for a thorough investigation. This also ensures that the company will be able to comply with document preservation obligations should a regulatory inquiry or a litigation arise out of the underlying matter.[10]

As a first step, counsel should identify employees who may have access to relevant information. In some instances, counsel may consider reaching out to non-employees such as directors, consultants, and former employees. The company should also suspend any automatic document destruction procedures (a so-called "silent hold").

Counsel should next issue a clearly written document hold notice that summarizes the documents that must be retained, including the time period covered. The document hold notice will often provide a summary of the matter, taking into account whether the company should limit knowledge of the investigation for sensitive investigations. The document hold notice should make clear the seriousness of failure to comply with the document hold notice and clearly note the consequences of document destruction. The document hold notice should also make clear that the categories of documents of interest are broadly defined and may include otherwise personal items—for example, cell phones, computers, or tablets—if used for company purposes. In most cases, the document hold notice should be sent by in-house counsel, which encourages compliance and provides a point of contact for employee questions.

Counsel should work with the company's Information Technology (IT) support on collecting potentially relevant documents and materials. Oftentimes, counsel may retain an e-discovery consultant who can assist in extracting the relevant data and loading it into an e-discovery platform, such as Relativity. While counsel should supervise this process, company IT and e-discovery consultants generally lead the process of locating and uploading documents and materials, which usually entails a search of email and other servers, cloud storage, hard drives, tablets, cell phones, and, in certain cases, employees' personal devices. In

[10] Pension Comm. of the Univ. of Montreal Pension Plan v. Banc of Am. Sec., LLC., 685 F. Supp. 2d 456, 466 (S.D.N.Y. 2010) (granting sanctions to defendants for plaintiff's failure to preserve documents for production, among other things).

addition, counsel should consider whether the company maintains certain discrete files, such as personnel files, documentation relating to projects, and company policies, that could be relevant to the investigation. While often beyond the scope of an initial document collection, counsel may begin having conversations about accessing the company's archived information, which may be hosted off-site, and whether forensic imaging of computer hard drives should be conducted. The latter is often employed if documents appear to be missing and there is suspicion that potentially relevant documents have already been deleted.

Counsel have a number of tools to reduce the burden and cost of document review. E-discovery consultants can help advise and run search terms to reduce the volume of documents to review. New technologies allow more efficient review through methods such as de-duplicating of duplicate emails; de-threading, which retains only the most inclusive email chain; and artificial intelligence-supported analytics, which can be used to identify responsive documents based on previously reviewed documents. Finally, documents that are subpoenaed by the government can easily be identified and sequentially numbered within the review platform for production to the government.

Preservation and collection of text messages have become increasingly common as companies, courts, and regulators have recognized that text messaging has become a dominant form of communication.[11] Text messages may be in the form of so-called "native" text messages, as well as through phone-based applications such as WhatsApp, Facebook Messenger, Signal, and other mediums. The document hold notice should specifically require the preservation of text messages and messages on other platforms, and employees should be asked about their use of messaging across platforms during collection.

Document review should be conducted with the anticipation that such documents may be produced to law enforcement, regulatory agency, or outside parties in civil litigation, as these actions often occur in advance of, simultaneously, or after an internal investigation. In many instances, it may be cost-effective to simultaneously conduct a preliminary privilege review alongside a responsiveness review of the documents.

VI. Employee Interviews

Employee interviews are a major component of any internal investigation, including ESG investigations. These are typically attended by outside counsel when retained, sometimes in-house counsel as long as impartiality is not a concern, and sometimes separate counsel for the employee.

At the outset of an investigation, it is worth giving some consideration to the order in which employees will be interviewed. At the initial stage of an investigation, witnesses may be interviewed to understand business operations, policies, and relationships. In a later stage

---

[11] *See, e.g.*, JPMorgan Sec. LLC, Exchange Act Release No. 93807, 2021 WL 5986789, ¶¶ 32–34 (Dec. 17, 2021); Paisley Park Enters., Inc. v. Boxill, 330 F.R.D. 226, 234 (D. Minn. 2019); Kan-Di-Ki, LLC v. Suer, No. 7937-VCP, 2015 WL 4503210, at *30 (Del. Ch. July 22, 2015). *But see* Lawson v. Love's Travel Stops & Country Stores, Inc., No. 1:17-cv-1266, 2020 WL 94078, at *1 (M.D. Pa. Jan. 8, 2020) (denying a blanket request for all text messages while suggesting that a more narrowly tailored request might be granted).

of an investigation, interviewers may seek to understand specific areas of concern, including individual or corporate culpability.

In light of these purposes, counsel often begin with interviews of lower-level personnel. Lower-ranking employees, while not privy to management decision-making, often better understand operations and the implementation of management decisions. Lower-ranking employees are often not implicated by fraud perpetrated by senior management and therefore may be more willing to speak to counsel. Lower-ranking employees may also be able to assist with obtaining key documents, as they are typically more involved in recordkeeping. Finally, lower-ranking employees also often have more time to assist with an investigation.

One exception to this general rule is if there is an internal whistleblower. Internal whistleblowers, in almost all instances, should be interviewed first regardless of seniority (see Section X for more detail).

Most counsel prepare outlines prior to conducting interviews. Alongside or within the interview outlines, counsel often also prepare a working chronology of events, which is supplemented as the case progresses. The chronology typically contains dates identified from the initial allegations, as well as key documents from any initial collection. These documents can often refresh employees' memories of events that may have occurred in the distant past. While counsel should not be wedded to their outlines, a good outline helps counsel stay organized during interviews and cover the issues as comprehensively as possible, as it is not always possible to conduct multiple interviews of the same witness.

Many, if not most, companies have policies requiring cooperation with a reasonable investigation, and failure to cooperate can often be a basis for disciplinary action, up to and including termination. That said, employee cooperation can vary widely, whether out of concern for their own culpability or other motivations.

VII. *Upjohn* Warnings

The *Upjohn* warning merits special consideration given its importance in preserving attorney–client privilege. Assuming that the interviewing attorney does not also represent the employee being interviewed, the attorney should provide an *Upjohn* warning before beginning the interview to put the employee on notice that an attorney–client relationship is not being created.[12] A standard *Upjohn* warning contains the following components:

1. The attorney represents the company and not the employee individually;
2. The attorney–client privilege belongs to the company, not the employee, as the purpose of the interview is for the attorney to provide legal advice to the company;
3. The company reserves the right to waive the privilege and disclose the substance of the interview to third parties, including law enforcement agencies, which the company may do without notice to the employee; and
4. The employee must not waive that privilege by disclosing—either inadvertently or intentionally—the content of the communications to third parties.

[12] Upjohn Co. v. United States, 449 U.S. 383, 394–96 (1981).

Care should be given, however, not to impede an individual from reporting a possible violation of law to a regulatory agency. For instance, the SEC brought a case against a company for requiring witnesses in certain internal investigations to sign confidentiality statements with language warning that they could face discipline and even be fired if they discussed the matters with outside parties without the prior approval of the company's legal department.[13] In particular, the SEC took issue with language in the form confidentiality statement stating:

> I understand that in order to protect the integrity of this review, I am prohibited from discussing any particulars regarding this interview and the subject matter discussed during the interview, without the prior authorization of the Law Department. I understand that the unauthorized disclosure of information may be grounds for disciplinary action up to and including termination of employment.

The SEC alleged that this language violated Rule 21F-17 enacted under the Dodd-Frank Act and ordered the company to cease and desist from future violations, in addition to imposing a $130,000 fine.

VIII. Written and Oral Reports

Counsel typically prepare a number of written or oral reports over the course of an investigation, including interim reports, witness interview memoranda, and final reports.

First, counsel are frequently asked to provide updates to the supervisor of the investigation, who may be in-house counsel or a committee of the company's board of directors, and to other stakeholders, including external auditors, who may have legitimate reasons (e.g., financial statement reporting) for wanting to understand certain aspects of the investigation or its results. Oral updates are common, especially if there is a risk of disclosure to opposing counsel in a litigation or to the government. Oral updates are often coupled with memorialization in meeting minutes, which should be labeled, as appropriate, as attorney–client privileged and work product. Counsel should make clear that any interim updates reflect interim conclusions subject to revision. In addition, with respect to external auditors, due care should be given to determining what aspect or findings of the investigation can be shared and still preserve attorney–client privilege and work product. This can be an especially sensitive and challenging situation, especially if the company is in the midst of a quarterly or annual review. At a minimum, experienced counsel should be interfacing with and conveying the necessary information in order to walk the fine line of protecting privilege while providing auditors with the information they need to complete their review.

Second, counsel commonly write memos following employee interviews to document what was learned in the interview. Such memos should take care to state that an *Upjohn* warning was given; that the memo is protected, as appropriate, by the attorney–client

[13] KBR, Inc., Exchange Act Release No. 74619, 2015 WL 1456619 (Apr. 1, 2015).

privilege and work-product doctrine; and that the memo contains the attorney's impressions of the interview and discussions of legal strategy. To the extent possible, the witness interview memo should avoid verbatim quotes or quotation marks.[14]

Third, counsel may prepare a written report at the end of an investigation, whether in the form of a memo or as a slide presentation. Access to such a report should be limited to the relevant individuals. Such a written report is frequently sought in discovery by the government or by opposing parties in a litigation.[15] Even if the report is privileged, counsel may be faced with a government demand to produce the presentation, and counsel may feel compelled to comply to show the company's cooperation. Thus, some counsel may prefer to deliver an oral report to the board of directors, audit committee, or other responsible party at the company rather than a formal report. As with interim updates, the final oral report may be summarized in meeting minutes with the appropriate caveats.

A final written report also may be prepared with the express purpose of disclosure to the government or a court with litigation in mind. For example, in a shareholder derivative suit, the report may be produced to show that an investigation was conducted and a particular course of action was recommended by management.[16] For these types of written reports, counsel should carefully consider and discuss with the company the possibility that the privileged information might be waived and the consequences of the waiver.

Regardless of the purpose of the report, counsel should take a number of steps to ensure a clear and accurate report. For example, the report should include a statement of the purpose of the investigation, a description of its scope and procedures, and any assumptions made in the report. Counsel should distinguish between facts and opinions, and assessments of credibility should be described as opinions. Discrepancies and conflicting evidence should also be noted. Finally, counsel should consider whether there is a risk of a defamation lawsuit brought by individuals who are not depicted favorably in a report.

IX. International Investigations

Given the interconnected nature of global commerce and the fact that ESG issues can often arise overseas where controls are weaker, investigations are increasingly cross-border. Such investigations bring unique challenges for U.S.-based counsel and often require the retention

[14] *See* United States ex rel. Cairns v. D.S. Med., L.L.C, No. 1:2CV00004 AGF, 2016 WL 7437919, at *5 (E.D. Mo. Dec. 22, 2016) (noting that fact-based work product, which may be discoverable, generally consists of "substantially verbatim witness statements contained in interview memoranda that have not been sharply focused or weeded by an attorney") (internal quotation marks omitted); United States v. Berkeley Heartlab, Inc., No. 9:14-cv-00230-RMG, 2017 WL 1533434, at *4 (D.S.C. Apr. 27, 2017) (requiring production of verbatim statements given by witnesses); *see also In re* Symbol Techs., Inc. Sec. Litig., No. CV 05-3923 (DRH) (AKT), 2017 WL 1233842, at *19 (E.D.N.Y. Mar. 31, 2017) (requiring production of interview memorandum containing factual summaries of confidential informants' interviews); *In re* John Doe Corp., 675 F.2d 482, 493 (2d Cir. 1982) (finding attorney notes of employee interview constituted only fact work product where "[t]he notes recite in a paraphrased, abbreviated form, statements by Employee A . . . to Lawyer").

[15] *See* United States ex rel. Wollman v. Mass. Gen. Hosp., Inc., No. 15-11890-ADB, 2020 WL 4352915, at *51, 57 (D. Mass. July 29, 2020); Sandra T.E. v. S. Berwyn Sch. Dist. 100, 600 F.3d 612, 615 (7th Cir. 2010).

[16] Ross v. Abercrombie & Fitch Co., No. 2:05-cv-0819, 2008 WL 1844357, at *2 (S.D. Ohio Apr. 22, 2008), *aff'd*, 2008 WL 3286346 (S.D. Ohio Aug. 8, 2008).

of local counsel. Jurisdictions frequently differ on a number of key areas: attorney–client privilege, data collection, employment, reporting of conduct, and substantive laws and regulations.

Privilege laws can be considerably complicated when working outside of the United States. For example, in some countries, the attorney–client privilege may not apply with respect to in-house counsel and may not apply at all in the context of an internal investigation.[17] In some legal systems, the communications of attorneys who are not licensed in the jurisdiction may not be privileged.[18] In addition, laws may differ on the waiver of privilege, which can affect strategic considerations in determining how to cooperate and potentially self-report with local jurisdictions' law enforcement.

Collection and review of documents internationally have become both easier with the advent of technology but also more fraught as different jurisdictions have promulgated data privacy regimes affecting how companies preserve, access, and produce documents. Most notably, the EU General Data Protection Regulation (GDPR) has established "rules relating to the protection of natural persons with regard to the processing of personal data and rules relating to the free movement of personal data" to protect "fundamental rights and freedoms of natural persons and in particular their right to the protection of personal data."[19] The GDPR and its implementation across the EU have created significant complexity and risk of substantial liability for counsel involved in document retention and production.

Counsel should be aware that documents located outside of the United States but brought into the possession of law firms located in the United States—for example, through a document review database—can become subject to subpoena.[20] Indeed, even access by U.S. counsel of document review platforms hosting documents overseas may bring the documents within the scope of a subpoena because of U.S. counsel's contractual control over the document review vendor or U.S. counsel's temporary electronic possession of a downloaded file.[21] Despite precautions taken by reviewing documents overseas, however, these issues may be moot: U.S. law enforcement can often obtain documents located overseas, although often

---

[17] Case No. C-550/07 P, Akzo Nobel Chems. Ltd. v. Comm'n, 2010 E.C.R. I-8301 (E.C.J. Sept. 14, 2010) (holding, in the European Court of Justice, that under European Union law, emails involving in-house counsel are not privileged).

[18] *Id.* (confining privilege to attorneys licensed to practice law within the European Union; communications between U.S. counsel and management in Europe are not privileged).

[19] Commission Regulation 2016/679, 2016 O.J. (L 119/1) 1 (EU).

[20] *See In re* Grand Jury Subpoena, 627 F.3d 1143, 1144 (9th Cir. 2010) ("By a chance of litigation, the documents have been moved from outside the grasp of the grand jury to within its grasp. No authority forbids the government from closing its grip on what lies within the jurisdiction of the grand jury.").

[21] *See, e.g., In re* Search of Info. Associated with [REDACTED]@Gmail.com that is Stored at Premises Controlled by Google, Inc., No. 16-mj-00757 (BAH), 2017 WL 3445634, at *17 (D.D.C. July 31, 2017) ("[W]here the evidence is stored or 'located' is irrelevant. Instead, the critical inquiry is whether the service provider has sufficient 'control' to retrieve and disclose the targeted records and communications in the United States."); United States v. First Nat'l City Bank, 396 F.2d 897, 900–01 (2d Cir. 1968) ("[A] federal court has the power to require the production of documents located in foreign countries if the court has in personam jurisdiction of the person in possession or control of the material.").

with some delay, through the Mutual Legal Assistance Treaties (MLATs)[22] or letters rogatory process.

Local labor laws also may limit the scope or conduct of employee interviews. Offering to provide employees with independent counsel may be advisable or even required in certain jurisdictions. Jurisdictions also differ on whether employees can be required to be interviewed and companies' ability to discipline employees for misconduct, including refusing to cooperate with an investigation. In addition, counsel should be aware of whistleblower and anti-retaliation statutes within that jurisdiction.

Laws on reporting of misconduct can vary greatly depending on jurisdiction. In addition to legally mandated reporting, local practices also differ for self-reporting; in many jurisdictions, law enforcement can serve as a mitigating factor and reduce potential civil and criminal liability.

Finally, counsel should be aware of local attitudes toward obstruction of justice. In certain countries, document destruction may not be sanctioned as seriously as in the United States, where the U.S. Department of Justice has aggressively pursued such destruction as obstruction of justice.[23] Counsel should ensure that clients understand the importance of preserving documents and avoiding the appearance of or engaging in anything that could be construed as hindering a law enforcement investigation.

X. Whistleblowers

Investigations, including ESG investigations, are often instigated by a whistleblower, whether reported internally or to the government. In recent years, the government has placed an increased emphasis on encouraging whistleblowing to the government. For example, some federal statutes incentivize whistleblowers by providing them with a share in any government recovery that results,[24] and numerous statutes protect whistleblowers against potential retaliation.[25] Given the high level of scrutiny over ESG issues, ESG issues are at front of mind for whistleblowers and the government, and whistleblowers represent a special area of risk for companies.

Individual regulatory agencies frequently have their own whistleblower office. One of the most active is the SEC's Office of the Whistleblower.[26] The SEC's Office of the Whistleblower

[22] Mutual Legal Assistance Treaties (MLATs) are agreements entered into between the U.S. government and the governments of foreign nations and provide for bilateral, mutual assistance in the gathering of legal evidence. Letters rogatory are a procedure whereby a court within the United States can make a formal request to a foreign court to serve a subpoena. *In re* Grand Jury Subpoena, 646 F.3d 159, 165 (4th Cir. 2011).

[23] *See, e.g.*, Press Release, U.S. Department of Justice, Auto Parts Industry Executive Pleads Guilty to Obstruction of Justice (Feb. 2, 2017), https://www.justice.gov/opa/pr/auto-parts-industry-executive-pleads-guilty-obstruction-justice (reporting on obstruction of justice charges against a former president of U.S. joint venture based in Japan for, among other things, deleting documents).

[24] The Securities Exchange Act of 1934 § 21F, 15 U.S.C. § 78u-6; 26 U.S.C. § 7623(b).

[25] *See, e.g.*, CAL. LAB. CODE § 1102.5 *et seq.*; 740 ILL. COMP. STAT. 174; N.J. CONSCIENTIOUS EMP. PROT. ACT; N.Y. LAB. LAW § 215; TEX. GOV'T CODE § 554.001 *et seq.*

[26] While there are many other state and federal whistleblower statutes that may pose risk to a company, we focus on the U.S. Securities and Exchange Commission's (SEC's) program given the SEC's attention on ESG issues.

was established pursuant to the Dodd-Frank Act, and the SEC promulgated rules favorable to whistleblowers. The SEC's whistleblower program has three core tenets: confidentiality, anti-retaliation protections, and monetary awards.[27] The existence of all three of these incentives make the SEC's program very attractive to would-be whistleblowers, including company employees who raised concerns via internal reporting mechanisms at their company and believe the company is not taking sufficient action on their report. To incentivize the reporting of possible securities law violations to the SEC, a whistleblower who voluntarily provides original information to the SEC that leads to a successful enforcement action with monetary sanctions exceeding $1 million may be entitled to receive an award between 10 percent and 30 percent of the collected money.[28] According to the SEC's Fiscal Year 2021 Whistleblower Program Annual Report to Congress, since the inception of the SEC's whistleblower program, the Commission has awarded more than $1.1 billion to 214 individuals.[29] Whistleblower tips were submitted in record numbers from all states in the United States as well as 133 countries worldwide. [30] Indeed, reporting to the U.S. regulator is a world-wide phenomenon.

Whistleblower information is increasingly becoming a predominant tool for the SEC's Division of Enforcement. When it announced the formation of its ESG Task Force in the Division of Enforcement, the SEC encouraged whistleblowers to submit information to the task force related to possible ESG violations.[31]

The SEC also has taken action against companies and individuals who have retaliated against an individual because they reported a possible securities law violation, and has brought enforcement actions for attempting to impede reporting out to the SEC. The actions were based on language in settlement agreements, confidentiality provisions, codes of conduct, training materials,[32] as well as verbal statements[33] and actions taken (such as cutting off access to the company's computer system).[34]

Given the increasing possibility that employees may report out to the SEC or other regulators related to ESG issues, it has become increasingly important for companies to ensure that their internal reporting mechanisms are well-publicized and that employees feel confident and comfortable reporting internally. In addition, healthy internal reporting systems are, in and of themselves, an important part of the "social" aspects of ESG. In FY 2021, more than 75 percent of corporate insiders who received awards through the SEC's whistleblowing

---

[27] The Securities Exchange Act of 1934 § 21F(h), 15 U.S.C. § 78u-6.

[28] *Id.* § 78u-6(b).

[29] SEC, 2021 Annual Report to Congress: Whistleblower Program 1 (2021), https://www.sec.gov/files/owb-2021-annual-report.pdf.

[30] *Id.* at 31.

[31] *See* Press Release, SEC, SEC Announces Enforcement Task Force Focused on Climate and ESG Issues (Mar. 4, 2021), https://www.sec.gov/news/press-release/2021-42.

[32] *See* Guggenheim Sec., LLC, Exchange Act Release No. 92237, 2021 WL 2581714 (June 23, 2021); Anheuser-Busch InBev SA/NV, Exchange Act Release No. 78957, 2016 WL 5404890 (Sept. 28, 2016).

[33] *See* Complaint, SEC v. Crumbley, No. 3:16-cv-0172-L (N.D. Tex. Jan. 21, 2016).

[34] *See* David Hansen, Exchange Act Release No. 94703, 2022 WL 112608 (Apr. 12, 2022).

program raised their concerns internally to supervisors, compliance personnel, or through internal reporting mechanisms, or understood that their supervisor or relevant compliance personnel knew of the violations, before reporting their information of wrongdoing to the SEC. Therefore, it is important that companies have appropriate mechanisms in place to identify, triage, and appropriately respond to whistleblower complaints.[35] Many times, whistleblowers report out to regulators or law enforcement because they do not believe the company took their complaint seriously.

A whistleblower's complaint should be acknowledged quickly—ideally the same day as it is received by the company. In an internal investigation, the whistleblower should be one of the first people, if not the first person, to be interviewed. Consideration should be given to touching base with the whistleblower during and at the end of the investigation. Companies will need to balance this with privilege and other considerations. Care should be taken to not, by words or actions, impede a whistleblower or any other individual from reporting to the SEC.[36]

Companies should have written policies and procedures for internal whistleblowers. An internal "whistleblower" is simply anyone who reports a possible violation of law to the company regardless of how small the issue appears at first glance. Whistleblowers do not always report via formal reporting mechanisms, such as hotlines or web forms. In many instances, whistleblowers tell their direct supervisor about the issue. Therefore, it is critical that line managers are trained to recognize when someone has reported an issue to them, who they should escalate the matter to, and how to avoid retaliating or impeding reporting to government agencies. Both policies and training should clearly prohibit retaliation, such as terminating, demoting, suspending, threatening, harassing, or otherwise discriminating against whistleblowers. Companies should also consider internal reporting frameworks, as changes in in-person, hybrid, and remote work may alter the effectiveness of whistleblower policies and procedures. Given the number of tips the SEC receives annually from overseas, companies should also consider training, policies, and reporting mechanisms for overseas operations where risk can be high. Employees should be assured that their allegations will be investigated and that any allegations of unlawful retaliation will be investigated impartially.

One difficult situation that may arise is when companies seek to discipline whistleblowers for legitimate, non-retaliatory reasons. In such instances, an employer should consider applicable law, follow the company's disciplinary policies and historical practices, and carefully document the application of policy and practice to the situation. Given the risk in this area, companies should consider seeking advice of counsel based on the specific facts and circumstances at hand.

Whistleblowers can be key in alerting companies to possible violations of law, including those related to ESG. Following best practices can keep the employment relationship on good terms and allow the company to investigate and remediate, if needed, before a regulator becomes involved.

---

[35] SEC, 2021 Annual Report to Congress: Whistleblower Program, *supra* note 29, at 24.

[36] *See, e.g.*, KBR, Inc., *supra* note 13.

Key Takeaways

The following is a non-exhaustive list of key takeaways to consider when conducting an internal investigation on ESG issues:

- Care should be given to determining the scope of the investigation. In the ESG context, a wide range of employees with special knowledge may need to be interviewed or consulted (e.g., director of sustainability, environmental specialist, human resources, external communications).
- Consider how to protect attorney–client communications and work product from disclosure. Counsel should always conduct, direct, or oversee the investigation.
- Determine whether outside counsel should be retained.
- Immediately take steps to preserve relevant documents and cast a broad net with document retention and preservation obligations.
- Give thought to the sequencing and content of witness interviews, and provide *Upjohn* warnings to all employees interviewed.
- Determine what facts or conclusions of the investigation, if any, should be shared in communications with external auditors or other stakeholders so as to strike a balance between legitimate stakeholder needs and the need to preserve attorney–client privilege.
- Take care in memorializing the investigation, and consider whether a written report is appropriate.
- In conducting an international investigation, research laws applicable to the local jurisdiction.
- Understand and be wary of special risks related to whistleblowers.

21

Monitoring Legislative and Regulatory Developments

David Skillman and Ryan Hartman

I. Introduction

Systematically monitoring and addressing potential legislative and regulatory developments can appear daunting to even an experienced general counsel or other practitioner, given the numerous federal, state, local, and international lawmaking, rulemaking, and other bodies that can attempt to exercise jurisdiction over businesses, the seemingly endless supply of proposals they may consider or enact, and the myriad of public and private interests constantly pushing (often out of public view) for them to do so.

This chapter explains how companies can monitor legislative and regulatory developments, with a particular focus on likely sources of U.S. federal legislative and regulatory activity, while setting out broader principles that apply across jurisdictions.

II. Monitoring Congressional Legislative Developments

Congress has followed ESG developments on a bipartisan basis but has yet to enact law regarding ESG disclosures or to respond to state-level ESG developments. Proposed legislative measures have moved through the House of Representatives but have yet to pass the Senate. The House passed, for instance, H.R. 1187, the Corporate Governance Improvement and Investor Protection Act, on June 16, 2022. The legislation would require publicly traded companies to periodically disclose information related to a wide variety of ESG performance metrics; it would also require a variety of reporting from the U.S. Securities and Exchange Commission (SEC), in part to facilitate the flow of capital to environmentally sustainable investments. The accompanying Financial Services Committee's report took favorable notice of a petition authored by Cynthia A. Williams of Osgoode Hall Law School and Jill E. Fisch of the University of Pennsylvania Law School, and signed by investors and associated organizations representing more than $5 trillion in assets under management. According to the House report, the petition[1] called on the

> SEC to develop a comprehensive ESG disclosure framework, and identified seven specific issues that the SEC could act on immediately: (1) climate risk; (2) annual ESG disclosures based on the Global Reporting Initiative (GRI) framework; (3) gender pay ratios; (4) human capital management; (5) human rights; (6) political spending; and (7) tax disclosure.[2]

The report, which aside from the minority views was drafted by the Democratic staff to the Financial Services Committee, set forth a rationale for passage of the Corporate Governance Improvement and Investor Protection Act. In turn, opponents of increased SEC disclosure (or ESG reporting in general) have described adherence to these rules as a politically motivated turn away from traditionally fiduciary rules. For instance, John Curtis (R-UT) described shareholders as "being duped, not knowing that those who are representing them aren't representing their financial interest."[3] This partisan split looks likely to continue and suggests that public companies should maintain a close watch on Congress to avoid surprise at legislative or public affairs developments.

Legislative activity is likely to increase as Congress continues its oversight of developments in this field. Public companies should establish plans to monitor Congressional hearings and related activity. In particular, Congress will continue its scrutiny of proposed SEC rules, corporate compliance, and any accompanying public discourse. Congress is also likely to continue its attempts to legislate in this field as well, though any such action will face the daunting procedural challenge of clearing both the House and the Senate. Companies, therefore, should carefully consider targeted Congressional monitoring and engagement. Such action can provide several benefits to a company's bottom line, including a knowledge of future opportunities and restraints, a sense of regulator focus, and the avoidance of public scrutiny. Such engagement can also influence regulator decision-making as regulators respond to Congressional inquiries.

III. What Authority Does Congress Have Over the Financial Services Industry?

Within the U.S. Congress, two standing committees are the primary—but not exclusive—overseers of the financial services industry. In the House of Representatives, the Financial Services Committee is assigned banks and banking (including deposit insurance and federal monetary policy), money and credit (including currency and the issuance of notes and

[1] Petition from Cynthia A. Williams, Osler Ch. Bus. L., Osgoode Hall L. Sch. & Jill E. Fisch, Saul A. Fox Distinguished Prof. of Bus. L., Univ. of Pa. L. Sch., to Brent J. Fields, Sec'y, U.S. Securities and Exchange Commission (SEC) (Oct. 1, 2018), https://www.sec.gov/rules/petitions/2018/petn4-730.pdf.

[2] H.R. Rep. No. 117-54 (2021), https://www.congress.gov/congressional-report/117th-congress/house-report/54/1.

[3] Nick Sobczyk, *Republicans Plan Legislative Assault on 'Woke' ESG Firms*, E&E Daily (June 7, 2022), https://www.eenews.net/articles/republicans-plan-legislative-assault-on-woke-esg-firms/.

redemption thereof), and securities and exchanges.[4] Under the standing rules of the Senate, the Banking Committee has substantially similar jurisdiction.[5] These rules provide those committees with primary jurisdiction to hear all bills, resolutions, and other matters relating to subjects within their jurisdiction. Thus, oversight of the issuance of particular rules by banking regulators will generally fall within the purview of these two committees. Their membership, on a bipartisan basis, therefore becomes important for any assessment of the likelihood of substantive Congressional action.

Depending on the nature of the inquiry or legislative subject, Congressional rules may assign some other standing committee primary jurisdiction. For instance, to the extent the subject relates to Congress's general oversight authority, the House Committee on Oversight and Reform "may at any time conduct investigations of any matter,"[6] notwithstanding the jurisdictional considerations of any other committee. Alternatively, where the particular ESG subject happens to align with the mandate of a particular committee, that committee can tailor its interest to the topic, such as Congressman GT Thompson (R-PA) targeting SEC disclosure rules as part of his concern that such proposed rules are part of a "regulatory assault on rural America"[7] during a hearing of the Committee on Agriculture.

Given the broad scope of ESG disclosures and the various interests these disclosures implicate, companies should endeavor to establish an awareness of ongoing Congressional interest in ESG and engage with the primary committees of jurisdiction to monitor legislative developments.

IV. What Types of Congressional Activities Are to Be Expected?

As a general rule, hearings are the primary tool to further Congress's legislative, oversight, investigative, and confirmation objectives.[8] ESG topics can arise in each of these types of hearings. Legislative hearings generally relate to gathering information on the topic of legislation or of considering and amending legislative proposals. Oversight hearings will often relate to the federal government's implementation of a particular public policy or the implications of a particular public policy at large. Investigative hearings will focus on the possibility of wrongdoing with regard to a particular public policy. Congress may compel individuals to appear, give testimony, provide documentary evidence and the like so long as it is "related to, and in furtherance of, a legitimate task of the Congress."[9] Given the ability of Congress to secure evidence and testimony, companies should assess the consistency of their public positions and statements on ESG topics and make efforts to respond to internal assessments of company performance on those measures.

---

[4] Rule X(1)(h), Rules of the U.S. House of Rep., 117th Cong. (2021).

[5] Rule XXV(1)(d)(1), Standing Rules of the U.S. Senate, 113th Congress (2013).

[6] Rule X(4)(c)(2), Rules of the U.S. House of Rep., 117th Cong. (2021).

[7] *The Role of Climate Research in Supporting Agricultural Resiliency: Hearing Before the H. Comm. on Agric.*, 117th Cong. (2022) (opening statement of Rep. GT Thompson).

[8] *See generally*, Cong. Rsch. Serv., No. 98-317, Types of Committee Hearings (2017).

[9] McGrain v. Daugherty, 273 U.S. 135, 187 (1927).

Confirmation hearings take place in the Senate to satisfy the Senate's Constitutional duty to provide "advice and consent" for certain nominations to high federal office. At such hearings, members of Congress scrutinize nominee positions, test out arguments, and assess support for their positions among their colleagues. During the confirmation hearing of Gary Gensler for Chairman of the SEC, for instance, Ranking Member Patrick Toomey emphasized his concern that "some . . . want the SEC to stray from its tradition of bipartisanship by using its regulatory powers to advance a liberal social agenda on issues such as climate change and racial inequality."[10] The regular sounding of similar arguments across a range of hearings and committees serves as a strong signal of the likelihood of Congressional action.

V. Examples of Recent Congressional Engagements on ESG Topics

Companies should also monitor legislative developments on ESG-related topics. While Congress has not enacted legislation governing ESG specifically, it has moved the legislative process forward. The House has passed some legislative measures. As described above, on June 16, 2021, the House of Representatives narrowly passed the Corporate Governance Improvement and Investor Protection Act (H.R. 1187). Democrats supporting the legislation argued that

> Investors have been demanding more—and better—disclosure of ESG information from public companies. Many investors view ESG information as important, not just for evaluating reputational risks, but for evaluating companies' financial performance as well as long-term viability.

Republican opponents of the measure, however, argued that the bill would damage the existing "materiality" standard, noting that "if ESG-related information is material to the investors of a public company, those companies are already required to make those disclosures under current law."[11] In this case, the House Democrats prevailed during floor consideration on a narrow 215–214 vote. Four Democrats voted no on the legislation, while no Republicans supported the measure. Given the continued narrow margins of Congressional control in the 118th Congress, it is unlikely the Senate will approve the bill. Rather, it serves as an example of policy measures Democrats are likely to champion should they regain power in some future Congress. Republicans have—so far—generally expressed skepticism regarding mandates to increase disclosure requirements.

On a more bipartisan basis, the House passed the Improving Corporate Governance Through Diversity Act (H.R. 5084) during the 116th Congress. The measure would require disclosures by issuers on the racial, ethnic, and gender diversity of their boards and executive officers; it would also establish a Diversity Advisory Group to report on strategies to increase gender, racial, and ethnic diversity among board members at the SEC. As with the Corporate Governance Improvement and Investor Protection Act, the Senate did not act on the measure.

---

[10] *Nominations of Gary Gensler and Rohit Chopra: Hearing Before the S. Comm. on Banking, Hous., and Urb. Affs.*, 117th Cong. (2021) (opening statement of Sen. Patrick J. Toomey).

[11] H.R. Rep. No. 117-54, *supra* note 2.

However, during the 117th Congress, similar provisions were included in the Federal Reserve Racial and Economic Equity Act (H.R. 2543), which passed the House on a partisan basis.[12]

Legislation tailored expressly to climate disclosure has also been introduced. The Climate Risk Disclosure Act of 2021 (H.R. 2570, S. 1217) would direct the SEC to require annual disclosure of climate change-related risks, including strategies to mitigate these risks. In particular, it would require reporting direct and indirect greenhouse gas emissions and fossil-fuel-related assets. In the House, H.R. 2570 has advanced out of the Financial Services Committee on a partisan basis.

Republican lawmakers have begun articulating a more aggressive opposition to these policies. For instance, in the wake of the SEC's issuance of its proposed climate disclosure rule, Republican members of the Senate Banking Committee (including former Chairman Mike Crapo [R-ID]) requested that the SEC preserve records related to the proposed rule, including emails and text messages between the SEC and the White House, U.S. Environmental Protection Agency, Financial Stability Oversight Council, and others.[13] This and similar requests suggest that a focus of Congressional oversight hearings, should Republican lawmakers take control over the Senate (they remain narrowly in the minority for the 118th Congress), will be the SEC's development of the disclosure rule, the costs it imposes on "oil, natural gas, and other energy industries,"[14] and the likelihood such a rule will aid "political pressure campaigns against companies to the detriment of shareholders." Such oversight could sweep up private companies depending on their level of involvement.

More broadly, Republican members have begun developing legislation that, beyond expressing concern about the costs of additional disclosure, would provide procedural protections for shareholder suits asserting that company actions are undertaken on a basis facially unrelated to the pecuniary interest of the company. Senator Marco Rubio (R-FL) has advanced the Mind Your Own Business Act of 2021 (S. 2829) as an example of such an approach. Such legislative efforts suggest an additional angle for Congressional scrutiny, as Congress monitors how companies navigate ESG considerations, attempt to accommodate SEC interest in increased disclosure, and respond to shareholder suits seeking contradictory outcomes.

As companies monitor these legislative activities and potential legislation, they should evaluate their controls related to ESG-related public disclosures. Beyond possible SEC evaluation, Congress—under control by either party—has demonstrated a political interest in company behavior with regard to ESG disclosures. Among other considerations, companies should assess how any ESG statements or actions fit within the company's business model and how it might affect the company image and brand to describe the activity before a Congressional committee. In particular, companies should assess any such statements for accuracy, consistency with past statements, and any underlying rationale to ascertain how it might be seen during public scrutiny.

[12] H.R. 2543, 117th Cong. (as passed by the House, June 15, 2022).

[13] Press Release, U.S. S. Comm. on Banking, Hous., and Urb. Affs., Banking Republicans Request SEC Records on Proposed Climate Disclosure Rule (June 16, 2022), https://www.banking.senate.gov/newsroom/minority/banking-republicans-request-sec-records-on-proposed-climate-disclosure-rule.

[14] Letter from Pat Toomey, U.S. Sen., et al., to Gary Gensler, Chairman, SEC (June 15, 2022), https://www.banking.senate.gov/imo/media/doc/banking_republicans_to_gensler_on_climate_proposal1.pdf (regarding the SEC's proposed rule on "The Enhancement and Standardization of Climate-Related Disclosures for Investors").

Lawmakers from both parties have indicated a willingness to legislate on these topics, with some—diversity, for instance—securing bipartisan support, and others—such as climate change—attracting heavy partisan criticism. Furthermore, recent passage of the Inflation Reduction Act (H.R. 5376), for instance, provides the Biden administration with support for executive branch actions both internationally, under the Paris Agreement (part of the United Nations Framework Convention on Climate Change), and domestically by executive order. Companies should assess these and similar developments for the risks and opportunities posed by possible Congressional scrutiny.

Sample of Recent Related Legislation

Passed the House:

- H.R. 2543, Federal Reserve Racial and Economic Equity Act, 117th Cong. (as passed by the House, 2022). Provides for a range of prohibitions to racial discrimination, including requiring financial institutions to report information relating to diversity policies and lending practices.
- H.R. 1187, Corporate Governance Improvement and Investor Protection Act, 117th Cong. (as passed by the House, 2021). Requires disclosure of information related to a variety of ESG metrics; establishes Sustainable Finance Advisory Committee that must recommend policies to the SEC facilitating the flow of capital to environmentally sustainable investments.
- H.R. 1277, Improving Corporate Governance Through Diversity Act of 2021, 117th Cong. (as passed by the House, 2019). Requires disclosures by issuers on the racial, ethnic, and gender diversity of their boards and executive officers.

Relating to Diversity, Equity, and Inclusivity matters:

- H.R. 9705, Promoting Diverse Investment Advisers Act, 117th Cong. (2023). Requires investment companies that register with the SEC to utilize "to the maximum extent possible" diverse intermediaries and broker dealers when contracting for asset management services.
- H.R. 2516, Promoting Diversity and Inclusion in Banking Act, 117th Cong. (2021). Requires federal banking regulators to rate financial institutions based on diversity and inclusivity using the Uniform Financial Institutions Rating System.

Relating to climate change:

- H.R. 2570/S.1217, Climate Risk Disclosure Act, 117th Cong. (2021). Requires the SEC to set mandatory, annual climate change-related risk disclosures for issuers that also clarify the issuers' plans for addressing disclosed risks.
- H.R. 1780, Paris Climate Agreement Disclosure Act, 117th Cong. (2021). Requires securities issuers to disclose information related to their greenhouse gas emissions on an annual basis.

Relating to over-inclusive actions/disclosures:

- Senator Marco Rubio (R-FL) introduced S. 2829, the Mind Your Own Business Act of 2021, 117th Cong. (2021), which would require corporations to defend the benefits of "woke" directives to their shareholders in order to avoid legal liability. He has reintroduced this legislation for the 118th Congress as well as S. 189.

VI. Monitoring Regulatory Developments

This section sets out general principles for monitoring regulatory developments, and specific observations regarding how regulators are likely to approach ESG.

A. General Principles

As suggested above, a single company or line of business can be subject to numerous overlapping regulatory authorities at the federal, state, local, and international level. To monitor and address regulatory developments systematically, it is critical that companies have a process for:

1. identifying and triaging key regulatory areas and agencies that are likely to impact them;
2. assessing the timing, likelihood, and materiality of potential regulations and their enforcement;
3. acting on opportunities to propose, shape, or defeat regulations before their enactment (whether individually or as part of an industry group or other collective); and
4. proactively adjusting business operations to facilitate compliance, promote efficiency, or create competitive advantages.

Companies enacting this process for the first time generally begin with a top-to-bottom assessment of the nature, scope, and location of their businesses; the high-impact, high-probability areas of regulation they may face; and the current state of their compliance. This may include ranking regulatory areas for follow-up in one of four quadrants based on a combination of their potential impact and likelihood of enforcement:

Regulatory Action Matrix

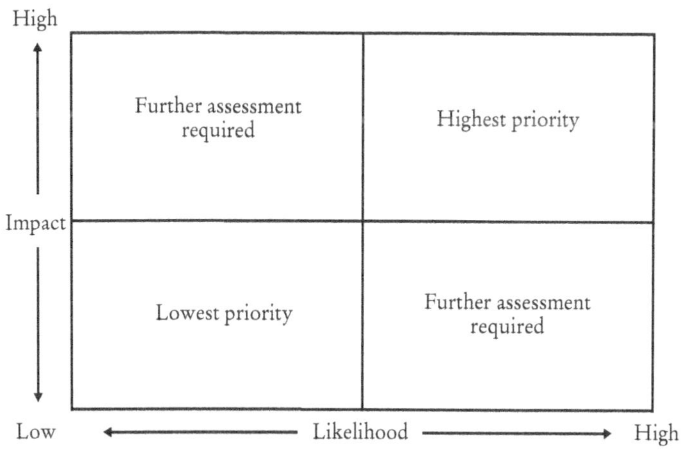

Companies with established processes have a deep understanding of these matters that instead allows them to devote resources to:

1. scanning the regulatory horizon for threats and opportunities, as well as allies and adversaries (e.g., political or advocacy organizations);
2. monitoring changes in their businesses such as new products, activities, lines of business, or geographic markets that alter their regulatory risk profile or bring them within the ambit of additional rulemaking bodies;
3. understanding regulatory enforcement trends applicable to them;
4. utilizing a network of local or specialist practitioners to ensure peripheral vision of developing areas around the world that are relevant to their businesses;

5. acting on internal metrics such as audit findings and risk assessments; and
6. taking proactive measures that go beyond reactive conformance to competitive advantage and regulatory advocacy.

B. Regulatory Approach to ESG

To monitor and anticipate regulatory actions on ESG, it is important to bear in mind two concepts. First, given ESG's prominence, many regulators are looking for the contribution they can make to supporting or diminishing its objectives, depending on their political viewpoint. Sometimes the link between ESG and a regulator's mission is clear, but not always, and not necessarily in every area of ESG in which they might attempt to deploy their rules and resources. Second, much like the observation that if one only has a hammer, every problem looks like a nail, regulators typically have a finite set of tools in their toolbox that they predictably use. Thus, regulatory views of and responses to issues are often shaped by the tools they have available to them.

The SEC provides an example of this. The SEC's longstanding mission has been "to protect investors; maintain fair, orderly, and efficient markets; and facilitate capital formation."[15] Within the ESG acronym, "governance" is clearly aligned with the SEC's remit, whereas "environment" is not. Nevertheless, one of the SEC's most consequential and controversial regulations proposed in 2022 is its Climate Disclosure Rule, which would require companies to disclose greenhouse gas emissions, climate-related financial data, and a host of related information. Unlike other agencies, regulating climate is not within the SEC's responsibilities. But the SEC has the power to promulgate regulations requiring issuers to disclose information that the SEC deems necessary or appropriate in the public interest or for the protection of investors.[16] In other words, the SEC's tool is disclosure, and the agency will use it to impact an area such as environmental performance that many would argue falls outside its responsibilities.

This is predictable because the SEC has used this same tool over decades to enact policy. At times, this has been at the direct request of Congress, such as the SEC's pay ratio rule requiring public companies to disclose the ratio of the compensation of its chief executive officer to the median compensation of its employees.[17] On other occasions, SEC staff have pursued agency or executive branch priorities through the lens of disclosure (for example, challenging U.S. issuers whose foreign subsidiaries that had financially immaterial business in sanctioned countries to disclose more information about that business based on purported qualitative rather than quantitative materiality to shareholders).

Companies can expect other regulators—whether proponents or opponents of ESG objectives—to look for the impact they can make on ESG and utilize the tools in their toolbox to do so. Those that understand what this may entail before their regulators or competitors do, and integrate this into their risk and regulatory management frameworks, will find themselves ahead of the steepening and sometimes conflicting ESG curves in these areas.

---

[15] *See, e.g.*, *Our Goals*, SEC, https://www.sec.gov/our-goals (Apr. 6, 2023).

[16] *See, e.g.*, 15 U.S.C. § 77g(a)(1) (2012).

[17] Press Release, SEC, SEC Adopts Rule for Pay Ratio Disclosure (Aug. 5, 2015), https://www.sec.gov/news/press-release/2015-160.

22

Differentiating ESG Investment Funds

Ellen Kaye Fleishhacker and Claire Frost[1]

I. Introduction

There has been rapidly growing interest in recent years in private investment funds with some form of an ESG focus, generally referred to as "ESG Funds." ESG Funds are different from other investment funds because they make investments with the intention of promoting a measurable environmental, social, or governance priority, *in addition to* seeking financial returns. However, there is a wide variety of vehicles that can be called ESG Funds. For example:

- There is a range of financial return outcomes that ESG Funds seek—from "return first" models that prioritize economic returns while still focusing on ESG-related factors as a way to drive those returns, to "return plus impact" models that seek to balance returns and impact, to "impact first" models that prioritize ESG-impact over returns.
- ESG Funds may invest broadly with an eye toward ESG factors generally or may focus on making an ESG impact under one of many possible themes (e.g., social themes, such as affordable housing, community health, and financial inclusion, and environmental themes, such as clean water, renewable energy, and sustainable transportation).
- Further, there is a wide variety of ESG Fund sponsors—from tax-exempt organizations and their for-profit affiliates, to specialized ESG Fund sponsors, to well-established private equity and hedge fund sponsors.
- Finally, there are many types of ESG Fund investors—ranging from sovereign entities to major institutional investors, to family offices, to individuals—and many possible ESG Fund structures to meet such investors' tax and regulatory needs.

[1] With thanks to William LeBas, a former associate at Arnold & Porter, for his work on an earlier iteration of this chapter.

This chapter provides a broad overview of the types of issues and considerations that matter to ESG Fund sponsors, investors, and their legal counsel. Please note that this chapter focuses primarily on closed-end private ESG Funds that pursue a single, targeted thematic ESG "impact" strategy. Although undeniably a significant part of the ESG Fund ecosystem, this chapter provides only some high-level observations regarding other types of investment products focusing on impact, including publicly traded funds and registered investment companies, private open-end funds that pursue liquid and semi-liquid investment opportunities, and private open-end and closed-end funds that pursue credit strategies, including lending funds and special situations or distressed credit funds.

A. Regulatory Context

Especially given that the regulation of ESG Funds is rapidly evolving along with their popularity, a detailed description of all of the regulatory considerations for ESG Funds is outside the scope of this chapter. However, we do touch on some of the recent U.S. regulatory scrutiny given to ESG Funds, and what it may mean for U.S. ESG Fund managers and their attorneys.

B. SEC Guidance Regarding an Interest in ESG

In a 2019 Interpretive Release, the U.S. Securities and Exchange Commission (SEC) made it clear that an advisor "may shape [its advisory] relationship by agreement, provided that there is full and fair disclosure and informed consent."[2] This Interpretive statement was widely taken to mean that sponsors can meet their fiduciary obligations to a fund client by considering other objectives as part of the fiduciary relationship—aside from economic returns—if full and fair disclosure of these common outcomes is contained in the fund's governing documents.[3]

While this fundamental emphasis on disclosure and process characterizes much of the U.S. regulatory scheme in the private funds space generally, it can be particularly challenging for managers raising ESG Funds to navigate this regulatory regime because the market is relatively new and market practice varies widely on issues (such as measuring and reporting impact) that are a key regulatory focus. Further, given the fluid nature of how ESG Funds may sometimes define ESG "impact," building credible documentation and rationales for investment decisions may require a significant amount of internal process.

This can be harder than it sounds because, at the agency level, not only has the SEC not specifically told market participants how they should define and measure ESG impact, but some SEC Commissioners have signaled that they do not believe that regulatory bodies should

[2] Commission Interpretation Regarding Standard of Conduct for Investment Advisers, Investment Advisors Act Release No. 5248, 84 Fed. Reg. 33669, 33671 (July 12, 2019) (to be codified at 17 C.F.R. pt. 276).

[3] Relevant for employee-directors who sit on portfolio company boards, there have also been helpful corporate developments in Delaware fiduciary law that give directors a greater ability to consider certain non-economic factors as part of the business judgment rule.

seek to define ESG and its impact at all.[4] Further, despite the SEC's public disagreement about the agency's role in defining ESG impact (and likely the wide difference of perspectives among SEC staff itself), it is notable that the SEC's Division of Examinations has indicated it intends to continue focusing on ESG issues through its exams of registered investment advisors.[5] In addition, on April 9, 2021, the staff of the Division of Examinations issued a risk alert[6] that highlighted their observations from recent exams of registered investment advisors, registered investment companies, and private funds offering ESG products. In the risk alert, they (1) encouraged sponsors promoting ESG investing to evaluate whether their ESG-related disclosures are accurate and consistent with internal firm practices, (2) noted that sponsors should ensure that their approaches to ESG investing are both implemented consistently and appropriately addressed in the firm's policies and procedures, and (3) noted that sponsors should also maintain records relating to important stages of the ESG investing process.[7]

Perhaps the SEC's focus should not be surprising given that ESG Funds—even more than other private funds—implicate unique disclosure, process, and measuring concerns. In this way, the SEC is seeking to ensure that managers do not abuse investor trust by overstating ESG efforts and impact, for which the SEC places the burden of proof on the sponsor.

Meeting this "burden of proof" in practice will require that managers be able to demonstrate—and, importantly, document—that they are abiding by relevant ESG- and non-ESG-related elements of their ESG process as stated in the fund's documents. For example, if a manager says the fund will evaluate certain criteria for fund investments, the manager should maintain internal checklists and/or high-level investment committee meeting minutes to document that such evaluations have occurred. Likewise, if a manager has promised that the fund will provide ESG-specific reporting on an annual basis, the manager will need to develop and deliver that reporting on the stated timeline and in the promised format.

As the regulatory environment in which ESG Funds operate continues to evolve, the SEC is also considering amendments to rules and reporting forms to promote reliable and consistent disclosure from funds regarding ESG factors. For example, on May 25, 2022, the SEC proposed certain amendments to rules and forms that would include the following:

- The proposed rule identifies three types of ESG Funds and states different requirements for each type:
    - For "Integration Funds," which consider ESG factors as well as non-ESG factors in their investment strategy, the funds would be required to describe how the ESG factors are incorporated into their investment process.

[4] *See* Hester Peirce, *Remarks by Commissioner Peirce on the Role of Asset Management in ESG Investing*, Harv. L. Sch. F. on Corp. Governance (Sept. 18, 2020), https://corpgov.law.harvard.edu/2020/09/18/remarks-by-commissioner-peirce-on-the-role-of-asset-management-in-esg-investing/.

[5] *See* Off. of Compliance Inspections & Examinations, U.S. Securities and Exchange Commission (SEC), 2020 Examination Priorities (2020), https://www.sec.gov/files/national-examination-program-priorities-2020.pdf [hereinafter 2020 Examination Priorities]; Div. of Examinations, SEC, 2021 Examination Priorities (2021), https://www.sec.gov/files/2021-exam-priorities.pdf [hereinafter 2021 Examination Priorities].

[6] Div. of Examinations, SEC, Risk Alert: The Division of Examinations' Review of ESG Investing (Apr. 9, 2021), https://www.sec.gov/files/esg-risk-alert.pdf.

[7] *Id.* at 7.

- For "ESG-Focused Funds," which consider non-ESG factors, but for which ESG factors are a significant, or the most-significant, factor:
  - The fund must provide detailed disclosure, including a standardized ESG strategy overview table.
  - The fund must disclose greenhouse gas emissions associated with its portfolio investments, unless the fund specifically discloses that it does not consider greenhouse gas emissions as part of its investment strategy.
- For "Impact Funds," which are ESG-Focused Funds that seek to achieve a specific ESG impact or impacts, the fund would be required to describe the specific desired impact or impacts and summarize progress towards achieving those goals, as well as disclose how the fund measures progress.

- Funds that use proxy voting or other engagement with issuers as a significant means of implementing their ESG strategy would be required to disclose information regarding their voting of proxies on particular ESG-related voting matters and information concerning their ESG engagement meetings.
- Funds would be required to provide ESG-related reporting on Forms N-CEN and ADV Part 1A.[8]

The May 25, 2022, proposal also included an update to the "Names Rule." Currently, the Names Rule requires that for investment funds whose names suggest that their investments are focused (1) on a particular type of investment (such as bonds), (2) on a particular industry (such as technology), or (3) on a particular geographic area (such as a particular country or continent), 80 percent of the fund's assets must be in this particular focus area. The May 25, 2022, proposed regulations propose several changes to the Names Rule, with the following proposed changes of particular relevance to ESG Funds:

- The scope of the Names Rule will be broadened to include names that suggest that the fund focuses its investment program on investments with particular characteristics, with ESG funds specifically covered in this category and therefore subject to the 80 percent requirement.
- Funds that consider ESG factors alongside non-ESG factors and do not weigh ESG factors more significantly (referred to above as Integration Funds) would not be able to use ESG in the name of their fund.
- Funds subject to the Names Rule would be subject to increased reporting ongoing requirements to demonstrate their compliance.[9]

[8] Press Release, SEC, SEC Proposes to Enhance Disclosures by Certain Investment Advisers and Investment Companies About ESG Investment Practices (May 25, 2022), https://www.sec.gov/news/press-release/2022-92.

[9] Investment Company Names, Securities Act Release No. 11,067, Exchange Act Release No. 94,981, Investment Company Act Release No. 34,593, 87 Fed. Reg. 36594 (proposed June 17, 2022) (to be codified at 17 C.F.R. pts. 230, 232, 239, 270).

It is important to note that the SEC Names Rule does not provide a safe harbor—a fund that is in compliance with the 80 percent requirement can still be found to have a materially misleading name.[10]

C. Regulatory Examinations and Investigations

Regulatory scrutiny of private funds primarily arises in the context of an exam (although in certain instances, it could arise as a result of specific fund investor complaints). For example, in March 2021, the SEC's Division of Examinations stated that it would "focus on" ESG products that registered investment advisors offer to investors.[11] Before that, in January 2020, the SEC's Division of Examinations announced that it had a "particular interest" in the accuracy and adequacy of disclosures provided by advisors offering clients new types of emerging investment strategies, such as strategies focused on sustainable and responsible investing, which incorporate ESG criteria.[12] In addition, in 2019 it was widely reported that the SEC staff had focused a sweep examination on the use of ESG criteria in certain advisors' investment processes. To that end, ESG Fund sponsors should expect that the Division of Examinations staff might ask for the following types of information (among other types) in future examinations:

- Processes for developing the definition of terms relating to ESG or impact (e.g., the use of any internal or third-party definitions);
- Written policies and procedures (e.g., related to determining whether an investment qualifies as an appropriate impact or ESG investment, and documentation supporting such decisions and recommendations);
- The manager's internal compliance programs (e.g., impact audits, annual reviews, and reports on impact compliance from third parties);
- Information on the systems or data the manager uses to evaluate or "score" ESG investments (e.g., whether they are proprietary or external measurements and how the manager uses the "scores" to make investment decisions); and
- Performance information related to impact investments (e.g., how financially profitable they are and how much "impact" they had).

In May 2022, the SEC charged BNY Mellon Investment Adviser, Inc. (BNY Mellon) for making misstatements related to ESG factors. Namely, the SEC found that BNY Mellon informed investors that a fund's investments had undergone an ESG quality review, but this was not the case for all of the fund's investments.[13] This charge is a reminder that, as with other disclosures and statements to investors, the SEC expects ESG Fund managers to do what they say they are doing related to ESG.

[10] Investment Company Names, Investment Company Act, Release No. 24,828 (Jan. 17, 2001) https://www.sec.gov/rules/final/ic-24828.htm.

[11] 2021 Examination Priorities, *supra* note 5, at 28.

[12] 2020 Examination Priorities, *supra* note 5, at 15.

[13] Press Release, SEC, SEC Charges BNY Mellon Investment Adviser for Misstatements and Omissions Concerning ESG Considerations (May 23, 2022), https://www.sec.gov/news/press-release/2022-86.

D. Other U.S. Regulatory and Legal Considerations

There are a host of other ESG-related regulatory and legal requirements that may apply to a fund depending on the nature of its investors. These include specific requirements that may apply to banking investors, government and state pension fund investors, charities and tax-exempt investors, and other institutions. For example, funds that seek investors that are subject to the U.S. Department of Labor's (DOL's) regulation under the Employee Retirement Income Security Act of 1974, as amended (ERISA), which may include corporate pension funds and other retirement and institutional investors, should be aware of both (1) the DOL's "ESG Investing Rule," which provides guidance on how and when ERISA fiduciaries may consider selecting plan investments to take into account non-pecuniary considerations, and (2) the "Proxy Voting Rule," which provides guidance on proxy voting for ERISA plans, including the duties of plan fiduciaries responsible for the economic interests of plan participants and beneficiaries in making voting decisions. ESG Fund sponsors seeking to attract investment by investors subject to ERISA will need to consider these complex rules when structuring, marketing, and operating their funds.

The DOL has issued guidance on ESG investments from time to time. Most recently, on December 1, 2022, the DOL released final regulations[14] that govern the circumstances in which plan fiduciaries may consider ESG factors when making investment decisions, including choosing an investment fund lineup in a participant-directed plan, without violating their duties of loyalty and prudence. Specifically, the final rule is not limited by its terms to ESG investments but would apply to a fiduciary's review of other factors. The rule allows ERISA plan fiduciaries to consider ESG factors when they are relevant to a risk/return analysis, or to serve as a tiebreaker between two investments that otherwise equally serve the financial interests of the plan. This rule makes clear, however, that plan fiduciaries may not prioritize "other objectives" over the financial interests of plan participants in their retirement outcome. The rule allows plan fiduciaries to consider participant preferences when selecting funds for an investment lineup for self-directed plans, but the fiduciaries will continue to be required to meet ERISA's duty of prudence. The rule does not provide a safe harbor for plan fiduciaries' consideration of ESG factors, and because the DOL has issued guidance on ESG investments in the past, fund managers will want to consider the latest DOL guidance as they structure funds.

1. *Defining and Measuring Impact*

One of the first decisions sponsors have in raising—and often step one in conceiving of—an ESG Fund is how they will define and measure ESG "impact." The sponsor's definition of ESG impact will drive nearly every other decision in the formation, marketing, fundraising, and investment activity of the fund. For some ESG Fund sponsors, this decision may be obvious. For example, managers that invest in affordable housing may define ESG impact based on the number of affordable units that the fund supports, develops, and preserves. Often, for

[14] Prudence and Loyalty in Selecting Plan Investments and Exercising Shareholder Rights, 87 Fed. Reg. 73822 (Dec. 1, 2022) (to be codified at 29 C.F.R. pt. 2550), https://www.federalregister.gov/documents/2022/12/01/2022-25783/prudence-and-loyalty-in-selecting-plan-investments-and-exercising-shareholder-rights.

ESG issues are often highlighted by news media when investors suffer sudden and substantial losses on listed equities—losses that are attributed to poor management of risks posed by one or more of these ESG issues. One example is the ongoing drought in California, which has increased the need for many businesses to consider water stress from agricultural farming to semiconductor manufacturing. Another example is climate change and the movement of investors away from fossil fuel assets that are finding expression in shareholder resolutions at the annual meetings of large oil companies, such as Shell. For investment management professionals, a key theme is that systematically considering ESG issues likely will lead to more complete analyses and better-informed investment decisions over the long term.

It is important to keep in mind that the consideration of ESG issues is a complement to (not a substitute for) traditional fundamental financial and investment analysis. For many investors, however, ESG issues remain relevant throughout the investment process—from the initial analysis to the buy/sell/hold decision, to ongoing ownership practices, the allocation of additional capital, and the disposition decision.

III. Overview of the Current SEC Disclosure Framework

The growing focus on ESG issues and related disclosures should be viewed in the context of the current disclosure framework under federal securities laws. Until recently, companies' disclosure obligations with respect to ESG matters were considered primarily in the context of reporting material risks to their businesses and known uncertainties that may materially impact their financial results. The SEC's view of materiality is discussed in further detail below.

At a more granular level, the SEC's current rules include required environmental-related disclosures in the context of identifying certain expenditures, such as a smaller reporting of company's costs and effects of compliance with federal, state, and local environmental laws.[1] They also require disclosure of supply chain information regarding conflict minerals.[2] With respect to social criteria, required disclosures are fairly minimal. For example, a company must disclose its human capital (HC) resources as part of Item 1 of the company's 10-K filing, to the extent that such information is "material" to the company's business taken as a whole.[3] This includes the number of persons employed by the company and any human capital measures or objectives on which the company focuses in managing the business.[4] With respect to governance, certain disclosures are required in a company's proxy statement. For example,

[1] *See* 17 C.F.R. § 229.101(h)(4)(xi).

[2] *See* 17 C.F.R. § 240.13p-1.

[3] *See* 17 C.F.R. § 229.101(c)(2)(ii). As one study on HC disclosures pointed out, "corporate HC disclosures are extremely heterogeneous in terms of their length, numerical intensity, tone, readability, and similarity with peer firms; they are generally not very numerically intensive, but they are very positively toned; and they inherit many of the properties of the firm's other Item 1 disclosures." Elizabeth Demers, Victor Xiaoqi Wang & Kean Wu, *Corporate Human Capital Disclosures: Early Evidence from the SEC's Disclosure Mandate*, SSRN, Aug. 2022, https://ssrn.com/abstract=4153845.

[4] *See* 17 C.F.R. § 229.101(c)(2)(ii).

a company must disclose information about its directors and their independence qualifications, the board leadership structure, board committee structures and responsibilities, and the process for shareholders to communicate with the company, among other things.[5]

A. The Materiality Standard

The SEC has traditionally required disclosure of financially material information. Regulation S-K provides a set of detailed disclosure requirements under both the Securities Act of 1933, as amended (the "Securities Act"), and the Securities Exchange Act of 1934, as amended (the "Exchange Act"), and is applicable to both public offerings and ongoing reporting obligations. Section 11 of the Securities Act,[6] Securities Act Rule 408,[7] and Exchange Act Rule 12b-20[8] generally require a registrant to disclose in its registration statements and periodic filings, in addition to the information expressly required by SEC regulation, any material information "as may be necessary to make the required statements, in light of the circumstances under which they are made, not misleading." The U.S. Supreme Court addressed the materiality standard in *TSC Industries, Inc. v. Northway Inc.*, and concluded that a fact is material if there is "a substantial likelihood that a reasonable shareholder would consider it important in deciding how to vote." The Court further ruled that an omission is material if "the omitted fact would have been viewed by the reasonable investor as having significantly altered the 'total mix' of information made available."[9]

Over the years, the SEC has provided guidance on materiality. For example, the SEC has stated that "[a] matter is 'material' if there is a substantial likelihood that a reasonable person would consider it important."[10] Further, "[t]he omission or misstatement of an item . . . is material if, in the light of surrounding circumstances, the magnitude of the item is such that it is probable that the judgment of a reasonable person relying upon the report would have been changed or influenced by the inclusion or correction of the item."[11]

B. Climate-Related and Investment ESG Disclosures

In recent months, the SEC has expanded its focus on companies' ESG disclosures. This expanded focus coincides with the Commission's decision to devote more resources to ESG enforcement. On March 4, 2021, the Commission announced the creation of the Climate and ESG Task Force in its Division of Enforcement (the "Task Force"), which is comprised of 22 enforcement attorneys and specialists whose initial focus will be on (1) gaps and

---

[5] *See* 17 C.F.R. § 229.407.

[6] 15 U.S.C. § 77k.

[7] 17 C.F.R. § 230.408.

[8] 17 C.F.R. § 240.12b-20.

[9] TSC Indus., Inc. v. Northway Inc., 426 U.S. 438, 449 (1976).

[10] U.S. Securities and Exchange Commission (SEC) Staff Accounting Bulletin No. 99, 64 Fed. Reg. 45150, 45151 (Aug. 19, 1999).

[11] *Id.*

misstatements in issuers' disclosures of climate risks and (2) disclosure and compliance issues relating to "investment advisers' and funds' ESG strategies."[12]

While the traditional disclosure framework relies on materiality as the basis for requiring various climate-related disclosures, there are no line-item requirements mandating such disclosures. Rather, in 2010, the SEC issued its Guidance Regarding Disclosure Related to Climate Change (the "2010 Guidance"), which addressed four items of Regulation S-K that could require disclosure regarding the impact of climate change: Description of Business, Legal Proceedings, Risk Factors, and Management Discussion and Analysis of Financial Condition and Results of Operations (MD&A). The 2010 Guidance identified certain climate-related issues that a company may need to consider in making its disclosures, including the physical impacts of climate change, direct and indirect impact of climate-related regulations or legislation, and indirect consequences of business trends, including changing demand for goods.

Although not released as an official regulation, over the past decade, the 2010 Guidance generally has been the primary clarifying guidepost for companies trying to discern which climate change risks require disclosure. The SEC has stated that while disclosures related to climate change have generally increased since 2010, the staff has observed "significant inconsistency in the depth and specificity of disclosures by registrants across industries and within the same industry" and that "disclosures in registrants' Forms 10-K frequently contain general, boilerplate discussions that provide limited information as to the registrants' assessment of their climate-related risks or their impact on the companies' business."[13]

In April 2021, the SEC's Division of Examinations provided additional guidance when it issued a Risk Alert detailing staff observations from recent examinations of investment advisors, registered investment companies, and private funds engaged in ESG investing.[14] These observations identified "some instances of potentially misleading statements regarding ESG investing processes and representations regarding the adherence to global ESG frameworks."[15] Following the issuance of this guidance, in May 2022, the Commission charged BNY Mellon Investment Adviser, Inc., with making false statements and material omissions related to its ESG investment representations.[16] Specifically, the Commission alleged that BNY Mellon "represented or implied in various statements" that its investments had all undergone an ESG quality review when in fact they had not.[17] To resolve the charges, the company agreed to pay a $1.5 million penalty along with a cease-and-desist order and a censure.[18]

---

[12] Press Release, SEC, SEC Announces Enforcement Task Force Focused on Climate and ESG Issues (Mar. 4, 2021), https://www.sec.gov/news/press-release/2021-42?utm_medium=email&utm_source=govdelivery.

[13] The Enhancement and Standardization of Climate-related Disclosures for Investors, Securities Act Release No. 11,042, Exchange Act Release No. 94,478, 87 Fed. Reg. 21334, 21339 (proposed Apr. 11, 2022) (to be codified at 17 C.F.R. pts. 210, 229, 232, 239, 249) [hereinafter Proposed Rule].

[14] Div. of Examinations, SEC, Risk Alert: The Division of Examinations' Review of ESG Investing (Apr. 9, 2021), https://www.sec.gov/files/esg-risk-alert.pdf.

[15] *Id.* at 3–4.

[16] Press Release, SEC, *SEC Charges BNY Mellon Investment Adviser for Misstatements and Omissions Concerning ESG Considerations* (May 23, 2022), https://www.sec.gov/news/press-release/2022-86.

[17] *Id.*

[18] *Id.*

The April 2021 Risk Alert also warned against the following corporate practices: "a lack of policies and procedures related to ESG investing; policies and procedures that did not appear to be reasonably designed to prevent violations of law, or that were not implemented; documentation of ESG-related investment decisions that was weak or unclear; and compliance programs that did not appear to be reasonably designed to guard against inaccurate ESG-related disclosures and marketing materials," despite claims to the contrary.[19]

C. Other ESG Disclosure Developments at the SEC

In September 2021, the staff posted a model comment letter that was sent to the largest public companies, reminding them of their existing disclosure obligations under Risk Factors and MD&A with respect to climate risk and warning against selective disclosure or utilization of non-SEC filed materials, such as corporate social responsibility (CSR) reports, to disclose material information on ESG matters.[20] Furthermore, among other items, the letter points to the following important observations: (1) the SEC may ask detailed questions related to climate risk factors, including regulatory and litigation risks; (2) the SEC appears focused on whether or not companies have fully accounted for the "significant developments in federal and state legislation and regulation and international accords regarding climate change" in their disclosures; (3) the SEC's sample letter asks companies to discuss in depth the "indirect consequences" of climate-related regulation and "business trends," including "decreased demand for goods or services that produce significant greenhouse gas emissions or are related to carbon-based energy sources"; and (4) the SEC may request further information from companies related to operational or financial impacts from the physical effects of climate change, including increased severe weather.[21]

Although the Task Force declared that its primary initial focus will be on climate risk disclosures and investment advisors' ESG representations,[22] the Task Force already has pursued alleged ESG misrepresentations and omissions beyond this scope. Moreover, the Task Force has made it clear that it will examine more than SEC filings in evaluating the accuracy of companies' ESG representations and also will consider companies' public reports and statements and information provided to the press. The Commission's willingness to look beyond SEC filings was highlighted when it brought charges in April 2022 against Vale, S.A., a publicly traded mining company based in Brazil. Among other allegations, the Commission alleged that the company misled local governments, communities, and investors about the safety of one of its dams through its ESG disclosures.[23] For example, the company's sustainability reports stated that it adhered to the "strictest international

[19] Div. of Examinations, SEC, *supra* note 14, at 4.

[20] *See Sample Letter to Companies Regarding Climate Change Disclosures*, SEC, https://www.sec.gov/corpfin/sample-letter-climate-change-disclosures (Sept. 22, 2021).

[21] *Id.*

[22] Press Release, SEC, SEC Announces Enforcement Task Force Focused on Climate and ESG Issues (Mar. 4, 2021), https://www.sec.gov/news/press-release/2021-42.

[23] Press Release, SEC, *SEC Charges Brazilian Mining Company with Misleading Investors About Safety Prior to Deadly Dam Collapse* (Apr. 28, 2022), https://www.sec.gov/news/press-release/2022-72.

practices" in assessing the safety of dams.[24] The Commission deemed this to be a misrepresentation because the company knew the dam at issue did not satisfy "internationally-recognized standards for dam safety."[25] The Commission also relied on alleged misleading statements in Vale's investor presentations, an ESG webinar, and verbal comments by company leadership.[26]

The Commission also has demonstrated a willingness to pursue companies making ESG-related misrepresentations that fall within the "social" part of ESG. Most recently, in July 2022, the Task Force charged a health insurance company, Health Insurance Innovations (HII) and its former CEO for failing to disclose consumer complaints about some of the company's health insurance products.[27] As evidence of a fraudulent statement, the Commission relied on the company's representations that HII "held its insurance distributors to high compliance standards, which prohibited distributors from making misrepresentations to consumers about health insurance products offered by HII."[28] In light of the "tens of thousands" of customer complaints that HII received related to distributor misrepresentations and other misconduct, the SEC concluded that HII's assurances about its distributors' compliance standards and its failure to disclose the customer complaints were misleading.[29] HII agreed to pay an $11 million penalty, and the former CEO agreed to pay more than $1 million in penalties.[30] The former CEO being charged along with HII as a result of the ESG misrepresentations is consistent with the SEC's and the U.S. Department of Justice's publicly reported focus on individual accountability. Companies can expect that going forward, the Task Force will not only be investigating whether ESG-related misstatements were made but also who was responsible for them.

Another anticipated area of "social" disclosure enforcement is disclosures related to workplace culture. For example, in September 2021, the Commission issued subpoenas to Activision Blizzard, a video game company, seeking "disclosures on employment matters and related issues."[31] The *Wall Street Journal* later reported that in early 2022, the Commission issued a second subpoena to Activision Blizzard related to the same investigation.[32] The Commission's subpoenas followed a lawsuit brought against Activision Blizzard by the California Department of Fair Employment and Housing in July 2021 related to alleged workplace

[24] *Id.*

[25] *Id.*

[26] Complaint, SEC v. Vale, S.A., No. 22 CV 2405 (E.D.N.Y. Apr. 28, 2022).

[27] Press Release, SEC, SEC Charges Tampa-Based Health Insurance Distributor and Its Former CEO with Making False Statements to Investors (July 20, 2022), https://www.sec.gov/news/press-release/2022-126#.

[28] *Id.*

[29] *Id.*

[30] *Id.*

[31] Press Release, Activision Blizzard, Activision Blizzard Provides Update on Workplace Initiatives, Company Continues to Work with Regulators to Resolve and Address Workplace Issues (Sept. 21, 2021), https://investor.activisionblizzard.com/news-releases/news-release-details/activision-blizzard-provides-update-workplace-initiatives.

[32] Kirsten Grind, *Regulators Widen Activision Blizzard Probes Over Workplace Issues*, WALL ST. J. (Feb. 17, 2022, 5:19 PM), https://www.wsj.com/articles/regulators-widen-activision-blizzard-probes-over-workplace-issues-11645136343.

culture issues at Activision Blizzard beginning as early as 2016. The complaint alleged, in part, that female employees at Activision Blizzard "were subjected to constant sexual harassment," and the company's executives and human resources personnel "knew of the harassment and failed to take reasonable steps to prevent the unlawful conduct and instead retaliated against women who complained."[33] The U.S. Equal Employment Opportunity Commission (EEOC) also filed a lawsuit against the company in September 2021 alleging, in part, that since in or around September 2016, Activision Blizzard employees were subjected to "sexual harassment that was severe or pervasive," and the company "failed to take prompt and effective remedial action reasonably calculated to end the harassment."[34] The value of Activision Blizzard's shares went down significantly in 2021 when the workplace culture allegations became public.[35] The current status of the Commission's investigation, including whether it will pursue charges against Activision Blizzard and its senior leaders for allegedly misleading investors about the company's workplace culture, is unknown, but the issuance of these subpoenas serves as a warning to companies that the Task Force may investigate potentially misleading statements or material omissions related to a company's workplace culture. Relatedly, there have been recent reports in the press regarding other companies under criminal investigation by federal authorities related to misrepresentations about their diversity program and their handling of whistleblower complaints related to gender and racial bias. As a result of these recent developments, it would be prudent for companies to incorporate workplace culture issues into their ESG compliance programs and for those programs to take a cross-functional approach to ensuring that workplace culture issues are properly addressed and disclosed.

IV. SEC Proposed Rule on Climate-Related Disclosures

Although the Task Force's expectations for ESG disclosures on some subjects will remain a gray area for the foreseeable future, the SEC has sought to provide clarity with respect to climate-related disclosures. On March 21, 2022, the SEC voted to approve a proposed 510-page rule to enhance and standardize climate-related disclosures for investors (the "Proposed Rule").[36] The Proposed Rule is the first time public companies in the United States (and foreign private issuers reporting in the United States) would be subject to such detailed disclosure requirements, though multinational companies face similar rules in Europe. Both the SEC's authority to issue a rule of this nature and scope as well as the detailed requirements of

---

[33] Press Release, Cal. Dep't of Fair Emp. & Hous., DFEH Sues California Gaming Companies for Equal Pay Violations, Sex Discrimination, and Sexual Harassment (July 21, 2021), https://calcivilrights.ca.gov/wp-content/uploads/sites/32/2021/07/BlizzardPR.7.21.21.pdf.

[34] Complaint, EEOC v. Activision Blizzard, Inc., No. 21 CV 7682 (C.D. Cal. Sept. 27, 2021).

[35] Samantha Subin, *Activision Blizzard Shares Drop After Report CEO Allegedly Knew About Sexual Misconduct*, CNBC (Nov. 16, 2021, 12:28 PM), https://www.cnbc.com/2021/11/16/activision-blizzard-shares-drop-after-reports-allege-sexual-misconduct.html; Nat Rubio-Licht, *Lawsuit Takes a Toll on Activision's Stock Price*, L.A. Bus. J. (Aug. 9, 2021), https://labusinessjournal.com/technology/activision-sexual-harassment-lawsuit-toll-stock/.

[36] Proposed Rule, *supra* note 13.

the proposal are controversial and likely to be litigated if adopted as proposed.[37] In light of recent Supreme Court decisions, including *West Virginia v. EPA*,[38] and the current makeup of the Court, the courts may prove to be an important battleground for opponents.

The primary elements of the Proposed Rule are (a) Corporate Governance, (b) Strategic Planning, (c) Risk Management, (d) Emissions Disclosures, and (e) Financial Statement Metrics. Specifically, the Proposed Rule adds a new subpart to Regulation S-K that would require a registrant to disclose in its registration statement and annual reports certain climate-related information, including climate-related risks that are reasonably likely to have a material impact on the registrant's business or consolidated financial statements. The Proposed Rule also adds a new article to Regulation S-X that would require a registrant to include certain climate-related financial statement metrics and related disclosure in a note to the registrant's audited financial statements.

The Proposed Rule exempts certain types of issuers, including, among others, issuers of asset-backed securities. The only small reporting company exemption is with respect to Scope 3 emissions disclosures, as discussed further below.

A. Corporate Governance

The SEC's Proposed Rule would require companies to disclose certain information regarding (1) the board's oversight of climate-related risks and (2) management's role in assessing and managing those risks. The Commission defines "climate-related risks" as the actual or potential negative impacts of climate-related events and conditions on a company's consolidated financial statements, business operations, or value chains, as a whole.

As proposed, companies may, but are not required to, discuss the board's and management's role in overseeing, assessing, and managing "climate-related opportunities." The SEC's Proposed Rule defines "climate-related opportunities" as the actual or potential positive impacts of climate-related conditions and events on a registrant's consolidated financial statements, business operations, or value chains.

With respect to the board's oversight, companies would be required to disclose, among other matters, any board members or board committee responsible for overseeing

[37] Attack on the Proposed Rule may take different forms. First, challengers may argue that the SEC lacks the authority to promulgate rules regarding climate disclosures, and thus is overstepping its statutory bounds. Second, those opposed to the rule may challenge the rule as arbitrary and capricious under the Administrative Procedure Act depending on the SEC's final explanation justifying the rule. Finally, opponents may argue that the rule violates the "major questions" doctrine, which is the theory that major policy decisions should be made by Congress, not singular agencies.

[38] *See* West Virginia v. EPA, 142 S. Ct. 2587 (2022). In *West Virginia v. EPA*, the U.S. Supreme Court addressed the Environmental and Protection Agency's (EPA's) authority to regulate greenhouse gas emissions under Section 111(d) of the Clean Air Act. Writing for the majority, Chief Justice Roberts relied on the major questions doctrine and concluded that it was "not plausible" Congress gave the EPA authority to adopt a regulatory scheme that would force a nationwide transition away from coal-generated electricity and that a "decision of such magnitude and consequence rests with Congress itself, or an agency acting pursuant to a clear delegation from that representative body." Following this decision, some have speculated the Supreme Court's reliance on the major questions doctrine could indicate a legal hurdle for other agencies with significant climate-related agenda items, such as the SEC and its proposal for mandatory climate-related disclosures.

climate-related risks. They also would be required to disclose the process and frequency by which the board or board committee discusses climate-related risks and the board's process in establishing and monitoring climate-related targets or goals.

With respect to management, companies would need to disclose whether certain management positions or committees are responsible for assessing and managing climate-related risks, as well as the processes by which the responsible individuals or committees are informed about and monitor climate-related risks (such as the use of third-party climate consultants). Additionally, they would be required to disclose whether and how frequently such individuals or committees report to the board about climate-related risks.

Key Takeaways

- Most, if not all, of the new requirements in the Proposed Rule can only be successfully complied with through an effective governance structure. Companies will need to evaluate their structures to identify any modifications necessary to comply with the SEC's new requirements and disclose the resulting modified structure.
- If not already done, companies should consider assigning responsibility to one or more board committees to define and assess the institution's climate-related risks, opportunities, strategies, and risk mitigation plans, as well as the institution's disclosures of such matters.
- Companies should define the management positions that will be responsible for climate risk management, climate data aggregation, and the new reporting requirement.
- Consideration should be given to the type and quality of climate-related data to be reported to the appropriate board committee, the management positions responsible for reporting such data, and the regularity with which the data is reported. Companies should be prepared to demonstrate that the board is receiving meaningful information required to effectively conduct its oversight responsibilities.

B. Strategic Planning

The SEC's Proposed Rule would require companies to disclose whether any climate-related risks are reasonably likely to have a material impact on the company, including on its business or consolidated financial statements, in the short, medium, and long term. The Commission considers a matter material "if there is a substantial likelihood that a reasonable investor would consider it important when determining whether to buy or sell securities or how to vote."[39] Moreover, with respect to potential future events, the materiality determination requires an evaluation of the likelihood that an event will occur and its potential magnitude or significance to the company. Consistent with the Task Force on Climate-related Financial Disclosures (TCFD), these climate-related risks include both physical and transition risks and encompass a company's business operations and value chain as a whole, including upstream

[39] Proposed Rule, *supra* note 13, at 21351.

and downstream activities related to the company's operations. Upstream activities include activities by a party other than the company that relate to the initial stages of a company's production of a good or service, such as materials sourcing and processing and supplier activities. Downstream activities include activities by a party other than the company that relate to processing materials into a finished product and delivering it or providing a service to the end user. Such activities could include transportation and distribution of the finished product, customer use of sold products or services, and investments. Companies would be required to differentiate between physical[40] and transition[41] risks and describe whether the risk is acute or chronic. In addition, for physical risks, companies would be required to identify the physical location(s) of the assets subject to the risk. Finally, companies may, but are not required to, disclose climate-related opportunities, such as any cost savings associated with reduced energy usage or greater demand for a company's services as a result of climate policy influencing market behavior.

If a company has identified any such climate-related risks, the company also must disclose the actual and potential impacts those risks have on its strategy, business model, and outlook. This includes, among other disclosures, effects on the company's operations, products or services, and suppliers or other parties in its value chain. Similar to the required disclosures regarding whether any such material climate-related risks exist, companies also would be required to disclose the time horizon for each disclosed impact, as well as the unit of measurement and any interim targets set by the company, among other items.

In the event a company uses carbon offsets or renewable energy credits or certificates (RECs) as part of its net emissions reduction strategy, the Proposed Rule would require disclosure of the role that carbon offsets or RECs play in the company's climate-related business strategy. In addition, a company must disclose, if used, its internal carbon price(s) and the rationale for selecting the carbon price used, as well as any climate-related targets or goals (e.g., net-zero goals) and information regarding how the company intends to achieve those goals.

The Proposed Rule would require a company to disclose any analytical tools it uses to assess the impact of climate-related risks on the company's business and financial statements or to support the resilience of the company's business model in light of foreseeable climate-related risks. One such tool is scenario analysis, a process for analyzing possible outcomes of future events under conditions of uncertainty.

---

40 "Physical risks" are both acute risks and chronic risks to the registrant's business operations or the operations of those with whom it does business. Acute risks are event-driven and may relate to shorter-term extreme weather events, such as hurricanes, floods, and tornadoes. Chronic risks relate to longer-term weather patterns and related effects, such as sea-level rise, drought, increased wildfires, decreased arability of farmland, and decreased availability of fresh water.

41 "Transition risks" are the *actual or potential* negative impacts attributable to *regulatory, technological, and market* changes to address the mitigation of, or adaptation to, climate-related risks, such as increased costs attributable to changes in law or policy, reduced market demand for carbon-intensive products, the devaluation or abandonment of assets, risk of legal liability and litigation defense costs, competitive pressures associated with the adoption of new technologies, and reputational impacts that might trigger changes to market behavior, consumer preferences or behavior, and registrant behavior.

Key Takeaways

- Companies will need to become educated in the various tools used by energy and manufacturing companies in assessing the impact of climate-related risk and proactively work with regulators to determine the tools that are most appropriate for their industry.
- Board committees and senior management should focus on internal diligence to obtain a good understanding of the company's climate-related risks and the internal resources needed to understand, measure, and manage those risks.
- Add climate to the company's overall strategic planning process or determine why this would not be appropriate for the company.
- Consider initial use of outside consultants to assist with the strategic planning process.

C. Risk Management

The SEC's Proposed Rule would require companies to make certain risk management disclosures, including (1) disclosure of any processes the company utilizes for identifying, assessing, and managing climate-related risks and (2) certain disclosures if the company has adopted a transition plan. With respect to risk management processes, this includes consideration of existing or likely regulatory changes, how the company determines the relative significance of climate-related risks compared to other risks, how the company evaluates materiality, and how the company determines whether to mitigate, accept, or adapt to a particular risk. As proposed, a "transition plan" means a company's strategy and implementation plan to reduce climate-related risks. The Proposed Rule would require companies which have adopted transition plans to describe the plan, including relevant metrics and targets used to identify and manage physical and transition risks, among other requirements. The SEC's Proposed Rule states that since transition planning "inherently requires judgments and predictions about the future," companies may be eligible to rely on the Private Securities Litigation Reform Act forward-looking statement safe harbors for forward-looking statements in discussion of its transition plan, provided that all other statutory requirements for the safe harbor are met.[42]

Key Takeaways

- Disclosure committees and audit committees of public companies should include ESG-related disclosure as an agenda item for discussion when developing, evaluating, and finalizing earnings releases, periodic reports, proxy statements, and other public disclosures. In particular, companies should recognize that the SEC is closely scrutinizing the use of generalities and should resist the temptation of "gilding the lily." ESG-related disclosures should have the same factual support as would be expected of all other public company disclosures.

[42] Proposed Rule, *supra* note 13, at 21362.

- Consider conducting a risk assessment review of ESG policies, procedures, and internal controls. In particular, consider developing or reviewing current policies and procedures related to ESG investing and testing internal ESG-related controls for adequacy and proper functioning. Ensure that compliance programs are reasonably designed to capture inaccurate ESG-related disclosures or marketing materials.

D. Emissions Disclosures

The SEC's proposed emissions disclosure requirement is primarily based on Greenhouse Gas Protocol (GHG Protocol) concepts. The Proposed Rule would require companies to disclose Scope 1 and 2 emissions. Scope 1 emissions are direct GHG emissions from operations owned/controlled by the company, and Scope 2 emissions are indirect emissions from generation of purchased/acquired electricity used by the company's owned/controlled operations. Of note, Scope 1 and 2 emissions disclosures are not tethered to a materiality requirement, unlike Scope 3, discussed below. Disclosure of total Scope 1 emissions must be separate from total Scope 2 emissions, and all scopes of emissions must be disaggregated as between constituent GHGs. The Proposed Rule would require reporting of emissions in *gross* terms, excluding any offsets purchased. The SEC has stated that disclosures of Scope 1 and Scope 2 emissions are important to investment-making decisions, easily qualified and compared across industries, and helpful in evaluating transition risks.

The SEC's Proposed Rule includes a disclosure requirement for Scope 3 emissions if material or if the company has set an emissions reduction target that includes these emissions. Consistent with the GHG Protocol, the Proposed Rule defines Scope 3 emissions as indirect GHG emissions that occur in upstream and downstream activities in a company's value chain that are not Scope 2 emissions. For financial institutions, the GHG Protocol defines Scope 3 emissions, or "financed emissions," to include the GHG emissions from which they lend to or invest in.[43] The Commission notes that emissions disclosures would likely include the emissions from companies to which the registrant provides debt or equity financing, thus including disclosures regarding all the corporate borrowers of a bank.

The Commission notes that a registrant's assessment of the materiality of Scope 3 emissions should include consideration of whether those emissions make up a large portion of its overall GHG impact. The SEC's Proposed Rule does not require a specific quantitative threshold, but the SEC notes that some companies use 40 percent as a benchmark for determining whether Scope 3 emissions are material.[44] As previously noted, smaller reporting companies are exempt from the Scope 3 disclosure requirements under the SEC's Proposed Rule. The Proposed Rule includes a safe harbor for Scope 3 emissions disclosures (e.g., Scope 3 emissions disclosures will not be deemed fraudulent statements unless made without a reasonable basis or in bad faith).[45]

---

[43] *Id.* at 21387.

[44] *Id.* at 21379.

[45] *Id.* at 21390–91.

For Scope 1 and 2 emissions, a company also would be required to include an attestation report and disclose information regarding the attestation service provider.[46] The Proposed Rule does not require attestation and assurances for Scope 3 emissions to the extent those must be disclosed. In years two and three after the Scope 1 and 2 emissions requirement takes effect, filers must provide limited assurance (e.g., equivalent to the review of a registrant's interim financial statements), and in years four and beyond, reasonable assurance (e.g., the audit rigor applied to a registrant's 10-K). The Proposed Rule would specify minimum attestation report requirements, minimum standards for acceptable attestation frameworks, and would require an attestation service provider to meet certain minimum qualifications. Requirements for the attestation provider include that it is "an expert in GHG emissions by virtue of having significant experience in measuring, analyzing, reporting, or attesting to GHG emissions" and independent of the registrant.[47]

Key Takeaways

- Disclosure of Scope 3 emissions will mean different things for different industries. Companies should stay apprised of disclosure trends and regularly assess what other companies in their industry are disclosing.
- Companies should carefully evaluate their upstream and downstream value chain activities and the third parties that may be implicated by the Scope 3 definition.
- Companies should identify potential data sources in their respective industries and value chains, and begin gathering and gaining an understanding of available data.
- Companies should start evaluating firms that could provide an attestation and the support required therefor.

E. Financial Statement Metrics

The SEC's Proposed Rule would require companies to disclose climate-related financial statement metrics that are mainly derived from existing financial statement line items. The three categories of information comprising this disclosure are (1) financial impact metrics, (2) expenditure metrics, and (3) financial estimates and assumptions.[48] In each case, registrants would calculate the proposed metrics using financial information consistent with the scope and applying the same accounting principles otherwise required in the preparation of the consolidated financial statements. Because the proposed financial statement metrics would be in the financial statements, they would be included in the scope of and subject to any required audit of the financial statements by an independent registered public accounting firm and within the purview of the registrant's internal control over financial reporting.

The SEC's proposed financial impact metrics include disaggregated information about the impact of (1) climate-related conditions and events and (2) transition activities, in each

---

[46] *Id.* at 21346.

[47] *Id.* at 21398.

[48] *Id.* at 21363.

case on any relevant line item in the financial statements.[49] As proposed, a registrant would be required to disclose the impact of climate-related events or transition activities on each line item of its financial statements unless the aggregate impact of such events is less than 1 percent of the total line item for the relevant fiscal year, determined by aggregating the *absolute value* of the positive and negative impacts on a line-by-line basis. Within each category (i.e., climate-related events or transition activities), impacts would be disclosed on an aggregated, line-by-line basis for all negative and positive impacts (separately).[50]

The proposed expenditure metrics refer to the aggregate amounts of expenditures expensed and capitalized costs incurred to (1) mitigate the risks from severe weather and other natural conditions and (2) reduce GHG emissions or otherwise mitigate exposure to transition risks.

Finally, registrants would be required to disclose whether any estimates and assumptions used to produce the financial statements were impacted by exposures to risks and uncertainties associated with, or known impacts from, climate-related events and transition risks (separately). If so, the company must provide a qualitative description of how, particularly where impacted by a potential transition to a lower carbon economy or any climate-related targets it has disclosed.[51] Companies would calculate the proposed metrics using financial information consistent with the scope, and applying the same accounting principles otherwise required in the preparation, of the consolidated financial statements. Financial statement metrics would be included in the scope of and subject to any required audit of the financial statements by an independent registered public accounting firm and within the purview of the registrant's internal control over financial reporting.

Key Takeaways

- Prepare to identify the appropriate sources of climate-related financial information in a manner subject to customary internal controls, especially where those quantitative figures intersect with the valuation of financial instruments.
- Evaluate the internal control framework and adjust as necessary to include appropriate processes and controls that will govern the collection, aggregation, and disclosure of the new metrics required by the new rule.

Additional Key Takeaways

- Client education is essential. Companies' boards, management, and compliance personnel must be knowledgeable about the company's ESG and climate-related practices, in addition to staying on top of key regulatory developments.
- Data evaluation, aggregation, and valuation is imperative.

[49] *Id.* at 21365.

[50] *Id.* at 21366.

[51] *Id.* at 21371–02.

- Start with governance—the key to effective regulatory compliance is a robust governance foundation. Establish a strong corporate governance framework to evaluate ESG factors throughout your organization. Attention should focus not only on identification of ESG risks but on the evaluation, monitoring, and strategic planning with respect to these risks and the escalation to the appropriate committees and/or the board.
- Evaluate talent, both at the company and in the market. The legal industry ultimately manages disclosure in addition to managing the risk along with risk professionals. Companies should leverage the expertise of outside counsel, as effective climate governance and regulatory compliance require a coordinated effort.
- Do not wait for the final regulations to assess your disclosure framework on climate risk. The SEC has clearly stated that the staff of the Division of Corporate Finance has current expectations on periodic reports, and the Enforcement Division is currently active.

24

Spotting and Navigating Antitrust Risk

Karen Rigberg, Francesca Pisano, and Tim Roche

I. Introduction

Companies throughout the world are ramping up their ESG efforts. And although these meaningful and important initiatives can cover a wide range of subject matter areas, from diversity to sustainability to worker rights, they often involve the following business activities, among others, which can raise potential antitrust risk:

- Information gathering and benchmarking
- Standard setting
- Working with trade associations and industry workgroups
- Lobbying and joint legislative actions
- Working with or influencing suppliers, vendors, customers
- Supply chain management
- Regional or local collaborations
- Joint ventures and strategic alliances
- Human Resource initiatives
- Licensing

These types of activities can potentially present significant antitrust risk, possibly resulting in criminal prosecution and civil liability for companies and their individual employees—even if the underlying purpose of the ESG activity is to "do good." Makan Delrahim, former Assistant Attorney General for the U.S. Department of Justice (DOJ) Antitrust Division, stated in 2019 that "[e]ven laudable ends do not justify collusive means in our chosen system" of antitrust law.[1] The current antitrust enforcers at DOJ and the Federal Trade Commission (FTC), Jonathan Kanter and Lina Khan, respectively, reinforced this view at a September 2022 Senate hearing, with Khan noting that "[the FTC has] seen firms come to us and try to claim an ESG exemption, and we've had to come to them and explain clearly that there is no such thing."[2] ESG efforts to impact competitor, supplier, vendor, or customer conduct are likely to involve "agreements" that may "restrain trade" within the scope of Section 1 of the Sherman Act—the question will be whether those agreements *unreasonably* restrain trade by leading to higher prices, reduced choice or quality, or other losses of concern to the antitrust laws.

Potential antitrust risks are only heightened by increasing state and federal political scrutiny of ESG activities. For example, in March 2022, the Arizona Attorney General announced an investigation into potential antitrust violations associated with a multi-entity pledge to achieve certain climate-related goals.[3] In August 2022, an open letter from several state Attorneys General warned that certain ESG commitments might constitute an antitrust violation.[4] And in November 2022, several U.S. senators warned a number of law firms in open letters that "[o]ver the coming months and years, Congress will increasingly use its oversight powers to scrutinize the institutionalized antitrust violations being committed in the name of ESG, and refer those violations to the FTC and the Department of Justice."[5]

The good news is that antitrust laws do not have to stand in the way of most corporate ESG initiatives. Instead, with careful planning and implementation, most ESG initiatives can be structured in a legal, safe, and procompetitive manner. This chapter provides practitioners with a step-by-step framework to help them identify and manage some common antitrust risks associated with ESG initiatives.[6]

A. Why This Matters

Free market competition is the cornerstone of the U.S. economy, and the antitrust laws focus on protecting and ensuring that competition. These laws collectively restrict business activities which may impede competition and, in turn, our free market economy.

---

[1] Makan Delrahim, *DOJ Antitrust Division: Popular Ends Should Not Justify Anti-competitive Collusion*, USA TODAY (Sept. 12, 2019, 7:31 PM), https://www.usatoday.com/story/opinion/2019/09/12/doj-antitrust-division-popular-ends-dont-justify-collusion-editorials-debates/2306078001/.

[2] *Oversight of Federal Enforcement of the Antitrust Laws: Hearing Before the Subcomm. on Competition Policy, Antitrust, and Consumer Rights of the S. Comm. on the Judiciary*, 117th Cong. (2022) (statements of Jonathan Kanter, Assistant Att'y Gen. for the Antitrust Div., U.S. Department of Justice [DOJ] & Lina Khan, Chair, FTC), https://www.judiciary.senate.gov/meetings/oversight-of-federal-enforcement-of-the-antitrust-laws.

[3] Mark Brnovich, *ESG May Be an Antitrust Violation: I'm Investigating a Coordinated Effort to Allocate Markets*, WALL ST. J. (Mar. 6, 2022, 4:40 PM), https://www.wsj.com/articles/esg-may-be-an-antitrust-violation-climate-activism-energy-prices-401k-retirement-investment-political-agenda-coordinated-influence-11646594807.

[4] Letter from Mark Brnovich, Ariz. Att'y Gen., et al., to Laurence D. Fink, Chief Exec. Officer, BlackRock Inc. (Aug. 4, 2022), https://www.azag.gov/sites/default/files/2022-08/BlackRock%20Letter.pdf. A response from other Attorneys General suggested that public statements in support of ESG goals without any actual agreement on concrete steps would not raise antitrust concerns. Letter from Karl A. Racine, D.C. Att'y Gen. & Rob Bonta, Cal. Att'y Gen., to Sen. Sherrod Brown, Chairman, Comm. on Banking, Hous. & Urb. Affs., et al. (Nov. 21, 2022), https://oag.dc.gov/sites/default/files/2022-11/ESG%20Letter_Final_11.18.22.pdf.

[5] Letter from Tom Cotton, U.S. Sen., et al., to Kenneth J. Markowitz, Akin Gump Strauss Hauer & Feld (Nov. 3, 2022), https://www.cotton.senate.gov/imo/media/doc/esg_letter.pdf.

[6] This chapter is intended to be a reference tool for attorneys and others who have little to no antitrust expertise. Where applicable, please consult additional legal resources or consult antitrust counsel to learn more.

In the United States, there are both state and federal antitrust laws, each complex in their interpretation and application. This chapter primarily applies the Sherman Act to ESG initiatives.[7] The Sherman Act prohibits agreements that unreasonably limit competition (e.g., price fixing) and monopolization, and attempts and conspiracies to monopolize. Sherman Act violations can, and do, result in significant penalties for both companies and individuals. The DOJ can prosecute Sherman Act violations as felonies, and companies can be fined up to $100 million per violation or an amount equal to twice the company's gain or twice the consumers' loss, if greater.[8] Individuals, including company employees, can be fined up to $1 million per violation and sentenced to up to 10 years in prison. And the threat of individual prosecutions is real: according to Attorney General Merrick Garland, the DOJ's "first priority in corporate criminal cases" is "to prosecute the individuals who commit and profit from corporate malfeasance."[9]

In addition to potential exposure to criminal penalties, antitrust violations can result in costly litigation, including class actions, brought by private plaintiffs. These lawsuits sometimes result in significant dollar settlements or verdicts.[10]

1. *The Important Difference between Unilateral and Concerted Conduct*

The antitrust laws are complex in their interpretation and application. However, there are a few big-picture concepts that can be applied to the facts of a situation to help identify the need for additional antitrust guidance.

One key question in assessing antitrust risk is whether a company is acting independently or with others. And, if acting with others, who are they? See Figure 1 for an example of this distinction.

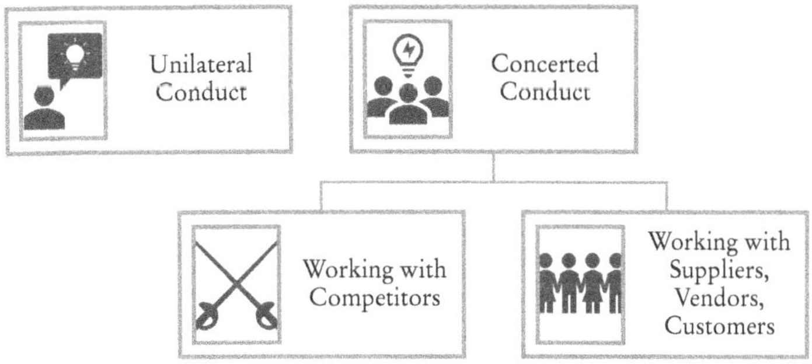

Figure 1

[7] 15 U.S.C. §§ 1, 2.

[8] To date, the largest such criminal fine imposed on a company is $925 million. *Sherman Act Violations Resulting in Criminal Fines & Penalties of $10 Million or More*, DOJ, https://www.justice.gov/atr/sherman-act-violations-yielding-corporate-fine-10-million-or-more (Feb. 3, 2022).

[9] Merrick B. Garland, Att'y Gen., DOJ, Remarks at the ABA Institute on White Collar Crime (Mar. 3, 2022), https://www.justice.gov/opa/speech/attorney-general-merrick-b-garland-delivers-remarks-aba-institute-white-collar-crime.

[10] Anna Wilde Mathews, *Judge Approves Blue Cross's $2.67 Billion Antitrust Settlement: Health Insurers Agree to Make Payments and Change Certain Practices Alleged to Limit Competition*, Wall St. J. (Aug. 9, 2022, 4:15 PM), https://www.wsj.com/articles/judge-approves-blue-crosss-2-67-billion-antitrust-settlement-11660075648.

A company's unilateral and independent conduct should present little to no antitrust risk unless it involves monopolization or attempted monopolization by using exclusionary conduct to foreclose competitors, which is discussed in further detail below.

2. *Two Types of Collaborations and the Importance of Understanding the Difference*

In general, the most common and significant antitrust risks arise when a company is collaborating with other organizations. As depicted in Figure 1, antitrust relationships and collaborations fall into two categories. In antitrust parlance, these two relationships are either "horizontal" or "vertical."

Figure 2 shows the difference between these two types of business relationships. Horizontal dealings involve competitors, including those in which companies directly compete for the sale or purchase of the same, or similar, products and services. Conversely, vertical dealings involve companies which do not compete, such as those at different levels of a supply chain (e.g., a buyer–seller relationship). Companies may stand in both a horizontal and vertical relationship with certain entities, such as when a firm sells through distributors (a vertical relationship) but also competes with those distributors (a horizontal relationship). This situation, called "dual distribution," is treated as a vertical relationship notwithstanding the horizontal element. Importantly, two companies may be competitors in some circumstances or areas, but customers/suppliers in others.

Notably, understanding whether two companies compete is not always as clear as Figure 2 may suggest. Companies compete in many different ways. For example:

- Companies selling different goods or services may be competitors for raw materials.
- Companies in different industries may be competitors for television advertising slots.
- Companies with seemingly nothing in common may be competitors for employees.

The distinction between horizontal and vertical relationships is crucial, as the antitrust laws place greater scrutiny on horizontal relationships than vertical ones.

Under the antitrust laws, certain horizontal agreements that coordinate or restrict competition are always, or "per se," illegal, which means that the conduct will be an antitrust violation even if the parties have low market share, legitimate business justifications for the agreement, or broader societal motivations, such as ESG.

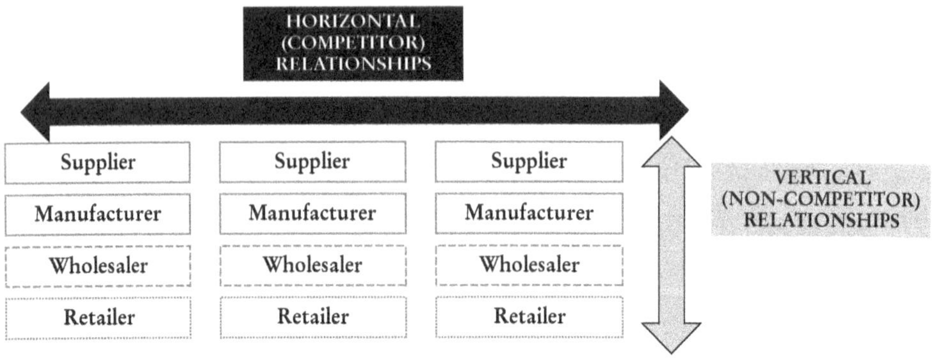

Figure 2

In the context of ESG, here are hypothetical examples of the most well-known "per se" competitor antitrust violations:

- **Price Fixing:** "Let's agree to charge at least $X for this product type to support minimum-wage efforts upstream."
- **Market Division or Customer Allocation:** "If you sell your 'carbon neutral' product to this set of customers, I'll sell mine to this different set of customers. That way we can support further carbon-neutral research and development."
- **Group Boycotts:** "Let's agree to not do business with X company, a known polluter."
- **Bid Rigging:** "If you agree not to bid on this request for proposal, we won't bid on the next one. That way we can each have a chance to win a big 'green' project."
- **No Poach:** "We will all be investing our resources in executive-level diversity training, so let's agree not to hire each other's people."

Looking at the big picture, competitors should not coordinate their commercial activities with competitors. The list of activities that might give rise to serious violations is broad, including current/future wholesale or retail prices, bidding opportunities, costs, capacity, terminating third-party relationships, research and development plans, freight or shipping costs, terms and conditions of sale, or employee hiring, compensation, or benefits.

In contrast, vertical agreements, which do not involve competitors, are analyzed under the more deferential "rule of reason," in which market share and business justifications (which might include ESG) are each considered when assessing the legality of an agreement, and conduct will not be condemned unless it leads to actual anti-competitive effects. For example, while it is very risky when competitors allocate sales territories among themselves, it is relatively less risky for a manufacturer to assign exclusive territories to resellers in its distribution network.

II. A Checklist for Assessing and Managing ESG Antitrust Risk

This section outlines a step-by-step process to help identify and manage the most common ESG antitrust risks, framed by three big-picture action items:

☑ **Action Item No. 1**

Define and continuously reinforce the stated goal of the proposed ESG initiative.

☑ **Action Item No. 2**

Anticipate the potential antitrust risks associated with different implementation activities.

☑ **Action Item No. 3**

Exercise care in monitoring and measuring ESG performance.

A. Action Item No. 1: Define and Continuously Reinforce the Stated Goal of the Proposed ESG Initiative

While defining the goal of an initiative may seem intuitive, it is one of the most important steps from an antitrust perspective and is often overlooked. Defining the stated goal will help assess antitrust risk, and should continuously frame and fence in the scope and implementation of the ESG initiative going forward.

1. *Evaluate the Antitrust Risk of the Stated Goal(s)*

Understanding at the outset whether the purpose of an ESG initiative presents potential antitrust risk will not only reduce the legal risk but can also help set expectations and save time, money, and resources later on. The last thing anyone wants is to rework a project midstream because of previously unidentified legal risk.

As a rule of thumb, if the proposed goal of an ESG initiative includes aligning any commercial business practices with another company—especially in the areas highlighted in the above section (including price, promotions, capacity, etc.)—this can present relatively more antitrust risk as compared to one company acting independently. For example:

Less Antitrust Risk	More Antitrust Risk
We will take this independent action . . ." • "We want to improve our corporate recycling program." • "We want our company to invest more in green technologies." • "We want our company to do more business with minority-owned suppliers." • "We want to set internal standards for who we hire."	*"We want others to change their business practices too . . ."* • "We want our industry to improve its collective recycling efforts." • "We want our suppliers to invest more in green technologies." • "We want the businesses in our city to do more business with minority-owned suppliers." • "We want our profession to set standards for who we each hire."

2. *Ensure That the Stated Goal Continuously Frames the Initiative*

Once the goal is defined and assessed for antitrust risk, it should frame the scope of all communications, discussions, and activities going forward. Otherwise, the activity can inadvertently veer into problematic areas. Here are two ways to help keep the project on track:

- **Instruct project participants on what is, and is not, the overall goal of the ESG initiative:** Many business people do not find the antitrust laws to be particularly intuitive and can quickly and inadvertently blur the lines between allowable and prohibited activities. Preparing a written mission statement or charter is helpful. Clear guidance distributed via email, intranet, and e-Training can also help ensure that all participants are on the same page.

- **Teach project participants to accurately represent the initiative and stay within its scope for the duration of the project:** Antitrust risk can be heightened where participants use shorthand or overly dramatic phrasing to characterize their activities. For example, if a company is considering ESG activities aimed at increasing transparency in a supply chain, the company's external and internal documents should reflect this overall goal. Internal company discussions that misstate this goal could subject the company to increased antitrust risk. For example, "Let's make sure no one does business with 'x' company" could appear to implicate problematic collective action to harm a disfavored supplier, increasing the overall risk that an ESG activity might be subject to antitrust challenge.

Depending on the duration of the project, participation may be a revolving door. If so, the initial team should prepare a plan for how future participants will be trained on the project scope and the antitrust risks of swerving outside of the guardrails.

B. Action Item No. 2: Anticipate the Potential Antitrust Risks Associated with Project Implementation

Once the ESG initiative has a clear purpose that falls within the desired antitrust guardrails, it is time to get to work. Below, we will discuss a few common types of ESG activities and their potential antitrust risks.

1. *Benchmarking and Information Exchanges*

Many ESG activities contemplate exchanging information or benchmarking with other industry participants, including to promote transparency and equity, gather "best practices" about how ESG initiatives are being implemented elsewhere, or identify "bad actors" in a supply chain.

However, sharing or receiving competitively sensitive information (e.g., prices, costs, plans, customers, hiring, compensation) with other companies can present antitrust risk because it can lead to illegal competitor coordination, the *appearance* of illegal coordination, or because access to competitively sensitive information allows firms to pull their competitive punches. So even if a company makes unilateral and independent business decisions about its own buying, pricing, hiring, or product launches, sharing related information with competitors can make even independent actions appear to be coordinated, or can be alleged to be unlawful where the agreement to exchange information itself causes harm to competition. Two ways to help manage the antitrust risks associated with information sharing include (1) assessing what type of information is being sought and (2) using lower-risk ways of obtaining that information.

- **Assess whether the information sought is competitively sensitive information:** Competitively sensitive information, or "CSI," is a subset of information which, if known by a competitor, would increase that competitor's ability to monitor or anticipate the other's business activities.

Typically CSI	Typically Not CSI
• Production/target volumes, capacity, inventories • Sales, sales plans, allocation, marketing, customers • Costs, prices, price changes, price formulas, differentials, markups, discounts, credit terms • Sales to, purchases from, or negotiations with suppliers such as bids, offers, contract terms, etc. • New product launches, capacity additions or closures, or changes in customers or territories • Current or future product specifications or costs • Purchasing information, including part purchasing prices, supplier information, sourcing studies, terms and conditions • Hiring, compensation, wages, and benefits practices and information • Expected reactions to market events or new government policies or regulations	• Business processes and key performance indicators • Quality standards and processes • Standardized workflows • Check sheets and evaluation forms used to document critical processes • Equipment manuals • Industry trends and best practices • Other high-level structures, checklists, and processes • Internal standards on how to place and train people • Inspection methods and best practices • Organizational charts

Obtaining information directly from competitors presents potentially significant risk and should be carefully vetted by experienced antitrust counsel to ensure that any information exchanged cannot be characterized as CSI because sharing or receiving competitor CSI can increase antitrust risk and can be prosecuted as an antitrust violation.[11]

- **Encourage the use of low-risk sources and methods to obtain competitor competitively sensitive information:** There are ways to obtain and share CSI that can mitigate antitrust risk. As a threshold matter, public materials (websites, analyst reports, press releases) and industry reports (from established sources who are using recommended best practices, below) are generally safe to use because information in those reports is generally not considered competitively sensitive if publicly available. If the information must be obtained from a competitor, the following best practices may reduce risk:
  - The exchange is managed by a third party, such as a vendor or trade association.
  - The information provided by participants is more than three months old (do not exchange current or prospective CSI).
  - The shared statistics are sufficiently aggregated that no participant can discern the data of any other participant (e.g., at least five participants provide the data for each statistic, and no single provider's data contributes more than 25 percent of the "weight" of any statistic shared).
  - The information is not obtained through dishonest actions or through actions that would violate confidentiality or other company policies or similar policies of the source of the information.

[11] Press Release, DOJ, Justice Department Requires Six Broadcast Television Companies to Terminate and Refrain from Unlawful Sharing of Competitively Sensitive Information (Nov. 13, 2018), https://www.justice.gov/opa/pr/justice-department-requires-six-broadcast-television-companies-terminate-and-refrain-unlawful.

- Internal documents are clearly labeled with the sources of any competitive information to reduce the likelihood of later confusion or ambiguity.
- Participation in information sharing is voluntary and not forced.
- The information shared is limited to only those types of data that are reasonably necessary—and narrowly targeted—at achieving the ESG goal.
- Participants receiving data each agree to abide by antitrust guidelines, not disseminate the data beyond colleagues who "need to know," and use the data only for the intended ESG purpose.

Importantly, given the increased focus by U.S. enforcers, there are significant risks to *any* exchange or benchmarking of competitor information, including that which is aggregated and anonymized or relates to employee compensation and benefits, regardless of the age of the information or the number of participants.[12] Firms should never communicate directly on these issues with competing employers, and experienced antitrust counsel should advise companies regarding the risks of participating in any wage or benefit benchmarking exercise conducted by a third party.

2. *Collaborating with Industry Competitors, Workgroups, or Trade Associations*

Many of the most impactful and wide-reaching ESG initiatives implicate companies in a particular industry, necessarily involving multiple competitors. However, these sorts of collaborations among competitors—including pledges, industry working groups, and trade association activities—can raise the most significant antitrust risk because they involve joint decisions made by competitors. Understanding how to manage the antitrust risks of competitor collaborations can directly affect the viability of any ESG initiative. Here are some ways to help minimize the antitrust risks of competitor collaborations:

- **Help participants understand what they can and cannot coordinate with competitors:** As outlined in Section I.A.2 above, competitors cannot coordinate their competitive business activities in certain areas. However, the antitrust laws recognize that competitor collaborations and joint ventures can be pro-competitive if they enable participants to offer goods or services that are cheaper, more valuable to consumers, or brought to market faster than would be possible absent the collaboration.[13] If an ESG collaboration implicates potential agreements among competing companies on price,

[12] *See, e.g.*, Doha Mekki, Principal Deputy Assistant Att'y Gen., Antitrust Div., DOJ, Remarks at GCR Live: Law Leaders Global 2023 (Feb. 2, 2023), https://www.justice.gov/opa/speech/principal-deputy-assistant-attorney-general-doha-mekki-antitrust-division-delivers-0; Press Release, DOJ, Justice Department Withdraws Outdated Enforcement Policy Statements (Feb. 3, 2023), https://www.justice.gov/opa/pr/justice-department-withdraws-outdated-enforcement-policy-statements; Press Release, Federal Trade Commission (FTC), Federal Trade Commission Withdraws Health Care Enforcement Policy Statements (July 14, 2023), https://www.ftc.gov/news-events/news/press-releases/2023/07/federal-trade-commission-withdraws-health-care-enforcement-policy-statements.

[13] FTC & DOJ, Antitrust Guidelines for Collaborations Among Competitors 27 (2000), https://www.ftc.gov/sites/default/files/documents/public_events/joint-venture-hearings-antitrust-guidelines-collaboration-among-competitors/ftcdojguidelines-2.pdf.

features, or innovation, antitrust counsel should be consulted early to help provide training and guardrails, as needed.[14]

To help manage the antitrust risks associated with any collaboration, participants should be regularly instructed and trained on the parameters and guardrails of a particular ESG project, including the following:

- Each participant's business decisions must be made unilaterally and independently.
- Any collaboration should not reduce competition between the participants.
- Participants should implement protocols to limit the sharing of competitively sensitive information.

Less Antitrust Risk	More Antitrust Risk
• Each competitor in the collaboration still makes its own independent commercial/business decisions.	• All companies in the collaboration decide on a course of action (such as commercializing a new product developed by the joint venture or not commercializing alternative products) jointly. • Companies agree to maintain "discipline" in marketing a new "second generation" product. • Companies agree to "stand down" on a "third generation" product so as not to cannibalize sales.

- **Establish collaboration ground rules early:** It is important to remember that not all industry participants will receive antitrust training or understand antitrust risk. So, at the outset of any competitor collaboration, the participants should set it up for success by developing a set of joint antitrust guidelines. These guidelines should, at a minimum, include the following sections:
    - The purpose and scope of the collaboration.
    - A statement of intent to comply with the antitrust laws.
    - A list of collaboration activities that fall within the scope.
    - A list of collaboration activities that fall outside of the scope (e.g., particularly risky agreements among competitors).
    - Information-sharing protocols to minimize antitrust risk.
    - Meeting protocols to ensure participants stay within antitrust guardrails, including the use of agendas, minutes, legal reviews, and attorney attendance.

Preparing and sharing this document *prior* to the start of the ESG collaboration will help ensure that all participants proceed with the same level of antitrust awareness from day one. Otherwise, well-trained company representatives can quickly find themselves amidst industry

[14] Press Release, Eur. Comm'n, Antitrust: Commission Fines Car Manufacturers €875.2 Million for Restricting Competition in Emission Cleaning for New Diesel Passenger Cars (July 8, 2021), https://ec.europa.eu/commission/presscorner/detail/en/ip_21_3581. For example, in mid-2021, the European Commission (EC) alleged that car manufacturers colluded on emission-reducing technological developments. Specifically, the EC alleged that the manufacturers agreed among themselves to avoid competition on the implementation of better emission cleaning standards. Although the car manufacturers defended the agreement on the grounds that it made it easier for the industry to develop and embrace new technology, they collectively paid the EC €875.2 million in fines. *Id.*

participants who are uninformed and are unknowingly "running with scissors," potentially introducing significant antitrust risk into the collaboration.

- **Leverage existing, well-run industry groups:** Sometimes an industry collaboration, including one involving ESG initiatives, will leverage the presence of an existing industry workgroup, roundtable, or trade association to manage or facilitate the collaboration. Working with groups that are broad-based and include multiple diverse stakeholders, such as suppliers, customers, and competitors, is generally preferable because competitor decision-making is diluted. But if such groups are not a feasible option, then operating through a well-managed trade association can be a potential pathway for competitors to develop industry-wide ESG initiatives. And while trade associations are not a "rubber stamp" for otherwise anti-competitive activity, trade associations can be used to help mitigate risk associated with other activities, such as benchmarking, as described in Section II.B.1. In doing so, however, it is important to remember that even working within trade associations or other existing groups, even if well-established, can present the same antitrust risks as any other competitor collaboration.

  When evaluating whether an existing industry association is well-managed, look for the following:
  - **Written antitrust policies and procedures that are continuously monitored and enforced.** Failure to have such safeguards should be seen as a red flag that the group does not understand the potential antitrust risks.
  - **Rules, codes of ethics, and bylaws that expressly allow members to compete with each other.** Trade association members must always remain free to compete against one another in all aspects of their business. Even if the association has antitrust policies in place, sometimes trade associations and other industry workgroups enact other rules which constitute an impermissible restraint on competition.[15]
  - **Fair and non-exclusionary membership criteria.** If a trade association has membership requirements or rules, these should be fairly drafted, based on objective standards, and uniformly applied. All industry participants, even one with a reputation as a "bad actor," should be allowed to apply for membership and given an opportunity to meet any required objective criteria. It would be much riskier to exclude such companies in an *ad hoc* manner, or prohibit certain organizations from applying for membership at all, which might open up the association and its members to an antitrust claim of boycott or exclusionary conduct.
- **Conduct competitor meetings with care:** A gathering of executives from different competitors can raise antitrust red flags regardless of whether the executives are discussing commercial or ESG initiatives. Company employees planning to attend an

---

[15] *See, e.g.*, Agreement Containing Consent Order, Music Teachers Nat'l Ass'n, Inc., FTC Docket No. 131-0118 (Oct. 25, 2013), https://www.ftc.gov/sites/default/files/documents/cases/121216musicteachersagree.pdf (consent decree in which the Music Teachers National Association, Inc., agreed to stop restricting or declaring it unethical for its members to solicit students from other music teachers).

industry meeting, even one focused on ESG, should be trained in best practices to ensure they do not open themselves or the company up to unnecessary liability. And, work should be done in advance of the meeting to confirm that the association has processes and best practices in place to mitigate antitrust risk. Any representatives of the company who will be attending the meeting(s) should be sensitized to antitrust risk, and in particular should be alert to:

- Ensuring that the discussion follows the agenda without "spilling over" into a more risky topic.
- Avoiding private or "side" meetings and understanding the obligation to leave the room if the conversation becomes more risky.

3. Collaborating and Competing for Employees

To the extent ESG efforts focus on diversity, inclusion, labor practices, and living wages, it is important to understand that the antitrust laws apply to labor markets the same way they apply to markets for goods and services. As shown by Figure 3 below, employees often move between employers in different industries. These employers are considered competitors under the antitrust laws. More competition for employees should lead to higher wages and better benefits. Less competition for employees will lead to lower wages and lesser benefits.

Figure 3

Put simply, individuals or companies that engage in no-poaching, non-solicitation or wage-fixing agreements can be subject to criminal or civil prosecution that could result in monetary fines and imprisonment.[16] Companies may also be subject to private litigation by affected employees, including class actions.

[16] In 2021, a federal grand jury returned an indictment against DaVita Inc., DaVita's former chief executive officer, and Surgical Care Affiliates LLC for agreeing not to solicit and hire each other's senior level employees. Indictment, United States v. Surgical Care Affiliates, LLC, No. 3:21-cr-00011-L (N.D. Tex. Jan. 5, 2021); Indictment, United States v. DaVita Inc., No. 1:21-cr-00229 (D. Colo. July 24, 2021). DaVita and its former chief executive officer were acquitted of all charges on April 15, 2022. Jury Verdict, United States v. DaVita Inc., No. 1:21-cr-00229 (D. Colo. Apr. 15, 2022). Additionally, in December 2020, a federal grand jury returned an indictment charging the owner of a therapist staffing company with conspiring to fix prices by agreeing with his co-conspirators to pay lower rates to

Companies that compete for employees can also trigger antitrust risk by sharing (directly or via a third party) hiring, compensation, wage, and benefits information. This is because sharing such information can lead not only to standalone liability for antitrust violations[17] but also to discussions and possible or implied agreements to coordinate.

- **Limit antitrust risk for human resources-related ESG initiatives:** Seek antitrust guidance if these activities occur or are proposed:
  - Coordinating compensation, benefits, or hiring with any other company, including business partners and vendors, such as setting a "floor" for wages to promote sustainability in the supply chain.
  - Expressing to any company that you should not compete too aggressively for employees.
  - Exchanging company-specific information about employee compensation or terms of employment with another company (this would be CSI as discussed in the previous section).
  - Participating in a meeting, such as a trade association meeting, where the above topics are discussed.
  - Discussing the above topics with colleagues at other companies, including during social events or in other casual settings.
  - Receiving documents that contain another company's detailed internal data about employee compensation.

To learn more about this area, a good place to start is by reviewing the DOJ and FTC Antitrust Guidance for Human Resource Professionals.[18]

4. Coordinating or Working with Customers, Vendors, and/or Suppliers

Many ESG initiatives (e.g., Scope 3 disclosures) are inherently intended to impact the conduct of one's suppliers and vendors. And while ESG collaborations with competitors raise the most significant antitrust risk, collaborations with a company's own suppliers or vendors can also raise unique antitrust risk. As a threshold issue, it is important to keep in mind that even a customer or a supplier can be a competitor in certain circumstances (e.g., competing to hire and retain talented employees).

---

physical therapists and physical therapist assistants. Indictment, United States v. Jindal, No. 4:20-cr-00358 (E.D. Tex. Dec. 9, 2020); First Superseding Indictment, United States v. Jindal, No. 4:20-cr-00358 (E.D. Tex., Apr. 14, 2021) (adding Davita's former CEO as a co-defendant). The defendants in *Jindal* were eventually acquitted of their alleged antitrust violations, with the jury finding *Jindal* guilty only of obstruction of justice. Jury Verdict, United States v. Jindal, No. 4:20-cr-00358 (E.D. Tex. Apr. 14, 2022).

[17] *See* Press Release, DOJ, Justice Department Files Lawsuit and Proposed Consent Decrees to End Long-running Conspiracy to Suppress Worker Pay at Poultry Processing Plants and Address Deceptive Abuses Against Poultry Growers (July 25, 2022), https://www.justice.gov/opa/pr/justice-department-files-lawsuit-and-proposed-consent-decrees-end-long-running-conspiracy (announcing DOJ lawsuit and subsequent settlement challenging an exchange of wage information among competing employers, including requiring $84.8 million in restitution payments).

[18] DOJ & FTC, Antitrust Guidance for Human Resource Professionals (2016), https://www.justice.gov/atr/file/903511/download.

In this section, we will discuss two notable risk areas that can arise even if a company is working with a supplier/customer in a "vertical" relationship (including dual-distribution relationships in which the supplier/customer is also a competitor): (1) supply chain ESG initiatives and (2) supplier/customer interactions that could involve other industry "competitors."

- **Customer/vendor/supply chain management and certifications:** Under the antitrust laws, companies generally have the freedom to unilaterally decide whether to do business with another company. Thus, if a company decides independently that it will only purchase goods from suppliers and vendors that meet certain criteria—e.g., those who pay their employees a certain wage, use certain sustainable harvesting methods, or have met certain diversity thresholds—it is typically free to do so.

  Even in this situation, however, antitrust risk can arise in two instances:
  1. If the company has a relatively high market share, there may be risk of a monopolization claim if the supplier or customer is also a competitor.
  2. If an independent decision could be misconstrued as coordinated competitor behavior, there may be risk of an antitrust investigation or claim.

i. Monopolization risk

With regard to the first risk, although it is true that a company can generally choose its business partners (or, to put it another way, choose certain standards by which it will or will not work with certain business partners), a company may face increased antitrust scrutiny if it has a relatively high market share (~30 percent) or some other form of "market power" and refuses to deal with a competitor. As a best practice, companies should exercise caution and seek antitrust guidance under any of the following circumstances:

- The ESG-minded company is the known "leader" or enjoys a high market share in a particular product, service, or geographic area.
- The ESG initiative could be viewed as "excluding" or "foreclosing" competitors, especially those that might not be able to meet a certain certification or standard.
- The ESG restriction prevents a competitor from gaining access to an essential product or input.

ii. Coordinated behavior disguised as individual conduct

As noted above, although collaborations with suppliers or customers ("vertical") present less antitrust risk compared to collaborations with competitors ("horizontal"), heightened antitrust risk can exist even in collaborations with suppliers/customers if competitive dynamics are implicated.

For example, a collaboration initially focused on a "vertical" relationship (e.g., supplier transparency requirements) can raise competitive issues if it becomes, or appears to become, an agreement among competitors. For example, as depicted in Figure 4 below, let's say that Company X unilaterally imposes ESG-related business requirements onto each of its suppliers. That would be vertical conduct. However, if the suppliers begin to enforce this same conduct on each other, it could become a horizontal restraint and a potential antitrust violation.

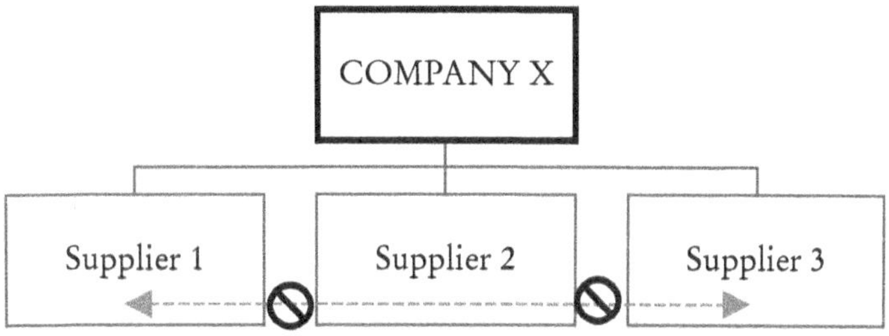

(COMPETING WITH EACH OTHER)

Figure 4

Similarly, if, as shown in Figure 5, Company X were to facilitate concerted conduct between its suppliers (such as by imposing the restrictions at the request of its suppliers), Company X could find itself prosecuted for its participation in and facilitation of an alleged horizontal conspiracy among the suppliers. This is known as a "hub and spoke" conspiracy—when a third party facilitates anti-competitive conduct among the competitors.

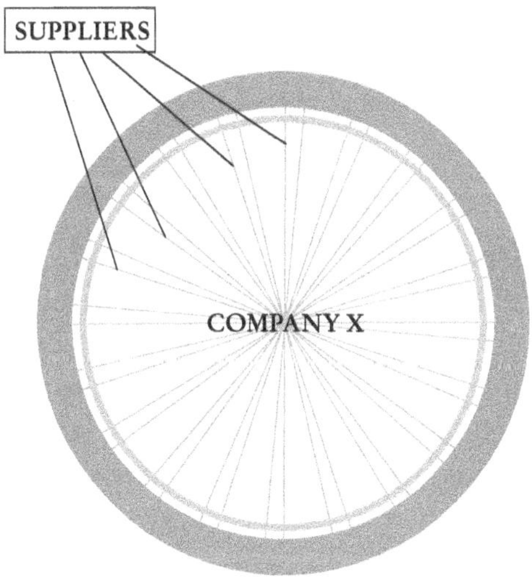

("HUB AND SPOKE" CONSPIRACY)

Figure 5

Here are some best practices to help navigate this situation:

- Adhere to information-sharing guidelines discussed in Section II.B.1.b, even with suppliers, vendors, and customers.
- Only share information with suppliers, vendors, and customers that they need to know.
- Be particularly cautious when sharing forward-looking information, especially if there is a risk the supplier, vendor, or customer may share the information with a competitor.

- Never share information obtained from one customer or supplier with other customers or suppliers.
- Never impose requirements upon groups of customers or suppliers at the request of those customers or suppliers.

5. *Working with Governments or Responding to Government Pressure*

ESG initiatives involving government (or regulatory) bodies can also raise antitrust issues. Generally speaking, companies who are coordinating with each other, even if they are doing so at the request of a governmental entity, are still subject to antitrust laws. The following chart outlines examples of coordinated activities that may raise antitrust risk:

Less Antitrust Risk	More Antitrust Risk
• Acting independently ("Our company will abide by this government standard.") • Issuing an independent ESG pledge • Joint lobbying (may be protected by the First Amendment, but seek antitrust guidance) • Situations in which a state requires and oversees a potentially anti-competitive activity (but seek antitrust guidance)	• Coordinating actions among competitors ("We all agree to abide by this government standard" or "We all agree to abide by this standard we are proposing the government adopt even before the government imposes it.") • Signing an industry-wide ESG pledge with multiple competitors • Jointly agreeing with competitors about how to commercially respond to a regulatory/legal change • Jointly agreeing among competitors on which company should win sole-source procurement contracts or become the government's contractor

6. *Working Alone/Independently*

As discussed throughout this chapter, it is typically safest from an antitrust standpoint to implement any business initiative—ESG or otherwise—unilaterally and independently. However, as discussed in Section I.A.2, even independent action may be subject to antitrust challenge (spurious or legitimate). To mitigate antitrust risk, it is good to remain mindful of two objectives: (a) avoiding potential monopolization/boycott claims and (b) avoiding even the appearance of collusion.

- **Avoid potential monopolization/boycott claims:** A company may face increased antitrust risk for its activities—even independent ESG activities—if the business has a relatively high market share (~30 percent) in a particular market. The relative risk in this area can vary significantly depending on the business's market share, the specifics of the industry, and the contemplated activities. However, a good rule of thumb is to be aware of these risks if the company has a relatively high market share and is engaging in some sort of activity that could be viewed as "excluding" or "foreclosing" competitors.
- **Avoid the appearance of collusion:** Although independent action is typically the "safest" course of behavior from an antitrust perspective, it is still prudent to take steps to ensure that independent action cannot be misconstrued (or twisted by an aggressive

plaintiff) to suggest that the company is engaging in collusive activity through otherwise independent and innocent ESG activities. Best practices include:

- Carefully crafting all company public statements—even when made independently—to avoid misinterpretation. These include conferences and earnings calls. The last thing anyone wants is having to "un-ring the bell" after a company executive pledges that the company will adhere to a price floor for a specific raw material and then calls on competitors to do the same.
- Be cautious about entanglements or interactions with competitors, even if through trade associations or nonprofits. If seeking to comply with board diversity requirements, seek antitrust counsel prior to nominating a board candidate who might be an executive or director at a competing company.
- Be thoughtful in business communications, including emails and texts. Avoid words that can be misconstrued, such as "dominate," "stifle," or "lock up."

C. Action Item No. 3: Exercise Care in Monitoring and Measuring ESG Performance

Once an initiative is up and running, it will be important not to "set it and forget it." Instead, monitoring, measuring, and, if applicable, enforcing ESG initiatives on third parties should be done in compliance with the suggestions discussed above. Here are some considerations:

- If the ESG team wants to benchmark the initiative's performance against similar ESG programs in other companies, be mindful of the information-sharing risks outlined in Section II.B.1.b.
- If an initiative includes disclosure or reporting obligations, companies should be sure to review guidance on best practices related to sharing CSI with competing companies.
- If trying to enforce an ESG policy on a competitor or supplier, it will be important to proceed in accordance with the antitrust laws.
- Consider seeking advanced guidance from the DOJ or FTC, as both have an informal opinion process, known as Business Review Letters or Advisory Opinions, respectively. This process can be complicated to navigate but has been used in the past for notable ESG-focused initiatives with enforcement mechanisms.[19]

[19] *See, e.g.*, Letter from Michael J. Bloom, Assistant Dir., Bureau of Competition, FTC, to Ezra C. Levine, Morrison & Foerster (Sept. 4, 2013), https://www.ftc.gov/sites/default/files/documents/advisory_opinions/money-services-round-table/130904moneyservicesopinion.pdf; *see also* Press Release, FTC, FTC Staff Issues Advisory Opinion that Information Exchange Program Proposed by United States Money Transmitters Is Unlikely to Harm Competition and May Enhance Consumer Protection Goals (Sept. 6, 2013), https://www.ftc.gov/news-events/news/press-releases/2013/09/ftc-staff-issues-advisory-opinion-information-exchange-program-proposed-united-states-money; Letter from Joel I. Klein, Assistant Att'y Gen., Antitrust Div., DOJ, to Kenneth A. Letzler & Richard M. Lucas, Arnold & Porter (Apr. 7, 2000), https://www.justice.gov/sites/default/files/atr/legacy/2006/10/31/4513.pdf.

III. Incorporate Antitrust Compliance into the "G" of ESG

Antitrust compliance is an integral part of good corporate governance, and every company should have a right-sized antitrust compliance program that is tailored to its specific market position and needs. An effective and comprehensive antitrust compliance program not only demonstrates a company's commitment to compliant governance but also carries the added benefit of potentially reducing potential charges and penalties should the DOJ or FTC come knocking.[20]

Key Takeaways

All of the above information is important for managing antitrust risk associated with ESG activities. Here are six key takeaways:

- ***Lofty goals do not confer immunity.*** Remember that ESG initiatives are not immune from antitrust risk. And, in some cases, those goals may make antitrust considerations even more important, such as efforts to influence competitors, suppliers, and vendors.
- ***Be mindful of risk.*** Antitrust investigations, whether originating from the federal government or a state attorney general, are costly and disruptive. This is the case whether or not the investigation (or any challenge) ultimately identifies a potential violation. Therefore, it is crucial to keep antitrust considerations in mind at all stages of ESG initiatives.
- ***Act independently.*** Independent action (as opposed to joint or industry-wide agreements) presents the *least* amount of antitrust risk. Instead of an industry-wide pledge, for example, consider a unilateral statement of the company's intentions.
- ***Coordinate cautiously.*** Be particularly careful when working with competitors in ESG activities. Seek antitrust guidance early, and remember that your company may compete against many other companies (even if the two do not produce the same product).
- ***Share with care.*** Sharing sensitive information can give rise to antitrust risk. Seek legal guidance before directly or indirectly exchanging even ESG-related data with competitors, and consider using firewalls and safeguards such as trade associations and other information-sharing intermediaries who will aggregate and anonymize the information.
- ***Prioritize antitrust compliance.*** Even in commercial activities, an effective and robust antitrust compliance program is crucial for a company's good governance. ESG-minded companies should be sure that they take proactive and effective steps to mitigate the risk of potential antitrust violations in both ESG and commercial activities.

---

[20] Antitrust Div., DOJ, Evaluation of Corporate Compliance Programs in Criminal Antitrust Investigations (2019), https://www.justice.gov/atr/page/file/1182001/download.

Acknowledgments

The editors gratefully acknowledge the assistance of Leigh Logan, a Specialist at Arnold & Porter. Leigh has provided invaluable assistance and support in the development of this manuscript. The editors also thank the 45 authors who contributed to this guide with their expertise, insights, and practical wisdom.

Finally, the editors are deeply grateful for the steadfast love and support of our families: Tsila, Miriam, Abigail, Einav, Jonathan, and Aiden (Brian); William, Kara, and Jonah (Ellen); and Daria (Terry).